CULTURAL
AMNESIA

CULTURAL AMNESIA

NECESSARY MEMORIES

FROM HISTORY

AND THE ARTS

CLIVE JAMES

W. W. NORTON & COMPANY

NEW YORK · LONDON

For information about permission to reproduce selections from
this book, write to Permissions, W. W. Norton & Company, Inc.,
500 Fifth Avenue, New York, NY 10110

Manufacturing by The Haddon Cratfsmen, Inc.
Book design by Chris Welch
Production manager: Anna Oler

Library of Congress Cataloging-in-Publication Data
James, Clive, 1939–
Cultural amnesia ; necessary memories from history and the arts / Clive James
p. cm.
Includes index.
ISBN-13: 978-0-393-06116-1 (hardcover)
ISBN-10: 0-393-06116-7 (hardcover)
1. Civilization, Western. 2. Intellectuals—Biography. 3, Artists—Biography. 4. Musicians—Biography. 5. Philosophers—Biography. 6. Intellectual life—History—20th
century. 7. Humanism—History—20th century. 8. Memory—Social aspects. I. Title.
CB245.J338 2007
909'.09821—dc22
2006036398

W. W. Norton & Company, Inc., 500 Fifth Avenue
New York, N.Y. 10110
www.wwnorton.com

W. W. Norton & Company Ltd., Castle House, 75/76 Wells Street
London W1T 3QT

3 4 5 6 7 8 9 0

To
Aung San Suu Kyi, Ayaan Hirsi Ali, Ingrid Betancourt
and to the memory of
Sophie Scholl

CONTENTS

S

T

U

V

W

Y

Z

All history is contemporary history.

— BENEDETTO CROCE

At certain times the world is overrun by false scepticism. Of the true kind there can never be enough.

— BURCKHARDT,
WELTGESHICHTLICHE BETRACHTUNGEN

One insults the memory of the victims of Nazism if one uses them to bury the memory of the victims of communism.

— JEAN-FRANÇOIS REVEL, *LA GRANDE PARADE*

In a universe more and more abstract, it is up to us to make sure that the human voice does not cease to be heard.

— WITOLD GOMBROWICZ, *JOURNAL*

We should esteem the man who is liberal, not the man who decides to be so.

— MACHIAVELLI

To philosophize means to make vivid.

— NOVALIS

Those are nearer to reality who can deal with it light-heartedly, because they know it to be inexhaustible.

— GOLO MANN

INTRODUCTION

I N THE FORTY years it took me to write this book, I only gradually realized that the finished work, if it were going to be true to the pattern of my experience, would have no pattern. It would be organized like the top of my desk, from which the last assistant I hired to sort it out has yet to reappear. The book I wanted to write had its origins in the books I was reading. Several times, in my early days, I had to sell my best books to buy food, so I never underlined anything. When conditions improved I became less fastidious. Not long after I began marking passages for future consideration, I also began keeping notes in the margin beside the markings, and then longer notes on the endpapers. Those were the very means by which Montaigne invented the modern essay, and at first I must have had an essay of my own in mind: a long essay, but one with the usual shape, a single line of argument moving through selected perceptions to a neat conclusion.

In the short term, many of my annotations went into book reviews and pieces for periodicals: writings which took an essay form, and which, when I collected them into volumes, I unblushingly dignified with that term. But there were always annotations that struck me as not fitting any scheme except a much larger one, to be attempted far in the future, probably towards the end of my life. By the time that terminus was in clear sight, however, I had begun to live with the possibility that there could be no scheme.

There could only be a linear cluster of nodal points, working the way the mind—or at any rate my mind, such as it is—works as it moves through time: a trail of clarities variously illuminating a dark sea of unrelenting turbulence, like the phosphorescent wake of a phantom ship. Far from a single argument, there would be scores of arguments. I wanted to write about philosophy, history, politics and the arts all at once, and about what had happened to those things during the course of the multiple catastrophes into whose second principal outburst (World War I was the first) I had been born in 1939, and which continued to shake the world as I grew to adulthood. Even in an ideal world, none of those subjects would be an easily separable category, and in the far from ideal world we had been given to live in they were inextricably mixed. Each of them, it seemed to me, could have no overt order at the best of times: its order could only be internal, complex, organic. And in the worst of times, which has become our time, any two or more of them taken together must show the same effect dizzily multiplied: the organic complexities intermingled into a texture so intricate that any order extracted from it could be called only provisional.

Well, that would fit. Modern history had given us enough warning against treating simplifications as real. The totalitarian states, the great sponsors of mass atrocity against innocent human beings, had been propelled by ideologies, and what else was an ideology except a premature synthesis? As the time for assembling my reflections approached, I resolved that a premature synthesis was the thing to be avoided.

SO THIS IS a book about how not to reach one. If I have done my job properly, themes will emerge from the apparent randomness and make this work intelligible. But it will undoubtedly be a turbulent read. The times from which it emerged were hard on the nerves, even for those of us who were lucky enough to lead charmed lives. I hope that the episodically intermixed account of direct experience from my own charmed life will alleviate the difficulties of a densely woven text, but I make no excuse for them. If this book were not difficult, it would not be true.

To younger readers who might find themselves wondering why it is so full of forgotten names, and takes such a violently unpredictable course, the first thing to say is: welcome to the twentieth century, out of which your century grew as surely as a column of black smoke grows from an oil fire. The second thing, though an adjunct of the first, is even more important: there is a lot at stake here. In the nineteenth century, in the time of the great philologist Ernest Renan, and despite the contrary evidence already provided by the French Revolution, *Studia humanitatis* was still thought of as an unmixed blessing. If the eighteenth century had meant to usher in the age of reason, the nineteenth century, with the cold snick of the guillotine ringing in its ears, meant to supply some of the regrettable deficiencies of reason by the addition of science. Apart from the prophets—Dickens, despite his inborn optimism, was one of them—few people with any aspirations to a philosophical view doubted that the extension of human knowledge would, in Renan's typically generous phrase, *élargir la grande famille*: produce a race of the enlightened to lead a life of mathematically calculable justice. By now, after the twentieth century has done its cruel work, that is exactly what we doubt. The future of science, Renan's cherished *avenir de la science*, can be assessed from our past, in which it flattened cities and gassed innocent children: whatever we don't yet know about it, one thing we already know is that it is not necessarily benevolent. But somewhere within the total field of human knowledge, humanism still beckons to us as our best reason for having minds at all.

That beckoning, however, grows increasingly feeble. The arts and their attendant scholarship are everywhere—imperishable consumer goods which a self-selecting elite can possess while priding itself as being beyond materialism; they have a glamour unprecedented in history—but humanism is hard to find. For that, science is one of the culprits: not the actual achievement of science, but the language of science, which, clumsily imitated by the proponents of Cultural Studies, has helped to make real culture unapproachable for exactly those students who might otherwise have been most attracted to it, and has simultaneously furthered the emergence and consolidation of an international cargo cult whose witch doctors have nothing in mind beyond their own advancement. By putting the humanities to careerist use, they set a bad example even to those who still love what they study. Learned books are published by the thousand, yet learning was never less trusted as something to be pursued for its own sake. Too often used for ill, it is now asked about its use for good, and usually on the assumption that any goodwill be measurable on a market, like a commodity. The idea that humanism has no immediately ascertainable use at all, and is invaluable for precisely that reason, is a hard sell in an age when the word "invaluable," simply by the way it looks, is begging to be construed as "valueless" even by the sophisticated. In fact, especially by them. If the humanism that makes civilization civilized is to be preserved into this new century, it will need advocates. Those advocates will need a memory, and part of that memory will need to be of an age in which they were not yet alive.

It was terrible, that age. Bright, sympathetic young people who now face a time when innocent human beings are killed by the thousand can be excused for thinking that their elders do not care enough, and indeed it is true that complacency tends to creep in as the hair falls out. But their elders grew to maturity in a time when innocent human beings were killed by the million. The full facts about Nazi Germany came out quite quickly, and were more than enough to induce despair. The full facts about the Soviet Union were slower to become generally appreciated, but when they at last were, the despair was compounded. The full facts about Mao's China left that compounded despair looking like an inadequate response. After Mao, not even Pol Pot came as a surprise. Sadly, he was a cliché.

Ours was an age of extermination, an epoch of the abattoir. But the accumulated destruction yielded one constructive effect, salutary even if solitary. It made us think hard about the way we thought. For my own part, it made me think hard about all the fields of creativity that I seemed to love equally, whatever their place in a supposed hierarchy. I loved poetry, but such towering figures as Brecht and Neruda were only two of the gifted poets who had given aid and comfort to totalitarian power. I loved classical music, but so did Reinhard Heydrich and the ineffable Dr. Mengele. I loved modern fiction in all its fearless inclusiveness, but Louis-Ferdinand Céline, the author of that amazing phantasmagoria *Voyage au bout de la nuit*, had also written *Bagatelles pour un massacre*, a breviary for racialist fanatics. On examination, none of these exalted activities was a sure antidote in itself to the poison of irrationality, which is inseparable from human affairs, but fatal to them if granted a life of its own. And for the less exalted activities, examination was scarcely necessary. I loved popular music, but one look at Johnny Rotten was enough to show you why even the SS occasionally court-martialled a few of its personnel for nihilistic behaviour beyond the call of duty, and more recently there have been rap lyrics distinguishable from the "Horst Wessel Song" only in being less well written. I loved the art sports, but so had Leni Riefenstahl, who also provided evidence that there was nothing necessarily humanist about the movies: *Triumph of the Will* is a spectacle everyone should see, but no one should adore. It would have been nice to believe that comedy, one of my fields of employment, was of its nature opposed to political horror, but there were too many well-attested instances of Stalin and Molotov cracking each other up while they signed death warrants, and there was all too much evidence that Hitler told quite good jokes. If there was no field of creativity that was incorruptibly pure, where did that leave humanism?

GRADUALLY I REALIZED that I had been looking in the wrong place. As a journalist and critic, a premature post-modernist, I was often criticized in my turn for talking about the construction of a poem and of a Grand Prix racing car in the same breath, or of treating gymnasts and high divers (in my daydreams, I astonish the Olympic medalist Greg Louganis) as if they were practising the art of sculpture. It was a sore point, and often the sore point reveals where the real point is. Humanism wasn't in the separate activities: humanism was the connection between them. Humanism was a particularized but unconfined concern with all the high-quality products of the creative impulse, which could be distinguished from the destructive one by its propensity to increase the variety of the created world rather than reduce it. Builders of concentration camps might be creators of a kind—it is possible to imagine an architect happily working to perfect the design of the concrete stanchions supporting an electrified barbed-wire fence—but they were in business to subtract variety from the created world, not to add to it. In the connection between all the outlets of the creative impulse in mankind, humanism made itself manifest, and to be concerned with understanding and maintaining that intricate linkage necessarily entailed an opposition to any political order that worked to weaken it.

SUCH WAS THE conclusion I had already reached after thirty-seven years of preparation. I was doing other things to earn a crust, but the book was never out of my mind, somewhere at the back of the building between the storeroom and the laundry. In the three years it took to compose the actual text, I was faced more and more, as it moved forward, with the consequences of not having isolated my themes. If I was determined on avoiding those broad divisions that I thought not only artificial but actively inimical to my view, the question was bound to keep on arising of where the book's unity was to come from. Answering that question over and over in the course of long days and longer nights, I had to intensify a faith that I had always kept throughout my writing life: the faith that the unity would come from the style. From the beginning of my career, whenever I had written an essay, it was most likely to come alive when its planned progression of points was interrupted by a notion which surprised me, and which could be brought to order only by making the manner of writing more inclusive instead of less. In other words, I took the same approach to prose as to a poem. When young and cocky, I had defined a poem as any piece of writing that could not be quoted from *except* out of context. Older but even more ambitious, I had the temerity to define prose in the same way: a prose work of whatever length should be dependent, in each part, on every other part of what was included, and so respect the importance even of what had been left out. From the force of cohesion would come the power of suggestion, and one of the things suggested should be the existence of other voices.

THERE ARE HUNDREDS of voices in this book, and hundreds more which, although not cited directly, are nevertheless present in the way its author speaks. In that sense, the best sense, there is no such thing as an individual voice: there is only an individual responsibility. The writer represents all the expressive people to whom he has ever paid attention, even if he disapproved of what they expressed. If anything in this book seems not to fit, it isn't, I hope, because it is irrelevant, but because I have written about it in the wrong tone, or the wrong measure. The polemicist has the privilege of unifying his tone by leaving out the complications. I have tried to unify it while encompassing the whole range of a contemporary mind. The mind in question happens to be mine, and any psychologist could argue persuasively that mine is the mind I am least likely to know much about. This much, however, I do know: it would not be a mind at all if its owner had allowed his multiplicity of interests to be restricted by a formula. He might have been more comfortable had he done so. But we have to do better than just seek comfort, or the Exterminating Angel will overwhelm us when he returns. He is unlikely to return at the head of a totalitarian state: even after the final and irreversible discrediting of their ideological pretensions, there are still a few totalitarian states left, but their days are surely numbered.

Totalitarianism, however, is not over. It survives as residues, some of them all the more virulent because they are no longer hemmed in by borders; and some of them are within our own borders. Liberal democracy deserved, and still deserves, to prevail—one of the aims of this book is to help stave off any insidious doubts on that point—but in both components of liberal democracy's name there are opportunities for the ideologist: in the first component lies inspiration for the blind devotee of economic determinism, and in the second for the dogmatic egalitarian. From within as well as without, the Procrustean enemies of our provokingly multifarious free society are bound to come, sometimes merely to preach obscurantist doctrine in our universities, at other times to fly our own airliners into towers of commerce. What they hate is the bewildering complexity of civilized life, which we will find hard to defend if we share the same aversion. We shouldn't. There is too much to appreciate. If it can't be sorted into satisfactory categories, that should make us take heart: it wouldn't be the work of human beings if it could.

There was never a time like now to be a lover of the arts. Mozart never heard most of Bach. We can hear everything by both of them. Brahms was so bowled over by *Carmen* that he saw twenty performances, but he had to buy twenty opera tickets to do so. Manet never saw all his paintings in one place: we can. While Darcey Bussell dances at Covent Garden, the next Darcey Bussell can watch her from Alice Springs. Technology not only has given us a permanent present, but has given it the furniture of eternity. We can cocoon ourselves, if we wish, in a new provincialism more powerful than any of the past empires. English is this new world's lingua franca, not because it was once spoken in the British Empire but because it is spoken now in the American international cultural hegemony. Born to speak it, we can view the whole world as a dubbed movie, and not even have to bother with subtitles. Should we wish, we can even savour the tang of alien tongues: a translation will be provided on a separate page, to be dialled up at a touch. We can be world citizens without leaving home. If that seems too static, we can travel without leaving home. The world is prepared to receive us, with all its fruits laid out for our consumption, and wrapped in cling film to meet our sanitary standards. Gresham's law, that the bad drives out the good, has acquired a counter-law, that the bad draws in the good: there are British football hooligans who can sing Puccini's "*Nessun dorma.*" It would be a desirable and enviable existence just to earn a decent wage at a worthwhile job and spend all one's leisure hours improving one's aesthetic appreciation. There is so much to appreciate, and it is all available for peanuts. One can plausibly aspire to seeing, hearing and reading everything that matters. The times are not long gone when nobody could aspire to that— not even Egon Friedell, a man once famous for being better informed than anybody in Vienna. In a city stiff with polymaths, he was the polymath's polymath.

Egon Friedell looms large in this book. Active from the early years of the twentieth century until the Nazis turned off the lights in Austria, the Viennese prodigy knew everything, or talked as if he did. There was nothing he could not talk about brilliantly. Some thought him a charlatan, but no charlatan is ever remembered for making clever remarks: only for trying to make them. One of the most famous cabaret artists of his day, Friedell in the 1920s combined his career in show business with a monkish dedication to his library, in which he produced a book of his own that must count as one of the strangest and most wonderful of the twentieth century: *Kulturgeschichte der Neuzeit* (*The Cultural History of the Modern Age*). A fabulous effort of style and concentration, a prestidigitator's trick box packed with epigrammatic summaries of all the creativity in every field of art and science since the Renaissance, a prose epic raised to the level of poetry, Friedell's magic show of a book remains a fantastic demonstration of the mind at serious play. At the time, he left people wondering if there was nothing he might not do next. That kind of expectation can easily breed envy. Though he did his best to be humble, there were many in his audience who thought him not humble enough. Friedell believed that an artist of his type needed "a magnetic field" in which to operate. He was well aware that he was surrounded by the kind of people whose only ambition was to cut off the electricity. They were Nazis, and he was a Jew.

On the day of the *Anschluß* in 1938, Friedell saw the storm troopers marching down the street, on their way to the building in which he had his apartment full of books. He was only a few floors up but it was high enough to do the job. On his way out of the window he called a warning, in case his falling body hit an innocent passer-by.

I CAN'T IMAGINE being brave enough to copy the way Egon Friedell made an exit, but there was something about the way he made an entrance that could be a model for us all. He came on as a combination of actor and thinker. We are all doomed to be actors, in the sense that our abilities and deficiencies will guide us, in certain ways if not in others, to becoming active participants in a productive society, whether we like that society or not. Alas, we will be participants even if we hate it: terrorism, which will not tolerate a passive audience, is already part of the show. But to palliate that condition, we are nowadays much more free to be thinkers than is commonly supposed. The usual division is to treat our daily job as the adventure and our cultural diversions as a mere mechanism of renewal and repose. But the adventurous jobs are becoming more predictable all the time, even at the level of celebrity and conspicuous material success. Could there be anything less astonishing than to work day and night on Wall Street to make the millions that will buy the Picasso that will hang on the wall of our Upper East Side apartment to help convince us and our guests that we are lucky to know each other? I have been in that apartment, and admired the Picasso, and envied its owner: I especially envied him his third wife, who had the same eyes as Picasso's second mistress, although they were on different sides of her nose. But I didn't envy the man his job. In the same week, I was filming in Greenwich Village, and spent an hour of down-time sitting in a café making my first acquaintance with the poetry of Anthony Hecht. I couldn't imagine living better. The real adventure is no longer in the job. In the job we can have a profile written about us, and be summed up: all the profiles will be the same, and all the summaries add up to the same thing. The real adventure is in what we do to entertain ourselves, a truth which the profile writers concede by trying to draw us out on our supposed addictions to shark fishing, fast cars, extreme skiing and expensive young women. But even the entertainment can no longer be adventurous if it serves a purpose.

It will be adventurous only if it serves itself. In other words, it will not be utilitarian. It has always been part of the definition of humanism that true learning has no end in view except its own furtherance.

What this book then proposes—what it embodies, I hope—is something difficult enough to be satisfactory for an age in which to be presented with nothing except reassurance is ceasing to be tolerable. As the late Edward W. Said wrote after the attack on the World Trade Center, Western humanism is not enough: we need a universal humanism. I agree with that. The question is how to get it, and my own view is that it can't be had unless we raise our demands on ourselves a long way beyond decorating our lives with enough cultivation to make the pursuit of ambition look civilized. When the doomed Russian poet Osip Mandelstam said that he was nostalgic for a world culture, he didn't mean that it would be a world culture if everyone could live in Switzerland.

THE IDEOLOGISTS THOUGHT they understood history. They thought history had a shape, a predictable outcome, a direction that could be joined. They were wrong. Some of them were intellectuals who shamed themselves and their calling by bringing superior mental powers to the defence of misbegotten political systems that were already known to be dispensing agony to the helpless. Young readers will find some of that story here, and try to convince themselves that they would have behaved differently. But the way to avoid the same error now is not through understanding less. It can only be through understanding more. And the beginning of understanding more is to realize that there is more than can be understood. As an aid to that end, this book is not a testament to my capabilities, but to the lack of them. Proust talked about "that long flight from our own lives that we call erudition." There is nothing inherently wrong with erudition: it's not as if we're drowning in it, and anyway Proust himself wrote the most erudite book in the whole of French literature. But this book is the reverse of erudite. It does not just record what I have learned. It also suggests what I have failed to learn, and now will probably never learn, because it is getting late. The student who flicks through these pages in the bookshop will see many strange names, and perhaps be impressed. But what impresses me is all the names that are missing. I would never have taken a note in the first place except out of the fear that what I was reading would soon slip away: a fear all too well founded. The Russian symbolist writer Andrei Bely once said that what we keep in our heads is the *sum* of a writer: a "composite quotation." But the only reason I still know that Bely once said that is that I wrote it down.

There was a time when I could fairly fluently read Russian, and get through a simple article in Japanese about my special subject, the war in the Pacific. I hope to get Russian back, but the written version of Japanese is the kind of language that you can study hard for five years and yet can't neglect for a week without its leaving you like a flock of birds. I hope they return as easily as they went, but I remember how long they took to arrive in the first place. I have always loved the title of Milan Kundera's *The Book of Laughter and Forgetting*. I hope this is a book of laughter, at least in places. But it is everywhere a book of forgetting. I am not urging young people to follow me on the path to a success. I am showing them the way to a necessary failure: the grim but edifying realization that a complete picture of reality is not to be had. If we realize that, we can begin to be realistic. Thinking otherwise, we doom ourselves to spinning fantasies, which might well be fluent, but could equally be lethal. Stalin and Hitler both thought that they could see the whole picture, and look what happened.

WHATEVER WE SAY, it is bound to be dependent on what has been said before. In this book can be heard the merest outside edge of an enormous conversation. As they never were in life, we can imagine the speakers all gathered in some vast room. Or perhaps they are on a terrace, under the stars. They are wearing name tags in case they don't recognize each other. Some of them recognize each other all too well, but they avoid contact. Thomas Mann, with the family poodle snuffling petulantly at his knee, would rather not talk to Brecht, and Sartre is keen to avoid Solzhenitsyn. Kafka tells Puccini that he would have approached him at the Brescia flying display in 1909, but he was too shy. Nabokov tells Pavlova that he never forgot the time he danced the waltz with her. Yeats has failed to convince Wittgenstein about the importance of the Mystic Rose. All over the place there are little dramas. Standing beside the piano, Stravinsky refuses to believe that Duke

Ellington is improvising. Robert Lowell has cornered Freud and is telling him that when he, Lowell, has a depressive phase he imagines he is Adolf Hitler. With barely concealed impatience, Freud mutters that Hitler spends very little time imagining he is Robert Lowell. Anna Akhmatova at her most beautiful, a catwalk model with the nose of an unsuccessful pugilist, has moved in on Tony Curtis at his most handsome, dressed for his role as Sidney Falco in *Sweet Smell of Success*. Curtis looks frightened. Akhmatova's friend and rival Nadezhda Mandelstam, on the other hand, seems delighted to have met Albert Camus: she distrusts the way he turns on the automatic charm even for an old lady, but she approves of his opinions.

Not all the figures are from the twentieth century. Some have been invited because what they said was prescient, or at least portentous. Heine and Wagner are getting on better than Nietzsche expected: neither has yet strangled the other. Montesquieu is doing his best to put up with Talleyrand. It is not a fancy dress party, but "come as you are" means that Tacitus has arrived in a toga, and the poet Juana Inés de la Cruz in a nun's habit. One of the great beauties of the seventeenth-century Spanish world, Juana Inés is a ringer for Isabella Rossellini. Tacitus seems quite taken with her, perhaps partly because she speaks fluent Latin. Never a million laughs, he tells her his story about the daughter of Sejanus: a story which the reader will find in this book. Tacitus thought it was the most terrible story he could imagine. We know what he doesn't: that in the twentieth century the story of Sejanus's daughter will be repeated several million times.

MY HEROES AND heroines are here. The reader will recognize some of their names: Albert Camus, Nadezhda Mandelstam, Thomas Mann, Marcel Proust, Franz Kafka. Other names will be more obscure: Miguel de Unamuno, Georg Christoph Lichtenberg, Leszek Kolakowski, Golo Mann, Arthur Schnitzler, Witold Gombrowicz, Manès Sperber, Raymond Aron, Hans Sahl, Jean Prévost, Stefan Zweig. My intellectual *bêtes noires* are here too, and the same division might apply. Everyone has heard of Sartre, Brecht, Céline. Not everyone has heard of Georg Lukács, Robert Brasillach, Ernst Jünger, Louis Aragon. There is a category of super-villain easy to assess: Hitler, Stalin, Mao. But although Hitler and Stalin both talked like maniacs from the start, Mao was capable of something like human reason early in his career; a fact to remind us that the merely verbalizing villains—those benighted intellectuals who truckled to power—were not always without a spark of reason. It might have been better if they had been: they would have done less damage. As it happened, not even Sartre could be wrong all the time, although he tried hard. And there were heroes who were not always right: Thomas Mann, in his youth, was terrifically wrong about militarized nationalism, and part of his later anguish was that he had lived to see the destructive consequences of a passion that he had once believed to be self-evidently creative. George Orwell thought, and said, that the bourgeoisie was the enemy of the proletariat, until the practical evidence persuaded him that anyone who believed the two classes could not be reconciled was the deadly enemy of both. When we talk about the imponderables of life, we don't really mean that we can't ponder them. We mean that we can't stop. Hence the conversation: a Sargasso of monologues that were all attracted to the noise.

Some of the voices are talking murder while thinking it to be medicine. Others, the blessed ones, are talking reason. Almost always it is because they know their own limitations. But unless they were born as saints, they had to find out they were not infallible by listening to the words of others. Most of the words were written down, and most of the listening was done by reading. Certainly it was in my case, during all those intervals in a busy life when I escaped to be alone in the café, and found that I was never alone for a moment. Because, as a journalist and television presenter, I travelled professionally for more than twenty years on end, the café was in many different cities: Sydney, London, Cambridge, Edinburgh, Florence, Rome, Venice, Paris, Biarritz, Cannes, Berlin, Munich, Vienna, Moscow, Madrid, Tokyo, Kyoto, Hiroshima, Bombay, Shanghai, Hong Kong, Singapore, Cairo, Jerusalem, Valletta, Los Angeles, San Francisco, New York, Chicago, Miami, Mexico City, Havana, Rio, Buenos Aires, Auckland, Wellington, Perth, Melbourne, Adelaide, Brisbane and Sydney again. But the café table always looked the same once I had piled it high with books. Out of the pages they came: those who thought they were wise and those who really were. So many of the first, and so very few of the second. Just enough, however, to make me thankful to have lived, and want to join them. If this book makes the reader want the same, it will have done its work. What I propose is a sum of appreciations that includes an appreciation of their interdependence: a new humanism. If I could put it into a sentence, I would say that it relies on the conviction that nothing creative should be excluded for the sake of any other conviction. Another way of putting it is this book.

—Clive James
London, 2006

MAINLY BECAUSE A thematic classification would be impossible, the essays are arranged in alphabetical order by author of the heading quotation. Any other rhyme or reason is meant to emerge in the reading. This might well be the only serious book to explore the relationship between Hitler's campaign on the eastern front and Richard Burton's pageboy hairstyle in *Where Eagles Dare*, but such an exploration is fundamental to its plan, which is to follow the paths that lead on from the citations, and try to go on following them when they cross. As for the citations, page references are given where a scholar might wish to check my interpretation. Otherwise, in the interests of readability, such notations have been kept to a minimum. Qualified linguists will quickly detect that I command only smatterings in any language except my own, but I remain convinced that tinkering with foreign tongues has stood me in better stead than concerning myself with literary theory, which would have taken just as much time and left me knowing nothing at all, instead of merely not enough. With a view to the impatience of the monoglot young reader I once was myself, almost every foreign phrase is translated on the spot; but the occasional single foreign word is left to stand alone when its meaning can be easily inferred. Sometimes a quoted phrase, or the account of an incident, is repeated when there seems a genuine benefit to be gained by seeing it from a different angle. (One of my models, Eugenio Montale, favoured that practice, and as a reader I was always grateful for it.) Fiction and poetry are seldom drawn upon for the heading quotations; partly out of a wish not to injure an organic context; mainly out of a conviction that it is in their ancillary writings that authors are more likely to state their opinions in a detachable form. (The argument that we should not want to detach the opinions of an artist is familiar to me: we shouldn't, but we do.) An autobiographical element is mixed in when the concrete information seems pertinent to one of the general themes.

Believing that "they" is no fit substitute for "he" in the singular, and finding "he or she" cumbersome, I have stuck with the traditional masculine dominance of the indeterminate gender. I have also availed myself of the European tradition by which sufficiently distinguished females are honoured through being referred to by their first names. I can quite see—or, anyway, I can almost see—how gallantry might be patronizing, but I don't see how confusion counts as a blow for justice. Nadezhda Mandelstam, for example, is actually insulted by being called just Mandelstam, because that surname belongs to her husband, Osip, in the first instance. I would rather convey my reverence for her by my argument than pay her the empty compliment of a modern formula that to me seems hollow.

Female readers can put all this down to unreconstructed chauvinism if they wish, but I don't think they will find their representatives slighted in this book: merely outnumbered. Female readers might find themselves grateful for that. This is a book about a world men made, and it taught plenty of us to wish that women had made it instead.

ACKNOWLEDGEMENTS

I SHOULD THANK Peter Straus, at that time Picador's chief editor in London, for listening to my first idea of this book and thinking it might be worth a try. Andrew Kidd, who succeeded to the command post at Picador, also deserves thanks for trusting me when I kept on saying that the only way I could define the book was that it would define itself. My deepest and longest thanks, however, must surely go to Robert Weil of W. W. Norton, who not only believed in the project from its formative stages, but gave it knowledgeable and detailed editorial attention from page to page as it steadily accumulated in his office on Fifth Avenue. If things got to the point that he had to schedule an editorial session for his flight back to New York from a conference in China, still he did not give up, and every comment he made in the margin was pertinent. In the spiritual sense, this book would not be the same without him: he was its ideal reader. In the physical sense, it would not be here at all without Cécile Menon. In her plural role as my secretary, assistant, *Webmeisterin*, chief executive officer and personal trainer, she found time, among her many other tasks, to teach me the computer skills without which any hypertext becomes a runaway train. In most cases, teaching me consisted in realizing once again that I was a hopeless case, and she simply pressed the buttons needed to save the day. To take a single point, it took her no more than two minutes to track down exactly what Cocteau said about the chameleon on the tartan. Thus she saved me desperate hours, and I can only hope that this book will be of as much use to her generation of hungry young culture-vultures as her brilliance and diligence have been to me. A final but vital acknowledgement should go to my copy editor, Trent Duffy, who, as well as spotting ambiguities lurking in the syntax, saved me from many serious blunders, including the results of my irritating mental habit of writing "Milos Forman" for "Louis Malle"—a conspicuous instance of the embarrassing phenomenon known to clinical psychologists as the Malle-Forman malformation.

A book of this kind can be especially taxing in its very last stages of preparation, when the correcting of details persistently adds more details to be corrected. But without the generous donation of time by family members and family friends, far too many blunders on my part would have been enshrined in print. It took Tom Mayer at Norton, however, to ensure that the process of correcting the corrections did not finish off the author along with the book, and I thank him with a whole heart, if not quite, any longer, a whole mind.

CULTURAL AMNESIA

VIENNA

I N THE LATE nineteenth and early twentieth centuries, Vienna was the best evidence that the most accommodating and fruitful ground for the life of the mind can be something more broad than a university campus. More broad, and in many ways more fun. In Vienna there were no exams to pass, learning was a voluntary passion, and wit was a form of currency. Reading about old Vienna now, you are taken back to a time that should come again: a time when education was a lifelong process. You didn't complete your education and then start your career. Your education *was* your career, and it was never completed. For generations of writers, artists, musicians, journalists and mind-workers of every type, the Vienna café was a way of life. There were many cafés, although in each generation there tended to be only a precious few that were regarded as centres of the action for the creative elite. The habitués might have had homes to go to when they wanted to sleep, but otherwise where they lived was in the café. For some of them, the café was an actual address. Most, though not all, of the café population was Jewish, which explains why the great age of the café as an informal campus abruptly terminated in March 1938, when the *Anschluß* wrote the finish—*finis Austriae*, as Freud put it—to an era. It also partly explains why the great age had come to fruition in the first place.

Even in Germany, where the Jews had full civil rights until Hitler repealed them, there was a de facto quota system in academic life which made it hard for people of Jewish background to be appointed to the faculty, no matter how well qualified they were. (The prejudice affected priorities even within the faculty: nuclear physics, for example,

featured so many Jewish personnel mainly because it was considered a
secondary field.) In Austria the quota system was built into every area
of society as a set of laws, limits and exclusions. As an inevitable result,
in Austria even more than in Germany there was a tendency for scholarship and humanism to be pursued more outside the university than
inside it. A case could be made—among the Austrian privileged class
you can still hear it being made—that the Jews thus benefited from
having doors closed against them. It would be a bad case. The humili-
ations were real and the resentments lasting. But there was one
undoubted benefit to us all. Whole generations of Jewish literati were
denied the opportunity of wasting their energies on compiling abstruse
doctoral theses. They were driven instead to journalism, plain speech,
direct observation and the necessity to entertain. The necessity to
entertain could sometimes be the enemy of learning, but not as often
as the deadly freedom to write as if nobody would ever read the results
except a faculty supervisor who owed his post to the same exemption.

In 1938, the flight from the *Anschluß*—and if only all of them had
fled in time—was not the first case of a Jewish intellectual community
scattering to the world. It had happened before, in the German cities
in 1933, and it happened before that, in Poland under Russian persecution, and in Russia both before and after the Revolution. In each
case, the suppression of liberalism worked like a shell-burst, with the
Jews as the fragments of the shell's casing, the fragments that travelled
furthest. These local disasters added up to a benefit for the world, so
we need to change the metaphor, and think of an exploding seed-pod.
In the reception of first-rate minds driven into exile, Britain and America were the most prominent beneficiaries, but we should not forget
smaller countries like my own, Australia. The intellectual and artistic
life of Australia was transformed by the arrival of those Jews who managed to make the distance. In New Zealand, the exiled professor Karl
Popper was able to develop the principles contained in *The Open Society and Its Enemies* because he was at last living in an open society, and
remembered the enemies. In those democracies that were sensible
enough to let at least some of the Jews in, the growth of a humanist
culture was immeasurably accelerated. It hardly needs adding that the
enforced new diaspora was an immense factor in turning Israel from an
idea to a burgeoning fact. The idea had earlier been developed in

Vienna, by Theodor Herzl. Just as Lenin's idea for a Communist nation left from Vienna for its long journey to Russia, Herzl's idea for a Jewish nation left from Vienna for its long journey to Palestine. Had history worked out otherwise, Herzl's idea might have retained the same status as Freud's ideas about the subconscious—a mere theory, though a seductive one. The same could even be said of Adolf Hitler, whose early years in Vienna confirmed him in his own idea: the idea of a world without Jews.

The Jews in the first half of the twentieth century were not the only persecuted minority on Earth, and indeed the time would come, after the foundation of the state of Israel in 1948, when they would begin to be regarded—sometimes correctly—as persecutors in their turn. As liberal Jews have had increasing cause to observe, one of the penalties for becoming another state was to become a state like any other. But the fate of the Jews, and its accompanying achievements, will be a recurring theme in this book for a good reason. There could be no clearer proof that the mind is hard to kill. Nor could there be a more frightening demonstration of the virulent power of the forces which can combine to kill it. There is some room for hope, then, but none for sentimentality. A book about culture in the twentieth century which did not deal constantly with just how close culture came to being eradicated altogether would not be worth reading, although there is an ineradicable demand for uplift which would always make it worth writing. There could be a feel-good storybook about Vienna called, say, *It Takes a Village*. But it took a lot more than that. As a place to begin studying what happened to twentieth-century culture, Vienna is ideal, but only on the understanding that the ideal was real, with all the complications of reality, and none of the consolations of a therapeutic dream.

Apart from the numerous picture books—which should never be despised as introductory tools, and in the case of Vienna are especially enchanting—probably the best first book to read in order to get the atmosphere would be Stefan Zweig's *Die Welt von Gestern*, which has been translated into English as *The World of Yesterday*. But there is lot of atmosphere to get, and with Zweig's memoirs you have to take it for granted that the great names did great things. A shorter and less allusive account, George Clare's *Last Waltz in Vienna*, is an admirably direct introduction to the triumph of Vienna and the tragedy that was waiting to ruin it. The triumph was a sense of civilization; a civilization that the Jews had a right to feel they had been instrumental in creating; and the tragedy was that their feelings of safe assimilation were falsely based. The triumph might have continued; the Nazis might never have arrived; but they did arrive, and everything went to hell. Clare's book is unbeatable at showing that one of the consequences of cultural success can be political naivety. The lesson still applies today, when so many members of the international intelligentsia—which, broadly interpreted, means us—continue to believe that culture can automatically hold civilization together. But there is nothing automatic about it, because nothing can be held together without the rule of law.

On what might seem a more exalted level, Carl E. Schorske's book *Fin-de-Siècle Vienna* brings on the first wave of great names: Freud, Herzl, Hofmannsthal, Klimt, Kokoschka, Karl Kraus, Adolf Loos, Mahler, Musil, Schnitzler, Schoenberg, Otto Wagner and others. It is an impressive work, deserving of its prestige, but tends to encourage the misleading assumption that greatness is everything. In the long run it might seem so, but in the shorter run, which is the run of everyday life, a civilization is irrigated and sustained by its common interchange of ordinary intelligence. After the turn of the century, in Vienna's case, this more ordinary intelligence began to make itself extraordinary through the essays and remembered wit that came out of the cafés. Of its nature, such a multifarious achievement is less susceptible to being summed up in a single treatise. Friedrich Torberg's memoir *Die Tante Jolesch* (*Aunt Jolesch*), published after World War II, looks back fondly and funnily on a vanished world. A peal of laughter ringing in the ruins, Torberg's book can be recommended with a whole heart. (It can also be recommended as a way for a student to make a beginning with German, because all the anecdotes that sound so attractive in English sound even more so in the original. Keep the original and the translation open beside each other and you've got the perfect parallel text.) But many of the names that shone brightest are destined to go on doing so from the far side of the language barrier. Half genius and half flimflam man, the polymath Egon Friedell—already mentioned in my preface, but being introduced twice fits his act—was a towering figure among the coffee-house wits. Somehow, in between cabaret engagements, Friedell found time to write *Kulturgeschichte der Neuzeit*, a mesmerizing claim to the totality of knowledge. It was translated, in three whopping volumes from Alfred A. Knopf, as *The Cultural History of the Modern Age* in 1931, but it never took on outside the German-speaking countries. (In those, it came back into print after the fall of the Nazis and has been in print ever since.) His omniscient tone of voice was at least partly a put-up job, but the universality of his gusto remains an enduring ideal. The finest wit of all, the essayist and theatre critic Alfred Polgar, has never been substantially translated, and probably never will be, because his prose has the compression and precision of the finest poetry. But both men can still be appreciated for what they represent, and their names will crop up often in this book. What they had in common was a brilliant sensitivity to all the achievements of culture at whatever level of respectability—although not even Friedell was receptive enough to realize that jazz might be music—and what all the coffee-house intellectuals had in common was that they knew Peter Altenberg, who by their standards hardly achieved anything at all. Altenberg was a bum, and I place him near the beginning of this book—preceded only by Anna Akhmatova, whom he probably would have hit for a small loan—not just because the initial of his name is at the beginning of the alphabet, but because he was living proof, in all his flakiness and unreliability, that the life of the mind doesn't necessarily get you anywhere. In his case it didn't even get him a job. Though he occasionally made some money from publishing his collections of bits and pieces, the money was soon spent, and he had to borrow more. But his very existence was a reminder to more prosperous practitioners that what they did was done from love.

Vienna feels empty now. You can have a good night at the opera, and in spring you can drink Heurige Wein in the gardens, and the Klimt and Schiele rooms in the Belvedere are still among the great rooms of the museum that covers the world, and on the walls of the Café Hawelka are still to be seen the drawings with which Picabia once paid his bills. But after World War II the eternally fresh impulse of humanism came back to Vienna only in the form of the zither playing on the soundtrack of the *The Third Man*. The creative spirit of the city had been poisoned by the corrupted penicillin of Harry Lime—the juice of irreversible psychic damage. Nor did Paris ever fully recover from the Occupation, although that contention can still buy you a verbal fight with resident intellectuals who are certain that it did. Humanism had a better chance of recovery in cities where its roots had never been deep enough to be thought part of the foundations. Post-war Berlin, whose civilization before the rise of the Nazis had been shallow and frantic, grew more fruitful than Vienna after the last Nazis of either city prudently shed their uniforms. In Tokyo, the pre-war coffee-house culture—so eerily mimetic of Vienna, even down to its brass-framed bow windows echoing the spare forms of Adolf Loos—melted in the firestorm of March 1945. But that culture had been the merest touch of the West, and before General MacArthur had barely begun his reign as visiting emperor, the influence of Western liberal creativity was back like a new kind of storm, a storm that put up buildings instead of knocking them flat, and turned on lights instead of switching them off, and accelerated, and this time in a less disastrous direction, the transformative process that had begun with the Meiji restoration in 1870, the process of a culture becoming conscious of itself—a process that will turn any culture towards humanism, even when its right wing, as Japan's does, gives up its convictions only at the rate of a tea ceremony in slow motion.

Today, in the second decade after the Berlin Wall came down, the still miraculously lovely Petersburg is only beginning to have again what it had before the Revolution: the magic of a poetic imagination on a civic scale. Moscow, which always had less of that, seems to have come further faster. If Rome was the only one-time seat of totalitarian power that recovered instantly a glory that it had before, it was because the Italian brand of totalitarianism was less total: its bullhorn rhetoric and slovely inefficiency left too much of the humanist tradition intact. But the great burgeoning, on a world scale, of the post-Nazi liberal humanist impulse, a burgeoning which continues in the new post-Soviet era, took place and is still taking place in London and New York. The subsidiary English-speaking cities—Los Angeles, Chicago, Dublin, Sydney, Melbourne and many more—follow those two, and of those two, even London must follow New York. The reasons are so simple they often escape notice. Outstripping even Britain in its magnetic attraction for those who fled, America had the greater number of creative refugees, especially in their role as teachers: in New York, to stay alive, they taught music, painting, acting, everything. And America had the GI Bill of Rights. The ideal teachers met the ideal pupils, and the resulting story made Eleanor Roosevelt, whose idea the GI Bill was, into the most effective woman in the history of world culture up until that time, and continues to make her name a radiant touchstone for those who believe, as I do, that the potential liberation of the feminine principle is currently the decisive factor lending an element of constructive hope to the seething tumult within the world's vast Muslim hegemony, and within the Arab world in particular. The secret of American cultural imperialism—the only version of American imperialism that really is irresistible, because it works by consent—is its concentration of all the world's artistic and intellectual qualities in their most accessible form. The danger of American cultural imperialism is that it gives Americans a plausible reason for thinking that they can do without the world. But the world helped to make them what they now are—even Hollywood, the nation's single most pervasive cultural influence, would be unimaginable without its immigrant personnel. One of the intentions of this book is to help establish a possible line of resistance against the cultural amnesia by which it suits us to forget that the convulsive mental life of the twentieth century, which gave the United States so much of the cultural power that it now enjoys, was a complex, global event that can be simplified only at the cost of making it unreal. If we can't remember it all, we should at least have some idea of what we have forgotten. We could, if we wished, do without remembering, and gain all the advantages of travelling light; but a deep instinct, not very different from love, reminds us that the efficiency would be bought at the cost of emptiness. Finally the reason we go on thinking is because of a feeling. We have to keep that feeling pure if we can, and, if we ever lose it, try to get it back.

A

❦ ❦ ❦

Anna Akhmatova

Peter Altenberg

Louis Armstrong

Raymond Aron

ANNA AKHMATOVA

❣ ❣ ❣

Born in Odessa, educated in Kiev and launched into poetic immortality as the beautiful incarnation of pre-revolutionary Petersburg, Anna Akhmatova (1889–1966) was the most famous Russian poet of her time, but the time was out of joint. Before the Bolshevik Revolution in 1917, Anna Andreyevna Gorenko, called Akhmatova, already wore the Russian literary world's most glittering French verbal decorations: her work was avant-garde, and in person she was a femme fatale. Love for her broken-nosed beauty was a common condition among the male poets, one of whom, Nikolay Gumilev, she married. After the Revolution, Gumilev was one of the new regime's first victims among the literati: the persecution of artists, still thought of today as a Stalinist speciality, began under Lenin. Later on, under Stalin, Akhmatova included a reference to Gumilev's fate in the most often quoted part of her poem "Requiem." ("Husband dead, son in gaol / Pray for me.") In the last gasp of the Tsarist era she had known no persecution worse than routine incomprehension for her impressionistic poetry and condemnation by women for her effect on their men. The Russia of Lenin and Stalin made her first a tragic, then an heroic, figure. After 1922 she was condemned as a bourgeois element and severely restricted in what she could publish. After World War II, in 1946, she was personally condemned by Andrey Zhdanov, Stalin's plug-ugly in charge of culture. She was allowed to publish nothing new, and everything she had ever written in verse form was dismissed as "remote from socialist reconstruction." Her prestige abroad helped to keep her alive at home, but also ensured that her life could never be comfortable: the security police were always on her case. In the 1950s she was rehabilitated to the extent that a censored edition of her collected poems was officially published. ("Requiem" was among the poems missing: Isaiah Berlin, who visited her in Moscow in 1946, was correct when he predicted that it would never be published in Russia as long as the Soviet Union lasted.) Unofficially, however, her work had always circulated, whether in samizdat or, in that peculiarly Russian tribute to greatness, from mouth to mouth, by memory. Akhmatova was the embodiment of the Russian liberal heritage that the authoritarians felt bound to go on threatening long after it had surrendered. As such, she was an inspiring symbol, but when a poet becomes better known than her poems it usually means that she is being sacrificed, for extraneous reasons, on the altar of her own glory. In Akhmatova's case, the extraneous reasons were political. It should be a mark of reasonable politics that a woman like her is not called upon to be a heroine.

This lyrical wealth of Pushkin . . .
—ANNA AKHMATOVA, "PUSHKIN'S
'STONE GHOST'"

SOME LANGUAGES ARE inherently more beautiful than others, and Russian is among the most beautiful of all. For anyone learning Russian, a phrase like "lyrical wealth" comes singing out of the page like a two-word aria from an opera by Moussorgsky. I noted it down as a soon as I saw it. In 1968 the West German publishing house that called itself Inter-Language Literary Associates produced a magnificent two-volume collection of Akhmatova's works in verse and prose. I bought those books in London in 1978, when I was in my first stage of learning to read the language. I never got to the last stage, or anywhere near it: but I did reach the point where I could read an essay without too much help from the dictionary. (Memo to any student making a raid on the culture of another language: essays are always the easiest way in.) Reading Akhmatova's essays, it was soon apparent that she would have been an excellent full-time critic of literature if she had been given permission. But of course she wasn't, which brings us immediately to the point.

If the 1917 Bolshevik Revolution had never happened, the cafés of Petersburg and Moscow would probably have dominated this book. Petersburg, in particular, would have rivalled Vienna. (If the Nazis had never come to power, Vienna and Berlin would have continued to rival Paris, but that's another matter, although one we are bound to get to soon enough.) The Russian cultural upsurge in the years before the Revolution was so powerful that after the Revolution it took a while to slow down. (In the emigration, it never slowed down, but it did thin out as time went on: whereas Diaghilev was a whole movement in the arts, Balanchine's influence was confined to the ballet, and Nureyev and Baryshnikov, though they could create contexts, did so mainly for themselves—wonderful as they both were, they were just dancers.) Largely because the new regime took some time to purge itself of apparatchiks with a taste for the artistically vital, the Revolution, inheriting an unprecedented cultural efflorescence, spent its first decade or so looking like the benevolent guardian of a realized dream. Left-leaning culturati in the West were able to fool themselves for decades afterwards that a totalitarian regime had somehow opened up new possibilities for making art a political weapon in the eternal struggle to free the people's creative will. The dazzle-painted agitprop trains and the snappily edited newsreels of Dziga Vertov were seen as signs of vigour, which they were, and of truth, which they were not.

Among the Soviet Union's apologists in the West, it was commonly supposed that, while the self-exiled Stravinsky no doubt enjoyed his personal freedom, Prokofiev and Shostakovich gained from being thought important by the power that paid them, and that this putatively fruitful relationship between creativity and a centralized state had been established in the early years after the Revolution. In reality, the intelligentsia was already doomed, simply because Anatoly Lunacharsky, the commissar for culture, wielded absolute power over the artists. He could wield it benevolently only with the indulgence of his superiors, which was withdrawn in 1929, the year the nightmare began to unfold unmistakably even to those who had been carried away when they thought it was a dream. (Awareness could be fatal: Mayakovsky, the poet most famous for transmitting state policy through works of art, shot himself not because he was mad, but because he was mad no longer—he had suddenly woken up to the dreadful fact that his creative enthusiasm had been used to cosmeticize mass murder.)

Akhmatova, to her credit, had always tried to stay aloof from the Revolution. But the Revolution was never likely to pay her the courtesy of staying aloof from her. As early as 1922, her poetry had been correctly identified as politically unhelpful, and she was forbidden to publish any more of it. The ban was relaxed temporarily in 1940, but we need to remember that Akhmatova, as a poet, was never really allowed to function. She earned her living mainly from translation and journey-work in prose. (As a consequence, a threat in 1947 to expel her from the Writers' Union was tantamount to a sentence of death.) Praising Pushkin, as she did in the essay that mentioned his "lyrical wealth," was as close as she was allowed to get to saying something subversive. As it happened, it was permissible to place a value on a poet's specifically poetic gifts as long as the poet was accepted as exemplifying—or, in Pushkin's case, heralding—the correct political direction. If she had been caught even thinking about the "lyrical wealth" of, say, Osip Mandelstam, she would have been in even more trouble than usual. Osip Mandelstam had been murdered by Stalin in 1938. There had been a time when Osip, like most of the male poets of his generation, had been in love with Akhmatova. She had returned his affection, much to the annoyance of his wife Nadezhda, who, in her essential book *Hope Against Hope*, can be found forgiving Akhmatova for alienating Osip's affections. Nadezhda Mandelstam knew that the glamorous Akhmatova, like Tolstoy's Natasha Rostova, needed to be adored: she was a vamp by nature. If there had been no revolution, Akhmatova could have made her seductive nature her subject, in the manner of Edna St. Vincent Millay but to even greater effect. History denied her the opportunity to sublimate her frailties. It made her a heroine instead. There were crueller fates available in Stalinist Russia, but that one was cruel enough.

What we have to grasp is that it needn't have happened to her. History needn't have been like that. That's what history is: the story of everything that needn't have been like that. We also have to grasp that art proves its value by still mattering to people who have been deprived of every other freedom: indeed instead of mattering less, it matters more. For the Russians, Akhmatova was iconic not just for what she had done, but for the majesty of what she had not been allowed to do. An admirer of Akhmatova, the writer and intellectual Nina Berberova, left the Soviet Union in 1921, the very year that Gumilev was shot and Akhmatova was proscribed. Written in her last years, Berberova's delightful book about her life in the Russian emigration, *The Italics Are Mine* (1991), traces the whole tragically fascinating experience of exile far into her old age (she died in America in 1993). In the book she tells the story of the Writers' Library, the bookshop in Moscow where the books of the old intelligentsia were traded for food after the Revolution. If there had been no revolution, the Writers' Library would have gone on being one of the most enchanting bookshops in the world. You could eat there, have a drink, write a poem, fall in love, and, above all, speak freely. It was a literary café. All too soon, there were no such places left in Russian cities. There was nowhere to lead the life of the mind except the mind. That thought would reduce us to despair if it were not for the evidence that humanist values are real, not notional: they persist even in conditions of calculated deprivation. 1947 was a particularly bad year for Akhmatova. Every effort was made to deprive her of almost everything except life. Yet she could call herself rich. With Pushkin to read, she still had "lyrical wealth." The belief that such wealth is our real and inextinguishable fortune is the belief behind this book.

PETER ALTENBERG

❣ ❣ ❣

In the café life that was such a feature of old Vienna from before the turn of the nineteenth century until the triumph of the Nazis, Peter Altenberg (1859–1919) was the key figure. His name now is not much mentioned outside the German-speaking lands, but for all the greater names on the scene who went on to acquire international reputations, Altenberg remained a touchstone, perhaps partly because he knew no worldly success at all. He had been born into a prosperous family but chose to be a panhandler. To his fellow Jews he was a *Schnorrer*: a borrower of money. He slept in flophouses and had no real address beyond his favourite café. But all the writers knew that he was carrying a treasure. He had an unrivalled capacity to pour a whole view of life, a few cupfuls at a time, into the briefest of paragraphs, and I am glad that his quotation appears so early on. It comes from an early World War I collection of his bits and pieces that I found in a warehouse on Staten Island in 1983, so when I sat down to read the book in a café on Columbus Avenue, this miniature masterpiece had been nearly seventy years on its journey before it hit me between the eyes like a micro-meteorite.

❧ ❧ ❧

There are only two things that can destroy a healthy man:
love trouble, ambition, and financial catastrophe. And
that's already three things, and there are a lot more.
— PETER ALTENBERG, *FECHSUNG*

ALTENBERG SPENT A lot of time scratching for a living, but when he wrote at all, he could write like that: a world view in two sentences. Sometimes he could do it in four words. One of Altenberg's many young loves had tearfully protested that his interest in her was based only (*nur*) on sexual attraction. Altenberg asked, *"Was ist so nur?"* (What's so only?) In Vienna before, during and after World War I, Altenberg was everybody's favourite scrounger, saloon barfly and no-hoper. Far outstripping him in prestige as recognized writers, Arthur Schnitzler and Hugo von Hofmannsthal both admired him. So did Robert Musil. The supreme stylist Alfred Polgar—later acknowledged by even Thomas Mann as the greatest master of German in modern times—often acknowledged a creative debt to Alternberg and edited his unpublished papers after his death. Kafka said that Altenberg could discover "the splendours of this world like cigarette butts in the ashtrays of coffee houses." The great satirist Karl Kraus, himself a Jew but equivocal about it, suspended his usual intolerance of Jewish-born writers in Altenberg's case, treating his mentally unstable protégé with patience, love and financial support. All these established writers had talents big enough to light a fire. Altenberg produced only sparks, but the sparks were dazzling.

Not many of Alternberg's writings extended for more than a few paragraphs, scribbled at the café table in the intervals between cadging drinks. More diligent writers and intellectuals cherished him as their other, less trammelled self, devoid of ambition and the obligations of honesty. He was an ideal for men weighed down with ideals. Later on in New York, the semi-mythical Little Joe Gould was celebrated by E. E. Cummings and Joseph Mitchell for the same reason, with the difference that Little Joe Gould was always "working on" a magnum opus that would never see the light of day, whereas Altenberg was a real literary figure. In the late twentieth century, Jeffrey Bernard played the

same part in London, but Bernard, by the end, was a man more written about than writing. Collections of Altenberg's scraps and shavings
were published regularly, even during World War I, and café-based
philosophers would quote the best bits.

Even by real scholars—the majestic polymath Egon Friedell was
only one example—Altenberg was much envied as a Falstaffian scholar
gypsy, and envied not least for his hit status with beautiful young
women. His deadbeat eyes, drooping moustache and chaotic personal
arrangements had their inevitable success with trainee bluestockings
inexperienced enough to want the mature male artist of their dreams
to look the part. Though he had a questionable taste for prostitutes,
and an even more questionable taste for underage working-class girls,
he did not withhold his attention from the aspiring young female intellectuals. Thus many a well-favoured daughter of good family was
inveigled back to his cheap hotel by Altenberg, where she would find
to her disillusionment that the scrutinizing of her poems was only the
second item on his agenda. Altenberg sugared the pill for his male
audience by making his amatory conquests sound like disasters, but
nobody was fooled. As a literary stratagem, however, self-deprecation
had the advantage of releasing him into comedy. With due allowance
for the intervening ocean, he was Ring Lardner's equal in getting a lifetime of failure into a short written span. You would think that there
could be no match for the compression of Lardner's question-and-
answer dialogue about the family in the car ("'Daddy, are we lost?'
'Shut up,' he explained"). But "What's so only?" is even neater.
Altenberg amply fulfilled Georg Christoph Lichtenberg's requirement
that the best writers should make passing remarks lesser spirits might
turn into a book. Altenberg made nothing except the passing remarks.
They were rarely aphorisms—too much like hard work—but they had
resonance. "What's so only?" resonates. He says just that much, but he
commands us to say more. The rest of the story is in our own heads. It
might be continued as follows.

The saying goes that men play at love to get sex while women play
at sex to get love. The second half of the antithesis is the more likely
to be found interesting, because the first sounds closer to the truth.
There are reasons, however, for questioning it further. Lenny Bruce
said, "A man will fuck mud." He also said that a man will have sex with

a venetian blind. He would not have got the laugh if it had not been a laugh of recognition. A lot of men will do a lot to get laid. But that doesn't necessarily mean they play at love. It seems far more likely that love plays with them. Theories of male genetic programming have long been under assault from feminists, who would like to believe that men's behaviour is socially determined, including the claims they make to be impelled by instinct. The belief is understandable and even commendable: justice benefits when a man can't blame biology after doing the wrong thing, even if it suffers when thinking the wrong thing becomes a crime too. But there can be no serious doubt, except from those who do not feel it, that the initial attraction of a man towards a woman is felt with the comprehensive force of a revelation. The sentimental view is not the romantic one, but the supposedly realistic one that love follows lust and grows through knowledge. It would be better for all concerned to admit that love hits with full force straight away.

Nor does the view that romantic love is a modern idea quite wash. Leaving aside Virgil's Dido and Aeneas, there is not much transcendental romantic love in Latin poetry. In Lucretius, lovers tear strips off each other, but with no hint of the spiritual either before or after. Propertius complained of how he was made to suffer. "Cynthia to my great undoing first ensnared me with her eyes / Though no other woman had ever touched me." Nobody was raised to a higher state unless you count Catullus, who, while he was clearly mad for women, never showed the same tenderness for any of them that he did for his dead brother. But there is at least one incandescent instance of it in Greek poetry, which came first. Troy burned because Paris was smitten by Helen's beauty: it is practically the first thing that happens in literature. It was to happen again often. David saw Bathsheba bathing and was ready to kill for her. The event is refined by Dante and Petrarch but the initial impact is the same: Beatrice, seen from a distance, inspires *The Divine Comedy*, and Laura, never possessed, possesses the author throughout the cycle of the *Canzoniere*, Petrarch's long series of incrementally varying viewpoints on the one event, written down as if he were walking very slowly around a diamond mounted for exhibition. And the two greatest Italian poets were not founding a tradition: they were giving a new impetus to one that already existed. The courtly love tradition, which has continued to our own day and at all levels—the most touching Tin Pan Alley and Broadway songs are about not getting the girl—has for its chief concern the stricken poet's *visione amorosa* of the woman who remains unknown. Love has not been increased through intimacy with her qualities and might well, had it happened, have been reduced by it. (Until Carmen made his life hell, Don Jose thought she was heaven on earth.) In Shakespeare, the reward for adoration is the interchange of enchanted speech, and for possession it is trouble and death.

Donne and Marvell get the beloved into bed, but lavish all their lyricism on reassuring her that she remains as attractive as she was when she played it coy. Pope's poetry might seem to scorn courtly love, but the poet's mockery of trivial young ladies is a clear attempt to offset the boggling effect of their beauty on a mind deprived of the bodily means to do anything else about it. His prattling sweethearts are so interchangeable that a part will do for the whole. *The Rape of the Lock* comes close to fetishism: a lock of hair has the same effect that a curved shape under the bed-covers had on Casanova if he thought it might be female. Pushkin felt the same way about a pretty woman's feet. Yeats, the great self-examining poet of modern times, fell in love often and with ease, granting his wife the cold comfort that he was unworthy of her steadfastness. On the strength of their appearance he would attribute qualities to his young companions that they did not really have: a common response, which would hardly happen unless the emotion were so complete in itself that the imagination had to be called in to help supply its object. The tendency for the love object to grow younger as the genius grows older was exemplified with embarrassing clarity by Goethe, who was in his seventy-fourth year when he fancied his chances with the nineteen-year-old Ulrike von Levetzow. The embarrassment was enormous, but one of the results of the embarrassment was the great poem we call "The Marienbad Elegy." The most intelligent man of his time was obviously in the grip of a soul-consuming passion that had not much to do with the intellect, which was an accomplice—he thought her mind as beautiful as her face—but scarcely the instigator. Instinct looks the more likely culprit: an instinct that can draw on the complete aesthetic apparatus of the brain. The greater the mind, the bigger the fool. Hazlitt's *Liber amoris* is an anatomy of the subject: an operation on himself, without anaesthetic.

Men who fall in love easily and often should do the world the favour of not taking their own passions personally. Above all they should do that favour to womankind. Albert Camus, in the week before he was killed, wrote to five different women and addressed each of them as the great love of his life. He probably meant it every time, but had long ago learned the dire consequences for those he adored of making them pay the emotional price for his laughably transferable fixation. His women forgave him because his unforced charm was infinite and when it came to a scene he was ready to concede that he was frivolous. A realistic self-appraisal brought with it the blessing of a fair-minded benevolence: he might cast a pretty young actress in one of his plays because she had gained his favour, but he never threw one out because she had lost it. George Balanchine, pitiably, was less civilized. The great choreographer ruled the New York City Ballet as a feifdom, with the *droit de seigneur* among his privileges. The older he became, the more consuming his love affairs with his young ballerinas. Often, by their own testimony, it was to their benefit, but his behaviour towards the sublimely gifted Suzanne Farrell was despicable. When Farrell fell in love with and married a young dancer, Balanchine dismissed her from the company, thereby injuring her career for a crucial decade. By the time she came back, it had become clear that he had injured his own as well. Still vivid in the dance world, the memory of Diaghilev's artistically ruinous paroxysm of jealousy about Nijinsky—previously Diaghilev's obedient lover, Nijinsky went straight in order to marry a ballerina, whereupon Diaghilev dismissed him from the company, thereby irretrievably weakening its future—should have told Balanchine he was making an unforgivable mistake. It probably did, but he made the mistake anyway. Balanchine being an undoubted genius, the fact that he could let even one among his many idealized passions dislocate his creativity is a sure measure of the brain-curdling intensity with which an old man can be drawn to a young woman. His great ballet for Farrell, *Don Quixote*, in which he cast himself as the Don, was a clear attempt to lay the ghost. The *pas de deux* in which the raddled hidalgo declares his hopeless love is sad beyond expression, although insufficiently expiatory: he should have lashed himself for penitence.

In our own day, Philip Larkin had the least courtly, or anyway least courtly-love, of mentalities: enslaving himself by handing his heart and soul to a female was the last thing on his mind. The submissiveness that began with the troubadors ended with him. When it came to love (or "love again" as he called it in his last years), he saved himself in advance, by writing a poem. Writing the poem was not his way in, it was his ticket out. But the revelatory power of love at first sight was one of his constant themes. "Latest face" meant what it said: just one more in a succession of beautiful faces was enough to make the whole tumult start again. Throughout history, all the literary evidence suggests that men are fools for beauty and will attribute every virtue to comeliness until experience disabuses them of the illusion. Acumen is no protection, because the initial effect is not assembled from particular judgements: it happens all at once, with the holistic suddenness of a baby reacting to its mother's voice. Female beauty has always been interpreted by men as the earthly incarnation of a divine benevolence. The occasional evil angel, from Salome to Kundry and from Lilith to Lulu, is a consciously perverse thematic variation, and would have no artistic value if the expectation were not the opposite. For men, the first and shamefully unthinking flood of worship is the opposite of casual. It is monumental, and Peter Altenberg got it in a phrase. What's so only? He had self-knowledge. He could have added the lack of it to his long list of the two things that can ruin a man's life.

LOUIS ARMSTRONG

Louis Armstrong was born in New Orleans in 1900 and died at home in New York in 1971, having done, in the intervening years, as much as anyone since Lincoln to change the history of the United States. The theory that art can have no direct impact on politics has the advantage of staving off wishful thinking, but it takes a beating when you think of what Armstrong did, or helped to do. Jazz would not have been the same without him, and the whole artistic history of the United States in the twentieth century, quite apart from the country's political history leading up to the civil rights movement, would not have been the same without jazz. There was no easy conquest, and Armstrong himself was the object of prejudice right to the end. He had to be brave every night he went to work. All the more edifying, then, that he himself was colour-blind when it came to the music he had helped to invent.

Those pretty notes went right through me.
—LOUIS ARMSTRONG,
TALKING ABOUT BIX BEIDERBECKE

B EFORE WE LET these words stir up bad memories, we should console ourselves with how they once started the long process of putting fallacies to rest. The first fallacy was that white men could not play
jazz. Bix Beiderbecke was white; Louis Armstrong was the strongest
creative force in the early history of the music; so if Armstrong thought
this highly of Beiderbecke, it follows that at least one white man could
play jazz. Everything was against Armstrong's forming an objective
judgement. Armstrong had good cause to believe that jazz had been
invented by black musicians, who had been systematically robbed of
the rewards. Segregation dictated that it would have been inconceivable for Armstrong to hold Beiderbecke's chair with the touring
orchestra of Paul Whiteman, whose very name might have been chosen
by a satirist to illustrate what black musicians were up against. Armstrong and Beiderbecke would never have been allowed to play together
in public. The magnitude of the insult would have excused a bitter view.
Yet Armstrong thought Beiderbecke was wonderful, and said so.

Nevertheless, and sometimes all the more, the fallacy lingered on
until long after World War II. At Sydney University in the late fifties I
was introduced to New Orleans jazz by well-heeled college students
who had been brought up listening to the shellac record collections of
their well-travelled fathers. These were still the early days of vinyl. The
definitive Jelly Roll Morton LP had just come out and was used as a
teaching aid by proselytes for New Orleans jazz, with the Louis Armstrong Hot Five and Hot Seven collections waiting further up the line
for advanced students. It was held to be axiomatic that you had to
appreciate the drive and syncopation of Morton's Red Hot Peppers
playing "Black Bottom Stomp" and "The Chant" before you could
move on to the challenging, ensemble-shattering solo subtleties of
Armstrong playing "West End Blues." It went without question that
jazz was black music. One of the set books of our informal jazz faculty
actually said so: *Shining Trumpets* by Rudi Blesh. In retrospect, Blesh's
book is a touching example of inverse racism: a white scholar, himself
from a beleaguered minority, he was claiming, on behalf of blacks,
exclusive rights to an art form. The white clarinettist Mezz Mezzrow
had done the same by immersing himself in a black culture: he did
everything but black up. It was Jim Crow in reverse. Mezzrow's barely
coherent book *Really the Blues* was on the course. Fated to supply the

dull passages in some of the finest records Sidney Bechet ever made, Mezzrow was an average player and a worse than average writer, but his sacrificial passion was food for thought.

Unfortunately the thought was likely to be scrambled by self-indulgent, unearned empathy. The emotion was admirable—disgust at racial inequality—but the speculative edifice that arose from it was painfully shaky on its base. Later on, Terry Southern questioned even the emotion, when he wrote a short story about a white jazz fan trying to make up for his inadequacies by hanging out with the black musicians. But it didn't need Southern to put the whole idea into doubt. The idea was Jim Crow—white prejudice against blacks—stood on its head, and would have seemed so from the beginning if there had not been such a concerted effort on the part of white liberal commentators to play a role in fighting Jim Crow when it was standing the right way up. The effort was commendable, but it depended on the suppression of evidence. Black creativity in jazz was everything the inverted racists said it was, and more. But white creativity was real, and could be discounted only at the cost of obfuscation—a high price to pay for feeling virtuous. By the end of my Sydney University years, the pre-war Benny Goodman small group recordings had been collected onto an LP and were among my regular listening. The crisp ensemble playing and the lilting sequences of short solos were just as dazzling as anything from Morton or Armstrong. Goodman was white. End of argument. But the argument had been over for more than thirty years. It was over when Armstrong went to hear Beiderbecke at the Savoy. If Armstrong hadn't known something was up, he would never have gone.

Even without Armstrong's generous testimony, it would be foolish to admit unquestioned the assumption of automatic black supremacy in a given musical art-form. It cuts out too much white achievement. You can still hear, from black ideologues and their white sympathizers, that Fred Astaire couldn't really dance. He is held not to have possessed the proper, syncopated improvisational skills of Bill "Bojangles" Robinson, who could lead and drag the beat with different strata of his body simultaneously. There might be something to it. Astaire rarely swayed a hip. Even in mid-miracle, the armature of his body was upright: underneath, he was strictly ballroom. But when you consider what Astaire could do, the idea that he should be measured by what he couldn't is absurd. It should have been patently absurd, but there was a political aspect, which applied beyond the kingdom of the dance to the world of American music in general. White men were in control, and they robbed the blacks. Armstrong never saw a dollar of royalties from all his Hot Five and Hot Seven recordings: there were more than sixty of them, they sold in the millions, but for too much of the rest of his life they didn't save him from a single week of one-night stands. His Hollywood earnings bought him the occasional vacation, but the royalties from his early masterpieces never materialized.

The white men not only took the money, they took the opportunites. Bojangles never got the chance to be Fred Astaire. Billie Holiday bravely refused the demeaning coon-turn roles that Hollywood offered her. On top of the ravages of her abused childhood, her frustrations as an artist drove her to drugs, and her whole tragedy—the tragedy of black talent in a white business—was part of the picture evoked by her signature tune "Strange Fruit." The song is about lynch law but so was her life. Bessie Smith, Charlie Parker, Charlie Christian—you could make a long list of victims just on the level of genius, let alone of mere talent. Even when you take due note of the equally long list of those who never lost control of their lives—Ella Fitzgerald is a long list all by herself—the cruel scope of the injustice still shrieks to heaven. The joy of the music is populated with unsleeping ghosts, and anyone who doesn't see them isn't using his eyes. But it's a bad reason not to use our ears, which will hear, if we let them, an awkward truth. Nothing can redress the flagrant inequalities of the past.

We can, however, refrain from compounding the insult. A man like Benny Goodman, for example, can't possibly be fitted into a schematic history that would base itself on the white exploitation of a black invention. He carried within himself the only answer to the conflict, and, as things have turned out, he presaged the outcome: a measure of tolerance and mutual respect, and at least a step towards a colour-blind creative world. He was born as poor as any black; he was Chicago, meat-packing poor; as poor as you could get. Being white, he was able to translate his prodigious talent into economic power: the very power to which black musicians, however successful, were always denied access. But Goodman used his power to break the race barrier. Though his mixed small groups existed mainly in the recording studios and only rarely on stage—the Carnegie Hall appearance with Count Basie was strictly an interlude—the music they made was the emblem of a political future, and in the aesthetic present it was a revelation. It is still a revelation, because in aesthetics the present is the only tense there is. There will always be a few diehards who deduce from those three-minute masterworks that Goodman's clarinet was metronomic compared to Charlie Christian's guitar. But the diehards were born dead. They have had no living thing to say since Armstrong heard Beiderbecke's pretty notes and saluted an equal.

If the two avatars had the same stature, how could they sound so different? It raises another question. Armstrong, with everything against him, knew how to lead an ordered life. Beiderbecke put as much energy into self-destruction as into creation. His father didn't want him to play jazz. Trying to prove to his father that his music would get him somewhere, the prodigal son sent home copies of all his records. His father never listened to them. You could call that a psychological obstacle: but there were no other obstacles that began to compare with what Armstrong had to put up with every day. The main reason Beiderbecke could not stop drinking was that he was an alcoholic. His short adult life was a long suicide. But the cautionary tale had an awkward corollary: his underlying melancholy got into his tone, and helped to make it unmistakable. Armstrong could play blues with unmatched inventiveness, but his soul moved in jump-time: a sharp, staccato attack was basic to him. Crackling excitement was his natural mode. Beiderbecke, on the other hand, was blue to the roots. Even his upbeat solos were saturated with prescient grief, and the slow numbers remind you of Ford Madox Ford's catchline for *The Good Soldier*: this is the saddest story ever told.

I listened to most of Beiderbecke's Jean Goldkette and Paul Whiteman sides before I left Sydney (even the most fanatical New Orleans purists among my friends seemed to have them on hand), but it wasn't until I was down and out in London in the early 1960s that I first heard "I'm Coming, Virginia." An Australian homosexual ballet buff—a lot of Australian homosexuals were still prudently sending themselves into exile in those days—persuaded me to sit down and listen to a piece of music he held to be the most beautiful thing in his life: better even than *Swan Lake*. (I wonder if he lived long enough to see *Swan Lake* danced by boys: I hope so.) For a while "I'm Coming, Virginia"—I used to make rude jokes about the title, but they conveyed my appreciation—became the most beautiful thing in my life too. The coherence of its long Bix solo still provides me with a measure of what popular art should be like: a generosity of effects on a simple frame. The melodic line is particularly ravishing at its points of transition: there are moments when even a silent pause is a perfect note, and always there is a piercing sadness to it, as if the natural tone of the cornet, the instrument of reveille, were the first sob before weeping. Armstrong could probably have done that too, but he didn't want to. He wasn't like that. Beiderbecke was, always: his loveliest-ever outpouring was an example of the artistic freedom that can be attained through being trapped in a personality. Perhaps for personal reasons, I took it as an encouragement. I wanted to write prose sentences that way, and lines of poetry: as a shining sequence of desolate exuberance, of playful grief. I loved the spareness of his technique: a wordless song with one note per syllable and no lapses into mere virtuosity. It helped me to conceive the notion that the only permissible obscurity is an excess of vividness, or the suggestive hiatus that comes from removing the connecting tissue between transparencies. In my last two years before I left Sydney I had moved on to bebop and modern jazz in general, but although I tried to enjoy some of the headlong *sprezzatura* stuff I always thought that it was only in the slow numbers that the virtuosi really showed what they could do. I liked it best when Thelonious Monk dragged his hands like tired feet in "Round Midnight," and my favourite Charlie Parker number was the last-ditch, half-ruined but drenchingly lyrical "My Old Flame." At Cambridge I was still listening to that one almost every night.

Mechanisms of influence are hard to trace. Writers tend to think that the way they write was influenced by literature, and of course scholars make a living by following that same assumption. But a writer's ideal of a properly built sentence might just as well have been formed when he was still in short pants and watched someone make an unusually neat sandcastle. He might have got his ideals of composition, colour and clean finish from a bigger boy who made a better model aeroplane. To the extent that I can examine my own case of such inadvertently assimilated education, I learned a lot about writing from watching an older friend sanding down the freshly dried paint on his rebuilt motorbike so that he could give it another coat: he was after the deep, rich, pure glow. But for the way I thought prose should move I learned a lot from jazz. From the moment I learned to hear them in music, syncopation and rhythm were what I wanted to get into my writing. And to stave off the double threat of brittle chatter and chesty verve, I also wanted the measured, disconsolate tread of the blue reverie. Jazz was a brimming reservoir of these contending qualities. Eventually I was listening to so much classical music that I left jazz aside, but I never thought that I had left it behind. Later on, when I took holidays from classical music, it was Tin Pan Alley and Broadway that attracted me, and there were years on end when I listened to everything happening in pop and rock. The second lustrum of the sixties was a particularly good time for that: you could slide a coin into a jukebox and hear Marvin Gaye singing "I Heard It Through the Grapevine," and wonder whether there had ever been, or would ever be again, anything quite so addictive as the triumphal march of a Tamla anthem.

Jazz, however, was always there underneath all that, and begging to be revisited. I couldn't muster an affection for John Coltrane or Sonny Rollins—I don't think I was meant to—but the tradition that led up to them still had many glories to reveal. The great period of Duke Ellington was a constellation of glories that made Berg and Webern seem very thin gruel. Listening on the same day to the Lester Young quintet and a string quintet by Ravel, I could hear no incongruity: they seemed comparable events to me, although there was not much evidence at the time to suggest that the same was true for anybody else. Such catholicity of taste has only recently become respectable. At the time when the divinely gifted and cruelly doomed cellist Jacqueline du Pré was breaking our hearts with Elgar, the boys around her were thought rather daring when they vamped and jammed a few jazz figures on their strings. But the argument about a supposed hierarchy of genres would have continued much longer if Leonard Bernstein had not put a stop to it. In the first chapter of his television series about music, after giving brief, instantly enchanting examples from the classical repertoire, Broadway, Tin Pan Alley, jazz, rock and pop, he said the only thing that mattered: "I love it all." He had jazz in his blood. His show song

"Lonely Town" is a melody that Bix Beiderbecke would have loved to play, and it would not have been composed in quite the same way if the broken heroes of jazz had not first lived their dangerous lives. The paradox was that the most persuasive witness to the lyrical distillation of Bix's broken life, Louis Armstrong, was a man whose life was never broken, even by the full force of America's most tenacious social malignancy, white prejudice. If it is a political nightmare no longer, Armstrong's shining trumpet certainly contributed to the wake-up call. But there is only so much art can do against injustice, and the blues, from which jazz took flight, were an embodiment of the sad truth that much beauty begins as a consolation for what can't be mended.

RAYMOND ARON

❣ ❣ ❣

Raymond Aron (1905–1983) began as a sociologist but made it clear from the start that the subject would not restrict him to social facts. Instead, it would release him into political analysis, and from there into general philosophy on the scale of Durkheim, Pareto and Max Weber. The strength of his voluminous theoretical work, however, would always be that his wider views were backed up by minutely observed concrete detail: his journalism was his bedrock. One of the few French thinkers who were equally at home in Germany, he saw during the Weimar Republic that the left intelligentsia hated capitalism, and hence social democracy as well, far too much to think that Nazism could be worse. As George Orwell did later, Aron realized that the professed enemy of Nazi totalitarianism was itself totalitarian. He carried this insight with him into exile in London during World War II.

After the war, he emerged as the great opponent of the French left wing, and especially of its most illustrious figurehead, Jean-Paul Sartre. Beyond their respective deaths, the contest between the two great names continued to define the frontiers of argument in French political thought right up to recent times. "Better to be wrong with Sartre than right with

Aron" is still meant to be a slogan testifying to political seriousness, rather than to intellectual suicide. For French
gauchiste thinkers, even after they had given up hope on the
Soviet Union, liberal democracy was fundamentally suspect
because it had capitalism for an economic motor. For Aron,
liberal democracy was the only way ahead to social justice: it
could be, and had to be, criticized in detail, but never dismissed in its entirety. Since ideologists of every stamp would
always attempt to do so, that made ideology itself the perpetual enemy of realism. Liberal democracy, based on an historic
consciousness, could afford to reveal even the most unpalatable truths, whereas ideology was bound to conceal them. Of
the comparatively small proportion of Aron's enormous body
of work that has been translated into English, *The Opium of the
Intellectuals* (1955) can still be regarded as the best introduction
to his thought, and indeed to modern intellectual history in its
entirety. For readers of French, he can be met more briefly, but
almost as effectively, in *Le Spectateur engagé* (1981), a long
interview of the type that French publishers do so well.

> ... the liberal believes in the permanence of humanity's
> imperfection, he resigns himself to a regime in which the
> good will be the result of numberless actions, and never
> the object of a conscious choice. Finally, he suscribes to
> the pessimism that sees, in politics, the art of creating the
> conditions in which the vices of men will
> contribute to the good of the state.
> — RAYMOND ARON, *L'OPIUM DES
> INTELLECTUELS*, P. 292

S UCH WAS THE central belief that put Aron on a collision course
with all the radical thinkers in Paris after World War II. He could-
n't have put it more clearly; and if he couldn't, nobody could. Essayists
who stake everything on writing the kind of spangled style that glitters
in the limelight near the top of the tent must sometimes wish, as they
sweat to keep a sentence alive, that the tightrope could be laid out

along the ground. There are essayists who write plainly and yet are duller still because of it. But the most enviable essayists are those who can write plainly and generate an extra thrill from doing so, demonstrating a capacity to clarify an intricate line of thought in their heads before laying it out sequentially on the page. Always matching a decorum of procedure to their weight of argument, they can make the more spectacular practitioner look meretricious. Foremost among these cool masters of expository prose must be ranked Raymond Aron.

Most of Aron's vast output remains untranslated in the original French, but enough of his books have been brought into English to give some idea of his importance, and some of those books are indispensable—most prominently *The Opium of the Intellectuals*, which remains to this day, after all the years since it first appeared in 1955, the best debunking of Marxism as a theology, and the most piercing analysis of why that theology, during the twentieth century, should have had so pervasive and baleful an influence in the free nations. Even now, every first-year university student in the world should read that book, if only because the poised force of Aron's prose style gives such a precise idea of the strength and passion of the consensus he was trying to rebut.

It should be said straight away that his clarity of view was not attained from a right-wing viewpoint. Though many a prominent figure of international anti-communism paid tribute to him after his death—Henry Kissinger, McGeorge-Bundy, Norman Podhoretz and Arthur Schlesinger Jr. were among the Americans who acknowledged his example—Aron himself began on the left and stayed there until the end. But he was always disgusted by the thirst of putatively humanitarian intellectuals for the lethal certitudes of Marxist dogma. As early as the 1950s he was proclaiming the need for a new party, *de la gauche non conformiste*. A sizeable party of the nonconformist left never really arrived, but the massed ranks of the conformist left were not fond of the idea that somebody so prominent had called for one. Many of his fellow French intellectuals never forgave him for his heresy. (Sartre, who respected Aron's credentials—Aron, unlike Sartre, had always been the kind of star student who actually read the books—took particular care to discredit his opinions: a potent endorsement.) A few of them were grateful, and they were among the best. Jean-François Revel, François Furet, Alain Finkielkraut and the small handful of other French writers on politics who have managed to defend their independence of thought while surrounded by a tenaciously lingering pseudo-progressive consensus have all had Raymond Aron as a fore-bear, and have usually been polite enough to acknowledge his pioneering faith in the strength, and not just the virtues, of liberal democracy.

There had always been plenty of intellectuals ready to pay lip service to the virtues, but they doubted the strength. Because, from the French viewpoint, liberalism had been able to do so little in staving off the Nazi brand of totalitarianism, it was thought that only another brand of absolute power—the Soviet brand—could fill the vacuum. The erroneous view that the Red Army had won the war all on its own helped to reinforce this illusion. In Czechoslavakia, in 1948, the same misguided humility led the whole liberal intelligentsia to abdicate from its responsibilities in advance. It never came to that in France, but it came close enough. At this distance it is hard to conjure up just how thick and poisonous a miasma of bad faith a man like Aron was trying to fight his way through, and just how honest, patient and brave he had to be in order to do so. He succeeded in the end. Though the French will probably go on thinking proudly of Sartre as the Victor Hugo of political philosophy—the most mentions, the most mistresses, the biggest funeral—Aron's name is nowadays quite often invoked by those who believe that there is an alternative to getting everything brazenly wrong. The alternative is to get a few things modestly right. Bernard-Henri Lévy will probably not find it expedient to drop his posturing slogan that it was better to be wrong with Sartre than right with Aron, but to the extent that Levy's political arguments are considerable, he sounds like Aron, not Sartre.

Aron is consequently the best reason for continuing to think of Paris as a capital city of political philosophy. As a Jew, he would not have survived the German Occupation long had he remained in France. Any possible illusion about what the Nazis were up to had been removed for him when he stood beside the historian Golo Mann in the Berlin Operplatz in 1933 and watched the storm troopers burn books. But when the Nazis reached Paris, Aron exemplified the one advantage of being a designated victim. His moral choice was made for him, and he could spend the war in London, with a relatively clear conscience. Sartre and Camus were only two of the many thinkers about politics who, being gentiles, could stay in Paris and think about politics there if they chose. It was a dubious privilege. The Nazis, operating with a subtlety rare for them, managed to corrupt nearly everyone in the Parisian literary world to some degree. The essential trick was to offer the intellectuals the opportunity to continue their careers if they kept their protests suitably muted. The first result was a widespread but tacit collaboration. The less common, overt collaboration could safely be denounced when the Germans packed up and ran. Claiming to be the instruments of *l'Épuration* (the Purification), self-appointed tribunals—"tribunal" is always a bad word in French history—dealt out the punishment. Such blatant collaborators as Robert Brasillach and Pierre Drieu la Rochelle had been asking for it, and one way or another they got it. But many of the denouncers had themselves collaborated in a less flagrant way. A pervasive sense of having been implicated, however passively, led to the second result: a long silence that really amounted to a cover-up.

What really happened under the Occupation is a story that, even sixty years later, is still coming out. For decades it didn't come out at all. The first accounts of any scope didn't appear until the 1980s, and the general conclusions have not yet been fully drawn. But one of them should be that the Propaganda Abteilung (Propaganda Division, also often called the Propaganda Staffel) succeeded in its main aim. Apart from the brave few who went underground and fought at the risk of their lives, the French intellectuals gave the Nazis little trouble, and were morally compromised as a consequence. Not even Camus, a writer whose stature depended on his very real capacity for translating his ideals of authenticity into action, was entirely untouched. But at least Camus had the grace to admit that his Resistance activities had not amounted to much, and at least he had the humanity to deplore the excesses of the post-Liberation witch-hunt against the more shameless collaborators. Sartre, whose underground activities had never amounted to anything except a secret meeting on Wednesday to decide whether there should be another meeting the following Tuesday, not only claimed the status of Resistance veteran but called down vengeance on people whose behaviour had not really been all that much more reprehensible than his own. The sad truth was that he, even more conspicuously than Camus, owed his wartime fame as a writer and thinker to Nazi tolerance, for which a price had to be paid. The price was to lace one's eloquence with a judiciously timed silence. The trick was to pay up and make it look like compulsion. So it was, but only if you considered your career as indispensable—something artists find it all too easy to do. They are even encouraged to, in the name of an ideal.

When you consider the mental calibre of the people involved, Paris under the Occupation thus becomes the twentieth century's premier field of study in which to reach the depressing conclusion that even the most liberal convictions buckle very easily under totalitarian pressure, unless there are extraordinary reserves of character to sustain them. The further consideration—that to deplore the absence of such fortitude might be illiberal in itself—is more depressing still, but should be faced. Apart from permanent outsiders such as homosexuals, petty thieves, and the very poor, only young people on their own had a real opportunity to be brave under the Occupation, and even they had to be saints to take it when death was the likely result. Behind the Nazi show of tact in Paris was the threat of absolute violence. The threat rarely had to be made actual. The threatened were too smart. Their smartness was well-known to the Nazis who ran the show, some of whom were great admirers of French culture. Receptions were held regularly at that most fashionable of restaurants, the Tour d'Argent. French cultural figures who turned up met Nazis who seemed well aware that Cocteau was more refined than anything they had at home. Cocteau, who attended more than once, was slow to realize that once should have been enough.

Wartime Paris was a moral crucible. Aron was out of it, and we don't even have to ask ourselves how he would have behaved had he been in it. (We have to ask ourselves about ourselves, but not about him.) He would have been dead. Untouched and untainted in England, he could prepare his comeback. He came back as a commentator in the newspapers and magazines, deploying his rare gift of making a nuanced, learned and unfailingly critical analysis attractive as journalism. Because of him, the advocates of the seductive fantasy that the imperialism of the West was the most ruthless imperialism affecting Europe did not have it all their own way. But it took a long, hard slog before the illusion began to be dispelled that somehow Sartre was the serious thinker about politics and Aron the dilettante. At the heart of the anomaly was the almost universally shared assumption that those who favoured the declaredly progressive consensus were working for the betterment of mankind, while those who believed that liberal democracy was a better bet were working against it. Helping to make Aron even more unpalatable to the entrenched pseudo-left was his expertise in sociology: he actually knew something, for example, about how industries ran, how houses got built, and how ordinary people earned the money to pay for their groceries. A respect for humble fact is one of the qualities that keep his prose permanently fresh. He could, alas, be very grand. All too often, and especially towards the end, he was a bit too fond of drawing himself up to his full height. But he never lost contact with the earth. He never lost sight of the imperfection that debars mankind from utopia.

> Communist interpretation is never wrong. Logicians will
> object in vain that a theory which exempts itself from
> all refutations escapes from the order of truth.
> — RAYMOND ARON, L'OPIUM DES
> INTELLECTUELS, P. 144

After World War II, Raymond Aron was the French philospher who did most to offset the more famous Jean-Paul Sartre's support for communism. Albert Camus tried to offset it also, but his scholarly qualifications were held to be dubious. Nobody doubted Aron's. From the moment he published *L'Opium des intellectuels* in 1955, the French left-wing thinkers knew that they had a real fight on their hands. They didn't give up easily. Some of them still haven't. Aron was obliged to go on plugging away at the same theme. He had already said, before the war, that the Communist version of socialism was a secular religion. What remains puzzling is why he said so little about it while the war was on. Self-exiled to London, he wrote a long series of brilliant articles for the Free French periodical *La France Libre*, which were collected after the victory into three books, nowadays themselves collected into a single volume, *Chroniques de guerre*. In the entire text, Stalin is mentioned exactly twice, and neither time derogatively. Writing in the same city at the same time, George Orwell risked his reputation and income by insisting on a distinction between the Red Army, which was making such a great contribution to defeating Hitler, and the lethal regime behind it, which was bent on the extinction of all human values. Why did Aron not do something similar?

Perhaps the best answer is that he considered himself debarred from attacking an ally. Most of the damning analysis he made of Hitlerite tyranny could have been transferred with equal validity to Stalin, but for Aron to have explicitly done so would have detracted from his first object as a French patriot and as a Jew—the defeat of Nazi Germany. As it happened, Aron underestimated the effects of Vichy's enthusiastic collaboration with the occupying power on the Jewish Question. (In reality, there never was such a question, hence the capital "Q": an early instance of falsification through typography.) Never a true pessimist, although always pessimistic enough to be a realist, Aron was not equipped by temperament to guess that a Final Solution was under way. But he had no illusions about the essential barbarity of Nazi anti-Semitic policies and the general nihilism of the assault on humanism by the psychotic authoritarian right—he hadn't since well before the day he stood with Golo Mann and watched the Nazis burn the books. As a man who loved France, he condemned the Vichy regime first of all for the false patriotism which allowed it to participate in the Nazi attack on the very thing that made French civilization what it was: its humanist heritage. Hence his reluctance to make distinctions between the various columns of the Resistance, one of the most prominent of which, after June 1941 at any rate, was Communist. He believed in de Gaulle, but not enough to disbelieve that the Communist *résistants* had earned a hearing. Nevertheless, after the Liberation, he could be heard—and can still be heard, in "*L'Avenir des religions séculaires*" (The Future of the Secular Religions), one of the last chapters of *Chroniques de guerre*—reminding himself and his readership that, despite the immense prestige won by the Red Army for Stalin's regime and the people of the Soviet Union, a system of belief which confused the desirable and the inevitable was still a dogma.

As the war came to an end, Aron, who was always a liberal more on the left than those on the left were liberal, was convinced that some form of socialism would be bound to prevail in all the European countries. He just didn't want any of those forms to be totalitarian. When it became rapidly more apparent that a different view prevailed in the Kremlin, he prepared himself to write *L'Opium des intellectuels*. Acting more from artistic intuition than solid study, the scholastically unqualified but piercingly sympathetic Camus anticipated Aron's central precepts by four years with the relevant chapters of *L'Homme révolté* (*The Rebel*), but Aron's is incomparably the more coherent work. Camus had appropriated much of his knowledge of Soviet reality from Arthur Koestler, along with the warm attentions of Koestler's wife. Aron had done his own research, in a colder archive. Camus's book was part of his romance, along with the vilification that it attracted. (The starting gun for the vilification was fired by Sartre, who tried to counter his upstart protégé's arguments by discrediting his qualifications: a reflex among established gurus that we should learn to look out for.) Aron's book was an impersonal treatise much harder to criticize in detail. The English translation, *The Opium of the Intellectuals*, was meticulously carried out by the doyen of London literary editors, Terence Kilmartin, who did for Aron's prose what he later did for Proust's—he caught its measure, which in Aron's case was always, throughout his career, the measure of sobriety, comprehensive sanity, and a sad but resolute acknowledgement of history's intractable contingency. Kilmartin himself thought that Aron in his old age overdid the last quality. One day in the Black Friars pub near *The Observer*'s old location at the foot of Ludgate Hill, and long before I knew that Kilmartin had been the English translator of *L'Opium des intellectuels*, I was loudly praising Aron— at that stage I had read about three of his books out of thirty—when Kilmartin warned me that my new hero had become, in his declining years, so cautious about social innovation that he was "a bit, um, *right wing*." Kilmartin remained "a bit left wing" until his dying day: a proper ideal for a generous man, and one to copy.

> In the course of the last forty years, the only part of the
> world that has enjoyed peace is the continent divided
> between two zones of political civilization both
> of them armed with atomic bombs.
> — RAYMOND ARON, *LES DERNIÈRES ANNÉES*
> *DU SIÈCLE* (THE LAST YEARS OF THE
> CENTURY), P. 68

It was always a bad mistake to suppose that Aron was some kind of Gallic Dr. Strangelove who had learned to stop worrying and love the bomb. The contrary was true: the annihilation of the defenceless was at the centre of his worries. The point to grasp is that he had already seen it happen. Hitler had dropped the equivalent of an atomic bomb on at least six million perfectly innocent people—a weapon more than sixty times more powerful than the one that obliterated Hiroshima. Stalin had dropped the equivalent of an atomic bomb a hundred times more powerful on his own citizens. Those bombs had gone off in comparative silence, but Aron had understood the repercussions. For an era in which mass extermination was already not just a possibility but a reality, he presciently drew the conclusion that mutual assured destruction would be the only possible guarantee against disaster. Arguments that it was a guarantee for disaster did not impress him. Hence he was free from the debilitating impulse to warn the world that the arms race was dangerous. Obviously it was: too obviously to need pointing out. While whole generations of intellectuals on the left exhausted their thin talents in an effort to say something that Kate Bush couldn't sing—she, too, daringly believed that a nuclear weapon was an offence against love and peace—Aron occupied himself with the more useful task of examining the peace that had finally come to Europe, guaranteed at last by no further armed conflict being possible, no matter how thoroughly each side might plan for just such an eventuality. In fact the more concretely they planned, the more the possibility retreated into the notional. Political conflict, however, was clear-cut as never before, and here, for once, Marx was proved right. Economics determined the outcome.

The conflict began and ended in Berlin, with not a shot fired except against unarmed people attempting to cross the killing zone between East and West. Nobody was ever shot trying to cross from West to East. When the Wall went up in 1961, its creators called it the Anti-Fascist Protection Barrier. There were no longer any fascists who mattered, but the need for protection was real. East Germany, and by extension the Warsaw Pact countries taken as a totality, all had to protect themselves against the glare from the shop windows of West Berlin. Soviet bloc propaganda, faithfully echoed by *gauchiste* theorists in the West, asserted from the beginning that a free Berlin could not be free at all: its materialist attractiveness was being artificially enhanced by American imperialism as a forward outpost of West Germany, which, in its turn, had been artificially bolstered by the Marshall Plan as a capitalist armed camp. In actuality, the *Bundesrepublik* would have outperformed the German Democratic Republic whatever the circumstances, merely through its not being burdened with a centralized economy. The propaganda was a fantastic response to a real and potentially lethal threat, already identified by Stalin before 1948, when he made his one and only military move: an armed blockade. Without the resulting Berlin airlift, he would have succeeded in reducing the city by starving and freezing its inhabitants—methods to whose human consequences he had already proved himself indifferent when applying them on a much larger scale against his own people.

Plane-loads of food and coal were the Allied response, which could not have been mounted without the threat of atomic war to back it up. When Stalin lifted the blockade, his battle was lost and the war along with it. From then on, the armed aggression of the East German regime was against its own citizens. In 1953, they had to be put down with tanks. The Wall was put up because too many of them had fled: East Germany was dying from its brain-drain. The Wall ensured only that it would die more slowly, from envy. The confrontation over a divided Berlin, a divided Germany and a divided Europe was one long war, which at any previous point in history would unquestionably have been fought with weapons. It was called the Cold War mainly in derision, by those who had managed to convince themselves that it was all an American idea. But Aron was surely right to view as peace a war in which the winning side made every effort not to fire a shot, and the losing side could have no recourse to its weapons even in despair. There were many thinkers who disagreed with him over the issue, especially among the French left. But he had more trouble with agreement from the right. He succeeded in detaching himself, however, from the addled notion that the long drawn out defeat suffered by the Soviet bloc was a victory for the American Way of Life. He was too clear-sighted for that, and the triumph of his lifetime's effort as a writer on politics was to demonstrate that the believer in liberal democracy, and not the believer in an autocratic utopia, is the one with the hard head. By now everybody realizes that the West's material abundance was decisive. Aron was the first to realize that the fight would have to be without weapons. That was what he really meant by his famous slogan "Peace impossible, war unlikely." He meant that there could be no settled peace without the threat of war, but that the war would probably not happen, and as long as it didn't there was a kind of peace anyway: the only kind available at the time.

> An aggressor would not be able to destroy them without
> killing American personnel, which is to say, without
> running a grave danger of reprisals.
> — RAYMOND ARON, *PAIX ET GUERRE ENTRE*
> *LES NATIONS*, QUOTED IN *LES DERNIÈRES*
> *ANNÉES DU SIÈCLE*

Aron's *Realpolitik* was distinguished by being real, as *Realpolitik* in the strict sense rarely is. When he reminds us of Machiavelli, he reminds us of Machiavelli's truly hard-headed style, and not of the would-be hard-headedness of his political philosophy—a philosophy that was essentially nihilistic. Machiavelli, perhaps encouraged into admiration by the ruthlessness with which the Medicis would eventually rack him, wrote an invitation to despotism. Aron was writing a prescription for democracy. But the prescription had to include a realistic assessment of the totalitarian challenge (a menace even though the opportunists who made a career from opposing it amounted to a menace in themselves) and in that department realism had to include an acknowledgement that a nuclear confrontation between West and East could not be wished away. In this particular passage, he makes a point which was so antipathetic to the proponents of unilateral disarmament that they were obliged to rewrite history in order to circumvent it.

European countries *wanted* American atomic bombs based on their soil, not just to fulfil their NATO obligations but because the weapons were accompanied by American personnel. A Soviet strike against the weapons would thus constitute an attack on the United States, which would be unable to remain uninvolved in the conflict. Hence there could be no localized nuclear exchange: only a global one. Unilateralists, unable to accept that it was in the interests of a European country to play host to American nuclear weapons, were obliged to argue that they were an imposition. By extension, this argument fitted a picture in which the U.S.A. was an imperialist presence in Western Europe, like the Soviet Union in Eastern Europe. (Even further to the left lay the belief that the U.S.A. was the *only* imperialist presence in Europe, the Soviet Union acting merely as a protective power against the further encroachment of a capitalist hegemony.) At this distance it is difficult to appreciate how thoroughly Aron's position went against the general trend of liberal sympathies. Stated on its own, this one point was enough to make him sound like Edward Teller, whose political programme—which had only parodic relevance to his practical ability as a scientist—amounted to building bigger and bigger bombs, and digging deeper and deeper holes in which to hide from the consequences. Teller being the principal model for Dr. Strangelove, it became easy to hint that Aron might share the same enthusiasms, even though his own right hand showed no tendency to shoot spontaneously skyward.

But Aron was right, and the effort the USSR made to back the unilateral nuclear disarmament movement in Europe proves it. With the American weapons in place, the USSR was unable to contemplate exerting military pressure in Western Europe in any circumstances. In *Paix et guerre* Aron made many other points of similarly unpalatable realism, the whole tract adding up to an advance on Clausewitz (one of Aron's passions: he wrote a two-volume commentary), in which Clausewitz's connection between diplomacy and war was extended into a further connection between perpetually imminent total war and the only possible form of peace—an armed truce. That the armed truce included an arms race was incidental, because the high cost was merely material, whereas the price of a shoot-out would have been the loss of everything. Salvation lay in the obviousness of this latter point to all. Aron's conclusion was an epigram: "Peace impossible, war unlikely." But it is the way his whole argument is laid out that needs to be appreciated. He was fully aware of the bitter irony inherent in reaching such a position from humanist principles, but he saw no paradox in the irony: if there was an apparent contradiction, history had enforced it. A real contradiction would have been to disarm in the hope that moral superiority would have prevailed. For Aron, such trust would have flown in the face of his basic geopolitical precept, which he held to be true for all time: that the nation states are in a state of nature with one another. It would also have flouted his reading of contemporary history, in which totalitarian nation states were bound to find it intolerable to cohabit with democracies unless forced to by the inevitable consequences of failing to contain their patience.

Personality affects thought—or at any rate affects the train of thought—and there can be no doubt that Aron's quiet but considerable *amour propre* got a boost from his being the only one in step. Near the end of his life, when his views became less unfashionable, he was at his least decisive. Jean-François Revel, recalling, in his book of memoirs *Le Voleur dans la maison vide* (The Thief in the Empty House), his time as editor of *L'Express*, complains sharply about the senescent vacillations of the paper's most distinguished contributor. Old men with many laurels often use them to lie down in. Aron was at his best when out of the swim, saying hard things—hard things that were made harder to say because they superficially echoed the unthinking right. During the war, for example, he had been no toady for de Gaulle, but when de Gaulle, in 1963, came back to supremacy on the promise to keep Algeria and then promptly gave it away, Aron clearly enjoyed saying that only de Gaulle possessed what the Fourth Republic had lacked, *l'héroïsme de l'abandon*—the bravery to renounce (*Démocratie et totalitarisme*, p. 11). There was always an element of sombre relish, of hushed gusto, in Aron's readiness to puncture liberal assumptions. But he himself was the very model of the liberal, and those on the left who persisted in believing that liberal democracy was itself ideological were bound to despise him, because he was the one who proved it wasn't. Liberal democracy was, and is, reality. No ideology can tolerate a full historical consciousness. Only realism can, and Raymond Aron's long shelf of lucid books will always be there to tell us why.

B

✞ ✞ ✞

Walter Benjamin

Marc Bloch

Jorge Luis Borges

Robert Brasillach

Sir Thomas Browne

WALTER BENJAMIN

❦ ❦ ❦

Walter Benjamin was born in Wilhelmine Berlin in 1892 and committed suicide on the Spanish border in 1940, almost within sight of safety. In the 1960s, when his work as a critic began to appear in English, he was hailed as an original contributor to the assessment of the position of the arts in modern industrial society, and by now he is taken for granted as one of the early giants of Theory, that capitalized catch-all term which is meant to cover all the various ways of studying the arts so as to make the student feel as smart as the artist. Benjamin is above all taken for granted as a precursor of postmodernism. It remains sadly true, however, that he is more often taken for granted than actually read. "The Work of Art in the Age of Mechanical Reproduction" is the Benjamin essay that everybody knows a little bit about. Whether its central thesis is true is seldom questioned, just as the value of his work as a whole is seldom doubted. His untimely death was such a tragedy that nobody wants to think of his life as less than a triumph. But there had already been many thousands of Jewish tragedies before his turn came, and what is remarkable for the historically minded observer is just how slow so brilliant a man was to get the point about what the Nazis had in mind. About the other tragedy, the one in Russia, he never got the point at all. This might seem an unpitying line to take, as well as a presumptuous one. Reinforced by the impressive density of his prose style, Benjamin's intellectual status is monumental, and it is bathed in the awful light of his personal disaster. As a critic devoted to the real, however, Benjamin deserves the courtesy of not being treated as a hero in a melodrama.

Far from inaugurating a purer sphere, the mythic manifestation of immediate violence shows itself fundamentally identical with all legal violence, and turns suspicion concerning the latter into certainty of the perniciousness of its historical function, the destruction of which thus becomes obligatory.
— WALTER BENJAMIN, SELECTED
WRITINGS, VOL. I, 1913–1926, P. 249

BUT LET'S BREAK the flow of eloquent opacity at that point and ask ourselves about its author. The essay is called "A Critique of Violence" and yields a lot more in the same strain. With Benjamin, "strain" was the operative word. Part of his sad fate has been to have his name bandied about the intellectual world without very many of its inhabitants being quite sure why, apart from the vague idea that he was a literary critic who somehow got beyond literary criticism: he got up into the realm of theory, where critics rank as philosophers if they are hard enough to read. Clever always, he was clear seldom: a handy combination of talents for attaining oracular status. More often mentioned than quoted, he has become a byword for multiplex cultural scope. But the unearned omniscience of post-modernism depends on its facility for connecting things without examining them, and the routine invocation of Benjamin as a precursor is symptomatic. In the under-illuminated conference hall where everything is discussed at once, everybody who matters knows his name, even if nobody seems to remember much of what he actually said. One of the few things Benjamin *is* remembered for actually saying is that his country was not Germany but German, meaning the German language. The idea poignantly harked forward to the unified New Europe which is now, we are assured, in the final stages of getting its act together. Populated by the merrily flush inhabitants of twinned towns, it will be the good New Place with no real borders except where languages meet. Unfortunately for Benjamin, as for nearly all the Jews of the Old Europe, he lived at a time when unity was being striven for by other means, and for other ends. In Hitler's New Europe, where all internal political frontiers had indeed been dissolved but only at the cost of surrounding the whole expanse with barbed wire, Benjamin, a French-speaking cosmopolitan who should have been at home everywhere, was safe nowhere. At the border between France and Spain, within hailing distance of freedom but without a proper visa, he took his own life because he was convinced that for him there was no getting out of Nazi territory. He had devoted his career to pieces of paper with writing on them, but he didn't have the right one.

Had he reached liberty, he might have written a classic essay about passports and permits. To write with scholarship and insight about the small change of culture was his calling card. He could have written an essay about calling cards: granted life, he would probably have got around to it. In the words of Ernst Bloch (from an encomium included in *Über Walter Benjamin*, a 1968 collection of tributes by various hands), Benjamin was blessed with a *Sinn für Nebenbei*: a nose for the lurking detail. The idea of studying cultural by-products wasn't new. His beloved Proust (of whom he was the first serious translator into German) had already said that when one reaches a suitable level of receptivity there is as much to be learned from a soap advertisement as from a *pensée* by Pascal. Mallarmé did not consider himself to be slumming when he got involved with women's fashion magazines. Baudelaire, less afraid of the ephemerally chic than of the stultifyingly elevated, presaged the tradition by which to this day the most high-flown French artists and intellectuals show little reluctance when asked to be guest editor of *Vogue*. Just try to stop them.

What was unique about Benjamin was not his readiness to take a side track, but the lengths he would go to when he took one. He would devote more attention to children's books than he did to books for adults. Even then, if all the side tracks had led downwards he would never have acquired his prestige. But enough of them led upwards to

give the totality of his work an impressive air of the intellectually tran-
scendent. Unlike Mr. Casaubon in *Middlemarch*, whose Key to All
Mythologies was as endless as a scheme for joining the stars, Benjamin,
we are encouraged to feel, really could see how it all tied up. He had
theories about history which still sound good even in the light of the
general agreement among practising historians after Arnold Toynbee
that any history written in conformity to a theory is likely to be bad.
Benjamin argued strenuously that science needs a theory, too: not just
theories but *a* theory, a theoretical background. The empirical evidence already suggested that it was a defining condition of science to
need no such thing. (Whichever way Einstein arrived at a theory of relativity, it wasn't by departing from a theory of science.) But Benjamin's
urge to validate his interest in concrete detail by elevating it with a suitably abstract lifting apparatus looked like a guarantee of seriousness
during the Weimar Republic, when the German tradition of cloud-
borne metaphysics was still strong. Posthumously and with renewed
vigour, the same urge helped again during the 1960s, when Benjamin,
like Gramsci, was rediscovered worldwide as a thinker about culture
whose Marxist emphasis could be regarded as unspoiled because he had
not stayed alive long enough to see everything go wrong in the Soviet
Union. (He had, in fact, but the significance of the 1937–1938 Moscow
trials was lost on him, perhaps because by then his own situation was
getting desperate.) For the semi-educated Beatles-period junior intellectual intent on absorbing sociology, philosophy and cultural profundity all at once and in a tearing hurry, Benjamin's scrappily available
writings constituted an intellectual multivitamin pill, the more guaranteed in its efficacy by being so hard to swallow. The various English
translations concentrated the effect by reproducing all the tortuous cer-
ebration of his original texts without any of the occasional poetic flair,
thereby forestalling accusations of frivolity. The less comprehensible he
was, the more responsible he was held to be. Here was no lightweight.

Benjamin's most famous essay, whose title might best be translated as
"The Work of Art in the Age of Its Technological Reproducibility," is
atypical for featuring a general point designed to be readily understood.
Unfortunately, once understood, it is readily seen to be bogus. Benjamin argued that an art object would lose its "aura" through being
reproduced. The logical extension of this line would entail that any

painting would retain aura through being a one-off, whereas any photograph would be deprived of aura through its capacity to be copied by the million. I made up my own mind about this seductive notion one afternoon in Los Angeles, during one of those breaks in filming that I had learned, over the years, were better devoted to self-improvement rather than to just lying down and praying for release. At the Getty Museum, which at the time was still in Malibu, I happened to look at the sumptuous but frozen Winterhalter portrait of a Sayn-Wittgenstein princess. The picture was hung so that she was gazing out to sea towards Catalina Island, and she looked as if she could afford to buy it. As an ancestress of one of the Luftwaffe's top-scoring night-fighter pilots, she was bound to attract my interest. She had some history ahead of her as well as, presumably, behind her: she was a bewitching glamourpuss. Or so, at any rate, Winterhalter was trying to assure us. He might have been trying to assure her as well, in which case he was worth the fee. But it was a pretty ordinary portrait, rather along the hagiographic lines of that other faithful servant to the aristocracy, Makart, except with a bit more light thrown on the subject. No doubt her price tag would have been in the millions, but she personally was a dime a dozen. Later on, back at the hotel, I was leafing through John Kobal's excellent coffee-table album *The Art of the Great Hollywood Photographers*. Not for the first time I was transfixed by Whitey Schaefer's spare but incandescent photograph of Rita Hayworth. The Sayn-Wittgenstein princess had looked very nice, but for aura, in any meaningful sense of the word, she came nowhere near the film star. *Which* painting, and *which* photograph? And what about all those lovely-looking books Benjamin collected and cherished even when he couldn't read them: what else were they but reproduced works of art, and why else caress them if not for their aura? Whenever Benjamin transcends his sense of the relevant detail, one's own sense of the relevant detail tends to punch holes in his abstractions. Luckily for his reputation, if unluckily for the world's sum total of mental health, his conclusions are seldom so separable from his relentless metaphysical vocabulary. A more typical essay is the one on Karl Kraus, of which Kraus confessed that the only thing he understood was that it was about him.

There is no arguing against all-inclusive obscurity except to say that the whole thing means nothing, which few of us dare to do. Kraus did.

Now that Benjamin's writings are at last being published in English in some sort of orderly sequence, there is all too much opportunity to conclude that Kraus might have had Benjamin's number. Kraus had his own limitations, but he had an infallible ear for the kind of rhetoric whose only real subject is its own momentum. Benjamin was a rampant case. Lest we doubt it, we can read on after the sentence already quoted. You will have noted that "the destruction" has "thus" become obligatory. But the "thus" is not enough. There is also "this":

> This very task of destruction poses again, ultimately, the question of a pure immediate violence that might be able to call a halt to mythic violence. Just as in all spheres God opposes myth, mythic violence is confronted by the divine. And the latter constitutes its antithesis in all respects. . . .

And that's only a sample. Thus, this very, might, just as—it's the prose equivalent of a velvet fog: breathe it in and you'll choke on cloth. Benjamin was young, but this style of argument was never to be long discarded. In the next volume, or perhaps the one after that, the critic grown older will be heard on more down-to-earth subjects, but invariably the attendant metaphysical speculation will send his treatment of them spiralling towards the ceiling, like the burnt paper wrapping of an amaretto cookie rising on its self-generated column of hot air. (The first time I ever saw that trick worked in an Italian restaurant, I thought immediately of a thin argument gaining altitude.) Apart from his remarks on the reproducible works of art and their lost aura, Benjamin's other widely known brainwave is about how the broad pavements of Paris favour café life. The observation is persuasive, if commonplace even for the time it was made, but the prospective reader should be warned that the disquisition it instigated was endless. Benjamin's aperçus about his ideal European city grew into essays which themselves went on growing, on their slow way to becoming a book which was left unfinished at his death and might never have been finished even if he had lived, since its obvious aim was to Get Everything In. Often supposed, by literati of the panscopic persuasion, to be one of the great lost books of the twentieth century, the completed work might well have turned out to be a teeming marvel. Indeed the fragment we have, published under the enchanting title of *The Arcades Project*, was greeted by some critics, notably George Steiner, as proof positive that the finished job would have been inexhaustibly miraculous. But for those of us who have been dismayed by the essays, the vanished prospect of Benjamin's magic syntopicon is less likely to bind us with a spell. There is no reason to believe, and every reason to doubt, that the fully realized *omnium gatherum* would have kept a reasonable proportion between its author's enviable knack for assessing the significance of what everybody else had already seen and his congenital propensity for inflating the results into a speculative rigmarole that nobody else would ever think or could even follow. The sceptical question lingers; how could a brain as sharp as his churn out so much mush?

His life story gives us the answer: he was cushioning reality. It needed cushioning. Reality was anti-Semitism. Born into comfortable surroundings, Benjamin nevertheless concluded at an early age that the Jewish bourgeoisie were kidding themselves about assimilation. The better they did in every field of the arts, science, the professions and commerce, the more they were resented. The more they fitted in the more they stood out. In other words, they were disliked for themselves. Before World War I, Theodor Herzl has drawn the central impulse of Zionism from no other assumption. (Victor Klemperer, in *To the Bitter End*, the 1942–1945 volume of his monumental diary, noted that a total rejection of assimilation for Jews was the point on which the arch-Nazi Hitler and the arch-Zionist Herzl were of the same mind: *les extrêmes se touchent*.) The idea was already in the air, but Benjamin, perhaps because he was struck with it so young, gave it a portentous twist. He chose to despise, not the goyim for their prejudice, but the Jewish bourgeoisie for their gullibility, and, beyond them, the bourgeoisie *in toto*. Wanting a more enlightened society, he saw its seeds in Marxism. Objectively (as the Marxists went on saying until only recently) he became committed to one of the two implacable forces that would combine their energies to undermine the Weimar Republic, which might conceivably have withstood the pressure from either the Communists or the Nazis, but was squeezed to death when attacked by both.

Well accustomed to travelling within Europe and setting up his desk anywhere, usually within sight of the sea, Benjamin was able to absent himself from Germany after the Nazis got their grip on it. Keeping a suitable distance should have been an aid to perspective, but he was hobbled in his capacity for political analysis by his pidgin Marxist conviction—which he shared with his friend Brecht—that the Nazi regime was somehow a logical consequence of bourgeois capitalism, instead of what it was, a radical force in itself. (In *Die vergebliche Warnung—The Unheeded Warning*—Manès Sperber said that when the Nazis finally came to power it never occurred to him that he was in danger as a Jew, only as a Communist. The Jews were capitalists, so why would the Nazis attack them?) Sooner or later, according to the Comintern general line, the coming crisis of capitalism would bring the Nazis down. The sooner became later and it never happened. If Benjamin had waited any longer he would have been caught at home, with the concentration camp as the inevitable consequence. When he finally ran, he was only just in time. If he had been better organized he might have made it across the border, but it would be a mistake to blame his unworldliness. Plenty of worldly people died from despair as he did, because the Nazis had taken care to ensure that the world was no longer worth living in. Mentioning Benjamin's suicide in one of her letters to Karl Jaspers (*Briefwechsel 1926–1969*, p. 77) Hannah Arendt made a point we should consider: "This atmosphere of *sauve qui peut* was hideous, and suicide was the only noble gesture." To go out nobly was the only way left to affirm life. It could be said that Arendt, who had got to safety in America, was asking a lot by suggesting that voluntary death was the only nobility left for those who didn't make it, but she was undoubtedly right about the hideous pressure exerted when ordinary civil existence was suddenly transformed into a case of every man for himself. The Devil took the hindmost, and one of them was Benjamin.

There was a subsidiary consequence of Germany's traditional anti-Semitism (the old, pre-Nazi brand that worked by exclusion rather than repression), a consequence which Benjamin might have examined if he had lived to write an autobiography. The autobiography would have had to be unsparing on the issue, because what affected him in a debilitating way was his acquiescence as much as his defiance. Benjamin never got the university post that he might legitimately have expected, but he allowed the rejection to haunt his work instead of giving it strength. Even as late as the Weimar Republic, the German universities retained their tacit quota system by which Jews found it hard to get a place on the faculty. Benjamin wanted a place on the faculty more than anything else in life. Other Jews of comparable critical talent, forced into journalism because the universities had shut them out, did what Benjamin could never bring himself to do. They accepted journalism's requirements of readability, and found ways of giving everything they had to the article rather than the treatise. The books they wrote had a general public in mind. In retrospect, the journalists can be seen to have enriched German-speaking culture by saving it from the stratospheric oxygen-starvation of the deliberately high-flown thesis. Their written and spoken conversations were informal seminars that turned the cafés into universities, even as the universities were hardening further into hieratic structures where nothing mattered except the prestige of position—a characteristic that made them fatally corruptible by political pressure. The journalists were well out of it, and the cleverest of them realized it: they took the opportunity to create a new language for civilization, a language that drew strength from the demotic in order to cherish the eternal.

Benjamin, on the other hand, even when he wrote for a newspaper, had a way of sounding as if he was still angling for a Ph.D. If he had reached safety he might have been obliged to change his ways, almost certainly for the better. To pine for more of what he had done already, you have to miss the glaring point that he had already done far too much of it. Take any essay by Benjamin and then place beside it an essay by, say, Alfred Polgar. In a Benjamin essay, there will be very few actual perceptions gleaming through the cloud of smoke. Some of them will be unique, but they will all be gasping for air. A Polgar essay is made of perceptions and nothing else, and the style is just the most elegant possible way of holding them together. Benjamin truly and touchingly loved Paris, but what did he ever say about it that is not left looking thin beside the wealth of observation that the journalist Janet Flanner could put into a single report, or the historian Richard Cobb into a single paragraph of an essay? Joseph Roth, the Jewish exile from Vienna who drank himself to death in Paris in the last days of its freedom, packed his every piece about the city with enough material to keep Benjamin speculating for a year. Examples could be multiplied, and always to Benjamin's detriment: the lowly journalism of others, then and since, leaves his paroxysms of verbiage sounding inarticulate.

None of this is pleasant to say, and is probably not pleasant to hear. There aren't so many truly comprehensive freelance scholars that we can afford to mock one of them just because he was a victim of his own style, and Benjamin was a victim of a lot more than that. Kicking a man when he is down is bad enough, and kicking him when he is unfairly dead looks like blasphemy. Considering the refinement of Benjamin's mind, his fate was a crucifixion. But we are talking about his reputation, the prestige he still has, and, for the humanities, the baleful encouragement he gives to the damaging notion that there is somehow a progressivist, humanitarian licence for talking through a high hat. There is no such licence. The wretched of the earth get no help from witch doctors, and when academic language gets beyond shouting distance of ordinary speech, voodoo is all it is.

MARC BLOCH

❦ ❦ ❦

Marc Bloch was born in 1886, fought in World War I, established himself as one of France's leading historians between the wars, and took up arms again as a Resistance fighter in World War II. He was caught, tortured and executed in 1944. His last, brief book, written while he was already in some danger ("The circumstances of my present life, the impossibility of reaching any large library, and the loss of my own books have made me dependent on my notes and upon memory"), is easily available in English as *The Historian's Craft* (1953). His more scholarly books, foundation stones in the *Annales* school of history, are for specialists, but his incidental commentary, like his life, is for everyone. There is an excellent account of his career by the Univeristy of North Carolina's Carole Fink, *Marc Bloch: A Life in History* (1989), a model of what an academic study can be, and a testament to the example of an heroic man.

❦ ❦ ❦

The nature of our intelligence is such that it is stimulated
far less by the will to know than by the will to understand,
and, from this, it results that the only sciences which it
admits to be authentic are those which succeed in

establishing explanatory relationships between phenomena.
The rest is, as Malebranche puts it, mere "polymathy."
— MARC BLOCH

ALREADY IN HIS FIFTIES, the historian Marc Bloch could have
dealt himself out of the French Resistance. But he dealt himself in,
and paid the penalty. The quoted sentence is the kind of wide-ranging,
narrow-focusing idea from Bloch which makes the reader, even at this
distance, grieve for his loss as if bereaved of a loved one. If Bloch had
not sacrificed himself, he would have had an incalculable but undoubtedly civilizing effect on the post-war intellectual life of France—a life
whose sophistication and global influence were attained at the high
price of a surreptitious retreat from humanist values. It could be said
that Bloch, as the founding *annaliste* historian, belonged to the bean-
counting school of Braudel, and might merely have added to the future
overstock of desiccated accountancy. But his subsidiary prose always
promised something better. It promised a broadly human view, and had
he lived he surely would have helped to sweeten an intellectual atmosphere turned sour by bad faith and fatigue. The literary critic Jean
Prévost, who suffered a similar fate, might have had a similar effect.
For both men, part of their lasting impressiveness resides in their
absence, the tangible quality of an untimely silence, the depth and
length of the If Only. Theirs are the voices that we miss. They were
killed because they were Resistance fighters, not because they were
scholars. In the light of that fact, their shared martyrdom was an accident, and not the result of a totalitarian conspiracy against humanist
culture. But it amounted to the same thing. Both men resisted because
for them the love of the European humanist culture that they themselves would come to represent was inseparable from their love of freedom. As true scholars, they refused to be drawn into the tacit, tentacular
bargain by which Vichy's cooperation with the invader was seen as a
pragmatic stratagem to preserve the eternal France. They could see
how that bargain attacked the eternal France in its essence. As true
heroes, they were not content to keep their heads down until it all blew
over: they guessed, correctly, that too much would be blown away.

So they fought. Prévost was lucky enough to die in battle in 1944.
Bloch was captured, and died horribly. In post-war France they were

further doomed to a long oblivion, and precisely because of the unequivocal bravery of what they did. If they had done less, and died in some other way except as warriors, their posthumous reputations might have flowered sooner. But the false heroes had too much to lose by the comparison, and those who knew better than to claim heroism for interior dissent were reluctant to be reminded that they had played for safety. We would all like to believe that acquiescence is inevitable in the face of overwhelming retaliatory violence. In Paris the occupying power devoted a lot of effort, skill and personal charm to persuading the French intellectuals that they could retain the luxury of a liberal conscience as long as they did nothing substantial to express it. If they acknowledged the inevitable, they could pursue their careers. The combination of ambition on the one hand, and ordinary human trepidation on the other, was so seductive that it conquered shame. The moral question posed by the judicious inertia of the intellectuals under the Occupation lay dormant for a long time after it was over, but shame was not the reason: the reason was that the shame itself lay dormant. Too much attention paid to men like Bloch and Prévost would have awoken it. Men of letters who had done nothing to resist preferred to admire those among their number who had done little, and safely late, rather than those who had done much, and dangerously early. The latter threatened to spoil the conspiracy by their mere existence. In the physical sense, luckily, Bloch and Prévost *had* no existence, and were thus deprived of a current voice to help remind the nation for which they had died that their spiritual presence was permanent. All they had was what they had written, and all that their writings could do was wait. The waiting worked, eventually. The sleepers woke, eventually. Their books came back into print, and then there were books about them. In that belated renaissance there is some encouragement, if small comfort. The heartening capacity of the tree of knowledge to replant itself in scorched earth does something to offset the depression induced by the spectacle of accumulated decades of bad conscience. The bad conscience was so bad that it would rather have undone its own culture than face itself. Paris, of all places, became the world's production centre for new ways of proving that the critical intelligence can operate with no fixed connection to reality. Marc Bloch believed exactly the opposite, but he wasn't there to say so: not then, not yet.

Elsewhere in the same chapter, Bloch went on to say that history must offer us a progressive intelligibility. For those with a vested interest in offering us a progressive unintelligibility—Lacan, Foucault, Baudrillard, Derrida *et hoc genus*—such a precept could not even be given the status of anathema: it could only be thought naïve. But in the naivety lay the purity and the robustness, and in the sophisticated mockery of it the pervasive malaise. Nevertheless, Bloch's idea that understanding holds the precedence over knowledge needs to be cut up before it can be swallowed without choking. He charts a desirable hierarchy of epistemology, but it would be disastrous if inculcated as a precept. It is commonly and truly said that young people who want to set the world to rights learn later to be grateful that the world is not worse than it is; but if they were convinced of that too early, we would lose their critical effect, and the world would be worse still. Similarly, it is true that most of our knowledge will drop away after we have condensed from it the principles which will connect into a view, but the principles can't exist to be extracted unless the knowledge is acquired in the first instance. Certainly the mind too impressed by knowledge will attain to nothing else. Ezra Pound famously said that culture begins when you forget what book that came from. Unfortunately he himself never forgot any citation that suited his mania, and his work as a totality is hopelessly vitiated by the half-witted diligence of the trainspotter. An edifying comparison can be made with Yeats, whose allegiance to the spiritualist claptrap of the theory of the Mystic Rose was at least as batty as Pound's to the pseudo-economic quackery of the theory of Social Credit: but Yeats could develop beyond his early lyrics because art, for him, was a system of solid knowledge by far transcending his own fads.

For Pound, the lyrics were as far as he went. I loved his early work too much to belittle it now. At my first café table, in the Manning House Women's Union of Sydney University in the late fifties, I read *Polite Essays* and felt that I was being injected with the ability to swim like Johnny Weissmuller, to dance with Cyd Charisse, to fly a Spitfire. But that first admiration was precisely the measure by which I found the rest of his career to be a tragic farce, and I think any honest critic feels the same. (I think Eliot felt it too, but he stuck by a friend.) Bulging with trifles passionately snapped up but invariably ill-considered, the *Cantos* are the wares of Autolycus, some of which, no doubt, were curiously interesting, but which meant nothing as a collection. Here and there, and for long stretches not at all, the *Cantos* have their beautiful moments, but those moments are wilfully beautiful, as if to admit that the dust heap needs decorating. (Even while the later *Cantos* were still coming out, there was an acute analysis of this discrepancy by Randall Jarrell, whose books of criticism, and especially *Poetry and the Age*, should be on the reading list of any student anywhere, and not just in his native America.) Pound vaunted his ability to make explanatory relationships, but it was the very thing he could never truly do, even though, like any other paranoid psychotic, he tried to all the time. Nevertheless he had the talent to demonstrate that to go mad for detail might yield something, whereas to go mad for generalization leads nowhere. Pound knew less than nothing about economics, one of his favourite subjects: but he could describe a coin, having looked at it long and hard, although never with comprehension. He thought he could judge an empire by the metallic composition of its small change, just as he thought he could extract the meaning of a Chinese ideograph from the way it looked. In both cases he was too far from the mark for sanity. But if he didn't get the picture, at least he could see it; and young readers will probably go on being excited when they are drawn into his emporium by the magnetic force of his conviction that the Thingness of Things is a destination as well as a departure point.

Pound's was a philosophical urge gone wrong. Thousands of even lesser philosophers are always with us to prove that it can go more wrong still, by trying to form systems out of no knowledge at all. Admirers of Ouspensky, Gurdjieff and Wilhelm Reich were all under the illusion that profundity can be attained by embracing principles with no basis in science. The occult and the mystically profound are perennial short cuts to a supervening vision: a world view without the world. Extreme authoritarianism is only a step away. Himmler was a mighty devotee of cabalistic flapdoodle, and Stalin, had he lived longer, would almost certainly have demonstrated an anti-Semitism rivalling Hitler's in its toxic fervour. The mass murderer is ever fond of theories that explain everything, and all the fonder if they can be acquired without study.

There is no reasoning someone out of a position he has not reasoned himself into. People are drawn into these enthusiasms by no mechanism that has anything much to do with rational thought. In their own minds, however, explanatory relationships between phenomena are exactly what they see. Bloch's precept is fulfilled in every particular. But of course he meant more than what he said. He meant that the knowledge must be real knowledge, which means that understanding must accompany it from the first moment, and can supersede it only on the condition that its chastening memory is never repudiated. Had he lived, he might have expressed himself more cautiously. Hitler had already shown the dangers of leaving knowledge behind too easily, and at least one of Hitler's victims, Egon Friedell, had amply proved that there need be nothing "mere" about a polymath, if the bearer of that title is one who exemplifies how the fields of knowledge are alive within one another, illuminating the world even in its cruelty—the cruelty that caught him defenceless, but surely not by surprise. Bloch, sadly, could not have been surprised either. He knew what he was up against. The drowning pool, the truncheon, the thumbscrew and the blowtorch: for an imagination like his, those things must have been almost as terrible in prospect as they were in actuality. But he risked it anyway. Appalled by the cost in mental treasure, we can even call him irresponsible, the more easily to live with his example.

JORGE LUIS BORGES

❦ ❦ ❦

Jorge Luis Borges was born in Buenos Aires in 1899 and died in Geneva in 1986, near the end of a century which he had lived almost all the way through and done a great deal to shape. If we now think of Latin American literature as central to the Spanish world, and of the Spanish world as a vitally renewed force in the world entire, it has a lot to do with Borges. As a twentieth-century master artist, he was celebrated even by nineteenth-century standards. Famous on the scale of Tennyson, Kipling and Mark Twain, he was reported like a natural phenomenon, a human volcano. By the end of his life his every spoken word got into print: dialogues with Borges appeared in *The New Yorker* as fast as they were recorded in Buenos Aires. His dialogues and essays can be recommended as an easy way into Spanish, a language which every student of literature should hold in prospect, to the extent of an elementary reading knowledge at least. (Borges's own, and much vaunted, knowledge of English was really not much better than that.) Once acquired, the Spanish language opens up a huge story, in which it will be found that Borges was not without rivals even in Argentina. His contemporary Ernesto Sabato, for example, wrote even better essays. Nor was the serene national treasure's apparently detached political position regarded as beyond cavil by other Argentinian writers who admired his art but questioned his relaxation into international eminence while his homeland was in the grip of terror. Before getting into all that, however, the beginner with Borges can find a seductive entrance to his enchantment through the short stories collected in *Labyrinths* (1962), which tranmsit his poetic magic irresistibly even through translation. *Borges on Writing* (1974) is a painless introduction to the incidental prose. (As early as that year, his writings had been translated into twenty-one languages.) The accessibility of the story-teller is no illusion— as with Kipling, the stories go to the heart of his vision—and his essays and dialogues turn his vast learning into an intellectual adventure guaranteed to thrill the young, as he meant it to do. Before questioning Borges on the political role of his artistic stature, it is wise, as it were, to go crazy about him first. But if he created a fairyland, he did not live in one, and even in the exalted last years of the blind icon there were voices among his countrymen ready to remind him that there had been times when he should have tried harder to use his ears.

The great American writer Herman Melville says
somewhere in *The White Whale* that a man ought to be
"a patriot to heaven," and I believe it is a good thing, this
ambition to be cosmopolitan, this idea to be citizens not of
a small parcel of the world that changes according to the
currents of politics, according to the wars, to what occurs,
but to feel that the whole world is our country.
—JORGE LUIS BORGES, "HOMENAJE A
VICTORIA OCAMPO" (HOMAGE TO VICTORIA
OCAMPO), IN *BORGES EN SUR* (BORGES IN
THE MAGAZINE *SOUTH*), P. 326

B Y *THE WHITE WHALE*, of course, Borges meant *Moby-Dick*. He was often very approximate about the details of his enthusiasm for literature in English. But our attention should be on the argument.

It's a pretty phrase, "a patriot to heaven," and nowadays it can doubt-less be tracked down "somewhere in" *Moby-Dick* by means of a search engine, without the necessity to re-read the actual text. In the language of book-bluff, "re-read" is often a claim to have read something that one has merely dipped into or even skipped entirely, but there was a period of my early life which I did actually occupy with getting through *Moby-Dick*. Perhaps spoiled in childhood by the narrative flow of *Captains Courageous*, I found Melville's ocean clung like tar. I wish I could believe that it was a masterpiece I wasn't ready for. Whoever said "Wagner's music isn't as bad as it sounds" was as wrong as he was funny, but there is surely a case for saying that the story of Captain Ahab's contest with the great white whale is one of those books you can't get started with even after you have finished reading them. It's not so much that I find his language contortedly and wilfully archaic: more that I find it makes a meal of itself, as if foretelling a modern critical age in which it is fated to be more taught than enjoyed. This idea of Borges's, though—that the whole world is, or should be, our country—was encapsulated shinily enough to be picked up like a bead in his untiringly darting magpie beak. So what I underlined was a quotation of a quotation, and I was wondering already if the idea, so attractive on the face of it to a displaced person like myself, was really quite right. Eventually it led me to the considerations that follow.

One of my exemplars, Witold Gombrowicz, would have had good reason to accept the idea: but he didn't, quite. Exiled in Argentina during World War II, he was reluctant to regard himself as the incarnation of Polish literature, but that was because he distrusted the whole idea of literature as a field of ambition, duty, or even of professional activity. After the war his forced exile continued, because he had correctly judged Poland's Communist regime as being only marginally less lethal to creative life than the Nazi slaughterhouse that had preceded it. He was under continual pressure to represent the true, liberal Poland, but he didn't believe in that either. He just didn't like abstractions. When it came down to it, however, he did not regard the land of his birth as an abstraction. He had all the qualifications of a world citizen, and often seemed to preach as one. But when finally cornered on the point he said there *was* a Poland, and that he, Gombrowicz, was it.

Under extreme conditions of forced exile from political extermination, all the expatriated artists of the twentieth century seem to have reached a similar conclusion. Thomas Mann behaved as if he were the eternal Germany, Stravinsky as if he were the eternal Russia. In London, Freud was still Vienna. Even the most assimilated to their new conditions found that they could not entirely change their minds. In America the possibilities were at their greatest to forget about origins and embrace world citizenship, just as long as American citizenship had been embraced first. Yet it was remarkable how the opportunity, even when it was taken up, always seemed to leave a mental loophole that led home. On the set in Hollywood, Billy Wilder and Marlene Dietrich cracked jokes in German. It was world citizenship, but it was also a way of reminding themselves that the melting pot had not boiled down their souls, which had been formed elsewhere, in a place that was really a place. "There are only two places where we feel at home," Milos Forman once said on television: "Home, and in America." Yet when Vaclav Havel visited the United States, Forman was one of the ringmasters for the new Czech president's welcome, and in Forman's excellent book of memoirs his lost country is perpetually rediscovered. Philosophically, the idea of the world citizen goes back through Erasmus at least as far as Eratosthenes the Stoic, who said he saw all good men as his fellow countrymen; which was only one step short of seeing his country as dispensable. But the modern refugees from totalitarianism, having been compelled to dispense with theirs, found it hard to let go of the memory.

The politically exiled artists thus proved, under laboratory conditions, that the concept of the *Weltbürger* has its limits. Borges was not in the same position. In 1979, when he wrote his homage to Victoria Ocampo (the founder of the cosmopolitan magazine *Sur*) in which this revealing passage appeared, the Argentinian junta was doing its obscene worst. Surrounded by horror, either he hadn't noticed or—a hard imputation, yet harder still to avoid—he knew something about it and thought it could be excused. But even if he was confident that the political Brahmanism he favoured could be pardoned for imposing itself by extreme means, he might well have detected an incipient challenge to his conscience. He had good reason—i.e., a bad reason but an urgent one—to suggest, if only to himself, that what was happening to his country was of secondary importance, because his first loyalty was to the world. But the world, not one's country, is the abstraction: an ideal that means nothing if one's first loyalties to truth, justice and mercy have been given up. The old man was pulling a fast one. I read the book, and made my marginal note, in 1999. But it was the date on the article that tipped me off: 1979. A reprinted article should always carry its original date, but you can see why writers and editors should sometimes find it expedient to leave it out. Otherwise an apparently impeccable sentiment might stand revealed as an opportunistic stratagem, or at the very least as a sign of obtuseness.

Self-exiled to Paris from his repudiated Romania, the fragmentary philosopher E. M. Cioran gushingly admired Borges's world citizenship. On page 1,606 of Cioran's monolithic Œuvres, we learn that the irresistible example of the Argentinian séducteur ("Everything with him is transfigured by the game, by a dance of glittering discoveries and delicious sophisms") helped the Romanian philosopher to formulate the device on his own mental shield: "Not to put down roots, not to belong to any community." But at the time Cioran said this (it was 1976), he was keen to give the impression that his native country had never meant much to him, while not keen at all to reveal that he had played a part in his native country's unfortunate fascist past. (The nice way of putting it is that he had been close to the Iron Guard, and the nice way of putting it when it comes to the Iron Guard is that their anti-Semitism, by Hitlerite standards, was hit-and-miss, although not many people they hit got up.) Cioran had even better reasons than Borges for suggesting that none of the rough stuff had ever had anything to do with him. Borges was never more than equivocally complicit in nationalist mania. Cioran, in that conveniently forgotten youthful period before he prudently took out citizenship in the world, had been in it up to the elbows. It is interesting that he thought a spiritual alliance with Borges might help to wash him clean.

At this point there is a key quotation from Ernesto Sabato that we should consider:

> From Borges's fear of the bitter reality of existence spring two simultaneous and complementary attitudes: to play games in an invented world, and to adhere to a Platonic theory, an intellectual theory par excellence. (*Ensayos*, p. 304)

In Buenos Aires after World War II, there were two literary voices of incontestable international stature. The main difference between them was that only one of them was known to possess it. The whole world heard about Borges. But to get the point about Sabato, you had to go to Argentina. Both inhabitants of a beautiful but haunted city, both great writers, and both blind in their later lives, Borges and Sabato were linked by destiny but separated in spirit: a separation summed up in this single perception of Sabato's, which was penetratingly true. Borges did fear the bitterness of reality, and he did take refuge in an invented world. When Gombrowicz called Borges's virtuosity "iced fireworks" he was arriving independently at the same judgement. There are no iced fireworks in Sabato, whose fantastic novels were dedicated to including all the horrors of the real world, and raising them to the status of dreams, so that they could become apprehensible to the imagination, which would otherwise edit them into something more easily overlooked. (His rationale for this process of saving reality from its own forgetful mechanisms is spread throughout his books of critical prose, but see especially *El escritor y sus fantasmas*.) Sabato's characteristic image is the tunnel. The tunnel is the area of concentration for the dreams. Most of the dreams we recognize all too clearly. He didn't need to search very far in order to find the stimulus for them. All he needed was the recent history of Argentina. In Sabato the reader is faced with that history often, but in Borges hardly ever. In Borges the near past scarcely exists: in that respect his historical sense, like his Buenos Aires, is without contemporaneity. His political landscape is a depopulated marble ghost-town remembered from childhood, spookily hieratic like the cemetery in Recoleta. Before he went blind he would still walk the streets, but usually only at night, to minimize the chance of actually meeting anyone. In his stories, the moments of passion, fear, pity and terror belong to the long-vanished world of the knife fighters. Death squads and torture are not in the inventory. The timescale ends not long after he was born. Why did he hide?

Probably because of artistic predilection, rather than human cowardice. There are always artists who place themselves above the battle, and in retrospect we don't regret their doing so. In World War II, André Gide took no overt position about the Occupation, the biggest moral dilemma that France had faced since the Revolution. Yet we would not want to be without his journals of the period. Safe in Switzerland, Hermann Hesse said next to nothing about the biggest events of any twentieth-century German-speaking writer's life: his dreamy novella *Morgenlandfahrt* (The Journey East) was the closest he ever came to making a comment on nationalist irrationality, and there was nothing in that skimpy book to which a Hitler Youth idealist could have objected. Borges openly loathed Peron, but fell silent on everything that happened after Peron was ousted—fell silent politically, but artistically came into full flower, an international hit even as his nation entered the tunnel of its long agony.

Though it would be foolish for an outsider to quarrel with his enormous creative achievement—one might as well take a tomahawk to a forest—there is reason to sympathize with those native Argentinians, not all of them Philistines, who can't help feeling that it was an accumulation of trees designed to obscure the wood. So much ancillary prose by and about Borges has been published since his death that it is a professional task to keep up with it all, but a casual student should find time to see *Antiborges*, a compilation of commentaries edited by Martin Lafforgue. (The contribution from Pedro Organbide, "*Borges y su pensamiento politica*," is especially noteworthy.) An instructive picture emerges of a visionary whose vision was impaired in more than the physical sense. Borges, alas, had no particular objection to extreme authoritarianism as such. The reason he hated Peronismo was that it was a mass movement. He didn't like the masses: he was the kind of senatorial elitist whose chief objection to fascism is that by mobilizing the people it gives them ideas above their station and hands out too many free shirts. When the junta seized power in March 1976, he took the view that they weren't fascists at all, because the helots weren't in the picture. Most of the intellectuals of the old conservative stamp declined to cooperate with the new regime, and Sabato behaved particularly well. (That a man as out of tune with the regime as Sabato should nevertheless have seen merit in the Malvinas adventure is a token of how indisputable the claim to the islands looked from the Argentinian side.) It need hardly be said that to behave well was not without risk: when everyone was aware of the hideous lengths to which the regime would go against ordinary people whose names meant little, there was never any guarantee that people of prestige would remain exempt. Fear took its toll in a fall of silence.

But there is no evidence that Borges ever felt the need to be afraid. His name and growing international renown were lent to the regime without reserve, either because he approved or—the best that can be said for him—because he was clueless. As the time arrived when not even he could claim blindness to the junta's war against the innocent, lack of information was what he claimed as an excuse for his previous inertia. Signing the round robin of protest that signalled the end of the regime's tacit support from the enlightened bourgeoisie—when *their* children were taken, they woke up—he said that he had not been able to find out about these things earlier. His impatient statement "*No leo los diarios*" (I don't read newspapers) became famous among his critics as a shameful echo of all those otherwise intelligent Germans who never heard about the extermination camps until it was all over. It was pointed out with some pertinence that his blindness had never stopped him finding out about all the literature in the world. There was a torture centre within walking distance of his house, and he had always been a great walker. It could be said that by then his walking days were over; but he could still hear, even if he couldn't see. There was a lot of private talk that must have been hard to miss, unless he had wilfully stopped his ears. He might well have done: a cocked ear would have heard the screams.

In 1983, after the junta fell, he was finally forced into an acceptance of plebeian democracy, the very thing he had always most detested. A decade of infernal anguish for his beloved country had at last taught him that state terror is more detestable still. It was a hard lesson for a slow pupil. On an international scale, Borges can perhaps be forgiven for his ringing endorsement of General Pinochet's activities in Chile: after all, Margaret Thatcher seems to have shared his enthusiasm, and John Major's Chancellor of the Exchequer, Norman Lamont, now wears a medal hung around his neck by Pinochet without any visible sign of chest hair set on fire by burning shame. But within Argentina, there are some distinguished minds that have had to work hard to see their greatest writer *sub specie aeternitatis* without wishing his pusillanimity to be enrolled along with his prodigious talent. Pedro Organbide, fully sensitive to the eternal literary stature of Borges, was being

restrained when he noted—with a sad finality it is hard to contest—
that his tarnished hero's behaviour was a living demonstration of how
political elitism depends on ignorance. There are not many great writers who oblige us to accept that inattention might have been essential
to their vision. Jane Austen left the Napoleonic wars out of her novels,
but we assume that she heard about them, and would have heard about
them even if she had been unable to see. Sabato's blindness, unlike
Borges's, was confined only to the last part of his life, but it was complete enough. His ears, however, remained in good working order, and
when the time came he was able to take on the cruel job of writing
about the Disappeared—the innocent people whose vanishing took so
long to attract Borges's attention.

ROBERT BRASILLACH

Robert Brasillach was born in 1909 in Perpignan and exce-cuted as a traitor in 1945. He is sometimes thought of, by wishful thinkers in France, as perhaps the most conspicuous example of the promising young all-rounder whose career would have been different if the Nazis had never come to Paris, although he had already been beguiled by what he thought of as their glamour when he visited Germany. But they arrived, and his nature took its course. As a regular con-tributor, during the Occupation, to the scurrilous paper *Je Suis Partout* (I Am Everywhere), he stood out for his virulence even among its staff of dedicated anti-Semites. His Jew-baiting dia-tribes were made more noxious by his undoubted journalistic talent. Most of the prominent French collaborators with the Nazis got into it because they were disappointed nationalists who thought their country had a better chance of becoming strong again if it stuck with the winning side. Comparatively few of them actually admired the Nazis. Brasillach was one who did. When the winning side became the losing side, he paid the penalty for having guessed wrong. Though there have been attempts, not always unjustifiable, to rehabilitate his reputation as a critic, few tears have ever been shed over his fate. By his rhetoric of blanket denunciation, he had been handing out death penalties for years. Whether the death penalty was warranted in his own case, however, is bound to be questioned by anyone who believes in free speech, however foul it might be.

❣ ❣ ❣

It is among them that I have found the most passionate defenders and they have shown a generosity which is in the greatest and most beautiful tradition of French literature.
— ROBERT BRASILLACH, *REMERCIEMENT AUX INTELLECTUELS*, FEBUARY 3, 1945, QUOTED IN PIERRE ASSOULINE'S *L'ÉPURATION DES INTELLECTUELS*

PREPARING HIMSELF FOR his imminent death, the condemned Robert Brasillach showed courage, but unless remorse had renovated his character it is doubtful if he realized just how generous his defenders had been. At the eleventh hour and the fifty-ninth minute, he can be heard enrolling himself amongst the greatest and most beautiful tradition of French literature, as if he still believed he had been its servant, instead of its betrayer. Whether he was a traitor to France was, and remains, a fine point of legal interpretation. There were plenty of people, including Marshal Pétain himself, who sincerely believed that to serve Vichy was the only legitimate loyalty, and later on they were able to argue from conviction that they had broken no laws. (During François Mitterrand's presidency it was revealed that his supposed career as a Resistance hero had been preceded by a verifiable career as a Vichy functionary. He contrived to imply, without being toppled from office, that there had been no alternative at the time, although of course he had been *preparing* himself for Resistance all along.) There were fewer people, although still far too many, who actively cooperated with the Nazis in the belief that the Third Republic had deserved its fate and that the alliance with Germany, even though compelled, would have been worth making voluntarily in the interests of European renewal and a France purged of liberal equivocation. There were

very few people who behaved like Nazis themselves, although even in
the literary world there were still more than a handful. Brasillach was
one of them.

He was given carte blanche by the Nazis to wield his poisoned pen
in the pursuit of Jews. On any scale of crime and punishment, a firing
squad could scarcely exact payment for the damage he had caused. But
he was shot anyway, and got out of his debt early. If the blindfolded
angel of Justice could have intervened, she would have sent him to Sigmaringen, the appropriately fantastic cliff-side haven on the Danube
where Louis-Ferdinand Céline and all the other unrepentant enthusiasts, taken away to safety by the Nazis, were even then sitting around
in plush chairs and boring each other to tears with the tatters of their
madcap theories. Their haven was soon overrun but the reprieve had
lasted long enough to save most of them from a death sentence. In his
disgusting book *Bagatelles pour un massacre*, Céline had murdered a
thousand time more Jews with his foul mouth than Brasillach had ever
accounted for by publishing names in the crapulous weekly newspaper
Je Suis Partout so that the Gestapo and the Vichy militia could add to
their lists over breakfast. Locking Brasillach in the same cell with
Céline for the next ten years would have been a far tougher punishment than shooting him. But the vigilantes, as always, were in a hurry,
so Brasillach died before he had time to entertain the possibility that
his real treason had been to the French humanist tradition he thought
himself to be part of.

He could have argued back, and said that Voltaire loathed Jews too.
But what would he have said about Proust? What did he think that a
pipsqueak like himself amounted to beside a man like that? Proust
might have been only half a Jew, but Brasillach was barely a quarter of
a literary figure, and in normal times would probably have measured
even less: the *Zeitgeist* lent him a dark lustre. He had some talent as a
critic, and could write forceful prose, even against the common run of
his own political position, whose banalities did not escape him. As late
as his 1937 visit to Germany, though he was impressed by the vault of
searchlights (the *Lichtdom*) at the Nuremberg rally and bowled over by
the sexy energy of the Hitler Youth, he could still describe Hitler as a
sad vegetarian functionary. (After the Nazis took over in Paris, Brasillach had to censor some of his own stuff.) But his fateful attendance at

the 1941 *Weltliteratur* pan-European get-together in Weimar put him over the top. It was the combination of poetry and daemonic power that did him in. No tenderness without cruelty! In occupied Paris, Brasillach knew that the Germanophile French writers were being had by the Propaganda Abteilung. But Brasillach wanted to be had. The Jewish Bolshevik peril was still there, and now it was there for the crushing. Here was the organized violence that could do it, and he could be part of it. Anger drove him, as it always drives the resentful. He had the kind of energy that could never widen its view. But it could certainly widen its scope, and the Occupation gave him the opportunities of a big game hunter set loose in a zoo: the targets had nowhere to run. His short career was the logical outcome of the nefarious, microcephalic intellectual trend that had started with the Dreyfus case and the foam-flecked symposium of Action Française: the idea that a cleaned-up, non-cosmopolitan, Jew-free culture could restore the integrity of France as the natural leader of Europe. Whether this glowing future was envisaged with the Germans or without them, it was always without the Jews.

But France was already the natural leader of Europe, and exactly because it had outgrown pseudo-hygienic notions of cultural purity. Paris had played host to Heinrich Heine when there was no home for him in Germany. As Nietzsche himself insisted, Heine was the greatest German poet since Goethe and one of the greatest in any language. Heine's presence in Paris had been a foretaste of the only cultural integrity that would ever matter: the hegemony of the creative mind that enriches nations but makes their boundaries transparent. The French anti-Semitic right was not just a political freak show, it was a cultural anachronism. From the veteran arch-nationalists Maurice Barres and Charles Maurras downwards to such bright young things as Drieu la Rochelle and Brasillach, its fluently virulent mouthpieces raved on about their nation's poisoned blood without ever realizing that they were the poison. Brasillach's goodbye note to a cruel world is just one more piece of evidence that they never got the point. Literature should have taught them better: but the real treason of the clerks has always been to suppose that their studies confer on them a power beyond the merely mortal, instead of revealing to them that merely mortal is all they are. If Brasillach had lived to repent, he might have found that out: although if he had, his conscience would have killed him anyway. He had too much blood on his hands. Thanks to his accusers, his is on ours. Some of them, like his defenders, were men of letters. They should have put it in writing. People who don't think that's enough shouldn't write.

SIR THOMAS BROWNE

Sir Thomas Browne (1605–1682) is one of those minor English prose writers whose reputations are always rediscovered in times of crisis, because they had a gift for rhythm that forecast the language of the future, and it is in times of crisis that the English language is most easily seen to be a treasure house of humanism. During World War II, European exiles in London—the future Nobel laureate Elias Canetti was one of them—learned to value Browne's style as an example of what English could do in a short space. Since written English can so easily run to specious prolixity, we can always use examples from the past to remind us that it doesn't have to be like that. The English language has always made its main initial impact through the turn of a single phrase. Book titles, when they catch our attention, are a constant reminder that this is so. One of the earliest unforgettable book titles was devised by Browne himself: *Urn Burial*. No sooner seen but memorized, even when you don't yet know quite what is meant.

Dreams out of the ivory gate, and visions before midnight.
— SIR THOMAS BROWNE, *ON DREAMS*

WHEN I FIRST read this magnificent line, the second half of it begged to be the title of a book. I copied the line into an early instalment of my journal, so it must have been when I was at Cambridge, where I had a brief period one winter of joining Browne's collected works in Pembroke Library after the early nightfall, as if those moulting leather-bound volumes were a gang of old drinking chums. At the time I had no idea what kind of book mine would be. The phrase was a cap looking for a head to fit. Later on, when I was assembling my first book of television criticism, it took me a while to remember that there was a suitable title all set to go. *Visions Before Midnight* seemed just right: the television programmes were visions, they happened before midnight, and the falling phrase had something in it of a civilization coming to an end, which was roughly the way the BBC sports commentators made me feel.

Since Thomas Browne thought of it first, I need not fear a show of immodesty in saying that "visions before midnight" is an exquisitely balanced phrase. Browne had an infallible sense of cadence that could operate through a whole sentence, making it a long poetic line. Characteristically the first half of the sentence rolled up the hill and the second half rolled down, so the second half had more momentum. "It cannot be long before we lie down in darkness," he wrote, "and have our light in ashes." In that sentence the first half itself falls into two halves. (One of those halves was borrowed by William Styron as a title: *Lie Down in Darkness*.) Another three-part two-parter should be more famous than it is. "Man is a noble animal, splendid in ashes, and pompous in the grave." Really there should be a colon after "animal," and everything after the colon is a single clause, soaring first and then coming in to land. Browne's section of *The Oxford Dictionary of Quotations* is full of lines like that, but they are best studied in context, in the oldest edition of his works that you can find. The musculature of his style should be appreciated through time, as the beauty of a leopard should be seen through trees. For a writer like him, an anthology is a zoo of the bad old kind, where the animals were stymied behind bars or on concrete islands.

Dreams out of the ivory gate—pause to consider the power of a single comma—and visions before midnight. I never contemplated stealing the first half of this particular sentence and thought that nobody ever would, but years later I found that someone already had. (These were still the days before "to Google" had become the infinitive that could search infinity.) There it was in a second-hand bookshop: *Dreams out of the Ivory Gate*, by J. B. Priestley. Why he picked the less dramatic half of the sentence is beyond comprehension, but he might have thought it the more poetic. I would call it the more poeticized, and thus the less durable. On its own, "dreams out of the ivory gate" sounds like an average moment from James Elroy Flecker's *Hassan* or *The Golden Journey to Samarkand*. Not that Flecker is without his covetable jewellery impatiently waiting for the right burglar. "Tonight or any other night / Will come the gardener in white / And gathered flowers are dead, Yasmin." As a title, all *The Gardener in White* so far lacks is a book to fit. It also has the virtue of being hard to misquote. Both in real life and in the media, I have had interlocutors wanting to talk about some obscure work called *Visions at Midnight*. Since they have probably been misled by nobody less than Shakespeare ("I have heard the chimes at midnight," says Falstaff, as if aware that Orson Welles will come along one day to borrow the last three words), I ought to feel complimented, but actually it drives me to distraction. Similarly, my novel *Brilliant Creatures* comes back to me as *Beautiful Creatures*. When I lifted that title from a poem by Yeats ("The Wild Swans at Coole") I thought it was fluff-proof. To hear it misquoted is like stealing a piece of Lalique glass for a high-maintenance girlfriend and then watching her drop it.

Book titles are not a true study, but they are a lasting interest. Often they are the first clue to the sensibility of the author who chooses them. In my novel *The Remake* (much excoriated by critics, and therefore cherished by me) I indulged myself with two separate passages of clever-dick dialogue in which characters vied with each other to name the best book titles ever. Before re-creating the game on paper I had played it many times in real life, and I am still ready to play it with all comers. From any contestant, the author most often drawn upon, as an adept of the seductive title, turns out to be Hemingway. Sylvia Beach, founding proprietress of the legendary Paris bookshop Shakespeare & Co., used to say that one of the secrets of Hemingway's commercial success was his unerring choice of titles, which resonated across the bookshop to ensnare the customers with their silent music. Some of his best titles, whether for novels or short stories, were made up: "A Way

You'll Never Be," "The Snows of Kilimanjaro," *Across the River and into the Trees*. (The last, probably his worst book, inspired a telling critical parody by E. B. White, "Across the Street and into the Grille," and after White came the deluge: every hack had a stab at the same construction—across the this, or these, and into the that, or those.) But a surprising number of Hemingway's best titles were borrowed from established literature, and among them were two of the very best: *The Sun Also Rises* and *For Whom the Bell Tolls*. Thus to establish a continuity with classic English prosody was not only clever of him, it was appropriate. Eugene O'Neill worked an appearance of the same trick with the title of his play *Mourning Becomes Electra*: the use of "becomes" hints at a hallowed archaism, and also, when the meaning is grasped, encourages you to emphasize the right word, thereby releasing from a short sentence its endless melody. William Faulkner went all the way by choosing a biblical quotation that had the Old Testament written all over it: *Absalom, Absalom!* But it was just as characteristic of him to call a book *Sanctuary*, bringing the browser close by opening up the echo chamber of a single word.

A knack for titles is not necessarily the prerogative of genius. Gifted journeymen can do it too. Raymond Chandler's titles were as good as his books: *The Big Sleep, The Little Sister, The Lady in the Lake*. Dashiell Hammett's were better than his books: *The Glass Key, The Thin Man, Red Harvest*. Ira Levin's can be poetic in the best sense: *A Kiss Before Dying*. Newly minted technical terms are an exploitable source for jobbing writers with no particular inspiration but a reasonable ear: *Fail-Safe*. The word "last" carries an automatically romantic charge which has made it too popular with title-seekers to be used now: *The Last Romantics, The Last Tycoon, Last Exit to Brooklyn*. The prolific inventor of the Saint, Leslie Charteris, got in early with the most lasting use of "last": *The Last Hero*. There have even been outright bad writers blessed by the visitation of a poetic title. Ayn Rand had one with *The Fountainhead*, and another with *Atlas Shrugged*: a bit of a mouthful, but nobody has ever spat it out without first being fascinated with what it felt like to chew. Yet if those were not two of the worst books ever written—the worst books ever written don't even get published—they were certainly among the worst books ever to be taken seriously.

A foreign title often loses something when brought over into English, but sometimes there is an even match—*Der blaue Engel* and *The Blue Angel*, *La Peste* and *The Plague*—and occasionally there is a substantial gain. Françoise Sagan got lucky in that respect: *Those Without Shadows*. So did Gabriel García Márquez: not for *One Hundred Years of Solitude*, a title I find as spongy as the book, but for *The Autumn of the Patriarch*. In the original German, *The Tin Drum* is *Der Blechtrommel*. Though it is always hard to judge the weight and balance of words in a language that is not one's first, it is just as hard to believe that Günter Grass lost anything there, because the English phrase gives you two clear beats on the drum, while the long German word sounds like someone choking. *If on a Winter's Night a Traveller* is a faithful rendition of the Italian original, and is therefore ridiculous, because no Italian of any real literary judgement believes that Calvino, when he conceived that title, was doing anything else except putting on the dog, plus a feather boa, a plumed hat and a pair of platform shoes. (This is not to say that long titles don't sometimes succeed: Elizabeth Smart's *By Grand Central Station I Sat Down and Wept* is still good, although it was never really a good book—it was an indulgence.)

When the language is so far away from English that the translator can afford to rebuild the title from the ground up, the results are more likely to be good, and in the case of Mishima they were marvellous. *The Sailor Who Fell from Grace with the Sea* is one of those ear-catchers that wear better than you think they might, and *The Decay of the Angel* is one of my favourite titles ever: desolate and lavish at the same time, like Cleopatra's barge at the breaker's yard. (The actual book, of course, has all the taste and judgement of a photo of Mishima in his posing pouch, pectorals oiled and motorcycle aching to be embraced between his bandy thighs.) Tanizaki, a far more important writer than Mishima, should have been as lucky with his titles, but apparently didn't care. The title of his masterpiece *The Makioka Sisters* is just as lacklustre in the original. If only he could have borrowed something by Mishima: *Spring Snow* would have been perfect. It would also have been irrelevant, but good titles often are. George Barker called one of his poetry collections *Eros in Dogma*. In the more than forty years since I first bought a copy in Tyrrel's second-hand bookshop in George Street, Sydney, I have found the title of the book as impossible to forget as the poems in it were impossible to remember.

The title that screams quotation is rarely right, although few go as wrong as Anthony Powell's notorious *O, How the Wheel Becomes It!*, which not only makes you not want to read his book, it makes you not want to hear anything else that Shakespeare's Ophelia ever said. (The same man, we should remember, invented a book title to beat the band: *Casanova's Chinese Restaurant*.) All the best quoted titles sound invented, with just a hint that someone else once coined the phrase: *A Long Day's Dying, The Strings Are False, All the Conspirators*. (The word "all" is too cheaply tempting: *All My Sons* turned out well, like *All the Brothers Were Valiant* and *All the Rivers Ran East*; but *All the Sad Young Cannibals* made all "all" titles suspect.) When writers take their titles from previous literature, the previous literature doesn't have to be all that previous: just as long as it is not contemporary. T. S. Eliot was still very much in business when Evelyn Waugh raided *The Waste Land* for one of his best titles: *A Handful of Dust*. But *The Waste Land* had been just long enough established as a canonical text for Waugh to pick a plum. Eliot's own idea of a terrific title was *Ara vos prec*: a sure-fire hit with any bookshop browser who spoke medieval Provençal.

Poetic titles ought to be easy for poets, but few of them make the effort, or notably succeed when they do. Auden made a point of choosing titles that would radiate art deco glamour even as they lay sideways on the thin spines of his early collections: the flamboyant side of his gift came in handy. *Look, Stranger!* is one of the best book titles in any genre. He took the title from one of his own lines: "Look, stranger, on this island now." His American publisher—at Auden's suggestion, strangely enough—pointlessly dissipated the effect by favouring the excerpt *On This Island*. (Decades later, the essayist Wayland Young, collecting a set of lectures about the state of contemporary Britain, realized that somewhere in the middle of the contretemps there was another good title going begging: *This Island Now*.) Another bank-raid title by Auden came straight out of the American colloquial language, in the same way that the Broadway lyricists picked up temptingly ambiguous phrases from conversations overheard in the street: *Another Time*. It means better luck next time, it means a different era, and it means regret. It also means that any reader who picks up the book can already feel his skin prickling before he opens it. I feel the same about the title of Galway Kinnell's great long poem—his great *short* long poem, an important consideration—*The Avenue Bearing the Initial of Christ into the New World*. Kinnell's title has the effect of a *trouvaille*: he probably found it attached to a painting of Spanish troops and priests advancing into a territory they were fated to lay waste. But it was an American find: a big find, the size of a house. Auden's finds were micromanaged, appropriate to his way with a phrase. When young he could invent phrases like "The earth turns over, our side feels the cold" and string them together in a headlong rush, thus producing his trademark early tension, between the locution begging to be pondered and the impetus declining to be stopped. In his later, austere manner, he invented less, but could hear just as well. What he wanted to hear was the plain statement with a wealth of implication behind it—well behind it, so that you had to dig. The idea that his American exile was poetically barren would be sufficiently rebutted by attention to one little poem: "The Fall of Rome." In my own mind, that title is etched as one of his richest, although there is almost nothing actually in it: everything is to come. The whole poem leads you back to it, and almost everything you read about in the daily news or hear about in your daily life will lead you back to the poem. The poem's "unimportant clerk" is you, here, today. Elsewhere in the world, the mutiny of "the musclebound marines" will affect you tomorrow.

As Auden's poetic corpus takes up its place in literary history, it stands ready to be mined for titles by later writers. I myself was one of the first in: the title of my autobiographical volume *Falling Towards England* came from an Auden poem that features Sir Isaac Newton watching his apple exemplify the law of gravity. (In a letter to me which is now in the State Library of New South Wales, Philip Larkin wondered why none of the reviewers had spotted the theft, and concluded that they were too young to have known the thrill of Auden's first impact.) Risking solipsism—not for the first time in my life—I can extrapolate from my own example to suggest that many writers feel the need to find their titles in the literary past, whether as a claim to seriousness, a desire for legitimacy, or just a childish wish to stick close to mother. There is also the consideration that if you pull off the heist successfully then at least one part of your book will be worth reading. Long ago, in the seedy heyday of Sydney's Downtown Push, I was told the story of an unrecognized but determined Push novelist who had completed a magnum opus bigger than anything by Tolstoy and thought she would have a better chance of getting it published if she could dig a good title out of an established masterpiece of English literature. On being told that Milton had been the author of several works that might conceivably be thought of as filling the bill, she searched his collected poems from end to end—as a slow reader, this took her almost a year—and finally announced that she had found something unbeatable: it encapsulated her theme, had an intriguing rhythm, came from an obscure secondary effort called "Lycidas," and nobody had ever thought of using it before. She would call her book *Look Homeward, Angel.* But there had been nothing wrong about her instinct. She just didn't know that Thomas Wolfe had got there before her, following the same instinct: to look for resonant phrases in the past, when writers like Sir Thomas Browne were minting new coin with everything they wrote.

C

❦ ❦ ❦

Albert Camus

Dick Cavett

Paul Celan

Chamfort

Coco Chanel

Charles Chaplin

Nirad C. Chaudhuri

G. K. Chesterton

Jean Cocteau

Gianfranco Contini

Benedetto Croce

Tony Curtis

Ernst Robert Curtius

ALBERT CAMUS

❧ ❧ ❧

Albert Camus (1913–1960) was born in Algeria just before World War I and never forgot his colonial origins, although he rose to stardom in metropolitan France, the homeland of the colonist. "Stardom" is the right word because from his first day as a published writer he was surrounded by the kind of glamorous aura that other writers are likely to resent. In Nazi-occupied Paris he took risks in support of the Resistance but was honest enough to admit later that the risks had not been very great. A fundamental honesty was his hallmark. It led him to question whether the horrors of Nazism in any way legitimized the horrors of communism. His answer to that question was his book *L'Homme révolté* (*The Rebel*), which appeared in 1951 and set him at odds with Sartre and the whole of the French left, although Camus, with good reason, went on calling himself a man of the left until the end. Raymond Aron found the book weak when not obvious, but that could have been partly because Camus had got into print first with ideas that Aron had held while Camus was still a boy. Those for whom Camus's thesis is still not obvious would do well to read the book: his novels *The Stranger* and *The Plague* deserve their reputations but give only part of the picture of a complex mind. The widespread notion that Camus's mind was not really very complex at all is the penalty he paid for being blessed with good looks, the Nobel Prize, too many women and too much fame. He even died famously, in a car crash featuring that most glamorous of all sports saloons, the Facel Vega. The fate of Algeria, his lost homeland, haunted him until his last day. Even at the height of his success, he was a *pied noir* in exile. To himself, his condition as a displaced person was a constant source of unease. For generations of admiring readers, it must count as the deep secret of his overwhelming charm. Bright young beginners will always be attracted to a man who could say that everybody's life looks to be in pieces when seen from the inside.

Tyrants conduct monologues above a million solitudes.
— ALBERT CAMUS, *THE REBEL*

WHEN I FIRST read *The Rebel*, this splendid line came leaping from the page like a dolphin from a wave. I memorized it instantly, and from then on Camus was my man. I wanted to write like that, in a prose that sang like poetry. I wanted to look like him. I wanted to wear a Bogart-style trench coat with the collar turned up, have an untipped Gauloise dangling from my lower lip, and die romantically in a car crash. At the time, the crash had only just happened. The wheels of the wrecked Facel Vega were practically still spinning, and at Sydney University I knew exiled French students, spiritually scarred by service in Indochina, who had met Camus in Paris: one of them claimed to have shared a girl with him. Later on, in London, I was able to arrange the trench coat and the Gauloise, although I decided to forgo the car crash until a more propitious moment. Much later, long after having realized that smoking French cigarettes was just an expensive way of inhaling nationalized industrial waste, I learned from Olivier Todd's excellent biography of Camus that the trench coat had been a gift from Arthur Koestler's wife and that the Bogart connection had been, as the academics say, no accident. Camus had wanted to look like Bogart, and Mrs. Koestler knew where to get the kit.

Camus was a bit of an actor—he thought, in fact, that he was a lot of an actor, although his histrionic talent was the weakest item of his theatrical equipment—and, being a bit of an actor, he was preoccupied by questions of authenticity, as truly authentic people seldom are. But under the posturing agonies about authenticity there was something better than authentic: there was something genuine. He was genuinely poetic. Being that, he could apply two tests simultaneously to his own language: the test of expressiveness, and the test of truth to life. To put it another way, he couldn't not apply them.

Though he sometimes fudged the research and often fell victim to the lure of a cadence, Camus was stuck with a congenital inability to be superficial: he could be glib, but would regret it while correcting the proofs. He is not being glib here. Over the course of more than forty years, this line of his must have come to my mind at least a thousand times. (I thought of it again in the first minute of realizing that I would one day write this book.) But the first time I ever read it was the time that really counted, because the idea didn't just strike me as true, it struck me as unbeatably well put. He didn't put it in English, of course, and at that stage I could read scarcely a word of French, so I had no way of checking up. But by a lucky break the line translates easily, and even sounds rather better balanced in English than it does in the original. It would probably sound solid even in Urdu, just as long as the second and third nouns matched for polysyllabic weight. What brings the idea to incandescent life is that the line itself is so attractive an example of the very thing the tyrant's monologue can never do: it's interesting.

The tyrant's monologue doesn't *want* to be interesting, and that's its point. Camus was among the first—almost as early as Orwell—to realize that the totalitarian overlord's power to bore was a cherished and necessary component of his repressive apparatus. Droning on without contradiction was a proof of omnipotence, Stalin had already proved it with his grinding speeches to the Presidium: speeches which had to be applauded at the end of each bromide, and for which the applause at the end had to be endless. (During the Great Terror in the late 1930s, the first person to stop applauding went in peril of his life: it was either bleeding hands or a bullet in the neck.) But Stalin's speeches were the merest rehearsal for the tedium of his writings. It was particularly brutal of him to call his personally penned missal on the theory and practice of communism *The Short Course*. There was nothing short about it except its length. Physically, his writings were not all that extensive. Spiritually, they extended into the life of his readers and suffocated everything that breathed. Lenin had already set the style, but with Lenin the occasional sign of an active mental capacity crept in to aerate the slogans. Stalin made sure that didn't happen even once, and from his earliest years in power until the Soviet Union finally crumbled, the tone of official prose never varied in its almost inspired dreariness. To take a late example, the official *Short Biography* of Brezhnev, nominally written as a group effort by the Institute of Marxism-Leninism, could have been dictated by Stalin's ghost.

In other Communist countries, the tyrant's monologue was equally a standard, all-pervasive, atmosphere-clogging item. Mao Zedong had a taste for Tang poetry and some qualifications as a poet himself. Western enthusiasts have even seen the virtues of Oriental miniature poetic forms in the component mottoes of his *Little Red Book*. But his speeches were an amalgam of squeal and scream that managed to extirpate from Mandarin its normally inalienable melody. His gift for the dogmatic tirade, lavishly decorated with scatological abuse, was faithfully reproduced by every party mouthpiece who ever addressed a meeting, until, in the Cultural Revolution, the official address was a recognized form of torture throughout the country. In Cuba, Fidel Castro's writings, such as they are, have usually appeared in the form of interviews given to the foreign media. They are not without brio, especially if you are learning Spanish, in which case it actually helps to have the same few themes hit from fifty different directions by the one hammer. The best example of a book-form Fidel interview is *Nada si podra deterner la marcia del historia*. Nothing can hold back the march of history, and he proved it with his mouth. The Swedish journalists who faithfully recorded his torrential flow also caught some of his charm, however, and you can't reach a realistic estimate of Castro unless you take his charm into account. I bought my copy in the book market in Havana, sat reading it in a café while staving off the heat with a *mojito*, and learned quite a lot of ordinary Spanish by reading from context: the context being, of course, the standard international revolutionary boilerplate, recognizable at a glance in any language with a Roman alphabet.

But Castro's more typical form of communication is the speech, and his speeches have to be experienced to be believed. Most of the jokes made about them are made by people who have never really listened to him: they have just seen footage of him tossing his beard about while jabbing his finger at the air. In real life, if it can be called that, Castro carries the leader's monologue to lengths that should be physically impossible: a dedicated scuba-diver, he can probably do without the oxygen tanks, because he must have the lungs of a sperm whale. Camus, who played soccer, would have admired Castro's sporting pro-clivities but might have found his oratory suspect. Offshore admirers of Castro's putative intellectual vitality are fond of explaining how the people of Cuba—happy, salsa-dancing folk whose simple minds can be read from long range—find his oratorical powers endlessly entertain-ing, but the emphasis should be on the endlessly, not the entertaining. A sceptic might note that Castro's supposedly spellbinding effect pre-supposes the absence of other forms of verbal entertainment, and indeed the absence of a substantial part of the Cuban population. Cubans who head for Miami with nothing but an inflatable inner tube between them and the sharks are unanimous on the point: Castro's speeches would have been enough to drive them out even if the regime's other promises of abundance had been kept.

From North Korea in its nightmare heyday, the writings of Kim Il Sung were exported to the West in container ships, but not even our most fervent advocates of an alternative to capitalism could generate within themselves a demand to match the supply. They should have taken a look: it would have been a useful education, although very painful. Our broadsheet newspapers frequently ran, as a paid advertise-ment, a full-page prospectus of the collected writings, quoting exam-ples of Kim's thoughts, or Thought. The prospectus was probably enough to make the fans postpone their enjoyment. The luckless inhabitants of North Korea, however, had no choice: they had to stay abreast of a stream of prose that flowed faster than they could read. Not a paragraph of it was of any interest whatsoever, except as an awe-inspiring demonstration of the great leader's prerogative to bore his people rigid, like the Chinese terracotta army he inspected on his tour of Shaanxi province in 1982. He must have thought that he had seen those glazed eyes before.

Examples from the Communist regimes could be multiplied—her

rhetoric was the other reason that Camus might not have relished an evening with Mrs. Ceaușescu—but the exercise would be without merit. The fascist leaders present a more problematic, and therefore more important, case. Mussolini was held to be an exciting speaker, but on any objective estimate you had to be an enthusiast to think so. Ezra Pound, who was otherwise such a fine judge of poetry that T. S. Eliot sought and accepted his suggestions for trimming *The Waste Land*, compared the spare shapeliness of a Mussolini speech to a sculpture by Brancuși. It is permissible to suspect, however, that Pound's demented politics (Mussolini's measures against the Jews were never enough to suit Pound, just as Pétain's were never enough to suit Céline) had affected his aesthetic judgement. Even at the time, there were plenty of native Italians capable of realizing that what was coming out of Mussolini's bag was wind, and later on, during the long hangover after the Fascist binge, dispassionate philologists subjected his rhetoric to a rigorous linguistic analysis, laying bare how he had worked his tricks. In the case of Hitler, German-speaking critics had identified his speeches as concerted trickery long before he came to power. (In pre-*Anschluß* Vienna, the coffee-house wit Anton Kuh published a persuasive dissection of Hitler's rhetorical hoopla, thus earning himself a high place on the Nazi death list.)

For the performance art of both Hitler and Mussolini—both of whom the young Camus heard regularly on the radio—the most you can say is that it was exciting stuff if you believed it, and abject tub-thumping if you did not. As a writer, Mussolini when young could turn out a reasonably rousing socialist polemic. Hitler as a writer gave us *Mein Kampf*, which is worse than boring: Rudolf Hess, who transcribed it as it poured from his hero's lips, would have been driven mad if he had not already been that way anyway. Had *Mein Kampf* been even halfway readable, more people would have actually read it, and the world would have been warned earlier. In their off-duty moments—their down-time, as it was never then called—Mussolini and Hitler were very different creatures. Mussolini, though he brooked no contradiction, could be entertaining because he could be entertained: an admirer of Fats Waller could never be entirely without bonhomie. But Hitler was boredom incarnate. A typical oratorical effort was his broadcast on the eve of the *Anschluß*: it lasted a full three hours. And if listening to him was hard work in public, it was living hell in private. As we have it in transcribed form, his table talk makes us long for Goebbels. In the salon of the Berghof, for hours after midnight, Hitler would keep his punch-drunk guests from their beds with an interminable monologue about his early struggles and the shining Nazi future: a *Ring* cycle minus the music. Secretaries who worshipped him fell asleep trying to write it all down, while amputee officers reporting to him from the eastern front longed to get back to the comparatively spontaneous entertainment provided by the Red Army's massed artillery.

Hitler had the con man's insight into other people's reactions and must have been well aware of what he was doing. He was proving himself. Or rather he was proving his position: proving his power. Tyrants always do, and Camus spotted it. If Mussolini strikes us as a partial exception, it was because he was a partial tyrant. In Fascist Italy, the idea of individuality never quite died among the people. The true political monster insists that, apart from a few hand-picked satraps, there shall be no individuals except himself. Everyone must be reminded, all the time, that solitude is all there is: solitude in the sense of helpless loneliness, awaiting its instructions from the leader's voice. It was probably Camus's own innate loneliness that permitted him the insight. For a would-be athlete with weak lungs, there was no amount of success that could detach him from his primal knowledge of what it feels like to be without power. It was a knowledge that helped to make him a great writer. The Gods poured success on him but it could only darken his trench coat: it never soaked him to the skin.

DICK CAVETT

❢ ❢ ❢

Dick Cavett was born in 1937 in Nebraska. In high school he was a state gymnastics champion and trained himself as a magician. After Yale, he began his television career as a writer for Jack Paar and Johnny Carson, and subsequently ruled as the small screen's most sophisticated talk show host from the early 1970s onwards. In America, the talk show format depends on a comic monologue at the top of the show, perhaps a few sketches, and then the star interviews. Cavett's format dissolved the humour into the interviews, and much of his wit was unscripted. The idea that one man could be both playful and serious was never deemed to be quite natural on American television and Cavett was regarded as something of a freak even at the time. Eventually he paid the penalty for being *sui generis* in a medium that likes its categories to be clearly marked. I should say for the record that his interview with me was one of the least amusing he ever did, and it was my fault. But I learned a lot from him and never forgot him. The book *Cavett* (1974), which carries on its title page both his own name and that of his friend and amanuensis Christopher Porterfield, is cast mainly in the form of a long interview with the star. One of the best books about show business ever published, there is nothing quite like it, just as there has never been anyone quite like him.

Howya gonna keep 'em down on the farm,
after they've seen the farm?
— DICK CAVETT, QUOTING ABE BURROWS

D ICK CAVETT may have heard this line from someone else and stored it away for future use, but was certainly capable of thinking it up for himself and delivering it on the spot. In lofty retrospect, the trick of the line seems obvious enough to rank as one of those *trouvailles* waiting to glorify whoever gets to it first. Abe Burrows merely got lucky. (Abe Burrows also shared the credit for the superb libretto of *Guys and Dolls*, which was scarcely a matter of mere luck; but that's by the way.) As a true sophisticate with a daunting intellectual range, Cavett was the most distinguished talk show host in America, if sophistication and an intellecutual range were what you wanted. Johnny Carson was an even bigger celebrity, but Carson was a comedian first and foremost. Cavett's mental life was so rich that he could do comedy as a sideline. The only persona that he bothered to, or needed to, develop for working to the camera was of a boy from Nebraska dazzled by the bright lights of New York. To fit that persona, he would freely help himself to ideas from his range of influences stretching back to W. C. Fields and beyond. But he also had the capacity to make up great new stuff at terrific speed. He began as a writer for the established hosts and he could write for anybody, matching not only their themes but their tone of voice. When he finally appeared on screen as himself, he had to match his own tone of voice. He found that harder, but soon got awesomely good at it. By the time he got to me, in 1974, he had already interviewed almost every household name in the country, and was ready for the more difficult challenge of interviewing someone whose name wasn't known at all, and of making something out of that. We were on air, I had hummed and hedged about my reasons for leaving Australia, and he suavely sailed in with his own explanation, which I reproduce above. The throwaway speed of it impressed me: if he had used the line before, he knew just how to make it sound as if he hadn't.

A small, handsome man with an incongruously deep voice, Cavett was deadpan in the sense that he had no special face to signify a funny remark. He just said it, the way that the best conversational wits always do. In conversation, "joke" is a deadly word: anyone who relishes improvised humour will duck for cover if he hears a prepared joke coming. Whether in private or in public, Cavett's style posed no such danger. He was by far the wittiest of the American talk show television hosts, most of whom have always been dependent on their writers. There is no shame in that: in Britain and Australia, most of the talk shows go on the air once a week for a limited season. In America it is more like once a day forever. The host's huge salary is his compensation for never being free to spend it. The schedule is crushing, and the top-of-the-show monologue, if the host were to write it on his own, would need a full day's work, with no time left over for all the other preparation he has to do. Before the American host sits down with his first guest, he must first be a stand-up comedian: a joke teller. Cavett, having started as a writer, understood that condition well. But in his career on camera he was always more interested in the stuff that came after the monologue: the conversation with the guest. In this he was different from Carson and anyone else who has followed in Carson's tradition, right up to the present day. Even Jon Stewart, who deserves his billing as a rare bird, is more like Carson than like Cavett.

Carson was most at home doing his annual, high-earning stand-up stint in Las Vegas. Sitting down on his show, he could be spontaneously funny if the guest opened an opportunity—the clumsier the guest, the more opportunities there were—but it was strictly counterpunching. When the guest provided no suitable stimuli, Carson's grovelling feed-man, Ed McMahon, chipped in and Carson counterpunched against him. Carson's successor on *The Tonight Show*, Jay Leno, does without the stooge but works essentially the same way: the core of his technique is stand-up joke telling, and he keeps in shape by taking cabaret dates all over America. (When he was my guest in London, Leno was in his element, firing off jokes one after the other. When I was his guest in Los Angeles, he did the same thing. I did my best to come back at him, but it wasn't a conversation: more like mouth-to-mouth assassination.) Of the star hosts currently operating, David Letterman comes closest to Cavett's easy-seeming urbanity, but Letterman, for all his quickness of reflex, needs, or anyway takes, a lot of time to tell a story—at the top of the show, he can take ten minutes to get two things said, with much eye-popping and many an audience-milking "Whoo!," "Hey!" and "Uh-*huh*!" Nor does Letterman really enjoy it when the guest threatens to be capable of completing a paragraph unassisted, and an eloquent woman races his motor to a frenzy: instead of interrupting after every sentence, he interrupts *during* the sentence. The interruptions can be very funny, and they increase our opportunities to admire him: but they reduce our opportunities to admire the guest. Among the current bunch, Conan O'Brien gave you, when he was starting out, the best idea of what Cavett's unemphatic poise used to be like; but O'Brien, as he completes his climb to stardom, gives himself an ever-increasing ration of havin'-fun hollerin'. It's an imperative of the business, and Cavett defied it at his peril. Cavett never mugged, never whooped it up for the audience, rarely told a formally constructed joke, and listened to the guest. To put it briefly, his style did not suit an American mass audience, and in the course of time a position that had never been firm in the first place was fatally eroded.

Perhaps he was too cultivated. His Upper East Side brownstone was full of good books, which the range of reference in his conversation proved that he had read. (At Yale he had been an erratic student, but one of those erratic students who somehow end up reading the whole of Henry James, probably because somebody advised him not to.) Though temperamentally a nervous wreck by nature, he seemed as much at ease among his civilized surroundings as Jay Leno seems at ease among his classic cars and motorcycles. I was in New York to promote my book *Unreliable Memoirs*, which I suspected at the start would have little chance of securing an American audience. It was just too hard to classify: most of the first wave of American reviewers had convicted it of trying to be truthful and fanciful at the same time. Since I had clearly had no other aim in mind, I read these indictments with sad bewilderment. The most powerful reviewer, in *The New York Review of Books*, had seized on my incidental remark "Rilke was a prick" in order to instruct me that Rilke was, on the contrary, an important German poet. These portents were not good. But Cavett had been so nice about the book on air that I allowed myself to imagine he had actually read it, so here was one American reader already in the bag. He asked me to lunch at the Algonquin, where he was delightfully fast and funny; and then later in the week he asked me home for drinks, where he was even better, because he was ready to talk his business instead of mine. I learned a lot from him in a tearing hurry. Discussing his disasters on air (self-deprecation was one of his charms) he put on a tape of an old show and fast-forwarded to an illustrative moment. I can't remember who the guests were or what they were doing—it could have been Truman Capote attacking Sonny Liston with a handkerchief—but I can remember exactly the question Cavett asked me. "Why did my voice get louder just then?" When I hazarded that it was because the sound engineer had racked up the level, Cavett rewound a minute of the tape and showed me the moment again. "It didn't get louder," he said. "The director cut to the close shot." Then he played me an example of a line getting lost because his director cut to the wide shot. Suddenly I saw it all: the closeness of the shot varies the volume. I had already done years of television without figuring that one out for myself. That was the night I learned to wait for the red light on my camera before launching a would-be zinger. The red light meant go. In later years, isolated individual tapes (called iso-tapes in the trade) did away with the problem, but at the time it was vital information. Cavett, who did a minimum of four shows a week, knew everything about talking in vision.

It made him famous. He was never as famous as Carson, but he was famous enough not to be able to go out except in disguise. With a fishing hat pulled down over his ears he walked me along to Fifth Avenue so I could hail a cab. In that area the sidewalks had just been relaid with a sprinkling of metal dust in the concrete so that they would sparkle under the streetlights. We were walking on a night sky. Years later I did his show again. He was just as welcoming but he had even less time to spare. His show was fighting for renewal. The network executives thought he was finished and they might have been right. Those hundreds of shows a year had worn him out. The joke-telling machines can take that kind of schedule because nothing troubles them in their interior lives except the problem of finding time to spend the money. Cavett's interior life was more complicated. For too long he had been questioning the value of what he did for a living. I think he really wanted to be a writer, but couldn't face the risk of failing at it. The idea that he was born for television secretly appalled him. One of his many on-air comments about his lack of inches—"Sony are making people"—had a bitter tinge.

But born for television he was. Even if he had never hosted a talk show, his comedy specials would have been enough to establish him as one of the most original small-screen talents since Ernie Kovacs. I particularly treasure the blissful moment when Cavett was being loomed over by a luscious six-foot blonde. Sheltering under her magnificent bosom, Cavett addressed the audience. "Allow me to present," he said, "Admiral Harvey Q. Beeswanger USN, master of disguise." He had the wit's gift of making the language the hero—the gift of playful seriousness. In America, however, play and seriousness make uneasy bedfellows. Even a supposedly urbane magazine or culture supplement will contract a severe case of editorial nerves if a contributor cracks wise on a serious theme, and in the general run of show business the two elements, as time goes on, grow more and more separate instead of closer together.

It might be said that the United States is the first known case of a civilization developing through disintegration. It *might* be said, but you wouldn't want to say it on an entertainment talk show. A licensed iconoclast like Gore Vidal could perhaps get way with it, but no host would dare try—or even, alas, be capable of thinking such a thing. There are special talk shows for that sort of stuff. Charlie Rose has the seriousness business all sewn up. There will be no Dick Cavett of the future. We should count ourselves lucky that there was one in the past. I count myself blessed that I knew him when he was still a small but seductive part of the American landscape. Eventually the American landscape seemed to change its mind about wanting to include him, but it is possible that he had the idea first. At one point, towards the end, he was scheduled to do a set of programmes in England, for later transmission in America. Booked as a guest and champing at the bit, I was one of the many admirers looking forward to his arrival: but he never showed up. Apparently he boarded the Concorde at Kennedy, had a breakdown before the plane took off, and was taken home. I never found out what happened to him afterwards, and have never tried to find out. He would always have been a melancholic if he had given himself time, and perhaps he finally had time. (At the Algonquin he had given me a copy of his marvellous book, *Cavett*, and on the contents page he wrote

"More in Seurat than in Ingres.") A man looking for oblivion should be allowed to have it. Like Dick Diver at the end of *Tender Is the Night*, Dick Cavett sank back into America. He had already taught me my biggest lesson about television, far bigger than the one about the light on the camera: doing television can be wonderfully rewarding in every sense, but if there is nothing else in your life, watch out.

PAUL CELAN

❦ ❦ ❦

Paul Celan was born in 1920 in Romania and committed suicide in Paris in 1970. A thumbnail sketch of his life would
include two main facts: he was a slave labourer under the
Nazis, and he wrote the single most famous poem about the
death camps, *"Todesfuge"* (Death Fugue). A more detailed
account of his life opens up into one paradox after another.
Anybody can understand *"Todesfuge,"* but to become acquainted
with the bulk of his other poetry is a much harder task, even
though there are admirers who say that the difficulties have
been exaggerated, and that he is hard to understand only
because he understood so much. But there are times in his
work when a purportedly deep penetration of reality looks
exactly like taking refuge in obscurity. Though the truth can't
always be told by sales figures, it is interesting that his first collection of poems, *Der Sand aus den Urnen* (The Sand from the
Urns), published in 1948, sold twenty copies in three years. If
one of the poems in it, *"Todesfuge,"* hadn't eventually caught
on, the world might have heard much less of him: and one of
the reasons it caught on was surely that it was, for him, so
unusually direct. He himself loathed the idea that his most
famous poem had become a media event. He thought that too

many Germans were using it to ritualize guilt. On the other hand he had time for Heidegger, who saw no cause for guilt about his own conduct under the Nazis. There is an excellent critical biography by Celan's chief translator John Felstiner, called *Paul Celan: Poet, Survivor, Jew*. There is also a question, however, to be asked about that word "survivor." If we can conclude that the only way he had not to be mad was to be dead, can he truly be said to have survived? He certainly survives as a poet, but one does not necessarily belittle him by saying that it all depended on one poem. Mervyn Peake, who was present for the liberation of Belsen, wrote a courtly love poem to one of its dying girls. The discrepancy between subject and vocabulary worked its ironic trick, but finally the properties and cadences of the nineteenth-century romantic heritage obtruded. Celan wrote a twentieth-century poem. He found a way of injecting the inescapable sweetness of the musically constructed poem with the necessary bitterness to fit the time in which it was written, thereby obeying the following instruction to himself.

Number me among the almonds.
— PAUL CELAN, QUOTED IN JOHN
FELSTINER'S *PAUL CELAN: POET,
SURVIVOR, JEW, P. 79*

AT THE TIME I noted this instruction down, I couldn't resist the unwritten addition: "And call me a nut." But I knew that a mental defence mechanism was at work to fend off the sense of being under-rehearsed that one is bound to have when reading about someone upon whom history came down with its full weight, thereby justifying any amount of eccentric behaviour later on. Celan's example will always be daunting to other poets. For one thing, it included suicide, which critics understandably tend to regard as a mark of seriousness. They would have thought him serious anyway, because most of the time his work was almost impossible to make sense of. It courts philistinism to say that Celan's best poem, *"Todesfuge,"* is also his most accessible, but there is no way around the risk. Celan's usual hermeticism, his obliquity that amounts to an insoluble encryption, was a necessity for the poet, not the poetry: there was never any reason poetry written in the dark light of the Holocaust should be indecipherable, and he wrote at least one poem to prove it. In *"Todesfuge"* you can tell exactly what is going on. He is titrating the language of the *visione amorosa* against the imagery of the *giudizio universale*. The poem is an amorous vision of the Last Judgement. To put it more simply, it is a love song from hell. When we pick its entwined melodies apart, which the poem demands that we do, we find that there are two kinds of amorous vision: one the exultant vision of the perpetrator, the other the anguished vision of the slave. Hence the fugue. Scholarship (but only scholarship: not the poem itself) tells us that the fugue started as a tango. In Majdanek the camp's pitiable tango orchestra was forced to play endlessly while the doomed prisoners were selected for the various ways in which they would be worked to death. The German masters were rather partial to the tango, perhaps because it was the smart music of the socially pretentious: Hitler and Goebbels were both entertained by a tango orchestra in 1941. Celan would have heard about the death-camp tango. He would have heard about it, but he would not have actually heard it. We should remember that he was never in Majdanek or in any *Vernichtungslager* as such, although as a forced labourer in Romania he might as well have been. Majdanek was liberated by the Russians in 1944 and Celan probably heard about its sinister tango immediately afterwards. After he had the idea for the two contesting visions of love, however, it had to be a fugue.

The "Death Fugue" (strictly, the death's-fugue, because *Todes* is possessive) is, if you like, the last love song. In that sense, Adorno's remark about the impossibility of poetry after Auschwitz is all too dreadfully true: after such knowledge, there might be forgiveness, but no more innocence. There could be no return to the joyful. But Adorno's remark was also false, in the sense that no such return had ever been possible at any time in the historical world. There had been Holocausts throughout history, which probably featured slaughter as its first multicultural activity. The Holocaust, "our" Holocaust, seemed to be unique for having emerged from culture itself. But that was a misreading: a misreading from professional readers, from whom emerge the misreadings of the most tenacious kind. Culture and the Holocaust were separate things, both of which emerged from history. In the long view—admittedly easier for us who had the privilege of growing to our intellectual maturity after the event—the two things are so separate that they define each other. George Steiner echoed Adorno's opinion, but didn't act on it. Emotionally, Steiner might, had he wished, have embodied the silence into which he suggested (in his early book *Language and Silence*) that language ought to beat a retreat. With a highly developed awareness of the richness of European culture, he had a sensitive knowledge of how extensive the damage was. But none of that stopped him becoming a student of Celan; a course which, logically, ought not to have been available to him; if there could be no poetry after Auschwitz, why look for it? Steiner's answer possibly lay in his seeming conviction that Celan's real poetry was in the encryptions, the meta-language that proclaimed, by its obscurity, the impossibility of dealing directly with the event. Leaving aside the consideration that academics might always favour poetic difficulty—it makes them indispensable—Celan's difficulty, and Steiner's endorsement of it, amount to a double endorsement for Adorno.

But "*Todesfuge*" undoes the whole thesis. The idea that lyric poetry might be rendered nugatory by an enforced awareness of evil will always have its validity as an emotional response. As the world goes, it would be a damned soul who did not feel the idea to be true every few hours: how can we write of love when women are being tortured? But to *think* it true is to defy reason. Even within the one man, there can be the capacity to see the world at its most destructive and still create. Celan proved it with "*Todesfuge.*" Though we are bound to say, and say in a hurry, that a beautiful poem is not the only thing it is, the poem would not be there at all if the tradition of courtly love had not at least been remembered—so the remembering of poetry is still possible, even in the light of the oven. Compounded with the echo of a biblical psalm, a new kind of courtly poem, embracing a more tragic concept of beauty, arises from the memory. Steiner was right about the death of tragedy as a form, but only to the extent that tragedy became formless by getting into everything, in the same way that the ash from the chimneys got into the landscape.

With "*Todesfuge*" the tragic ash got into the lyric poem. It always had done, by implication—there was never a poem about the idea of love that didn't get its force from the fact of death. (Anthony Burgess, in *Nothing Like the Sun*—one of the few books about Shakespeare that a young student should read while he is first reading Shakespeare—paints a convincing picture of Shakespeare being inspired to lyric composition while watching an execution at Tyburn.) But no poem ever got quite so much force, from quite so much death, as "*Todesfuge.*" There are no points to be scored by calling it a great poem: of course it is. What is harder is to risk opprobrium by saying that Celan might have written more poems of its stature if he had not written so many poems about himself. His hermetic poetry no doubt reflected, and possibly controlled, his mental distress. Judging from his biography, it was a sufficient miracle that he could concentrate at all. But "*Todesfuge,*" by reflecting the physical destruction of its beautiful girls, got him out of himself. It got him away from the condition that Mario Vargas Llosa usefully calls *ensimismamiento* (being wrapped up in yourself), and Hannah Arendt defined as the tendency to identify one's own mind with the battlefields of history. Paul Celan had a perfect right to inhabit that condition, but it worked against his best talent, and might even have have helped to convince him, in the long run, that his best talent was not the best part of his mind, thus leaving his conscience free to condemn his own survival. There are no simplistic rules for poets: if there were, any duffer could write poetry. There are, however, rules of thumb, and one of the best is that getting the focus off yourself gives you the best chance of tapping your personal experience. For anyone with a personal experience like Celan's, of course, detachment from the self would be an impertinent recommendation. But it remains fascinating that in this one instance he achieved it, and wrote the poem by which most of us define him: the man who came out of the flames with a love song that redeems mankind in the only way possible, by admitting that there is no redemption.

CHAMFORT

Known, to his contemporaries and to posterity, always and only by his pseudonymous single name, Chamfort was born Sébastien-Roch Nicolas in 1741 and forecast the modern age by the reason for his death. He committed suicide in 1794 because the Revolutionary authorities had made it clear that they planned to reward his irreverent wit with a visit to the guillotine. In the rich tradition of French aphorists, Chamfort was the one who paid with his life for the knack of getting reality into a nutshell. It was because he lived at the wrong time. The Revolution had given birth to ideological malice in a form we can now recognize, but it was not recognizable then. It was still discovering itself. Chamfort, by the time that he ran out of luck, had already defined some of its characteristics, but not even he had guessed that it couldn't take a joke. In the twentieth century both of the main forms of totalitarianism were united in promoting the jokers to the head of the death list.

If it wasn't for me, I would do brilliantly.
— CHAMFORT, QUOTED IN JEAN-FRANÇOIS
REVEL'S *FIN DU SIÈCLE DES OMBRES* (AT
THE END OF THE CENTURY OF SHADOWS)

*S*ANS MOI, *je me porterais à merveille*. Chamfort said this after a bungled attempt to kill himself. His real name was Sébastien-Roch Nicolas, but he lived, and lives on, as Chamfort the wit. He had other ambitions, some of which brought him worldly success. His theatrical works were well enough thought of to gain him admission into high society. Tall, handsome, and a mighty lover of women, he said that he would never get married, "for fear of having a son like me." He was admitted to the Academy in 1781. In today's textbooks, however, Chamfort's sentimental plays are remembered for the thoroughness with which they have been forgotten, and he is classed with Rivarol as one of those pre-revolutionary minor philosophers who haunted the salons, made a night of it, and put too much of their effort into clever talk. But Chamfort's posthumously published *Maximes* took their place in literature for those connoisseurs of the aphorism who positively liked the idea that there was a wasted lifetime behind the wisdom. Though initially all in favour of the Revolution, Chamfort would probably have had the same chance as Camille Desmoulins of surviving the Terror, and for the same reason: he was a known critic and parodist of the hypocrisy prevalent among humanitarians, and the humanitarians were in charge. Desmoulins was executed because he had made a joke about Saint-Just. (In the tumbril, Desmoulins was heard to say "My joke has killed me," and his last witticism was already spreading by word of mouth even as his clever head fell into the basket.) Unlike Desmoulins, however, Chamfort tried to anticipate the guillotine. In a piquant forecast of Egon Friedell's flight from a window in Vienna 144 years later, Chamfort chose himself as an executioner. He made a frightful mess of it, but luckily died of his wounds, leaving the memory of his deliciously sardonic intelligence free to do its work. Chamfort was the one who supplied the lasting definition of *fraternité*: "Be my brother or I will kill you." That, in fact, was the joke that killed him: he was arrested soon after making it.

Jean-François Revel is only one of the many subsequent students of politics to admire Chamfort. Mirabeau borrowed from him freely, and Talleyrand more than freely, because Talleyrand didn't even acknowledge the debt. In London, Chateaubriand read Chamfort's complete works. Pushkin, the Goncourt brothers and Schopenhauer all thought Chamfort exemplary. From Ernst Jünger's Caucasus notebooks we can tell that he was reading Chamfort attentively in November 1942, with American bombers already over Germany in broad daylight and the Stalingrad disaster in the final stages of preparation. In de Gaulle's memoirs, Chamfort is quoted to fascinating effect: "Those who were reasonable have survived. Those who were passionate have lived." Evidently Chamfort helped de Gaulle to believe himself a bit of a devil. It is possibly the secret of the attractive wastrel, as a type, that reasonable men see in him the road not taken: his seemingly effortless charm allays momentarily the consideration that for them the road might never have been open. Some of the admiration heaped on the talented goof-off is gratitude to the sacrificial goat. Writers in general are happier if one of their number wastes his gifts, especially if the gifts are conspicuous: the way is left open for his tone to be borrowed, not to say plagiarized. But Chamfort might not have needed his overdeveloped taste for social life in order to marginalize himself. Purporting to find the whole business of securing a reputation sufficiently off-putting to justify a career of cynicism, he seems to have suffered few agonies of shame in writing his romantic entertainments. It was the serious literature that he found, or claimed to find, repellent. "Most books of the present have the air of being made in a day from the books of the past." It will do as well as anybody else's aphorism as a warning against making books out of books, although—as I have tried to argue elsewhere in this book made out of books—there is something to be said for the practice, as long as what is said is something true.

Chamfort had a way of getting something true said memorably without making it look laboriously chiselled. "I am leaving a world," he said, "in which the heart that does not break must turn to bronze." Few wits bow out with a throwaway line, and if they try to, the line is seldom as good as that. Even from such masters of elision as La Rochefoucauld, La Bruyère and Vauvenargues, too many French aphorisms come equipped with a marble slab. Chamfort favoured the paper dart. There is an easy, wristy flourish to his phrasing, which an artist-journalist like Revel is qualified to appreciate, because he can do it himself. "Systems of literary criticism," Revel wrote in his little book *Sur Proust*, "are made to satisfy the devouring lack of interest in literary works that calls itself a thirst for culture." If that sentence turned on "calls itself a thirst for culture" it would just be a Wildean paradox. But *dévorante* gives it savour, because the consuming energy of the deafness to art that goes into a critical system is always one of its distinguishing features—distinguishing it, that is, from the decently reticent poise of a sensitive response.

Chamfort got the vital extra word from his lyrical talent. With the aphoristic statement as with any other measure of prose, a nose for poetry helps. "For this magician of the epigram," wrote Revel of Chamfort, "the crystal and the music of a phrase are what matter most." A hidden corollary might be that the truth and the justice are what matter least; but there can be no doubt that a suggestive enchantment, always in shorter supply than rational exposition, is more likely to get our attention first, if not to hold it longest. Chamfort reaped all the rewards open to the quick wit, and almost convinces us that it was the only way to live. But if he had really believed that, he would have written down nothing at all. He did do brilliantly in the end, and all because he was himself, and not in spite of it.

COCO CHANEL

❣ ❣ ❣

Never pretty but always beautiful, Gabrielle "Coco" Chanel (1883–1971) embodied, during the course of her career, two important themes relevant to the story of the humanities in the twentieth century: one of them was the capacity of the popular and applied arts to influence culture at its highest level, and the other was the frailty of creativity under moral pressure. As a designer, her invention of the "little black dress" shifted the centre of attention from *haute couture* to *prêt-à-porter*: before her, the height of fashion had been priced out of the reach of any except the wealthy. From the fortune she made from her inventions, she was able to further exercise her infallible taste by patronizing the avant-garde: she wrote cheques for Diaghilev and Stravinsky. During the Occupation, however, her tastes, if not her taste, led her to accept the protection of a German official, with consequences for her reputation that would have been disastrous if her talent had not been regarded, correctly, as a national treasure. She lives on as a brand name: a perpetually bankable guarantee of elegance. The name tells something of the truth, though not all of it.

☟ ☟ ☟

Luxury is a necessity that starts where necessity stops.
— COCO CHANEL (ATTRIB.): A LINE
WRITTEN FOR HER BY PIERRE REVERDY,
AS QUOTED IN *CHANEL*,
BY EDMOND CHARLES ROUX

CHANEL MADE A profitable habit out of keeping a tame poet on hand to coin aphorisms that could be put into circulation attributed to her. As a general rule, the best aphorisms are truisms, but are true about subjects too scandalous to receive regular treatment. The truth of this one was most piquantly confirmed in Chanel's capital city. In Paris under the Occupation, the rationing of luxuries did not stop the women dressing as well as possible. Indeed they tried harder: it was something to take their minds off the grinding boredom, and the competition for the few available men was fierce. Paris was probably the first wartime capital in which the shortage of sheer stockings was compensated for by painting the legs, with a seam pencilled up the back of the leg for verisimilitude. The outbreak of fashion extravagance after the war—the New Look made far more news all over the world than the New Deal ever did—was a generational revenge for shortages of cloth, colour and silk lining.

When I was young enough to be dressing up in my mother's clothes while she was out—I had my transvestite phase at the age of seven, as I remember—the next most fascinating thing after the propelling lipstick was the look of the sequins on her one and only best dress for evening. Their glitter still affects the way I see Sydney Harbour in oblique sunlight. My mother's clothes were her sole connection with a better life, and they were vital. Her clothes and mine: the day when she left the hot iron for too long on the trousers of my first proper blue suit was one of the worst days of our lives. We had enough, but not a lot: not enough for it not to matter. Although Sydney was a long way from the worst of the war's hardships, it did not escape the global law that elevated everything pretty to the status of a rarity. It was only decades later, however, that I fully realized how those few fine things my mother had to dress in had been the true expression of a spritual value.

"Philosophy is about people in clothes," said the British philosopher
T. E. Hulme, "not about the soul of man." It's about both those things,
but he was right to insist that the first mattered.

The next level up from bare necessity is where the life of the soul
begins. As the war neared its end, the goods of the American military
PX were the world's first international currency. Girls in Germany
could be bought for a bar of chocolate. Less directly but just as effectively, cartons of Lucky Strike and Camel cigarettes bought the affections of women in Britain and Australia. For our fighting men, the
superior uniforms of the American service personnel amounted to one
of the most soul-destroying aspects of the war. American enlisted men
were better dressed than our officers. It hurt worse than German
bombs or Japanese bayonets: with those you could take your chances,
but the opulent small change of American culture you simply had to
take, and taking it was hard.

Years had to go by before those discrepancies ceased to be painful.
People's morality was judged by how long they had held out against the
lure of material goods. Chanel's borrowed axiom had a wide and lasting application—a sociological principle raised to the level of science.
Unfortunately her own principles were too easily compromised by it.
During the Occupation she chose the easy path. She took on a powerful German protector. It paid off in a big way in the early stages: she
would not have wanted for butter and sugar. Later on, when the Germans themselves ran out of luxuries, the deal no doubt held less attraction at the material level. Perhaps she deserves some credit for sticking
with him. The censorious committees of *l'Épuration* (the Purification)
would not have seen it that way. If she hadn't decamped to Switzerland
she would undoubtedly have had her head shaved: a new hairstyle that
even she would have been hard-pressed to make fashionable. The film
star Arletty spent two years in purdah for collaborating a lot less blatantly. Finally Chanel was allowed back, because she was one of the
keepers of the great secret of couture, which the French correctly saw
as the first chance of national recovery. A perennial guarantee to the
world that Paris held the secret of a stylish life, couture was already
helping to regenerate the French economy when the Citroën DS19
was still being designed. No matter how elegant the cars and airliners
(and there was never a more classy looking aircraft than the Caravelle),

it was the clothes that sold the world on the idea of a uniquely French combination of artistry and design. Nevertheless, Chanel sensibly kept her head down until, in 1954, inspired by the presence in Paris of the beautiful American model Suzy Parker, she went back into the rag trade.

In the West during the twentieth century, the blockade of the German-speaking countries in World War I, the post-war waves of inflation, the Depression throughout the free world, the war in Europe and the Pacific and its long rationed aftermath everywhere except in America—they all contributed to a laboratory for the study of the connection between materialism and the spirit. But it was in the heartland of dialectical materialism that the laboratory provided measures for the whole of existence. In the Soviet Union, nothing mattered more than access to the special stores, which were reserved for the *nomenklatura* and its chosen favourites. The special stores were where the luxuries were, some of them poignantly elementary: toothpaste that did not corrode teeth, toilet paper that did not cut, scissors that did. The vast majority of the people were condemned to the ordinary shops, where the command economy proved its efficacy by providing a standard of living only one rung up from the Gulag. Except for the brief burst of the New Economic Policy under Lenin, it was like that for seventy long years: the society that had proposed to abolish the gap between rich and poor made it an unbridgeable chasm. In Moscow in 1976 I was with a party of tourists who stayed at the Metropol hotel, famous scene of many a midnight visit in the late 1930s, when foreign Communist dignitaries would go to bed with all their clothes on in case their number came up. One of my fellow tourists, a lecturer in sociology at an English university, told me solemnly at dinner that it was a relief to be in a country where the gap between rich and poor was not blatant. He didn't see our Intourist guide slipping some leftover blinis into her plastic leather-look handbag. In Cuba in 1986 the security man in charge of my party of journalists—we were there to help generate publicity for the Varadero resort project—told me that if I really wished to reward him for his help I could use a few of my dollars to buy him a bottle of good rum from the special store. He was a government agent in a country famous for manufacturing the stuff, and in his whole adult life he had never been able to get a taste of it except at the lowest grade.

Except in periods of deliberately induced famine, nobody starved in the Soviet Union, or died of thirst or went unclothed. But they ate, drank and dressed at a level too low to leave them untouched by a desolate envy of the capitalism they were supposed to despise, and finally it was that corrosive spiritual deprivation that brought socialism down. The deprivation was comparative, not absolute: but the comparison was real. Thoughts of it filled the day, the week, the month, the year and the whole wasted life. In the West, someone obsessed with material things is correctly thought to be a fool. In the East, everyone was obsessed with material things from daylight to dusk. It was the most sordid trick that communism played. Killing people by the millions at least had the merit of a tragic dimension. But making the common people queue endlessly for goods barely worth having was a bad joke. At the Paris *prêt-à-porter* collections in 1982 I met Viktor Sichov, a photographer who had managed to defect from the Soviet Union and bring his whole archive with him. He thought he had spent his life photographing Soviet women in their moments of joy, passion, suffering and defeat. In Paris he finally realized that the true subject of his photographs had been their clothes. The edge of the crime, where it shaded into ordinary life, was the area in which the sadness became most palpable. In the centre it was too intense to grasp. Soviet consumer goods were the small-arms fire of the government's relentless economic assault on the people. Soviet consumer goods were an insult. They were already rubbish when they were fresh from the factory, and the fate of the people who had slaved, saved and stood in endless lines to buy them was to find that they could not even be cherished, because they were already falling apart. Meanwhile, the tastes of the ruling elite gave the game away. No Soviet diplomat based abroad ever returned to his homeland without a few bottles of Chanel No. 5. So Coco Chanel, who had rolled over for the Nazis, played her part in discomfiting the next dictatorship that came along.

CHARLES CHAPLIN

For most of his life, which stretched from 1889 to 1977, Charles Chaplin was world-famous, and for much of the early part of his career, up until the end of the silent movie era, he was, if measured in terms of recognizability and media coverage, by far the most famous person in the world. Readers of his stilted *My Autobiography* might assume that it all went to his head. The facts say that it didn't. The object of adulation on a scale that would have embarrassed Louis XIV, Chaplin nevertheless maintained his identification with the common people from whom he emerged. His progressive politics were genuinely felt, and his embarrassment at the hands of Red scare witch-hunters during the McCarthy era—the persecution drove him into exile—was an episode in modern American history of which his adopted country had no cause to be proud. In his later and less successful movies of the sound era, there were signs of disabling conceit in his determination to take every major credit including that of composer, but nobody had a better right to consider himself an artistic genius. He knew, however, that he wasn't a genius about everything else as well. Hitler, who awarded himself credentials for peculiar insight even into science, was thus a perfect subject for Chaplin's

comic gift. *The Great Dictator* (1940) was a study of megaloma-
nia by an essentially humble man.

> They cheer me because they all understand me, and they
> cheer you because no-one understands you.
> — CHARLES CHAPLIN TO ALBERT EINSTEIN
> AT THE 1931 PREMIERE OF *CITY LIGHTS*

O N THE BIG night, both of the great men looked good in their
tuxedos, but the film star was undoubtedly the more adroit at
social charm. He said exactly the right thing. He wasn't quite right,
however, about the "no-one." Contrary to the lasting myth—generated
by a *New York Times* reporter keen to sex up the story—every physicist
in the world understood the theory of special relativity straight away,
even if they thought it might be wrong. By now, almost every literate
person can recite the equation $E = mc^2$, and even give a rough account
of what it means. They might not be able to do the same for the multiple equations of the theory of general relativity, but they have some
idea of what the theory deals with. To give a rough account, however,
is not the same as giving a precise one, and having some idea is not the
same as understanding. It remains true that only the scientifically competent can fully know what is involved. Everybody else has to take it on
trust. Chaplin's remark nailed down a discrepancy between two kinds
of knowledge: the artistic and the scientific.

The discrepancy had already been there when Goethe rejected
Newton's theory about the composition of light because it didn't strike
him as artistically satisfactory. The discrepancy was there, but it wasn't
obvious. (Certainly it wasn't obvious to Goethe.) By the time Chaplin
and Einstein both went to see *City Lights*, it was obvious to all but the
insane. Most of science, for those of us without mathematics, is a
closed book. But some of the book's contents can be transmitted in a
form we can appreciate, and there is consolation in the fact that the
humanities unarguably constitute a culture, whereas whether or not
science is a culture is a question that science can't answer. When the
British scientist cum novelist C. P. Snow gave his lecture called *The Two
Cultures* in 1959—his main point was that literary people who didn't

know something about science couldn't know enough about the modern world—he started a quarrel that he was bound to lose, because the dispute could be conducted only within the framework of written argument. There was no way of conducting it by experiment, or stating it in symbols. It could take place only in language—on the territory, that is, that the humanities have occupied throughout history.

Science lives in a perpetual present, and must always discard its own past as it advances. (If a contemporary thermodynamicist refers to the literature on phlogiston, he will do so as a humanist, not as a scientist. Nor did Edwin Hubble need to know about Ptolemy, although he did.) The humanities do not advance in that sense: they accumulate, and the past is always retained. The two forms of knowledge thus have fundamentally different kinds of history. A scientist can revisit scientific history at his choice. A humanist has no choice: he must revisit the history of the humanities all the time, because it is always alive, and can't be superseded. Two different kinds of history, and two different kinds of time. Humanist time runs both ways: an arrow with a head at each end. If Homer could be beamed up from the past, taught English, and introduced to Braille editions of the novels of Jane Austen, he would be able to tell that they were stories about men, women and conflict, and more like his own stories than not. Much of the background would be strange to him, but not the foreground. A couple of millennia have done not much more to make the present unrecognizable to the past than they have done to make the past unrecognizable to the present. Science, on the other hand, can make its own future unrecognizable in a couple of decades. If the most brilliant mathematicians and computer engineers of 1945 could be brought here now and shown an ordinary laptop, they might conceivably be able to operate it, but they would have no idea of how it worked. Its microprocessors would be insoluble mysteries. The power of science is to transform the world in ways that not even scientists can predict. The power of the humanities—of the one and only culture—is to interpret the world in ways that anybody can appreciate. Einstein knew that science had given Chaplin the means to be famous. Einstein also knew that Chaplin could live without a knowledge of science. But as Einstein told Chaplin on many occasions, he himself, Einstein, could not live without a knowledge of the humanities. Einstein loved music, for example, and was so wedded to the concept of aesthetic satisfaction that he gained added faith in his general relativity equations from finding them beautiful, and frowned on the propositions of quantum mechanics because he found them shapeless. On the latter point he turned out to be wrong, and physicists in the next generation were generally agreed that his aesthetic sense had led him astray. The two different kinds of inspiration almost certainly connect, but only at a level so deep that nobody inspired in either way can ever know exactly how he does it. Whoever was inspired to invent the tuxedo, however, did the world a service: on the big night, the two different geniuses looked like the equals that they were.

NIRAD C. CHAUDHURI

Born in East Bengal in 1897, Nirad C. Chaudhuri lived for a hundred years, which meant that for almost the whole of the twentieth century one of the great masters of English prose was an Indian: and of Indian masters of English prose, Chaudhuri was by a long way the most distinguished. He was granted that title even by other writers of Indian background who might well have claimed something like it for themselves: V. S. Naipaul, Anita Desai, Zulfikar Ghose. They revered him even when they disagreed with him. Chaudhuri himself never set foot outside India until 1955, for a trip to the centre of the old British Empire—rapidly shrinking at the time—that he had always infuriated many of his compatriots by more admiring than not. His short book about that short visit, *A Passage to England*, gives us the essence of his limpid style and historical range. But readers should not be afraid to tackle at least two of his longer books. *Thy Hand, Great Anarch!*, his account of the crucial years in Indian history between 1921 and 1952, is one of the indispensable historical works of the century, and *The Autobiography of an Unknown Indian* is rich in self-examination, unfailingly hard-headed in its liberal sweep, and true in every detail except its title. If ever there was a known Indian, it was

Chaudhuri. His decision to live out the last act of his life in
Britain had profound impliciations for some of his fellow
Indian intellectuals. Many of them resented it. But his belief in
India's importance to the world remained beyond question.

❣ ❣ ❣

My notion of what is proper and honest between
Englishmen and Indians today is clear-cut and decisive.
I feel that the only course of conduct permissible to either
side in their political and public relations at the present
moment is an honourable taciturnity. The rest must be left
to the healing powers of Time.
— NIRAD C. CHAUDHURI, *THE
AUTOBIOGRAPHY OF AN UNKNOWN INDIAN*,
P. 502

IN EARLY 2002, British Prime Minister Tony Blair might have profited if his Foreign Office brief had included this quotation. He might
have been a bit less ready to lecture his Indian and Pakistani opposite
numbers on the advisability of cooling down. The advice was received
with polite disdain: the best that could be hoped for. It was Blair's lucky
day. After the Indian Mutiny, cheeky Sepoys were tied across a cannon's mouth preparatory to its being fired. The hankering for a comparable decisiveness must surely linger. Another use for the quotation,
and one we can all put into effect, is to remind us that Chaudhuri,
while he valued the connection with Britain, had no rosy view of its
effects: he was never a lickspittle for the Raj. In *Thy Hand, Great
Anarch!* he recounts how Britain manoeuvred to get India's cooperation
during World War II without having to promise independence. On the
other hand, he came down hard on the counterproductive intransigence of India's political parties, especially of the Congress party. If
Congress had cooperated with Britain during the war, he says, it might
have prevented partition afterwards. Nehru, not Gandhi, is Chaudhuri's villain. In Chaudhuri's picture, Gandhi retreats into the background while Nehru, between 1939 and 1947, stands forward as "the
wordmonger par excellence."

The Indian intelligentsia, says Chaudhuri, wanted Britain weakened but not defeated. Like the Trinidad-born writer C. L. R. James, whose message to the Third World was that it should learn from the First, Chaudhuri offered no automatic comfort to the old Empire's self-renewing supply of angry radicals. Most of Chaudhuri's political talk means discomfort for someone, usually for India's intellectuals. Many big subcontinental names have admired him, but you can't imagine any of them not dropping the book and whistling at some point, especially when he reaches the conclusion (and his writings *in toto* reach no other) that Britain made India possible. The best reason to whistle, however, is the quality of his prose. Ten pages into *The Autobiography of an Unknown Indian*, he's already snared you. "The rain came down in what looked like already packed formations of enormously long pencils of glass and hit the bare ground." If he had lived long enough, W. G. Sebald would probably have got the Nobel Prize for writing like that. Chaudhuri's prize was to live for a hundred years, retain a rock-pool clarity of mind, and spend his extreme old age in England, surrounded by the foreign language he loved best, and of which he was a master.

Chaudhuri and Sebald might seem a strange coupling, but more united them than their choice of England as a place of voluntary exile. Chaudhuri was a character from one of Sebald's books: like Austerlitz in *Austerlitz*, Chaudhuri could develop a philosophical theme out of a long study of practical detail. Similarly, Sebald was a character out of Thomas Mann. If you ever find yourself wondering where you have heard Sebald's infallibly precise memory speak before, think of the enchanting and omniscient Saul Fitelberg in *Doktor Faustus*. There are tones that connect authors in exile, and that give them a single country to inhabit: the country of the mind. The difference is in the timing. Chaudhuri and Sebald were looking back on shattered civilizations. So was Thomas Mann, but with Fitelberg he could make the character prescient. In *Doktor Faustus* the end has not yet come. The character can foresee it because the forces that will lead to disintegration are the first he feels. Chaudhuri's prescience was about a future that had not yet happened, and is happening only now. By the mere act of writing such a richly reflective prose, he suggested that a civilization continues through the humane examination of its history, which was its real secret all along.

G. K. CHESTERTON

G. K. Chesterton (1874–1936) published so many books that his posthumous reputation is almost impossible to sort out. He would have been famous just for his Father Brown stories. He would have been famous just for his novels *The Napoleon of Notting Hill* and *The Man Who Was Thursday*. He would have been famous just as a literary critic: his monographs on Browning and Dickens are still required reading for serious students of those authors. Above all, he would have been famous just for his journalism: the thing he is least well-known for now. The essays he contributed to periodicals were at the heart of his talent for subversive observation. His vice was wilful paradox, but his virtue was for asking the awkward questions about current liberal fashions. The virtue itself had a drawback: as a Catholic convert, he valued theological tradition to the point of embracing some of its blemishes, one of which was an abiding suspicion of the cosmopolitan. Anti-Semitism reared its head, although not as blatantly as in the work of his contemporary Hilaire Belloc. But generally Chesterton's collections of essays and casual pieces are well worth seeking out in second-hand bookshops. There are a thousand brilliant sentences to prove that he was the natural opponent of state power in any form, so there can be no real doubt about the stance he would have taken had he lived longer. He defined true democracy as the sum total of civilized traditions. It was a conservative approach, but it could never have become a fascist one, since the idea of a civilized tradition was exactly what fascism set out to dismantle.

To set a measure to praise and blame, and to support the
classics against the fashions.
— G. K. CHESTERTON

WHEN I COPIED this sentence into a workbook about twenty years ago, foolishly I neglected to note the provenance. The sentence does not appear in *The Oxford Dictionary of Quotations* but that, alas, is no surprise: its entry on Chesterton consists almost entirely of scraps torn from his poetry, whereas all his best remarks were in his prose, which the editors of the Oxford book obviously did not get around to reading. It is hard to blame them for that, because catching up with Chesterton's prose is the work of a lifetime. He wrote a lot faster than most of us can read. Chesterton published many, many books, and at one time I was trying to collect them all. (My shelves containing Chesterton still outdistance my shelves containing Edmund Wilson, but with Wilson I know my way around almost to the inch, whereas there are cubic feet of Chesterton's output where I can't find my way back to something I noticed earlier: a slipshod disorientation, which I could have avoided by taking proper notes.) I saw myself as his champion. Other journalists feared him because he was so productive. Mainstream writers feared him because he wrote too well. He was my favourite kind of writer, scaring everybody because he had talent to burn, and no sense of calculation to make his talent decisive.

His critical writings struck me as particularly valuable among his output: rather more valuable, in fact, than the nominally creative work, in which *The Man Who Was Thursday* was widely proclaimed to be his masterpiece by people who had no intention of finding out what else he wrote. I thought *The Man Who Was Thursday* dreadfully windy and most of the poetry less thrilling than its own craft. Is "The White Knight" really that good, even on the level of a *recitativo* party piece?

In Sydney in the late fifties I knew at least one Catholic poet who thought "The White Knight" a deathless text, but he (my friend, not Chesterton) was very Catholic, and no great reciter himself. In my experience, fuelled by many a shouted evening among young men educated by Jesuits, the awkward truth became apparent early: Chesterton the Catholic poet was outstripped even by Belloc, and both were left for dead by Hopkins. But it was just as apparent that some of Chesterton's criticism was excellent. Dickens and Browning are not the only names he can bring alive in a short monograph. As an enthusiast for Chaucer he is only just less inspiring than Aldous Huxley, and he had a gift for the critical essay that could survive even his mania for paradox. Somewhere among the paradoxes there was always a considerable plain statement, and the statement quoted above is a prime example.

On the whole, Chesterton's paradoxes merely asked for trouble. His seemingly plain statements were real trouble. I think I knew that at the time, or I would not have written this one down. If I had taken it straight, I would have regarded it as a truism, and left it unremarked. But there was something unsettling about it. Pretending to just lie there inert, it glowed, fizzed, and shovelled piquant smoke, as a lot of Chesterton does. With a new century crowding in on London's journalistic world, I can recommend Chesterton's teetering example to Grub Street hacks on their last legs, facing oblivion in the current equivalent of the Cheshire Cheese, going home to a mansard room full of unmarked files, yellowing tear-sheets and—impossibly dated now, fading to nothing in ordinary daylight—the carbon copies that were once called blacks. *Nil desperandum.* We just might live. After all, did Chesterton ever look at an article and think: this is the one? No, he never knew.

The second part of the sentence is the more immediately awkward part. The first part apparently takes care of itself. Critics who overdo either the praise or the blame are soon rumbled: sooner still if they overdo both. But the apparently unexceptionable exhortation to support the classics against the fashions conceals a genuine dilemma. All the classics were fashions once; new classics have to come from somewhere, and might be disguised as fashions when they do. The neatest deduction that can be made from the advice is about the advisability of finding out what makes something classical, whether it is new or old: and of supporting that, presumably by praise, while blaming anything that pretends to the same condition without the proper qualifications. So the two parts of the motto connect at that point. They connect more closely when we consider that a classic might be tainted by fashionable components, or that a fashion might be enriched by classical ones. Such a possibility is not likely to arise with accepted classics from the past: unless, paradoxically, we find out too much about them. Suppose we knew everything about popular entertainment at the time of Ovid: it might turn out that tall stories about metamorphosis were a craze at fashionable dinner tables, the hot topic at the saturnalia. Or suppose we knew everything about theology at the time of Dante (some scholars almost do): it might turn out that some of Dante's points of doctrine were the merest run-of-the-cloisters debating points. Benedetto Croce, indeed, working like that very basic Australian device the milk separator (it left the cream on top of the milk, like a golden duvet on a heap of sheets), divided the *The Divine Comedy* rigorously between *poesia* and *letteratura*, and by *letteratura* Croce meant the stuff that belonged to its time—a concept which sounds more like fashion than like anything else. Still, most of us never get to know that much. Knowing about the background is what we either don't get to do or else forget about in short order, and for us, the common readers—who are, in modern times, the uncommon people still interested even though the examinations are no longer compulsory—every ancient classic remains classical right through, even when impenetrable. Homer's most vivid translator in recent times, Christopher Logue, knows that the Homeric poems are classics, even though he can't read them in the original. That's why he feels compelled to bring all his talent to the task of finding an English equivalent for them, with results that might very well prove classic in their turn.

But with contemporary classics we are involved with the same dichotomy from the jump. It is hard to think of a creative mind so pure that it would not be affected by popular notions to some extent. Also it is hard to think of any modern classic in any field that has not been affected by the popular arts. Some modern classics began as popular arts, and in very recent times an assumption has grown up—not easily to be laughed off—that there is no better way for a modern classic to begin. Certainly, in the English-speaking countries, a modern classic song is more likely to come out of a centre for a popular genre—Tin

Pan Alley, say, or Broadway, or the Brill Building, or Nashville—than out of the "art song" tradition. In France, the "art song" tradition has some important classical composers at the foundation of it (Fauré, Reynaldo Hahn, Duparc, etc.) and carries prestige as a consequence; but one of the reasons the *chanson* heritage is relatively strong is that the popular genres have always been relatively weak; and anyway, Prevert, Brel, Brassens and a dozen other names are scarcely thought of as members of an academy. In literature, a writer as good as W. G. Sebald is safe from selling millions of books, but he would not be disqualified from seriousness if he sold hundreds of thousands, which he is nowadays quite likely to do, given time. No theorist about literature could any longer get away with the proposition that best-sellerdom is an automatic disqualification from quality. Louis de Berniere's *Captain Corelli's Mandolin* might not be quite the masterpiece it was thought to be by many of those who chose it for their one hard read of the year, but it is not inconsiderable either: millions of man-hours on the holiday beaches were well enough spent in reading it, although the heart quails at the thought that those same readers later fell for the unalleviated stupidity of *The Da Vinci Code*. In Germany, the critic Marcel Reich-Ranicki's uncompromisingly taxing autobiography *Mein Leben* was at the top of the best-seller list for most of the millennium year. No doubt there was a fashionable element in its reception—some of the people who bought it to decorate the hall table might have been establishing their tolerance, refurbishing credentials vis-à-vis the cloudy past, etc.—but there was no fashionable element to the book itself, a literary work of the first order. Chesterton was actually alive when his principle was used against Puccini, and if Chesterton had been active as a music critic he might well have used it himself. Apart from Shaw, most of the writers on opera at the turn of the century loftily regarded the Italian operatic heritage as a branch of popular music. ("The music's only Verdi but the melody is sweet.") Puccini's overwhelming popular success was interpreted as a fashion by his detractors. Until very recently it still was. When I was an undergraduate at Cambridge, a prominent Wagnerian among the dons tried to tell me several times that Wagner's stature as a classic confirmed Puccini's as a fashion.

The same don has since turned into one of our best, most receptive and conscientious opera critics, but he didn't do it by following up on Chesterton's principle, which turns out, for its second half, not to be a principle at all. Either in life or in the mind, there can be no such rigid division of the classical and the fashionable. A work of art has to be judged by its interior vitality, not by its agreed prestige. Prestige alone was never enough to keep an acknowledged classic alive: if it had been, Petrarch's long poems in Latin, which he thought were his real claims to fame, would still be read today. The response to vitality brings us back to the first part, and reveals it, at last, to be an even bigger conundrum than the second. Without a capacity for blaming the sterile, there can be no capacity for praising the vital. Those without a gift for criticism can't be appreciative beyond a certain point, and the point is set quite low, in the basement of enjoyment. (Being mad about Mantovani is *not* a good qualification for the appreciator of Beethoven: Albert Einstein, who in his role as a dinner-party guru enjoyed introducing ignoramuses to classical music, would use Mantovani as bait, but he never thought the bait was a living fish.) On the other hand, those who are too critical are apt to run out of appreciation at the crucial time. Stravinsky, who was never comfortable about attention paid to other composers even if they were long dead, took most of his adult life to get around to the appreciation of Beethoven's late quartets, and gave the impression that his own life had to be almost over before he could hear what Beethoven was trying to do at the end of his. (It was also Stravinsky, however, who finally and incontrovertibly gave Tchaikovsky the praise that was due to him, and thus rescued him from a hundred years of being denigrated as Easy Listening.) All we can be certain of is that such oscillations between praise and blame, whatever their amplitude, show no discontinuity. Praise and blame are aspects of the same thing. The capacity for criticism is the capacity for enjoyment. They don't have to be kept in touch with each other. They are a single propensity that has to keep in touch with itself. Chesterton's plain statement is like one of his paradoxes without the simplicity: but that's a paradox in itself. It's an area that the dear, bibulous, chortling old boy gets you into. He invited being patronized, but it was a stratagem. He was serious, always. He just didn't seem to be.

JEAN COCTEAU

❣ ❣ ❣

The role of Jean Cocteau (1889–1963) in French twentieth-century culture was to be the wonder boy in perpetuity. He should be commended for it: some of his untiring precocity continues to amaze. Diaghilev's famous instruction to him ("Astonish me") was one he fulfilled by astonishing everybody. For Diaghilev, during World War I, Cocteau put together the ballet *Parade*, with music by Satie, décor by Picasso and choreography by Massine. No single production did more to advance all the arts at once. That they needed advancing was a principle Cocteau never questioned. In that sense, he was dedicated not to the private experience of art, but to its public impact. Unlike other troublemakers such as the Dadaists, however, he was not making up for shortage of talent. Cocteau went on astonishing everybody in a dozen different fields. He was poet, dramatist, graphic artist, novelist and film-maker, practising every art form at a high level. His love for the doomed young novelist Raymond Radiguet resulted in a cycle of tragic poems fit to dispel any illusion that he might have been a dilettante. But he had a dangerous taste for showing off to the exalted, and during the Nazi Occupation of Paris it led him astray. Receptions thrown by the Propaganda Staffel of the occupying power at the Tour d'Argent were too often graced with his exquisite profile. Compounded with an addiction to opium, his compromised reputation led to a spiritual decline after the war. Even then, though, he managed to produce the work by which he is most easily approached now: the film *Orphée*, which after sixty years still looks original despite all the originality it inspired from everybody else. ("Cinema is the form of modern writing whose ink is light" was a typical epigram.) There were other Cocteau films, most notably *Beauty and the Beast*, but *Orphée* gives the best sense of *tout Paris* making a home movie. If not the first, it was certainly the most sensational updating of a classic myth into modern dress. Orpheus, with immaculately cut pleated trousers instead of a toga, was played by Jean Marais, Cocteau's young lover. The leading actress, Maria Casares, was Albert Camus's mistress. French intellectual life was the world's biggest small world, and everyone in it thought of Cocteau as the arbiter of elegance, even when they despised him. Sympathetic biographies by Francis Steegmuller and Frederick Brown have the facts, and the right judgement. Cocteau's all-embracing multiplicity was a kind of unity, even if moral weakness was one of the things that it embraced. The best writer of all on "the banquet years," Roger Shattuck, often brings Cocteau on as light relief, but doesn't underestimate his importance. By and large, the well-funded and often highly qualified American students of French culture after the Belle Époque were ready to forgive all in their aim to understand everything. A humane attitude, as long as it doesn't lead us into the illusion that a man as intelligent as Cocteau didn't know what collaboration meant. He did: he just thought he could find a style for it. After the war, Cocteau's old friend Misia Sert (the tasteful patroness who serves as the nominal subject for one of the best of the many books about *tout Paris*, Arthur Gold and Robert Fizdale's *Misia*) threw a string of soirées for which she invited both those who had collaborated and those who hadn't. She invited

the two groups on different nights. So Cocteau never had to
meet the people who wouldn't stay in the same room with him,
because they weren't there.

Too many milieux injure an adaptable sensibility. There
was once a chameleon whose owner, to keep it warm, put it
on a gaudy Scottish plaid. The chameleon died of fatigue.
—JEAN COCTEAU, *LE POTOMAK*

I UNCONSCIOUSLY PLAGIARIZED this idea on two separate occasions
before discovering, when searching through my journals, that it
belonged to Cocteau. If I had remembered, I would have flagged the
borrowing: it is bad manners to do otherwise, and bad tactics too,
because usually you will be found out. My excuse would be that
Cocteau, though no end of a dandy and in many respects a posturing
water-fly, had the knack of hitting on expressions that were so neat they
seemed without a personal stamp, like particularly smooth pebbles on a
pebble beach. He once said to an interviewer that you couldn't teach a
young artist anything: all you could do was open the door and show him
the tightrope. I loved that idea and kept it in my memory. In his film
Orphée there are ideas that I loved and kept in a different way: the cryp-
tic phrases used by the angels—the phrases were based on coded BBC
radio calls to the French Resistance—became recognition signals for
my group of writers at Sydney University in the late fifties. "The bird
sings with its wings," we would intone to each other, in smug ecstasies
of knowingness. No doubt we were being very precious, but so was
Cocteau: *Orphée* is the apex of preciosity, and therefore, appropriately,
the distilled projection of Cocteau himself. In life, far from being
Orpheus, Cocteau was an Osric with an infinite range of hats, too many
of them by Schiaparelli. In World War I, when he visited the front in a
party led by Misia Sert—muse and patroness to all the artists—Cocteau
wore a nurse's uniform of his own devising. In World War II he was a
cocktail-party collaborator, mainly because he couldn't bear to be out of
the swim. At the Propaganda Staffel receptions, with cocktails and fin-

ger food, Cocteau was a fixture, if a chameleon crossing a swastika can be called that.

While not exactly despicable—nobody died because of him—his behaviour was not admirable. He can be classed with Sacha Guitry, Arletty and Maurice Chevalier among the top-flight artists who gave themselves a free pass because of their art. Only Chevalier was subsequently crass enough to hint that he had really been an Allied spy risking his life to gather information, but Cocteau came close to the same kind of vulgarity when he evoked the call signs of the Resistance in *Orphée*. All he had the right to evoke was a simpering air-kiss aimed at the Gestapo. There was, however, another, deeper Cocteau: this one, the Cocteau who invented the exhausted chameleon. This was the quickly whittling and fletching phrase-maker who could say and write things that would travel through time like untiring arrows. "Victor Hugo was a madman who thought he was Victor Hugo." A crack like that doesn't end the discussion, but it certainly starts one.

This, I think, was the Cocteau whom Proust loved: not the stylish poseur but the true stylist, a living concentration of art and intellect, of taste and daring. The moment in *À la recherche du temps perdu* when St. Loup runs along the top of the banquette in the restaurant is probably based on one of Cocteau's carefully calculated displays of his show-stopping knack for creating memorable scenes by stealing them. And in the long run, St. Loup's unlikely conversion to homosexuality was probably justified in Proust's mind by Cocteau's nature. Probably there were several real-life models for St. Loup, but at the end the model for one of the character's dramatic moments took over the character's inner being, if only because Proust's inner being had the same bent. It would scarcely have happened, however, if Proust had not genuinely admired Cocteau, who was impossible to admire if one did not envy his talent. This remark about the chameleon comes from the aspect of Cocteau's gift that will always remain enviable: the combinative power that underlay his protean knack for special effects. (The book *Le Potomak*, from which the quotation comes, was named not after the American river but after a creature he made up: a deep-sea fish that rises to the surface and dazzles everyone with its polychromatic, scintillating brilliance. Clearly he was talking about himself.) Endlessly pirouetting to get himself into profile, Cocteau was tiresome in the extreme, but mainly because the froth and fizz of his superficial behaviour made you nostalgic for the underlying man, whom you guessed correctly to be classical in his perceptions despite his self-denigrating mania for originality. It could be said that anyone who admired the looks of Jean Marais, the rebarbative star of both *Orphée* and *La Belle et le bête*, had the same classical perceptions as a Las Vegas hotel designer, but the late 1940s were a long time ago, and Marais's bouffant hairstyle was the first ever seen in a serious context. Elvis Presley was not yet there to be copied. Cocteau thought of his own images. He really was as innovative as his admirers said. Their only mistake was to imagine that novelty was an ethos.

GIANFRANCO CONTINI

❦ ❦ ❦

Gianfranco Contini (1912–1990) was the most formidable Italian philologist of his time. As a scholar of Dante and Petrarch he was crucial to the modern Italian tradition of studying the literary heritage on a rigorous textual basis. But he was also intimately involved with contemporary creativity, as a friend and sounding board to such poets as Eugenio Montale and Pier Paolo Pasolini. (His little collection of articles on Montale, *Una lunga fedeltà*, A Long Faithfulness, is a classic of the genre.) Vast in his learning and uniquely compressed in his prose style, Contini, even for the Italians, has a reputation as a *scrittore difficile* (difficult writer), and to translate his major critical articles into English would be a task for heroes. But beginners with Italian will gratefully discover that when giving an interview he could talk with clarity and point on cultural topics, some of them with wide resonance outside his own country. Regarded as a collaborative venture, the literary interview has a long and distinguished tradition in Italy. Contini collaborated with one of his pupils, Ludovica Ripa di Meana, to produce an outstanding example of the form, with a disquisition on education that has general relevance for all countries now suffering from the effects of having reduced the demands on memory.

> Unfortunately, the custom of learning by heart has disappeared in the schools, and as a consequence the very use of memory has gone with it. Nobody knows how to read verse. My best students, notably gifted philologists, can't recognize by ear whether a line is hendecasyllabic or not: they have to count on their fingers.
> — GIANFRANCO CONTINI, QUOTED IN *DILIGENZA E VOLUTTÀ* [DILIGENCE AND ENJOYMENT]: *LUDOVICA RIPA DI MEANA INTERROGA GIANFRANCO CONTINI*, P. 190

CONTINI WAS NEAR the end of his long, fruitful life when he did this book-length interview, which can be recommended for beginners with Italian as a fast track into the national discussion of the humanities. Just as, in the case of Argentina, interviews with Borges and Sabato—and sometimes they had interviews with each other— bring you straight to the top level of the subject, so, in the case of Italy, the dialogue with a protagonist is apt to save you from the perils of over-compression that come with his written prose. This latter advantage is especially important in the case of Contini, whose prose could be so compact that even his best students had trouble picking it apart. In Florence in the mid-sixties, a standard spectacle at the university was a football huddle of his students over their lecture notes after a silently frantic hour of listening to him whisper. Most of the students were female. A few of his best pupils were male but it took an especially daunting breed of woman—we used to call them the *continiane*—to summon the required pertinacity.

Ludovica Ripa di Meana is a classic *continiana*. When she interviewed her erstwhile teacher in 1989, Contini was in his frail seniority, but his mind was still working at full speed. Her registration of the old man's delivery is a scrupulous job, made easier, perhaps, by the fact that he wasn't speaking formally in the lecture hall, but conducting a seemingly ordinary conversation. There aren't very many ordinary conversations, however, that have so much to say about the humanities as this one; and on this particular point, about memory, he goes right to the heart of the topic. If you think of the humanities as an activity in which the mode of appreciation and the means of transmission are versions of one another, there could hardly be a more pertinent complaint than this: he was looking the death of his beloved subject right in the face.

There is an untranslatable Italian word for the mental bank account you acquire by memorizing poetry: it is a *gazofilacio*. Contini believed that an accumulation of such treasure would eventually prove its worth even if it had to begin with sweated labour. He confessed that not all of the teachers who had made him memorize a regular ration of Tasso's epic poetry had been inspired. Some of them had held him to the allotted task because they lacked imagination, not because they possessed it. But in the long run he was grateful. Most readers of this book will spot the sensitive point about modern pedagogy. Readers my age were made to memorize and recite: their yawns of boredom were discounted. Younger readers have been spared such indignities. Who was lucky? Isn't a form of teaching that avoids all prescription really a form of therapy? In a course called Classical Studies taught by teachers who possess scarcely a word of Latin or Greek, suffering is avoided, but isn't it true that nothing is gained except the absence of suffering? In his best novel, *White Noise*, Don DeLillo made a running joke out of a professor of German history who could not read German. But the time has already arrived when such a joke does not register as funny. What have we gained, except a classroom in which no one need feel excluded?

The questions are loaded. Few of us enjoy the thought that the younger generation has escaped our miseries, and I suppose it was a misery when one of my first teachers, a stalwart of the then pitiless Australian school system, made me stand up to recite "I come from haunts of coot and hern." Thus I paid the penalty for having memorized the first stanza more quickly than the rest of the class. More than half a century later I still know the line that comes next ("I make a sudden sally") and the one that clinches the stanza ("I bicker down a valley"). The third line has turned into a bit of an um-um canter, like Nigel Molesworth's approximate rendition of "The Charge of the Light Brigade" in Geoffrey Willans's *Down with Skool!*, a classic spoof that depends for its effectiveness on at least an indirect memory, if not a direct one, of the old teaching methods of the British private school. Though Molesworth never got anything right, he knew he was supposed to try. ("Harfleag, harfleag, harfleag onward. All in the Valley of Death rode the er.") But there are still poems, drilled into me in the classroom, that I can recite in chunks. If I get myself started on "I love a sunburnt country," sooner or later I will get to the rugged mountain ranges, the droughts and flooding rains. I will not always get to the name of the poet. In my uncaring recollection, Henry Kendall, Dorothea McKellar and many other Australian poets all shared the one elasticized identity until they were superseded by Shakespeare. But hundreds of their lines got into my head, and with them came the measures of English verse, the most common rhythmic structure being the iambic pentameter. (In Italian, the equivalent is the eleven-syllable line, which is why Contini picks it out.) Even before my first celebrated classroom appearance as a Lady Macbeth shrilly demanding that her milk be taken for gall, I had the shape, weight and length of the iambic pentameter in my mind, as a sort of sonic template. A long time later, in Cambridge, I abruptly realized what a blessing this early inculcation had been. In the practical criticism classes, the American-affiliated students were incomparably better informed than the locals—incomparably more intelligent all round, to put it bluntly—but the one thing the Americans could not do to save their lives was recite the verse in front of them. Whether it was by Donne, Herbert, Fulke Greville, Lovelace, Marvell or Dryden, it came out like a newsflash being read sight unseen by Dan Rather. They had no feeling for a line of iambic pentameter whatever. On their being quizzed about this, it transpired that they had never been required to remember one.

In Italy at any one time there is always someone who can recite the whole of *The Divine Comedy* by heart. Usually he is of humble clerical occupation: if the man at the post office who goes off to get your parcel fails to come back, that might be what he is doing. Contini wasn't impressed by that kind of feat, the mental equivalent of lifting a grand piano with the teeth. Contini said that where memorizing Dante was concerned, the important thing wasn't to release a torrent at the touch of a button, but to have the poem in your head as an infinite source of ready reference for the events of every day. It was true for him and he valued the same capacity in others. He was a quiet man and it was hard to make him laugh aloud, but his delighted smile was a rich reward for a Dante reference appositely supplied.

One night in Florence in the early eighties, my wife and I accompanied Contini to the opera. He was already pretty frail by then and you got the sense that he was choosing his remaining nights out for their concentration of the qualities: nothing was being left to chance. He had certainly judged well that night. The opera was *Adriana Lecouvreur*, conducted by Gianandrea Gavazzeni. For Contini as for his friend Eugenio Montale, Gavazzeni was the ideal maestro. After the performance it was raining so heavily that Contini accepted a lift home, with my wife at the wheel of our worn-out Mini. He was in the front passenger seat and I was folded in the back. They talked scholarly stuff. As a *continiana* of impeccable credentials, my wife was well qualified for the colloquy, but she was no better than anyone else at driving blind. The rain was so heavy that we ended up going the wrong way. I remembered, and recited, a tag from Dante: *Ché la diritta via era smarrita*. Because the right way had been lost. Contini smiled from ear to ear, and when I added my regrets that I hadn't written the line myself, he laughed aloud. My timing hadn't been *that* good, but the pedagogue had been pleased to the depths of his soul. This was what he had been in business to do all his life: spread the word about culture across cultures. And one of his aesthetic beliefs, acquired as an inheritance from Croce, was that Dante had been in business to do the same. It was the universal conversation, conducted through memory, and it had happened right there beside the Arno, in the dying echo of the music.

Though it can be overdone, there is nothing like a trading of quotations for bringing cultivated people together, or for making you feel uncultivated if you have nothing to trade. Nowadays very few people can quote from the Greek or would think to impress anyone if they could, and even quoting from the Latin—still a universal recognition system in the learned world when I was young—is now discouraged. Quoting from the standard European languages is still permissible at a suitably polyglot dinner table: I was once at a dinner in Hampstead with Josef Brodsky when we both ended up standing on restaurant chairs clobbering each other with alexandrines. If the audience (they had started off as our dinner companions, but had grown resigned to being an audience) had been mainly monoglot, the performance would have been less forgivable. But even if all present understand only English—even if the day comes when the whole world understands only English—memorized poetry would still be the surest way of signalling a love of language.

The proof that the English critic Frank Kermode and the Australian poet Peter Porter inhabit the same mental world—the same civilized tradition and the same literature—is in the treasure chamber of memorized poetry that each carries with him, in the number of valuable items that each *gazofilacio* holds in common with the other. Either of them could supply the next line to any poem by Auden or Empson or Wallace Stevens that the other quoted. It is on the basis of such universally shared memories that a generation builds its range of allusion. One of the most conspicuous differences between the British and American literary worlds is that the American periodical editors discourage the assumption of a range of allusion shared by the readership, even when they themselves—the editors—do share it. The American editors are not necessarily wrong to have their eye on democracy. There is such a thing as putting the frame of reference at a height where preciousness drives out plain sense. Before World War II, learning poetry by heart was a requirement in American schools. Steadily, between 1945 and 1960, that requirement vanished from the culture, as far as the common run of pupils was concerned. But the uncommon run, those interested in literature, remained; and on the whole it is surely better if writers and editors can trust the reader to be as well informed as they are. In English, a general familiarity with the poetic heritage ought not to be too much to assume. After all, no language in the world is as richly blessed.

It certainly ought not to be too much to assume among poets. But sometimes you wonder. The only thing I have to say against most modern poetry is that so much of it avoids all verse conventions without rising to the level of decent prose. Decent prose has a rhythmic pulse which, if it comes in the first instance as a gift, must be schooled to attain reliability, and there is no way to school it except to take in the rhythmic resources of the language as they have already been discovered by the poets over the course of centuries. By reading and memorizing their predecessors, the poets are set free from the standardized contemporary patterns in which meaning is bonded to syntactic forms.

They might not even especially remember what someone once said. What they remember is the pace and lilt of how he said it: what they retain is more likely to be a rhythmic measure than a paraphrasable expression. In this manner, a poet studies his own language as if it were a foreign one. Eliot found out a lot from Donne because Donne was more foreign to him than Shakespeare: the lines and phrases went in directions he did not expect and could not predict. When Eliot said that good poetry in a foreign language could communicate before it was understood, he probably meant, or meant at least partly, that the movement in the lines of the French poets after Victor Hugo was opening up new patterns to him in his own language. (Dr. Leavis, through being reasonable for once, thoroughly misunderstood Eliot's seeming preference for Dante over Shakespeare, and said that Eliot had underestimated what Shakespeare had to offer him. Eliot would have agreed that Shakespeare had a lot to offer, but might have said that only a foreign writer can offer you a lesson in how your own language is put together at a deep level.)

Reading Shelley, you can see that in the last of his few allotted years he had saturated his rhythmic sense with the forms of Dante and Petrarch. He doesn't echo their meanings: he echoes their structures. Similarly, Racine absorbed the structures of Latin poetry; and it is a nice question whether he is closer to Catullus, some of whose lines he mirrors property for property, than to Virgil, whom he does not materially transpose so much as imitate in his pulse and balance. These sonic templates, as they might be called, are transferable through time even when an instigator is unknown to a beneficiary. Dante gets effects from Virgil that Virgil got from Homer, but if we didn't know that Virgil had come in between, we would have to swear that Dante knew the Homeric poems intimately, whereas he couldn't, in fact, read them. It is doubtful whether poets, in order to know each other at this level, need to set out to memorize poems. The memorizing comes automatically with the intensity of engagement. And so, ideally, it ought to do with all of us. We memorize something because we can't help it, and the thing we memorize was written with that result in mind. Poetry is written the way it is in order to be remembered.

It can't always be remembered precisely, which is still the best reason for writing it down. Robert Robinson, one of the last of the

over-qualified presenters to grace BBC television in its best years, once
contributed to a BBC2 TV programme about Auden (those were the
days) with a recital of "The Fall of Rome." Reviewing the programme, I
could tell that Robinson had recited the poem from memory. In the most
beautiful stanza of one of the most beautiful poems in modern literature,
the stanza about the reindeer that, "altogether elsewhere," move across
the golden moss, Robinson said "run" instead of "move." The misquota-
tion illustrated our common habit of literalism, which will often, in the
memory, substitute a concretely specific word just when the poet wants to
be abstractly vague. (Auden himself worked against the tendency when a
misprint in proof gave him "the ports," instead of "the poets," having
"names for the sea." He found the mistake more interesting, and let it
stand.) It seems a fair guess that the capacity to remember always entails
a certain amount of adaptation to set mental patterns. Robinson had made
his error out of a trick played by familiarity. I twitted him about it in my
column, and when we next met he told me that he had at first not believed
that he could have made a mistake about something he knew so well, but
that he had looked it up and been mortified to find out that he had got it
wrong. The excellence of his memory had caught him out.

Leaving aside the occasional freak cursed with total recall, a good
memory is in the possession of a personality, not of a machine, and personalities impose their own perceptions, altering their recollection of
even the most cherished things in order to fit inner critieria. Italo
Calvino traces the process enchantingly in his book *Why Read the Classics?* Impeccably translated by Martin McLaughlin, *Why Read the Classics?*
is not only the best single book for approaching Calvino, but might well
be the best single book for approaching the whole idea of reading for
pleasure at a high level. One could praise the book's virtues for pages on
end, but perhaps the best way to demonstrate them would be to single
out the first of its two essays on Eugenio Montale. In that essay, Calvino
shows why, as a student, he found Montale's poetry impossible not to
memorize—and also shows why it was hard to memorize accurately. The
reader's mind has its expectations, which the poet will play upon in order
to defeat. Somewhere in that interplay of expectation and contrary strategy is the reason that scholarship had to evolve the principle of *lectio dif-
ficilior*—the idea that in any crux, the more difficult reading is likelier to
be the true one. Calvino's reminiscences about the workings of his own

memory—remember that I have remembered—have many implications, but the one we need to make explicit here, for the benefit of our children if not ourselves, is that the future of the humanities as a common posses- sion depends on the restoration of a simple, single ideal: getting poetry by heart. Far from democratizing poetry, there can be no surer way of reducing it to the plaything of an elite that to write it and read it as if it made no claim to be remembered. A man like Gianfranco Contini stud- ied poetry at the very highest level, but could do so because of his ear for its primal movement: for him, the subtle heartbeat in the eleven-syllable line was like the movement of the music I once watched him listening to in the opera house in Florence. He knew what was coming next—he had known that music all his life—but you could tell by the tiny noddings and shiftings of his head and shoulders that he was hearing it afresh. If he had not, it would not have been art, which would have a hard time surprising us if it did not first give us something easy to remember.

> The departure point for inspiration is the obstacle.
> — GIANFRANCO CONTINI, *VARIANTI*

This idea, variously expressed, comes up in almost every article Con- tini wrote about Dante. The emphasis is on a principle: that lyricism, for Dante, was the opposite of an indulgence. Though the principle is especially true of *The Divine Comedy*, Contini isn't just saying that for Dante the *terza rima* was a necessary discipline. Contini means that for Dante the whole business of writing poetry was a discipline. In Italian a rhyme scheme, even a constantly demanding one like the *terza*, is no great challenge, because Italian is so rich in rhymes. An English poet who tries to write even a short stretch of *terza rima* in his own language will soon find out how poor in rhymes it is: even Louis MacNeice, an awesomely competent verse technician, was driven to the half rhyme in his long *terza rima* composition *Autumn Sequel*. His results were dis- tressingly approximate. He would have done better to stick with the flexible forms, firmly based on classical measures, that he developed for his earlier work *Autumn Journal*, but perhaps they were too demand- ing to be repeated. *Autumn Journal*, which he wrote in the year follow- ing the Munich crisis, is the best thing of its kind in the twentieth century, and one of the reasons for its supremacy is the confidence of its interior movement, which depends entirely on a seemingly free choice of rhythms being held together overall by a classically trained sense of form. No discursive poetry has ever seemed more liberated, or been less loose. The whole poem, in all its richness of incident and observation, fully conforms to Eliot's proviso that no verse is entirely free to someone who wants to do a good job.

In saying that, Eliot could have been answering Robert Frost, who said that poets who wrote free verse without rhyme were playing tennis without a net. Philistines understandably elevated Frost's aphorism to the status of unarguable truth. (An aphorism is never that: unless there was a genuine collision of views, nobody would be moved to a calculated terseness.) Not only by redneck editors but by desperate academics self-assigned to hold the fort against modernism, Frost was thought to have pinpointed the line of division between discipline and anarchy. But the division is purely notional. There have been poets who wrote in strict rhymes and yet were slack in all departments— from the Victorian through into the Georgian era, the dullest poetry was remarkable only for its technical proficiency—and there have been poets who, without rhyming at all, achieve an alert tension in every line and an unfailing sense of coherence in the strophe. As Philip Larkin fondly recorded in his introduction to *The North Ship*, Vernon Watkins once said that good poetry doesn't just rhyme at the end of the lines, it rhymes all along the line. He thus left the way open for the possibility that lines might not rhyme at their ends at all, yet be so calculated, in all their parts, as to contribute to a form, or at least not detract from it.

Montale spoke several times about the salutary effects of avoiding rhyme—not just the easy rhymes into which Italian always tends to slip, but any kind of end-rhyme at all. In the mainstream of his lyric poetry it is quite hard to find even internal rhymes longer than a syllable: he goes always for the hard sonorities. Mallarmé recommended the same in French: "*Il faut rimer difficilement.*" Mallarmé, like Montale later, was out to provide something grittier than the too-smooth heritage of established tricks. Poets today should have the same determination. But it's an emphasis, not a rule: the much despised "moon" and "June" can rhyme successfully as long as, in each case, the line leading up to the last word is sufficiently intense. The most difficult way to rhyme is not to rhyme at all, and yet maintain coherence. The hard part of doing that is to square unrelenting vigilance with the free play of the mind that will let a new idea break through to the surface. (Strict rhymes *force* new ideas to the surface, as depth charges do to a submarine.) Established rhyme schemes leave more room to relax, which is probably why they are best for comic verse. But Dante didn't choose the *terza rima* in order to set himself a simple technical requirement so that he could relax when not fulfilling it. He made every passage of verse a technical requirement throughout; made it evident that he was doing so; and made part of his poetry from making it evident. As Contini says (*Varianti*, p. 320), a constant of Dante's literary personality is continually to make technical reflections on poetry. The technical reflections amount to an ordering of natural wealth. Contini calls Dante's verbal talent "lexical magnanimity" (*Varianti*, p. 322). When I was young, the department in the *Reader's Digest* called "It Pays to Increase Your Word Power" caught my restless attention. While still in very short pants I learned a lot from that department, and still can't see much wrong with the term "word power"; but "lexical magnanimity" is better because it gets the generosity in.

Generosity, however, can be gush when uncalled for. Even in Dante's time, Italian ran easily to gush. Dante pretty well invented the Italian language we read and hear today. The ideal version of the Italian language, say the Italians, is Florentine Italian spoken by someone from Siena. The Sienese are less likely to murder the "c" sound by aspirating it. But the language they speak with such melody is the one invented by Dante and his friends in or near Florence. Even then, though, it could be a torrent like the Arno in flood, and especially when aspiring to the lyrical. As Contini explains, Dante saw how part of the task would be to keep his *lirismo* in check rather than to let it rip. Much later on and in another country, we find that Laforgue liked the same thing about Tristan Corbière, who was a wild man, but used common speech—sometimes very common, from the gutter or the brothel—to chasten the worn-out lyrical effects that not even Victor Hugo was able to render obsolete all by himself. Poeticized poetry will always crop up again of its own accord; you can tell it is a weed because it looks too obviously like a flower, and grows again during the night. Ernst Robert Curtius (in his book of collected essays, *Gesammelte Aufsätze*, p. 312) borrowed Laforgue's idea to praise the prosaic stretches in Eliot's *East*

Coker, the poetry that was not like poetry. In our time, the greatest exponent of deliberately prosaic poetic diction was Philip Larkin. Recently in Melbourne, when I was trying to tempt a young admirer of Larkin's poetry to begin learning enough Italian to make a start with Dante, I told her that the dialogue in the Paola and Francesca scene in Canto V of the *Inferno* sounds as natural as Larkin's narrative tone in "Dockery and Son," and that when Dante stands back to deliver a clinching moral, the sonorities are just like Larkin's: magisterial because unaffected, the same language intensified without being notably heightened—a dignified squaring of the shoulders rather than a climbing onto stilts. With so finely calibrated a control of tone, Larkin could have written verse forever without rhyming even once. It is very interesting that he usually chose otherwise, and rhymed solidly throughout the poem. The big, matched stanzas of his showpiece poems like those in *The Whitsun Weddings* are, without striving to prove it, technically challenging beyond anything attempted by the Thomas Hardy he so much loved. Larkin got them, in fact, from Yeats: another self-disciplinarian on the grand scale. In some of Larkin's later poems, he will take the *ottava rima* stanza and deliberately make the rhymes approximate, but the structure is still strictly present behind the altered façade. Compare Larkin's "Church-Going" with Yeats's "Among School Children" and look for the contrast. There isn't one.

BENEDETTO CROCE

❧ ❧ ❧

Benedetto Croce (1866–1952) was the philosopher of twentieth-century Italy. One says "the" philosopher because nobody else came close, and even those intellectuals who disagreed with him most violently—Giovanni Gentile, who pledged allegiance to Fascism, was one of them—were obliged to take account of what he said. A practising politician as well as a political theorist, Croce was impressed by Mussolini in the beginning but soon saw the threat to liberalism. He went into internal exile and continued with his writing. After the war Croce was offered the presidency of Italy but declined, although in other respects he was crucial to the rebuilding of the country's liberal institutions. Lending him almost irresistible force as a thinker was the riverine flow and clarity of his prose style, fully equal to Shaw at his best, but without the paradoxes. Unfortunately no comparable stylist ever tried to translate him, and although some of his central works were brought over into English, they never had the influence that was their due. (An admirer of R. G. Collingwood would object to these assessments, but few admirers of Collingwood are aware that his indebtedness to Croce attained the level of mimicry, which always belittles the original.) In the 1960s I

learned quite a lot of Italian by reading almost everything
Croce wrote, and emerged from the experience with a lasting
admiration for his range of understanding. When he didn't
understand something, however, he brought all his powers of
expression to bear on saying the wrong thing: a salutary lesson
in the relationship between style and substance.

❧ ❧ ❧

Attempts to determine the place of art have, until now,
looked for that place either at the peak of the theoretical
spirit or in the vicinity of philosophy itself. But if, so far,
no satisfactory result has been obtained, might it not be
because of the obstinacy of looking too high? Why not
turn the attempt on its head, and instead of proposing the
hypothesis that art is one of the highest grades, if not
the highest grade, of the theoretical spirit, propose instead
the inverted and opposite hypothesis, that it is one of
the lowest, even the lowest of all?
— BENEDETTO CROCE, *PROBLEMI DI ESTETICA*
(PROBLEMS IN AESTHETICS), P. 13

A S ALWAYS, CROCE defeats ordinary expectation by looking for
the creative impulse in the natural instinct rather than in the
developed mind. The secret of his fecundity as a thinker was to open
up possibilities rather than close them off, and he always did so by
demoting the adept. According to him, a heart in the right place, rather
than a mind in a high state of training, was the more likely source of
truth, and the only source of creativity. Art, far from being the further-
most refinement of intelligence, came before thought, and was as natural as breathing. Croce's guess was that the first human beings sang
before they spoke. He was certainly right that they drew before they
wrote, and wrote poetry before they wrote prose.

Such propositions from Croce, when taken all at once, can sound
like paradox-mongering. But he made them consistent. Over the vast
range of his fundamental works—leaving the incidental works aside,
which it takes a separate room to do—the key concepts are thoroughly
and concretely worked out, abetting each other without friction. The

best way of summing up their effect is to say that they show how the instinct to live and grow is channelled through creativity towards mentality. If he had given the mind the precedence over art, he would have been inhibited in his explanatory powers. He did the opposite, and released them. Released, they could give a reasoned account of what he saw in the street: all the busy littleness that was so astonishing in its prodigality and variety of imagination. He always thought that there must be something wrong with an overarching concept if a necessary mental activity withered in its shadow. For a philosophy to be true, he believed, its proponent had to be able to write history. (One of the reasons he thought religions were incomplete philosophies was that no religion can tell the truth about the past.) For an aesthetic to be valid, its proponent had to be able to write criticism. That second idea was especially valuable to his successors. Its effect was to humanize in advance the Italian critical tradition as it extended without a notable break into the modern period. Italy's left-wing theorists, for example, unlike those in other countries, have always felt obliged to show due tact when treating the arts as a political expression, thereby acknowledging Croce's warnings against doing such a thing to any degree at all. (Not even the red radical Gramsci could afford to ignore Croce.)

One of Croce's precepts was paraphrased by Eugenio Montale when he said: "It isn't the man who wants to who continues the tradition, it's the man who can, and sometimes he's the man who knows least about it." It was one of the sentences that made Montale almost as famous a critic as he was a poet, but he would not have been able to write it if he had not read Croce first, and Montale's very next sentence was one that Croce could have written himself. "To this end, programmes and good intentions are of little use." Montale's echo of Croce—or, if you like, Croce's presaging of Montale—is an example of the continuity that makes Italian literary culture so satisfying in its coherence. We should remember, however, that there are Italians who find it too coherent, to the point of being hidebound. They would prefer a story big enough to get lost in, in the way that we get lost in ours. We don't feel obliged to read our philosophers before we read our critics. In Italy there is one philosopher whom everyone has to read before they read anything else, down to and including the instruction manual for a new washing machine.

TONY CURTIS

❧ ❧ ❧

Like many film stars, Tony Curtis (b. 1925) was already pretending to be someone else before he landed his first Hollywood role. As a Jew raised in the New York Upper East Side district he later called "Nazi land," Bernard Schwartz already knew what World War II was about before he went to it. He emerged from the war with his first professional credentials already established. He had kept his buddies laughing. A further education in drama was made possible by the GI Bill: once again he was the class clown. As an apprentice Hollywood leading man, under his new name Tony Curtis, he caused more laughter for his accent and his hairstyle, but his box office appeal for a young audience was immediate. The rest of the story—mainly about his long and eventually successful quest for credibility—is told in a better than average ghosted autobiography (*Tony Curtis*, 1993). Necessarily it leaves out the wider context, which would concern just how the equivalents of Tony Curtis in the European countries failed to make the same impact internationally. American cultural imperialism might look like the answer, but the term explains nothing in itself. American dominance of the world's big screens worked by consent. The effort that went into the product was hard to match. Part of the effort was the quality of the human material that was actually on view. Behind the camera there were refugees from all nations, but most of the faces on screen were Americans. The newer faces, however, knew more about the world than any previous generation. The war changed every-thing, even the pitch of performance from the established leading men. James Stewart came home from the war a more naturalistic actor than he had been before he left, and the younger men, for whom the war had been not an interlude but an overture, avoided histrionics from the start. Paul Newman and Lee Marvin were conspicuous examples. This naturalism was apparent even in the otherwise frenetic exuberance of Tony Curtis. In his first movies, he looked human even when he hammed it up. He had "only in America" written all over him. But also written all over him was "America is every-where," and that infinitely exportable quality of confident savvy stayed with him to provide the basis of his charm in the distinguished roles of his later career.

Yonder lies the castle of my father.
— TONY CURTIS (ATTRIB.), *THE BLACK SHIELD OF FALWORTH*

NO, OF COURSE Tony Curtis didn't write his most famous line. It was written by the otherwise unsung screenplay writer, Oscar Brodney. But Tony Curtis said it, in the accent of the only recently reconstructed Bernie Schwartz, and nobody ever forgot the high-flown speech bubble from a chivalric comic book recited in the cadences of the Bronx. "Yonder lies duh castle of my fuddah." Back there at the Rockdale Odeon in Sydney I heard him say it, and I didn't laugh. Along with the girls in the audience, I was too struck with his beauty. I had already guessed that only America was big enough to produce Gene Kelly, and here was another living god, not quite as good-looking per-haps, but with an even more acute case of the stylish energy that the Americans had so much of they could hand it out virtually free to the less lucky nations. If I knew that Australia was an almost equally lucky nation—and in some respects even luckier—I forgot it that day. I even liked the way he said the line. I was practising his intonation when I went home to my muddah.

Actually there were already good reasons for admiring Curtis's way with the words. He might not yet have been getting some of the consonants right, but he was always spot on with the emphasis and the impetus. (From his first movies, I assumed that it was an Italian ethnic background he was surpressing. It didn't occur to me that it was a Jewish one, and that Bernie Schwarz had become Tony Curtis for the same reason that Julius Garfinkle became John Garfield. Nothing mattered except the enchanting way that the tormented phonemes seemed to give an extra zing to the American demotic.) In the last year of the war, trapped in the Pacific on a submarine tender, Curtis had entertained his fellow sailors by supplying voices for the movies that they were running with the sound off because they were sick of them. For men whose expectations of life varied between endless boredom and a kamikaze attack, he must have been good to have around, if harder to stave off than a Japanese suicide plane flown by someone with a different idea of glory. Bernie Schwartz was relentless. Like the character in the epigraphs to *The Waste Land*, he did the police in different voices.

The practice stood him in good stead. With due allowance for the castle of his fuddah, his work in the movies was always marked by his precise way of pointing a line. When he made the whole world laugh in *Some Like It Hot*, it was surprising to find that some of the critics were surprised. He was also very funny in *Operation Petticoat*. Playing opposite Cary Grant, no mean speaker himself, Curtis held his own in a mentor-prentice interchange that was worked out in dialogue as much as in action. (Later on, in *The Great Race*, the same director, Blake Edwards, stuck Curtis with a role that had very few good lines, so we have nothing to remember except his white driving suit and the starry glint superimposed on his smile—an early case of a special effect substituting for the effects that really count.) Curtis always excelled as the apprentice: he was in the same relationship with Burt Lancaster in two more films, *Trapeze* and *The Sweet Smell of Success*. Since Lancaster was a genuine athlete and Curtis knew how to look like one, the first film is ridiculous only when Gina Lollobrigida pretends to fly; and the second film is a masterpiece, with Curtis, in his role as the hustling press pimp Sidney Falco, raising sleaze to the status of poetry. Burt Lancaster once told me in an interview that in his position as co-producer of *The Sweet Smell of Success* he had come close to firing the director from the movie. The director was Alexander Mackendrick, who worked meticulously with the director of photography James Wong Howe to give the film's visual style a fluency unseen since the heyday of Max Ophuls, who set the standard for filming a whole scene in one elaborate—and therefore expensive—take. But such workman-ship took time, and Lancaster, who was counting the financial cost, grew impatient. If he had fired Mackendrick, he would have removed the only force that could rein him in. Lancaster gave a controlled per-formance because for once someone else was in control. (In *Atlantic City* it happened again, thanks to Louis Malle.)

But Curtis needed no control. His Sidney Falco is one of the defin-itive performances of the American cinema: the galvanic answer to the perennial question of what makes Sammy run. There is something marvellous about the way he varies the pace of his dialogue between the cockiness he parades among his fellow grifters and the servility he lavishes on Lancaster's magisterially ruthless J. J. Hunsecker. It takes a lot of self-discipline to develop such possibilities, and they are mainly developed through his way of pointing the line. Doing so, Curtis helped to found a classic school, in which serious delivery avails itself of comic timing. In *Tootsie*, Dustin Hoffman is meant to be desperate when he delivers the speech about the endive salad: but he doesn't let his desperation get in the way of the words, and sounds all the more panic-stricken for the precision of his delivery. Curtis would have delivered the speech the same way: words first, emotion second. Robert De Niro, coming from the method school, works in the oppo-site direction. Though he can turn in a precise verbal performance when tightly directed—*Wag the Dog* is a good example—he can swal-low the script when left to himself, especially when he doesn't trust it. The two different emphases are glaringly on view in that wreck of a blockbuster *The Last Tycoon*. Curtis's cameo as the swashbuckling hero of silent movies who has lost his confidence works perfectly in two reg-isters: he falls apart when he is closeted with the studio boss, and he jumps in and out of powerful automobiles when he is on public view. De Niro works in one register, and the puzzled audience spends the whole picture trying to figure out which one it is. The effect is of Tony Curtis giving Robert De Niro an acting lesson. Alas, the ingénue, Ingrid Boulting, who really did need an acting lesson, was never given one. But she might have got one later, when she saw Curtis up there showing what can be done with a few lines.

When it comes to *Some Like It Hot*, Billy Wilder's justly celebrated hit comedy of 1959, we find out why a screen star like Curtis is worth all that money. First of all, there is what he does on screen. Again, his way with dialogue is the key factor. Hobbling in a pair of 1920s high heels along the station platform, he looks as funny as Jack Lemmon, but so would Arnold Schwarzenegger. Not even Lemmon, however, could deliver the lines like Curtis. By that stage Lemmon was already indulging himself with the stuttering false-start technique that less funny actors have since made the mistake of thinking funny in itself. (In *Ally McBeal*, Calista Flockhart restarts every sentence half a dozen times before she gets through it: she isn't just padding the part, she is picking up on a mannerism that Lemmon helped to launch.) Curtis delivers his lines with a clean bite that would have made Cary Grant proud of his pupil. When Curtis is actually imitating Grant, in the seduction scene opposite Marilyn Monroe, his story about the two astigmatic lovers whose bodies had to be brought up from the canyon by mule is a copybook example of how to pace and point a comic extravaganza. Billy Wilder and I. A. L. Diamond, his screenwriting partner, must have been hugging each other as Curtis brought it off. He would have had to bring it off many times, because Marilyn Monroe is often in the two shot. Her presence reminds us of the second reason Curtis was worth his money. As Wilder told him, with Monroe on the case there would be multiple takes, and he, Curtis, would have to get it right every time, because the take when she finally got it right would be the one they would print. Like Lemmon, Curtis had to keep on delivering the goods over and over in every scene that involved Monroe throughout the movie. Curtis's scenes with her are far more complicated than Lemmon's. In private, Curtis execrated Monroe for her lack of professionalism, but on the set he never wavered. He might easily have been worn down. Marlon Brando, a kind of male Marilyn Monroe when it came to the actual business of learning the lines or getting the shot, always dominated the screen no matter how strong the cast, but he dominated it for a single reason: he needed so many takes that the other actors got tired. He just wore them to a frazzle. Opinions differ about whether he did it deliberately. There is only one opinion about Monroe: she was helpless. But Curtis wasn't, and he is the actor at the centre of one of the funniest pictures ever made.

After that tour de force, some of Curtis's later triumphs should not have come as a revelation, but they always did. When he dominated the screen in *The Boston Strangler* or stole it in *Insignificance*, there were always otherwise intelligent critics who congratulated themselves for originality by calling him talented. Nobody would ever have called him anything else had he been less disarming. Like the eloquent man who gets no points for the poetry he writes because he talks well anyway, Curtis was always downrated for his accomplishment because of his screen presence. Throughout his career, he has been one of the most convincing proofs that the secrets of screen stardom must always lie beyond complete analysis. There are actors like Alan Arkin who can do anything except dominate the screen, and there are other actors who dominate the screen yet can do almost nothing. To the extent that screen stardom can be broken down into separate gifts, however, Curtis, apart from a physical beauty that was built to last, had another gift that was rare and precious. He was a writer's actor. When he spoke it, the language came alive. Somewhere under the quiff and eventually the rug, Tony Curtis weighed a line for its rhythm and melody, and said it as if it could be said in one way only, and no uddah.

ERNST ROBERT CURTIUS

Ernst Robert Curtius (1886–1956) was the most eminent medieval romance philologist of his time. After World War I he tried to build bridges between the German and French humanist worlds, deploring the extent to which they had been separated. In 1932, when it was clear that the Nazis had a chance of power, he published *Deutsche Geist in Gefahr* (The German Spirit in Danger). When the danger became an actuality, however, he made no further combative moves. Nor did he choose exile. He withdrew into his library, emerging after the war to publish, in 1948, his capital work *European Literature and the Latin Middle Ages*, which was universally hailed as one of the great scholarly books of the century. He also continued with the series of literary essays through which he is most easily approached by the non-scholarly reader. (They were posthumously translated and collected, as *Essays on European Literature*, in 1973.) So it looked as if he had done the best he could. But there was a lingering question. With his lifelong emphasis on cultural continuity, what did he really think about the greatest blow that the Nazis had struck against it?

> When the German catastrophe came, I decided to serve
> the idea of a medievalistic Humanism by studying the
> Latin literature of the Middle Ages. These studies
> occupied me for fifteen years. The result of them
> is the present book.
> — ERNST ROBERT CURTIUS, IN THE
> INTRODUCTION TO THE 1952 ENGLISH
> TRANSLATION OF *EUROPEAN LITERATURE
> AND THE LATIN MIDDLE AGES*

SEVEN YEARS HAD already gone by since Hitler's fall, and still the most revered scholar in Europe wasn't saying very much about what the catastrophe had actually entailed. (In the original, German edition of the book that had come out in 1948, he had said even less.) The lacuna wouldn't have mattered so much had he been less magisterial. At his best, that was the only word for him. When I was first a student at Sydney University in the late 1950s, my teacher George Russell, himelf a scholar of the Middle Ages, placed his copy of Curtius's masterpiece on a lectern, opened it as if it were a holy text and said: "This is a great book." At the time I had no means of knowing whether he was right. Years later, when I had finally swallowed the hint and began to take on board some of the preliminary knowledge (such as who Dante was) necessary to appreciate what Curtius had written, I found that the book read like a thriller. Curtius had the invaluable knack of not getting bogged down in his own scholarship. His Dante, like the Dante of Gianfranco Contini (Curtius and Contini were friends), lived and breathed. They were agreed that Dante was a great mystifier, but to that fact they both posted the necessary qualification. He was, but not as much as he wasn't.

Dante set problems that only scholars can tackle: a reason for them to love him. But if Dante had not done much, much more than that— if he had not written in a way that invaded the memory and imagination of people with no scholarly qualifications at all—there would be no *Divine Comedy* for scholars to study. Curtius is a tacit, benign and unusually creative proponent of a line of thought that can be vocal, malignant and sterile: the idea that scholarship and criticism are essential to culture. But they are not: they are essential to civilization, just as culture is. Culture on the one hand, and the study of culture on the other, are inseparable only in the sense that they both belong to something larger. The idea that the professional student of culture is some kind of creative collaborator easily grows into an assumption that the professional understanding of culture is part of culture's driving force. It is, after all, the professional understanding that establishes the culture's tradition. For Curtius, tradition was a key concept. "Culture without tradition," he wrote, "is destiny without history." For him, a threat to tradition was a threat to life. In the Nazi era it was understandable that he should feel that way: understandable and commendable. To help stave off the threat, he wrote *European Literature and the Latin Middle Ages*. He did the work for it while the Nazis ruled, and published it not long after they were gone. Even more than Erich Auerbach's *Mimesis*, Curtius's *summa* looks like an act of creative regeneration: a timely and triumphant effort to reintegrate the shattered mental world. At this distance, to equivocate seems churlish. But there are aspects of Curtius's position that require comment, and at least one that ought to be questioned closely.

Not long after peace broke out, Curtius and André Gide met at a café in Cologne, within sight of the ruined cathedral. They could congratulate themselves for having survived, and trade reasons for pessimism. Both had seen the culture of their beloved Europe brought to the same condition as the city around them. The spectacle of disintegration must have been especially discouraging in the case of Curtius. After World War I he had done more than any other German to further the interchange of mental life between France and his own country. The first serious study of Proust to be published in Germany was from his hand. It was contained in a 1925 collection of essays called *Französischer Geist im neuen Europa*, which is among my treasures: an elegant book bound in crimson polished linen, solidly printed in Bodoni bold, the true typeface of the modern Europe after World War I. He also wrote the best German book about Balzac. Victor Klemperer (now justly famous for his Nazi-era diaries but still a minor figure at the time) was in the same field. A two-volume study of French pre-Revolutionary literature was among Klemperer's early publications. But nobody in the Francophone departments of the German academic world had quite the cachet of Curtius. Always a scholar of the far past, he was keen to apply his curatorial standards to the creative present.

(Later on, his admirer Contini was to be the Italian exemplar of the same double competence.) Curtius was also the first German translator of *The Waste Land*. A valued contributor to Eliot's magazine *The Criterion*, Curtius kept up with Eliot's poetry and knew all of it by heart. He trusted his memory of it at least once too often: in his posthumously published *Gesammelte Aufsätze* (Collected Essays) we find "April is the cruellest month of the year," a line that Eliot never actually wrote. But the slip proves that Curtius took literature in as a living thing.

In his role as a representative of European cultural unity, as it had once existed under Christendom and might conceivably one day exist again in a new political synthesis, Curtius could hardly have done a better job. History, however, caught him out: not cruelly, as it did the Jews, but ironically, in the way that it so frequently did to those Aryan scholars who thought they could keep a shred of civilization going by sticking to their tasks. On the right wing of French intellectual life, there were quite a few writers and scholars who dreamed that French culture might get together with German culture in a beautiful union, with the new, strong Germany as a political facilitator. (The recurring emphasis on the idea of "strength" should have tipped them off that the unitary concept had less to do with *Kultur* than with *Macht*, but wish fulfilment was doing its deadly work: World War I had cost France so much to win that nobody believed there could be a war again.) Though the part of the French right wing that took its tune from Action Française was resolutely German-hating like its founder Charles Maurras himself, there were plenty of others who believed that an integrated Euro culture was at hand. After the Germans occupied Paris, the Propaganda Abteilung encouraged that belief. Some of the second rank of French writers fell for the invitation to tour Germany. (The farcical results were recently well recorded in François Dufay's *Le Voyage d'automne*.) The higher orders were less pliant, but there was a brand of quietism ready to believe that cultivated Frenchmen and cultivated Germans could make a civilized common cause over and above the sordid level of mere politics.

Gide was one of the Frenchmen and Curtius was one of the Germans: the meeting in post-war Cologne was not their first contact, although during the war it had been through an intermediary. We learn from Gide's *Journal 1939–1949* that on 15 March 1943, he met a "*très aimable jeune officer allemand, étudiant l'histoire de l'art, ami d'Ernst Robert Curtius.*" (A very amiable young German officer, a student of the history of art, and friend of Curtius.) "He simply said, at the beginning of our conversation, how uncomfortable he was made to feel by his uniform." "*Il parle chaleureusement aussi de Jünger.*" (He also spoke warmly about Jünger.) Like Ernst Jünger, Curtius was one of the eternal Germany's living, breathing examples of a cultural continuity that the current unfortunate episode in history had no doubt compromised but could scarcely obliterate—or so their theory went. The deeper their commitment to the richness of the past, the slower their acceptance of the fact that there was nothing the Nazis could not obliterate. Later on, Curtius soft-pedalled this part of his career, but there is no reason to suppose he had anything much to hide. Curtius was no Heidegger: he never gave the Nazis any vocal support. He and Gide were guilty of nothing except a wishful, wistful thought: that there could be a cultural unity in conditions of political barbarism. Most of our wishful thinking is about what we love. If there were to be condemnation for that, we would all be condemned sooner or later. But if we are to learn anything from catastrophe, it is wise to remember what some of the men who shared our passions once forgot.

Curtius forgot that continuity is not in itself an inspiration for culture, merely a description of it. Similarly, a tradition is an accumulation through time of inspired works, created by people who do not have tradition on their minds. If they have anything on their minds, it is their own uniqueness: the ways in which they do not fit in, not the ways they do. The critic and the scholar, when they are properly qualified, spend at least as much time dismantling their own continuity as reinforcing it. In the twentieth century Natolino Sapegno, the Dante scholar *in excelsis*—and rivalling even Contini as a scholar of the fourteenth century in general—dismantled the Romantic critical tradition which had given Dante's Paolo and Francesca the saving grace of an eternal love, a free pass valid even in the winds of the *Inferno*. Dante, Sapegno pointed out, wanted the lovers punished: the poet's morality was at the heart of his originality. Scholarly emphasis on cultural continuity—including scholarly emphasis on scholarly continuity—will always attempt to erode the very idea of originality. But originality is more than an idea: it is the closest description of the creative impulse. Curtius would never been the great scholar he was if he had not known that all along. Indeed he would have thought it a truism to say so. But in his work there was also the tacit assumption that, with scholarship's help, art grew out of art.

Art grows from the individual vision. It always has, when political circumstances make individuality possible. The Nazis were dedicated to the self-imposed task of removing individuality from the world. By one of the twentieth century's most vicious paradoxes, Hitler did more than any of his all-conquering predecessors to integrate Europe politically. Luckily he never completed the job, but he got far enough to prove, by negative example, that a civilization is inseparable from a measure of liberalism. In the past, artists have worked for tyrants and done great things, but only because the tyrants, in the exceptional case of the artists, allowed a bubble of freedom. The civilization we know most about, and which we still inhabit, has institutionalized freedom to the point where the connections between art and the study of art are sometimes hard to see. But the central catastrophe of the century gone by served to show us that any such connection between them depends entirely on their both being joined in the first instance to the civilization itself. In the light of that demonstration, Curtius the universal scholar is left looking depressingly restricted, and humanism is left with its besetting weakness on display—the temptation it carries within it to reduce the real world to a fantasy even while presuming to comprehend everything that the world creates.

It is comprehensible and forgivable that Curtius said nothing about Nazi atrocities during the war. Incomprehensible and unforgivable is that he said nothing about them after it. At the height of his prestige, with the whole international scholarly world for a worshipping audience, he never alluded even once to the extermination camps. George Steiner was right to point out that Eliot's post-war *Notes Towards the Definition of Culture*, by neglecting to mention what had just happened to Europe, disqualified itself from being a definition of culture. The same objection can be made to Curtius's thunderous silence. Writing in his defence, Christine Jacquemard-de Gemeux, in the closing pages of her 1998 monograph on Curtius, touchingly contends that he did not wish to comprehend the tragedy, because to comprehend it would have been to approve it. ("*Il refuse de chercher à comprendre le phenomene parce que le comprendre serait une maniere de l'approuver.*") It is hard to see why. The sad truth is that Curtius lived out his studiously untroubled years still stuck with the decision he had made in 1933, when he condemned Thomas Mann for going into exile. Curtius thought that Mann had been unfaithful to his country. Curtius thought that the true Germany could survive within the Nazi state. Mme. Jacquemard-de Gemeux, generously attempting to make a point he never made for himself, would have us believe that he thought there was such a thing as an interior intellectual life to which Hitler was exterior. In the same way she might have argued that the worm in the apple's core was exterior to the apple. In the café across from Cologne cathedral, Curtius and Gide no doubt found the heaps of rubble a sad comment on their uncivilized times. But the ruins were a sign that the civilization they valued had been fought for, and saved against the odds.

D

❦ ❦ ❦

Miles Davis

Sergei Diaghilev

Pierre Drieu la Rochelle

MILES DAVIS

♪ ♪ ♪

Demanding to be heard but not always inclined to make the listening easy, the famous long, slow trumpet solos of Miles Davis (1926–1991) were a follow-on from bebop, the post-war musical development which tried to ensure that jazz would no longer be the spontaneous sound of joy. Whether any art form can really develop is a permanent question, but there is a partial answer in the fact that some of its most adept exponents will often believe it should. A master of his instrument, Davis could play anything he wanted. What he wanted to play was sometimes immediately attractive—often enough to give him some of the all-time most successful jazz albums—but much of it was deliberately parsimonious and oblique, like the soundtrack of a Noh play that had closed out of town. Students of race relations in America are generally agreed that the exponents of post-war jazz were determined, with good reason, to present themselves as challenging artists rather than tame entertainers. Davis had the personality to fit that ambition. Preceding Bob Dylan in his readiness to ignore the audience if he felt like it, he differed in his capacity, when talking offstage, to say something both brief and funny at the same time. He

could never be imagined laughing it up like Louis Armstrong.
But he still had a cutting wit.

If I don't like what they write, I get into my Ferrari
and I drive away.
— MILES DAVIS (ATTRIB.)

I HAVE NO SOURCE for this oft-quoted line except my memory, but it
is probably written down somewhere. I first heard it from a jazz
musician who held Miles Davis in awe, no doubt for excellent reasons.
As a mere listener, I tried hard to feel the same way, but somehow could
never quite make it. Always a sucker for the sweet shout of the open
horn, I never much liked even the most famous work of Davis, because
his trumpet sounded as if it had been shrunk within to the diameter of
a drinking straw. Scholarly devotees assured me that his long solos
were bringing an art form to its ascetic apex. I thought he was using a
pipette as a kazoo. I couldn't see that it made much difference when he
chose to sit playing away from the customers, because he had sounded
as if he were doing that even when he played towards them.

But if I had ever felt the necessity to say such things in print, I would
have tried to remember the Ferrari. His wealth was his whip hand. The
concept can be recommended to aspiring artists in all fields; it is the
same principle that applies to feminism; if you are vulnerable economically, you are vulnerable all along the line. If you have pleased the public enough to have transferred some of its money into your own bank
account, however, you can afford to ignore your detractors. Humphrey
Bogart called it his "fuck you" money: with enough in the bank, he
wouldn't have to take a bad deal. The point ought to be obvious,
although it is not often enough made when the question comes to a sad
turn in an artist's career: he might have been forced into it by lack of
the wherewithal to give Bogart's instructions to the proponents of a
doomed project. What I like about the way Davis put the axiom is the
neatness of the illustration. The Ferrari says what matters: he's got one
and his critics haven't. A similarly vivid illustration marks the standard
anecdote about the Manchester United soccer star George Best. So

brilliant that he was marked out of the game by opponents who had been specifically assigned to kick him in the ankles, Best might have taken to drink anyway, but it is more likely that he was simply a born alcoholic. To him the stuff was poison, and that's it. In the sad aftermath of his glory he was a reliable sad-sack act on television talk shows: a wreck who thought he was a rascal. But he had a story up his sleeve that always gave him the victory even if he looked as if he had fallen into the chair he was threatening to fall out of. It is doubtful if he made the story up all by himself: it is too well crafted, and Best's talent, though enormous, was never for words. But one way or another the story got written, and its hero got to recite it. The story is about a room-service waiter in a luxury hotel who pushes a trolley laden with caviar and lobster into Best's VIP suite, only to find Best in bed with Miss World and a bottle of Bollinger. The waiter says: "George, George, where did it all go wrong?"

On closer examination, Miles Davis and George Best were not saying quite the same thing. Davis was talking about the invulnerability conferred by his money. Best, by that stage, had no money. But he had the right to imply that his remembered glory ensured he would still do better than a waiter. A wise artist, however, will be careful to bank his windfalls, because any glory he acquires will soon be compromised if the cash runs out. Money buys control over your career. Without money, your career will control you. But money can't buy you a career in the first place, and inheriting wealth is almost invariably a bad way to start one. Among the screen stars, Jan Sterling and Cliff Robertson were both born rich, but neither would have got anywhere without talent. Jan Sterling, indeed, didn't get as far as she should have, and is nowadays forgotten: later on, Grace Kelly found it easier to be a Lady in Hollywood. The poet James Merrill, who had Merrill Lynch behind him for a rainy day, was free to write exactly as he liked. His poetry might have been less demanding, and more in demand, if he had had to establish himself in an open market. The point can't be pushed too far, of course: Carly Simon, who was brought up as a privileged child in a publishing family of enormous wealth, nevertheless deserved her hit songs, and no doubt took genuine satisfaction out of making money by herself.

But if too much money is made on the job, it can be almost as dangerous as an inheritance. When popular musicians turn to self-indulgence, it is because they can at last afford to do what they would have done anyway. Their early hits, written under the constrictions of compulsory crowd-pleasing, are usually seen in retrospect to be their best work, and often the most adventurous as well. (With the singers, it is always a very bad sign when they start to talk instead of sing. Diana Ross's recorded speeches became the litany of Tamla-Motown in its downhill phase. She was proving that she no longer needed to please the public: a point all too easily made.) Higher up the scale, serious artists are too often exempt from enquiries about the role of money. Tom Stoppard was refreshingly candid when, after the successful premiere of *Rosencrantz and Guildenstern Are Dead*, he was asked what the play was about: "It's about to make me a lot of money." Those of us who attend upon artists with our scholarship, criticism and admiration are apt to forget that the gifted people who give us a glimpse of the sublime are not immune from mundane cares, which, by no paradox except the deviltry of economics, can multiply with success. Mainly because of the glamour involved and the ever present temptations, the arts in all fields seem exactly designed to vaporize even the most exalted practitioner's stipend as fast as he earns it, and the larger the faster. The mere cost of having your money professionally looked after, for example, instantly becomes an overhead. In his *Paris Review* interview, S. J. Perelman enjoyed showing how hard-headed he was about the writing business. The trick in Hollywood, he said, wasn't to make the loot, but to get it out. He said that the "fairy money" they paid you had a way of evaporating as you headed east.

Books about the finances of the painters are often written, because the money involved is big if the painter becomes fashionable—especially, strangely enough, if the painter belonged to the anti-bourgeois avant-garde before he clicked with the buyers. Painters have to buy materials and pay a large percentage to their galleries, so they are rarely as rich as we tend to think, but when they do break through, they break through on an industrial scale. For writers the financial rewards are comparatively small-time, but a good book dedicated to nothing except the money would be very useful. It might help to explain behaviour that is puzzled over on the metaphysical level when there are concrete explanations that have not been considered. When Nazi Germany cancelled the distribution of Hollywood movies, MGM faced a loss of only a small proportion of its income. Thomas Mann, when he finally realised the necessity of cutting himself off from publication in his homeland, faced the loss of nearly all of his, because although he was internationally famous, his central audience was in Germany. In the Soviet Union, royalties existed only in the form of privileges—an apartment, a dacha, the chance to be published at all—but the privileges were decisive. The threat of their being withdrawn was enough to make almost anyone think twice about speaking against the state. Without this point in mind it is fruitless to go on speculating about why Pasternak, for example, was so slow to dissent in public, and was so equivocating when he did. Lovers of the arts should be slow to despise the cash nexus on the artist's behalf: the niggling difficulties of securing and handling one's personal finances are nothing beside the pressures of state patronage. Going to hell in your own way has everything over being sent there at a bureaucrat's whim.

Was Miles Davis speaking for black America? Yes, of course, although he shrugged off the black man's burden: he wasn't Martin Luther King Jr. But Martin Luther King couldn't have recorded *Kind of Blue*. Davis had his real trouble not with acceptance as such, but with drugs. In the past—the immediate past, let's not forget—black musicians were robbed blind by white businessmen as a matter of course. Davis robbed himself, incidentally showing us the difference between a weakness and a vice. He had a weakness for women, but nobody has ever proved that he played worse for his prodigious sexual appetite. His appetite for drugs was another matter, and it would be a brave defender who claimed that drugs never affected his playing. Charlie Parker was explicit on the subject: "Anyone who says he is playing better either on tea, the needle, or when he is juiced, is a plain, straight liar." Sadder than a falling phrase from "My Old Flame," the line is quoted on page 379 of *Hear Me Talkin' to Ya*. Edited by Nat Hentoff and Nat Shapiro, it is a book as rich in precepts as in anecdotes, and one which should never be allowed to go out of print. Students in all fields of creative endeavour need a copy of it nearby, to instruct them in the unyielding nature of bedrock. Not long ago I heard a man playing the most beautiful tenor sax. I could tell he had absorbed everything Ben Webster and Lester Young had to teach, but his gift for assembling his phrases into a long legato line was all his own. He was terrific. But he was playing at the bottom of the escalators in Tottenham Court Road tube station. No Ferrari for him.

SERGEI DIAGHILEV

Born in Novgorod and buried in Venice, Sergei Diaghilev (1872–1929) became famous to the world as the impresario of the Russian opera-and-ballet export drive that turned fashionable Paris upside down before and during World War I. He was already famous in Russia as the brilliant young connoisseur whose lavishly mounted exhibitions rediscovered the country's tradition of religious icons and secular portrait painting, and as the editor of the truly wonderful magazine *Mir Iskusstva* (The World of Art), in which Benois, Bakst and other Russian names that later became bywords made their first appearances. The gift Diaghilev demonstrated in Paris of attracting all the most celebrated artists of the day (Picasso, Stravinsky, Cocteau, Satie, Poulenc and many more) to join his enterprises had already been demonstrated at home. But at the height of his powers, home was lost to him. After the Revolution he stayed abroad, and the Soviet authorities, once it became obvious that he could not be lured back, condemned him in perpetuity as an especially insidious example of bourgeois decadence. Soviet historians of art wrote him out of their picture of the past for more than sixty years. When, in 1982, a two-volume collection of his pre-revolutionary writings on art was published in Moscow, it was a sign that the confident rigidity of official ideology was starting to bend, because any move towards telling the truth about the past was likely to be a prelude to telling the truth about the present. But it was just a sign. Only in retrospect was the change certain. What the astonished reader could be sure of at the time, however, was that Diaghilev had been a great critic—the discriminating impulse at the heart of his uncanny ablity to bend the talented to his will. They felt that he understood them. He almost always did.

Why should I waste my imagination on myself?
— SERGEI DIAGHILEV (ATTRIB.)

AS A LIFELONG admirer of Diaghilev I am easily impressed by anything he is said to have said, but when I first read this I was so impressed that I neglected to make a note: I knew I would remember it always. I could have sworn that I read it in *Theatre Street*, Tamara Karsavina's radiant little sheaf of memoirs. (Karsavina, previously the darling of the Maryinsky company in Petersburg, danced the very first *Firebird*, in Paris in 1910.) Probably the best single book ever written about dancing, it also has general application to the whole world of the arts: if I were making a list of ten books that art-crazy young people should read to civilize their passion, *Theatre Street* would be on it. But when I searched through the book to find this quotation, there it wasn't. The conversation was there, but only in reported form: no inverted commas. Did I read it in that mighty balletomane Richard Buckle's book about Diaghilev? I couldn't find it there, either: nor in the fascinating interview with Karsavina contained in John Drummond's fine compendium *Speaking of Diaghilev*. Anyway, unsourced though it is, the remark is too resonant to leave out. The location was Diaghilev's small apartment in Petersburg—as the city was then still called, and now, happily, is called again. Karsavina, very young at the time and bowled over by Diaghilev's sophistication, noticed that his tiny bedroom had almost nothing in it except a bed. She said she was surprised, and Diaghilev replied with the rhetorical question quoted above. The remark comes straight from the centre of his personality and helps to define it, as the arthritic Renoir defined his own personality when he said, "Tie the brush into my hands" and the senescent Richard Strauss when he screamed at the orchestra, "Louder! Louder! I can still hear the singers!"

Diaghilev, an artist whose art-form was to combine the art-forms, gave everything to the world and kept little for himself. His hotel bills could be immense and he dressed to kill, but otherwise he did not need artistic surroundings in his personal life. Other impresarios have been less monastic. Lincoln Kirstein, whose taste made possible the whole coruscating pageant of Balanchine's career at the New York City Ballet, kept his Manhattan apartment full of beautiful things. Widening the scope to directly creative artists, we can see the same contrast. At one extreme, some pour all their creativity into their art and don't care how they live. At the other, there are those who have to arrange their personal lives at a certain aesthetic level before they can function. Perhaps the most easily chosen paradigm case of the first kind would be Beethoven, whose working environment was elementary, not to say squalid. (In Erica Jong's debut novel *Fear of Flying*, which does not deserve the neglect that has followed its best-seller status, there is a convincing passage where the narrator, visiting a mock-up of Beethoven's music room, is "moved by the simplicity of his needs." I quote from memory, but a writer has always done well when you feel the urge to do that.) Keats exemplified the second kind, if only for one memorable moment, when he put on his best clothes before he sat down to write a poem. In order for inspiration to strike, Wagner had to be living in velvet splendour, no matter what it cost him and others. He lived beyond his means on principle, as if imbued with the divine right of kings. It took a king, Ludwig II of Bavaria, to keep him in the style to which he had no intention of becoming unaccustomed. Verdi, on the other hand, paid his way and expected his possessions to do the same: he lived in comfort and the vineyards he could see from his house were all his, but they were a business proposition. Comparable figures in the imperial magnitude of their achievements, the two giants are at odds in this: Verdi could have slept in Diaghilev's spartan bedroom and got up in the morning to compose. Wagner would have thought he was in gaol.

Goethe kept a grand drawing room to impress his guests and a spartan bedroom because he did not need to impress himself: in him, the economy of imaginative effort attained the level of poetry. Yet he might have lived chaotically and written no less well. The connection between highly organized work and an impulse towards a life of order is frequent, but not necessary: a fact amply proved by the slobs. Ford Madox Ford's accumulated literary achievement is a shambles of scrappily realized catchpenny projects dotted with masterpieces, but two of those—*The Good Soldier* and the first three volumes of *Parade's End* taken as a totality—are triumphs of precise arrangement. Yet his personal circumstances were so disorganized they looked like a deliberate challenge to Oblomov. Ford would spend all day in a dressing gown stained with bacon fat. That same ingredient of breakfast food was also a theme in the life of Cyril Connolly, an important critical writer whose once high reputation is in a continuous position of never quite being restored, and partly because his epicurean tastes are found repugnant. Connolly's books (mainly collections of essays) were testaments to the cultivated high life, which he tried to live in reality, mortgaging a notional future income to keep himself in champagne, *foie gras*, upmarket women and first editions. But he could use a cold rasher of cooked bacon as a bookmark, especially if the book belonged to someone else. In all of literary history as we know it, perhaps the most outstanding slob was W. H. Auden. The man whose lyrics were showpieces of carpentry—try to imagine a poem more accurately built than "The Fall of Rome"—kept a kitchen that could have doubled as a research facility for biological warfare. Worse, he treated other people's houses the same way. Mary McCarthy, when a guest, earned a bad reputation by taking a long shower with the curtain outside the bath instead of inside: the host would receive no apology for the subsequent inundation. From Auden, a mere flood would have counted as a thank-you note: he left his benefactors under the impression that they had been visited by the Golden Horde. Auden lived long enough for me to see his tie. I thought it had been presented to him by Jackson Pollock until I realized it was a plain tie plus food. It put the relationship of writer to the written in a new light. How could his poems be so neat and clean, and he so otherwise? Rimbaud, of course, had raised the same question long before. His teenage masterpiece *Bâteau ivre*, among all the other things it is, is a perfect construction, architecture on paper. But the young man who wrote it was also capable of composing a poem on a café table using, as a substitute for ink, his own excrement, delivered fresh into his hand specifically for the purpose. When any acquaintance made the mistake of offering him hospitality, he trashed the place on principle. Why Verlaine waited so long to shoot him is a great mystery. (In his biography of Rimbaud, Graham Robb—whose books on Balzac and Victor Hugo are likewise models of the form—does his best to give us an answer, but I still don't get it.) Later on in a short life, the prodigy sobered up sufficiently to suggest, by example if not in a written testimonial, that while an adolescent he might have been a crackpot. Certainly it would be nice to believe it. Auden, however, although on a less destructive scale, was a mess for the long haul: a career scumbag.

Exquisite work is no sure sign of a fastidious worker. If you knew them only from what they wrote, you would expect both Proust and Rilke to be dandies. Proust wasn't: his clothes sense was considered weird even before he started to pad his shirts with insulation, and his handwriting was barely legible. Rilke was, except that the word "dandy" is inadequate to the fanaticism of his everyday display of taste. Everything about him, right down to his notepaper, was faultlessly chosen. His handwriting was so beautiful that his merest thank-you note would look like a work of art even to someone who couldn't read. The whole performance of his personal life cost money, some of which he had. When he had to cadge, he was a lot more subtle than Wagner. A supreme master of the bread-and-butter letter, Rilke was continually invited by great ladies to honour their estates by creating his poems in rent-free accommodation. Once again, the way he managed his circuitous trajectory from one finely appointed ambience to the next was a work of art in itself. Taste justified everything. Taste was his world. He behaved as if art were taste elevated to the highest possible degree. The armigerous chatelaines who played hostess were happy to believe it, since the idea made them artists too.

But even Rilke was self-denying in the only area that counts: he served his art and nothing but. He created the conditions for himself in which he would not be distracted. Absurd though it may sound, Wagner was doing the same. The *Ring*, after all, did get written. The test is not whether the surroundings seem crassly extravagant, but whether what gets created within them seems worth the expenditure. Did Stravinsky keep a needlessly grand household? Not if he needed it: and the precisely discriminating, colour-coded penmanship of his manuscripts was a sure sign that his well-chosen furniture enabled him to concentrate like a monk. (Diaghilev paid him late: behaviour which Stravinsky interpreted, correctly, as bohemian, in the sense that a bohemian's ability not to worry about money always starts with your money rather than his.) The requirement of stately circumstances applied also to Thomas Mann: always grand in his way of life, he followed Keats's principle in every respect, right down to his fingertips. Without a proper manicure, Thomas Mann couldn't write. But he wrote: the second part of *Joseph und seine Brüder* and the whole of *Doktor Faustus* cost a small fortune in buffed nails at Brentwood prices, but we got the books. An artist crosses the line only when the way he lives gets in the way of his work. When Scott Fitzgerald spent his way into debt, he sinned against himself and us, because to write beneath himself was the only way out of the trap, so the escape route led to the worst trap of all. *Tender Is the Night* would have been an even better book if he had known how to give himself time, and admirers who think that *The Last Tycoon* is much more than a pitiful sketch must have a strange idea of what makes *The Great Gatsby* a masterpiece. But the self-destructive artists who scare us by the profligacy of their capital outlay can do so only because we know what they are really worth. Orson Welles only appeared to destroy himself: he was still Orson Welles. Plenty of men have been big eaters on borrowed money but we never heard of them. A better comfort, though, is that Diaghilev, when he borrowed money, was rarely thinking about how he could spend it on himself, and almost always about how it would help finance his next miracle of imagination.

PIERRE DRIEU LA ROCHELLE

❦ ❦ ❦

Pierre Drieu la Rochelle (1893–1945) was the tall blond darling of the French right between the wars. Brought up in a
bourgeois family with royalist beliefs, he emerged from World
War I with with the kind of loathing for capitalism that found
the right more congenial than the left. Later on he said that he
had been a fascist all along, Although he didn't officially
declare his allegiance until 1934, he had decided quite early
that there were only two sides, fascism and communism. A
much-admired poet when young and an effective prose stylist
always, he would have been regarded as an adornment of
French culture if not for his politics. As things turned out, only
his politics lend him lasting interest. (A direct route to the centre of his agitated political consciousness is *Pierre Drieu la
Rochelle: Secret Journal and Other Writings*, translated and introduced by Alastair Hamilton, a valuable student of the fascist
intellectuals right up until the day of their total disappearance
at the end of World War II.) Drieu was convinced that French
culture had been toppled from its rightful pre-eminence by the
corrosive influence of liberals and Jews. Giving a warm welcome to the idea that France might be restored to strength by
an alliance with Germany, he saw France as the woman and

Germany as the man in a partnership that for him always had sexual overtones. His personal beauty was important to him. He was the kind of man who takes it to heart when he loses his hair. Since he looked more like a blond barbarian Nazi god than most of the Nazis did, his alliance with the invader had the stamp of destiny. More than ready to collaborate with the Nazi Occupation, he accepted the editorship of the *Nouvelle Revue Française* after the parent publishing house, Gallimard, made a deal with the Germans by which it would censor itself in order to stay in business. To do him what little credit he had coming, Drieu became disillusioned with the occupiers, but his annoyance was mainly because they proved themselves less keen about the strength of French culture than he was. The measures against the Jews didn't bother him.

Nevertheless he must have been aware that he had not only chosen the losing side, but behaved badly enough to attract vengeance, because when the Liberation came he attempted suicide instead of standing up to argue for his views. The failure of his quest to eliminate himself raised the question of what to do with so embarrassingly gifted a leftover, but finally he managed to do the right thing, although scarcely for the right reason. "We played and I lost," he said in the farewell address he called Final Reckoning. "Therefore I demand the death penalty." But we don't demand the death penalty because we lose. We demand it because we have done the wrong thing.

And above all, I am not interested enough in politics to let
them encumber my last days.
— DRIEU LA ROCHELLE, QUOTED IN PIERRE
ASSOULINE'S *L'ÉPURATION DES
INTELLECTUELS*

O N THE FACE of it, Drieu's valedictory testament was absurd. It was 1944, after the liberation of Paris; he had never made any secret of collaborating with the Nazis; his deeds were done and his time had run out. And his whole personal disaster had been because of his interest in polics. Already resolved to suicide, he was attributing a deficiency to himself in the very area where he had been most obsessed. It is an instructive demonstration of the lengths to which self-deception can go. In the thirties he had been the golden boy and even looked like one. His hulking personal beauty was certainly enough to make some extremely civilized women forget his politics. (Visiting from Argentina, the bluestocking heiress Victoria Ocampo, future editor of the literary magazine *Sur*, welcomed him into her bed, and decades later she was still forgetting his politics, writing fond articles of reminiscence in which his intellectual proclivities featured as charming quirks at worst.) But his political passions, which included a visionary anti-Semitism, had led him all the way to treason, by a series of steps that had begun with his disgust at the inability of France to unite Europe in a crusade against the liberal democratic heresy. Since he thought Nazi Germany could do a better job, he welcomed the German invasion. It is important to remember, on this point, that he was not coming from the direction of Action Française. Maurras hated the Germans. What united the two different strains of collaboration was that they both hated the Jews.

As editor of the *Nouvelle Revue Française* under the tutelage of a compromised regime, Drieu was effectively a collaborator for as long as he held the chair. But here the difficulties begin. The picture becomes less clear than we might like. Drieu found out, on closer acquaintance, that he didn't think much of the Nazis either: they weren't really serious about the transformation of culture. Feeling that, he was able to nurse within himself the belief that he still had the interests of a greater France at heart. (The fate of the Jews, it need hardly be said, he was able to ignore: i.e., tacitly approve.) Had he chosen to live, he might eventually have been able to put up a case for his past behaviour. As a collaborator on the practical level, he had not done much more to favour the oppressive power than many of the late-flowering literary *résistants* had done against it. It had been Rebatet and Brasillach, after all, who had helped to direct the hunt against the Jews. Punish those two, by all means. But Drieu had been a cut above all that vulgarity, had he not?

He might even have been able to carry the point about politics: the thoroughness with which he had got them wrong was, after all, a kind of proof that they had never held his interest, which had been expended on his purely intellectual vision of a properly authoritarian Europe. In other words, he might have proved himself incompetent. Some of his contemporaries later ventured the cynical but all too plausible opinion that if he had stayed hidden for a couple of years he might have resurfaced as a minister in the provisional government, where he had friends and admirers. It wasn't just his old Nazi pals who tried to get him to safety. When he revived in hospital after his first suicide attempt through an overdose of Luminal, he found a passport good for Switzerland under his pillow. The documents were almost certainly put there by Lt. Gerhard Heller of the Propaganda Abteilung. Heller was still busy in the corridors of Paris even as the German troops were pulling out and the high-echelon collaborators were settling into their supposedly safe new billets in Sigmaringen. But Heller's efforts were duplicated by Emmanuel d'Astre de la Vigerie, minister of the interior in the provisional government, who also thought that Drieu and Switzerland were a good match. There were plenty of eminent literary figures who considered Drieu as one of them, and thus too important to be sacrificed on the altar of *l'Épuration*. They had a point, about it if not about him. All too quickly it had emerged that the purgative courts would be used as a means of settling old scores. The unspeakable Louis Aragon (a long-time apologist for state terror as long as Stalin was in control of it and not Hitler) shamelessly tried to nail doddery old André Gide. Gide's collaboration had amounted to not much more than a judicious reticence, eked out with the occasional soirée for Ernst Jünger where both men could deplore the barbarism that made it so hard to concentrate on one's art. But Aragon, as a Communist bonze, had never forgiven Gide for his pioneering pamphlet *Retour de l'URSS*, which had revealed Stalin's regime for what it was.

Luckily Aragon's vindictive spite did not prevail. Nor, thank God, did Picasso's stupidity: to his everlasting shame, the greatest of all modern painters allowed his studio to be used as a meeting point for vigilantes preaching havoc against those who had compromised themselves with the foe—a strictness that came oddly from Picasso, who had eaten in black market restaurants throughout the Occupation and never run a single risk. It was a time for fake virtue: a time in which there was no sure sign of real virtue except diffidence. The fair-minded François

Mauriac (some said he had to be fair because his brother had been a *collabo*) put in a good word for the unsavoury Henri Béraud, who throughout the Occupation had kept up an unrelenting barrage of vituperation against Communists, the Popular Front, England and, always and above all, Jews. Mauriac was brave enough to defend even the choleric Jew-baiter Robert Brasillach as "*ce brillant esprit*," large praise for someone who had asked for his fate in open print by telling the Gestapo which doors to knock on. Brasillach's execution by firing squad was generally regarded at the time as the least he had coming, but Mauriac was prescient in guessing that a saturnalia of rough justice would produce a lasting hangover. Mauriac simply disliked *l'Épuration*, and in retrospect he seems right. A good moral test for the business is that while Camus saw that there had to be a reckoning but thought it should be done regretfully, Sartre was an untroubled enthusiast. If Drieu had faced trial straight away, a death sentence might well have been on the cards. But it could be that he had already sentenced himself. In March 1945 he finally succeeded in committing suicide. He used gas. Since he almost certainly knew the truth about what had happened to the Jews deported from Drancy, perhaps he thought the means of his own exit appropriate.

E

✻ ✻ ✻

Alfred Einstein

Duke Ellington

ALFRED EINSTEIN

❦ ❦ ❦

Not to be confused with his physicist cousin Albert Einstein, the musicologist Alfred Einstein (1880–1952) was born in Munich and went into exile after 1933, first in Italy and then in London. He devoted much of his life to scholarship, of which the principal results were his three-volume history *The Italian Madrigal* and his reworking of Köchel's Mozart catalogue. He also produced the standard monograph on Mozart —still the best single book to read on the subject—and an authoritative survey of the golden period in Vienna, *Music in the Romantic Era*. Abetting these major works were some superbly compressed essays, the best of which are collected in *Essays on Music* (1958), the book through which he is most easily approached. At a time when biographies of great composers so often run to many volumes (the trend began well with Ernest Newman's *Wagner*, but by now it is out of hand) it can be a revelation to discover how much Einstein could say in a single paragraph. He had both wit and a sense of proportion. The second thing is not always accompanied by the first, but the first is impossible without the second.

❦ ❦ ❦

> If we let our imagination roam, it is difficult to conceive
> what might not have happened in the realm of music if
> Mozart had lived beyond the age of thirty-five,
> or Schubert beyond thirty-one.
> —ALFRED EINSTEIN, "OPUS ULTIMUM," IN
> ESSAYS ON MUSIC

LATER IN THE same essay, the musicologist gives a brief list of what Mozart did with the few years of extra life he had that Schubert hadn't: "*Figaro, Don Giovanni, The Magic Flute*, the three great Symphonies and the last four quartets." The musicologist thus refocuses an eternally nagging question. The question isn't about what Schubert would have done if he had lived as long as Beethoven. The question is about what Schubert would have done if he had lived as long as Mozart. Einstein doesn't actually ask the question in that form, but he makes sure that we do. Einstein says that the word *frühvollendet* (too early completed) is often "strangely and mistakenly" applied to composers who were never completed, because they were interrupted.

For the twentieth-century Jewish scholars of the arts, the idea of a truncated creative life was an ever imminent reality. First in a disintegrating Europe and then later in American exile, Alfred Einstein wrote his books about musicology in the shadow of a looming threat to culture. With persecution always a danger, his view of the past was inevitably tinged with pessimism. One of the elements that make his monograph about Mozart a great book is this projected sense of cultural fragility. He makes Mozart's prodigious outpouring a race against fate. He treats Mozart the gentile as a *Luftmensch* with a tenuous claim to a place on Earth. He did the same for Schubert, and was surely right. Schubert's career—what in German would be called his *Laufbahn*, the road he ran—was one of busy contentment. Though the occasional romantic radical of today sometimes paints him as an embattled rebel, Schubert was in fact very much at home in bourgeois Vienna, surrounded by friends, a byword for merriment. But he was also an avatar. If he had climbed out of a flying saucer, he could not have been less of this world.

How do we account for such genius? The first question to deal with is how its prodigality did not interfere in any way with its quality. In a conversation I had with the Australian poet Peter Porter, who has a vast knowledge of classical music, he argued that this is nearly always so with the great composers. Modern literature since Flaubert might lead us to cherish the paradigm of a few perfect products slowly refined over a lifetime, but the main tradition of music from Bach through to Mahler allows of no such ideal. The composers churned the stuff out, and it was all good. There would have been no better Bach cantatas if he had written a hundred fewer of them.

But even among his prolific ancestors and heirs, Schubert was something else. My own way into his sonic universe was through the piano sonatas, played by Artur Schnabel. Theoretically my main interest was in the *Lieder*, but I found that the words got in the way. The better I got at understanding German the less I liked most of the texts. (With the French *chanson* tradition at its height there is no such restriction, because Fauré, Hahn, Duparc and the rest took care to set first-rate texts; but with Schubert that was less often so.) Schubert's wordless works presented no such barrier: there was no verbosity to interfere with the eloquence. After a while I could place any phrase from any of the sonatas to the correct sonata, and the time arrived when I could do the same for the symphonies. At Cambridge I knew the future musicologist Robert Orledge. We were in Footlights together—he was musical director for several of the revues I produced on the Edinburgh Fringe—and it would not have surprised me at the time to be told that he would one day be one of our leading musical scholars. (It was a pity he did not compose more: the future student of Duparc could write melodies fully as beautiful as those of his hero.) One evening we had a long discussion about music in which we brandished at each other the names and opus numbers of all our favourite works by the great composers. Orledge admired them all, but Schubert, he said, was beyond admiration. He was surprised that I had not yet heard the Quintet in C Major, and predicted that when I did hear it for the first time it would be one of the great days of my life.

He was right. I heard it played by the Amadeus quartet plus one, in a performance that I later judged to be too lush with the *rubato*; but a certain amount of over-interpretation probably helped the initial impact. (Over-interpretation does some of your reacting for you: you hate it later, but it can help you on the way in.) I had thought that nothing could be more wonderful than Beethoven's late quartets, but the *adagio* of the Schubert Quintet in C Major contained them all with room to spare. Thirty years later, I listen to the Quintet only rarely: it takes me back too far and too deep, and anyway I already know it note by note. But I can already see that I might listen to it many times in my last years, and might even die to it—during the *adagio* for preference. I was not surprised, merely satisfied, to find Wittgenstein referring to the Quintet in C Major in one of his letters to the British linguist C. K. Ogden. In language unusually fervent for so cool a hand, Wittgenstein hailed its "*fantastic* kind of greatness." The italics were his, and well judged. No more measured words will do. But here, at the moment of rapture, is the exact time to return to Einstein's formulation. If Schubert had lived even four more years—the difference between his lifetime and Mozart's—he would have written not just a few more works of the same complexity, but dozens, perhaps hundreds. It is like thinking of the Bellini operas we lost because of a simple sickness. (The same sickness took Bizet, but he was three years older: if he had been the same age, it would have cost us *Carmen*.) It is not like thinking of the Aristophanes plays we lost because someone mislaid them, or of the missing books of the *Annals* of Tacitus that took with them the story of how Sejanus came to ruin: those works were composed, they existed. But Bellini's lost operas, like Masaccio's lost frescoes and Seurat's lost paintings, were lost because they never happened. Their creators were not early completed: they were interrupted.

And the creator who was most catastrophically interrupted was Schubert. It could be said that Masaccio, who died at twenty-six, was an even more grievous loss. Young trainee appreciators of art who stand astonished in front of Masaccio's frescoes in Florence can comfort themselves with the thought that Michelangelo once stood in the same spot and was equally daunted by Masaccio's transformative genius. Masaccio's untimely death switched off a miracle. But there is the consideration that he had probably already worked all the revolutions he could, and what we would have been given had he lived would have been more of the same—bigger and better, perhaps; even monumental on the scale of Michelangelo's ceiling and the Raphael Stanze; but surely within the limits of representational art. He would not have gone all the way to impressionism, cubism and abstraction. But Schubert might have gone anywhere. There is just no telling. Einstein's contribution to criticism was to remind those of us who practise it that we have an inbuilt tendency to freeze the past into position with an injection of the shaping spirit.

Poetic sensitivity, like poetic creativity, is fraught with the sense of an ending. But the tradition we cherish could have been very different: a fact that the twentieth century brought home to us with anachronistic violence. The whole of modern Polish literature, in which Witold Gombrowicz and Czeslaw Milosz are only two of the most luxuriant flowers, might have had an utterly different layout if some Nazi thug, in 1942, had not put a bullet through the head of Bruno Schulz, who, although already fifty, was probably only at the beginning of what he would have written. And as a painter, Schulz was only one of a whole Jewish generation who never got as far as their first exhibition. When we look at the single easel painting by Schulz that survived, we are clearly looking at the start of a magisterial creative outpouring. But the start is all we get to see. Such possibilities were always on Alfred Einstein's mind. As a young scholar, he had the Nazi nightmare still in his future, but he had the eastern pogroms in his memory. It's the Jewish contribution, and a very dubious privilege: to restore to the past the sense of happenstance that its great works contrive to obviate. But of course the great works contain it too, or they could never have been created. Proper criticism brings it out: the play of chance, the capricious fate that energized the inevitability, the number of strokes of luck it takes to make something that will last.

DUKE ELLINGTON

Edward Kennedy "Duke" Ellington was born in Washington, D.C., in 1899. His musical training was a compound of piano lessons and an early exposure to the heady cocktail of church music and burlesque theatre. His career as an orchestral leader began when he organized small bands for parties. His first professional band, the Washingtonians, had only half a dozen players when it reached New York in 1923. At the Cotton Club in Harlem, the size of his band increased to ten players or more, on its way to the later standard aggregate of sixteen— the full Ellington orchestra (usually billed as the Famous Orchestra) was usually no bigger than that. But it could create its own world, and the truest statement ever made about Ellington's supremacy was that his orchestra was his instrument. There was not only an Ellington era, there were Ellington eras, of which perhaps the most fruitful was the period of the 1940–1941 band, when every sideman was a star. After making initial contact through his Newport Jazz Festival LP of 1956, my own appreciation of Ellington started with the recorded works of that pre-war (pre-war for America) flowering in the early 1940s, and in the following set of notes I try to reflect how, when I later ranged backwards and forwards in his work, I started always from that sure base. Beginners now, I think, would do best to start there too, so as to be never in doubt that they are dealing with a genius. When he died, he took with him a secret that no other modern composer, whether in jazz or in more formal music, has ever quite recaptured—the secret of combining other people's individual creativity into a larger vision. The best comparison, perhaps, is with Diaghilev. A prophet honoured in his own country—partly because of Richard Nixon, who invited him to the White House and played the piano beside him—Ellington died in 1974.

Jitterbugs are always above you.
—DUKE ELLINGTON, QUOTED IN *HEAR ME TALKIN' TO YA*, EDITED BY NAT HENTOFF AND NAT SHAPIRO

ELLINGTON LOVED THE dancers, and he was appalled by the very thought that jazz might "develop" to the point where they could no longer dance to it. When he said "jitterbugs are always above you" he wasn't really complaining. They might have kept him awake, but he wanted them to be there. He was recalling the sights and sounds of New York life that he got into "Harlem Airshaft," one of his three-minute symphonies from the early 1940s. If he had put the sounds in literally, one of his most richly textured numbers would have been just a piece of literal-minded programme music like Strauss's *Sinfonia Domestica*. But Ellington put them in creatively, as a concrete transference from his power of noticing to his power of imagining. Ellington was always a noticer, and in the early 1940s he had already noticed what was happening to the art-form that he had helped to invent. He put his doubts and fears into a single funny line. "It don't mean a thing if it ain't got that swing." Characteristically he set the line to music, and it swung superbly. But under the exultation there is foreboding. Ellington could see the writing on the wall, in musical notation. His seemingly flippant remark goes to the heart of a long crisis in the arts in the twentieth century, and whether or not the crisis was a birth pang is still in dispute.

For Ellington it was a death knell. The art-form he had done so much to enrich depended, in his view, on its entertainment value. But for the next generation of musicians the art-form depended on sounding like art, with entertaiment a secondary consideration at best, and at worst a cowardly concession to be avoided. In a few short years, the most talented of the new jazz musicians succeeded in proving that they were deadly serious. Where there had been ease and joy, now there was difficulty and desperation. Scholars of jazz who take a developmental view would like to call the hiatus a transition, but the word the bebop literati used at the time was all too accurate: it was a revolution. The *ancien régime* was kept as a foundation only in the sense that it was pounded into the earth. Thousands of paired examples could be adduced to make the difference audible. A simple case is the contrast between Ben Webster and John Coltrane in their respective heydays. As a sideman for Ellington, Webster played short solos on some of the three-minute-miracle records made by the 1940–1941 band. It was the most star-studded yet best-integrated ensemble Ellington had in his whole career. Every soloist was encouraged to give it everything he had in a brief space, with no room for cliché or even repetition: riffs were discouraged in favour of a legato flow which, though improvised at the time, could have been written down afterwards and shown not a single stutter. Musicians of the calibre of Johnny Hodges, Cootie Williams and Rex Stewart customarily packed more into their allotted few seconds than they later deployed in a whole evening when they were leading their own orchestras. But nobody packed more in than Webster. When I first heard him in action with Ellington I thought he left even Coleman Hawkins sounding tentative. Webster's solo on "Cottontail" was my favourite. After a few hearings I could hum and grunt every note of it, and fifty-five years later that line of notes is still in my brain like the sonic equivalent of a neon sign on a nightclub with a long name, and I can even remember the exact texture of his tone, substantial and burred like Sean Connery snoring. The name Ben Webster got into my head beside the other Webster, the one who was much possessed by death. Ben Webster, I thought, was much possessed by Melody's incestuous love affair with her brother Rhythm. As an adjective, "Websterian" took on a new, modern meaning, with modernism taken in the sense of the age of drama happening again, in a new form and in our time, but with all the primordial vitality of the poetic emerging from the savage. From Ben Webster's recorded works of that period, and especially when he was with Ellington, there was not a bar that I could forget. To remember it was effortless. To be remembered was what it demanded. As Lester Young was for Count Basie, Ben Webster was for Ellington: the sideman in whose tone the orchestra's entire texture was concentrated and projected.

Now put "Cottontail" aside, take a couple of decades to regain your breath, and listen to John Coltrane subjecting some helpless standard to ritual murder. I won't waste time trying to be funny about John Coltrane, because Philip Larkin has already done it, lavishing all his comic invention on the task of conveying his authentic rage. (For those who have never read Larkin's *All What Jazz*, incidentally, the references to Coltrane are the ideal way in to the burning centre of Larkin's critical vision.) There is nothing to be gained by trying to evoke the full, face-freezing, gut-churning hideosity of all the things Coltrane does that Webster doesn't. But there might be some value in pointing out what Coltrane doesn't do that Webster does. Coltrane's instrument is likewise a tenor sax, but there the resemblance ends. In fact it is only recognizable as a tenor because it can't be a bass or a soprano: it has a tenor's range, but nothing of the voice that Hawkins discovered for it and Webster focused and deepened. There is not a phrase that asks to be remembered except as a lesion to the inner ear, and the only purpose of the repetitions is to prove that what might have been charitably dismissed as an accident was actually meant. Shapelessness and incoherence are treated as ideals. Above all, and beyond all, there is no end to it. There is no reason except imminent death for the cacophonous parade to stop, a fact which steadily confirms the listener's impression that there was no reason for it to start. In other words, there is no real momentum, only velocity. The impressiveness of the feat depends entirely on the air it conveys that the perpetrator has devoted his life to making this discovery: supreme mastery of technique has led him to this charmless demonstration of what he can do that nobody else can. The likelihood that nobody else would want to is not considered. It wouldn't have been true, either: nothing is more quickly copied than virtuosity, and Coltrane had a hundred clones. They didn't swing either.

Here made manifest is the difference between the authoritarian and the authoritative. Coltrane made listening compulsory, and you had to judge him serious because he was nothing else. Webster made listening irresistible. But such enchantment was bound to be suspect for a new generation that was determined not to be patronized. The alleged progession from mainstream to modern jazz, with bebop as the intermediary, had a political component as well an aesthetic one, and it was the political component that made it impossible to argue against at the time, and makes it difficult even now. The aesthetic component was standard for all the arts in the twentieth century: one after another they tried to move beyond mere enjoyment as a criterion, a move which put a premium on technique, turned technique into subject matter, and eventually made professional expertise a requirement not just for participation but even for appreciation. (In architecture, the turning point came with Le Corbusier: laymen who questioned his plans for rebuilding Paris by destroying it were told by other architects that they were incompetent to assess his genius.) The political component, however, was unique to jazz. It had to do with black dignity, a cause well worth making sacrifices for. Unfortunately the joy of the music was one of the sacrifices. Dignity saw enjoyment as its enemy.

Swing was the essence of the enjoyment. In the late thirties the word "swing" was appropriated to a category of big band jazz, which later became the music of the American war effort, and thus went on to conquer the world: in Japan, the first bobby-soxers appeared so soon after the surrender that they might as well have been dropped from the B-29s. But swing had always been a staple component of jazz in any category, because jazz began as dance music, and without a detectable beat the dancers would have been stymied. It need hardly be added that without a detectable beat there can be no variations on it: for syncopation to exist, there must first be a regular pulse. No matter how complex, subtle and allusive it became, jazz had always contained that energizing simplicity. Unfortunately bebop had the technical means to eliminate it. The highly sophisticated instrumentalists of the rhythm section were encouraged to display their melodic invention: in the hurtling fast numbers, Charlie Parker and Dizzy Gillespie played showers of notes that deliberately suffocated any rhythmic pulse, while the rhythm instruments that might have contained the cascades within a palpable tempo were instead intent on claiming equal status by implying the beat instead of stating it. All the implications rarely added up to the explicit. The word "departure" was often heard in approval: everyone in the band departed as far as possible from a predictable measure. (In classic jazz, there had never been anything metronomic about the predictable—syncopation took care of that—but the compulsive innovators thought the essential expendable, as a brain grown too self-conscious might become bored with the regularity of its own heartbeat.) The result of the abandonment of a basic linear propulsion was a breakneck impetus with no real excitement. Only in the slow numbers could the listener tell if the instrumentalists were in command of anything except their technique. The upbeat stuff was a business simultaneously frantic and arid, a desert preening itself as a sandstorm; so it was no wonder that Ellington, a cool customer full of the authentic juice, thought it a fraud.

Listening in much later from a long way across the Pacific, I was very glad to agree with him. I found bebop a fascinating area when I began to explore it, but I was always worried by how seldom I felt compelled to tap my foot. I loved the Thelonious Monk slow numbers and even some of the fast ones, but it was partly because they swung. (In his last phase, which I saw something of, Monk was so stoned that he would occasionally grab for a chord and miss the piano altogether, but in better times his left hand rocked along no matter how oblique his right hand got in its dialogue with the infinite.) The bop that didn't swing drove jazz towards the unflowering graveyard where pretension gets the blessing of academic approbation. It was a destination towards which the exhausted higher arts had spent a hundred years looking for refuge, but what was disconcerting was the way the popular arts headed for the same terminus almost as soon as they were invented. Even without the politically inspired character of bop—let's play something they can't steal—jazz would probably have taken the same course as the movie musical, in which a magically equipped performer like Gene Kelly sadly proved that if he were left to himself he would ditch the self-contained show numbers and turn the whole movie into a bad ballet. The fatal urge to be taken seriously would still have been there even if the musicians had all been white. But the best of them were black, and status was a matter of life and death.

Not even Ellington was immune to its lure. He was a superior being, but it took the Europeans to treat him like one. In Europe he sat down with royalty, as if his nickname were a real title. In America no president before Nixon ever invited him to the White House. In America he had to keep his orchestra on the road, and some of the roads led near enough to the South for Jim Crow to be waiting. Ellington did his best to stay out of all that, but it remained disgracefully true that there was plenty of humiliation available even in the north. It had to be faced: the tour was the key to his economics. He met the payroll as a bandleader, not as a composer. It was understandable that composition should become, in his own mind, his ticket to immortality. As a lover of his creative life I tried hard to agree, but on the evidence of my ears I found the large-scale works smaller in every way than the three-minute miracles. For one thing, the large-scale works didn't swing, except in selected passages that seemed to have been thrown in as sops to impatient dancers who shouldn't really have been in the hall. The set-piece suite of his last years on the world tour, the Sacred Music Concert, was the etiolated culmination of his adventures in large-scale composition—the end point of a long development in an art-form for which his own best work had proved that "development" was an inappropriate word. I attended the Sacred Music Concert in Great St. Mary's at Cambridge while I was an undergraduate. It was a privilege to see the grand old man still in command of his destiny and his charm, but there was too much sacred and not enough music. When the sidemen rose for their solos, showers of notes were no substitute for the carved phrases of their forgotten ancestors. Ellington must have known it: he was conducting a tour of his own tomb. Later on, outside in King's Parade, I saw him ease himself into the limo with his old-time bass saxophonist Harry Carney, sole survivor from the days of glory, the only Ellingtonian sideman who was ever allowed to ride in the car with the chief, instead of in the bus with everyone else.

From the limo before it pulled away, Ellington smiled and twiddled his fingers at the fans, the bags under his eyes like sets of matched luggage. (I got a wink from him, which I filed away among my best memories.) He had seen mobs in his time who would have wanted his blood if he had shown his face, but there was no wariness in his glance. There was not much energy either. I guessed that it was goodbye, and indeed

Ellington retired not long afterwards; but the sad truth was that the creative spirit I had so admired was long gone. It had already started to go at the time when I first heard his music on record, in the late fifties. At the 1956 Newport Jazz Festival, the Ellington band's long disquisition on the theme of "Diminuendo and Crescendo in Blue," with its marathon tenor solo from Paul Gonsalves, had made world headlines on the music pages. A rejuvenation for Ellington's career, the performance was transferred to a long-playing record—it was pretty well the first time that the LP had been exploited to show what a jazz band could do in a space longer than three minutes—and in Sydney we played "Diminuendo and Crescendo in Blue" over and over, making learned comments. Scholars among us knew which Joe Jones it was, plain Joe Jones or Philly Joe Jones, who was slapping the edge of the stage to flog Gonsalves onward for yet another chorus. The debating points were made in mid-dance: nobody listening was stationary, even if he was sitting down. The whole number swung so hard that you had to hit something: sometimes it was your neighbour.

Driven by that sweet stampede of rhythm to a belated acquaintance with what Ellington had done before, I realized only in retrospect that the rot had already set in. The possibility of more room for the band to breathe was tempting him away from the delicious intricacies he had been forced into when time was tight. Though the large-scale suites from the past all turned up on vinyl along with their more recent companions—"Such Sweet Thunder" began its life that way— it was all too evident that three minutes on shellac had been his ideal form from the start: he was a sonneteer, not an epic poet. The standard was set in the Cotton Club days, when cars still had running boards. As the LP Ellington anthologies came out, I built up a library that went all the way back to his recorded beginnings. Bar by bar I drank in the wa-wa sonorities of Bubber Miley and Tricky Sam Nanton, for both of whom the effect would have been dissipated if they had gone on longer than a chorus or two. As Ellington's various ensembles succeeded each other, with the personnel always changing but a few always seeming to come back at the right moment, the soloists provided one of the connecting threads. There was a particularly tremendous Ellington band in the mid-thirties, with Rex Stewart playing open horn to complement Cootie Williams and his sour manipulation of the plunger mute: two different kinds of shining trumpet, one a golden bell, the other a wail in the night. The way those two voices would call to each other was quintessential Ellington, for whom the sounds of the city—"Harlem Airshaft," "Take the A Train"—were a collective inspiration for a melodic urban speech that no poet could ever match, not even Hart Crane in *The Bridge*, or Galway Kinnell in his wonderful mini-epic *The Avenue Bearing the Initial of Christ into the New World*. But Ellington's toughest connecting thread was the compactness of the head arrangements: as precise as if it had been scored yet as loose and easy as jam session, the section work never even riffed without varying and developing the figure. The word "development" fitted for once, and in the only way it should: to mean a deepening, an enrichment. Those inspired soloists, each of them a composer in himself, built the transparent bridges between the dense passages of ensemble voicing, and always with an unfaltering, rhythm-driven melodic surge even when the pace was slow. When he was holding down a chair for Ellington, the most lingering alto sax solo from Johnny Hodges was never boring for a moment. Anyone who thought that Hodges's honey sweet tone could never be boring anyway was at liberty to find out otherwise by listening to the space he gave himself on recordings of the orchestra he made the capital mistake of trying to lead under his own name.

Ellington gave his superbly self-trained horses enough time—just enough time and no more—to perform every trick they knew, but they had to do it inside the corral. The result would have sounded like confinement if the rhythmic pulse, the swing, had not made it sound like freedom. As Nabokov said of Pushkin's tetrametric stanza, it was an acoustical paradise. The 1940–1941 band was Ellington's apotheosis, and as a consequence contained the materials of its own destruction, because all those star soloists wanted bands of their own. Hodges wasn't the only one who found out how hard it was to be the man in charge, and ever and anon the chastened escapees would make their way back to Ellington, but never again were enough of them available at once to recapitulate the hallucinating complexity of those beautiful recordings. I memorized every bar of every track, and without trying. Vintage Ellington was a language: many-voiced, a conversation in itself, but a language none the less, or rather all the more. The most wonderful thing about the Ellington language was that it could be listened to only in the way it was created, through love.

Scholarship and biography, too often twinned in this regard, are always trying to break up Ellington's language by analysing it to pieces. In his later years, Ellington became more and more the subject of learned enquiry, and on the whole it did him little good. (He had long before tried to warn the world against too much analysis: "That kind of talk stinks up the place.") Once it was established that Billy Strayhorn's contribution as an arranger had been underestimated, it was soon discovered that Ellington's contribution had been overestimated. Out on the road, Ellington had freed himself from the dominance of any single woman by sleeping with them two at a time. Now they were old and ready to talk. Thus we heard of the barbarism behind his suave façade. It could now be deduced that, as a cynical stroke of self-exculpation, male chauvinism had expressed itself as sentimentality: "Mood Indigo" was a midnight flit by Don Giovanni. But scholarship and biography could never add enough irrelevant nuance to dilute the truth, which was that the great man had no flaws within himself which he could not transmute into a living song. The flaw that he could not control was in the country he lived in. Even he, a man born to rule, had to fight for prestige, the only armour against perpetual insult. He did it by expanding the lateral scope of his inventiveness beyond its natural compass, in the effort to become yet another American composer, like Aaron Copland, Samuel Barber or Charles Ives. He felt that as a necessity, but the necessity was merely political. Acting from an inner necessity, he was already *the* American composer, having taken jazz to the point where no further satisfactions could be added in order to make it different. They could only be subtracted. The new boys had to go somewhere. Ellington was too generous not to realize that one of the reasons they went there was because of him, so he was careful never to criticize them too hard. He made a joke of it: it don't mean a thing if it ain't got that swing. But the joke was true, and by extension it is true for all the arts.

F

❧ ❧ ❧

Federico Fellini

W. C. Fields

F. Scott Fitzgerald

Gustave Flaubert

Sigmund Freud

Egon Friedell

François Furet

FEDERICO FELLINI

❧ ❧ ❧

Federico Fellini (1920–1993) was born in Rimini but dreamed of Rome, where he arrived in time to see the Fascist regime launch itself on the final adventure that ensured its ruin. His gift for drawing caricatures was his ticket to the big smoke. Mussolini banned American comic books in 1938 but for Fellini's generation the damage was already done. Fellini's early work in the comic-strip medium was heavily influenced by American models: he drew bootleg versions of *Flash Gordon* and *Mandrake*. After the war the American comic strip, no longer officially frowned upon, became more powerful in Italy than ever, to the extent that not even Communist intellectuals, in the 1960s, saw anything incongruous about poring over the monthly comic-strip anthology called *Linus*, after the *Peanuts* character. It remains a safe bet, however, that Fellini's ability, in his formative period, to fight off the siren call of the revolutionary left, had something to do with his mental immersion in an imaginary America. All of Fellini's movies, whether sooner or later, culminate in his masterpiece *8½*, and the hallucinatory imagery of *8½* begins in the comics: one of the most conspicuous examples of how, in the twentieth century, the popular and high arts established an intimate connection. Other low-life forms that Fellini scraped a living from early on were vaudeville and radio drama. The story of the great director's unsophisticated origins is told well by John Baxter in his *Fellini* (1993). My own essay "Mondo Fellini," collected in *Even as We Speak* (2001) and *As of This Writing* (2003), is an attempt to record the formative impact that a man accustomed to pleasing millions of people at a time could have on a single life.

When I was a little boy I believed I looked a little bit like Harold Lloyd. I put on my father's spectacles and to make the resemblance even closer I took out the lenses.
— FEDERICO FELLINI, *INTERVISTA*, p. 76

ONE WOULD LIKE to have seen Fellini's Harold Lloyd impersonation. Did he do stunts on the dizzying cornice of a *palazzo*? Most of Harold Lloyd's apparently death-defying stuff was done with camera angles and false perspectives, and at least once he used a double; but it is easy to imagine the young Fellini trying it for real, not yet having figured out that cinema is an illusion. On a similar impulse, at the age of eleven I almost killed myself imitating Batman leaping from the roof of a building site into a sand-pit. If I hadn't landed flat on my back I might have been worse than winded, but at least the world would have been deprived of no more than a writer, a species of which there are always many. A world deprived of Fellini would have had something more rare to mourn: a true director, *il regista*, the master of the revels. "*È una festa, la mia vita*," says Guido in *8½*: my life is a party. It was true, and he invited everybody.

Fred and Ginger is merely the most obvious case of Fellini's debt to American popular culture. Even when they don't look it, his works are saturated with its influence, right down to their visual style. After Italy pulled out of World War II, Fellini had his beginnings in Italy's teeming subculture of comic strips and *fumetti*, which were essentially comic strips made up from posed photographs. Before the war that whole subculture had been inspired by America's example, and not even the Fascist regime, when it put an end to the syndication of American comic strips, felt it had the power to cancel Mickey Mouse. Under his

Italian name Topolino, Mickey continued his adventures. (After the war, his name was given to Fiat's most popular small car.) Near the end of his career, Fellini cooperated with the brilliantly accomplished pornographic cartoonist Marinara to produce a *bande dessinée* called *Voyage à Tulum*, a sort of free-form sequel to *8½* and *La Città delle Donne*. Marinara's phantasmagoric style took a lot from the American comic-strip tradition that started with Little Nemo and ran right through the parodic *Mad* magazine period in the 1950s to its self-consuming apotheosis in the extravagant layouts of the head comix in the 1960s. But in *Voyage à Tulum*, when he celebrated Fellini's big-screen extravaganzas, you can see how well Marinara found a match between the initial purity and the culminating sophistication. He found it by getting back to their common ancestor. Fellini, too, started with the American visionary tradition that grew from the restless mind of *Little Nemo*. The big pictures of Fellini's mature period, from *La Dolce Vita* through to *E la Nave Va*, all look like something that Winsor McCay's little boy Nemo dreamed of, and could wake from only by falling out of bed. In his introduction to the published script of *8½*, Fellini said that the Marcello Mastroianni character, vis-à-vis the same actor's character in *La Dolce Vita*, had to grow in stature because his enemies were more dangerous. But the enemies were all in his mind: his obsessional neuroses.

When Fellini said that in *8½* he found a pretext for putting in everything that had been tormenting him for years, he meant everything that had been tormenting him all his life. Critics have searched in vain for literary precursors of Fellini's grandiose Freudian dreams. Proust? Joyce? The answer lies much closer to hand. In *8½*, Mastroianni is dressed like that because his director is remembering Mandrake the Magician. The American comic strip was the first art-form to exploit the image-generating possibilities of a sleeping mind on its endless journey through the caves and hallways of dreamland. (Tenniel had merely illustrated Lewis Carroll: he didn't take off on his own.) Fascism was a kind of dreamland too, as Fellini emphasized in *Amarcord*. But the dreamland turned to a nightmare while he was growing up. Nazism and Soviet communism combined to drown the ceremony of innocence. Fellini kept his innocence, but it was bound to look like childishness. It was Italy's fate to have its social fabric poisoned first by the Fascists, then by the Nazis and finally by the Communists, whose propaganda campaign against the liberating allies, and especially against the Americans, attained a level of virulence hard to imagine from this distance: reading what the Communist newspapers said about the bombing of Cassino, you would have thought that Guernica had been bombed again, and never have dreamed that the war against Germany was not yet over. Post-war Italian cinema was left-wing because the left was almost all there was: under the pressure of Communist ambitions, the intelligentsia as a whole was polarized between party-line orthodoxy and the independent left, but further to the right there was next to nothing except the wilfully eccentric. Nominally an alumnus of neo-realism, Fellini looked as if he had gone to school in a party frock. Even among those who lauded him for the richness of his imagination, it occurred to nobody that he was the director with the most penetrating social vision. Such an estimation became possible only in retrospect, after it became apparent that no universal plan for society could be compatible with the autonomy of art. The artist who made it most apparent was Fellini himself. The advantage of those lensless spectacles was that he could see an untinted reality. He might have looked like a clown, but from his side of the empty frames he could see the world as it was, and so transform it into fantasies that would last.

W. C. FIELDS

William Claude Dukenfield (1879–1946) was known to the world as W. C. Fields. He began as a carnival juggler. As the magicians Johnny Carson and Dick Cavett discovered in a later era, the accompanying patter was more in demand than the act, although Fields, until the end of his career, was still able to do some of the most difficult conjuring tricks in the book. But there were other conjurers who could do them too. Nobody could equal him for his patter. He was a success in silent movies from his debut in *Pool Sharks* (1915) until sound movies arrived, but when they did, he was one of the few silent stars who actually gained from the change. It was because he could both write his own material and speak it inimitably: a winning combination. *The Bank Dick* (1940) is the movie that his admirers know line by line. In real life he was a self-destructive drinker, but he would have been the first to discourage any large theories about his essentially subversive talent having suffered in the context of Hollywood conformity. He had a drinks trolley at the side of his tennis court.

Is Mr. Michael Finn in residence?
— W. C. FIELDS, *THE BANK DICK*

WOODY ALLEN AND Steve Martin have a common ancestor, and
his name is W. C. Fields. A greater prodigy of comedy even than
Chaplin, Fields could create dialogue for himself that was as funny as
his physical presence. (Chaplin's abiding limitation was that he
couldn't: the real reason that he wanted to stay silent forever.) In *The
Bank Dick*, the question about "Mr. Michael Finn" is Fields's way of
advising the barman in the Black Pussycat Saloon that a Mickey Finn
should be slipped to the visiting bank inspector, Pinkerton Snoopington. The pesky Snoopington having been duly rendered incapable,
Fields helps him through the foyer of Lompoc's leading and only hotel,
The New Old Lompoc House. (Once having established the name of
this hostelry, Fields abbreviates it to "the New Old"—a typically
bizarre stroke of verbal economy.) From the right of frame, Fields ush-
ers the barely mobile Snoopington across the foyer and up the stairs on
the left, which lead to the room where Snoopington will be safely
stashed. The camera doesn't move. Nothing happens. Then Fields,
alone, rushes across the frame from left to right. After a pause, he once
again slowly propels Snoopington across the frame from right to left,
heading for the stairs. We in the audience deduce that Snoopington
must have fallen out of the window of his room once Fields had got
him up there. Without having seen it happen, the audience is con-
vulsed at the phantom spectacle of the paralytic Snoopington plunging
into the street.

The scene is all action with almost no dialogue, but Fields could
write wordless physical comedy the way he wrote words: with
unequalled compactness and suggestiveness. The direction is already
there in the script, and there is every reason to think of Fields as one
of the great directors of comic films, even if he seldom took a formal
credit. He certainly knew more than the producers: one of them
wanted to cut the moment in *The Bank Dick* when Fields shows his
minion Og Ogilvy the warning signal he will use if Snoopington
threatens to queer the pitch. If that preparatory moment had been cut,
Fields's later use of the signal would have lost half of its effect. (A sure
sign of a director who should not be fooling with comedy is when he

gets the urge to cut the preparation so as to increase the pace.) Fields knew everything there was to know about comic construction: an important point to remember. Even his appreciators tend to think that because his life was an inspired chaos his work was too. In fact he was disciplined to the roots. The same effort he had put into his vaudeville juggling routines—he would practise until his hands bled, hence the kid gloves—he put into his inventions for the cinema. The most portable of those inventions was his way with the single subversive line. Every Fields fan can recite at least half a dozen of them, and make a fair show of imitating the master's drawling delivery, which could make even an abstract fragment of surrealist delirium as funny as a crutch. ("Rivers of beer flowing over your grandmother's paisley shawl.") It is easy to think that the lines came to him in a dream, but the awkward truth is that they were poetically crafted. When the top hat that fell off Fields's head ended up standing on the edge of its brim on the point of his shoe, it didn't happen by magic, and neither did a line like "What do you mean, speak up? If I could speak up, I wouldn't *need* a telephone." Just think of all the ways that idea could be written down differently, and not be funny. Magicians do not use magic. "Thou know'st we work by wit and not by witchcraft," says Iago, "and wit depends on dilatory time." Iago's business was duplicity, but one of his weapons was straight sense.

Everyone knows that censorship closed off the future for Mae West. Less well-known is that it did the same for Fields. It wasn't alcohol or old age that ensured his decline, but a sudden, fatal limitation on what he was allowed to say. (Nevertheless alcohol helped: one of his best throwaway lines in *My Little Chickadee* was written from the heart. "During a trip through Afghanistan we lost our corkscrew and were compelled to live on food and water.") *The Bank Dick* is a great movie, but it might have been greater still if the censors hadn't read the script first; and there would almost certainly have been more Fields movies to equal it. When a poet is denied one word, it casts a pall for him on all the others; and Fields was a poet—a poet of innuendo. In private life, nobody cared if he said "Filthy stuff, water: fish fuck in it." But in the movies he was not allowed to go on getting away with advising little girls against playing "squat-tag in the asparagus patch." Nor could he any longer say to his Little Chickadee, "I have a number of pear-shaped ideas I would like to discuss with you." Restricted by the new regulatory codes, the Hollywood film-makers did not necessarily abandon their intelligence. Some of the screwball comedies, made when studio censorship was in full force, remain among the most intelligent films ever. The terse eloquence of films like *My Man Godfrey* and *His Girl Friday* has been matched since the lapse of censorship but not exceeded. There was, however, a certain range of verbal playfulness that went disastrously into abeyance. It became impossible to be suggestive about sex. One could be amusingly evasive about the broad fact of it, but never suggestive about its detail. For Fields, especially in his later years, being suggestive about sex was at the heart of speech, because the discrepancy between his raddled body and his intact lusts was the secret of his screen personality. All his best dialogue came from a mental underworld of sensual indulgence. Hence we have to live with the cruel paradox that sound movies silenced him. What we see of him on screen is just the beginning of what he might have done: a daunting thought if you are one of those people who find his every audible moment even funnier than the way he looked when struggling with a wilful hat, or walking upstairs on the wrong side of a banister. Though he exaggerated his early deprivations when he told tales of his upbringing, Fields was certainly the man out of place: one of those people who are born exiles even if they never leave home. For some reason such misfits seem to favour the notion of verbal economy, as if turning ordinary language into the kind of compressed code that unfolds into a wealth of meaning when you have the key.

F. SCOTT FITZGERALD

❦ ❦ ❦

F. Scott Fitzgerald (1896–1940) is a cautionary tale, but the tale is about us more than about him. Tormented by a glamorous marriage that went wrong, drinking himself to destruction while doing second-rate work to pay the bills, lost in a Hollywood system guaranteed to frustrate what was left of his ability, he became the focal point of numberless journalistic stories about the waste of a literary talent. He himself gave the starting signal for that approach with the self-flagellating articles later collected by his friend Edmund Wilson in *The Crack-Up*. Faultless in its transparent style and full of true things about the perils of the creative life, it is certainly a book to read and remember, but not until we have read and remembered (indeed memorized) *The Great Gatsby* and *Tender Is the Night*. Otherwise we might get the absurd idea that one of the most important modern writers spent his career preparing himself for a suitably edifying disintegration. The inevitable effect of a biographer's hindsight is to belittle the subject's foresight. As his two great novels prove, Fitzgerald was well aware that the culture of glamour was a drawback of democracy, a levelling mechanism calculated to give us comfort by turning gifted lives into manageable legends. If he had written nothing else at all after *The Great Gatsby*, we would still be faced with one of the prophetic books of the twentieth century. Fitzgerald guessed where celebrity, if pursued for itself, was bound to end up: as a dead body in the swimming pool.

A good style simply doesn't *form* unless you absorb half a dozen top-flight authors every year. Or rather it forms but instead of being a subconscious amalgam of all that you have admired, it is simply a reflection of the last writer you have read, a watered-down journalese.
— F. Scott Fitzgerald in a letter to his daughter, quoted by Edmund Wilson in *The Crack-Up*, p. 296

MORE THAN FORTY years after I first read them, these two sentences from the ailing writer to his teenage daughter still arouse that thrill of delighted approbation that once took the form of the word "yes!," uttered while one stood up suddenly before walking around the room. Nowadays I stay in my chair, but in the metaphysical sense I am no less moved. Fitzgerald wrote this letter in 1940. Propelled by his alcoholism, he was far gone in his decline by then: so far gone that he could actually believe his stints in Hollywood were getting him out of trouble instead of further in. (We should hasten to note that it wasn't the place's fault: other writers could work the double trick of staying true to their gifts while still doing what the studios wanted, but Fitzgerald was cursed, or blessed, with an incurable lack of savvy about conserving his energies.) He was not so far gone, however, that he didn't feel the need to impress his daughter by presenting himself as a wise man. In the long run, of course, there was a cosmic joke: he *was* a wise man. Great failure had made him so. It takes a great artist to have a great failure, and F. Scott Fitzgerald was so great an artist that he could turn even his fatal personal inadequacies into material for poetry. The magazine articles collected in *The Crack-Up* were worth the crack-up: the moment when his mind came closest to disintegrating was the moment when his prose style came closest to a perfect coherence. That was quite a thing for it to do so markedly, because it had always been coherent. Fitzgerald, seemingly from his apprentice years, had wielded a style of inclusive fluency, his because it was nobody else's: the ideal natural, neutral style, so finely judged in its musicality it convinces its readers that their own melodic sense is being answered from phrase to phrase, sentence to sentence and paragraph to paragraph. Can we really believe that he arrived at his style only after reading many other great stylists, absorbing and synthesizing their various influences, and somehow contriving to eliminate the residues, even of the latest one? The belief comes hard.

Edmund Wilson guarded and nurtured Fitzgerald's reputation: helped, in fact, to bring it back from almost nowhere. The precious miscellany we call *The Crack-Up* was Wilson's editorial work, and was prefaced by his magnificent valedictory poem to Fitzgerald that begins "Scott, your last fragments I arrange tonight . . .": in my view one of the touchstone modern poems, all the more valuable for being anachronistic. *The Crack-Up* also contains the selection of letters in which I first read this quotation, at a time when I was still unrecovered from being overwhelmed by *The Great Gatsby* and *Tender Is the Night*. By those two books one is always impressed, but their first impact turns the world into Fitzgerald's creation: one is unduly receptive to any news about him, and in those days—the late fifties—it was almost exclusively Wilson who was reading the news. Wilson made no strictures about Fitzgerald's talent. But Wilson did make Fitzgerald out to be a bit of a lummox scholastically, not unlike the footballer Bolenciecwcz in Thurber's college memoir: the footballer who, "while he was not dumber than an ox he was not any smarter." In that regard, the picture Wilson painted of Fitzgerald in maturity and later life seemed not very different from the young Princeton student who had played the language by ear and thrown together his first books under the obvious influence of nobody more exalted than Compton Mackenzie. Looking back on it, in fact, Wilson's generous tributes to his academically clueless classmate add up to a bit of a backhander: he praises the marvellous boy, but only on the understanding that a boy is what the marvellous boy remained. According to Wilson, Fitzgerald, although fully gifted, wasn't fully serious. Making the usual contrast between Fitzgerald and Hemingway—it was always usual, although Wilson was among the very first to draw upon it for didactic purposes—Wilson said that Hemingway was the one who could starve for his art. Hemingway, it was implied, had the stuff in him that the high life could not distort. Hollywood might make silly stories out of Hemingway's books; and Hemingway might even write a silly story so that Hollywood would get lucratively interested; but at least Hemingway guarded himself against the temptation or the necessity to work *in* Hollywood. Hemingway was serious about literature. He knew more about literature. Hemingway and Fitzgerald were both writers, but Hemingway was the reader.

Looking further into Fitzgerald's letters to his daughter, Frances, one is inclined to agree. Fitzgerald asks her whether she has read any good books lately, and supplies, over the course of a series of letters, what amounts to a "such as" list. There are some good names on it, and Fitzgerald has obviously read among them to a considerable critical depth: Henry James, Turgenev, Dreiser, Balzac, Dostoevsky, Ibsen, D. H. Lawrence, Flaubert and Thomas Mann are all sifted, analysed and compared. But in other respects the list is pretty scrappy. In the context of the chic leftism then prevalent in Hollywood, *The Communist Manifesto* is a plausible inclusion, but when he recommends *Ten Days That Shook the World* you start to wonder. If Fitzgerald was belatedly reading up on modern political events in order to repair the lucanae in his own education, there might have been some reason to favour such a book in order that his daughter might be better informed from the beginning; but as a measure for style, *Ten Days That Shook the World* is devoid of beneficial properties. There were American journalists and non-fiction writers of the period who could be studied for their prose: Wilson, Mencken, even George Jean Nathan when his frenzy to decorate did not weigh down his architecture. There were cultural reporters who have since dated hopelessly because what they reported has been absorbed, while the way they reported it was never interesting enough in itself to ensure their survival: you could put Gilbert Seldes in that camp, and the wonderfully curious James Gibbons Huneker. (Paul Rosenfeld, much favoured by Edmund Wilson, should, in my opinion, be left to rest: though he wrote quirkily and well about modern music, he essentially believed that jazz would never amount to anything while it remained in the hands of black people.) But John Reed, even at the time, fell into the category of those who could barely write at all. In *Ten Days That Shook the World* he had the biggest story on earth to tell, and no gift to tell it with. He ended up buried in the Kremlin wall, but the reader feels the same weight. To Fitzgerald, this discrepancy between task and talent must have been apparent at a glance. It follows, damagingly, that Fitzgerald felt he *ought* to rank Reed's celebrated kludge as a good book, presumably because of the line it spouted. One is forced to conclude that Fitzgerald not only declined to take his own literary judgement as an absolute, he thought there was another absolute that he ought to conform to, if only he could figure out what it was.

What Fitzgerald says is true, but its truth is more in our possession than his. In the circumstances from which he speaks, self-deception is not far away, nor is the bombast that goes with it. Fitzgerald was such a drinker that when he was drinking nothing but beer he thought he was on the wagon. (American beer at the time was low on alcohol but he ordered it by the crate.) Similarly he might have convinced himself that he had always been a dedicated student of his art, just because he remembered how, during all those parties, he had made plans to start some systematic reading the next morning, and had made the same plans again during the hangover. Hemingway had better claims to the title of serious reader, even though he flourished his credentials with a bluster that emphasized just how modest in the matter Fitzgerald was. In *Green Hills of Africa* there is some ludicrous posturing around the campfire as Papa announces his intention of going toe to toe with Tolstoy. The embarrassment factor is off the scale, but the implied claim to a fellow craftsman's intimacy with Tolstoy is nothing but the truth. Hemingway knew Tolstoy almost by heart, and there were less obvious tastes in which he showed the same loving diligence—which, it should be remembered, can't be had without humility. When Hemingway praised Ronald Firbank, it was no mere flirtation. Critics as disparate in their origins and interests as Edmund Wilson and Evelyn Waugh both spotted that Hemingway's tricks of arranging dialogue had been quietly lifted from Firbank. Hemingway the bull-necked ruffian and Firbank the pale exquisite sensitively hiding behind the sofa: they were such different writers that a connection seemed unlikely. But it was more than a connection. In the direction from Firbank to Hemingway it looked like the kind of influence that Fitzgerald was talking about in his letter—an absorption. The subtext of Fitzgerald's homily is that you must be influenced by a lot of exemplars to be influenced properly. If you are influenced by only one, there will be traces, and the essence of an absorption is that you don't see the traces. One continues to suspect of Fitzgerald, however, that the reason he showed no traces is that he was never really influenced: he was more or less born writing in his characteristic manner and is recommending school to his daughter because he played hookey himself, and is all the more ashamed because he got away with it.

Fitzgerald's self-schooling in prose style consisted mainly of eliminating arabesques. Montesquieu, in his formative years, did the same: he was temperamentally susceptible to the superficial charm of those virtuoso performers whose spectacular effects he was designed by his artistic nature to supersede with a dignified exposition limpid even when condensed. A case could be made that such powerful writers don't need to be influenced by any model: they need merely to encounter examples of the unadorned expression to which they should aspire, the capacity for which they already possess within themselves. If Fitzgerald can be said to have absorbed and amalgamated all the excellent stylists in English, then it was probably because he was already like that, deep down. His fellow-feeling for Keats (the title of *Tender Is the Night* is only one of the signs) reminds us of a question: where did Keats get it from? Keats's touch and tone (we notice his excesses because they are *his*, not because they are borrowed) had always been fully formed: though he read prodigiously throughout his short life, he seemed mainly in search of reassurance that he was not as unique as he felt. Fitzgerald was like that, except that he was seldom alone long enough to find out that he was lonely. Quite early on, he ceased to sound like anybody else. The young Hemingway sounded like Gertrude Stein, and later on he sounded more and more like Hemingway, in a dreadfully hypertrophied example of the self-imitation we call mannerism.

Fitzgerald was never mannered except in his attitudes, and not even they became predictable until, with his final curtain already falling, the set of sketches we call *The Last Tycoon* assembled them in the one place. For all we know, the principal influence other writers had on Fitzgerald lay in the effort he took to avoid echoing their rhythm and tone. If genius is inherently absorptive, that might always be the principal influence: whereas weak writers sound instantly and comically like the writers they admire, strong writers take care not to, as part of their strength. In *The Great Gatsby*, Fitzgerald's well-manicured dreamland on Long Island has something in it of a Booth Tarkington small-town idyll. Jay Gatsby carries distant echoes of Penrod Schofield. The echoes would be louder if Fitzgerald had not known how to suppress his memories of Tarkington's slick-magazine romanticism, and the memories might have been harder to suppress if they had not been so powerful and thus easy to identify. For any writer, the writers he reads when young open up possibilities of subject matter, drama and psychology. It is quite possible that some of the writers who open up the most to him in these areas will not be artists at all; but if they are, they will inevitably also open up possibilities of diction, rhythm and narrative tactics. The strong talent will be less likely to echo these than will the weak talent. Now justly forgotten, the busy 1950s journeyman Robert Ruark, in books like *Horn of the Hunter*, wrote in abject homage to Hemingway. He wanted to live like Hemingway, shooting every animal in Africa. Fatally for his achievement as well as for the animals, he also wanted to write like Hemingway, copying all his cadences. He would never have tried to copy Fitzgerald. But copying Hemingway seemed easy to do—for at least a generation, every mediocre American writer lapsed automatically into Hemingwayesque incantation—and Ruark did it with a thoroughness that established him unchallengeably in the position of Hemingway's second most helpless unintentional parodist. The first, alas, was Hemingway himself. Sounding more like his own imitators as his works became more empty, he provided an annihilating illustration of why style and substance are separable concepts after all.

It can be argued—indeed, it is hard to argue otherwise—that ever since Shakespeare, every writer in English literature has had to devote a huge effort to not aping him. The chief reason there can't be another Shakespeare is that he never had to waste time doing the same. Shakespeare created a permanent imbalance in every traditional field of subject matter and expression, so that it will never be possible to escape his influence, especially not by ignoring it. (The fallacy in the idea that purity of expression can arise from untainted ignorance lies right there.) The process of submission and avoidance is so deep-seated and long lived that it is hard to examine. But developments in technology and social organization continually make it possible for someone to make a green-field discovery. A new range can be opened up, and ways of exploring it can be developed, but the fresh seam can be mined only as far as the individual artistic personality allows—and that individual artistic personality is the thing to keep in mind when talking of style, tone, diction and influence. Hemingway, in his short stories, could equal Tolstoy's writing about warfare in the Caucasian forests and at the bastions of Sebastopol. For modern times, Tolstoy opened up a field—the field of civilized men taken back to natural savagery by warfare. In late 1942, Ernst Jünger in his Caucasus notebooks consciously echoed Tolstoy's effects and cited his name to prove it. Hemingway didn't need to mention the name: the forests and the closely wooded creeks of his early stories ring with Tolstoy's rifle shots and the snort of his horses. Hemingway took on board every technique that Tostoy ever devised. But in all of Hemingway there is nothing like the relationship of Anna Karenina and Vronsky. In *The Sun Also Rises*, Hemingway could imagine himself as an emasculated man; but he could never imagine himself as a weak one, and the idea of a strong man weakened by an emotional dependency was not within his imaginative compass. (It might well have been within his life, but that would have been the very reason that, for him, it was not something he cared to imagine.) For Fitzgerald, on the other hand, Anna and Vronsky were well within range. In *Tender Is the Night*, the mere existence of Nicole does to Dick Diver what the mere existence of Anna does to Vronsky. Fitzgerald nowhere sounds like Tolstoy, but his themes, and especially his love themes, are everywhere comparable. Their minds are alike, and one might as well say their talents are alike: because in art the mind is the talent, although just how the artistic talent-mind is constituted might be destined to remain a mystery, in the sense of being inherently impossible to analyse to any depth beyond the outermost surface, which is the art itself. With Fitzgerald, however, the place to start analysing it is not in *The Crack-Up*, which, although certainly a work of art, shows only the perfection his prose could attain when his larger creative powers were disintegrating. The place to start is one or the other of the two major novels, where those powers are integrated.

When the talent-mind of the artist exists and has the conditions to express itself, it seems to develop with great speed and daunting ease. On this subject, scholarship can be misleading, and the formal history of the plastic arts can be especially misleading. For long periods and over wide areas, primitivism reigns, but that might only mean that the wrong people are painting the pictures, carving the logs and throwing the pots. The idea is hard to kill that the natural condition of graphic art is to be not very impressive: after all, the idea fits what we ourselves can do, who can barely draw a man standing sideways. But those cave paintings in France, if they didn't come out of nowhere, certainly came out of a very short tradition. In the eye of history, perfection was reached in a trice. The animals on the walls make ruins of all developmental theories. No higher development is possible: there is nowhere to go except abstraction. There are good reasons for thinking this to be the natural condition not just of graphic art but of all the arts, even music: that something which needs to be expressed will quite rapidly gather towards it all the technical means it requires. It might be said that it takes a while to marshal a symphonic tradition to the point where Beethoven can write the *Eroica*. And so it does, because there are practical considerations: for one thing, all the instruments have to be invented, and very few instruments were invented just to be in an orchestra—most of them were invented for separate purposes. But Bach needed few predecessors in order to write *The Well-Tempered Clavichord*, and he didn't even need a very highly developed clavichord: it just had to be well tempered.

None of this line of thought is meant to simplify the question of the individual talent and its composition. On the contrary: one is trying to complicate it, by rendering it even less explicable than it was. Explicability is inimical to it. Talent can be dissected, but not alive. The elegant yet conversational cadence of Fitzgerald's prose is unmistakable precisely *because* it can't be analysed. The creative talent is probably the most complex phenomenon a non-scientist will ever have to deal with, and to deal with it the non-scientist needs first of all to realize that there is only one thing he can borrow from the scientist, but borrow it he must—the scientist's unsleeping attention to the question of what constitutes evidence. Just because someone says that he has been influenced by someone else, for example, doesn't mean that he has, and just because someone doesn't say that he has doesn't mean that he hasn't. In philosophy, an area where gifted people try hard to tell the truth, few practitioners have ever been able to provide plausible reports of their own interior workings. In the creative arts, where fantasy is at a premium, introspection is even less likely to be reliable. Advice, rules of thumb and cautionary tales from established artists are always worth hearing—Goethe certainly thought that such talmudic material was worth providing—but there is no guarantee that those artists ever followed the same path themselves. What they are giving you might be the sum of their experience, but could just as well be a schematized form of what they had by nature. They might be trying to teach you what they had no need to learn.

There is no small print, unfortunately, to warn us it might be impossible to teach. We guess, and probably guess correctly, that if an artist acquires technical ability beyond the requirements of what lies within him to be expressed, the result can only be mannerism. The same guess should lead us to the possibility that the technical expertise artists really do need they will be driven to acquire by the demands of talent. If there is a class, whether for music or for painting, the best students in it know what they want; and it is doubtful whether a class for creative writing can teach anything at all except remedial reading. We shout "yes" to Fitzgerald's advice because what he recommends is what we were doing anyway: reading dozens of the best writers we could find, including him. As things turned out, Fitzgerald's daughter did become a writer: but never one like him, because what he had could not be transmitted.

The same was true for Rilke and his letters to a young poet. *Briefe an einen jungen Dichter* is a toy-town book for the magic doll's house of the mind, but before we choke up with twee gratitude for its impeccably balanced cracker-mottoes we should remember that the young poet to whom they were addressed turned into a boring old businessman whose only masterpiece was his impeccably balanced account book. Rilke and Fitzgerald were two different versions of the same neurotic wreck, and both would have given a lot, in their darker hours, to be blessed with the ordinary ambitions of the youngsters they advised. But the avuncular advice, as always, ran exclusively in the wrong direction, from those in need of consolation to those who could not benefit. An effective letter from Fitzgerald's daughter to her desperate father would have had too much to cover: it would have had to tell him to get out of Hollywood, to go back in time, to stop imagining that he could hold his drink, to visit the fashionable world for material but never think that he could live in it, and above all to marry someone else—someone he could not damage, and who would therefore not damage him.

He wouldn't have listened anyway. When a man on a cross is told to save himself, he can do so only at the price of seeming to admit that it was all for nothing—he knows better than that. Concerning Fitzgerald, there is a principle that can't be taught in a creative writing class and is hard enough to teach in the regular English faculty, but it's worth a try: his disaster robbed us of more books as wonderful as *The Great Gatsby* and *Tender Is the Night*, but we wouldn't have those if he hadn't been like that. Fitzgerald's prose style can be called ravishing because it brings anguish with its enchantment. He always wrote that way, even when, by his own later standards, he could as yet hardly write at all. He could still write that way when death was at his shoulder. He wrote that way because he was that way: the style was the man.

GUSTAVE FLAUBERT

❦ ❦ ❦

Gustave Flaubert (1821–1880) was adopted by twentieth-century modernists as a precursor, especially if the modernists wrote in English. Among his fellow French writers, Flaubert's first fame was for his bad grammar. But his untiring quest for factual accuracy and the right word (the untranslated French expression *le mot juste* got into English mainly because of his influence) eventually, and justifiably, formed the basis of an international reputation, mainly because *Madame Bovary* can be seen to be charged with meaning in every sentence even when translated into Japanese. The reputation was buttressed by the lengths he would go to in order to keep his art uncorrupted by the allegedly sentimental expectations of the bourgeoisie. Flaubert himself looked on the bourgeoisie as the sworn foe of art, even though he and most of his readers were of bourgeois origin. In the following century his hatred of cliché was eagerly taken up by right-wing critics—principally Ezra Pound—disdainful of democracy's supposedly weakening influence on language, and his view of the bourgeoisie as the class enemy of art was equally eagerly taken up by left-wing critics with an anti-capitalist programme. The most conspicuous among the latter was Jean-Paul Sartre, who devoted much of the later part of his career to a mountainous critical biography of Flaubert which should certainly be sampled by any student of ideology on the rampage, but not before that same student has read *Madame Bovary* and at least one of Sartre's own novels, which prove, although not quite as thoroughly as Flaubert's do, that a living work of fiction is a vision of what the world is, and not just of what the author thinks society should be.

No cries, no convulsions, nothing more than a face fixed in
thought. The gods no longer existed, Christ didn't exist
yet, and there was, from Cicero to Marcus Aurelius,
a unique moment in which man was alone.
— GUSTAVE FLAUBERT, IN AN 1861 LETTER
TO MME. ROGER DU GENETTES
(TRANSLATED INTO SPANISH BY MIGUEL DE
UNAMUNO IN *ENSAYOS*, VOL. 2, P. 1022)

THIS PASSAGE IN one of Flaubert's letters has fascinated two great essayists, Miguel de Unamuno and Gore Vidal. For Unamuno, the apostate Catholic in a permanent spiritual crisis about his repudiated faith, it was one of the great texts of his life. In interviews, Vidal has said several times that Flaubert's godless hiatus was the historical period in which a sane man would have been glad to live. Obviously the idea appealed to Unamuno in the same way. It never appealed much to me, which is probably why I didn't underline it in Francis Steegmuller's magnificently edited translation of Flaubert's letters. (A well-edited translation of such an archive is often more useful than the original, because the editor is more likely to supply copious annotation: witness our privileged access, in English, to Mozart's letters and Cosima Wagner's diaries.) But because it appealed to Unamuno, suddenly it appeared striking, so I underlined it there. Unamuno preceded Vidal in his distrust of the religious impulse, and Flaubert preceded both of them. Those of us who came easily to our paganism will find it hard not to think all three of them correct.

But really the idea that mankind would do better if atheism were universal is only an idea. Some of us would now like to think that Islam will destroy itself, and possibly us along with it, unless it develops a secular culture strong enough to offset the comforting strictness of fundamentalism: but we had better be right. There is also the question of whether Flaubert was factually correct. The two questions are linked. In his preferred interregnum between polytheism and monotheism, it is more likely that people believed everything than that they believed nothing. Flaubert has pinpointed a brief age in which superstition, far from being absent, was almost certainly paramount. In those circumstances, the last thing you could say, whether in French, English or Spanish, is that man was alone. Even theoretically, man had no refuge from the judgement of his fellow men. You can't be less alone than that. A society in which all the pressures are social is the one dreamed of by totalitarians. In *Julius Caesar*, one of them pricked Cicero's name on a list. Shakespeare, with typical sensitivity to an historic turning point, recorded the sub-zero temperature of the unique moment, although he did not show us how Marc Antony made the proscription: he only showed us how Cassius heard about it, rather put out that Brutus already knew. If Shakespeare took such a roundabout course to make the point, it could have been because of his irrepressible awareness that he was living at a totalitiarian period in history, all the more insidious for being apparently exuberant. In the time of Good Queen Bess, it meant death to be Catholic.

Eventually, in the West, we emerged from the age in which people paid with their lives for a religious allegiance. We emerged into another age in which they were murdered by the million for other reasons, but not for that one. Though the religious might hate to hear it said, the West graduated from its nightmare only because religion ceased to matter in any way except privately. At the time of writing, we are in the uncomfortable position of hoping that the same thing can come true for Islam, and do so in a briefer time than the span of centuries it took to come true for us. While we are waiting, it might be of some help, although of little comfort, to realize that an Islamic fundamentalist doesn't have to share the psychotic certitudes of Torquemada in order to be dangerous: it is enough for him to share the civilized attitudes of Queen Elizabeth I, who wanted every invading priest tortured as soon as caught, and gruesomely executed soon after that. It's the general view prevailing within a religious culture—the general view usually described as being "moderate"—that matters most. When she was growing up in Somalia, Ayaan Hirsi Ali was taught that Salman Rushdie deserved death because he had blasphemed against the holy book. She was taught it, and she believed it, as did everyone she knew. It was the moderate view. Now, as a member of parliament in Holland, and after her Dutch friend Theo van Gogh was murdered in the street by an Islamic extremist, she believes differently. But how extreme was the extremist? Until the whole of the Islamic world repudiates him, we will be forced to believe that its moderate views are dangerous in themselves, if only for what they condone. We will be forced to believe that there is something crazy about all those people actually *believing* all that stuff; and wish that their belief could become more unbelieving, like ours; and not a few centuries from now, but right now. Such a quick transformation doesn't seem very likely. Perhaps it would be better to wish that their religion could be reinforced, in that area where, so we are told, Islam means peace and tolerance. Certainly there were times in history when Islam meant that, much more than Christianity did. But our understandable hope that every Muslim male of fighting age, if exposed to a sufficiency of Western culture, might transform himself into Flaubert sounds very like wishful thinking; and it is quite likely that Flaubert was thinking wishfully in the first place, when he posited a wonderful ancient time in which nobody had any Gods to worship. He searched the far past, and lo! He found a new dawn.

SIGMUND FREUD

❣ ❣ ❣

Sigmund Freud (1856–1939) was first a neurologist, then a psychopathologist, in which second role, and based in Vienna, he developed the technique of conversational "free association" that we now recognize as the distinctive feature of psychoanalysis, psychotherapy and counselling in whatever form we might happen to encounter them. Since at one time or another most of us will spend hours telling our troubles to somebody we hardly know, this is a very widespread influence for a single thinker to have had. On an academic level, Freud's theories about human personality will always be argued over, as they were when they were being developed. The quarrels of his disciples with him and among themselves are interesting studies in how animus and outright hatred can arise from purely mental differences. The driving force of any ideology stands revealed: it can't be coherent without being intolerant. What there can be no argument about is Freud's stature as an imaginative writer. Quite a lot of it comes over into English— *The Psychopathlogy of Everyday Life* (1904) is a good place to start—but in the original German his body of prose is poetically charged almost without equal. When the Nazis came to power in Germany in 1933, they banned psychoanalysis straight away. After they took over Austria in 1938, Freud was lucky to escape. In London he lived for a further year before succumbing to cancer. His house in Hampstead retains his wonderful collections of books and sculpture. The Freud name, through his descendants, is still prominent in British cultural life.

❧ ❧ ❧

Finis Austriae.
— SIGMUND FREUD, AN ENTRY IN HIS
DIARY, PROBABLY MADE ON SATURDAY,
MARCH 12, 1938

ALL THE ENTRIES in Freud's diary of his last decade are short. Very few are more than one line long. On the day he began to keep the diary in 1929, he signalled his intention on the first page with the underlined heading "*Kürzeste Chronik*" (Shortest Chronicle). The entries are explicated ably in a Hogarth Press coffee table book, *The Diary of Sigmund Freud 1929–1939*, edited by Michael Molnar: a punctilious effort which can be recommended, not least for its lavish iconography. As picture books go, it's a page-turner. But a longer and more sensitive explication of this particular entry would have been useful. Austria's chancellor, Kurt von Schuschnigg, had resigned, Hitler was already in Linz, and the *Anschluß* was inevitable. Its advent could be measured in hours. This was indeed the end of Austria. But why did the great seer say so in Latin?

One reason might have been that *The Times* of London had already said it in Latin. True to the paper's appeasing form in that period, the *Times* leader writers had behaved despicably right up to the crucial moment, but when the catastrophe finally looked inevitable even to them, they summoned the courage to admit that the end might indeed be near. (Up until then, they had run endless assurances about Hitler's benevolence.) Because *The Times* was read religiously in Vienna, and especially by the Jewish intellectuals, the imported Latin tag had been circulating for a week. But there was no reason for Freud to pick up on it. He probably did so to give the moment an automatic historical perspective, and thus claim for himself, through speech, an oracular viewpoint. Shakespeare did the same for Julius Caesar: *Et tu, Brute?* At the moment when all is lost, Caesar reverts out of his everyday language (which in the play, of course, is English) to the formal language of his schooldays, which for Shakespeare would have been Latin. Shakespeare, a psychologist far more intuitive that Freud himself, knew that people revert under pressure. (Even trained singers, when things are going wrong, will suddenly retreat into the shallow breathing that was once all they knew, and any professional in whatever field could tell a similar story.) In the case of Caesar, Shakespeare was probably helped to the idea by Suetonius. In Suetonius's account of Caesar's life, Caesar, when he receives the last blow, reverts out of Latin into Greek: *kai su, teknon.* The effect is not just of a retreat to youth but of a distancing, as if history has inevitably led to this, and the moment must be given its dignity as a point in the flow of time.

The irony in Freud's case is that his tendency to an historical perspective on modern European politics was portentous for himself and potentially lethal to his family. The Nazis emerge slowly in the last years of his diary: too slowly, as it turned out. From the historical viewpoint, the diary is not a proportionate account, because the history that really mattered is barely mentioned. No doubt in his everyday conversation he said much more, but in the diary he said so little that the paucity can be assessed as a kind of inverted *Sprachfehler*—one of those linguistic slips in which he saw so much when they were made by other people. In the years of Austria's final and fateful destiny, he had been working on two culminating trains of thought. One train of thought is captured in *Die Zukunft einer Illusion* (The Future of an Illusion), his most intense evocation of the destructive impulses in mankind. In that book, he defined civilization as the overcoming of nature, with the implication—and the implication was fully worked out—that mankind's natural state was destructive. It was a powerful argument brilliantly articulated, and remains to this day one of the most magnificent condensations of a world view into a prose style. But there was a penalty to be paid, and he paid it. The growing threat to civilized Austria seemed nothing special. He even seems to have seen nothing special about the Nazis themselves. Did he think civilization would contain this destructive force in the same way as, recently at any rate, it had contained all the others? Or was he fatalistically resigned to the catastrophe?

If he was fatalistically resigned, his other important train of recent thought might have played a part. It was in these years that he brought to a climax his theories about the libido and its typology: erotic, narcissistic and obsessional. Everyone, he thought, shares all three departments, with an emphasis on at least one of them at the expense of the other two, and possibly on two at the expense of the third. The narcissistic-obsessional was the most creative combination. Those blessed with it, or cursed, could do great work. But beneath it all, as Philip Larkin was later to put it, desire of oblivion runs. Thanatos, the death wish, was much on Freud's mind. It is possible to say—although it might be wiser to say something else—that he looked forward to personal extinction. He was suffering badly from his cancer by then, and might well have longed for a crisis that would release him. He could not seriously contemplate oblivion as a thing of his own will, because his mother was not yet dead. (He called that "the barrier.") But he might have contemplated it for his country, which, if it went down to destruction, would take him with it.

What makes that line of argument seem unwise is the terrible array of facts that would have to be counted as its cost if it were true. When the reign of terror finally arrived, Freud, with help from abroad, was able to get away to England. But four of his sisters were trapped. All of them were in their eighties, but none was allowed to die of old age. (Marie and Pauline went to Treblinka, Rosa to Auschwitz and Adolfine to Theresienstadt.) In Freud's beloved Vienna, Jewish contemporaries who almost equalled him in eminence suffered the tortures of the damned. Thanatos was no gentleman, and he came not to rescue minds from their torments, but to torment bodies until minds collapsed. Thanatos was a raving maniac, not a mental principle. How was it that Freud, of all people, could not foresee this? Hannah Arendt and E. H. Gombrich, among others, have reminded us that in the German-speaking countries the assimilated Jews thought of themselves as nationals first and foremost: that there was never really any such category as the Jews until Hitler invented it. But Hitler had already invented it. From Germany, the news had been coming in for five years at least. Everyone in Vienna who knew anything about politics was well aware of what might be in store. But to Freud, it might all have been happening to the Hittites and the Assyrians. His historical perspective was everything but actual.

He was a bit like that. There was always a naivety underlying what he knew. An unquenchable naivety is part of an artist's power, and that Freud was an artist should never be in doubt: he was one of the great prose writers in German, which would be worth learning to read for him alone. But his naivety had a way of coming to the surface even in his most subtly elaborate formulations. He thought there was something psychologically wrong with his rich female Viennese patients who did not want to sleep with their husbands. Schnitzler's writings would have taught him better if he had known how to read them. Schnitzler's writings should also have told him about the potential danger to the Jews. But Freud, the master psychologist, was not equipped to receive the message. Freud took holidays at Berchtesgaden without being much troubled by the demeanour of some of its newer visitors. Stefan Zweig, who had a house in Salzburg from which the activities in Berchtesgaden could be observed, was less confident. With the top Nazis in plain sight, Zweig guessed what was coming all too well, but if he ever told Freud, Freud didn't take it in. Freud's sensitivity to his fellow masters of prose was at the level of the ego. When Thomas Mann published a testimonial piece about Freud's scientific achievment, Freud was miffed to note that it was really a tribute to his literary style, with the stuff about science tacked on at the top and tail. He was sensitive enough on that level. But he was cut off from the cultural information that the writers were providing as the situation in Europe steadily deteriorated. He would have been more likely to view them as neurotic. His attention was focused on personalities and their individual neuroses, not on politics and its collective disease. The real psychodrama was too big for him to see.

He could have escaped so much sooner, and from exile he could have saved all his relatives in good time. There would have been no financial problems: from the beginning of the post-war inflation, he had always based his finances on the hard currency brought in by foreign patients. Moving to where the patients were would have boosted his income. Leaving early would have been a better way for him to love

Vienna. Alas, he seems to have believed that the Nazi irrationality was just one more instance of the destructive impulse like any other, and could be contained in balance with the impulses to order, continuity and creativity. (At a meeting in his Hampstead house, I once heard a letter of his quoted in which he said, months after he had reached safety, that the Catholic Church would probably be able to sort the whole matter out.) He never grasped that Nazi destructiveness was a complete mind in itself. Surely he was the victim of his own poetry, which was so vivid that he took it to be a map of reality. From the realm of the human spirit he had banished God and the Devil, and replaced them with a family of contending deities bearing proud Greek names. They were household gods: aided by judicious therapy, they would one way or another always reach an accommodation, in a world where people like his old sisters, even if they were not happy, would die in bed. But the Devil came back. The Devil had never been away.

EGON FRIEDELL

❦ ❦ ❦

Egon Friedell (1878–1938), a student of natural sciences who graduated to the twin status of cabaret star and polymath, was a figure unparalleled even in Vienna, where there were several learned cabaret artists and even a few funny polymaths, but nobody else who could be both those things on such an heroic scale. To think of an equivalent in an English-speaking context is impossible: you would have to imagine a combination of George Saintsbury, Aldous Huxley, Peter Ustinov, Kenneth Clark and Isaiah Berlin. Translated into English in 1930, the three-volume set of his *Cultural History of the Modern Age* was such a publishing disaster that it simply vanished. Today it can be obtained only from a dealer in rare books. In the original German, however, *Kulturgeschichte der Neuzeit* turns up second-hand all over the world, because it was a talisman for the emigration: the refugees took it with them even though, in its usual format of three volumes on thick paper, it weighed more than a brick. Of the several copies I own, the most beautifully printed, which I bought in Buenos Aires in 2000, was put out as a single volume on thin paper by Phaidon Press in London in 1947, for export back to the newly democractic Germany and Austria. (Phaidon also ensured that the book's unfinished companion piece *Kulturgeschichte des Altertums—The Cultural History of the Ancient World*—was published with fitting splendour.) The scholars and book lovers of the emigration gave Friedell's capital work a context, which could be picked up on by the German publishers after the war. I own three copies of the handsome, single-volume post-war edition put out by Beck. My intention was to use one of them as a workbench, and put into its endpapers the notes that have gone into this book. But I ended up defacing my beautiful Phaidon edition, perhaps guessing in advance that my graffiti would be labours of love. It's that kind of book: it makes you feel civilized. The best explanation for Friedell's continued presence in the German-speaking countries, and his absence everywhere else, is that they needed him. His writings give the comforting illusion that the historical accumulation of knowledge makes some kind of steadily increasing, and therefore irreversible, sense. He himself might have thought differently by the time of the *Anschluß*, when he anticipated his inevitable arrest by jumping out of his window, calling a warning as he descended: a cry whose lingering echo contains an era, with all its promise of a just world, and the despair of that world cruelly lost.

❧ ❧ ❧

Of all the good wishes I received for my fiftieth birthday,
it was yours that delighted me most.
—EGON FRIEDELL, QUOTED BY FRIEDRICH
TORBERG IN *DIE TANTE JOLESCH*, P. 195

EGON FRIEDELL'S POLITE message doesn't sound witty at all until you are supplied with the information that it was sent as a printed card. The recipients must have loved it. You can imagine them considering themselves members of an exclusive club for the rest of their lives. A lot of Viennese wit was like that: shared jokes that travelled in a collective memory, and often didn't get into print until a long time later. Friedrich Torberg's retro-guide *Die Tante Jolesch* (Aunt Jolesch) is full of such moments, all recorded after the war, when the

Anschluß, the deportations, the mass murder and the rigours of exile had trimmed the cast of characters to a random few. (One of them, the publisher Lord Weidenfeld, put me on to *Die Tante Jolesch*: like Alfred Brendel, he never sent me away from a conversation without a reading list.) The minor Hungarian literatus Friedrich Karinthy has vanished into obscurity but his eternal question remains unanswered: "What can you make out of a day that starts with getting out of bed?" Ferenc Molnár, the internationally successful playwright, had an acute business sense to go with his enviably marketable talent, but he was much put upon by women. When he and his ex-wife, the actress Sari Fedak, were both in American exile, she traded on his name by billing herself as Sari Fedak-Molnár. He published a brief but effective newspaper advertisement declaring that the woman calling herself Sari Fedak-Molnár was not his mother.

Molnár's quietly delivered bombshells always dug in deep before they went off. One famous compulsive fabulist, the Jeffrey Archer of his time, never recovered what was left of his credibility after Molnár said: "He's such a liar that not even the opposite is true." As happens in any literary circle, some of the Viennese writers were better in conversation than they were on paper. The journalist Anton Kuh (who later died of a broken heart in New York, unable to survive out of his café context) wrote pointed articles and sketches that are well worth reading today, but his talk, by all accounts, was on another level: too good to miss and therefore, alas, too fast to catch. One of his few lines to survive is a definitive physical description of Stefan George: "He looks like an old woman who looks like an old man." Most writers would be pleased with themselves if they could get even one crack like that into an article. Kuh talked like that all the time. A lot of them did. The main reason more of the stuff wasn't written down was because everyone was Johnson and nobody was Boswell. It was the stuff of common interchange. The sense of something precious came after the collapse.

Although most of the Jewish figures in Vienna's intellectual life were secular and assimilated, the rabbinical tradition was strong. The wisecracks were concentrated wisdom, and the verbal thumbnail sketches that were treasured, polished, elaborated and passed on had a moral background. The unrolling scroll of illuminated talk was a continuously enriched compendium of edifying stories: an unwritten literary text, a spoken Talmud. Wit and point were taken for granted. When everyone was a famous talker, there were no great individual reputations that could be marketed to a wider public. The contrast with pre-war New York could not be more complete. The Algonquin Round Table wits prepared their epigrams with the intention of being quoted in newspapers and magazines. The results, even at best, sound strained: they hark back to Oscar and Bosie at the Café Royal rather than to Friedell, Karl Kraus, Peter Altenberg and Alfred Polgar at the Café Central, or Hermann Broch, Robert Musil, Franz Werfel and Joseph Roth at the Café Herrenhof. The tradition began in the 1890s at the Café Griensteidl, where Arthur Schnitzler and Hugo von Hofmannsthal were both regulars. But really it can't be confined to the cafés: in the whole culture right through until the Nazis turned out the lights, talk was a way of being, and it was universally understood that the best talkers had the right to talk it all away. When the distinguished and wildly eccentric legal advocate Hugo Sperber played cards, people would take turns to stand behind him so they could overhear his running commentary: the queue would stretch down the aisle between the tables all the way to the door of the café. Talk was one thing and literature was something else. Even the feuilleton, a demanding genre that reached a high state of development in Vienna, was commonly thought to be more talk than literature. Alfred Polgar, the supreme master of the form, was praised to his face by Molnár as the world champion of the one-metre sprint.

For more than forty years in Vienna, talk was a way of life, and then it ended. In 1938, just before the Nazis took over, there were about 180,000 Jews in the city—down from about 201,000 in 1923. (As George Clare tells us in his exquisite memoir *Last Waltz in Vienna*, it was already a dying community, but nobody wanted to admit it.) After 1945 only 10,000 came back, and most of the rest, of course, had not chosen to be absent: they were absent because they had been slaughtered. But even in the great period not all the participants were Jews, and post-war, it has been argued, the tradition might well have revived, even if in restricted form. Torberg contends that there was more than one reason it didn't. In the old days, people concerned with literature and journalism had time for a café existence even when they were busy. Peter Altenberg was only one of the many literati who did everything but sleep in the café, although he might have been unique in having it as his only address: P. Altenberg, Café Central, Wien 1. Novelists and critics wrote in the café, impresarios made their plans there, publishers read manuscripts and corrected proofs. Today, people use machinery to write, and need a telephone right in front of them, instead of in a little booth downstairs next to the lavatory. They write at the studio or in the office. They might meet for lunch at the café, but a lunch hour isn't long enough to get the unimportant things said. The talk that counts is the talk that doesn't matter, and to get that you need time to spare.

So argues Torberg, and there is reason in what he says: but there is also an unintended pathos, like a nervous whistle in the dark. In Vienna, the Jewish café habitués had no other real home. They were assimilated, but mainly in a technical sense: except for the café, where they could pay for a place by the hour, there was nowhere they belonged that was not overseen by a watchful landlord—the *Blokleiter* of the future. They could feel comfortable only in public. They could feel *private* only in public. Torberg tells a poignant story of seeing, in the Café Herrenhof in 1960, Leo Perutz and Otto Soyka still pursuing their no-speak policy from the years before the *Anschluß*. Soyka had returned to live in Vienna but Perutz was merely visiting, from his new home in Haifa. The only reason the Herrenhof was still open was that its proprietor, Albert Kainz, thought there should be a meeting point for anyone who came back from the past. These two had, but they refused to meet. Their time-honoured vendetta—some ancient business of an unexpiated insult—continued long after its context had disappeared. In the café thronged with the voices of contentious ghosts, no literary Jews remained alive except them. Their quarrel was all they had left, and no doubt they preserved it as a way of pretending that this much, at least, had not altered.

Horrific evidence suggests that the Austrian Nazis, when their armbands were still in their pockets, put the café talk high on their long list of Jewish intellectual pursuits to be trampled out of existence when the great day came. The future firebrands and executioners had been listening in for years, probably inflamed as much by sincere disapproval as by thick-witted jealousy. After a single orgiastic day of violence in March 1938 there was no-one left who had anything to say worth hearing. Hugo Sperber, already worn out from too many years of living on thin pickings, was thrown to the ground and kicked until he fell silent for good. Fritz Grunbaum, one of the stars of the *Simplicissimus* cabaret, was arrested within hours of the takeover, shipped to Dachau, and beaten to death. Whether in Austria or Germany, it had never been the fault of the Jews that they were so slow to realize the catch in the assimilationist ideal: the more indispensable to culture they became, the more they were resented. Hitler needed no telling that there were a lot of brilliant Jews from whom German-speaking culture had gained lustre. That was what he was afraid of: of a bacillus being called clever, and of the phosphorescence of decay being hailed as an illumination. For him, as for every racial hygienist, the whole thing was a medical problem, and the last thing he was likely to contemplate was that the medical problem might lie within himself. He didn't know he was sick. He thought he was well. Convinced racists think they are healthy: their conscience can't be appealed to, they have no better self that might repudiate the lesser one, and they bend all the powers of human reason to the unreasonable, without reservation. For the Jewish intelligentsia, cultivated to the fingertips, it was very hard to grasp the intensity of the irrationality they were dealing with—the irrationality that was counting the hours until it could deal with them. Even in Auschwitz, some of the enslaved musicians must have thought that Schubert's writing for strings would melt Dr. Mengele's heart, as it had always melted theirs. And it did melt his heart. It just didn't change his mind. Similarly, there were probably crypto-Nazi kibitzers who laughed at the running commentary of Hugo Sperber as he played cards. But that was exactly why they wanted him dead. They wanted *their* jokes to be the funny ones, and they got their wish.

It should be said that Friedell's great book, for much of its enormous length, does not use wit for its texture. But it always has wit for a basis. The Viennese tradition of the enlightening wisecrack is there underneath, supporting a prose narrative that never loses its geniality even when talking about the Black Death. Friedell didn't always feel compelled to be funny. But he was never unfunny, in the sense of straining to amuse, and missing the mark. For him the whole target was a bullseye, and he could let fly at his leisure. He saw the same quality in Shaw, whom he admired, perhaps to excess. When Friedell dedicated the English translation of *The Cultural History of the Modern Age* to Shaw, the dedicatee was already a known admirer of the dictators. Friedell would never have been capable of such a misplaced enthusiasm. He would have been a valuable voice in the English-speaking world if he had ever been taken up, but his name was never well-known in Britain or the United States except to the German-speaking refugees. Today it is so thoroughly forgotten that he is not even listed in the excellent *Chambers Biographical Dictionary*, which finds room for Finnish playwrights of the second order, and is usually good about those who once were prominent but are so no longer. Friedell, however, was never there to be forgotten. But if we know nothing about him, he, true to form, knew a lot about us. He was a student of British cultural history and wrote one of the best appreciations of Lord Macaulay. Typically playing himself in with a witticism—Friedell the cabaret artist always knew how to buttonhole the audience—he said that Macaulay was so highly regarded in Britain that his book of collected essays was included in any list of classics. In the English-speaking countries, Friedell pointed out, a list of classics was regarded as a guide to books that should be read, and not, as in the German-speaking countries, to books that should be avoided. It's easy to imagine that idea starting its life at a café table. Harder to imagine is how the giant could walk away from his laughing friends, climb the stairs to his apartment, and settle down for another day's lonely work on his strange and wonderful attempt to get the whole of creation into a nutshell.

> Electricity and magnetism are those forces of nature by
> which people who know nothing about electricity and
> magnetism can explain everything.
> — EGON FRIEDELL, *KULTURGESCHICHTE
> DER NEUZEIT*, VOL. 3, P. 225

In his great book, Egon Friedell regales us with thousands of lines like this. If they were fully separable from their context, they would be aphorisms: we could pick them out like jewels from a crown. But they are more like threads and knots in a tapestry, and can't be pulled loose without violating the texture. Suitably aware, however, that we are doing his masterwork an injury, we can memorize some of his best moments and reproduce them in conversation, although morality demands that we should acknowledge the borrowing. After all, he did. This line is one of the many he lifted from someone else. Friedell gives the provenance: one Gustav von Bunge said it in his *Lehrbuch* (Textbook) *der Physiologie*, and it wasn't his line either. He was quoting a professor of physics who said it in a lecture. Thus, all the way back to anonymity, we can follow the trajectory of a shining notion. The tapestry analogy breaks down. Friedell's mighty gathering place of a text is a game park, a menagerie, an aviary and an aquarium. Sentences live in it as our dreams are populated with fragments of experience, often including experience we have not yet had, and may never have. It follows that the importance of always identifying a source lies not only in common justice, but in truth to life. Whether we like it or not, individuality is the product of a collective existence. Few writers have ever had a more identifiable tone of voice than Egon Friedell. But the tone was a synthesis of all the voices he had ever heard, and so is ours. If we had never heard anyone else, we would not sound more like ourselves; we would sound like Kaspar Hauser the savage infant, on the day he was rescued from solitude. In the matter of style, freedom lies in all the ways we have been a prisoner of someone else's example. He might only have been a school bus conductor with a gift for sardonic verbal abuse. She might only have been the woman who stamped your card at the lending library. But they gave you the gift that comes next after the gift of speech: the gift to give it shape.

Obviously, in wit, there are degrees of humour, from intense to nonexistent. What is funny is a matter of dispute, but I have always found the anonymous humour of Hollywood immensely funny. Nobody knows who first said: "She'd be a nymphomaniac if only they could slow her down." But whoever thought of that line knew a lot about humour: probably he worked in it professionally, in some branch of the film business, although I doubt if he was a writer. (If he had been, he would have a found a way of letting us know who he was.) One day, perhaps on the spur of the moment, he—or, come to think of it, more likely she—came out with a witty line that was also creasingly funny. Slightly lower down the scale of tickled ribs, there are witty lines that make you smile with appreciation—the smile that acknowledges how you almost laughed.

On that level one can place many of Oscar Wilde's best epigrams:

the ones that are condensed without being leaden, and fashioned without being laboured. "Meredith is a sort of prose Browning, and so is Browning." But much of the most valuable wit forms at a level where laughter is neither induced nor sought, and even a smile is not required: the level where a sense of rightness combines with a sense of neatness, and a nod of the head is enough to acknowledge the blend. It's possible to say that on this level all wits sound the same. They are not monotonous—quite the reverse—but they do share a tone: the enviable tone of something put with sufficient cogency to make the listener feel that if he can't remember exactly how the thing was said, he won't remember exactly what the thing was. It is as if there were one precisely codified set of manners operating, which all its adepts know equally.

As a result, it's easy to mistake them for one another. As an illustration, I once quoted several aphorisms by Hugh Kingsmill, capped them with a single aphorism by Santayana, and defied the reader to spot the difference. In my memory, the one by Santayana is "A fanatic redoubles his effort when he has forgotten his aim." But I would not be surprised to be told that it is by Kingsmill. It is not so much that the memory plays tricks: rather that, in this area of distilled truth, there is not all that much difference between personalities. "We are asleep," says Baptiste to Garance in *Les Enfants du Paradis*, "but sometimes we wake up just long enough to realize we are dreaming." "If all the people who lived together were in love," says Wittgenstein, "the earth would shine like the sun." It is easy to imagine the attributions reversed; and indeed, without your permission, I just reversed them; it was in Jacques Prevert's screenplay that the shining earth appeared, and the moonlit line about the dreaming sleepers came from the thin-lipped mouth of the sad philosopher.

Vauvenargues the unlucky aristocrat is a larger spirit than La Bruyère the rising bourgeois, and both would have been more fun to meet for a drink than La Rochefoucauld, whose contempt for mankind would have been unlikely not to have included us. They were three very different minds, but you would need to know an awful lot about the treasury of the French aphorism never to misattribute a coup by one of them to either of the others. The same applies even on the dizzy level where wit becomes funny: in the brief span that the Italians use-

fully call a *battuta* there is not much room for an individual personality
to show up, so all the wits sound like the one sparkling soul, and on our
deathbeds—if we do much laughing there—it will probably be a matter of hearing the jokes that go past our ears rather than of seeing the
people who cracked them go past our eyes. When forgetfulness confers
anonymity, it could well be that justice will be restored. I doubt if Lib-
erace was the first to say "I cried all the way to the bank." It sounds like
Old Hollywood, and could very well be Old Vienna. Dorothy Parker
might not have been the actual inventor of the joke about the woman
who injured herself sliding down a barrister. Except for Flann O'Brien,
there was never a new pun, although always an alert plagiarist. Dorothy
Parker could think the stuff up, but you can tell that it took effort: in
her theatre reviews, she could barely manage one real zinger each time,
even when it was expected of her. A wit under pressure to produce is
very apt to borrow on the sly.

Friedell could go on and on being wise because he didn't feel compelled to be funny. He thought it sufficient to be interesting: a desirable condition for a writer to be in. Comedians do not enjoy the same
luxury, although they always aspire to it: given the chance, they will
construct a framework in which character makes the points, so that
they can relax. The necessity to go on throwing a double six is nerve-
racking and eventually not even amusing. A commentator probably
does better to accept that too many wisecracks are a mistake. Even
Mark Twain soured some of his early travel writing in Europe by dragging in a vaudeville routine when he should have been focusing his
observations, which were always the most interesting features of his
pieces, and often the funniest.

Friedell was one of those enchanted spirits who are observant over
the whole range of human experience from everyday behaviour up to
the most exalted level of creativity: indeed he scarcely recognized the
hierarchy, and took it all as an isotropic universe of delicious excitement. Finding everything significant, he was in a good position to
appreciate the perennial charm of the charlatan, whose expertise is to
convince the hayseeds that they share the same propensity for universal insight. It is not enough for the mountebank to unleash a theory
that explains everything: to be successful, he must convince his gormless onlookers that the same theory has always been in their possession,

but now stands suddenly revealed. They reward him for what he has discovered in them, and buy his snake oil as a vote of thanks.

Memories from childhood tell me that it can be deeply disturbing to be addressed by an adult in the grip of such all-encompassing certitude. It sounded like madness even before I could tell sense from nonsense, and ever since, through a life now blessedly stretching to some length, I have been periodically rocked to meet otherwise normal-sounding people who are suddenly taken over by the same rhythmic rant. Those in the grip of an all-encompassing Answer soon make it clear that the desire to be so enlightened has more to do with personality than intelligence. Few men were more intelligent than Arthur Koestler, for example. He was one of the first prominent international commentators to develop a case of clear-sightedness about what was going on in the Soviet Union. During the Spanish Civil War, savage maltreatment by the NKVD helped to open his eyes. He stopped believing in communism as an Answer. But he started believing in everything else: one fad after another until the end of his life. He thought the world was going to be put to rights by science fiction, by J. B. Rhine's researches into the paranormal, by a Lysenko-like offshoot of Lamarckian evolution. Finally he asked his ageing but loyal audience of intellectual supermarket browsers to fall to their knees in wonder when they heard a word on the radio at the same time as they were reading it in a book—to be impressed, that is, by mere coincidence. Throughout this stentorian career of waxing and waning enthusiastic, Koestler always maintained his solid capacity for realistic observation and cosmopolitan savvy. He was hard to fool, except when the boondoggle was big enough, and sounded like science. If you want to read an essay whose humour attains the level of a cosmic joke, read P. B. Medawar's demolition of Koestler's theories about the inheritance of acquired characteristics. Medawar put his fastidious finger exactly on the throbbing point of the fervent amateur's psychological problem: Koestler was science-struck. Untrained in science himself, he had a taste for it—the fatal proclivity for magnetism.

As Robert Musil said in praise of Alfred Polgar, our only *idée fixe* should be the determination to avoid one. But the bonnet-filling bee is a tireless migrant, and can even show up in fields nominally concerned with the rational employment of the brain. Apart from the sharpness of the disappointment, there should be no surprise in the fact that the philosopher's stone has always made its most prominent appearance in philosophy itself, where its looming outline is the surest mark of incompetence. But monomania would be easier to deal with if the sufferer were of one mind: we could just avoid him. Unfortunately it is quite possible for the subtle visionary and the shouting dunce to inhabit the same skull, so that Wagner the anti-Semite will always be there to help convince aspiring race scientists that they know something about politics, and perhaps even something about music. Newton's celestial mechanics constitute a mental achievement sublime beyond estimation. But those same exalted capacities of ratiocination spent years plugging away at a system of chronology whose fraudulence was self-evident to any shopkeeper. From the evidence supplied by history's teeming reservoir of minds simultaneously clear and crazed, the logical inference can only be that we probably all suffer—somewhere on the pathway winding through our heads there is a philosopher's stone waiting to trip us up. But as long as we don't hit anyone else with it, we are probably doing well. One of the loveliest women I ever knew was a believer in colonic irrigation as an aid to beauty. She was mad enough to think that it had worked for her. But she wasn't mad enough to suggest that it might have worked for me. On that showing, I would have pronounced her sane, but I wouldn't have wanted to stand surety for how she might have behaved if the Moonies had got hold of her. Fifty years before, it might have been Reich's orgone box, and fifty years before that it might have been the theories of Madame Blavatsky. When the beautiful Magda Rietschel met her future second husband, she had just finished being passionate about Buddhism. Before that, it had been Zionism. In order to marry Josef Goebbels, she became equally passionate about National Socialism. Her latest and last enthusiasm made even less sense than the others, but there can be no doubt it convinced her: she not only killed herself for it, she made certain that her children died too. And so on, all the way back through history, in which the beautiful women, because they get written about, are forever cropping up in the grip of the latest explanatory fad, whose essential property is to console them for having been picked out from other mortals, and thus made to feel so mortal. Friedell caught the essential truth about people prone to catch-all theories: they aren't in search of the truth, they're in search of themselves.

> Mankind in the Christian era possesses one huge advantage
> over the ancients: a bad conscience.
> — EGON FRIEDELL, *KULTURGESCHICHTE*
> *DER NEUZEIT*, VOL. I, P. 132

Friedell wrote this not long before the Nazis arrived in Vienna. Had he survived the onset of the new barbarians, Friedell might have modified an unwarrantably uplifting sentiment. He must have been revising it in his mind long before he went out of the window, because it had already turned out that he had chosen too confident a grammatical form for the verb. Mankind in the Christian era *ought* to possess a bad conscience. By the time of his wisely chosen suicide, the evidence had already been coming in from Germany for the previous five years that Christianity was in for a comprehensive rewrite, the main aim being to jettison its moral encumbrances, of which the bad conscience was the most burdensome.

Even if the Nazis had stayed where they belonged, at the ragged edge of politics instead of in the centre, the same sort of evidence would still have been coming in from Russia for a full twenty years. A conscience of any kind, good or bad, was never listed as an item of a Bolshevik's mental equipment. Loyalties beyond the state's declared aims were thought to be inimical, and an *a priori* set of values carried within the mind could have no higher status than that of a psychological problem. Since Christianity was the main source of the problem, the elimination of Christianity was a state aim from the word go. The state could have lived with the icons and the incense. The icon, in fact, was about to come into its age of gold, even if the gold was the light gilded alloy of the badges that bore the images of Lenin and Stalin, and which always startled you by weighing no more that snowflakes when you picked them up.

But the Soviet state could never live with spiritual values. Strangely enough, the Nazi state could, as long as the spiritual values were aimed in the right direction, along the path of Parsifal, or of Siegfried on his journey down the Rhine. Compared with the Soviet state, which was a monolith, the Nazi state was a bucket of eels, with conflicting values of individual conscience having validity independently of the programmes of state power. Even near the top, departments were in contention. There were even different departments to interpret orthodoxy, so that Alfred Rosenberg, the cultural "expert" on policies towards foreign populations in the East, would have ideas on race that other top Nazis thought stupid. To get a ruling was hard: Hitler would have preferred it if all his subordinates were in conflict with each other, always. Only the paper-pusher Martin Bormann ever succeeded in imposing hegemony, and he could do so only as an exercise in pure bureaucracy, after Nazi power to influence events had ceased to be a reality. The Nazi state got its act together when it could no longer act. There was always room in the upper reaches of the Nazis' earthbound Valhalla for dreamers to imagine they were following the true path—for an appeal to spiritual values of chivalric dedication. Himmler brought it down to pentagrams and runes, but even among the SS there were would-be Teutonic Knights in the picture. It was possible to dream of being Parsifal—Parsifal standing upright in the turret of a Tiger tank. Siegfried could carry a flame-thrower charged with Wotan's magic fire. The mark of sentimentality it is to be all choked up with feeling about nothing, and the mark of black-and-silver ceremonial was to upgrade sentimentality to the religious plane by working towards a future in which nostalgia for the supposed purities of the heroic past would become real. The time and treasure that the Nazis put into mumbo-jumbo was one of the marks of their regime. Other racist regimes have been more pragmatic. In post-war South Africa under apartheid, when it became expedient to make the Japanese racially acceptable, they were simply declared racially acceptable. Under the Nazis, when it became expedient that the Japanese should be reclassified as Aryans, Himmler poured a lot of the Reich's money and effort into proving the point scholastically. Cynicism could have worked the trick in an instant, but sincerity demanded evidence. Nothing except the fervour of religious belief can explain such a rush of blood to the head.

After the defeat, the Nazis vanished completely. Officers of the occupying powers forgivably got the idea that the party membership had consisted of nothing but opportunists. Some of the opportunists were among the hierarchs. Goebbels stood out for his willigness to accompany Hitler to oblivion. Himmler and Goering were both ready to forget the whole thing. But we should not overlook the dreamers: there were many men who looked back on their duties not just as a dedication of moral effort, but as a sacred rite. Those quondam mass executioners who talked about "the task" were the Nazis we should not write off. Many of them, after the war, grew comfortable enough to wear fleece-lined car coats, drive a big Mercedes, and die in bed, and some could not resist telling the television reporters how sad it was to see a new generation of young people who believed in nothing and had no respect for values, because they had never done anything hard and clean. There is no reason to believe that those terrible old men were faking their disgust. They remembered their lives as a crusade.

The religious trappings of the Nazi movement were kitsch, like all its art: but as with the art, they left a long echo in the mind for as long as the mind had nothing else in it. It was by no great act of cynical calculation that Nazi liturgical material could be pitched unerringly at the kind of people who were genuinely moved by tripe. It was concocted by the same sort of people. Bad taste gives aesthetic expression to the aspirations of upstarts, and part of the appeal of Nazism was in the way it turned social mobility into a path of adventure rewarded with decorations at every step. The kind of women who could pin a diamond studded swastika to a bias-cut jersey silk evening dress were thrilled by the kind of men who had learned just enough about Wagner's Siegmund to fancy the idea of impregnating Sieglinde. When the years of power were over, there was plenty to be nostalgic about. The memorabilia market was soon in the position of having to manufacture souvenirs: there are probably more SS ceremonial daggers in existence now than there were in 1945. In the Soviet Union, by contrast, nobody ever felt the same way about the paste cookies cranked out by the state medal factories. A Soviet officer at general staff rank was covered with medals like a pangolin with scales, to no lasting effect except on the spectator's funny bone. The Soviets knew nothing about rarity value, whereas the Nazis made sure that the ascending grades of a high decoration all occupied the same focal space—the Knight's Cross was worn at the neck, and so was the Knight's Cross with Oak Leaves, the Knight's Cross with Oak Leaves and Swords, and the Knight's Cross with Oak Leaves, Swords and Diamonds. The "Diamonds" was referred to in the singular and almost invariably conferred by Hitler personally. The aim was to stress quality over quantity, and once again the trick worked particularly well on people who had not been brought up to know the difference. After the Berlin Wall came down I bought a KGB cap (it was from a clerical branch of the KGB: no rough stuff, and therefore not very glamorous) at a stall near the Brandenburg Gate for a few dollars. An equivalent SS cap would have cost a hundred times as much, and I would have had to buy it in Islington. In Germany, the stuff is so precious it either circulates in secret or is crated for export to America's alarming abundance of people who find the Nazis glamorous. The big question, in Germany, has always been whether the hard-eyed sentimentality would live on into the next generation. The question was hard to answer because the older generation was so slow to go away. Nobody lives longer than those old men who got tough from killing children. They can ski until they're ninety. They don't even lose their hair.

It can be said that the Nazi brew of Nordic saga, Wagnerian fable and elfin tomfoolery had little to do with the Christian concept of conscience. There is truth to that, although we ought not to leave out the consideration that for many centuries a Christian conscience was no obstacle to the most hideously comprehensive persecution of unbelievers. Nevertheless the liberal conscience, the conscience we really value, would never have arrived in the world unless the Christian conscience had preceded it; so Christianity can be conceded the primacy.

When Friedell talked about a bad conscience, he meant the mind that was capable of seeing that might and right were not the same thing. The Nazis were dedicated heart and soul to observing no such discrepancy. Their superstitions served merely to make them feel better about it. If the Communists had managed to come good on their declared aim of abolishing all superstitions, they would have been even more frightening than the Nazis. It is a weird kind of consolation, but at least it is something, to have evidence that they couldn't keep up the secular momentum beyond the death of Lenin. Already during Lenin's life, his writings and sayings had been awarded religious value, like the poetry of Virgil, which for a large part of the Christian era was consulted as an oracle. Even as late as the seventeenth century, and in a country as civilized as England, people were still poking a finger at random into the *Aeneid* to be given a portent of an upcoming battle. Lenin was awarded that treatment while he lived, having given the lead by the way he treated the writings of Marx. After Lenin's death, the embalming fluid was an interior anointment presaging the divinity to come. Stalin's act as the Son of God depended on Lenin's continuing as God, so the corpse remained safe. The superstitions attached to Stalin need not be rehearsed. Though they generated boredom on an intercontinental scale, they remain interesting to the extent that he agreed with them: the great realist really seems to have believed, for example, that he knew something by instinct about economics, biology and military strategy. Stalin's capacity to join in the superstitions centred on his person is the gateway to the larger subject of how an utterly cock-eyed metaphysics guaranteed that the Soviet experiment could not possibly succeed even though the men who led it were ready to murder the innocent en masse.

It was hell; nor were they out of it; and the fuel that fed the flames was superstition of the most unsophisticated kind. The superstition which held that bread and wine turned into the body and blood of Christ always had a poetic justification even when men were burning each other in disagreement about whether it really happened, and on a practical level it scarcely matters whether it is true or not, because only the spiritual life is, or should be, affected. But the superstition that Soviet agriculture would do better if it were collectivized by force was one that killed people by the millions, and none were more certain to be victims than those who looked as if they might know the truth. There is a great danger, here, in ascribing the whole disaster to Stalin's personal mania. Young people today who find it thrilling to flirt with the notion that they might be Trotskyites should know that Trotsky's voice was the very loudest in calling for a more thorough "militarization" of the struggle against the reactionaries on the land: by which he meant that the peasants weren't being massacred in sufficient numbers. It can be concluded, however, that agriculture was an area in which Stalin was particularly loopy. Almost certainly it was the importance of biological research to agriculture that made Stalin see the attractions of putting the ineffable T. D. Lysenko in charge of biology.

Lysenko preached the kind of biological theories that Stalin could understand: i.e., they were poppycock. Stalin gave Lysenko the power

of life and death over a whole field of science. The result was the collapse of Soviet biology and the permanent ruin of Soviet agriculture,
which never again produced enough grain to feed the nation. (The difference was made up by importing part of the American surplus at a
knock-down price, a *sub rosa* agreement which continued throughout
the Cold War.) But lest it be thought that Lysenko was the invention
of Stalin and Stalin alone, it should be noted that it took the intervention of Andrei Sakharov, then still at the height of his prestige as the
golden boy of Soviet physics, to persuade Khrushchev against favouring Lysenko's comeback. The dreadful truth was that the superstitions
had reached so deep into the fabric of the Soviet polity that nothing
except a complete collapse could get them out. The notion that a government can plan a whole economy, for example, was already known to
be a superstition at the time of Marx. By the time of Lenin, there were
no serious economic theorists in the world who thought that a command economy could exist without a large area of private enterprise.
Stalin spent his whole career in power proving that a state could plan
every detail of an economy only at the cost of terrorizing a large part
of the population which might have hoped to benefit from it.

By the time of Brezhnev, the Soviet Union had effectively given up.
The Twenty-fifth Party Congress in 1976 decreed that the quality of
consumer goods would be raised. I was there at the time and saw the
decree hoisted into position on every second building, in red letters
anything up to six feet high. The Soviet Union certainly knew how to
make signs. But nobody knew how to raise the quality of consumer
goods. Brezhnev's own consumer goods were all bought abroad, like
his cars. Brezhnev bought his shoes in Rome because no shoe factory
in the Soviet Union could produce a pair of shoes that didn't leak—a
state of affairs which Stalin's era had long ago proved as *especially* likely
to come about if you threaten to shoot the official in charge. By Gorbachev's time, the party hierarchs were no longer making a secret of
having their tailoring done abroad. (When filming in Rome, I had a
jacket made by the celebrated tailor Littrico, and found out that I had
the same measurements as Gorbachev: they were on file in Littrico's
office.) Even while it was still a qualification for membership of the
Politburo that the old dreams should be paid earnest lip service as if
they still had some life in them, Andropov, head of the KGB, was

preparing his organization for the novel concept of *not* ruling by terror. Sakharov had tried and failed to tell the Party that unless the Soviet Union embraced the concept of freedom of information there would be no way to continue. U.S. Secretary of State George Shultz tried to tell Gorbachev the same, with pie charts. But Andropov didn't need telling. The intelligence community in the Soviet Union were the people who knew from experience that information and superstition were different things. The story of how the Soviet Union backed out of its historical cul-de-sac is adequately told in Scott Shane's *Dismantling Utopia*, but it would be a blessing if John le Carré could occupy himself with the biggest single mystery ever to come out of Moscow Central—how the men charged with State Security managed to conspire against the state without becoming victims of each other merely for suggesting it. In his last years, I. F. Stone, an erstwhile sympathizer turned unyielding scourge, developed an elaborate theory to prove that the Soviet apparatus of control could never voluntarily dismantle itself. Before the eminent sociologist Aleksandr Zinoviev was expelled from Russia, he had already developed a similar theory, taking it so far as to suggest that even dissident writings like his own had come into existence only to support the structure by acting as a safety valve. There would be no retreat. It couldn't happen.

It couldn't happen, but it happened. The story is hard to summarize and of course it isn't over yet, any more than history is over. Since the Soviet Union's nuclear weapons are even more dangerous now than when the state was making sure they were chipped free of rust, it is quite possible that the end of history is in the offing, but not in the way that Francis Fukuyama was talking about. It was yet another superstition to believe that the collapse of one of history's most complete totalitarian dystopias would be succeeded automatically by a functioning democracy, as day follows night. In politics, it is more likely that a deep enough night will be followed by a lot more night, and then by nothing at all. But to be too confident about that happening in this case would be yet another superstition, and would lead us away from the fascinating question of where men like Andropov got their bad consciences from. They grew up in an atmosphere of unrelieved moral squalor. Through bad faith, they flourished; and good faith would have held them back. The system had been designed so that they always stood to benefit personally from the decay around them. If the whole thing had gone to the dogs, they would have been all right. Yet they chose to dismantle the system that had given them their careers. Most men bend with the breeze: which is to say, they go with the prevailing power. But a few do not. With or without Christ's help, they grow a bad conscience. Thank God for that.

FRANÇOIS FURET

❦ ❦ ❦

François Furet (1927–1997) was one of the most valuable liberal voices in France, where they were in short supply. As a general rule, the liberalism of ex-Communists always needs to be searched with a careful eye for any signs of the original extremism's having been transferred to a new domicile, but Furet passes that test well. One of the first attempts to treat the effect of Communist ideology on a global basis, his book *Le Passé d'une illusion: Essai sur l'idée communiste au vingtième siècle* (1995) is a touchstone, and partly because he himself had once been caught up in the illusion. Apart from his powers of realistic observation, one of the forces that shook him loose from his first allegiance was the conclusion he drew from his studies of the French Revolution that its dogmatism was not just incidentally lethal, but necessarily so. New students can get the essence of his two-volume *La Révolution française* (1965, written with Denis Richet) in the sheaf of articles he wrote subsequently in defence of his view, published posthumously as *La Révolution en débat* (1999). His views needed defending because almost everyone on the established left attacked them. For *gauchiste* thinkers, Furet's position on the Revolution required that he be discredited, but it was hard to do: he wrote too well.

The most accessible evidence of his journalistic brilliance is
the lifetime collection of articles put together after his death by
Mona Ozouf: *Un Itinéraire intellectuel* (1999). Admirers of
Jean-François Revel will find that Furet, as both thinker and
writer, was in the same league, with something of the same sardonic tone. But they will usually remember that Revel, before
he championed liberation, had no illiberal position to repudiate. Furet had; and whether his personal history gave him the
advantage of experience is an abiding question, for him as for
other lapsed believers.

> In this clinically pure fascism, reduced to its own cultural
> elements, the central point is racism, and the idea of race,
> impossible to think about clearly, is made up from an anti-
> image, that of the Jew. . . . Constituted at this level of
> psychological depth, the fascist ideology is completely
> impermeable to historical experience.
> — FRANÇOIS FURET, *UN ITINÉRAIRE*
> *INTELLECTUEL*, P. 258

THE AUTHOR OF the best book in French about the history of
Communism was part of the history. François Furet had been a
Party member himself. Jean-François Revel has many times warned us
about the tendency of belatedly reformed *gauchiste* intellectuals to
high-hat those who never fell for the drug in the first place. Furet,
however, was too fine an analyst to flaunt his superior experience. He
could, had he wished, have flaunted his superior insight. In recent
times France has been blessed by the presence of a gifted plain-
language philosopher, Alain Finkielkraut, who writes almost full-time
on the problem posed by the anti-Semitic heritage of modern France.
But part of France's recent run of good luck—it needed some, in view
of what the past was like—is that a philosopher like Finkielkraut has
been accompanied, abetted and often preceded by older journalists,
commentators and historians who were forced to some of his conclusions by the weight of events. Furet never sat down to argue in a systematic way about nationalism and racism, but he had a knack for

turning in the remark that opened the subject up. Talking about the noxious collaborator Lucien Rebatet, who managed to blame the Jews for their own deportation, Furet said that the right-wing ideologue has nationalism in order to legitimize racism. It is always useful to be reminded that if an ideology contains a prejudice, the prejudice is likely to have been there first, like the splinter in the fester, if not the speck of grit in the pearl.

Furet would have attracted far less opprobrium if he had stuck to criticizing the right. But his criticism of the left was too uncomfortable to bear. His most irritating device, from the viewpoint of progressive orthodoxy, was to pick out the big lies of the past that were still resonating in the present. Talking about the Stalinist terror in the late 1930s, Furet noted how Stalin made use of Hitler. Because Hitler was anti-Communist, Stalin was able to say that anybody else who was anti-Communist must be a fascist. He could intimidate his liberal adversaries *"en répandant le soupçon que l'antisoviétisme est l'antichambre du fascisme"* (by spreading the suspicion that anti-Sovietism was the antechamber to fascism) (*Le Passé d'une illusion*, p. 266). Such a point from Furet put his *gauchiste* contemporaries on the spot, because they were still using the same tactic, calling anyone who opposed left-wing orthodoxy an enemy of "democracy," a word they employed only as a decoy. They inherited the usage from Stalin. The Soviet Constitution of 1936 proclaimed the Soviet Union as the only true democracy. The proclamation was a musical prelude to the grinding of machinery, as the Great Terror was put into gear.

For Stalin, liberal democracy was always the chief enemy, with Nazism coming a distant second. Stalin never cared what crimes Hitler committed, as long as they were committed against the democracies. The Molotov-Ribbentrop pact was designed to keep the Soviet Union safe while Hitler wiped out the democracies in the west. Furet is particularly good (i.e., subversive) about the Soviet liberation of Auschwitz in January 1945. The Soviets said nothing about what they had found there, and when they were finally obliged by British pressure to make an announcement in August, the Jews didn't get a mention. Stalin didn't think they mattered. It was a perfect example of how the two totalitarianisms were aspects of each other. Furet's most important book, the book about the passing of an illusion that still hasn't passed, is crammed from beginning to end with such unsettling perceptions. But making it even richer is his answer to your question of why anyone was ever fooled. He was. How? Not just because he was young and clueless, but because he cared so much about humanity that he couldn't believe that the destruction of innocent millions could be without a constructive result. Having grown older and learned better, he put his finger on the reason otherwise decent and compassionate thinkers could stick with a discredited ideology so long: their reluctance to accept that so much suffering could be wasted.

G

❢ ❢ ❢

Charles de Gaulle

Edward Gibbon

Terry Gilliam

Josef Goebbels

Witold Gombrowicz

CHARLES DE GAULLE

❧ ❧ ❧

As the single most dominant figure in twentieth-century France, Charles de Gaulle (1890–1970) has inspired a whole library of commentary, much of it written by him. After absorbing William L. Shirer's classic *The Collapse of the Third Republic*, the student of modern French politics, in order to follow everything that happened afterwards, could safely settle down to read nothing but books by, about, for and against de Gaulle. The argument about whether the so-called Man of Destiny was a despot or a guardian angel will never be over. But there can be no argument about his status in French literature. He was a prose stylist in the grand manner, with a force of argument that was held in respect even by his most bitter opponents. His four volumes of autobiography are all available in English. A beginner with French, however, could do worse than become acquainted with them, although he might get the impression that French is a language for and about demigods. All four volumes can be kept easily on the bathroom shelf in the neat little Pocket Presse boxed set from Plon. Jean Lacoutre's three-volume biography *De Gaulle* is likewise available in a boxed set. It makes a good story: misunderstood youthful genius, the proof of battle, the rebuffed redeemer, years in the wilderness, eventual triumph. The three volumes of the general's wartime speeches, *Discours de guerre*, are likewise a compulsive study, although they should be sipped at rather than wolfed down: the reader doesn't want to end up talking in that style. Reading in that style is already grand enough. It is a good rule in life to be wary of the company of people who think of themselves in the third person, no matter how well justified they might seem to be in doing so. We can spend only so much time with the sculpted busts of Louis XIV and Napoleon before our own heads start to swell. In almost all his aspects, de Gaulle had a marmoreal momumentality. But he did have one vulnerable point, and it helped to keep him in touch with the ordinary human world.

A spirit has been set free. But the disappearance of our
poor suffering infant, of our little daughter without hope,
has done us an immense pain.
— CHARLES DE GAULLE, WRITING TO HIS
DAUGHTER ELISABETH ABOUT THE DEATH
OF HER SISTER ANNE; QUOTED BY JEAN
LACOUTRE IN *DE GAULLE*, VOL. 2:
LE POLITIQUE, P. 326

AFTER A LIFE OF misery, Anne de Gaulle, who had a severe case of Down's syndrome, died choking in her father's arms. She was twenty years old. At her funeral, de Gaulle is reputed to have said, "Now she is like the others." The awful beauty of that remark lies in how it hints at what he had so often felt. Wanting her to be like the normal children, the ones who couldn't help noticing that she was different, must have been the dearest wish of his private life. Knowing that the wish could never come true must have been his most intimate acquaintance with defeat. For us, who overhear the last gasp of a long agony, there is the additional poignancy of recognizing that the Man of Destiny lived every day with a heavenly dispensation he could not control. But to be faced from day to day with a quirk of fate not amenable to human will is sometimes the point of sanity for a man who lives by imposing his personality—the point of salvation, the redeeming weakness. Hitler's will power was sociopathic: his instinct, when faced with frailty, was to kill it. Stalin's will of iron came from a heart of ice: his response, when asked to consider what his son might be suffering in German hands, was to blame his son. Roosevelt and Churchill were both paragons of will power but they had great, living countries behind them. De Gaulle's country was dead. He had to resurrect it, providing an example of political confidence unmatched in the democratic politics of the twentieth century. (Undemocratic politics, alas, was staffed by a full range of would-be national leaders who had the same virtue of never giving up until their dreams came true; but when the dreams did, the virtue tended to be offset by what happened next.)

Establishing himself in London after the French defeat in 1940, de Gaulle had few resources beyond his prestige—he always said that prestige counted for more than anything—and his gift of persuasion. He drove Churchill to distraction and Roosevelt wanted nothing to do with him, but the antagonism he aroused in foreign leaders served his purpose as long as it helped to rally his countrymen. Once he had secured their allegiance, he extended his intransigence even to them. Intellectuals of the French left wing who had seen the Communist element in the Resistance as the precursor of a post-war socialist France were doomed to disappointment. So were the Algerian *pieds-noirs* who expected, when he came back to power in 1958, that France would retain its sunlit colony. Having ruthlessly and correctly decided that Algeria had been kept only through weakness and that giving it away would be an act of strength, he gave it away. When the Secret Army tried to assassinate him, he never doubted that they were traitors to their country. *Je fais don de ma personne à la France*. Who did he think he was? This is my body, which is broken for you!

The presidential system he bequeathed to his successors had the flaw of placing more power in the hands of friends and favourites than of elected officials. The flaw showed up early, and the constitutional set-up of the Fifth Republic already looked like a well-tailored tyranny even during the reign of its founder. De Gaulle decided off his own bat to pull out of NATO in 1966: he told only three ministers, and consulted not even them. The French have a word for it: *égocratie*. Such an identification of man and nation would have been monstrous if it had been made only by the man, but the nation, on the whole, thought the same, including a large part of its liberal element, which had not been the case in the love affair between Hitler and Germany. When the French nation ceased to make the identification, the Man of Destiny fell from power. In 1968 he used television as a megaphone instead of an ear trumpet. It was a miscalculation, but it lay within his nature, and whether his ascendancy had ever amounted to more than a protracted constitutional crisis remains a moot point. What can't be disputed is his grandeur. Had he been a true megalomaniac, he would have been less impressive. Napoleon, owing allegiance to nothing beyond his own vision, was petty in the end, and the fate of France bothered him little. De Gaulle behaved as if the fate of France was his sole concern, but the secret of his incomparable capacity to act in that belief probably lay in a central humility. This might have been imposed by his awkward height, progenitor of the shyness that made him seem aloof. (Even in the communal bathhouse of his World War I prison camp, nobody ever saw his private parts—he must have been as dextrous with a skimpy towel as Sally Rand was with her fans.) A more likely answer, however, is that the touchstone of his humanity was his poor daughter. Nothing is more likely to civilize a powerful man than the presence in his house of an injured loved one his power can't help. Every night he comes home to a reminder that God is not mocked: a cure for invincibility.

EDWARD GIBBON

❧ ❧ ❧

Edward Gibbon (1737–1794) wrote a book that inadvertently raises the question of whether English prose style can be, or even should be, an end in itself. *The Decline and Fall of the Roman Empire* encapsulates—in a very large capsule—his idea that history is "little more than the register of the crimes, follies and misfortunes of mankind." The reader can decide whether it is or it isn't, and might very well decide that it is both. But about the style of the book, the question is not so clear-cut. Praised already at the time as one of the unchallengeable artistic creations of the eighteenth century, Gibbon's prose style was still held up as example in the nineteenth century even when Lord Macaulay became popular for writing history in a far more conversational manner. In the twentieth century, there were still historians who praised Gibbon's style as their true model. But in fact they all tried to write like Macaulay, and by now nobody could expect to echo the balanced Gibbonian period without being laughed at. Since much of the most substantial expository prose of modern times can be found in the writings of historians, it is perhaps worth looking in detail at the characteristic innovations within Gibbon's prose, and at least entertaining the possibility that the reason

most of them did not catch on was that they did not deserve to.
At a time when one of the dangers facing liberal democracy
is a loss of confidence, there is an easy reflex by which it is
assumed that the powers of expression of the English language
are in decline. A possible, and desirable, contrary opinion
would be that the worst writers do indeed write worse than
ever, but that the best writers write better. If they do, one of
the reasons they do is that they have learned from ancestors
who had an ear for ordinary speech. But to call that a desirable
object, we have to do something about Gibbon, whose desires
were quite otherwise.

❧ ❧ ❧

To resist was fatal, and it was impossible to fly.
— EDWARD GIBBON, *THE DECLINE AND
FALL OF THE ROMAN EMPIRE*, P. 73

ONCE READ, IMPOSSIBLE to forget; and I have used this line ever
since, but always in the sad knowledge that Gibbon provided very
few like it. I expected him to. I came to him late, and spoiled: spoiled
by Thucydides and Tacitus, by Machiavelli and Montesquieu, by Pieter
Geyl and Lewis Namier, by Mommsen and Gregorovius, by Napier's
History of the War in the Peninsula and Prescott's *Conquest of Peru*, by
Stephen Runciman's set of books about the Crusades and finally by—
one of the great long historical reads in the world—Shelby Foote on
the American Civil War. I expected Gibbon to provide me with a heap
of those readily detachable judgements that all the serious historians
seem able to generate at will as a qualification for their trade.

No such luck, alas; and after twenty years I am still getting to the
end of Gibbon's long book—longer than its admirers admit, I think,
because not as good as they claim. No doubt the quoted sentence
translates itself from the eighteenth-century page to the twentieth-
century mind with such ease because the modern condition is in it. Gibbon was talking about an empire that filled the known world, so that
when a tyrant was in charge there was nowhere for the victim to run:
and that was the kind of empire that Stalin, Hitler and Mao all brought
into existence. Mao's version, indeed, though admittedly in attenuated

form, is still here to distort the lives of more than a thousand million human beings. But the modern condition is in any pregnant sentence from any time: current possibilities are what a classic sentence is pregnant with. In Tacitus and Montesquieu there are few paragraphs without a sentence that seems written with us in mind, and few chapters without a paragraph. Sometimes there is a whole chapter: even in Tacitus, let alone Montesquieu, there are times when time collapses and the past seems very near. You would swear, when some vengeful emperor's proscription is raging in the *Annals* of Tacitus, that you were reading the secret diary of the daughter of a Prussian landed family after the botched attempt against Hitler's life on July 20, 1944—the atmosphere of prying doom is so similar. One way or another, the modern age is always there in the best moments of the old historians: we can tell by the way the construction of the prose suddenly ceases to sound anachronistic, or even constructed.

Gibbon, unfortunately, seldom ceases to sound any other way. From him, this quoted sentence is rare first of all for its relatively natural cadence. Yes, it is consciously balanced around its caesura and makes us feel that it is: but no, it is not typical of him, because his usual classicism was neo-classical by way of the Baroque, and what he wrote rarely lets you forget that it has been written. Had he been an architect, his buildings would never have ceased to remind you that they had been built. He is one of the four master dwarves of the Rococo, but unlike the other three—Pope, Lichtenberg and Cuvilliés, the court architect of the Wittelsbachs—he can't make you forget his injuries, which dulled, instead of sharpening, his sense of proportion. Would his capital work have ever acquired its huge reputation if it had not been a harbinger of imperialist dominance, a proof that Britain could own, not just all the new worlds, but the ancient world as well? Now that the wave of history has retreated, the book is left looking like a beached whale. A more compact version could have been the written equivalent of Sir John Soane's Museum. Instead, Gibbon produced a hulking forecast of St. Pancras Station. But a shorter book, to seem so, would have needed less elaborate sentences: at their original length, even a single page of them is a long haul.

There are parts of Gibbon's autobiography to prove that a simple declarative sentence was not beyond him. In *The Decline and Fall of the*

Roman Empire, for some reason, it was. Having chosen a tall theme, the small man got up on stilts, and stayed elevated for twenty years. Not the least of his heroism was that he could make a single page seem like an eternity. His secret was—we had better say is—to make you read so many of his sentences twice even while you think you are reading them only once. His aim might have been compression and economy, but the compression was a contortion and the economy was false. In a single sentence, two separated adjectival constructions often served the one noun, or two separated verbs the one object, or two separated adverbs the one verb, and so on through the whole range of parts of speech: it was a kind of compulsive chess move in which a knight was always positioned to govern two pieces, except that the two pieces governed it. Whether this conspicuous stroke of ingenuity ever really saved time is debatable, but when properly done it added the value of density, or at any rate seemed to. Take this observation about the two sons of Severus and Julia, the "vain youths" Caracalla and Geta: "Their aversion, confirmed by years, and fomented by the arts of their interested favourites, broke out in childish, and gradually in more serious, competitions . . ." (volume 1 of the Modern Library edition, p. 111). There is more to the sentence, but all we need note here is that "childish" and "more serious" both qualify "competitions"; and that there is no great hardship in following the train of thought, because we don't imagine that a noun to fit the adjective "childish" will fail to arrive eventually. Gibbon worked this forking manoeuvre over and over, but it was a dangerous habit, especially if the first adjectival construction could be mistaken for a noun. After Caracalla's oppressive tax had made a mess of Rome's finances, the "prudent liberality" with which Alexander restored them attracted Gibbon's admiration. But Alexander was still left with the problem of how to meet the expectations of the troops, and Gibbon with the problem of how to mirror Alexander's perplexity. Gibbon would no doubt have packed my previous sentence into a smaller space, but he might well have made it as awkward in its compactness as this one of his: "In the execution of his design the emperor affected to display his love, and to conceal his fear, of the army" (vol. 1, p. 133).

By now the danger needs no explaining, because you have just tripped over it. Until you read further, there is nothing to say that the first comma might not as well be a full stop; and the same applies to the second comma; so you must get all the way to the end before you read back again and make the proper sense of what you previously mistook. When you have been long enough with Gibbon you learn not to mistake it, and always wait for a re-reading before settling on what must be meant; but it is a tiresome necessity, and makes for the kind of stylistic difficulty which leads its admirers to admire themselves, for submitting to the punishment. There was never much to the assumption that a sentence is only ever read diachronically from left to right with never a backward glance: the eye doesn't work like that and neither does prose. But there is still something to the assumption that a sentence, however the reader gets to the end of it, should be intelligible by the time he does, and that if he is forced to begin again he has been hoodwinked into helping the writer do the writing. Readers of Gibbon don't just help: they join a chain gang, and the chain gang is in a salt mine, and the salt mine is reached after a long trip by galley, during which they are never excused the feel of the oar or the snap of the lash.

Gibbon was quite capable of working his favourite bipartite effect of pretended compression twice in a paragraph and sometimes three times. In one of his best early chapters of summary, chapter XVI (A.D. 180–318), he has a paragraph that begins very promisingly. "History, which undertakes to record the transactions of the past, for the instruction of future ages, would ill deserve that honourable office if she condescended to plead the cause of tyrants, or to justify the maxims of persecution" (vol. 1, p. 453). This is almost good enough to remind you that Montesquieu was alive at the same time, although by now the reader has recognized Gibbon's favourite stylistic device to be a nervous tic, and the tic has transferred itself from the writer's quill to the reader's face, so that he flinches while wondering if the word "future" should not have a comma after it too, in case "past," like "future," is not a noun but an adjective sharing the task of qualifying the noun "ages." I suppose that if Gibbon had meant that, he would not have put a "the" in front of "past," but it gets hard to give him the benefit of the doubt after you have realized that he was in the grip of mania. The proof is only a little way away in the same paragraph, where three sentences in a row are all lamed by the same hobble.

But the princes and magistrates of ancient Rome were strangers to those principles which inspired and authorised the inflexible obstinacy of the Christians in the cause of truth, nor could they themselves discover in their own breasts any motives which would have prompted them to refuse a legal, and as it were a natural, submission to the sacred institutions of their country. The same reason which contributes to alleviate the guilt, must have tended to abate the rigour, of their persecutions. As they were actuated, not by the furious zeal of the bigots, but by the temperate policy of legislators, contempt must often have relaxed, and humanity must frequently have suspended, the execution of those laws which they enacted against the humble and obscure followers of Christ.

When I first read this the name of our redeemer had already sprung to my lips before I saw it in print. In a way I am still reading it: years have gone by but the anguish in the brain has not abated. Gibbon has that deadly combination of talent and determination which can put jagged awkwardness into your head as if it were a melody, and keep it there as if it were a splinter of shrapnel.

Talented he was; a genuinely superior individual; but he wanted his readers to be optimates like him. He was continually testing them. Especially he tested their powers of memory. Quite often he expected them to remember the layout in detail of one sentence while they were reading the second. Take this for a first sentence. "Like the modesty affected by Augustus, the state maintained by Diocletian was a theatrical representation: but it must be confessed that, of the two comedies, the former was of a much more liberal and manly character than the latter" (vol. 1, p. 332). Got that? You will need to have done, because the next sentence depends on it. "It was the aim of the one to disguise, and the object of the other to display, the unbounded power which the emperors possessed over the Roman world." Just to make it feel like Groundhog Day, the second sentence has the familiar two-part forking routine as well; but in the long run the reader—who will either develop a more muscular attention span or, more likely, postpone into old age his commitment to what the counsellors call closure—is obliged to accept the memory test as an equally inescapable, if not equally frequent, event.

How did you do? You had to look back? But of course you did. Everyone has to, all the time, and it makes reading Gibbon a long business, which some of us never seem to quite finish. An expert will judge from my citations that I have got not much beyond a third of the way through. Actually, over the years, I have several times gone further: but I could do it only by ceasing to make notes, and for one of the few times in my reading life I have skipped and tasted, in the manner that the egregious twentieth-century British politician R. H. S. Crossman unwarrantably dignified with the name of "gutting." As well as the Modern Library edition, which is ugly but strong and therefore good for travel, I also own Bury's handsome but fragile seven-volume edition of 1902, and at home, in fits of fire-lit studiousness during a cold winter, I have sometimes dipped into the later volumes, hoping to find some uncluttered going, but always in vain. The one passage everyone quotes is indeed a standout, and that's just the trouble. "Twenty-two acknowledged concubines, and a library of sixty-two thousand volumes, attested the variety of his inclinations, and from the productions he left behind him, it appears that the former as well as the latter were designed for use rather than ostentation." Roguish Gibbonians assure us that the younger of the two Gordians has thus been impaled unforgettably on the skewer of satire. By Gibbon's usual standard it certainly counts as a moment of light relief, and indeed it isn't a bad gag even with its donnish dressing: you could just about say that the elevated diction multiplied the mirth. But even here, you need Quiz Kid retentiveness if you aren't to be driven back to the beginning of the sentence to sort out which was the former and which the latter. *The Decline and Fall of the Roman Empire* is a Grand National with a fence every ten yards, each to be jumped backwards as well as forwards; and you have to carry your horse. At one stage I skipped all the way to the end, and found the pages about Cola di Rienzo blessedly free of most of Gibbon's most irritating tricks. But not even Wagner can be fully boring about Rienzo, and in Gibbon the road to the final excitement is very long.

Is it worth the struggle? Yes, certainly. I still don't think Gibbon is the Virgil with whom to take your first journey into ancient history. If it takes multiple volumes to make the effort feel valuable, about Greece you can do well with Grote, and about Rome you can do very well with Mommsen. And there are single-volume histories that have served schools well for decades, through telling the story first, before getting down to the implications. In Gibbon the narrative would be hard to retain even if he wrote as fluently as Macaulay, and nowhere, not even in his autobiography, does Gibbon even look like doing that. (When you hear Macaulay's style belittled, guard your head: there is an owl in the room, and it is not Minerva's.) What Gibbon does give you is not ages past in summary, but his own age in one of its several cordials. He gives you contrivance. In him we can study the arrangement of prose pushed to its limit—not to the limit of prose, but to the limit of arrangement, where a trellis weighs like a bronze door. Though the intention might be the opposite, there is a risk of turning the permanent into the evanescent.

Gibbon had a knack for the permanent. It showed up when he was simple. The epithet "vain youths" is a token of what he could do: it was understatement, precisely calculated to sound that way, as a sign that the facts were too extreme to be evoked. After Probus imposed peace on the vanquished nations of Germany he used German troops to reinforce the legions throughout the empire, "judiciously observing that the aid which the republic derived from the barbarians should be felt but not seen" (vol. 1, p. 288). That is good, plain narrative, and this is better: "The feeble elegance of Italy and the internal provinces could no longer support the weight of arms." The two-word coupling "feeble elegance" is excellent: a thought compacted but not crippled, it encapsulates the theme for the chapter and indeed for the whole work, which is the story of an empire dying from the poisonous fermentation of the fruits of its initial success. That there is something feeble about Gibbon's own elegance is an idea his admirers would resist. I think there is: but I am in no doubt about the elegance, or at any rate about the initial fruits that lay behind it, before the mania of his stylistic ambitions began to waste them. A proof of the gift he began with is that he could often revert to it, so long as the occasion was sufficiently unimportant. His footnotes, for example, are almost always better than the main text. "With regard to the times when these Roman games were celebrated, Scaliger, Salmasius, and Cuper have given themselves a great deal of trouble to perplex a very clear subject" (vol. 1, p. 300). What a pity that the same was true of Gibbon. Not that he always had to take trouble: sometimes he could create confusion through ordinary carelessness. His otherwise exemplary tirade about the decline of Roman jurisprudence and the rising tide of lawyers (vol. 1, p. 536) is ruined by a sentence in which there is no sorting out the personal pronouns except by guesswork. "Careless of fame and of justice, they are described for the most part as ignorant and rapacious guides, who conducted their clients through a maze of expense, of delay, and of disappointment; from whence, after a tedious series of years, they were at length dismissed, when their patience and fortune were almost exhausted." Who, after the semicolon, is dismissed, and whose patience and fortune are exhausted? We will have to read it again.

We will always have to read it again, but sometimes the requirement is a blessing. "The same timid policy, of dividing whatever is united, of reducing whatever is eminent, of dreading every active power, and of expecting that the most feeble will prove the most obedient, seems to pervade the institutions of several princes, and particularly those of Constantine" (vol. 1, p. 540). If only he had written like that all the time. He scarcely ever did: a fact made more galling when we find out that he could. We want more than enjoyment from our historians; but it is hard to make do with less, and to find them tedious is no sure sign that they are thorough. There are eminent readers who say they wallow in Gibbon. They are hard to believe. When that old showman Harold Macmillan retired into his valetudinarian role as Lord Stockton he noised it quietly abroad that he was occupying his slippered hours with reading Gibbon "again." He got away with saying that. When Lady Thatcher let slip that her idea of cloistered intellectual satisfaction was a second reading of *The Day of the Jackal* she attracted scornful laughter. John Major knew just how high to pitch his claims: in retirement he allowed it to be known that he was closeted with Trollope, whom he had always always loved, but could now read properly. Stockton sounds to me like the odd man out: i.e., the one who was dressing the set. It is fitting that a retired Tory prime minister should punish himself with hard reading, as a belated participation in the sufferings of the poor. But if we ever hear that the old man was propelled into slumber by every second Gibbonian period, I will be no more surprised than Gibbon was in that famous moment when a blind man felt his face and thought it was a baby's bottom. Gibbon was resigned to the absurdity of his appearance. His true absurdity, however, is that he tried to make up for it with the dignity of his style, and his style was never enough at its ease to be truly dignified. It could have been: but in the great work on which he staked his reputation it died from the strain of hauling on its own bootstraps.

TERRY GILLIAM

❦ ❦ ❦

Born in Minnesota in 1940, Terry Gilliam, after pioneering his personal graphic style as a resident artist for Harvey Kurtzman's *Help* magazine, reached international fame by way of Britain, where his visual inventiveness, based mainly on the silent wit of animated collage, was an important part of the *Monty Python* television series. In his subsequent career as a film director he earned an unjustified reputation for extravagance when his *Adventures of Baron Munchausen* left its budget behind and sailed off into the unknown. On the level of cold fact—always hard to regain once a myth has taken hold—he has proved, with several Hollywood projects including the extraordinary *Twelve Monkeys*, that he knows exactly how to bring in a movie on time and on budget. These undeniable achievements availed him little, however, when his film of *Don Quixote* had to be abandoned. A measure of his idiosyncratic creative energy is that even a documentary about that film's abandonment—*Lost in La Mancha*—is required viewing. Really he doesn't fit the Hollywood frame at all, and needs his own country of which to be a representative writer-director, like Pedro Almodóvar or Lars von Trier. If he had been born in Montenegro instead of Minneapolis, today there would be an annual Gilliam Festival on the shore of Lake Scutari, although his tendency to giggle at a solemn moment might still queer his pitch. Gilliam came nearest to inventing his own country with *Brazil* (1985), one of the key political films of the late twentieth century. There is an excellent interview book, *Gilliam on Gilliam*. It takes some effort to see past his laughing façade to the troubled man within. His best work depends on an audience that can do so, which will always be in short supply.

❣ ❣ ❣

No no no no no no no no no. . . .
— TERRY GILLIAM, *BRAZIL*

THE TEXT MEANS exactly what it says, but it needs a lot of decoding. A meek, distinctly non-glamorous secretary is taking dictation through earphones. She types up everything she hears in the next room. In the course of time, the viewer of the film deduces that she is compiling an endless transcript of what the victim is saying in the torture chamber. Even if he screams it, she types it up as if he has merely said it. She herself says nothing, and her face betrays no emotion as the words quietly take form. Her boss, the torturer, is played by Michael Palin in the full, sweet spate of his bland niceness. This is the *ne plus ultra* of torture as an everyday activity. Still revealing its subtleties after a third viewing or a fourth, *Brazil* is one of the great political films, an extraordinary mixture of Fellini and Kafka, with a complex force of synthesized image which belongs to Gilliam alone. The torture surgery contributes one of the most brain-curdling of the film's many disturbing themes. The suggestion seems to be that a torturer, except for what he does, need be no more sinister than your doctor. That's the picture we take away. But how true is the picture?

In modern history, which is most of the history that has ever been properly written down at the time, there is plenty of evidence that the torturers are people who actually enjoy hurting people. What was true in medieval Munich was true again in the cellars of the Gestapo HQ in the Prinz-Albrecht Strasse, and what was true under Ivan the Terrible was true again in the Lubyanka and the Lefortovo. The frightening thing is that any regime dedicated to ruling by terror so easily finds a sufficient supply of lethal myrmidons, and even Americans, on those occasions when they bizarrely conclude that the third degree might expedite their policies instead of hindering them, never suffer from a shortage of volunteers: at Abu Ghraib, the dingbats were lining up to display their previously neglected talents. On the whole, the man in charge is not a sadist himself, presumably because it would be a diversion of his organizational effectiveness if he were. Beria obviously enjoyed conducting the occasional interrogation personally, but Himmler would have fainted dead away, as he did on his sole visit to a massacre. Ceaușescu gave his dreadful son a torture chamber for his birthday. No doubt daddy knew what went on in it: but again, regular attendance at the frightfulness he encouraged is not known to have been among his pleasures. The same was true for General Pinochet. His critics, still trying to convince us that he was a homicidal mediocrity despite all the evidence that he was nothing else, write about him as if the dogs that were trained to rape women were trained by him. He probably never saw it happen. He didn't need to. All he had to know was that the state commanded unspeakable powers of savagery.

In his huge and definitive political biography of Juan Peron, the esteemed Argentinian historian Felix Luna gives us a once-and-for-all illustration of how the author of a state that rules by terror can detach himself from the brute facts. First, Luna chillingly describes the actuality that festered at the base of the Peronist dictatorship. (The description starts on page 253, but a preliminary stiff drink is recommended.) Luna takes the view, which to us might seem quixotic, that the torturers were just doing their job. He calls them *tecnicos*, and certainly they were technicians of the *picana*, the electric torture which was invented in Argentina, and was therefore one of Peron's gifts to the world, along with a good role for a soprano in *Evita*. Luna describes the subtleties of the technique, which on the torturers' part did indeed require a certain lack of passion if the victim was to survive for long. If Luna gets you wondering how he knew so much about it, your questions are answered a few pages later, where he records a conversation he had with Peron in 1969. "But in your time," said Luna, "people were tortured." Peron said: "Who was tortured?" Luna said: "Plenty of people. Me, for example." Peron said: "When?" We are at liberty, I think, to marvel at the detachment of an historian who could confine to a few pages out of a thousand a personal experience that might have left him incapable of being detached about anything ever again.

Luna had been a victim of torture sanctioned by the state: a legitimization that adds outrage to injury. Weber actually defined the state as the entity holding a monopoly of legalized violence. But the terror state goes beyond that. The terror state aims to command a monopoly of legalized horror. As long as its hierarchs can safely assume to be in charge of that horror, they don't have to see it to enjoy its fruits. Saddam Hussein was regarded as a madman even among other tyrants for his habit of specifying the details of punishment. Hitler seldom did. He just let the sadists get on with it, and he might even have been proud of being so powerful that he didn't need to know the minutiae of what was going on in the Gestapo cellars in the major cities, and in the political block at Dachau. It is doubtful if, in his mind, he ever reached the point where he enjoyed the idea of inflicting pain for its own sake. Mad enough to think himself sane, he was under the impression that the sufferings he sanctioned had their justification as condign punishment. In 1937, when a child molester was convicted in the courts and given a long sentence, Hitler personally intervened to ensure that the prisoner would be tortured first, but that was a rare instance. It is known that he watched films of the July conspirators strangling in their wire nooses, but he seems to have taken his satisfaction from the spectacle of a just punishment being inflicted, rather than from the hideous pictures of a slow agony. To do his colleagues what little credit they have coming, Hitler watched the films pretty much on his own. It was Goebbels's idea to have the conspirators hanged, but for once he didn't turn up for a screening.

With due allowance for Luna's emphasis on their clinical indifference, the maniacs who do the work seem mainly to come from the unfortunately plentiful supply of those who do enjoy inflicting pain for its own sake. "In what pubs are they welcome?" Auden asked rhetorically. "What girls marry them?" It is a nice question how large the supply would be if circumstances did not create it. Alas, the circumstances seem often to be there. Many of the Nazi torturers enjoyed their omnipotence on the strict understanding that without their place in the regime they would have been nothing: hence the tendency to go on tormenting their prisoners even after Himmler called a halt. They faced going back to where they started, which was nowhere.

Similarly, in the Soviet Union, the security "organs," under whatever set of initials they flaunted at the time, were always, at the brute force level, staffed by otherwise unemployable dimwits. The opportunity to inflict torment gives absolute power to the otherwise powerless, and must be a heady compensation for those with a history of being the family dolt. The Japanese army of the twentieth century was based on the Prussian model of strict discipline. Combined with the traditional violent streak of the samurai culture, in which an accredited warrior could decapitate any peasant who failed to bow at the correct angle, the bushido version of Prussian browbeating produced a fatal cocktail. Among the enlisted men, every rank could hit the rank below in the face until finally the wave of intimidation got as far as the lowest rank, whose members had nobody to hit except prisoners and civilians. The unsurprising result was a daily nightmare for POWs and for those Asian people that the Japanese imperial forces had supposedly come to liberate from European colonialism. The details are still hard to credit, and people of a squeamish temperament would prefer to believe that reports were exaggerated. Such a belief continues to be encouraged by the Japanese educational system. Japan's post-war ministry of education was eager to soft-pedal the bad memories, mainly because it was a bolt hole for high-level perpetrators who had escaped being prosecuted. As a sinecure for the judiciously silent, the education ministry made sure that the next generation learned nothing from the school textbooks about what the army had done to disgrace itself. German school textbooks were already talking about the Nazi disaster by the mid-1950s. In the late 1980s, when I was spending a lot of time in Japan, the one and only author of a school history text who had attempted to mention the 1937 Nanking incident (in which something like a quarter of a million innocent people perished, many of them in hideous circumstances) was in peril of his life, and his book had still not left the warehouse. The situation is better today—mainly because NHK, the Japanese public-service television network, was brave enough to grasp the nettle—but the Japanese right wing still regards any mention of those old embarrassments as a provocation.

In the Italian transit camp of Fossoli during the Republic of Salo (the last stage of Mussolini's Fascist regime, with the fanatics well in charge), there was a female officer who indulged herself in the Dantesque experiment of packing a cell with victims and keeping them without nourishment of any kind until they ate each other. Many of her victims were women. She seems to have had a social problem: she was cutting prettier, wealthier women down to size. In Latin America, the torturers were all men, but even the qualified medical practitioners among them seem to have been motivated by a similar urge to assure their victims that the boot was now on the other foot. On the disheartening subject of how sadism and sexuality might be connected, Argentina has the dubious privilege of having produced a key document. In a short story called "*Simetrías*"—a creative work which unfortunately has ample documentation in fact—Luisa Valenzuela tells us how some of the male torturers would take out their victims for an evening in a café or a nightclub. The wounds caused by the electrodes would be covered with makeup. (The story appears in *Cuentos de historia argentina*, a collection published in Buenos Aires in 1998.) In Brazil after that country's nightmare was over—it took place roughly at the same time as Argentina's—a book came out called *Cale a boca, jornalista!* (Shut Your Mouth, Journalist!) (São Paulo, 1987). The book enshrines the testimony of journalists who had the sad privilege of seeing the big story from close range: too close. Survivors recall being woken up in the middle of the night by the cold barrel of a .45 automatic applied to the nose, as a preliminary to a long encounter with the electrodes. There were journalists who never came back to say anything. Unsurprisingly, silence soon reigned.

In the years since the silence broke, documentation has piled up. Too many of the most terrifying pages reveal that the torments were an end in themselves. Torture, especially when the victim was a woman, went on far beyond any use it might have had as a means of extracting information, and even beyond what was needed to create a universal atmosphere of abject terror. Films like *Kiss of the Spider Woman* and *Death and the Maiden* have done their best to face what happened in Latin America, but finally, if we can bear to look at what is happening on screen, we have been spared the worst. The general picture in Latin America squared up badly with the picture of torture evoked in an impeccably realistic film like Gillo Pontecorvo's *The Battle of Algiers*, in which the decent young paratroopers did not really want to be doing that kind of thing. (Alain Resnais's *Muriel*, without showing the horrors, made the same point by implication.) In Latin America the torturers did want to be doing that kind of thing. Which brings us back to Brazil, and hence to *Brazil*. Were they ever the same place?

In the film called *Brazil*, Michael Palin is the torturer as the civil servant who might conceivably have been doing something else, such as selling life insurance. In the country called Brazil, the same role was usually played by a psychopath. (The key document proving this is *Brasil: Nunca mais*—Brazil: Never Again—published in São Paulo in 1985. By the time I bought my copy in 1988, it had gone through twenty printings.) We know from the fascinating long interview published as *Gilliam on Gilliam* that the Palin character in the movie was slow to take shape. The first three drafts of the script were written by Tom Stoppard. Finally Stoppard and Gilliam parted company because of disagreements over some of the characters. One of the characters in question was the torturer. The way Stoppard wrote the part, Michael Palin would have had the opportunity to play against type: he would have embodied evil. Palin is a very accomplished actor and could undoubtedly have done it. But Gilliam insisted on Palin's full, natural, non-acting measure of bland benevolence: the same set of teeth, but they would be bared only to charitable effect. On the set, Gilliam gave Palin mechanical things to do while acting—eat, for example—so that Palin would be distracted from developing any nuances on top of his natural projection as Mr. Nice Guy. It is a moot point which of them was right, Stoppard or Gilliam. In the long run, the Banality of Evil interpretation of human frightfulness is not quite as useful as it looks. It helps us appreciate the desirability of not placing ourselves in a position where the rule of justice depends on natural human goodness, which might prove to be in short supply. But it tends to shield us from the intractable facts about human propensities.

White settlers of America were horrified to discover that the Apaches would torture their prisoners slowly to death on the assumption that the captor would gain spiritual stature as the captive lost it. The student would prefer not to think that a primitive people was thus showing us what was once universally true, and came from instinct. It would help if mankind were the only animal that tortured its prey: we could persuade ourselves that only a social history could produce such an aberration. Unfortunately, cats torment mice until the mouse turns cold, and killer whales play half an hour of water polo with a baby seal before they finally put it out of its misery by eating it. We can do better than the cats and the killer whales, but it might be a help to admit that the same propensity is widespread, and could even be there within ourselves. In that respect, the film *Three Kings* was a rare feat for the American cinema. Educated in a hard school of bombed refugee camps, the Arab torturer was trying to show his clueless American victim what it felt like to be helpless. It is possible that all torturers are attempting to teach their own version of the same lesson. But in that case we are bound to consider the further possibility that anyone might be a torturer. The historical evidence suggests that on the rare occasions when a state begins again in what a fond humanitarian might think of as a condition of innocence, a supply of young torturers is the first thing it produces. Certainly this was true of Pol Pot's Cambodia.

If, as seems likely, Pol Pot would never have come to power had not the U.S. Air Force first devastated Cambodia, then Henry Kissinger has a lot more than the disaster in Chile on his conscience. He has the disaster of the Khmer Rouge torture camps. Of 17,000 people who were interrogated in the S-21 camp in Phnom Penh, 16,994 died in agony. The half dozen people who survived were questioned again, by journalists, but they had been too badly injured to say much. The writing on the wall probably says all that we need to hear. "While getting lashes or electrification you must not cry at all," said Security Regulation No. 6. The other regulations were no less terrifying, but there is something unique about Regulation 6, as if Swift and Kafka had both had their brains picked by a lethal child. There was a variation on the same instruction: "During the bastinado or the electrification you must not cry loudly." But "not cry loudly" leaves room to cry softly, whereas "not cry at all" has the perfect lack of logic which reminds us, as we will always need reminding, that the Khmer Rouge torturers were not an example of a system of thought decayed into a perversion: they were pre-thought, and thus had a kind of childish purity.

Another Khmer Rouge regulation is almost charming: "Don't try to hide the facts by making pretexts this and that. You are strictly prohibited to contest me." The charm is in the waste of effort: the prisoner can give only one answer, so why didn't the interrogator just write it down and sign it with a mark, especially since the prisoner's eventual signature wouldn't make much sense anyway? Unfortunately for our hopes of innate human goodness, all the evidence suggests that the torturers were keen to get on with the job even if it was meaningless. All the evidence was still there afterwards, including photographs taken at every stage of the torment. Whether the Khmer Rouge torturers were psychopaths is a question for psychiatrists. The question for general students of human affairs is about the reputation of the Khmer Rouge in the West. Their own mad frenzy did not last long, but while it lasted there were sophisticated Western apologists who made some marvellous pretexts this and that. It was notable, however, that in this one case the apologetics had no staying power. One of the first Western publications to blow the whistle was *The New York Review of Books*, which could normally be depended on to suspend judgement as long as possible in such cases. Access made the difference. If we had known as little about what went on in the Killing Fields as we knew about, say, North Korea, the example of Pol Pot's Cambodia ("Hands off democratic Kampuchea!") might have rallied the West's faithful dupes a lot longer. But the story got out straight away, mainly because a pack of adolescents were in charge. Adults are cannier.

Back in the late 1950s, on the sleeve of the *Beyond the Fringe* record album, Jonathan Miller made a dark joke about his worst fear: being tortured for information he did not possess. The assumption behind the joke was that if he had something to reveal, the agony would stop. He was looking back to a world of polite British fiction, not to a world of brute European fact. In the Nazi and Soviet cellars and camps, people were regularly tortured for information they did not possess: i.e., they were tortured just for the hell of it. Kafka guessed it would happen, as he guessed everything that would happen. In his *Strafkolonie*, the tormented prisoner has to work out for himself what crime he has committed, and is finally told that it is being written on his body by the instrument of torture into which he has been inescapably locked. Kafka was there first, but he wasn't alone for long, and now we must all live in a modern world where the words "No no no no no no no no" can be recorded with perfect fidelity for their sound, yet go unheeded for what they mean.

JOSEF GOEBBELS

☿ ☿ ☿

Josef Goebbels (1897–1945) began as a professional student (he was enrolled at eight different universities) and would-be literary figure. He ended as a corpse in the Reich Chancellery, having achieved, in the interim, the distinction of being minister of public enlightenment and propaganda in the Nazi government, and a ranking second only to Goering's among those closest to Hitler. During the war, after Goering's prestige waned, Goebbels moved up to the vacant second spot, and was effectively in charge of the country in the final period when its most terrible crimes were being carried out: the idea that Himmler acted without Goebbels's knowledge does not bear examination. A crippled schizophrenic, Goebbels was easy to make fun of at the time by those safely out of his reach. Now that we all are, we should perhaps try to remember that as a young man he was interested in the arts, loved the movies, saw the power of advertising, studied the techniques of publicity, and favoured the idea of politics as a spectacular drama. A lot of what we think normal now, he thought of first: so we need to be very sure that we have a different slant on it. Even his anti-Semitism began as an intellectual pose: he took it up while he was on a scholarship.

☛ ☛ ☛

Since Stalingrad, even the smallest military success has
been denied us. On the other hand, our political chances
have hugely increased, as you know.
—JOSEF GOEBBELS, QUOTED IN HIS OFFICE
ON JANUARY 25, 1944, BY WILFRED VON
OVEN IN *MIT GOEBBELS BIS ZUM ENDE*,
VOL. I, P. 178

AMONG THE NAZIS who got away to Argentina after the war was
the future author of what would be the world's funniest book, if it
did not take your breath away so thoroughly that laughter is impossible. After a notable beginning as a war correspondent reporting Nazi
victories in Poland, the West, the Balkans and in Russia, Wilfred von
Oven spent the late part of the war as press secretary, personal assistant
and tireless sounding board for Goebbels. At the Propaganda Ministry
in Berlin, Goebbels would think aloud by the hour while von Oven
wrote it all down. Von Oven was on the spot when Goebbels micro-
filmed his personal diaries and made them safe for posterity.

But the papers in von Oven's own keeping were even more precious.
In Argentina von Oven typed up his reminiscences as if they constituted a world historical document, which indeed they did, and still do.
They were published in two volumes by Dürer-Verlag in Buenos Aires
in 1949. My set dates from 1950, when the work achieved a second
printing. (They had an awful lot of coffee in Brazil, and they had an
awful lot of Nazis in Argentina.) I bought the set second-hand in that
same city fifty years later. The twin volumes were in good shape:
bound in yellow cardboard with orange cloth spines, they had never
sprung their hinges, and the paper, though of low quality, had not yet
begun to crumble. I took my find to my favourite café in San Telmo,
sat down to read, and almost instantly realized that I was in the presence of an unrivalled comic masterpiece. In Mel Brooks's *The Producers*, the berserk playwright in the helmet admires Hitler as one psycho
admires another. But von Oven is funnier than that. He thinks
Goebbels is the soul of reason, a great intellectual, a philosophical and
creative genius whose visions are frustrated only by unfortunate circumstances. Making it even funnier is that van Oven himself shows few

signs of being exceptionally stupid. Like his boss, he was able and industrious. He didn't miss a trick. All he missed was the point.

If we ever doubted that Goebbels did the same, the evidence is here. Goering knew that the game was up when the first P-51 Mustang long-range escort fighter appeared over Berlin. Even Himmler started looking for a way out. But Goebbels kept the faith. Though finally it got to the point where not even he could keep his faith in victory, he still kept his faith in Hitler. Even as it became clear that the insurmountable obstacle to any political solution was the existence of Hitler himself, it never occurred to Goebbels that his loyalty to Hitler could be abandoned. After the attempted coup of July 20, 1944, it was suggested to Goebbels that the cause might still be saved if Hitler could be sidelined in favour of a Goebbels-Himmler duumvirate. Though Goebbels held Himmler in high respect ("immaculate," "a paragon of character"— vol. 2, p. 301) he could see no choice: he was for Hitler, even if it meant that Germany and Hitler would go down together. As the end neared, the only reproach Goebbels made against Hitler was that the Führer had not been sufficiently true to himself, having allowed himself to be surrounded by a gang of opportunists, time-servers and mediocrities. There was certainly some truth in that. Goebbels had good reason to think of himself as the genuine Nazi article. The comedy lies in his unintentional revelation of what being a genuine Nazi entailed. One thing it entailed was a huge, incapacitating overestimation of the world's tolerance for Nazi policies of territorial aggression and mass murder. Goebbels was right to believe that Stalin threatened civilization in the West with a similar disaster. But he was wrong to believe that the Western allies, when they realized this, would see Nazi Germany as a bastion against the threat. He couldn't let it occur to him that the unlikely global alliance against Nazi Germany was held together by the existence of Nazi Germany itself, and would be maintained until Nazi Germany was gone. For him it was a thought too simple to be grasped. He was too clever for that.

Goebbels's cleverness was diabolical. Faithfully transcribing the master propagandist's torrential paroxysms of inspiration, von Oven was right to be awed. The man who invented Horst Wessel (a Nazi thug beaten to death by Communists, Horst Wessel was turned by the creative staff in Goebbels's office into the hero of a song) never ran out of ideas. But the diabolical cleverness all served a self-deception. In September 1944 we find the Minister (von Oven always calls Goebbels the Minister or the Doctor) favouring his assistant with a long tirade about how the situation could be saved if only he, instead of Ribbentrop, were in charge of foreign policy. "I would work in both directions," Goebbels explains. "The English way of thinking is congenial to me. I could bring into play my good and friendly connections with many important Englishmen. But I would also start talking to the Bolsheviks. It is not for nothing that I count as the representative of our party's left wing. What possibilities! What visions!" *Der Minister seufzt und lehnt sich in seinen Sessel zurück* (vol. 2, p. 145). The Minister sighed and leaned back in his chair.

Once again, what makes it funny is that there was something to it: just not enough. Before the war, Goebbels had indeed charmed the pants off many of the visiting Englishmen: he had long heart-to-hearts with the Duke of Windsor, Sir John Simon and Lord Halifax. Even Beaverbrook, later tiresomely active on Churchill's behalf, had seemed to understand Germany's sacred mission against Bolshevism. But Goebbels could never grasp that everything was transformed from the moment Churchill took office. The accommodating opinions of all these influential people either had ceased to matter or had changed, so that now, while they might all have been variously influential, they were united in having no power to favour Germany even if they had wanted to. Predictably, Goebbels's interpretation of this otherwise unaccountable turn-up for the books was that a small, Jewish-inspired clique had taken over.

On the question of the Jews, von Oven does his best to employ the soft pedal on the Minister's behalf. Even in post-war Argentina, where Nazi refugees could voice their old opinions virtually unchecked, it was thought prudent to go easy on the mania. But a true mania has a way of seeping through any amount of reasoned argument, and so it proves here. Though von Oven's post-war preface to the complete work assures us that he had never known anything about gas chambers or exterminations, in the body of the transcript the guileless amanuensis can't hide even his own real opinions, so his master's are bound to come out eventually. On October 3, 1943, von Oven delivers himself of the prediction that some of the Nazi hierarchs will soon start looking for alibis: "they will manufacture a connection with some resistance group, or they will pretend that they helped some Jew (*etwa einen Juden*) escape from Germany." Now why should some Jew have wanted to do that? In volume 2 von Oven lets the Minister, in his role as Doctor of all the arts, rave on for three solid pages about the slyness with which the Jews pulled off the confidence trick called Modern Art, but von Oven is still careful to confine the discussion to aesthetic matters. On a later page, however, both he and the Minister stand revealed as fully aware of what has been going on. Goebbels "wonders" if Himmler, fine fellow though he is, might not have let the concentration camps (in German, *Konzentrationslager*, or KZ) get a little bit out of hand. Previously, says the Minister, one was able to assume that the conditions in the KZs, "though they might have been hard, were correct and humane. Hard work, strict discipline, but everything that a man should have: adequate food, medical care, even some entertainment." The Minister goes on to lament, however, that under wartime conditions the KZs might have become a touch less entertaining than they used to be. "Just imagine how it would look if the camps in their present condition are discovered by the enemy!" In that case, predicts the Minister, even the German people will say no more about the blessings that Germany has enjoyed since 1933: blessings which have ensured that even during the war there has been "no unrest, no strikes, no uprisings, no rowdies, no Jews. . . ." At which point, there is no more game to give away.

There is a kind of poetry to it: the poetry of evil, a destructive lunacy so fluent that it soars to the level of the creative, as if Mephistopheles, as well as appearing in *Faust*, had actually written it. Compared with Goebbels, Hitler himself was earthbound. With the aid of Albert Speer, Hitler conjured gargantuan visionary cities to be made real in brick and marble, but he would never have thought of a concentration camp that provided entertainment along with the adequate food. Goebbels really was some kind of artist, which is why he should interest us: even more than Speer, Goebbels was the Nazi who talked the talk of an intellectual. As for the way he walked the walk, in von Oven's masterpiece the Minister's bad foot goes largely unremarked. As we can tell from Goebbels's diaries, it never went unremarked in the mind of the man on whom a cruel trick of birth had inflicted it. Byron's bad foot, we are told, did not make him limp: but he might have felt as if it did. Goebbels's bad foot never let him feel any other way. Only one thing could make him forget it. His measure of a suitably passionate mistress was how she could liberate him from that dreadful awareness. "I forgot my foot." Goebbels, though always a family man, awarded himself an artist's privileges with women, and his position of power ensured that he did not have to restrict himself to the demimonde— where, indeed, he got so involved with an actress that Hitler had to call a halt to the affair.

Things could be more discreetly managed among the upper orders, with the usual proviso that too much discretion tended to stifle the action. During an official visit to Nuremberg, the Minister drove out to the countryside to take lunch with the Gräfin Faber-Castell, an accomplished, gracious twenty-six-year-old beauty who clad herself in a dirndl for the occasion. After the war the Faber-Castell firm was still making most of the pencils produced in Germany; in Australia as a schoolboy I had a whole box of them in various grades, and very fine pencils they were. (In Solzhenitsyn's long narrative poem *Prussian Nights*, the invading Russian soldiers marvel at the perfection of the Faber-Castell pencils: the very kind of reaction to Western goods that Stalin was afraid of, and obviated retroactively by purging his victorious army, nicely calculating how long a stretch in the Gulag it would take to forget a centrally heated house or a flush toilet that worked.) As pioneering participants in the post-war *Wirtschaftswunder* (economic miracle), the Faber-Castell dynasty saw no reason to change the firm's name, and indeed they hadn't done anything. They had just made pencils; and made Goebbels welcome. After lunch, there was a cultural interlude. When the Gräfin played and sang *Lieder*, her illustrious visitor joined her at the piano for a four-handed, two-voiced recital. If not a passionate physical relationship, it was certainly a passionate spiritual one. She was his upper-class muse and point of solace: the same supporting role that was played for Goethe by Anna Amalia Herzogin von Sachsen-Weimar-Eisenach, a parallel that Goebbels would have been well equipped to draw. The Gräfin Faber-Castell's exalted name crops up repeatedly as the end approaches. It was already approaching on the day of that cosy little combined lunch and *Lieder* concert. It was June 6, 1944.

After D-day Goebbels gave up smoking, probably because he was on a psychological high. He really did think, or said he thought, that the chances of working a political master stroke were going up as the military situation deteriorated. By July 1, however, he was smoking again. We have to admit the possibility that his mind was working at two levels. He was the pre-eminent Nazi advocate of Total War (he was surely right that if he had been allowed to institute it earlier, Germany would have done better) but he was also a realist; although we should always remember that he was a realist in a surreal world, the madhouse he had helped to create. There was a significant development on June 11, 1944: von Oven's help was required in a comprehensive reordering of the Doctor's personal library. All the standard party literature was thrown out and the remaining books were arranged purely according to literary standards (*nach literarisches Masstaben*). There is something touching about that. Goebbels wasn't getting out of the Nazi party. He thought that the Nazi party would be eternal, even if it were reduced to two members, him and Hitler. But he seems to have decided that all this ideological junk had nothing to do with the real thing. He might have also been trying to get back to his essential, untainted self, all unaware—or perhaps only almost unaware—that the taint *was* his essential self. Nevertheless there had been a day when, as a young student, he had it all before him. It was a day when he had respected his Jewish professors, saw a literary future for himself, and had not taken the Nazis seriously. A day before he met Hitler. Perhaps now, with the roof falling in, he hankered for the lost past, at a level he could not examine. But the reordering of his books did the examining for him. A man's relationship with his books tells you a lot about him, and in the case of a man like Goebbels we should pay close attention, because a crucial early choice he made was one that continually faces any of us who read at all. He chose a life of action, and his life would have been different if he had not. It could be said that the lives of millions of innocent people would have been different too, but there we should be equally alert to the danger of optimism. The only thing different might have been that he would have had a job like von Oven's. He might have been merely reporting on the insanity instead of helping to create it, but the insanity would still have been there. Hitler wouldn't have needed to find someone else. Someone else would have found him. When absolute power is on offer, talent fights to get in.

The Nazis had no tragedies: they caused tragedies for other people. In tragedy there must be a fall from high degree, or at least from the level of common humanity: and the Nazis had nothing to fall from. The tower they built was subterranean. But we can sympathize with their children. Near the end of the second volume Frau Goebbels speaks; and when she speaks, laughter dies. It is the April 22, 1945, and the Russians are already in the U-bahn tunnels under Berlin. She tells von Oven that she and her husband have already said goodbye to life. They had lived for Nazi Germany and would die with it. "But what I can't wish away is the destiny of the children. Certainly my reason tells me that I can't leave them to a future in which they, as our children, will be defenceless before the Jewish revenge. But when I see them play around our feet, I just can't reconcile myself to the idea of killing them."

When the time came, she managed it. It probably never dawned on her that her innocent children were following at least one and a half million other innocent children into the same poisoned oblivion, and for the same reason—no reason. (Once again, incidentally, von Oven forgets to explain why the Jews should have wanted revenge. Had something bad happened?) In all the literature about the Nazis, there is nothing quite like *Mit Goebbels bis zum Ende* to tell you that the whole vast historical disaster was a figment of the imagination. If only we could return the dead to life and the tortured to health, we would be able to see it as a comic extravaganza. Goebbels was the limping, shrieking embodiment of the whole thing. He was not a fool. In many respects he was very clever. He even had creative powers. But his creative powers were all at the service of Hitler's destructive powers. So everything the most eloquent of the Nazis said was a joke. If the joke had all happened within his study—if the Doctor had remained what he was, a dreaming student walled in by books—the laughter would never end, and we might even sympathize. The way things turned out, the most we can do is try to understand. As for Wilfred von Oven, his long post-war career provided evidence that a Nazi past could count as a sort of qualification if you could hang in long enough. In Argentina he was prominent in the circle around Hitler's favourite Stuka pilot

Hans-Ulrich Rudel, the bunch who always knew where Eichmann was. Having never been deprived of his German citizenship, von Oven went back to Europe as often as he liked, and as late as 1998 he was loudly active in Belgium with an outfit dedicated to winning back separate nationhood for the Walloons. For his fellow agitators, his curriculum vitae, going all the way back to service with the Condor Legion in the Spanish Civil War, was a powerful indicator that he knew what he was talking about. And on top of all that, he had known Goebbels personally!

WITOLD GOMBROWICZ

❢ ❢ ❢

In Poland between the wars, Witold Gombrowicz (1904–
1969) became a successful writer of a recognizable type, principally because of his surrealist novel *Ferdyduke* (1938). After
he went into exile in Argentina, however, he gradually transmuted into a type of writer that we are only now starting to
recognize: the writer who doesn't write in established forms,
but just writes, and who, not belonging anywhere, makes
everywhere belong to him. When Poland ceased to suffer
under the Nazis, Gombrowicz declined the opportunity to go
home and see it suffer under the Communists. In the many
volumes of his *Journal*, *Varia*, correspondence and memoirs (all
available in French, but only some, alas, in English) he worked
out a position by which he himself was Poland, and the
detailed description of his flight from artistic form was the
only art-form to which he felt responsible. On this latter point
he differed from his fellow Polish-speaking exile Czeslaw
Milosz, who practised all the literary art-forms as if they were
one. In his long final phase, Gombrowicz practised none of
them, and wrote about how he didn't. But the way he wrote, in
a prose teeming with observed detail and subversive perceptions, was a continual fascination, and went on being so after

his death: volumes of his casual-seeming writings continued to
appear, and his widow, Rita, became the curator of his reputation as it rose inexorably to fame. At his death he was called
"the most unknown of all celebrated writers." Two decades
later, in the year that the Berlin Wall came down, the first
uncensored edition of his complete writings finally appeared in
Poland. His country had come home to its most obdurate
world citizen.

I find that any self-respecting artist must be, and in more
than one sense of the term, an émigré.
— WITOLD GOMBROWICZ, *VARIA*,
VOL. I, P. 203

"EVERYONE," SAID DR. JOHNSON, "has a lurking wish to appear
considerable in his native place." If he had been blessed with
clairvoyance, he might have added: "Everyone except Witold Gombrowicz." Having spent most of his writing life in exile, Gombrowicz
was under some compulsion to judge the experience vital to his cast of
mind: but he seems not to have been faking. He might possibly have
gone back to Communist Poland if its literary authorities had not been
so stupid as to attack him before he got there instead of afterwards. In
his *Journal Paris-Berlin* we find him merely nervous about going back.
He is not yet refusing to. But things worked out as they always did,
with one of Poland's most talented writers confirmed in his course of
having as little as possible to do with Poland and its immediate concerns. It seems fair to say that he liked it better that way. He wasn't just
making the best of a bad job. Over the course of a writing life spent far
from home, he took the opportunity to examine just how closely a
national writer must be connected to his nation. In *Journal* I he asked:
is the life of an exile *really* more fragmentary? In *Journal* II he said that
the more you are yourself, the more you will express your nationality—
with the implication that it was easier to express it if you were free of
nationalist pressures. In Nazi Germany, he had noticed, the citizens
had become *less* typically German, *less* authentic. (It should be said that
in the writings of Gombrowicz the frequently employed word "authen-

tic" has an authenticity that it never has in the context of Sartre's existentialism, where it essentially means having the chutzpah to do what it takes so that you may suit yourself—not quite the same thing as being true to yourself.) In *Journal* II Gombrowicz said: "I want to be only Gombrowicz": i.e., a country all by himself. He could see the attendant danger: "*mon moi gonfle*"—my self inflates. "Because the trivial concerns oneself, one fails to see it might be boring." But in the end, he said in *Testament*, to lose one's country is a release. In Empson's famous poem, the companion piece to the line "It seemed the best thing to be up and go" is "The heart of standing is you cannot fly." If Gombrowicz had not been able to fly, he would probably have ended up dead. But it is not impossible, just difficult, to imagine him choosing a quiet life from the start, and writing his diary in secret. It is impossible, however, to imagine him not leaving home if given the choice. The idea he spent his life refining—that art was its own kingdom—was an idea that he was born with.

Nobody got closer than Gombrowicz to making the idea of the "world citizen" seem exalted, the ideal condition that we should all seek, the only way that a mind can come home. But it is important to remember that he had only *lost* his country: he never forgot it. Poland is one of his constant themes—more so than Argentina, his land of exile—and he continually defines himself in relation to it. "I want to be only Gombrowicz" is transmuted into various versions of "I am Poland": pretty much the way de Gaulle felt about France, Stravinsky about Russia or Thomas Mann about Germany. The surest guarantee of Gombrowicz's deep feelings about his country is that he went on writing in its language. Under their various titles, the journals, which amount to his masterpiece, were written in Polish, not Spanish. We owe it to the French publishing house Christian Bourgois Editeur that the Polish was translated into French. Year after year in the late eighties and early nineties—the years when the East was coming back from the dead—I would stop in at the Polish bookshop on Boulevard St. Germain to see if there was a new volume of Gombrowicz. There almost always was. It was a pity that the same did not happen in London or New York. The complete Gombrowicz journals are still not available in English. Thus we pay the penalty for the too-long lingering policy of publishing in an expensive hardback edition first. The

French, publishing directly in paperback, found an out-of-the-way writer like Gombrowicz a less suicidal commercial proposition. After all, they had at least one customer they could be sure of. Gombrowicz would have liked the idea of an Australian resident in London looking forward to a trip to Paris so that he could buy the latest book of a Pole resident in Buenos Aires, take it to a café, gather together his rudimentary French, and start construing the text line by line, with much note-taking in the endpapers after copious use of the dictionary. The spectacle would probably not have inspired Gombrowicz to large approving statements along the lines of Vargas Llosa's *cosmopolitanismo vital*. But Gombrowicz might have been pleased by the evidence that the individual personality is at the centre of the art, and gets through.

> It is isn't easy to make someone who hasn't experienced it
> understand what it feels like, this martyrdom of being
> judged, devalued, disqualified, and misrepresented by
> journalists writing in haste who are bored by reading and
> who, for that matter, hardly ever read anything anyway.
> — WITOLD GOMBROWICZ, *VARIA*,
> VOL. I, P. 105

He was making the classic complaint of those who would rather be famous than not, but find fame an instrument too blunt to leave their refined views uninjured. As a man without a country, Gombrowicz was good copy for international style-section journalists, and he admitted the advantages of the accruing prestige even as he deplored the psychological effects of being hailed by the uncomprehending. He brought the theme to a nodal point in *Journal* II, with a disquisition on "*le sex-appeal des messieurs d'un certain âge.*" Perhaps indulging in wishful thinking—although in his own case the wishful thought seems to have often come true—he said that a man no longer young, but with a certain lustre for his achievements, will soon find the second factor outweighing the first in the matter of attracting youthful admirers. One might as well lie back and enjoy it. The thing to do, he added, is to enjoy it without believing it. Gombrowicz thought that Thomas Mann *did* believe it, and that the result was "a complacent dignity . . . parading in its cardinal purple." Calling Mann an old cocotte, Gombrowicz couldn't let his victim go, and those pages of the second *Journal* in which he toys with Mann's reputation can be recommended as a paradigm example of one great literary exile getting on another's case.

Gombrowicz probably had the right of the argument: even if glory is justified by talent, nobody can remain fully genuine "*dans cette dimension supérieure.*" (Gombrowicz cheekily suggested that Mann would have made an extra contribution to literature if he had recorded how his growing grandeur had made him more bogus.) But it was Mann who went on adding to his roster of novels. Though Gombrowicz never quite gave up on himself as a novelist, he did give up on putting his main imaginative effort into fiction. Instead he persuaded himself—with what success it is up to us to judge—that his factual work was imaginative. The question remains (and is bound to remain, because he wanted it to remain) of whether the journals, taken all together, are a true literary work. I think they are, but they are a true literary work of the second order—the second order of ancillary writings which, as he said when singing a bitter hymn to his lost country in *Souvenirs de Pologne*, is a measure of a nation's culture. On that last point he was surely right. A nation can boast masterpieces while having no culture. The Soviet Union, had it wished, could have claimed that it had produced Shostakovitch, but it could never have produced the equivalent of *Singin' in the Rain*, even if it had wished to. Gombrowicz had spotted a new, ideologically determined and therefore wholly modern kind of aridity, in which first-class art was up for display but had no general effect in everyday life.

Gombrowicz would never have become himself if he had not escaped from the requirements of a literary career: if he had not dismantled his own reputation as fast as it threatened to form. (His chief rule for getting this done was never to make an expected move.) The escape is part of his fame. What he did not do is part of what made him Gombrowicz—a name that means an attitude. Without the attitude, there would never have been the name. He woke up to this specific form of celebrity quite slowly, and was probably far embarked on his journals before he ever realized that they were destined to be his capital work. After her chandelier-shaking first night in Paris before World War I, Karsavina, the very first Firebird, sat up until all hours darning her stockings as usual, until a friend told her that she would have to stop doing it. "And he brought me the papers, and for the first time I learned that I was Karsavina" (John Drummond, *Speaking of Diaghilev*). From all those boring journalists who tracked him down and trailed him around, the diarist in exile learned that he was Gombrowicz. He had staked his life on the idea, but kept repeating it as if he didn't yet believe it. After the dullards agreed, he was able to believe it. Goethe said that Ovid remained classical even in exile: he found his unhappiness not in himself, but in his distance from the capital of the world. Gombrowicz avoided even the unhappiness, by deciding that *der Hauptstadt der Welt* went with him wherever he went. Or anyway he appeared to avoid it: some of his art might lie in the pretence.

> Bizarrely, I am convinced that a writer incapable of talking
> about himself is not a complete writer.
> — WITOLD GOMBROWICZ, *JOURNAL*
> VOL. I, P. 69

But not even Gombrowicz talked about his complete self. As Ernesto Sabato complained when Gombrowicz was safely dead, the endlessly self-revealing exile never talked about his homosexuality. Sabato was an unquestioned feature of Argentina's literary landscape and Gombrowicz was always and only the questionable visitor, but the two men admired each other. From Gombrowicz's *Testament* we learn that he was struck by Sabato's *Sobre heroes y tumbas* (*On Heroes and Tombs*), It was, however, by no means a perfect match. In his reputation-making pre-war surrealist novel *Ferdyduke*, the young Gombrowicz had proclaimed that the artist's aim was never to grow up. "*Notre élément, c'est l'éternelle immaturité.*" Our element is eternal immaturity. Gombrowicz stuck to that idea all his life: he came closest to outing himself when he proclaimed, in terms that would have seemed familiar to Thomas Mann, that age could be refreshed only by involvement with youth. No idea could have been further from Sabato's mind. Sabato, unlike Gombrowicz, had not given up on the surrealist novel. Sabato thought the dreamwork could be a work of maturity, not just an effusion of youth. Sabato did not play it young, nor did he ever hide. Gombrowicz, though his stance was to talk about himself without self-censorship, probably thought that it couldn't be done unless something was held back. Favouring the Latin tag *lavartis prodeo*—I advance in a mask—he drew attention to Goethe's proper location, which was behind Faust. (In his *Testament* Gombrowicz said, *"Je m'avance masqué"*—a straight translation from the Latin.) We are left with the daunting prospect that there is another, real Gombrowicz who is not in the voluminous journals—or we would be left with it, if we thought that the secret man was the real one. The chances are low, however, that we are dealing with the Constantine Cavafy of Buenos Aires. Gombrowicz seems to have simply done what he said: drawn refreshment by surrounding himself with youth. In the sumptuously illustrated memorial volumes edited by his widow, Rita (*Gombrowicz en Argentine 1939–1963* and *Gombrowicz en Europe 1963–1969*), the photographs are selected to show Gombrowicz well supported by a cast of stunning young women. At ease on an *estancia* in Argentina during some comfortable weekend, he can be seen bathing in the worship of three beautiful blonde Grace Kelly lookalikes all hanging on his every thickly accented word. It was the main story. It just wasn't the whole story.

> Any pipsqueak can roar like a lion on paper, because grand
> words cost little, whereas delicacy—the delicacy of Chopin
> for example, persevering to the extreme, tense, elaborate—
> requires effort and character.
> —WITOLD GOMBROWICZ, *SOUVENIRS DE
> POLOGNE*, P. 141

When Rubinstein was in America making his great Chopin recordings after World War II, Gombrowicz was in Argentina writing the first of his *Journals*. It was Poland's fate that its artists had no home, especially if they were still in Poland. Their best way of keeping their country alive was leave it. In that sense, Gombrowicz was just another Polish artist of his time. He shared the dubious benefits of a thorough education in powerlessness. First the Pitsudski right-wing regime, then the Nazis, then the Communists: it was a long course of instruction in what happens to civilization when it is deprived of a political dimension. It becomes a dream based on its surviving personalities, who are forced to live in a world of their own. The constant temptation for the powerless is to daydream of super-strength. Gombrowicz's originality was to realize so clearly that his powerlessness would be his subject.

Elsewhere in the same book, he retroactively defines his aim as "to transform weakness into force, the defeats into values. If I was not sufficiently authentic, not linked enough to reality, it was precisely that which could become my rich and authentic drama." The same explicit statement of his mission was made again in *Varia* II: "in the end, the weakness becomes the strength." The sign of deadly seriousness in the quoted passage is the mention of Gombrowicz's revered Chopin. In the previous century, Chopin had been a pioneer of what was to become every talented Polish exile's historical position: he was under continuous pressure to represent his country. Chopin had represented it by living for his art in Paris, where he could play in private. In Poland he could play only in public. Gombrowicz served the eternal Poland by being Polish in Buenos Aires, and didn't even serve his art in the accepted sense; he abandoned even that, and made a point of refusing to create. Writing his decision down, however, he seems to have realized, by the way he felt compelled to return to the subject and draw out its nuances, that his refusal to create was a new kind of creation. And so it proved. The twentieth century was rich in journal writing, but not even Gide or Julien Green brought the formless form quite to the pitch of informal intensity achieved by Gombrowicz, who would have his name on his discovery if his name had been less . . . well, less Polish.

H

William Hazlitt

Hegel

Heinrich Heine

Adolf Hitler

Ricarda Huch

WILLIAM HAZLITT

✧ ✧ ✧

William Hazlitt (1778–1830) was the writer who put the English essay into the mainstream of English literature, and did so as much by his commentary on public affairs as by his attention to poetry, drama and literary history. He thus supplied the English-speaking countries (including America, where Henry Adams wrote very much like Hazlitt) with a new tradition of higher journalism that could be exploited to the full in the twentieth century, during which the dignity and worth of the essay form were taken for granted. (Other countries were less lucky: in Spain, for example, when Ortega said that the essay written for a newspaper or a periodical could be a vital form, he was thought provocative, because the heritage wasn't there to back him up.) Hazlitt's comprehensive grasp of contingent reality had a lot to do with his capacity for self-examination: his emotional life, for example, was a succession of disasters about which he had the courage to come clean, at least in part. "Well, I've had a happy life," was a large-hearted thing for him to say when he died poor. Although he could be acerbic when on the attack, he was rarely vicious, and generosity will be the main impression he gives to the beginner, who would be advised to start with his later collections of pieces, because

Hazlitt got better as he got older, his powers of reflection having more of his own experience on which to reflect. The volumes *Winterslow* and *Sketches and Essays*, both published posthumously, contain some of his best things, and nobody who reads them will succumb again to the seductive notion that a wide-ranging concern with all forms of creativity is a specifically modern, or post-modern, propensity.

> Burke's style was forked and playful as the lightning,
> crested like the serpent.
> — WILLIAM HAZLITT

WHAT AN ELECTRIFYING thing to say. I not only thought so when I first read it, but the actual word "electricity" came into my mind, no doubt because the word "lightning" was already there on the page. It didn't bother me that I couldn't think of many crested serpents. A cobra, perhaps, with those bits at the side of its head quivering; or perhaps he meant the arched neck crested like a wave as the serpent gets set to strike. Possibly there was a crested serpent somewhere in Shakespeare, and Hazlitt was making a subtle reference; or Shakespeare might have had a crested *servant*, and Hazlitt was remembering a sequence of sounds rather than a specific meaning. ("Be thou my crested servant, bear my shield / As token of two prides, both mine and thine" as the Duke of Alpacino does not say in *The Good Woman of Sienna*.) What mattered was the balance between the two pictures. The first picture was of things happening very quickly at random, and the second was of a pause, a poise. These pictures were matched by the two contrary movements of the sentence, prancing up to the comma, and then turning deliberate after it. Hazlitt had paid Burke's style the double compliment of contesting it with a well-crafted sample of his own.

There can be no doubt that Burke (1729–1797) deserved it. As the greatest combined statesman, parliamentarian, philosopher and prose stylist of the century before Hazlitt's, he was a fitting object for admiration even by a man of Hazlitt's talents. We would scarcely need to say so if it was not for the suspicion that Hazlitt can sometimes arouse when singing in praise. Hazlitt made his living as a freelance journalist, and there has always been a tendency, for a man in that occupation, for the pen to run off on its own. Nobody tried harder than Hazlitt to keep the pen in check. His standards for his own originality were high. In his lecture on Shakespeare and Milton, he says, about *Paradise Lost*, one of his best ever things: "Wherever the figure of Satan is introduced, whether he walks or flies, 'rising aloft incumbent on the dusky air,' it is illustrated with the most striking and appropriate images: so that we see it always before us, gigantic, irregular, portentous, uneasy, and disturbed—but dazzling in its faded splendour, the clouded ruins of a god." The trouble with that is that it is too good. It is detectably better than anything he has been able to quote. Plenty of quotation from Milton decorates the lecture. Quoted lines helped to fill the hour, but decency demands we should presume that Hazlitt liked them. He found it hard, however, to point out any phrase from Milton that looms and resonates like the clouded ruins of a god. It looks exactly as if he coined the phrase to get himself interested.

With his writing about Burke, the same suspicion does not intrude. He has no secret reservations: he admires with a whole heart. We can tell that because he writes at his whole ease. Writers are at their best when they can do that—when they can do it at all. On the whole, writers find other writers hard to be enthusiastic about, even when the other writers are safely dead. It takes security in one's own talent on top of generosity of soul. Philip Roth and Milan Kundera are both wonderfully admiring of Kafka: real generosity in both cases, because each entered Kafka's territory, and must have felt him to be a competitor. It is easier to admire someone who is nothing like you, as Hemingway admired Ronald Firbank. Martin Amis's praise of Saul Bellow is especially valuable because the younger writer is continually faced, when reading the older one, with things he himself would like to have said. In admiring Burke, Hazlitt showed magnanimity as well as taste, because Burke had the stature as a public figure that Hazlitt, in his own eyes, lacked. In our eyes, of course, his lack of pomposity is part of his dignity. But he was not to know that he would come so well out of his age—an age in which he was not even a poet, when almost everybody else was. As for the general principle contained in this encomium to Burke, it can hardly be followed as a recommendation, because it is too general. Laforgue wrote rather the same way about de Musset. These are recommendations to the reader's attention, not incitements to action. The chief merit of the praise is that it does not fall short of its object. But it doesn't really tell you anything specific. In the visually lavish but linguistically impoverished film *Titanic*, Leonardo DiCaprio is not really much less informative when he draws Kate Winslet's attention to Monet's "use of colour." Everyone with a considerable prose style varies the pace, picks up on the unexpected, rises to the occasion. That is what a style does. Burke's style just did a lot of it. More important—as Hazlitt doesn't forget to point out—Burke's style didn't do those things for their own sake. In other words, he was not just a stylist. But there again, nobody with a considerable style is.

None of this means that style and content are ever wholly separable. But neither are they so closely integrated that they can never be discussed separately. In the twentieth century, the United States became the laboratory for Frankenstein experiments in expository prose. In Britain after Bernard Shaw—or during Bernard Shaw, when you consider how long his fluent blarney set the pace—there was only so much sky left overhead for the forked lightning to be playful in: even T. S. Eliot, who abominated Shaw's every opinion, acknowledged him as a master of prose style. (The only contemporary who ever did a convincing job of analysing the cliché content in Shaw's prose was Flann O'Brien, and O'Brien had caught his giant compatriot in windy old age.) In America it was open house. Consider the jump from that lone bounty-hunter of a cultural journalist James Gibbons Huneker to the vaudeville double-act billed as H. L. Mencken and George Jean Nathan. Huneker knew all there was to know about modern art, Europe and modern art in Europe: three linked subjects that he diligently made one. But his prose had no more interior life than John Reed's. In *Ten Days That Shook the World* Reed made the Russian Revolution sound dull, but Huneker could make the whole modern upsurge in the arts sound dull—an even harder task.

With Mencken and Nathan, co-editors of *The American Mercury* and twin commentators on everything that roared in the Roaring Twenties, you are abruptly in a different world, where each man tries to embody his intellectual excitement in his style: to make his journalism, in fact, part of the creative outburst. Nathan overdid it to the extent that nobody now reads him, but Mencken at his best—in his reportage, in his memoirs and in his loving scholarship about the American language—worked the enviable trick of being always identifiable without wearing out his welcome. If admirers of his *Prejudices* had known what some of his prejudices were really like—his anti-Semitism would have earned a tick of approval from Alfred Rosenberg—they would have stopped reading soon enough, but a guardian angel riding in his forehead made sure that the stuff from his brain's bilges didn't get through from his secret diaries to the public page. Unlike the true nutty pamphleteer, Mencken could be selective about the application of his unbounded energy. Thus equipped, he set the standard for the individual voice in upmarket American journalism. Most remarkably, and right to the end, he managed to preserve, despite the tendency of American periodicals to over-edit, his unique individual rhythm.

Rhythm is never effortless. To achieve it, you must start rewriting in your head and then continue rewriting on the page. The hallmark of a seductive style is to extend natural speech rhythm over the distance of a complex sentence. In speech, Gore Vidal has always been a famous wit; and probably a well-rehearsed one, like Disraeli or Oscar Wilde. The rehearsed epigram is a piece of writing in itself. Kingsley Amis loathed the prepared epigram, but his own aphoristic remarks in conversation, though they sounded spontaneous, frequently bore the telltale signs of having been made ready: they were well made like an army bed, the polished kit precisely arranged on a blanket stretched tight, with hospital corners. Vidal chose the right place, where he could be properly overheard, to launch his salute for the nuptial arrangements of two Broadway artistes: "The rocks in his head fit the holes in hers." But he didn't choose just the delivery point, he chose the syntactical balance. Developed over a lifetime, this mastery of construction finally yielded a prose style that could express the most complicated argument as if it were being spoken. Many of his juniors, of whom I am only one, learned a lot from his example—and at a time in our own careers when we thought that we had already learned everything. But one of the things I learned incidentally was that Vidal's transparent style could transmit a false argument as persuasively as it could express a true one. Vidal was at the height of his written eloquence when he began to advance his thesis that the United States provoked Imperial Japan into a war in the Pacific. The kind of proof he offered was on a par with

Hitler's proof that Poland had provoked Germany into a war in 1939, but the way he offered it was dazzling. Vidal's bizarre *démarche* has quite serious implications for the world outlook of my own country's intelligentsia—who should, in my view, be on their guard against any attempt to give aid and comfort to Japan's recidivist right wing—but what matters here is that there could be no more cavernous discrepancy between the thing said and the way of saying it. The two things really are disjunct, and can be made to seem otherwise only by craft. Hazlitt, when he praised Burke's style, was appreciating an artefact, and probably knew that he was. The penalities for not knowing are very large. When we start believing that a statement must be true simply because it is arrestingly put, we are in the first stages of being spellbound, and the later stages are a kind of slavery.

> What is the use of being moral in a night-cellar,
> or wise in Bedlam?
> — WILLIAM HAZLITT, "ON THE
> DISADVANTAGES OF INTELLECTUAL
> SUPERIORITY," IN *TABLE TALK*, P. 280

This reproduces the cadences of Sir Thomas Browne's "splendid in ashes, and pompous in the grave." The comma is the giveaway; it is placed at the same point of balance, as a fulcrum; and then the beam tips, as if your glance had weight. Echoes of a predecessor's rhythm, pace and melody are rarely accidental. Hazlitt had read Browne's sentence and remembered it. The words might not match, but everything else does. These underlying templates are the true transmission tunnels of influence from writer to writer through the ages, and the hardest thing for scholarship to get at. In painting, the echoes of shape are easier to detect. Kenneth Clark writes convincingly about Rembrandt's absorption of every striking outline in the Renaissance: Rembrandt took in the shapes, rather than the iconography. It is the means, rather than the meaning, that travels through time.

HEGEL

❣ ❣ ❣

The philosophy of Georg Wilhelm Freidrich Hegel (1770–1831) was a departure point even for those later philosophers who disagreed with his version of idealism. Croce, for example, was as much in debt to Hegel as he was to Vico. But most of the miasma that retroactively surrounds Hegel's name was generated by those who agreed, or thought they did. The Communist theory of dialectical materialism was a toytown model of Hegel's dialectic, as set out in the two volumes of his *Wissenschaft der Logik* (*The Science of Logic*) between 1812 and 1816. Similarly, his later theories about the state as a perfectible creative expression appealed to those who saw Germany in a leading role, and the long residue of that idea was available to those pre-Nazi nationalist thinkers who helped pave the way for the Nazis, who scarcely thought at all. (Unfortunately their sleep-walk towards destiny fulfilled Hegel's prediction of what the right people might one day do: he just hadn't guessed that the wrong people would do it.) Helping to confuse the issue about Hegel was a prose style that became steadily more impenetrable as his thought developed, thereby encouraging, among his numerous epigones, the damaging notion that obscure is the way philosophy should sound.

It should be remembered that Hegel, early on, after his academic career was interrupted by Napoleon's victory at Jena in 1806, did time as a newspaper editor and a headmaster. He was not without experience of practical affairs, and his art criticism shows that he could stick close to an issue. But he had an undoubted natural tendency to ascend to higher realms, building towering systems of thought that were attacked in the twentieth century (notably by Moore and Russell) as castles in the air. Those who believe, however, that all German philosophy is necessarily as abstruse as Hegel's should read one of his predecessors, Georg Christoph Lichtenberg, whose resurgent reputation after World War II might have had something to do with a widely felt desire to re-attach German philosophy to the concrete reality from which Hegel's influence had worked to separate it.

❧ ❧ ❧

The owl of Minerva begins its flight only
in the gathering darkness.
— HEGEL, QUOTED BY EGON FRIEDELL,
KULTURGESCHICHTE DER NEUZEIT, VOL. 3, P. 79

HEGEL'S PROSE COULD be very beautiful, like this. After his death, his prose became famous for being unyieldingly opaque; and indeed much of his later prose was; but the best reason for believing that the tangles he got into were legitimate is that he could have an idea as delicately suggestive as this and write it down without breaking it. The theme is that the *Zeitgeist* can be understood only when its time is over. There is a piquant appeal in that for us; and part of the appeal might arise from a syllogism with an undistributed middle term; we would like to take, as proof that a bad time is over, the fact that we have begun to understand it. I, for one, would dearly like to believe that this book is a flight by Minerva's owl; in the sense that I would like to believe a terrible era has so finally and unarguably come to an end that even I have begun to understand it. I would like to believe that, but I can only hope it's true; and since September 11, 2001, even the hope has come to seem silly. The period when "the end of history" sounded

like an attractive idea can now be recalled as being very brief: a hump
in the hallway, a thirty-second seduction by language. In the dark light
of recent events, Hegel's owl of Minerva might be heading anywhere.
Following the sound of its flapping wings, we can perhaps say a few
things about where beautiful language can lead, when it unexpectedly
shows up somewhere in the course of a reasoned argument.

The poetic line plucked from a philosopher might provide us with
only the illusion of understanding what he has to say, but the range of
implication feels real for a good reason—it might not be under our
control, but it is not under his either. By saying something so resonant,
he made a lucky strike, and part of the luck is that it can reach us by an
indirect route. The rich saying gets passed on. It was at the end of
Edgar Wind's classic set of 1963 Reith Lectures, *Art and Anarchy*, that
I first read about Kant's dove—the dove which, on being told about air
resistance, thought it could fly faster by abolishing the air. If I had had
to wait to hear about the dove from Kant himself, I might have grown
old and grey. As things were, I was handed in good time an analogy that
has served me well for the ambitious artist who hopes to express himself more easily by ignoring technique. I even have a picture of him: a
gormless bird disappointed by its own slowness as it flaps in the opposite direction to Minerva's owl.

Walter Benjamin, by way of Hannah Arendt, supplied another flying paradigm for a mental skyscape growing crowded like one of those
airborne avenues in *Blade Runner*. In her collection of essays *Men in
Dark Times* Arendt cites Benjamin's angel of history, which flies backwards with its hands raised to its face, appalled by the spectacle of the
ruins piling up constantly before its eyes. Benjamin, it might be
objected, was not a philosopher. Well, he was when he wrote that: or
else he was the kind of poet who, writing only in prose, has moments
of explanatory intensity for which the word "poetry" is hard to withhold, unless we call them philosophy instead. As for the systematic
philosopher, he might try, as a matter of professional etiquette, to avoid
speaking in quiddities, but is most likely to be cogent when he finds
that imputation hard to dodge. If he has poetic moments, they will not
necessarily be throwaway: often they will happen at the focus of the
argument, as a natural consequence of trying to get a lot said at once.
The same happened even for Croce, who preferred to lay out an argu-

ment throughout a whole book at an even pace, with an unvarying transparency. He preferred a texture as serenely even as a snowy plateau in the Antarctic. But just as the snowy plateau in the Antarctic is studded with meteorites like chocolate chips in vanilla ice cream, so Croce's long, smooth stretches are riddled by sentences heavier than the surrounding texture. Reading Croce day after day in the Biblioteca Nazionale in Florence the year after the 1966 flood, I picked out and stored hundreds of sentences as attention-getting as Hegel's twilight owl. If I had to choose a favourite, it would be because it chose me: for reasons I can't be sure of, although I am sure they go deep, it's the one about the history of the flowers. Croce was saying that all living things have a history: having a history and living are the same process. Even the flowers, he said, have a history, although only they know it.

I can remember sitting back and shaking my head, to clear it from too much clarity. *Although only they know it* was the speeding point of light that rang the bell. The wave-particle of prose that rings the bell does what poetry does. Poetry just does more of it, and one of the ways we measure greatness in poetry is by how it organizes, to an even higher degree, everything that great prose does in the same space, gracing it with the additional splendour of a festival. Shakespeare, nearly three hundred years before Croce was born, did that for the flowers.

> *How with such rage shall beauty hold a plea*
> *Whose action is no stronger than a flower?*

I saw it said in some newspaper profile that this is Seamus Heaney's favourite moment in Shakespeare. A favourite moment in Shakespeare is a concept that could make sense only to a cultural journalist with a deadline. One can imagine the journalist's question, and the poet's politely suppressed groan of despair. Yet if one were forced to choose on pain of death, this moment would not be a bad choice. We might think it could not be added to, but Croce added to it, because one of the things meant by what he said is: *and no weaker*. These connections between phrases, sentences and lines across time might seem tenuous, but I know nothing more surely than that the collective mentality of humanism is made up of them. They give the mentality of humanism its coherence and independence: two of the characteristics which the totalitarian mechanism always makes it an early business to destroy. Sooner or later, and usually sooner, the jealous mind of the tyrant decides that pleading beauty must be brought under strict control, even when it presents itself in the unspectacular form of a philosopher's passing remark. In normal times, the aim of scholarship is to bring out the meaning of a seemingly passing remark in its full richness. In dark times, the aim is to confine meaning to a sanctioned path, or eliminate it altogether. In 1939, the German state came to knock on the study door of Hegel. He wasn't in, but the Nazis knew how to make even a dead man change his story. There was an irony in that, because Hegel thought civilization had reached its purpose and apogee in the ordered Prussian state. But the Nazi state, though it had received some of its impetus from his ideal of order, was something else. In 1939 Alfred Kroner Verlag in Stuttgart put out a handy one-volume selection from Hegel on the subjects of *Volk, Staat* and *Geschichte* (the people, the state and history). Poetic suggestiveness was rigidly eschewed: this little book meant business. (The Kroner pocket books always did: they were the hard-bound German equivalent of the English Pelican series in later years.) The editor of the Hegel volume was one Friedrich Bülow. My copy, which I bought in Munich in 1992, was first owned by Dr. H. Linhardt of Münster. He bought it in Rothenburg on May 19, 1940— a time of Hitlerite triumph. (Rotterdam was blitzed five days before, and the King of the Belgians capitulated nine days later.) There is a bravura passage in paragraph 373 which we hope was not music to Dr. Linhardt's ears. It certainly would have been to Hitler's, at any time before those final hours when he decided that the German people had been unworthy of their destiny. Hegel speaks of the *Volk* destined to rule an epoch. This *Volk* carries the development-stage of the world-spirit (*Entwicklungsstufe des Weltgeistes*), against which other peoples have no rights: in world history they no longer count.

As far as I know, Dr. Linhardt's activities during the war made little mark on world history. One hopes they were benign. We know what happened to Hitler: in Hegelian terms, he died cursing the German *Volk* for their shortage of development-stage. But the name to notice is that of Friedrich Bülow. His name was still there on the title page of Kroner's 1955 reissue of Hegel's *Volk. Staat. Geschichte.* Though the reissue was in the same reliable Kroner format, there was a notable change to the exterior. The word *Volk* had disappeared from the spine, which now read *Recht. Staat. Geschichte.* The people had been quietly replaced by the law. But on the inside of the book, the ecstatic passages about the people chosen by history to carry the development-stuff of the world-spirit remained intact. There was no footnote to warn of the presence of toxic waste, and perhaps there should not have been. Though I think the West German government was right to ban *Mein Kampf* even at the certain cost of its becoming a bootleg hit with neo-Nazis, on the whole the revived democracy's educational authorities were wise not to attempt a new tampering with established texts. The Nazis had done that, usually by banning them if not burning them: and it hadn't worked. Some of Hegel's thinking had lethal tendencies, but the times had to become lethal before the tendencies became obvious; until then, those bits looked merely silly. In 1940 Dr. Linhardt made marginal notes against any of the editor's comments that he found too liberal (*grund falsch!*) but that was because the Nazis had so distorted *Staat* and *Recht* that they had convinced a nonentity like Dr. Linhardt he was enrolled with Hegel as a member of the world-historical *Volk.* Hegel's celebration of unopposed and inexorable power had become temporarily relevant, but it was never right. On that subject he had set Minerva's owl flying too early. In the long run, had he lived, his poetic perceptiveness would have shown him what had gone wrong with his political theories. Great writers supply us with the strengths to measure their weaknesses; but the latter are always there, to generate the air through which the dove flies, dreaming of freedom.

HEINRICH HEINE

Heinrich Heine (1797–1856), one of the greatest writers in German, spent only the first third of his mature creative life being a great writer in Germany. Already famous for both his poetry and his prose, he went into exile in Paris in 1831, never to return. In 1825 he had volunteered for the Christian baptism that a Jew then needed if he were to gain German citizenship; and he had incurred the derision of some of his fellow Jews as a consequence; but it was his revolutionary political opinions that made emigration advisable. In Paris he continued with the travel journalism that he had already pioneered as a serious form, and added a body of miscellaneous writings recommending a closer identification of French and German intellectual achievement. On whatever subject, he wrote a clear prose whose wide-ranging play of thought has never gone flat: on every page will be found something relevant now. As a cosmopolitan democrat he eventually incurred the disapproval of the more incendiary revolutionaries, and might easily have died in a duel. Instead, he was condemned to the long agony of spinal paralysis, which kept him in bed for the last seven years of his life, during which he wrote and published books and collections that can be seen in retrospect to express the romantic age at its height. His status as a displaced person, and a prophetic statement—that those who burn books will one day burn people—combined to place him, politically, a hundred years before his time. Nietzsche thought him second only to Goethe among the German poets. Beginners who start with his poem about the slave ship ("*Die Sklavenschiff*") will get the immediate and correct impression of a brave liberal intelligence combined with a vaulting lyric gift. Both characteristics transferred readily to his prose, making it one of the first and finest models for what we now see as desirable in literary journalism.

I take pride in never being rude to anyone on this earth,
which contains a great number of unbearable villains
who set upon you to recount their sufferings and
even recite their poems.
—HEINRICH HEINE, *REISE VON MÜNCHEN
NACH GENUA*, CHAPTER I, P. 193

THE JOKE STILL rings true. Hearing a man recite his poems unbidden remains even worse than hearing him recount his sufferings. So Heine's sarcastic crescendo is as funny as ever after more than 150 years. But the statement as a whole has been overtaken by time. The possibility of choosing not to be rude has long vanished. It was already vanishing when Yeats said, "Always I encourage, always." A few years later, and Yeats's prominence on the radio would have ensured that the heaps of unsolicited manuscripts he was already receiving would have increased to teetering hills that he could no longer consider being polite about. The mass media, even when a literary figure did his best to avoid their embrace, eventually made it certain that there could be no natural, human connection between the illuminated exemplar and the solicitous disciple. There is no real relationship, for example, between ordinary letters and fan letters. In the pre-celebrity-culture world, an important writer received a lot of letters, but they all, in some way, had to do with his work, even when the correspondent's own work was the subject under discussion. Later on, in the celebrity age we now all inhabit, the fan letter is connected only with the addressee's fame: it has nothing to do with his achievement. If it has, it is not really a fan letter: it is an ordinary letter buried in the pile of fan letters. Circumstances dictate that it will be buried deep.

A woman much more original than she is often given credit for, Greta Garbo was one of the first international celebrities to spot what was going on. Joan Crawford answered every fan letter she was ever sent: she was under the illusion that they were ordinary letters, and that there were just a lot of them. Garbo never answered a single fan letter in her whole Hollywood career. She ordered them destroyed before they reached her. The few that did reach her she threw into the fire. She was acting on the defensible assumption that they had already done their work simply through having been sent. She also showed acute insight in divining that there was no appropriate response. The sort of person who might send a fan letter would take any form of personal reply as the beginning of a relationship. It was not given to one person to maintain even a small proportion of those possible relationships in a single lifetime. Dismissing the prospect was thus the only way of dealing with it. As the most famous woman in the world, only Garbo could know that the sole means of behaving politely was to subtract herself from the whole monstrously amplified anomaly.

It will be argued that Heinrich Heine was not Greta Garbo. But he practically was. Heine was famous on the scale of Byron and Victor Hugo. If there could be a twentieth-century equivalent to his kind of literary prominence—you have to imagine a Philip Larkin as famous as Jeffrey Archer—he would be snowed under with correspondence that had no clear instigation except his fame. As things were, the flow of attention was on a scale that, though great, allowed him to think he still had a choice. Even in retrospect, however, it is remarkable that he chose not to be rude. His nature must have been uncommonly sweet. It might also have been perilously gullible. The sheer volume of correspondence with which any literary figure, no matter how obscure, is nowadays inundated has the dubious advantage of uncovering a full taxonomy of the literary aspirant. The correspondence from the obvious maniacs bears a disturbing resemblance to the correspondence from the apparently sane. The disturbing element springs from the dreadful suspicion that the normal-sounding ones might not be quite

all there either. Leaving aside the typical appurtenances of the nut letter—the many closely written or typed pages, the numerous cut-out
inserts, the documentary evidence to illustrate some rankling item of
litigation—the things that the psycho supplicants want are wanted also
by the sane. They want you to read a manuscript. Often the manuscript
is huge, but they want you to read it. Some of them, verging on the
nutty, want you to help write the next draft. A few, nutty but perhaps
not irreversibly so, will generously suggest that after you have arranged
for its publication, the title page might carry your name. A very few,
nutty on a career basis, will insist that it carry both your names, and
there will be the occasional one—the supreme nut, the dingbat *in excelsis*—who thinks *your* next book should carry *his* name. Backing up all
these suggestions, in all their varieties, will be the general argument
that the publishing industry, as at present constituted, is not favourable
to the individual talent. The publishers have formed a conspiracy
against any fresh voice.

To the occasional sane-sounding letter informed by the same
assumption, it is possible, if one has the time, to reply with the truth.
The truth ought to be so obvious that it needs no pointing out to anyone not mentally unbalanced, but there is always the chance that your
correspondent has lost his judgement temporarily just from the fact of
knowing you, and knowing you to be a writer—as you yourself might
temporarily lose your judgement just from knowing somebody and
knowing him to be a doctor. If you have ever found yourself describing
your symptoms to a new acquaintance who had until then been under
the impression that he was meeting you in social circumstances for a
few drinks, you will see how it happens that people who have been in
your life for years—good, solid friends, sometimes—can be struck
simultaneously with the unfortunate urge to write (the sudden disease
that Dr. Johnson, following Juvenal, called *scribendi cacoethes*) and the
capacity to forget common manners. Anyway, whatever the reasons,
and without warning, someone you thought you knew well is telling
you that he requires your assistance in getting his manuscript past the
usual barriers thrown up by publishers to ward off original talent. It is
made clear that a recommendation, to your agent if not to your publisher, is the very least favour expected. What do you say?

You say the truth: there are no such barriers. Publishers are in busi-

ness to publish a marketable manuscript, and go to some expense
employing professional readers in order to ensure that such manuscripts may be found, among the mountain ranges of unmarketable
ones. (A single glance at the clogged throughput of this traffic in any
publisher's office would be enough to convince the independent
onlooker that the old saw about the average novel is nothing but the
truth: the average novel does not get published.) Recommendations
never work: publishers are too well aware that whoever does the recommending might be under pressure, and anyway an author's personal
marketability is no proof of his capacity to detect it in others. You
might be sincerely passionate on behalf of a friend, but sincerity will
not do: a good publisher will sometimes be prepared to lose money on
a writer he believes in, but not on one that *you* believe in. Just making
these simple points will take you at least a page of prose, which will
make you impatient of lost time, so try to remember that it's your
friend, and not you, who has tested the friendship. Blame him, not
yourself. Getting harder not to be rude, isn't it? Things will be easier
all round if he has included his manuscript, because the awesome bulk
of its presence will help you reclassify him in the screwball category
where he belongs.

For a close friend, a phone call is probably the best way out of it.
Don't hesitate to sound as if you are too short of time to write. You are:
you are a writer, and so time spent writing without financial reward is
time worse than wasted—unless you are writing for pleasure, which in
this case you most certainly aren't. For everyone else, a form letter is
probably the best course. It should say that you get hundreds of such
requests. You won't be exaggerating by much: over a lifetime, even the
most determinedly hermetic poet will receive a few score unpublished
novels and autobiographies, which can find their way to an igloo, a
shack in the desert, a hut on the beach. Make the point that publishers
do not listen to recommendations, they employ readers: and add the
point that agents almost invariably do not. This will defuse in advance
the standard hint that if your correspondent could be recommended to
your agent it would smooth his path. If the unjustly neglected manuscript has not turned up with the first letter, it will almost certainly turn
up with the next, so to ward off that dreaded eventuality your first letter should make the crucial point that you are under legal advice not to

read unsolicited manuscripts. If this is not strictly true, it ought to be; because if you sought legal advice, that is the advice you would get. Anyone self-obsessed enough to hand you his manuscript is more than self-obsessed enough to sue you if he thinks a future work by you is based on his idea. In Hollywood, which has a full century of experience as the laboratory for every legal aspect of handling literary property, no written material, in any form or at any length, is ever dealt with for five minutes unless the legal rights attached to it are beyond dispute. There is nothing perverse about such caution. It is the logical consequence of everyone—including your admirably sane friend—honestly believing that the idea he just wrote down is unique.

Heine, with his fatal pride in his own politeness, sounds as if he might have trouble with modern autograph hounds. In his day their activities were restricted by limitations on transport, and on the technology to follow through after an initial refusal. Today, an autograph nut can travel hundreds of miles in a short time to catch you at your latest location before you can move on, and has several routes through which to forward his requests. He doesn't even have to confront you in order to pester you to distraction. A modern Heine should be smart enough to keep his own address out of *Who's Who*. He should also keep his agent's address out of it. (Anyone who needs his agent's name in *Who's Who* is lucky to be in *Who's Who* in the first place.) But his publisher, unless instructed not to, will forward requests from autograph freaks, and is even morally obliged to if they are marked "Personal: Please Forward." Straightforward requests for an autograph to add to the correspondent's world-beating collection can be binned with a clear conscience if a self-addressed stamped envelope is not included. If there is an SASE, there is probably also a heart-rending account of how little time the correspondent has left to live, owing to a progressive disease inexorably depriving him of the strength to do anything except (he forgets to say the next bit) send mad requests for autographs to every minor celebrity on Earth. After struggling with his conscience and losing, Heine will probably send off his name. After struggling with mine and winning, I usually bin the letter and keep the stamp, but that's probably why I haven't written anything as tenderly humane as "*Das Sklavenschiff*" lately. All letters from dealers, SASEs included, should be burned immediately, as if infected. As a clue, people asking you to sign first-day covers are always dealers. Never believe they are philatelists. And anyway, how sane is a philatelist?

Met in person, autograph hounds are a big problem with no easy solution until your fame fades, whereupon their absence might make its disappearance less painful. Even when his worldwide instant recognition factor was at last blurring at the edges, Cary Grant, if asked for an autograph, invariably said "Go get Elvis Presley's." He was being courageous even in those days, and today it would be folly to turn down any such request so abruptly, because there is now no way of knowing how many of the people you rebuff are homicidal maniacs—all you can be certain of is that there are far more of them about. It is sometimes wise to cut things short when assailed by an aggressively rude man, but never when he has a child with him. Though he may demand that you sign everything including the child, a man shamed in front of his offspring won't forget it, and you should try to follow the rule of never making an enemy except deliberately. Of the regulars who hang around the stage door, the door of the Ivy and any other door that a celebrity might come out of, the genuinely banged-up man in the wheelchair should have your signature, for what it is worth. (If it is Madonna's it will be worth a substantial amount: but yours he might conceivably want for itself.) The others are merely head cases and if you waste time standing in the rain to write in their books, so are you.

When asked to sign his own books, Heine will be on safer ground. If someone bearing a well-thumbed copy of an author's book conveys the impression that the addition of a signature to its flyleaf or title page will raise it to the status of the Rosetta Stone or the shield of Achilles, the author will find it hard to disagree. But Heine will need to keep his wits about him. At book signings, and especially after readings, there will be people in the queue carrying every book he ever wrote. Most of them will be genuine admirers, but some of them will be dealers, and it is often hard to tell the difference. Either way, they should be sent to the end of the queue, so that people who have actually purchased your book are not kept waiting. When the person with the teetering armful finally gets his turn, the question arising is no longer about whether to sign, but about how. For safety, the author should put the current date after his name. Harold Pinter once asked a man who proffered a first edition of one of his early plays for signing: "I suppose if I didn't date this," (pause) "it would look as if I'd signed it *at the time*," (pause) "and that would make it more valuable," (pause) "wouldn't it?" The man could not disagree, and Pinter wrote the current date. Heine might not mind helping a dealer make money, but most authors do: they remember too vividly how little they earned from an entire print-run to enjoy seeing some stranger cash in from a single copy of it.

Some authors are armoured against signing anything at all except the initial presentation copies, and when a successful author finds out how valuable that makes *them*, he might cease doing even that much, and just include a card. (The best method anyway, because it means that the recipient, if he wants to, can sell the book without embarrassing you both.) Another famous playwright of my acquaintance was once given free board and lodging by the illustrious director Mike Nichols in Los Angeles, and wanted to pay back his host by presenting him with a full set of Anthony Powell's *A Dance to the Music of Time* novels, which Nichols much admired, and presumably would have admired even more if he had been regaled with a set of first editions all signed by the author. At great expense and trouble, the famous playwright got a set of firsts together, but Powell would not sign them. He was well aware of who was asking and of whom the gift was for, but his pen stayed in his pocket. That was his principle and he stuck to it, even though a set of first editions of *A Dance to the Music of Time* which had provably passed through the hands of the famous playwright, of Mike Nichols and of Powell himself would have been an association copy fit for a museum. It could have been, however, that Powell was afraid of exactly that: becoming a museum piece. There is something unsettling about being sought out for one's name; as mummies in the mummy cloth are wound, one feels wrapped up in documentation; breathing comes hard. I quite understand why some writers try to get out of public life altogether. Perhaps Heine today would take J. D. Salinger's route to privacy, although Heine's blessed sense of the absurd—still scintillating after all this time—might tell him in advance that solitude is no guarantee of being left alone.

But really there are no rules except rules of thumb, and for a quiet life it is probably better just to sign everything put in front of you, even bare skin, and try to think of something useful while you are wasting the energy. After all, back there at the start you wanted to be well-known. Even Heine did. He just didn't want to pay the price of being a good poet: hearing bad poetry. But if he had built up an infallible early-warning system to ensure that no ninny could ever reach him he would have been less human than he was, and therefore less of a poet. So it all worked out in the end. It usually does. Unless you actually get killed, you have handled fame as well as can be done. At the Australian Grand Prix in Adelaide I once saw George Harrison staving off the autograph hounds with the brilliantly enigmatic explanation "It's Thursday." I thought it a marvellous technique: funny enough to satisfy the normal, and plausible enough to soothe the sort of psycho who had already accounted for John Lennon. George Harrison did as good a job as an unmanageably famous man can do to stay sane. But the man who broke into his house and stabbed him to the point of death had never stayed sane at all.

If Heine were here with us, he would have something new to write about, and it would be edifying to hear his conclusions. My own guess is that he would find, now as then, no alternative to being polite, while being obliged to admit that some of the unbearable villains nowadays come armed with more frightening weapons than the well-rehearsed grievance and the tritely rhymed poem that doesn't scan. The admission would soon lead him to the real subject: what happens to the women. Heine had a tender heart, and for any man with one of those the real and abiding questions about modern fame concern the completeness with which it takes famous women back to the primeval forest. There are some famous men who pick up a female stalker: but there are no famous women who do *not* pick up at least one male stalker, and very famous women pick them up by the platoon. The only reason you hear so little about the restraining orders the women have to take out is that they are doing their desperate best not to attract any more copycats. Stalking is mainly a male preserve because, for men, love is an aesthetic event in the first instance. Though the stalker's mentality is a long way from the mentality of a lyric poet, it is not impossibly far. Stalkers are murderers—they all are, without exception—whose killer instincts are triggered by beauty. Garbo guessed that fact by another instinct, the one for survival: through those finely flared nostrils, she had correctly sensed that a man ready to rob a woman of her peace would just as easily take her life if given the chance. Heine's politeness depended on the idea that it is right to be nice to strangers. It is a civilized idea, but it is not always correct, because life is not always civilized. Once upon a time, it never was, and being rude to strangers was the only way to stay safe. The truly awful thing about the celebrity culture is how far it takes us back.

ADOLF HITLER

❧ ❧ ❧

Adolf Hitler (1889–1945) should need no introduction. Statistics suggest, however, that a large proportion of young people now emerging from the educational systems of the Western democracies either don't know who he was or have only a shaky idea of what he did. One of the drawbacks of liberal democracy is thus revealed: included among its freedoms is the freedom to forget what once threatened its existence. Granted the uncontested opportunity to do so, Hitler would have devoted himself to eliminating every trace of free expression that came within his reach. The awkward question remains of whether, on his part, this propensity precluded any real interest in the humanities. The awkward answer must be that it didn't. Though it is tempting to think of him as illiterate, he could quote Schopenhauer from memory. Hitler's love of music was passionate, to the point where some believed that his admiration for Wagner was a sufficient reason in itself for dismissing that composer from musical history. Hitler the would-be painter never lost his interest in the plastic arts. His projected art gallery in his home town of Linz was one of his most dearly cherished dreams for Nazi Europe after the inevitable victory, and just because he thought Menzel the best of the German painters is no good reason for thinking Menzel inferior. Above all, Hitler was moved by architecture, which brings us to the central point; because he wasn't just moved by it, he was mad about it. He had no sense of proportion in any of his ostensibly civilized enthusiasms. His interests lacked the human element, so they could never have amounted to a true humanism. But though his connection with the civilized traditions was parodic at best and neurotic always, there was still a connection: in that respect, he stands above Stalin and Mao, and should therefore, by the scholar, be handled with even greater caution, because far more poisonous. Many of his more cultivated victims used their learned resources to deny that Hitler had a mental existence. Some of the last aphorisms written by the great Robert Musil were devoted to summarizing the pathogenic nature of Hitler. Beautifully crafted statements, they had no effect on Hitler whatsoever. The finest minds in Europe devoted their best efforts to proving that their mortal enemy had no mind at all. But nothing they said was of any avail. Hitler could be defeated only by armed might: i.e., on his own terms. Whole libraries written to his detriment didn't add up to the effect of a single Russian artillery shell. This ugly fact should be kept in view when we catch ourselves nursing the comforting illusion that there is a natural order to which politics would revert if all contests of belief could be eliminated. There is such a natural order, but it is not benevolent.

Books about Hitler are without number, but after more than sixty years the first one to read is still Alan Bullock's *Hitler: A Study in Tyranny*. Familiarity with the events that it recounts should be regarded as an essential prerequisite to the study not just of modern politics, but of the whole history of the arts since its hideously gifted subject first demonstrated that a sufficient concentration of violence could neutralize any amount of culture no matter how widely diffused. It is not possible to be serious about the humanities unless it is admitted that the pacifism widely favoured among educated people before World War II very nearly handed a single man, himself something other than a simple Philistine, the means to bring civilization to an end. The lessons of history don't suit our wishes: if they did, they would not be lessons, and history would be a fairy story.

> You have everything that I lack. You are forging the spiritual tools for the renewal of Germany. I am nothing but a drum and a master of ceremonies. Let's cooperate!
> —ADOLF HITLER AT THE JUNI-KLUB,
> SPRING 1922, AS QUOTED IN JEAN PIERRE
> FAYE'S *LANGAGES TOTALITAIRES*, P. 30

RESPECTABLY SITUATED in Berlin's Motzstrasse, to the south of the Tiergarten, the Juni-Klub, or June Club (the name breathed defiance at the Treaty of Versailles), was a twenties talking shop for right-wing intellectuals concerned with revolutionary conservatism. The consciously oxymoronic idea of revolutionary conservatism had almost as many forms as it had advocates, who found it easy to mistake their dialectical hubbub for the clanging forge of a new order. Of the one hundred and fifty members, thirty were present on the afternoon Hitler dropped in. They thought he had come to hear what they had to say, and they found out that he had no intention of listening to any voice but his own. Their scholarly qualifications counted for nothing. Best qualified of all was Arthur Moeller van den Bruck. Before World War I, Moeller had been a translator of Baudelaire, Barbey d'Aurevilly, Defoe, De Quincey and the complete poetry of Edgar Allan Poe. He had written essays on Nietzsche, Stefan George, Hofmannsthal, Büchner, Strindberg and Wedekind. With Dmitriy Merezhkovsky and others he had edited the first complete German-language edition of Dostoevsky, published in Munich in 1905. He knew Paris well, and spent time also in London, Sicily, Venice, the Baltic countries, Finland, Russia, Denmark and Sweden. For cultivation he was up there with Ernst Jünger, one of Germany's most gifted modern prose writers and likewise a revolutionary conservative. As a kind of back-to-the-future movement, revolutionary conservatism depended for its force on advocates who embodied established values. Moeller embodied learning the way Jünger embodied storm-of-steel militarism. Both had their rationale for a conservative revolution worked out in detail, with all the nuances duly noted. Possibly because of this meeting at the Juni-Klub, Moeller was the first to grasp that Hitler didn't care about any of it.

Moeller's revolutionary conservatism was meant to safeguard the nation's *Wesens-Urgestein* (the original essential stone) from the corrosive encrustation of *Blutmischung* (mixed blood). Nominally, the tainted blood he was most concerned about was the Latin blood of the German south. (In France at the same time, the future arch-collaborator Drieu la Rochelle had the identical bee in his bonnet about blood from the south: he thought even the south of France was dangerous.) Some of Moeller's colleagues thought that Hitler might have picked up the dreaded southern infection from spending too long in Bavaria. But it hardly needs saying that Jewish blood was the real bother. If anyone is still looking for the linking factor between the resolutely thuggish Nazi movement and all those long-forgotten, highfalutin nationalist groupuscules that superficially seem so much more refined, anti-Semitism is it. To Ernst von Salomon, one of the assassins who found so many excellent reasons, that same year of 1922, for murdering Weimar Germany's most creative politician, Walther Rathenau, Jünger actually said it: "Why didn't you have the courage to say that Rathenau was killed because he was a Jew?"

What we should say to Jünger's ghost is still in question. When, during World War II, he finally allowed himself to find out exactly what the Nazis were doing to the Jews in the east, he was suitably devastated. But during the twenties it never seemed to concern him much that all the various nationalist groups—even the national Bolshevist group fronted by Ernst Niekisch—always seemed to have this one characterisitic, anti-Semitism, in common. Not, of course, that it would have come to anything much if Jünger and the rest of the intellectuals had been left to themselves. It wasn't mass murder that they had in mind: just the purification and protection of the folk heritage, brought to the point of irreversible decay by the curse of liberalism. Like Niekisch, who was coming from the other direction but with the same prejudice, Moeller thought that the nineteenth-century theorist of Prussian conservatism Julius Stahl was not convervative enough. Stahl was baptized a Lutheran, but he was Jewish. So the objection was racial, although Moeller would have resisted being defined as a mere racist. He had bigger ideas than that. The biggest of them was that liberalism was the real enemy. To the Juni-Klub's collective testament, an album by many hands called *Die neue Front*, he contributed a fragment of his forthcoming book. The fragment was called "Through Liberalism Peoples Go to Ruin." The book, published in 1923, carried a title which would gain in resonance beyond his death: *The Third Reich*.

I have a copy of *Das dritte Reich* in front of me as I write. An ugly little volume bound in paper, it was put out in 1931 by the Hanseatische Verlaganstalt, a Nazi publishing outfit based in Hamburg. This particular example was purchased in Jena in 1934 by someone signing himself Wm. Montgomery Watt. Presumably he was a Scot, because I found the book in a dust pile in the back of an Edinburgh second-hand bookshop. Whether in approval or disapproval it is hard to tell, but Wm. Montgomery Watt was a great underliner. You soon spot that he underlined the same point over and over. It was the point Moeller couldn't help making: he got around to it whatever the nominal subject. The point was that Germany had never lost the war, except politically. Militarily it had triumphed, and all that was now needed was a revolution in order to put reality back in touch with the facts. It just never occurred to Moeller that to say Germany had never lost the war except politically was like saying that a cat run over by a car had never died except physically. It never occurred to hundreds of thousands of present and future Nazis either, but Moeller was supposed to be an intellectual. So was Jünger, whose book *Der Arbeiter* was also published by the Hanseatische Verlagsanstalt, with a resonant line of publicity material: "Jünger sees that bourgeois individualism, the cult of personality, the conceit of the ego all belong to the nineteenth century, and are now visibly melting before our eyes through the transformation of separate people into a collectivity." (Memo to a young student of cultural flux: when you buy old books, keep the wrappers if you can. Nothing gives you the temperature of the time like the puffs and quotations.) All these finely articulated arguments were going strictly nowhere, because nobody in the Nazi hierarchy ever found much time to read them, and certainly Hitler never read a single line. What continues to matter, however, is not where the arguments were going, but where they came from. They came from the same source that gave the chance of action to the thugs who used them as a warrant: the chaos, the dislocation and the demoralization of a civil order. To that extent, and to that extent only, superior minds like Moeller and Jünger were right. They were like Groucho Marx turning up his nose at any club that might admit him as a member: a society that led them to write such stuff had no future.

At the end of the meeting in the Juni-Klub, before Hitler set off on foot through the Tiergarten to doss with an old comrade, Moeller politely offered him a free subscription to the club's monthly magazine *Gewissen* (Conscience), but was later heard to say that Hitler had understood nothing. If, as seems likely, Hitler had given nobody time to speak except himself, it is hard to see how there could have been anything to understand. Finally, however, Moeller understood Hitler in the only way that counted. The following year, the Munich putsch was a fiasco, but it caused enough uproar to show Moeller the difference between well-polished words in small-circulation magazines and raw charisma in the streets. Suddenly Moeller remembered Hitler's little farewell speech. Shouting feebly from the sidelines, Moeller made the classic obeisance of the man of letters to the man of action. "Beat the drum, drum of nature!"

With a brief pause for unsuccessful psychiatric treatment, Moeller committed suicide in 1925, so he never had to see what became of his subtle theories. What became of them was nothing. They had never mattered. What mattered was the stuff he took for granted: anti-Semitism, and his certainty that the Weimar Republic had only one destiny—to be destroyed. It was the second of those two things that turned out to be crucial, and the steady subversion from men like him that helped to make it happen. After Moeller's death, the Juni-Klub was succeeded by the Herrenklub, the gentlemanly conservative ambience of which provided a support group for von Papen, who in turn thought that he had found a suitable ruffian to clear the way for a return to the traditional ascendancy. Hitler, the suitable ruffian, could never have done it on his own. He could never have done it with all his party. He needed a climate of belief—the belief that Weimar was a problem requiring a solution. Having solved it, he was free to answer his version of the Jewish Question—the question that the intellectuals had fooled with on paper. Only the madmen among them had ever thought it needed to be answered with fire. But the sane ones had helped open the door for the avenger that the madmen had dreamed of. Moeller was lucky he didn't live to see the results.

When intellectuals conspire to undermine vulgar democracy in favour of a refined dream, it might seem unfair to condemn them for failing to foresee the subsequent nightmare. And Moeller, though outstandingly qualified, was only one among many. But there were too many: that was the point. Too many well-read men combined to prepare the way for a pitiless hoodlum who despised them, and they even came to value him for being a hoodlum: for lacking their scruples, for being a drum of nature. Among the revolutionary conservative intellectuals, Jünger is the real tragic figure. Unlike Moeller, Jünger was condemned to live. He saw the light, but too late. In his notebooks he gradually de-emphasized his call for a conservative revolution led by men who had been "transformed in their being" by the experience of World War I. In 1943, in Paris, he was told the news about the extermination camps, and finally reached the conclusion that he had been staving off since the collapse of the Weimar Republic he had helped to undermine: one of the men whose being had been transformed by their experience of the Great War was Adolf Hitler. The quality Jünger valued most had turned out to be the only one he shared with the man he most despised.

RICARDA HUCH

❦ ❦ ❦

Ricarda Huch (1864–1947), the first lady of German humanism in modern times, can be thought of as a bridging figure
between Germaine de Staël and Germaine Greer. Poet, novelist and above all historian of culture, she started out as the very
model of the stylish female troublemaker, the upmarket bluestocking as inveterate social bugbear. Breaker of many male
hearts, including those of her husbands, she began her career
of role reversal as one of the first female graduates from Zurich
University, where she studied history, philosophy and philology. (The universities of her native Germany still did not
admit women.) Her books on romanticism retain their position as key works. Her historical novel *Der dreissigjahriger
Krieg* (The Thirty Years War) richly demonstrates her uncommon gift for talking about the powerless as if they had the
importance of the powerful. She got into history herself in
1933, when she publicly rejected the blandishments of the
Nazis, who were keen to co-opt her prestige. After quitting her
position as the first woman ever elected to the Prussian
Acadamy of the Arts, she went into internal exile in Jena. A
lifelong rebel against the class structure of capitalist society,
after the war she stayed in the East, spending her last years as

a figurehead: in the year of her death she was honorary president of the First German Writers Congress in Berlin. If she
had lived to see the regime ossify, she would probably have
written yet another book that her would-be masters would not
have liked. But she was an old lady, and her studies of history
had given her everything but clairvoyance.

❣ ❣ ❣

> To save Germany was not granted to them; only to die
> for it; luck was not with them, it was with Hitler. But
> they did not die in vain. Just as we need air if we are to
> breathe, and light if we are to see, so we need noble
> people if we are to live.
> — RICARDA HUCH, *FÜR DIE MARTYRER DER
> FREIHEIT*, MARCH/APRIL 1946, CITED IN
> *BRIEFE AN DIE FREUNDE*, P. 449

BEFORE WE SPEAK about the old lady who wrote this, we should
recall the doomed bravery of the young men she was writing
about. For those involved in the July 20, 1944, plot against Hitler's life,
martyrdom was always a possibility, and in retrospect, naturally
enough, it looks like a certainty. A successful coup d'état would have
required far too much to go right. Even if the conspirators had succeeded in killing Hitler, their own lives would have been forfeit:
Himmler had the exits covered. With martyrdom secured, canoniza-
tion duly followed, especially on the conservative right. Many of the
plotters had been aristocrats and it was felt—felt because wished—that
they had expressed a long-standing repugnance among people of good
family towards the vulgar upstart Hitler.

Actually it had never been as simple as that. When some of the condemned young officers had been even younger, Hitler had looked to
them like a saviour, a new Bismarck. Nor was it only the Wehrmacht
that benefited from well-connected enthusiasm. Aristocratic recruits to
the SS were plentiful: promotion was rapid, and there were opportunities to ride horses. (Funding an SS equestrian team was one of Himmler's master strokes.) Most of the young officers who developed doubts
about Hitler had close friends who never developed any doubts at all.

Critics on the left who would like to deny saintliness to the high-born conspirators will always have a lot to go on. But the papal voice, the voice that matters most, spoke early. The voice belonged to the distinguished scholar Ricarda Huch, the bearer of a resounding title given to her by no less an authority than Thomas Mann. He called her the First Lady of Germany.

When the Nazis came to power in 1933, Ricarda Huch, by then heaped with laurels but still glamorously prominent as an enfant terrible, was the kind of illustrious Aryan name they wanted to keep enrolled in their academic institutions to help offset the gaps left by the expelled Jews. Already of a certain age but with plenty of a glittering career left in her, she nevertheless, and without hesitating for a moment, found the courage to tell the Nazis where they could put it. The composer Max von Schelling, president of the Prussian Academy of the Arts, received a letter from her in which she insisted that the "Germanness" the Nazis kept talking about was not her Germanness: *nicht mein Deutschtum.* Her point made, she retired into private life. It was a mark, of course, of Nazi Germany's relative porosity vis-à-vis the Soviet Union that it offered bolt holes in which it was possible to lie still and say nothing, as if silence were not treason. Had the regime lasted longer than its brief twelve years, Himmler's steadily growing SS imperium and Bormann's always more enveloping bureaucracy would have probably closed off the last chances of tacit dissent: as under Stalin, vociferous affirmation would have been the only survivable posture. But under the Third Reich a woman of Ricarda's age and authority could get away with holding her rulers in contempt, as long as she wasn't vocal about it. The housebound matriarch survived the war and resumed her career afterwards, living long enough to find her early works forgotten. With the relentless, and largely justified, left-wing critique of the old institutions increasingly establishing an unchallenged ascendancy, a scholarly achievement like hers was thought too bourgeois to be valuable. The First Lady of Germany was quietly lowered into the tomb of her own respectability. The Germans have a word for it: *Todgeschweigen.* Killed by not being mentioned.

But there was a paradox in the deathly hush, because the First Lady, when young, had been the First Vixen. Born too grand to be impressed by high society, Ricarda became an establishment figure only by default and by the lapse of years: as a girl she was a rebel, not to say a bit of a raver. Intellectually, she had begun as an admirer of Mussolini, not for his Fascist hegemony but for his rowdy anarchist origins. She had admired Bakunin for the same reason. Emotionally, she was a feminist role-reverser *avant la lettre*. In Wilhelmine Germany, at a time of stifling conformity when the marriageability of young women was the quality that mattered most, she managed, by sheer force of character, to dish out to men the kind of treatment she would ordinarily have been expected to take. If women got in her way, they too were given short shrift. She stole her sister's husband without compunction and usually made a point of getting engaged to her suitors before giving them the elbow, just to ensure that they would have the humiliation to remember. She was a social revolutionary in the deepest sense: no party, not even the Sparticists, had a programme to match her behaviour. She was on her own. For her spiritual equivalent in modern times, you would have to imagine a combination of Germaine Greer, Billie Jean King and the London bluestocking Barbara Skelton, the fiery amalgam eventually cooling into the general shape of Muriel Spark, with overtones of Camille Paglia after the second cocktail.

It is doubtful, however, if the wild girl's pilgrim soul was ever tamed, even by time. One modern parallel that won't work is to attribute to her a Jane Fonda–like anabasis from one mould of progressive conformity to the next. Ricarda was never a conventional spirit looking for the display case of a radical context: she was always a genuine solo act. Her opinions were entirely hers and often uncomfortable to even the most wide-ranging liberal hierophant, as if she had been some kind of clerical surrealist out to shock with decontextualized opinions instead of sliced eyeballs and soft watches. In June 1943 she recorded in writing her profound enjoyment of her first air raid. It was the same month that Hamburg was incinerated. Thoughts of doom and retribution would have been more suitable, but Ricarda could not repress her delight that the full-colour spectacular had come to a cinema near her. "Finally Jena has had a sensation." In Berlin after the war she wandered the world of ruins—the *Trümmerwelt*—where it would have been permissible for the author of one of the most important books on the Thirty Years War to weep heavy tears for the downfall of a civilization. She loved it. Her aesthetic enthusiasm for the gutted buildings and heaped rubble was boundless. She was in her eighties at the time.

And that was the time when she wrote her encomium to the suicidal young nobles of July. It would do us good to remember that the old lady had lived a long life as they had not, and that she had lived it with originality as they might never have done. They were exactly the kind of stiff-necked, tight-trousered cadets to whom she had once so enjoyed giving the runaround. If she could salute them, so should we. She was, after all, absolutely right on every point in the paragraph. The boys never had a chance. Even if the apprentices had managed to kill their sorcerer, they could not have saved *Grossdeutschland*, which was going down to unconditional surrender no matter who led it. But even if they had known in advance that a coup would not work, they would still have been right to try. Henning von Tresckow, who knew more about the Killing Hitler business than anybody, guessed that the July 1944 plot was doomed but said it should go ahead anyway. He could only have meant that he saw it as a ceremony: a moment of honour that would be remembered when there was nothing else to remember except shame.

Ricarda was well aware that there were other and less charismatic people in the conspiracy apart from the glamorously uniformed *Hochadel* scions whose consciences had developed few notable doubts until military defeat became a certainty. There were obscure common- ers who had seen through Hitler from the beginning. What she meant by nobility was the sacrificial spirit that joined, in this one instance, the beautiful young men from the *Almanach de Gotha* and the plodding minor bureaucrats from the local council. She could take such a large view of nobility because she was noble herself. One of the marks of the natural aristocrat is that the brain, the centre of rationality, does not become detached from the viscera, the seat of moral judgement. As a student of German history—and a reader of her book on romanticism will wonder if there was ever a better student—she was well placed to assess the condition her country was in during the Weimar Republic, and to understand the appeal that a strongman might have to those con- servative forces who feared a Bolshevik insurrection beyond anything else. But she had only to see the Nazis in action to know exactly what they were, and when they invited her to join them she had only one answer to give. Millions of dead bodies later, those who equivocated were slow to mention her name. Their reluctance was understandable, and remains easy to share. Conscious that we, too, might have found no uncompromising path through a moral maze, we would all like to believe that there was no easy answer. And indeed there wasn't. But there was a clear one. It was to tell the Nazis to go chase themselves.

All it took was courage. But courage is hard to come by: as Ricarda's rococo c.v. suggests, to have buckets of guts you need to be a little bit mad. Hence the discomfort which haunts any of us who write about the subject: the malaise comes from our self-doubt, and the self-doubt is the surest sign that the murderers in black uniforms are still with us. It is almost as disturbing that a woman like Ricarda Huch is still with us, but if we seek reassurance about human dignity instead of mere acceptance of human weakness, we must face up to her, and try to remember why Judas found it so hard to look into the face of Christ—not because of the divine serenity that was there, but because of the self-seeking calculation that was not.

✶ ✶ ✶

Ernst Jünger

ERNST JÜNGER

‼ ‼ ‼

Ernst Jünger was born in Heidelberg in 1895 and reached maturity just in time to volunteer for service in World War I, during which his bravery won him the Pour le Mérite, Germany's highest military decoration. After the war, his book *In Stahlgewittern* (*Storm of Steel*) launched him on a literary career that amounts to as big a problem for the student of twentieth-century humanism as Bertolt Brecht's. In Jünger's case, however, the problem came from the other direction. Jünger emerged from the trenches as a believer in national strength, which he thought threatened by liberal democracy. Though he never gave his full allegiance to the Nazis, he was glad to accept military rank in the Wehrmacht, and wrote approvingly about the invasion of France, in which he accompanied one of the forward units. After the plot against Hitler's life in July 1944 he fell under suspicion, but his prestige and his Pour le Mérite made him untouchable. Never an active conspirator, he thought he was fulfilling his duty to civilized values merely by despising Hitler. The thought of killing him did not occur. In his post-war years, Jünger wrote contemptuously against the apparatchiks of the East German regime, who found it easy to condemn him for his right-wing track record, describing him in their official literary lexicon as "an especially dangerous exponent of West German militaristic and neofascist literature." Having missed his first chance to identify a totalitarian enemy in good time, he didn't miss the second. Demonstrating powers of compression and evocation that could pack a treatise into a paragraph, his two collections of linked short essays, *Auf den Marmorklippen* (*On the Marble Cliffs*) and *Das abenteuerliches Herz* (The Adventurous Heart), are the easiest introduction to his literary talent and political vision. The talent is unquestionable. The vision is quite otherwise. But when he finally realized what Hitler had done in pursuit of the same ideal of strength that he had himself cherished, even he was obliged to consider that his espousal of Darwin (the struggle for existence) and Nietzsche (the will to power) might have depended on some sort of liberal context for its rational expression. He died in 1998, his name much honoured, with good reason, and much in dispute, for a better one.

> Things like that belong to the style of the times.
> — ERNST JÜNGER, *KAUKASISCHE
> AUFZEICHNUNGEN* (CAUCASIAN NOTES)

WHEN IT COMES to a great offence, a phrase like "the style of the times" can be self-serving, because it removes the obligation to place blame. Even before Hitler launched Germany on a catastrophic war, Jünger should have been able to assess the toxicity of the Nazis by the intellectual quality of some of the people who were trying to get beyond their reach. In retrospect, his phrase "the style of the times" enrols itself among many euphemisms that served to sanitize the effects of the Nazi impact even on the learned professions. Jünger, as an Aryan, was safe from that impact. He should have cared more about what happened to those less privileged. A learned man himself, Jünger knew all their names: even the names of the minor figures, the spear carriers and walk-ons. In the late 1930s, in a race for a foreign chair of philology, the obscure Victor Klemperer was beaten to a safe seat in Ankara by the illustrious Erich Auerbach. If Klemperer had secured the prize instead, and got away to safety, it is unlikely that he would have written anything with the bold scope of Auerbach's *Mimesis*. We should not romanticize Klemperer because of what he went through: millions did. But we are compelled to admire him for what he made of it. Compared to Auerbach, Klemperer was a plodder. Fated to stay where he was, however, he was granted the dubious reward of experiencing from close up what the Nazis did to the German language: an instructive, if disheartening, philological field. Some of Klemperer's conclusions are loosely distributed through his indispensable two-volume diary, published in English as *I Shall Bear Witness* and *To the Bitter End*. But most are tightly contained in a separate book assembled after the war out of the notes he somehow managed to make and keep during it: *LTI*. (The initials stand for *Lingua tertii imperii*—Language of the Third Empire—a bitter scholarly pun.) As a Jew in the Third Empire, Klemperer was allowed no new books or newspapers. He wasn't even allowed to listen to the radio. But he picked up the new usages at second hand. Reading his analysis, we can only conclude that the Nazis wrecked the language they had usurped. They wrecked it with euphemism: they spoke and wrote the officialese of slaughter.

But we should not delude ourselves that an Aryan non-Nazi, no matter how exalted his intellect, could exercise the privilege of remaining uninfected. Ernst Jünger is a case in point: perhaps *the* case in point, because he was incomparably the most gifted writer to remain on the scene. In his wartime diaries, the strange usage isolated in my opening quotation keeps on cropping up. It centres on a single word. The word is *Zeitstil*: "the style of the times." In early December 1942 we find Jünger visiting the Russian front. He hears about dreadful things happening to Russian prisoners. First of all he convinces himself that the prisoners are partisans, and can thus expect no quarter. When this thesis starts to look shaky, he convinces himself of something else: that both sides are behaving dreadfully, and it all belongs to "the style of the times." Later on in the same month, he hears from a general (the generals were always at home to Jünger, whose prestige was immense) that the Jews are being slaughtered. Jünger's reaction is: "The old chivalry is dead: wars from now on will be waged by technologists." Once again, it is the style of the times. And so it was, but not in the way he meant it.

Jünger had lent his literary gift to the idea of German militaristic renewal. Until the news about the extermination camps was finally and unmistakably read to him by a German general in 1943, no amount of horrifying truth could induce him fully to admit that he had made a mistake. His way out of such an admission was to blame the style of the times: i.e., to console himself with the belief that everyone was at it, led back to barbarism by the modern spirit of technology. The style of the times was a powerfully useful idea. It didn't even need to be put into words. It could be put into silence. In his elegant, learned and finally disgraceful *Notes Towards the Definition of Culture*, published in 1948, T. S. Eliot simply declined to admit that the Holocaust might be a pertinent topic in a discussion of what had happened to Europe. Closer to the scene but equally untouched, Eliot's admirer and colleague Ernst Robert Curtius achieved a similar feat of inattention. If pressed on the point, both savants would have blamed the new technological order: the style of the times. But there was no such thing as the style of the times, except in the sense that they themselves personified: a style of not concerning themselves with the catastrophic results of a political emphasis they had been given ample opportunity to recognize as the first and most deadly enemy of the humanist culture they claimed to represent. The humble Victor Klemperer, if they had been forcibly reminded of his name, would have been dismissed as small beer by both of them. Ernst Jünger would have behaved better. To give him the respect he has coming, he finally realized that the massacre of the Jews could not be wished away. But he never quite gave up on the airy notion that the style of the times was to blame for things like that.

K

❦ ❦ ❦

Franz Kafka

John Keats

Leszek Kolakowski

Alexandra Kollontai

Heda Margolius Kovaly

Karl Kraus

FRANZ KAFKA

❧ ❧ ❧

Franz Kafka was born in Prague in 1883 and died in Berlin in 1924. In his brief four decades alive he created a body of work that has influenced almost everything written since: not even James Joyce had such an impact. Kafka was trained as a lawyer and was first employed in Prague's Workers' Accident Insurance Institution. This experience probably laid the foundations for his evocation of bureaucracy and the plight of the individual caught up in the remorseless logic of an irrational system. (J. P. Stern's short book about Kafka is predicated on the view that Kafka's supposedly fantastic vision was largely an account of reality; and it is a measure of the unsettling power generated by Kafka's magic spell that Stern's view is commonly regarded as wilfully paradoxical.) As a Jew, Kafka also had first-hand knowledge from birth of how it felt to be faced with exclusions and unpassable tests with ever-changing rules. But his vision of state terror lay deep in a psychology personal to him. Since the Nazi era need never have happened, to say that he prophesied it is actually a belittlement of his creative achievement, and only one step up from saying that he caused the whole thing. But nobody could now read *The Trial* without thinking of the Soviet show trials, or the short works *Metamor-*

343

phosis and *In the Penal Colony* without thinking of death camps. The novels for which he is now most famous—*The Trial, The Castle* and *Amerika*—were all published posthumously, against Kafka's wishes that they should be destroyed. (Often derided as a giftless and interfering parasite on Kafka, his friend Max Brod was in fact responsible for ignoring Kafka's instructions, preserving his books, and thus giving us the genius that we know today.) Kafka's very order for the immolation of his work could have been missed by the keepers of *The Castle*, a book which has been usefully defined as a *Pilgrim's Progress* whose pilgrim does not progress. Beginners reading in English can place sufficient trust in the translations by Edwin and Willa Muir to be sure that they will get something vital from reading *Metamorphosis, In the Penal Colony* and *The Castle*. But just how Kafka should ideally be translated remains a question, best tackled by Milan Kundera in the relevant sections of his *Testaments Betrayed*. Philip Roth is another important novelist who writes illuminatingly about Kafka. Writings on the subject by scholars and critics are without number, but perhaps the best single short essay is by George Steiner, collected in Louis Kronenberg's indispensable *Brief Lives: A Biographical Companion to the Arts*. The best way to approach Kafka, however, is probably just to plunge into *The Castle* and get lost. Getting lost and staying lost is the whole idea of the book, and a matchless symbol for how, according to Kafka, we really feel underneath, when we momentarily convince ourselves that we know what's going on, while still suspecting that the momentary conviction might be part of the deception.

How short life must be, if something so fragile
can last a lifetime.
— KAFKA

KAFKA WAS TALKING about a young woman's body. Along with the anguish, there is an unmanning tenderness in the statement, and the tenderness should be remembered when we consider what a tangle the whole business of sex was for Kafka, who never quite got away from the idea that the consummation of sexual desire, if it should ever happen, would be *Schmutz*—something dirty. We need to remind ourselves that a man can be in that condition and still find inspiration in desire. If that had not been so for Kafka, he would never have said this. Anything Kafka said gained so much weight in the light of events that it is hard to extract it from history. Here is one thing he said, how-ever, that has its true setting in eternity. History tells us that many of the pretty female bodies on which he helplessly doted were consumed by fire before their time. Eternity tells us that he would have been right anyway, even if the disaster had never happened. The heavenly expres-sion before us will last only as long as a life.

"Just so long," as Louis MacNeice put it, "but long enough." Desire can be repressed to the point of extinction, but it is still the wellspring. As we saw when discussing Peter Altenberg, there is nothing "only" about it. Nietzsche said that sexuality saturates the consciousness all the way to the top. In European literature, ever since the poetry of courtly love first codified the *visione amorosa*, the identification of desire and revelation has been common currency. We can think of Wagner's emphasis on redemption as an attempt to separate the flower from its roots, but he could have had no such aim if he had not felt the connec-tion as a fact. If the fact is a myth, it is a myth that all cultivated mankind shares, so it is a fact anyway. When we stumble across another literature in which the fact is lacking, we tend to find that literature perverted rather than primitive. Our assumption is that the whole idea was there from the beginning, one of the first things in the mind, perhaps even before religion: primordial. We might even think that civilization began at that point, when the individual was first seen to embody the univer-sal. It brought endless trouble: when Menelaus and Paris both burned for Helen, Troy burned with them, and Pascal was making a powerful point when he suggested that history might have turned out differently if Cleopatra's nose had been a different length. Men have always been fools for beauty. But without being bowled over in the first place, they would never have begun to be wise. Sex, the most powerful instinct, generates the most closely focused attention: so that we see, in the desired other, the proof that creation is a miracle. Men who see the proof ten times at every pedestrian crossing are no doubt foolish, but men who see it only in their own shaving mirrors are generally agreed to be suffering from a case of arrested development.

For the narrator of *The Castle*, the girl Frieda is his only connection with a sane order of events as he reluctantly but steadily realizes, in the opening section of the book, that the castle has a mind of its own, and the mind will marshal infinite resources to shut him out. In Frieda's arms he can momentarily believe that she, at least, is not doing what the castle wants. The lovers soon find that they can't go to sleep together without expecting to find spectators gathered around them when they wake up. Even during their first sexual encounter there are probably other people in the room: it is hard to tell, but one of the novel's mechanisms is not to permit us to rule out such a possibility. Much later, in *Nineteen Eighty-Four*, Orwell reprised the same relationship of physical love to hopeless odds. Orwell wanted the tenderness reduced to raw sex: Winston Smith presses Julia to admit that the act itself is enough, as if Orwell was looking for a touchstone, an irreducible impulse that the totalitarian state cannot eliminate even by control. But for Kafka, the touchstone is the tenderness. Presciently, Kafka's nightmare state is even more controlled than Orwell's. "You ask if there are control officials?" asks the *Vorsteher* (superintendent) rhetorically. "There are *only* control officials." But Kafka creates Frieda as a whole personality, not just a symbol. As a personality, she wilts under the pressure of what she and K. are up against: her beauty fades. Under the influence of the *Wirtin* (innkeeper's wife), Frieda reinterprets K.'s involvement with her as a stratagem for getting nearer to the castle. K. rebuts her, but he can't refute her. How can he be sure? All he can be sure of is that he is robbing her of her vitality. Merely from the psychology of Frieda's accusations—which any man who has stood accused by a woman will recognize—it would be one of the great scenes in Kafka, and thus in all modern literature. But to see how magnificent it is, we should look through it, into Kafka's heart. K. hates having reduced her to this, and it is because he loves her. Rather than see her destroyed, he is even ready to contemplate that she might regain her position with Klamm—the inexorable and suitably mysterious figure of authority—thus to restore her credit with the castle. K. knows that he spells danger for Frieda, and he wants her safe.

Allegorical interpretations of Kafka's major novels are no doubt valid—with the usual proviso that if they are all valid they might all be irrelevant—but for once the biographical element begs to be brought in. In real life, Kafka sent his imagination to rest in the minds of women. If he had not done so, his fiction would have been less different: more like ordinary fiction, and less like fact—the facts that were yet to happen. There are good reasons for believing that he could prophesy the nature of the totalitarian state because as a Jew he had already lived with its mechanisms of exclusion, the first parts of the totalitarian state to develop: he knew them so intimately, and thought them to be so pervasive, that he came to agree with them, providing one of our most tragic examples of self-directed *Judenhass*. But much of the prophetic element in Kafka comes from his extreme sensitivity to evanescence, and that sensitivity was centred squarely on what time could do to a woman's life. Milena Jesenská, the woman worthy of his intellect, was wooed from the distance at which she was kept. Felice Bauer (on whom the Frieda of the book was probably based) never had a chance: even if a marriage had followed upon the repeated engagements, nothing would have happened. Kafka thought sex was a disease. But he also thought that it was a gift, or he would not have asked himself, only a short time before his death: "What have you done with the gift of sex?" (*Was hast du mit dem Geschenk des Geschlechtes getan?* You can hear the integrative rhythmic force of his prose even at the moment of resignation.) We hope that Dora Dymant, with whom he shared a brief spell of happiness in Berlin, would have said that he had done at least something with it. And he would never have written to Milena with his desperate complaint about the certainty of their never living together *Körper an Körper* (body to body) if he had not wanted that above all things, even in his consuming fear of the wish coming true.

JOHN KEATS

❡ ❡ ❡

John Keats (1795–1821) exemplifies the difference between the past and yesterday. Wordsworth and Coleridge are in the past. Even Browning, who came later and who in so many ways was a prototype of what we call the modern, is still in the past. But Keats, like Byron, is just yesterday. Every modern poet is obliged to have a view on Keats, as if he were part of the living competition. Sometimes an adverse view is even more packed with cherished information than an approving one. (Collected in his deliberately provocative book *What Became of Jane Austen? And Other Questions*, Kingsley Amis's essay on Keats is a fine example of the critical attack that brings out every virtue.) A searching critique of Keats could be built up just from what he wrote about himself, especially in his *Letters*, collected into a book which outstrips even Rilke's *Letters to a Young Poet* as a document that goes to the centre of the poetic life. Keats's observation on the unnecessarily high quality of Shakespeare's "bye-writing" is an example of how the young writer could bring to the examination of language the same analytical intensity with which he examined the world. It was a quality he shared with Pushkin: their lives overlapped, but they didn't know about each other. They might, however, have shared the one mind when it came to precocity of technique, the technique beyond technique, the technique that includes every modulation of the natural speaking voice; and with both it is necessary to remember that they died at the beginning of their careers, not at the end. The forbearance that we bring to Shelley; the astonishment that we bring to Büchner and Radiguet; the sense of being robbed by fate that we bring to Masaccio and Bizet; we must bring all these things to Keats, or miss the full point about the arbitrary fate that leaves us thinking of him as a promise only partially fulfilled. We should also remember that Keats, like Chekhov and Schnitzler later on, was trained in medicine at a time when medicine could not yet cure tuberculosis: he lived and died, that is, in a time when it was normal for talent to be killed at random. In the modern age we don't regard that as normal, even when it is common. Hence our outrage when it happens, and the permanent indignation with which we find it so much harder to come to terms than our ancestors did with mere regret.

Nothing is finer for the purposes of great productions than
a very gradual ripening of the intellectual powers.
— KEATS TO HIS BROTHER,
JANUARY 23, 1818

COMING FROM KEATS, the remark was either generous or nervous. On any objective estimate, he was a prodigy: and a prodigy not just on the level of raw verbal talent, but in the breadth and reasonableness of his mind. (There is a striking contrast here with Shelley, who was rarely reasonable even when brilliant.) Given all the qualities at a young age, it would have been large of Keats to envy the plodders who acquire them, if at all, only over time. Or it would have been large of him had he known how blessed he was. But perhaps he thought he wasn't, in which case he was being jumpy. We tend to think he was jumpy, because we tend to believe Byron had something when he mocked Keats for letting bad reviews get to him: the mind, that very fiery particle . . . snuffed out by an article. (Because the rhyme clicked, the barb stuck: a couplet, like a caricature, can set the terms of discussion far into the future.)

But nobody who lacked a solid inner artistic confidence could have written the Odes. When I was first in London, a fair copy in Keats's best hand of the "Ode to a Nightingale" was on display in a glass cabinet in his house. His best hand was a thing of sculptural beauty, like Petrarch's, Rilke's or Rimbaud's. Though the ink looked barely dry, the ode might as well have been chiselled into a slab of marble. Lack of confidence was not his problem. He would just have liked to live, thrive and grow wise. There is no good reason to believe that he would not have gone on developing: there are reasons, but they are all bad. Kingsley Amis left that consideration of Keats's possible future development aside, as if it didn't matter. Not normally prey to obtuseness, Amis should have taken warning from a previous example. F. R. Leavis had done the same for Shelley, with plainly ludicrous results, because the unastonishing conclusion of Leavis's essay was that Shelley was not as good as Shakespeare. A Swiftian method of textual comparison was used to establish this. Leavis's owlish judgement obviously meant nothing without a consideration of whether Shelley, had he lived, might not conceivably have got a bit better. Amis at least conceded that Keats's initial charm was Shakespearean in its buttonholing melodic effect. Amis, indeed, said that no English reader could know much about poetry who did not think at some time in his life that Keats, because of the initial impact of his verbal music, was the greatest poet in English after Shakespeare. But Amis definitely meant that it had to be an early time in the reader's life: that an enthusiasm for Keats was a callow enthusiasm, because the poetry was callow poetry. Even if Amis was right on the point, it is hard to see why Keats's poetry, had he lived, should not have grown more mature. Keats might have had everything, but he still needed time. He knew that within himself. Only twenty-six years old, he died knowing it, and should surely be granted the validity of his own insight. Today's young tourists of a literary bent, when they pass, on the Spanish Steps in Rome, the window of his last resting place, are being granted an insight into the fearful realities of a world without antibiotics.

Degas said he was more interested in talent at forty than in talent at twenty. We think the remark good because of our general conviction that anyone who credits himself with a vocation should prove it by staying the course. Keats's remark fits into that view, so it, too, wins our approval. But in fairness we should not forget the artists who reached such an intensity and complication of achievement at an early age that we can think of them as fulfilled even if they died young. Masaccio and Seurat are the two clearest cases in painting. In literature the French seem to specialize in the phenomenon of the nonpareil prodigy: during the Revolution they had André Chénier, whose neo-classical measures were certainly the complete product even if he himself was not, and in modern times they had both Radiguet and Alain-Fournier. The German language boasts the most amazing literary prodigy of all: Büchner, whose *Dantons Tod* sums up the lifetime's political experience of a man sixty years older than its author—Burckhardt might have written its last act. In music, Mozart and Chopin were old stagers compared with Schubert and Bellini, dead at thirty-one and thirty-three, respectively. Speculation about what Schubert and Bellini might have done had they lived can continue for ever, but despite Alfred Einstein's warning that we ought not to think of the brilliant young dead musicians as in any way complete, we do in fact think of them as complete artistic personalities: we don't think, "Well, that was a beautiful piece from the man who one day would have been Schubert" or "What a pity that '*Prendi l'annell' ti dono*' betrays none of the restrained coherence that a fully developed Bellini might have given it." We think of them, that is, in the same way as we think of Rimbaud, who lived out his life; but who, as an artist, really was *frühvollendet*, to use Einstein's word—completed early. The question is whether Keats would have been the same: a prodigy who, had he lived, would have gone no further. Surely our only reason for entertaining that notion is that he was so very, very good, and we find it uncomfortable to contemplate how rich his career might have been had he been allowed to live it through. It might have realigned the whole history of English literature by giving it a second apex: a turn-up for the books.

There is also the consideration that when we go back even so short a distance as to the early nineteenth century—only a few generations— we have already moved out of our time, the time of arbitrary premature death from politics, and entered something even more frightening by our standards, the time of arbitrary premature death from disease.

The American philosopher Charles Pierce, in the title of his best-known book, had a phrase that captured the resulting dilemma: *Values in a Universe of Chance*. Looking back to the long pre-modern human era when life was valued at a pin's fee, we should be careful, as critics of the arts, not to take with us our sense of a reasonable expectation of health and longevity. We need to cultivate a feeling for the suddenness and randomness of God's wrath, because it is almost certainly true that the urge of genius towards artistic coherence was in reaction to exactly that. With Keats, though the age of preventive medicine was arriving—as a physician, he would have been part of it—we are still in that old continuity. When we see, as his powers of evocation make us bound to see, the mental picture of his nymph's filmy clothes sliding down her body on the Eve of St. Agnes, we are seeing the living body with such intensity because of the intensity with which he saw dead bodies in the dissecting room. The dark knowledge behind his light moments was once the constant background radiation behind all creative life. As Louis MacNeice said of the ancient world, "It was all so unimaginably different, and all so long ago." But we have to imagine it, or else lose our grip on the past. What we need is a trick of the mind, unobtainable with any known drug, by which we can imagine how it must have felt when the only possible way to view reality without the benefit of religious faith was to despair. Imagining that, we will find it easier to realize why Lucretius committed suicide, although even harder to believe that he should have composed the presciently realistic *De rerum natura* before he subtracted himself from the game of chance whose full arbitrariness he had so bravely faced. Many poets before Keats had caught his tone of realism, but he sustained it, and one of the most remarkable of his many precocities is that he intensified it, all the way to the end. The end came too soon and much of his realism was veiled in romance, but underneath the romance he saw things as they were, and wrote them down as if to record the texture of life were his deepest compulsion. He probably felt the same way about dying, but he could no longer lift his pen.

LESZEK KOLAKOWSKI

❦ ❦ ❦

Leszek Kolakowski was born in Radom, Poland, in 1927. As an unduly inquisitive professor of philosophy at the University of Warsaw he was first of all ejected from the Communist Party in 1966 and finally expelled from academic life in 1968. In exile he was variously a visiting professor at the universities of Montreal, Yale and California (Berkeley), and, in the long term, a Fellow of All Souls College in Oxford. His three-volume treatise *Main Currents of Marxism* is one of the most important, and luckily also one of the most readable, twentieth-century books on the theory of politics. (Students who find Karl Popper's *The Open Society and Its Enemies* a hard and repetitious slog will have no such difficulties with Kolakowski.) The three volumes of *Main Currents* progress chronologically from Marx's own lifetime to those crucial years after Stalin's death when the dream, somehow deprived of energy by the subtraction of its nightmare element, was already showing signs of coming to an end, in Europe at least. In its third volume, entitled *The Breakdown*, theory is backed up with the harsh realities of practice, because Kolakowski is talking about the period he himself lived through, and was lucky to survive. In this repect, Kolakowski's observational scope will remind the

reader of the Russsian professor of sociology Aleksandr
Zinoviev, another academic who was obliged to carry with him
into exile a bitter first-hand knowledge of his subject.
Kolakowski's analysis of Marxist logic is as penetrating as Raymond Aron's in *The Opium of the Intellectuals* but it attains a
wider resonance by extending itself to the individual personalities of those thinkers who espoused the cause and were distorted by it. Prominent among these was Georg Lukács: the
potential student could start with the pages on Lukács and
arrive straight away at the fulcrum of Kolakowski's view. Like
many a political analyst who was born to serve a socialist hegemony but lived to question it, Kolakowski developed and har-
boured an increasingly rich nostalgic regard for the lost civil
order. His slim but rich *Le Village introuvable* (1986) puts a
Burkean emphasis on the indispensibility of an inherited social
fabric and insists that the so-called global village will always
remain a pipe dream: a cautionary message that applies to our
cybernetic future just as much as to his collectivist past. The
beginning reader should not be too quick to assume, however,
that an argument billed as an anti-Marxist polemic must automatically favour social conservatism: some of Kolakowski's
principles are radical enough, the most subversive of them
being that the individual intellect, whatever its learned scope
and range of interpretation, has no inbuilt safeguards against a
hardening into sclerotic orthodoxy. He thus gives any university student not just a licence, but an imperative, to stay on the
alert against authority.

> Lukács is perhaps the most striking example in the
> twentieth century of what may be called the betrayal of
> reason by those whose profession is to use and defend it.
> — LESZEK KOLAKOWSKI, *MAIN CURRENTS*
> *OF MARXISM*, VOL. 3, P. 307

I F KARL POPPER had not traced the irreparable faults in the cir-
cuitry of Marxism, Leszek Kolakowski would have done it. In his

Main Currents of Marxism, the third volume (the one to read first) sums up what happened to Marxism in the twentieth century, and proves it to be a case of Marxism happening to defenceless people. Georg Lukács was Hungary's gift to the international delusion (slow to die even though Stalin didn't like it either) that serious literary studies might serve progressive ideological ends. In the Communist world there were hundreds of thousands of intellectuals who were doomed to the status of victim, but Lukács rated even above the Soviet cultural commisar Lunacharsky (who, in the 1920s, was first of all given the job of encouraging the avant-garde artists and then, later on, the job of bringing them to heel) in the sad category of intellectuals doomed to the status of perpetrator. What made Lukács doubly pathetic was that he could never quite stop trying to talk himself into it even after he had done it: a trick of the mind which Kolakowski analyses with a fine touch. Kolakowski makes such an example of Lukács because Lukács was a true intellectual: an intellectual of real culture in a context of dogmatists without any. Bukharin counted as a thinker among the old Bolsheviks because he could make a general statement about the connection of music to economics: nobody would be able to play the piano, he pointed out, if there were no pianos. Compared with that sort of thing, Lukács was a humanist. But he was a Jesuit humanist, which was what Thomas Mann made him in *The Magic Mountain*, where the character called Naphta reflects Lukács's insatiable need for a totalitarian system in which he could immerse himself by developing a theoretical justification for its hegemony. (Briefly serving as minister of culture in the Imre Nagy government of 1956, Lukács was duly deported to Romania by the Russians and had a ringside seat while almost all his colleagues were murdered. His conclusion was that Stalinism was a mere aberration in the triumphant story of socialism.) Kolakowski can assess the range of Lukács's culture, and therefore measure the depth to which he sank.

Kolakowski's combination of critical rigour and humane sympathy is yet another reminder of what we owe Poland. If history could begin again, Poland's contribution and sacrifice would both be too much to ask of any nation of so small a size. (For Poland to escape its fate, geography would have to begin again: between Germany and Russia was simply the wrong place for a smallish country to be.) Poland gave us too many examples of what the twentieth century could do when all its destructive forces were unleashed at once. Some of the losses were our gains. Poland gave us a set of glittering literary exiles: Witold Gombrowicz, Czeslaw Milosz and my personal favourite among all the world's literary critics, Marcel Reich-Ranicki. But, in his best-selling autobiography *Mein Leben*, Reich-Ranicki reminds us about the Polish literati whom we never got to hear of even vaguely. One of them was Julian Tuwim, a poet of "incomparable many-sidedness" who, while he escaped being murdered, did not escape oblivion—the world still hasn't heard of him. Unnamed young Polish mathematicians gave us the first clues to the Enigma machine, and thus to the Ultra secret that saved Europe from Nazi domination. Other losses were dead losses: the world gained nothing except cautionary tales. Poland gave us Bruno Schulz, perhaps the single most unbearable modern example of talent laid waste in midlife. It gave us the Katyn massacre: a whole generation of gifted young men wiped out at once, and buried without even the opportunity of rest, because one of the only two forces physically capable of such a deed spent decades befouling the air by trying to pin it on the other. (The Russians did it; the Nazis accused them of it; and for decades the Russians were exonerated because it was the Nazis who did the accusing.) But as Michael Burleigh reminds us in his essential book *The Third Reich*, we should not always be looking at the talented.

In Poland the whole of ordinary life was distorted: everything that had given rise to a civilization and helped to sustain it was rooted out. After the collapse of the Soviet bloc, there was a general expectation in the West that there would be a sudden cultural efflorescence in the East. It was thought that Poland would produce a dozen young versions of the film director Andrezj Wajda, for example. Only gradually was it realized that things don't work that way. A figure like Wajda was never a precursor of a free-market future: he lived in an air pocket of the liberal past which had somehow managed to hold itself together in the surrounding miasma. The films that made him famous were made in the rare periods when the grip of the regime relaxed. (By the time that I first watched *Ashes and Diamonds* in the late 1950s, the comparatively tolerant conditions that had allowed Wajda to make the film were already hardening again into orthodoxy.) The merit of Kolakowski is that he tells us where the miasma came from. Karl Popper, Raymond Aron and the other sociological analysts show how Marxism affected everything at the practical level. Kolakowski does an even better job than Isaiah Berlin of showing how it affected everything at the mental level. Except to the extent that a clear explanation always offers a kind of encouragement, volume 3 of *Main Currents of Marxism* makes depressing reading: but it can be recommended for all those of us who grew up in sheltered circumstances. It was an encouraging sign, towards the end of the twentieth century, that Kolakowski's conclusions got into the general conversation about politics—and especially about constitutional politics, in which the effect of his sceptical view of holistic intellectual innovation was to encourage a salutary dab on the brake pedal.

> "We rebelled by criminal methods against the
> joyfulness of the new life."
> — LESZEK KOLAKOWSKI QUOTING BUKHARIN
> AT HIS TRIAL, IN *MAIN CURRENTS OF
> MARXISM*, VOL. 3, P. 82

Kolakowski is surely right to pick this confession by the Old Bolshevik Bukharin as the definitive moment of the 1938 Moscow show trials. Onlookers who fell for Bukharin's big moment would fall for anything. There were sharp onlookers who did, however. Dorothy Parker, the once and future drama critic and lifelong analyst of bogus language, thought that the trials were authentic. More interestingly, there were sceptics who still fell some of the way. Arthur Koestler, whose *Darkness at Noon* was really based on the Bukharin case, thought that Bukharin could have told such a lie only out of the belief that it might benefit the cause. Koestler's novel, nominally dedicated to discrediting the Soviet Union, thus held out a crumb of comfort to its admirers in the West: there must have been a cause to believe in. The crumb of comfort helped to sustain sympathizers for another eighteen years, until Khrushchev, at the Twentieth Party Congress in 1956, revealed that no such sophisticated interpretation of Bukharin's performance had ever been necessary. The Old Bolsheviks' ludicrous confessions had been beaten into them. (Bukharin, apparently, did not need to be tortured: a threat to the lives of his wife and little son was enough to do the trick.)

After Khrushchev blew the gaff, the international left intelligentsia had
no choice but to give up on the idea that the terror in the late 1930s
had been at some level a necessary stage in the building of socialism.
But there was still, and still is, a reluctance to believe that the Soviet
Union had been like that from the beginning. Bukharin had always
been well aware of the horrors that underlay the joyfulness of the new
life. During one or another of the Party purges, Brecht delivered himself of the opinion that the more innocent the Party members were, the
more they deserved to suffer. The charitable, and probably correct,
interpretation of his remark is that he meant there was no such thing
as an innocent Party member: if they had faithfully done their duty,
they were necessarily guilty. (An uncharitable interpretation must follow the charitable one: if Brecht realized that the Party conspired
against the people, why did he support it?) Though Bukharin's lifeless
prose style pioneered the *langue de bois* that Stalin would later bring to
an eerie perfection, he was certainly a shining light of humanism compared with the rest of the top echelon of the Old Bolsheviks. Surviving
members of the pre-revolutionary intelligentsia thought he might
intervene for them or their relatives if only he could be reached. But
he helped to build the nightmare, whose countless innocent victims
have a far better right than he does to be spoken of in tragic terms.

ALEXANDRA KOLLONTAI

❧ ❧ ❧

Alexandra Mikhaylovna Kollontai (1872–1952) was born and raised in comfortable circumstances in old St. Petersburg; rebelled against her privileges on behalf of women and the poor; and was exiled to Germany in 1908. During World War I she travelled in the U.S.A., preaching socialism rather in the manner that an American feminist like Naomi Klein would nowadays preach against globalization when travelling in Europe. Upon the outbreak of revolution in Russia in 1917, Kollontai returned home, where she served the Soviet government first as a commissar for public welfare, then in a succession of foreign ministerial and ambassadorial posts. She was the regime's recognized expert on women's rights: special rights, that is, in a state where there were no general ones. She was thus the twentieth century's clearest early case of the fundamental incompatibility between feminism and ideology. Feminism is a claim for impartial justice, and all ideologies deny that such a term has meaning. Kollontai managed to live with the contradiction, but only because she was unusually adroit when it came to aligning herself with the prevailing power. Her dogged service to a regime that condemned large numbers of innocent women to grim death has rarely resulted in her being criticized by left-wing feminists in the West. The pattern, alas, continues today, especially when it comes to the spurious alliance between feminism and multiculturalism, an ideology which necessarily contains within itself a claimed right to confine women to their traditional subservience. Against the mountain of historical evidence that left-wing ideology has been no friend of feminism, there is some comfort to be drawn from the fact that fascism was even less friendly: Hitlerite Germany, in particular, did little to release women from their traditional typecasting. But it remains sad that women who seek a release for their sisters from the crushing definition of a biological role have always found so many bad friends among those theoretically wedded to the betterment of the working class. Readers of Spanish might care to look at a file of Cuba's *Bohemia* magazine for 1959, the year of Castro's revolution. The yellowing pages are full of stories about the heroic women who fought and suffered beside all those famous beards for the liberation of their island from tyranny and backwardness. How many of those women ever became part of the government? At least Kollontai got a job, and perhaps she and the Soviet Union she so loyally served both merit a small salute for that.

> The masses do not believe in the Opposition. They greet
> its every statement with laughter. Does the Opposition
> think that the masses have such a short memory? If there
> are shortcomings in the Party and its political line, who
> else besides these prominent members of the Opposition
> were responsible for them?
> —ALEXANDRA KOLLONTAI, "THE
> OPPOSITION AND THE PARTY RANK AND
> FILE," IN *SELECTED WRITINGS*, P. 313

A FAMOUS FIGURE AMONG the Old Bolsheviks, Alexandra Kollontai was a sad case, and sadder still because it is so hard to weep for her. Her career is a harsh reminder that feminism is, or should be, a demand for justice, not an ideology. It should not consider itself an ideology and it should be very slow to ally itself with any other ideology, no matter how progressive that other ideology might claim to be. Kollontai was an acute and lastingly valuable analyst of the restrictions and frustrations imposed on women by the conventional morality of bourgeois society. Fifty years later, Betty Friedan and Germaine Greer did not say much that Kollontai had not said first, even if they said it better—as they were bound to do, because they were proposing feasible modifications to a society already developed, whereas she was trying to make herself heard over the roar of chaos. Armed with her hard-won awareness of how injustice for women had been institutionalized in the bourgeois civil order, she thought that the Russian Revolution, the universal solvent of all institutions, would give feminism its chance. She spent the next thirty-five years finding out just how wrong she was. From the viewpoint of the slain, the best that can be said for her is that she backed the regime for a good reason. Unfortunately she backed the regime no matter how murderous it became. This outburst from 1927 is really a declaration of faith in Stalin, making an appearance under his other name, "the masses." "The Opposition" were those brave few among the Old Bolsheviks who still dared to question him, starting with Trotsky. As always, it is advisable to note that Trotsky, the butcher of the sailors at Kronstadt, was no humanitarian. Only a few years further up the line, he actually thought that Stalin's treatment of the peasants sinned through leniency. But it was obvious at the time that any conflict among the leaders had nothing to do with principle: it was a power struggle, with absolute power as the prize. Kollontai was weighing in unequivocally on the side of an infallible party with an unchallengeable leader.

A textual scholar might say that she was taking a conscious risk when she wrote: "If there are shortcomings in the Party and its political line . . ." It is quite easy to imagine a Lubyanka interrogator asking her: "Oh yes, and what shortcomings are those?" But the interrogation never came. Kollontai managed to stay alive, partly by spending as much time as possible on diplomatic duties in Norway, Sweden and Finland. (Talleyrand said, "He who is absent is wrong." In the Soviet Union, however, being absent was often the key to survival.) She died in 1952, shortly before her eightieth birthday, with two Orders of the

Red Banner to her credit, if credit that was. The terrible truth was that the only real equality made available to women in the Soviet Union of her time was the equal opportunity to be a slave labourer. Her dreamed-of principle was "winged Eros," love set free. The Soviet actuality of love set free was a one-size-fits-all contraceptive diaphragm, with the overspill taken care of by serial abortions. In her early writings—just as charmless as the later ones but a touch more personal—she was already exploiting the standard *langue de bois* technique of speaking as if she herself were the incarnation of the proletariat. She probably hoped that if she sounded like the Party line, the Party line might be persuaded to incorporate her views. A sample:

> The proletariat is not filled with horror and moral indignation at the many forms and facets of "winged Eros" in the way that the hypocritical bourgeoisie is. . . . The complexity of love is not in conflict with the interest of the proletariat.

In the event, she found winged Eros a hard taskmaster. In a touching forecast of the policy declared by Germaine Greer forty years later, Kollontai favoured the notion that a non-academic but suitably vigorous proletarian might be a fitting partner for a female high-brow. But either the muscular young lovers she chose for herself did not understand that in offering them freedom she required their respect, or else she found parting from them hurt more than it was supposed to. It would be cruel not to sympathize, and patronizing too: even while she was earning her decorations she was in fear for her life, and during the Yezhov terror in the late 1930s she thought every trip back to Moscow might be her last.

Our real sympathy, however, we should reserve for those who were not spared. An impressive proportion of them were women, even within the Party itself, where they were seldom given high office, but certainly had unhampered access to the status of victim. If Kollontai had been sent to the Gulag and somehow survived it, she might conceivably have written a book along the lines of Evgenia Ginzburg's *Into the Whirlwind*, although it is hard to believe that any amount of deprivation and disillusionment would have given her Ginzburg's gift for narrative. Kollontai wrote boilerplate even on the few occasions when she felt free to speak. Besides, she already had the disillusion: she didn't have to be locked up to have that. A single week in the company of the regime's high-ranking thugs and boors would have been enough to tell her that there was no hope. We should not go so far as to greet her every statement with laughter, but we should try to rein in our pity. Pity belongs to the countless thousands of her sisters who were sent to the unisex hell that lay beyond Vorkuta, where they aged thirty years in the first three months unless they were granted the release of a quicker death. Did she know about all that? Of course she did. Women always know.

HEDA MARGOLIUS KOVALY

❧ ❧ ❧

Heda Margolius Kovaly (b. ca. 1920) could have been sent into history specifically to remind us, after we have read about an initially worthy but fatally compliant apparatchik like Alexandra Kollantai, that there really can be such a creature as an incorruptible human being, and that it quite often takes a woman to be one. The broad details of Kovaly's life are outlined in the short essay below. Harder to evoke is the personality that sets its healing fire to every page of her terrible story. Reading *Prague Farewell* is like reading about Sophie Scholl, the most purely sacrificial protagonist of the White Rose resistance group in Munich in 1942; like reading Nadezhda Mandelstam's *Hope Against Hope* in its saddest chapters of resignation; like reading one of the interviews that the Somali-born Dutch politician Ayaan Hirsi Ali gave just after her friend Theo van Gogh was murdered in an Amsterdam street by a fanatic who took exception to her views about the subjection of women under Islam. Examples could be multiplied. Unfortunately, for some reason, they have hardly ever been codified: either the modern encyclopedia of feminist heroism has not yet been assembled, or else it has never been made popular.

Almost certainly the reason is that ideology gets in the way. An uncomfortable number of the heroines achieved their true bravery by questioning the political cause they first espoused, and a chronicler who still espouses it is not likely to tell their story well, or at all. The real opportunity—to evoke a set of humanist values that lie beyond the grasp of any single political programme, and thus form a political and ethical ideal in themselves—remains untouched. Yet it would be a poor man who could finish reading Kovaly's book without asking himself how an experience like hers could ever have been thought to be subsidiary. Why, he must surely ask himself, isn't this the central story? If the world can't be ruled by the values that come naturally to a woman like her, how can it be worth living in?

A few miles out of Prague, the limousine began to slide on the icy road. The agents got out and scattered the ashes under its wheels.
—HEDA MARGOLIUS KOVALY, PRAGUE FAREWELL, P. 180

GIVEN THIRTY SECONDS to recommend a single book that might start a serious young student on the hard road to understanding the political tragedies of the twentieth century, I would choose this one. The life of Heda Margolius Kovaly is not to be envied. If we had to live a life like hers in order to come out of it with her spirit and dignity, we would be better off not living at all. But her life did have one feature that we can call a blessing. It dramatized, for our edification, the two great contending totalitarian forces, because they both chose her for a victim. As a Jewish teenager in Czechoslovakia she was fated to be swept up by the Nazis, and subsequently went right through the mill, starting with the Lodz ghetto and going all the way to Auschwitz, where she wound up in a block for young girls. Mercifully, in evoking her girls' dormitory, she restricts herself to one scene. The girls had to kneel all night on the parade ground waiting to see one of their number punished the next morning for having tried to escape. Any of the kneeling girls who fell over was taken away to be gassed, so they had to hold each other up. In the morning, the recaptured escapee had her arms and legs broken in front of their eyes.

Emerging by sheer chance from that most hideous of grand tours, Heda walked home to Prague in good time for the next disaster. Between 1945, when she got back from Auschwitz, until 1948, when the Communists came to power in Czechoslovakia, there was a brief interlude, during which she had ample opportunity to realize that those who have made compromises under an occupation in order to survive are reluctant to meet anyone tactless enough to return from oblivion. But there were still some people left who had retained the rare combination of integrity and energy, and one of them was the man she married. All too soon, Rudolf Margolius was asked to be a minister in Klement Gottwald's Communist government. Rudolf had his doubts, but as an honest and conscientious man he felt he couldn't turn the job down. He threw himself into the task, ignoring the warnings of less gifted but wiser friends that he was throwing himself into a pit. His intelligence and ability earned their inevitable reward. In the Slánský show trial, Rudolf was one of the eleven Jews on the list of fourteen accused. The rehearsed confessions were extracted, or rather instilled, under torture. They were well down to the standard of the pre-war Moscow trials. All the prisoners were found guilty of the crimes they had accused themselves of and most of them were duly hanged, including Rudolf. The bodies were burned and the bags of ashes were driven away to be distributed in the woods. But there was ice on the roads. Now look again at the quotation above.

For the murdered idealist's young wife, what happened next was, if possible, worse. The classic Russian techniques of making life impossible for the family of a people's enemy were in full swing, with additional refinements made possible by Czech inventiveness. Heda was thrown out of her job and her apartment, and then additionally persecuted for being unemployed and homeless. After Khrushchev finally blew the whistle on the Stalinist system in 1956, Poland, Hungary and Bulgaria all rehabilitated their show trial victims before Czechoslovakia did. Not until 1963 was the truth told, and even then the information was officially restricted to the Party itself. Heda would have been justified in giving up on her country. She has hard things to say about its educated class, too many of whom knew all about the horrors of Soviet communism but thought that the Czech version would turn out more civilized because its apparatchiks—they had themselves in mind—would be more cultivated. But she found many examples of instinctive decency among the common people. She has, however, no sentimentality about anyone, and the most valuable aspect of a valuable book is how she is able to count heads in order to trace the insidious transition from one political catastrophe to another. According to her, there were plenty of democrats in Czechoslovakia after the war who realized the danger of yielding up their country to the next absolutism. But they were guilty about having yielded up their country to the last one. Abandoned by its supposedly liberal allies, the republic had let the Nazis in. During the Nazi occupation, the democrats had been demoralized by fear. The Nazis had crushed them and the Russians had saved them: they had done nothing for themselves. They felt powerless. Perhaps, they reasoned, it would take a new authoritarianism to create and preserve a just order. So they swam with what felt like the tide of history, trying to convince themselves that it was taking them somewhere even as it sucked them under.

All this is recounted in an exemplary amalgam of psychological penetration and terse style. In her few years of relatively normal existence before the 1968 Prague Spring and its bitter aftermath disrupted her life all over again, Heda earned a slim living as a translator from English. Raymond Chandler and Saul Bellow were two of her authors: perhaps their lively example got into her prose. The only fault in the book is that some of the remembered dialogue is too specifically dramatized to be credible. She would have done better to paraphrase it. Otherwise, everything is as neatly done as the sentence about the ashes. Her book should never have had to be written; but, since it had, we are lucky that it was done so well. American readers should note that in the U.S.A. it was called *Under a Cruel Star*. A Google search reveals that the book is on the course in several colleges, but it deserves to be lot more famous than that.

KARL KRAUS

❦ ❦ ❦

Karl Kraus (1874–1936) was the satirical voice of Vienna from the *Jahrhundertwende*—the turn of the century that marked the last glorious epoch of the old Austro-Hungarian Empire—to the eve of the *Anschluß*, which luckily he did not live to see. As a Jew whose comprehensive contempt for bourgeois complacency also embraced virtually every Jewish artist whom he suspected of a taste for success, Kraus had found abundant material for mockery in the old society as it decayed. During World War I he had been tirelessly eloquent on the subject of how the debased language of patriotic journalism had helped to feed lambs to the slaughter. But when the time came, he had comparatively little to say about the advent of the Nazis, and lived just long enough to confess that Hitler struck him dumb. *"Mir fällt zu Hitler nichts ein,"* he confessed in July 1933. He followed the confession with a 300-page essay about "the new Germany" which J. P. Stern later called "one of the greatest political and cultural polemics ever written," but it remained true that Hitler's personal success left Kraus speechless, because it was beyond satire. Even with due allowance for the famous satirist's waning powers, this was a remarkable, if tacit, admission of a failure of imaginative energy to match a new reality. The new reality was at least as absurd as the old one, but it left him with less occasion to expose its hidden purpose, mainly because the purpose wasn't hidden: instead, it was blatant. The open face of Nazi evil left Kraus wrong-footed. Published, edited and largely written as a one-man enterprise, Kraus's magazine *Die Fackel* had worked mainly as a *sottisier* of all the self-deluding things said in the newspapers and periodicals; his cabaret act had worked in the same way; and so had his endless, endlessly self-renewing epic play *The Last Days of Mankind*. But even at the time, the debunking emphasis of Kraus's effort raised the question of whether his satirical view of society was really all that informative, since any society that allows free expression of opinion is bound to spend a lot of time talking foolishly anyway, and can be quoted against itself without limit, and indeed, if it is free enough, without penalty. After Kraus's death the question came rapidly to a head when the Nazis, far from needing to wrap up their intentions in fine phrases, proved that they could be quite frightening enough by saying exactly what they meant. The problem posed by Kraus's high reputation as an analyst of language was repeated later on with the advent of George Orwell, who so convincingly identified the misuse of language with fraudulent politics that it became tempting to suppose the first thing caused the second, instead of the second causing the first.

Today, Kraus's satirical vision, far from being an intellectual lost cause, is a show-business success story: the continuous and unrelenting mockery of the language of official power is institutionalized in the liberal democracies, and especially in the United States, which, since the heyday of Mort Sahl and Lenny Bruce in the 1950s, has teemed with political and social satirists, many of them holding stellar positions in the media. It is now part of the definiton of a modern liberal democracy that it is under constant satirical attack from within. Unless this fact is seen as a virtue, however, liberal democracy is bound to be left looking weak vis-à-vis any totalitarian impulse. An ideology, especially when theocratic, runs no risk of demoralizing its young adherents through questioning its own principles, because it never does so. A bright child of his time, Kraus was unusual for his capacity to express his disgust that a free society could be full of things that intelligent people might not like. If, at this distance, he looks naïve, it is only because of the devastation wrought since by systems which suffered much less from disunity. We have come to value, in other words, the humanist approximations that made him impatient. One of them was the female aspiration towards personal liberty. He found the idea embarrassing, forgetting that all aspirations sound shrill until they are fulfilled.

A liberated woman is a fish that has fought its way ashore.
— KARL KRAUS

B UT KRAUS NEEDED a woman to liberate him. He found her in the person of the Baroness Sidonie Nadherny von Borutin, the great love of his life. He had loved the beautiful actress Annie Kalmar and after her pitiably early death he never forgot her: but he worshipped her as a symbol. She fitted his idea of the sensual woman whose eroticism would provide the fuel for the intellectual man. Another actress, Bertha Maria Denk, was harder to fit into the same frame because she was very bright, but Kraus managed to talk his way free. From Sidonie there was no escape. Sidonie was the living woman, and didn't even need his money. (Kraus had a private income, but Sidonie's wealth was on a different scale.) The luxury of her company offered him the chance to become fully himself: to live like a prince, lose himself in a passion, cry on a fine-boned shoulder. Knowing that, we can see why so much of his supposedly scorching satire now strikes us a fire in straw. There were people at the time who thought the same, and not all of them were his victims. He had admirers who spotted that by giving the society he lived in more scorn than it warranted he might have too little left over for something worse. His satirical attack was based on the analysis of clichés: in politics, in the arts and above all in journalism. He did for German what Swift had once done for English, and Flann O'Brien would do again. Nothing got past him. He was a one-man watch committee, the hanging judge of the *sottisier*. Anyone who let slip a loose phrase lived to rue it if Kraus caught him. As the self-appointed scourge of self-revealing speech, he was a linguistic philosopher before the fact, a blogger before the Web.

But the world is made up of more than language, and a truly penetrating view, if it is to have scope as well as depth, must get through not just to the awkward facts beneath the lies, but to the whole complexity of events that give the facts their coherence, and to the networks of necessary human weaknesses that even the most developed civilization can't realistically hope to eradicate. The archimandrite of a linguistic monastery, Kraus found human beings guilty of being human, and society of allowing them to be so. The Austro-Hungarian Empire was a monument to theatricality, and it was certainly true that hyprocrisy was universal, especially in matters of sex. But at least hypocrisy was human. He was unable to envisage what a society would be like that eliminated the human factor altogether. The Nazi future was not yet available to tell him, but he might have found instruction in the despotic past, had he been historically minded.

He conspicuously wasn't. He belittled the forces that held his world together because he was not sufficiently educated by the incoherence within himself. Had he been, he would have expressed it. His whole stance was to say the unsayable. If he didn't say it, it was because he hadn't thought it: or, having thought it, couldn't face it. Hence his confident ability to say a thing like this: a rock through a window. There are a thousand other Krausian moments like it. He is made up of such moments. The complete run of his magazine *Die Fackel*—given to me by a cultivated young Austrian aristocrat in expiation for what his country has never been able fully to admit, it occupies a whole shelf of my library in Cambridge—is an asteroid belt of pebbles that have passed through glass. They all share the same unfaltering tone of the self-elected elect: the oracle who can see everywhere except into its own being, and sees through everyone because it has no insight into itself.

Kraus's self-assurance was a pose that he believed was real. If he could have admitted it as a pose, his work would have more to astonish us with than its glowing surface. The golden bowl was cracked, and its richest secrets were in the flaw: but he could not go in there. Schnitzler, whom Kraus had the arrogance to patronize, could interpret the world through knowledge of his own failings. Klimt, another of Kraus's targets, was being lastingly self-exploratory in the very paintings that Kraus found cliché-ridden and sentimental. (The Nazis, with their gift for practical criticism, paid Klimt the tribute of pulverizing his greatest set of murals, in which they saw what Kraus had missed: an unashamed celebration of desire.) It never occurred to Kraus that his vulnerable contemporaries had something to gain through not being self-protective. The loophole in his own armour was his love for Sidonie, but he did not, and obviously could not, make it an energizing subject for his main work. He shunted it aside into his lyric poetry, which is weak precisely because it contradicts his prose without complementing it. Man's love is of man's life a thing apart: Byron meant that as an emphasis. Kraus meant it as an axiom.

What finally happened between the two lovers will always be a secret. The long affair ended too gradually to bequeath the memory of a revealing crisis. ("K.K. so kind, so good," Sidonie told her diary in English, while Kraus was tearing his hair out waiting for a letter.) But it seems fair to suggest that he put on too much pressure, and it was all the wrong kind. He wanted to own her. She wanted to be free. ("I want freedom, solitude. . . .") She told him that his enslavement enslaved her. All the usual things happened. When he showed signs of taking back his independence, she enslaved him again. She was no stranger to guile. But her heart was good—on the testimony of her many friends, she was one of those aristocrats with all the bourgeois virtues—and Kraus, given a modicum of acumen, should have been able to drink from the fountain of her loving kindness for the rest of his difficult life. One would prefer to blame Rilke, who had his eye on Sidonie's sumptuous estate at Janowitz as a plush staging post in which he might one day write a cycle of poems. Rilke was always scouting the country seats of the great ladies for a suitable ambience in which to connect himself with eternity. As his nauseating letters to Marie von Thurn und Taxis Hohenloe reveal, Rilke knew no shame in such pursuits. His bread-and-butter letters are always hard on the reader's stomach. But to shut Kraus out from his possible claims on Sidonie's hospitality, Rilke truly disgraced himself by hinting to her that she courted degradation by keeping company with a Jew. (In his letter of February 21, 1914, Rilke carefully avoided the word "Jew," but she knew exactly what he meant when he warned her that Kraus could only ever be a stranger: to help her figure it out, Rilke underlined the adjective *fremd*. Admirers of Rilke's spiritual refinement will find the letter quoted on page 52 of the second volume of Friedrich Pfafflin's two-volume edition of Kraus's letters to Sidonie.) Kraus, all unknowing that he had been betrayed, went on helping Rilke's literary career, and Rilke went on accepting the help.

Rilke reminds us of the young man who wanted to be a suspect when he grew up. Alas, Kraus looks like a better bet as the culprit. He wanted all the social credentials that an official alliance with an aristocrat would have brought him; and the wish seems understandable, if not particularly edifying. But he didn't want to modify his exalted stance as the seer who needed no other viewpoint than his own. When he went to her he was on holiday, and by marrying her he wanted only to make the holiday official. The biographers seem agreed that she grew to want less of him. It might have been equally possible, however, that she wanted more: some evidence of a change of heart, an expansion of sympathy that she might have ascribed to her own influence. She knew how she inspired him to poetry, but there was nothing of her in his prose, which from first to last was one long tirade of self-assertion. Clearly he felt free to fall apart when safe on her estates: that was the attraction of her comfortable ambience. But he always put himself back together in the same form, and returned to work as the universal castigator of *The Last Days of Mankind*. Too much is made of the discrepancy between the *grande dame* and the self-despising Jew, and not enough of a more usual difference, between the housekeeper and the nihilist.

Later on, when the Nazis came to Schloss Janowitz, she met some real nihilists and must have had cause to look back fondly on a warrior violent only with words. But in view of her intrinsic worth she had been right to freeze him out. He had loved her for her beauty, position, charm, cultivation and *savoir faire*. But her intrinsic worth went deeper than that. She was the product of a social order, which Kraus had admired only for its accoutrements: i.e., he wanted its benefits without understanding their provenance. Though he was pleased to appropriate the concept of gentility as a talisman against modern opportunism, he had no real capacity for valuing *noblesse oblige*, which is the long-gestated product of a society of obligations, not of rights, and is almost wholly unwritten. Kraus lived in the written world. He thought that the misuse of language was an incitement to crime. (In his tireless analysis of the bad journalism that came out of the war, he came very close to suggesting that the war had been caused by bad journalism: if only it had been that simple.) But there were worse incitements to crime than misused language, and if he had lived a little longer he might have been caught up in a crime it was beyond his powers of reason to predict. All the politicans and journalists whose bad prose he had laughed at were unexpectedly silenced by a new range of orators who meant exactly what they said, and who took their satisfaction from mangling a lot more than syntax and vocabulary. He would have found that there are forms of speech to which satire does not apply. He lived just long enough to entertain the possibility, and we can be sure that the possibility did not entertain him. When he said that he had nothing to say about Hitler, he was really saying that his life's work had come to nothing.

Famous while he lived, Kraus is cited now as a byword for hard-headed wit by people who have never read more than few paragraphs: his name is invoked rather in the way that Cole Porter invoked Dorothy Parker's, as shorthand for a quality. It's the same sort of lazy journalistic reflex that once made him spit tacks. So was his career a waste of time? Not really, although he might have died thinking so. Though to read him for long at a stretch is like trying to make a meal out of Mexican jumping beans, some of his aperçus are more than enough to make you see why the scholarly commentators should enrol him *honoris causa* among the Vienna school of philosophers. Anyone who reads a few random pages of Kraus will write more carefully next day, with fear of his blue-pencil eyes as the spur to revision. He knew how to cut the inessential. "Female desire is to male desire as an epic is to an epigram." Try saying the same thing quicker. It was a production in English of *The Last Days of Mankind* that led Niall Ferguson to learn German, and so helped him towards laying the learned foundations of his fine book *The Pity of War*, in which Kraus's debunking of patriotic rhetoric is frequently acknowledged. The whiplash speed and snap of Kraus's reasoning can be heard even through the language barrier.

But his negative example is the one that lasts. He embodied the unforeseeable tragedy—made actual only by a cruel trick of history—of those bourgeois Jewish intellectuals who caught out Jewish artists for their bourgeois vulgarity: by helping to undermine the bourgeoisie as a class, and by helping to establish Jewish origins as a classification, the intellectuals unwittingly served two future masters whose only dream was to annihilate them. Above all, his supreme mastery of verbal satire served to prove that satire is not a view of life. It can be a useful and even necessary by-product of one, but it can have no independent existence, because the satirist hasn't either. Any writer who finds the height of human absurdity outside himself must find the wellspring of human dignity inside, and so lose the world. The secret of a sane world view is to see virtue in others, and the roots of chaos within ourselves. Kraus had the secret right in front of him, in the soul and body of Sidonie. She was his best self, come to save him. He had his arms around her, but he lost her. We will never know quite how, but there is something about this deadly little aphorism to make us think it more plausible to blame him than to blame her.

Georg Christoph Lichtenberg

GEORG CHRISTOPH LICHTENBERG

† † †

Georg Christoph Lichtenberg (1742–1799) stands at the beginning of German modernity, and right in the centre of the country's post–World War II concern with the recovery of liberal thought from historical catastrophe. If it was felt necessary to pump the mystique out of the whole idealistic heritage of German philosophy, Lichtenberg was the prototype of a German thinker who could be seen as the level-headed smallholder waiting back at the beginning, looking once again like an attractive prospect, now that the smoke had cleared. Mainly owing to Hegel and his long influence, German, as a language of thought, had acquired a bad reputation for the higher nonsense of self-generating transcendentalism. In truth, however, German has as good a right as French to be thought of as essentially terse. (All of its most able prose writers, from Goethe through Schopenhauer to Freud, Schnitzler, Kafka and Wittgenstein, found the aphorism a natural form.) Just as Pascal, in French, began a tradition of compact concrete statement even about the spiritual, so did Lichtenberg in German. He came later, but then the whole of Germany came later. Germany is a young country, and Lichtenberg is one of the reasons that it can still feel that way for anyone who can push

back through the curtains of tosh, much of it woven by patri-
ots who believed that only the solemn could be truly serious
and only the impenetrable profound. One of those valuable
faculty members (he was a professor of physics, astronomy and
mathematics at Göttingen) who never lose the trick of talking
like a brilliantly amusing graduate student—we can imagine
Robert Oppenheimer at Los Alamos, or Richard Feynman at
CalTech—Lichtenberg was critically minded about the language of others, unfailingly scrupulous about his own, and
never content to settle into a formula. Barred by physical
deformity from any easy participation in the passionate emotional life he saw as central to existence, he was nevertheless
wonderfully sympathetic to the realities of love and sex: with
every excuse to turn away from the real world, he kept its every
aspect always in plain sight. Finally it is his detailed and
unflinching awareness that astonishes the reader. Scattered
through his scores of "Waste-Books" and manuscript notebooks, Lichtenberg's innumerable observations add up to a
single demonstration of his guiding principle: that there is
such a thing as "the right distance," a sense of proportion. He
is the thinker against hysteria, the mind whose good-
humoured determination to avoid throwing a tantrum provides us with a persuasive argument that the tantrum might be
the motive power of political insanity. In German there are
numerous selections and collections, but most of the very best
moments are in J. P. Stern's excellent *Lichtenberg: A Doctrine of
Scattered Occasions* (1959). Nutshells packed as cleverly as an
old soldier's kitbag, Lichtenberg's sayings are quoted in the
original where that seems helpful, are always sensitively translated into suitably colloquial English, and are thoroughly
annotated, from the body of humanist knowledge about shattered Germany that Stern built up after the war. (Born and
raised as a Czech, Stern also wrote one of the best short books
about the man who shattered it, *Hitler: The Führer and the People*, in 1975.) Stern first encountered Lichtenberg's name in the
pages of Karl Kraus's magazine *Die Fackel*. It would be a mistake, however, to confine the question of Lichtenberg's long

delayed but highly welcome influence merely to the sardonic paragraph. His clarity and concision set a standard for expository prose, at whatever length, in the whole of his language, and, by extension, in all languages.

> It was impossible for him not to disturb words in the
> possession of their meanings.
> — LICHTENBERG, *APHORISMEN*

LICHTENBERG IS DESCRIBING a bad writer. There are bad writers who are exact in grammar, vocabulary and syntax, sinning only through their insensitivity to tone. Often they are among the worst writers of all. But on the whole it can be said that bad writing goes to the roots: it has already gone wrong beneath its own earth. Since much of the language is metaphorical in origin, a bad writer will scramble metaphors in a single phrase, often in a single word. From a made-for-television film called *The Movie Murders* I noted down this perfectly bad line of dialogue: "A fire is a Frankenstein when it's let out of its cage."

A fire can be a caged animal if you don't mind a cliché. But a caged Frankenstein is worse than trite. Frankenstein was not the monster, he was the monster's creator: so the use of his name is an inaccuracy. By now the inaccuracy has entered the language, like the juggernaut that serves us for Juggernaut's car: but one of the things good writing does is to fight a rearguard action against this automatic absorption of error. For example, a competent writer would look twice at "rearguard action" to make sure that he means to evoke a losing battle, and check "automatic absorption" to make sure that it falls within the range of phenomena against which a battle might conceivably be fought. He had better also know that "phenomena" should not be used in the singular, although that knowledge, too, is becoming rare. Competent writers always examine what they have put down. Better than competent writers—good writers—examine their effects *before* they put them down: they think that way all the time. Bad writers never examine anything. Their inattentiveness to the detail of their prose is part and parcel of their inattentiveness to the detail of the outside world.

In a television interview, Francis Ford Coppola said "hoi polloi" when he meant "elite." There is no reason to think that he would not commit similar solecisms in one of his screenplays if he were to put himself beyond the reach of expert advice, which the more bankable film directors—the ones whose films are marked as being "by" them— are increasingly apt to do. (This tendency, by the way, arises less from the conceit of directors than from the paucity of writers: screenplays depend more on construction than on dialogue, and experienced writers with those priorities are hard to find.) Most of us write "the hoi polloi" when we should leave off the "the" because "the" is what "hoi" means, but that is a point of usage. Using "hoi polloi" to mean "elite" is an outright error, indicating that the speaker has either misunderstood the term every time he has read it, or, more likely, that he has not read much. Unblushing semi-literacy is quite common among film directors, especially those who fancy themselves to have so powerful a vision that they grant themselves not just the final word on the structure of a script but the privilege of creating its language from line to line. We have to forgive them for this: the ability to put a movie script together takes such rare qualities of generalship that the person who can do it is almost bound to succumb to hubris. James Cameron's screenplay for his film *Titanic* is no doubt a mighty feat of construction. It is also linguistically dead from start to finish. If pressed on the point, he would be able to say that his film made more money faster than any other film in history. He could also say that the visual narrative matters far more than the dialogue, and that his mastery of the screen image would be alone sufficient to refute the charge of inattention to the texture of reality. But there is a clear connection between the film's infantile characterization—which for any adult viewer entirely undoes the effect of the meticulously reproduced period detail—and the dud dialogue the characters are given to speak. None of this would be germane to the issue if the director did not consider himself a writer. But he does, and he is a bad one: a bad writer by nature.

Macaulay's review of the hapless poetaster Robert Montgomery is the classic analysis of the naturally bad writer who gets everything wrong because he is sensitive enough on the question of style to attempt to lift his means of expression above the ordinary. When Montgomery evoked a river that "meanders level with its fount,"

Macaulay pointed out that a river level with its fount can't even flow, let alone meander. Macaulay had uncovered the connection between the inability to notice and the inability to transcribe: the double deficiency that Montgomery's highfalutin diction was invented to conceal. Mark Twain did the same for, or to, James Fenimore Cooper, who thought that "more preferable" was a more impressive way of saying "preferable": the clumsily elevated language, Twain argued, was closely linked to the deficient power of observation that made the action of Cooper's Leatherstocking books absurd. When a bad writer borrows locutions from past authorities, he characteristically takes the patina but leaves the metal. Biblical pastiche is a standard way for a mediocre stylist to attempt distinction. Attempting to define the sensationalism of the press, Malcom Muggeridge came up with the slogan "Give us this day our daily story." A doomed effort, because all it did was remind the reader that the King James Version of the Lord's Prayer was better written than an article by Muggeridge. He would have been better off just saying that the press needs a new story every day. Gombrowicz in his *Journal* (specifically, vol. 2, p. 164) notes that when a writer complicates a truism it is a sure sign that he has nothing much to say.

Julius Caesar wrote with invariable clarity, whether about Gaul being divided into three parts or about building a bridge. Frederick the Great wrote about falconry from direct observation, with no hearsay, and in a plain style. Queen Victoria's letters are models of compact accuracy: she wrote better than Queen Elizabeth I, which is saying a lot. Such practical expository prose by people with non-literary day-jobs should give a measure for would-be professional writers wise enough to build a solid base in their craft before trying to make an art out of it. They will soon discover that even the most down-to-earth of practical writers can scramble their meaning when they are in a hurry, so it must be a craft, and not just a gift. In addition to *A Genius for War*, his excellent biography of Gerneral Patton, the eminent American military historian Carlo D'Este wrote two essential books surveying whole campaign areas in World War II, *Decision in Normandy*, about Operation Overlord, and *Bitter Victory*, about the Allied invasion of Sicily. But a third book, *Fatal Decision*, is much less satisfactory than the other two because it squanders their chief virtue, which is to record and weigh the facts in a transparent style. D'Este knew all there was to know about the Anzio campaign, but while trying to tell the reader either he got so excited he forgot how to write or else—more likely, alas—he received less than his usual quota of editorial help. Thus we are regaled with his paraphrase of Churchill's strategic view "that the 'soft underbelly' of the Mediterranean is Germany's Achilles heel" (p. 12). But such a blatantly mixed metaphor at least enables you to divine what is meant. Metaphorical content is mixed more inextricably when a standard idiom is unintentionally reversed in meaning, thereby infecting the whole sentence. "For the next eight weeks there was a standoff in the northeastern corner of the beachhead as the 504th were forced into trenches that for sheer misery had nothing on their World War I counterparts" (p. 176). Here "had nothing on" is used for "yielded nothing to," but they do not mean the same thing. When an important book is infested with deeply lurking solecisms, it has to be read twice while you are getting through it once. A less important book, of course, is quickly cast aside.

If language deteriorates in journalism, the damage will be felt sooner or later in writing that pretends to more distinction. In my time, to take one out of a hundred possible examples, it has become common among cultural journalists to use "harp back" for "hark back." If "bored of" should succeed in replacing "bored with" there will be no real call to object, except from nostalgia: "of" does the job at least as well as "with" and anyway such changes have happened in the spoken language since the beginning. But "harp back" scrambles the separate meanings of "harp on" and "hark back," and thus detracts from the central, hard-won virtue of the English language, which is to mean one thing at a time. The solecism gets into the paper because the subeditors no longer know the difference either, so to see it cropping up in books is no surprise, although a great disappointment. David McClintick's *Indecent Exposure* is one of the best books about moral turpitude in modern Hollywood. The constant and unavoidable struggle between creative freedom and the necessity for cost controls, with the consequent oscillation between daylight robbery and ecstasies of bean-counting precision, could not be better explained. But the otherwise savvy author uses "flaunt" for "flout," thereby injuring two words at once: "To Cliff Robertson, Columbia's reinstatement of Begelman was not only a brazen flaunting of justice, but also a deep insult to Cliff personally." In a single sentence, an author who has convinced you that he could write anything leads you to suspect that he has read nothing. In the normal course of events, a tactful copy editor might have corrected the error. But by now the barbarians are within the gates, and there seems to be no stopping the process of deterioration even in America, whereas in Britain the cause is lost irretrievably. Backs-to-the-wall raillery from established authors is fun, but won't work. As Kingsley Amis acutely noted, the person who uses "disinterested" for "uninterested" is unlikely to see your article complaining about the point, because the person has never been much of a reader anyway. There is evidence, however, that writers can read a great deal, among all the best exemplars, and still not take in the power to discriminate on critical points of grammar, derivation, usage, punctuation and consistency of metaphor. Prescriptive initial teaching probably helps, but the capacity for such an alertness may be more in the nature of an inborn propensity than a possible acquisition.

The propensity can even appear in hypertrophied form, to the writer's detriment. A good writer of prose always writes to poetic standards. (One of the marks of poetry in modern times is that the advent of free verse opened the way for poets who could not write to prose standards, but that's another issue.) The good prose-writer's standards, however, should include the realization that he is not writing a poem. Henry James was not being entirely absurd when he complained that Flaubert was unable to leave his language alone. (Proust's qualified praise of Flaubert comes down to the same point.) It is possible to be an admirer of Nabokov while still finding his alertness to cliché overactive, so that passages occur in which we can hardly see for the clarity: and with James Joyce it is more than possible. Somewhere between Tolstoy, who was so indifferent to style that he did not mind repeating a word, and Turgenev, who would sooner have died than do so, there is an area where the writer can be economically precise without diverting the reader's whole attention to his precision. Lichtenberg would have included that area in his key concept of "the proper distance," which he thought crucial to the exercise of reason. Rembrandt, in a reported statement Goethe was fond of, said that people should not shove their noses too close to his paintings: the paint was poisonous.

One drastic side effect of an overdeveloped vigilance is the counter-

productive attempt to make description answer the totality of observation. In *Troilus and Cressida*, Alexander has a phrase for it: "purblind
Argus, all eyes and no sight." Attention is necessarily selective: if it
were not, we would spend most of our waking hours paralysed by the
impact of what we see. The secret of evocative writing is to pick out the
detail that matters, not to put in all the detail that doesn't. Consider
Joan la Pucelle's lines in *Henry VI, Part 1*: lines which might not be by
Shakespeare, but which were certainly written by someone who knew
what he was doing.

> *Glory is like a circle on the water,*
> *Which never ceases to enlarge itself,*
> *Till by broad spreading it disperse to naught.*

In reality, when something makes a splash there is always a *set* of rip-
ples. There can never be just one circle. But the playwright needs only
one, so he leaves the others out. If he had been concerned with rendering the natural event, he would have got in the road of the Homeric
simile. The simile, not "the object," was his object. More than two
thousand years before, the same was true for Homer, who could render an object in passing (the twanging string of a silver bow is rendered
in a single onomatopoeic stroke, argurio*io* bio*io*) and was always hunting bigger game. Ezra Pound, typically, was hammering away at a nail
whose head was already flush with the wood. There is the occasional
good writer who is not a good describer, just as there is the occasional
good painter—Bonnard, for example—who can't draw a horse, but in
general the ability to register the reality in front of him is a *donnée* for
anyone who writes seriously at all. When Joseph Conrad said the aim
of the writer was "above all, to make you see," he meant a lot more
than what the writer saw in front of his eyes. He was also talking about
what was going on behind them: the moral dimension. In the novella
Typhoon, when the narrator is thrown suddenly sideways, Conrad
makes you see how the stars overhead turn to streaks: "the whole lot
took flight together and disappeared." A scintillating descriptive
stroke, but for him not hard. In *Lord Jim*, he makes you see Jim's
shame: much, much more difficult.

It is better to err on the side of too much scrupulosity than too little, but it remains a fact that good writers are occupied with more than language. The fact is awkward; and the most awkward part of it is that for metaphorical force to be attained in a given sentence, the metaphorical content of some of its words—which is an historic content provided by their etymology and the accumulated mutability of their traditional use—must be left dormant. Our apprehension of the Duchess of Gloster's mighty line in *Richard II*, "Thou show'st the naked pathway to thy life," would be blunted, rather than sharpened, if we concerned ourselves with the buried image of a naked person instead of with the overt image of an unprotected path, and our best signal for not so concerning ourselves is that Shakespeare didn't, or he would have written the line in a different way. (Simultaneity of metaphor becomes a feature of his later plays, but the complexity which is almost impossible to understand at first hearing—and surely, as Frank Kermode boldly notes, must have been so at the time—would not be worth picking at if we gave up on our conviction that Shakespeare himself must have understood the strings before he tied the knots.) To make an idea come alive in a sentence, some of its words must be left for dead: the penalty for trying to bring them all alive is preciousness at best. If such preciousness is not firmly ruled out by the writer, there will be readers all too keen to supply it. In modern times, critics have earned a reputation for brilliance by pushing the concept of "close reading" to the point where they tease more meaning out than the writer can conceivably have wanted to put in; but it isn't hard, it's easy; and the mere fact that their busy activity makes them feel quite creative themselves should be enough to tell them they are making a mistake.

With the majority of bad writers the question never comes up. As Orwell points out in his indispensable essay "Politics and the English Language," they write in prepared phrases, not in words, and the most they do with a prepared phrase is vary it to show that they know what it is. Usually they are not even as conscious as that, and their stuff just writes itself, assembling itself out of standard components like a spreading culture of bacteria, except that most of the components are too faulty to be viable. Our real concern here, however, is not with the writing too bad to matter, perpetrated by writers who have nothing in mind except to fill a space. What troubles us is the writing imbued with enough ambition to outstrip its ability. It faces us with the spectacle of a failed endeavour. Somewhere back there, we wanted a world in which everybody would be an artist. Now we are appalled when the duffers actually try. But there is still some point in striving to provide, by precept and example, the kind of free training that the veteran Fleet Street literary editors used to dish out as part of their jobs. When suitably trained, a decent writer edits himself before the editors get to him. An outstanding creative talent is always an outstanding critic, of his own work if of nobody else's. Pushkin lamented the absence of proper criticism in Russia not because he needed help in judging his poems, but because he wanted to write them in a civilized society. *Eugene Onegin* is a miracle of lightness in which every word has been weighed. When Pope called genius an infinite capacity for taking pains, that was what he meant. The greatly gifted have almost everything by nature, but by bending themselves to the effort of acquirement they turn a great gift into great work. Their initial arrogance is necessary and even definitive: Heinrich Mann was right to say that the self-confidence of young artists precedes their achievement and is bound to seem like conceit while it is still untried. But there is one grain of humility that they must get into their cockiness if they are ever to grow: they must accept that one of the secrets of creativity is an unrelenting self-criticism. "My dear friend," said Voltaire to a young aspirant who had burdened him with an unpublished manuscript, "You may write as carelessly and badly as this when you have become famous. Until then, you must take some trouble."

> It is a common failing of all people with little talent and
> more learning than understanding, that they call more on
> an artistic illustration than a natural one.
> — LICHTENBERG, *APHORISMEN*

Lichtenberg was late to the game with this manifold idea, although he might have been the first to get it into a nutshell. Shakespeare's clever dolts, spouting their studious folderol as if it were wit, provided a lasting measure of how erudition can drive out sense. *Love's Labour's Lost* offers not the only, merely the mightiest, confrontation between brainsick bookmen, as Don Adriano de Armado and Holofernes spend four-fifths of the action warming up for the showdown in which they bury each other with verbiage. ("They have been at a great feast of languages," says Moth, "and stolen the scraps.") In play after play, the typical encounter between two or more such zanies is a disputatious colloquium in which each participant levitates on a column of hot air. A hallmark of Shakespeare's people of substance is never to do the same except in jest. Iago, wise when not jealous and "nothing if not critical," scorns "the bookish theoric" whose talk is "mere prattle, without practice." Clearly Iago speaks for Shakespeare even as he plots against Othello. Ben Jonson's plays teem with mountebanks who raid the tombs of scholarship while picking the pockets of the suckers. The great playwrights infused our language with a permanent awareness of the difference between desiccated eloquence and the voice of experience. English empirical philosophy began in the inherited literary language. That was how the English-speaking nations, above all others, were armed in advance against the rolling barrage of ideological sophistry in the twentieth century. The Soviet craze for assembling a viewpoint out of quotations from Marx and Lenin reminded us of men in tights defending the indefensible with chapter and verse.

Even without Shakespeare (supposing that such a precondition were possible) subsequent English literature would have been well populated with satirical examples to ward off casuist flimflam. In Restoration comedy, the division between true wit and false turned on the same point: true wit might have contributed to a new book, but false wit was always quoting an old one. Molière's typical scam artist talked like a library, but Molière on his own was not enough to inoculate the French language against the pox of learned affectation. The English language had the benefit of repeated injections. The *folie raisonnante* that ruled Swift's flying island of Laputa was fuelled by book learning, and Thomas Love Peacock, the great student of the connection between high-flown diction and mental inadequacy, made post-romantic nineteenth-century England the focus of the topic: just as Peacock in real life undid Shelley's vegetarianism by waving a steak under his nose when he fainted, so Peacock in his quick-fire novels riddled the inflated language of romantic soul-searching. In Peacock's crackpot masterpiece *Melincourt*—one of a whole rack of strange books, it stands out by being even stranger than the others—that compulsive classicist the Rev. Mr. Grovelgrub, poised on a high rock with

Lord Anophel Achthar as they both face imminent death, quotes Aeschylus in the original Greek and Virgil in the original Latin, while Lord Anophel curses him in the original English. (Peter Porter, himself a mighty quoter, though a sane one, has a soft spot for the Rev. Mr. Grovelgrub.) The idea—an idea built into the English language over centuries of comic richness—is that learning and knowledge must be kept in balance. In *Love's Labour's Lost*, Shakespeare's King of Navarre summarized it in advance when he commended Biron: "How well he's read, to reason against reading!"

In Lichtenberg's language, which was the lightly conversational version of German, Schopenhauer extended the same idea by favouring real observation over erudition, and stated confidently that the second sapped the first. German is a language supposedly given to the airy building of conceptual castles, but there is a use of German given to the opposite: those who find Hegel wilfully impenetrable would do well to look at his art criticism, where they will find him down-to-earth, fixed on the object and responding to a work of art as if it were an event in nature. (Kant could never do that: he conjured Spanish castles about aesthetics without ever having seen a painting.) In Italy, the vast edifice of Benedetto Croce's aesthetic theory was erected on the basic proposition that true creativity is a primary function, not to be derived from formal knowledge. He thought the same about formal knowledge: unless acquired through passion, it would count for nothing. Egon Friedell, perhaps the biggest bookworm of all time, deplored bookworms. He could make it stick: he read, and wrote, from a personal hunger that had nothing to do with emulation. But knowing himself to be vulnerable on the point, in his crowning work *Kulturgeschichte der Neuzeit* (*The Cultural History of the Modern Age*) he was always careful to identify sclerotic erudition as a sure sign of decadence in any historical period. In our time, Philip Larkin warned against the consequences of trying to make art out of art. Larkin thought the later Auden had done that, and there is evidence that Larkin was right. But Auden, both the earlier and the later, always presented his artistic enthusiasms as if they had forced their way into his busy head: he wrote as if learning had pursued him, not he it. In his critical compendia, even the most abstruse speculations are given as the workshop know-how of a master carpenter. If he wrote a poem about a painting, it was because the painting had hit him like a force of nature, as an everyday event. Stefan Zweig, in his book *Begegnungen* (Meetings), squeezed the theme into a single antithesis when he said that in Goethe's life and career there was seldom a poem without an experience, and seldom an experience without the golden shadow (*ohne den goldenen Schatten*) of a poem. First the experience, then the golden shadow. It would be easy to contend that the same is so for all of the art, and all of the thought, that has ever mattered. But is the thought itself quite true?

If it were, this book would be a folly. It might well be the product of more *Belesenheit* (bookishness) than *Talent*: as I remember it across the decades, I wrote more fluently when I knew nothing, and may have been talentless even then. But a primary impulse and a lifelong disposition are the very things that tell me Lichtenberg is fudging a point for one of the few times in his life: in a naked proposition there is a hidden assumption. He assumes that an explanation drawn from art can't be natural. The antithesis is false. Art is a part of nature. Art is one of the most natural things we do, and to care about art, and to draw our examples from it, is as natural as caring about our personal experience and drawing our examples from that. It can even be more natural, because it gets more experience in: other people's as well as ours. If we were to say, "I almost had it figured out but Nola Huthnance from next door interrupted me and by the time she finished yakking I lost my train of thought," we would be speaking from personal experience. But if we were to say, "I almost had it figured out but I was interrupted by a person from Porlock," we would be speaking not only from our experience, but from Coleridge's; and being more specific instead of less, because we would have incorporated a recognition that such an event is universal. We would have also conveyed the suggestion that the thing we were on the verge of figuring out was pretty important, perhaps on the scale of the masterpiece that *Kubla Khan* might have been if Coleridge's flying pen had not been stopped short by a passing dullard. If we didn't want to lose Nola Huthnance, we could just add the poetic reference to her prosaic name (". . . but Nola Huthnance from next door did a person from Porlock . . .") and get two benefits for one. Increasing our range need not cost us our focus: quite the reverse. The person without a range of reference is not more authentically human for being so. He is just more alone.

The root of the matter lies in whether art and learning are loved, or merely used. Among the thirty or forty missing plays of Aristophanes, it would be surprising if there were not three or four well populated with pretentious halfwits: there were men of learning in those days too, and wherever learning is valued there are arid scholiasts who seek merit by flaunting its simulacrum. Pointless erudition has always been ripe for parody. Proust's Norpois puts his audience to sleep by quoting endlessly from diplomatic history, but what makes him funny is that he knows nothing about life, not that he knows everything about diplomacy. (We conclude that he must have been a bad diplomat, but that's by the way, and might not be right.) If Talleyrand had quoted from diplomatic history at the same length as Norpois, Talleyrand could have sold tickets. People who crank out their knowledge of the arts in a mechanical manner gained it the same way. Some of them came to it late, as a social accomplishment. Others were unfortunate enough to be born as Philistines into a cultivated household. (At Cambridge I met one of these: he knew everything about all the arts in many languages, but had a way of proving it that made you want to enlist in the Foreign Legion.) Most of us were luckier, and took in our first enthusiasms as we took in our first meat and drink, with a scarcely to be satisfied hunger and thirst. Choosing one case out of a possible thousand, I first encountered Toulouse-Lautrec in Sydney, in the year 1957. He had died in Paris in the year 1901, but suddenly, and with overwhelming enchantment, he was alive again for me. There were no actual paintings by Lautrec on public display in Australia at that time, but the Swiss publishing firm Skira had just produced its first series of little square books bound in coarse white cloth, with tipped-in colour plates. Eventually I owned them all, but the Lautrec was the first. Not much bigger than postage stamps—big postage stamps from South American countries, but still postage stamps—those little reproductions occupied my eyesight for a week. I could see nothing else. But when I was finally ready to see the world again, I kept meeting Lautrec's characters from the cabarets of Paris—Yvette Guilbert, Jane Avril and la Goulue—in the streets of Sydney. I saw the rubber-legged dancer Valentin le Desosse bonelessly jumping off a Manly ferry at Circular Quay. It wasn't art instead of life: it was as art as well as life, and the art in life. Years later, when I got to Europe, I was ready for the real Lautrec paintings because I already had some idea of what was coming. And I was immeasurably more ready for Paris itself than I would have been without my scraps of book learning that had given me the living ghosts of Montmartre and Montparnasse. It had never been book learning, really. It was passion: a sudden, adolescent, everything-at-once passion for shape, colour, the permanent registration of the evanescent, the singing stillness of a captured movement, the heroism of an injured man who had forged a weapon to fight time. And fighting time, it collapses space: because of the sumptuous concentration of capital works by Lautrec in the Art Institute, the streets of Chicago are haunted for me by his small, bent but unbroken form. Twenty years ago, filming there very late one night by the lake, I thought I saw him. A beautiful set of roller-skating blonde twin girls came hurtling out of the dark along the esplanade, streaked carelessly through our laggard lights, and were gone before we could catch them. He would have caught them.

And that was just Lautrec. Gauguin did the same for me before I could pronounce his name. (I called him Gorgon.) Degas I gave an acute accent over the "e," not realizing that the "De" was an honorific prefix: "duh" would have been closer to the right sound, and certainly would have conformed to my general reaction when faced with his genius. Adding tear sheets from magazines to a small stack of thin books, I built up an archive of reproductions, calling him *Day*-ga until a kind woman from Vienna at last corrected me. (She ran a little coffee house in the Strand Arcade. How young and foolish of me not to quiz her on the story of her life.) From then on, I never laughed at anyone who mispronounced an artist's name, because it usually only meant that what he had read had run far ahead of what he had heard, and I knew too well how that can happen. When you are learning a new language, there is a blissful moment when, from not knowing how to, you pass to not knowing how not to. The second phase is the dangerous one, because it leads to sophistication, and one of the marks of sophistication is a tendency to forget what it was like to be naïve. But it was when we were still naïve that we knew most intimately the lust of discovery, a feeling as concentrated and powerful as amorous longing, with the advantage that we never had to fear rejection. Art will always want us. It finds us infinitely desirable. Beethoven's late quartets waited for me for more than thirty years after I first went mad for the *Eroica* symphony, and when I finally deigned to notice them they didn't even look peeved.

For anyone who loves it, art is as personal as that. The works of art have personalities: they are another population of the Earth. They even behave like people. After Barbirolli prepared the way with his Berlin concerts at the end of World War II, Mahler's symphonies, which had never been played while Hitler ruled, entered the conversation of music lovers in Berlin and were gossiped about as if their sumptuous attractions were a delicious scandal. Under Stalin, one of Shostakovich's most sublime creations took on a secret identity and hid out until the world got better. It holed up in the soundtrack to a Soviet film called *The Gadfly*, where I finally tracked it down only a few years ago, after hearing it by accident as the theme of a television series entitled *Reilly, Ace of Spies*. A middle-aged man by then, I found it to be the dreamed-of companion of my youth, a melody I would have been pleased to hum and whistle to an early girlfriend, although whether she would have been pleased is another question. But if the works of art have personalities, their creators are a human race in themselves: one that never ages, nor, unlike the Struldbruggs, grows tired of immortality. When you are young, and first meeting them, the artists seem more than human. But to hail the superhuman is always to keep bad company. (Yeats not only should have known better, he did know better: but he couldn't resist the cadence—the reason that Plato wanted to banish poets from the Republic.) Luckily a more thorough acquaintance is bound to teach us that the artists are more than human only in the sense of being even more human than us. It is an important lesson to learn because there is a severe penalty to be paid for the belief than an artist should be beyond personal reproach. We are paying it now, in the cultural press, where too many half-qualified reporters are continuously busy proving to us that our idols have feet of clay. The fault, a double fault, is in the arrested psychological development and the ruinously abbreviated education of the reporter: a propensity to vindictiveness drives him to the task of cutting down to size people who were never giants in the first place—not in that sense, anyway.

Few artists were ever fully well, so it is no great trick to prove them ill. There are commentators who can't get interested in Caravaggio until they find out that he killed someone. They are only one step from believing that every killer is Caravaggio. But we must all be alert to the potentially deleterious effects of letting in too much light on art. It is an essential political study, for example, to examine just what a treacherous piece of work Bertolt Brecht was, to his friends, to his loved ones and to civil society. But the study will lead to nothing if we fail to keep in mind that he was a great poet. Our innocence can't be regained: once we start finding out how our heroes and heroines lived and what they did, we can never go back to our first pure infatuation with what they made. But our innocence should never be forgotten: and if it is remembered, infatuation matures into admiration, as we blend our knowledge of the creators' failings and vicissitudes with our gratitude for what they created. Art is for adults, even when it is made by children. Children, left to themselves, tear up each other's stuff.

Because Lautrec was one of my first great loves, I often think of the very first artist, painting in the cave, as a man with withered legs. Unable to go out hunting, he would probably have been killed off if he hadn't turned out to be so entertainingly good at drawing a bison with a burnt stick. What were his feelings? They were primitive: almost as primitive as the instinct that sent the first hunters hunting, instead of just lying around to die when the edible roots ran out. But the painter, like the hunters, was doing something that was not in the natural dispensation. And as soon as he did it, it was. Though Sigmund Freud's reputation as a scientific thinker is in constant dispute, there can be no dispute about his stature as a writer. He was a very great poet in prose, and he was on top of his form in his essay "*Die Zukunft einer Illusion*" (The Future of an Illusion) when he said that culture's characteristic reason for being (*ihr eigentlicher Daseingrund*) is to protect us against nature (*uns gegen die Natur zu verteidigen*). He might have added, however, that protecting ourselves against nature is the most natural thing we do: the thing that makes us human. The arts, and learning about the arts, are not additions to life: they are life itself, an expression of life that feeds back into it and helps to make it what it is—and, above all, to *show* it what it is, to make life conscious. But Lichtenberg knew all that. Dozens of his other aphorisms prove it. He wrote this one on a bad day. Some bookish twerp must have got up his nose.

If reason, the daughter of heaven, were to judge what is
beautiful, then sickness would be the only ugliness.
— LICHTENBERG, *APHORISMEN*

Lichtenberg is saying more than that we should not judge by how people look. He is also saying that we can't help doing so. The operative word of the aphorism is the first word, "If." (*Wenn Vernunft, die Tochter des Himmels, von Schönheit urteilen dürfte, so wäre Krankheit die einzige Hasslichkeit*: you can see that my English has dampened the lilt of his rococo German, but it's the best I can do.) We are closer to being reasonable, then, for not caring about appearance; but we are further from instinct. In men, the instinct to admire personal beauty is traditionally held to be more powerful than in women, and women are thus traditionally held to more reasonable on that issue, if on no other. The tradition answers the facts: the only question is whether the facts are biologically determined. Late-twentieth-century feminism put a lot of effort into arguing that a cult of female beauty had been imposed by a consumer society. But presumably a consumer society was not imposing anything on the Greeks when they made Helen's beauty the ignition point for the war that brought the topless towers of Ilium down in flames. It makes more sense to admit the instinct than to deny it. All the evidence of literature, painting, sculpture and the dance suggests that men see divinity in beauty. Except for opera and ballet, music is the art where personal beauty has no value, and is perhaps the most consoling form of art because of that. E. M. Forster was brave enough to say that music lovers—of whom he, of couse, was one—were not a very attractive lot. He was stepping carefully in a minefield. He might have said it more boldly. On that point, music, when not allied with opera and ballet, is fair always. Other art forms very seldom are.

Admitting the instinctive response gives us our best chance to examine it. By saying the instinct does not exist we are merely saying it should not, and condemning even the unattractive to lie. Kingsley Amis, in *Take a Girl Like You*, pulled one of his boldest strokes when he launched the incurably awkward Graham into a stricken aria about what it is like to be shut out from companionable access to female beauty. The strength of the episode depends on our recognition that he is saying what he feels. We can argue that he ought to think differently, but we can scarcely ask him to feel differently. (The beautiful Jenny Bunn, his interlocutor over the doomed dinner table, does ask him to feel differently, and finds to her consternation that he is almost as angry with her as he is with fate.) We can't begin to be reasonable on the subject until we concede that our response to beauty is unreasonable in the first place. Tolstoy dramatized the truth incomparably— incomparably even for him—when he made Pierre fall in love with the pulchritude of his future wife even while she was busy proving that her head was full of air. Pushing the theme to its outermost artistic limit, Tolstoy shows Pierre obsessed with the shapeliness of her breasts at the same moment when she is obsessed with the shapeliness of her own arm. Translated into a dumb-bunny vocabulary of sighs and silence, she incarnates the neo-Platonic idea of Shelley's that catapulted him to one of his wildest flights of vision: "I am the eye with which the universe / Beholds itself and knows itself divine." Pierre is heading for trouble. He has committed his soul to the care of Candy Christian, whose only real love affair is with a mirror.

Candy would be a much less interesting book if it were merely pornographic. If Terry Southern and Mason Hoffenberg had wanted to make their little masterpiece hornier, they would have given their heroine a sex drive. As it is, she can be aroused only by men driven mad with need. In a key scene, two Greenwich Village poets (called Jack Katt and Tom Smart as a tactical alternative to calling them Terry Southern and Mason Hoffenberg) fight like animals for the right to possess her. Their right to possess her is merely notional, because she has already been spirited away for intimate examination by one of the book's endless line-up of randy doctors. In the book the doctors are best equipped to assess her physical perfection. But the fighting poets are a tip-off to an apparently frivolous work's deep reservoir of subversive truth. Southern, working solo this time, made another breakthrough with *Blue Movie*, which was based on the premise that a serious director like Stanley Kubrick might want to make a pornographic film in which the protagonists were beautiful and the proceedings therefore genuinely arousing instead of disgusting. (The book is dedicated to "the great Stanley K." who, at the end of his career, actually did make a film something like the one in the book, although nothing like as interesting.) As a novel, *Blue Movie* fatally dispenses with the saving grace of *Candy*, where the sex scenes are played for laughs. *Blue Movie* too often plays them straight, falling into pornography's usual trap of trying to show what can only be felt. But the idea that sexual commerce is only accidentally, and not necessarily, divorced from the aesthetic impulse is a valid one.

It would take a scholar in the field (like Dr. Krankheit in *Candy*) to work his way through the world's complete catalogue of pornographic videos: there must be thousands of them. But any late-night channel-surfer in hotel rooms around the planet will be all too aware that there is a hierarchy of physical attractiveness even in the strange universe of sexual performance on demand. At the bottom of the pile—she sometimes literally is—will be a woman who seems to be held together only by Band-Aids, tattoos and metal pins. In the middle range, emanating mainly from California, there are women whose body parts have been artificially enhanced to the point where the cameraman has to back out of the room to fit it all in. But at the top of the range there are some women you might, at first glance, conceivably like to know. The men you would never like to know: if you ever doubted that there could be a specific physiognomy of stupidity, these men are there to set you right. They are at their most frightening when fully clothed, struggling with their challenging role as the man who has come to repair the garbage disposal, or the psychologist who must check the tactile sensitivity of a female astronaut just back from space. You have to see them act to realize how dumb a man can look. With their clothes off and their virile members contractually erect, they are merely competitors in some sort of international caber-tossing competition in which they are not allowed to use their hands. The women, as always, provide the interest. Some of them look almost normal: no collagen in the lips, no silicone in the breasts, a thoughtful air of having spent the previous night with a good book, or anyway with *The Da Vinci Code*. What are they doing there?

The quickest answer is that the market has expanded to the point where they can earn millions for spending a couple of hours a day wrapping themselves around an oaf. A slower answer, but perhaps closer to the essential truth, is that they are almost invariably without any acting talent whatsoever. Neither do they look quite as good as Cindy Crawford, so the modelling option is not open. (It probably was, when they were starting off: apparently the progression from almost-made-it model to porno princess is a classic route to the pay dirt.) But they look pretty good. In fact some of them are outright fetching, and this awkward fact understandably multiplies the effect. If the effect of watching pornography is to leave a man who is alone in a hotel room feeling even lonelier, he can expect to feel as lonely as the Man in the Iron Mask. There she is, an Aphrodite de Melos with arms, and they are wrapped around a reasonably plausible businessman with his pants around his ankles. The actor playing the businessman is one of the few male porn stars with a forehead higher than a box of matches lying on its side. He arrived at Aphrodite's mansion in a black BMW and a blaze of sunlight. When he got out of the car, the sun went in. When he rang the doorbell, the sun came out again. (Even in the highest grade of porn video, introduced by David Duchovny in more penurious days, the lighting and the sound tend to be variable in consistency: if she takes her shoes off, stick your fingers in your ears before the shoes hit the floor.) But now he is in character up to the hilt. Even for the critical viewer, it is hard not to envy him. Just as long as she doesn't say anything. Unfortunately she does. Oh no, don't say that. And don't do that with your face. Just do nothing. Alas, they never do nothing. The dream is always spoiled.

Maybe it's that kind of dream. Here is appearance detached from personality, and put to the service of nothing but sex. But in real life, appearance is never detached from personality for long, and there is no such thing as nothing but sex: if there were, there would be nothing in the bordello except naked women. As things are, the women can hardly get into the bordello for the props: uniforms, whips, trapezes, leather masks, torture instruments, plunge baths full of custard. Imagination will not be denied, and least of all when ecstasy is for sale. Everyone wants a relationship. Even if the girl does everything for your eyes, she must also do something for your mind's history. Buñuel, the man who knew most about these matters, condensed them into a single moment in *Belle de Jour*. For the large customer from the Orient, it is not enough to be given Catherine Deneuve in a peignoir. She must carry a little box which, when opened, reveals some nameless atrraction that he has always wanted. We don't know what it is. As he revealed in his excellent memoir, Buñuel doesn't know either: that's the point.

So Lichtenberg is only half right. He is right that reason does not judge beauty. He is wrong in his implication that the instinct which does do the judging is uncomplicated. It is complicated by our dream world, which complicates reason too. Indeed it is on this very matter that we are given our clearest demonstration of how we can never have a purely reasonable response to the world. Reason is poetic: it carries our personal history folded into it. We probably do best to accept that the poetry and the desire can't be separated. In his memoir *Die doppelte Boden*, Marcel Reich-Ranicki tellingly quotes Kurt Tucholsky. "*Entweder du liest eine Frau oder du umarmst ein Buch.*" (Either you read a woman or you embrace a book.) But he doesn't tell us what Tucholsky meant. I think he meant that the two kinds of experience were not just compatible, but intimately involved with one another. At the turn of the nineteenth century, long before an age of political correctness would have punished him for it, George Saintsbury, probably the best-read man on Earth at the time, reached for a simile adequate to the effect on our minds of a successful lyric poem: he said it was like seeing "the face of a girl."

Homosexual men are unlikely to agree. For the heterosexual man, male homosexuality is not impossible to imagine—most of us have an early history of it, in some form—but male homosexual promiscuity *is* impossible to imagine. Even sensitive souls like Christopher Isherwood seem to have been decathletes of the Turkish bath. Cavafy probably wasn't, but his poems prove that he dreamed of nothing else. The number of sexual contacts enjoyed by the cruising homosexual man in the pre-AIDS era doesn't even sound like enjoyment: it sounds like the history of a pinball in a machine rigged to play forever. Can all these targets have been seen as beautiful? Perhaps it is a hint of what the purely reasonable world would be like: the world in which anybody could be attractive. It might be tough on the women. In the most ruthless set of laboratory conditions we know about, Lavrenty Beria and Mao Zedong, two men who had absolute power to do whatever they wanted in the sexual sphere, confined their attentions only to women they thought beautiful. Beria routinely picked up any pretty girl he saw in the street and took her home to be raped. Barely pubescent girls whom the senescent Mao liked the look of were given the privilege of keeping him young by licking off the dirt that he never removed by any other means. (The story is told in a fascinating book by Mao's doctor, Zhisui Li: *The Private Life of Chairman Mao*.) If both men had lived in a world where judgement was the preserve of reason, no woman would have been safe.

One assumes that in the world of promiscuous homosexual men, there are aesthetic criteria that limit the score to something this side of the astronomical. Oscar Wilde notoriously dished himself in court by saying there was a young man he had not kissed because he (the young man) was too ugly. One can further assume that for some homosexual men the aesthetic consideration is paramount and even disabling. Thomas Mann's writings, from first to last, were full of the *visione amorosa*: carefully immured in his various castles of domesticity, he sent his imagination on endlessly repeated flights to the ecstatic, which could be found only in the revelation of a young male face. *Death in Venice* is one of the most powerful expressions of the amorous vision in all literature. For Aschenbach, young Tadzio standing caught by the light in the shallows of the Lido is a message from heaven. But Mann exchanged scarcely two words with the original boy. In *The Confessions of Felix Krull*, the hero's attractions may well have something to do with the Australian tennis champion Lew Hoad, a hero of my youth, although not quite in the same way: Mann kept a picture of Hoad on his desk, for purposes of inspiration. (The picture is reproduced in the useful iconographical album *Thomas Mann: Ein Leben in Bildern*, but the player is not identified. I offer his name as my contribution to Mann scholarship.) Had they met at Wimbledon, Hoad would probably have been safe from anything beyond a handshake. As far as we can tell, Mann's extramarital love life was mainly a thing of dreams: a significant glance from the young waiter, an ambivalent smile from the new pool cleaner. From the angle of actual fulfilment, the great writer was out of it: except in his mind.

But the mind is where it is. Even when the body finds its satisfaction, the mind does not find rest. We know this was true for Lichtenberg himself, whose own sexual history was a thing for wonder and pity. A cruelly crippled hunchback dwarf, he found love and marriage, but on a crooked path. Yet he found out enough to become a student of the passions. If he had not been such a student, he could not have composed this aphorism. From the way it is written, we can tell he was a step ahead of its apparent conclusions. He was always a step ahead. He was one of those people who have every excuse to tell us that life is valueless, and yet who love life so much that they can even forgive, if not forget, the fate that condemned them to their long anguish.

> There is no surer sign of a great writer than when whole
> books could be made out of his passing remarks. Each in
> his way, Tacitus and Sterne are both masters of this quality.
> — LICHTENBERG, *APHORISMEN*

When Lichtenberg wrote this, Sterne was practically his contemporary, so by yoking Sterne with Tacitus he was perpetrating a deliberately shocking boldness, as if we were to say that same lessons could be drawn equally from the letters of Madame de Sévigné and the diaries of Bridget Jones. It is an attention-getting way of promulgating a truth, but the truth had better be true. This truth was. Making marks in the margin of his Shakespeare, Keats noted the quality of Shakespeare's "bye-writing": the local intensities that were better than they needed to be. The awkwardness of Lichtenberg's principle—and really all his principles are awkward—is that it subverts any idea of artisitic unity. Ideally, nothing in a written work should show signs of wanting to hive off and start another work. Practically, it happens all the time, and not always in expository prose, although naturally a discursive argument is more likely to provide instances of a subsidiary statement that asks to be followed up. In *The Gulag Archipelago*, there is a great moment when prisoners are sweltering in a black Maria while Jean-Paul Sartre is standing a few feet away on the footpath proclaiming the wonders of the Soviet Union. It could conceivably be the start of a different book about the stupidity of philosophers, but in fact it fits. There is another great moment, however, that doesn't. On a prison train, Solzhenitsyn is jammed into the floor of a compartment with about an inch of air to breathe in, and suddenly realizes he is happy. It doesn't fit at all: it is the start of another work, about mysticism—a work that could have been written by the mystical philosopher Nikolay Berdyayev. It could be said that if Solzhenitsyn had not been capable of such moments, *The Gulag Archipelago* would not be one of the great books about lost possibilities, so it fits after all: but it dangerously leaves the way open to the thoroughly misleading conclusion that extreme conditions have a justification in mystical experience.

The problem of the passing remark crops up most often in novels, and especially in the greatest novels. Theoretically, a great novel should meet a poem's standard of containing nothing extraneous. In practice, great novels are always sinning against that standard, and are usually the better for it. In *Madame Bovary*, the socially aspiring Emma, invited to the grand ball at the country house, notices that aristocrats are glossier than ordinary people. The observation begs to be the starting point for a sociological treatise on differential nutrition, but it just doesn't sound like her conclusion: it sounds like Flaubert's. If he had said that she *didn't* notice, and had made the observation his, he would have been telling us more about her. In *The Great Gatsby*, the scene where Gatsby shows Daisy his beautiful shirts fits as perfectly as the shirts. Gatsby has nothing else to woo her with except the proofs of his wealth: flaunting the shirts, he makes the material spiritual—the key to his character, and the clue to how Fitzgerald can get poetically interested in the Philistine he has chosen as a hero. (The putative mystery of Gatsby's identity is no mystery at all: he is what Fitzgerald would have been if he had had no talent.) When Daisy's coldly amoral friend Jordan Baker moves her golf ball, she tells you everything you need to know about her character. But Fitzgerald was also capable of the passing remark that doesn't fit at all. His narrator Nick Carraway's gift for the aphorism makes you wonder if he was studying Pascal when he was learning to sell bonds. "If personality is an unbroken series of successful gestures," Nick says of Gatsby, "there was something gorgeous about him." It was the first line of the book I learned, but I learned it because it broke off from the book. Similarly, Nick's avowal that "Any display of complete self-assurance draws a stunned tribute from me" is a bit too good, because the man who says it is displaying complete self-assurance. None of this means that *The Great Gatsby* is less than what it is: a masterpiece. But it does mean that one of the characteristics of a masterpiece might be its composer's ability to get in extra stuff without us noticing the strain of the shoehorn. Even in *The Great Gatsby*, you can tell that Fitzgerald was a notebook writer. Things would go into the notebook that were too good to leave unused, and one way or another he would get them into the novel. Hemingway worked in the other direction. A really good Hemingway short story is an episode from the novel he did not make the mistake of trying to pack around it. By extension, a really bad Hemingway novel is the accumulated sets of notes for short stories he did not write.

In Anthony Powell's *A Dance to the Music of Time*, there is a tremendous moment just after the lumbering anti-hero Widmerpool, at the height of his pomposity and power, has delivered a boring lecture about an immensely valuable vase. The beautiful but dangerous Pamela comes along and vomits into it. You need to have followed both characters through several novels of the sequence to see the perfection of the coincidence. It fits together like the components of a Rolls-Royce Merlin engine from two different shadow factories. But I can remember a line from the narrator, Nicholas Jenkins: something like "Nothing beats the feeling of an interesting woman being interested in us." I thought it sounded like an aphorism from one of Powell's notebooks. I have searched the novels and can't find it, and I can't find it in the notebooks either. Perhaps I heard him say it. I knew Powell well enough at one stage for us to have talked about such things. He was terrific on the mechanics of his craft, but it should be remembered that he found almost everyone clumsy except himself. He has been mocked for that. The truth is that most writers feel the same, because they read other writers professionally and are always on the lookout for a muffed trick.

In *Lucky Jim* Kingsley Amis is consistently wonderful at separating Jim's particular viewpoint from the narrative. The French have a term, *style indirect libre*, for the narrative prose that is coloured by the character's viewpoint because the character is in the scene; but the trick of the technique is that the writer's frame of reference must not get into the character's head. In the tour de force comic scene near the end of *Lucky Jim* when Jim, if he is not to lose Christine forever, must get to the railway station and everything conspires to stop the bus, we are laughing too hard to notice that Jim makes the wrong conjecture about why the bus driver is apparently slumped at the wheel. Had he been struck, Jim asks, by the idea for a poem? Jim does not write poems and so would not know that getting an idea for a poem can render a poet catatonic. It is something only the narrator would know. But at the time, for one reader at least, the anomaly didn't matter, and indeed it still doesn't. I think it is probably the funniest scene in all of literature, so if there is a blemish, it must be part of the beauty. Written works of art aren't perfect. They create the air of being so, but they are too full of life to keep all their own implications within the perimeter. Lichtenberg was warning us against a Procrustean ideal of perfection. No writer, not even Chekhov in his short stories, can be Vermeer. A painter can leave you with nothing left to say. A writer leaves you with everything to say. It is in the nature of his medium to start a conversation within you that will not stop until your death, and what he is really after is to be among the last voices you will hear.

M

❦ ❦ ❦

Norman Mailer

Nadezhda Mandelstam

Golo Mann

Heinrich Mann

Michael Mann

Thomas Mann

Mao Zedong

Chris Marker

John McCloy

Zinka Milanov

Czeslaw Milosz

Eugenio Montale

Montesquieu

Alan Moorehead

Paul Muratov

NORMAN MAILER

☀ ☀ ☀

Norman Mailer was born in Brooklyn in 1923, educated at Harvard, saw action in the Pacific, and returned to write one of the three American novels that made the war the subject of a serious best-seller, with the word "serious" used in both senses. James Jones wrote *From Here to Eternity*, Irwin Shaw wrote *The Young Lions*, and Mailer wrote the book that was most commonly, and correctly, greeted as a modern classic, *The Naked and the Dead*. The unarguable stature of his novel established him immediately in the twin roles of media celebrity and literary hope: an inherent conflict which it suited his personality to dramatize, and which it suited his talent to make a subject, thus opening up a whole new avenue of creative expression that can be summed up by one his titles, *Advertisements for Myself*. Ever since his dazzling beginnings, for a half century and more of unceasing fame, Mailer the holding company and corporate brand-name has mainly been in competition with himself, pitting Mailer the novelist against Mailer the anti-novelist, whose principal incarnation is the writer of non-fiction. The novelist Mailer, as if in flight from his own talent, has always made a point of writing barely readable books—from *Barbary Shore* to *Ancient Evenings*, they

stretch out in a line that only a tenured academic could love—
but he occasionally re-emerges from disaster with a substantial
new success: *Harlot's Ghost* was the fictional effort most like a
complete return to form. If there had been whole row of such
completely worked-out novels he would have ranked unquestionably with Philip Roth, John Updike and Saul Bellow
among the novelists giving us the imaginative account of
America's post-war emergence as the world's dominant cultural power. It could be said that he chose to do something
more interesting, although it is possible that burgeoning
alimony requirements chose his course for him. For whatever
reason, he preferred to extend the career of the other Mailer,
the journalist. Unlike his television sparring partner Gore
Vidal, he has never—to his loss and ours—bothered to master
the standard set form of the pointed and reasonably brief essay.
But he has invented other forms in profusion, some of them
running to volume length. In his books of non-fictional prose,
such as *The Armies of the Night* and *Of a Fire on the Moon*, are
to be found some of his most astonishing stretches of imaginative prose. Tom Wolfe, in his entertaining book of essays *Hook-
ing Up*, is within his rights to contend that his own novel *A
Man in Full*, which took him ten years of research, well
deserved its commercial success, the hit parade result that the
average, dashed-off novel or glorified think-piece by Mailer
fails to achieve. But Wolfe is on dangerously yielding ground
when he supposes that the assiduous fidelity of his own social
observation is automatically a more interesting quality than
Mailer's irresponsible extravagance. Wolfe's diligent reportage
is good at observed detail, and he knows how to dress it up
with exaggeration, invective and mimesis, but Mailer's prose,
even at its most slipshod, has access to moments of poetry
beyond the ken of a busy dandy in a white suit. Everything that
the cult of celebrity in America can do to destroy an artistic gift
has been done to Mailer. Much of the damage he has either
connived at, or else has taken an indecent pleasure in recording, as in the wonderfully awful *The Prisoner of Sex*. But the
fame machine is right to recognize him as a talent, as if talent

can exist as a potential, without solid achievement. It can. As when Orson Welles sat on television doing nothing except reminisce about films that were never even made, the creative imagination can prove it exists merely by suggesting itself. Literary talent, especially, will out even when its owner goes nuts. It might come only in flashes, but without the flashes there was never a true fire. It must be firmly said, however, that the hints demand to be followed back to their source: every student should be familiar in detail with *The Naked and the Dead*, the book in which an abundant gift fulfilled its duty to history, at the precise moment when American cultural imperialism became, for good or ill, the world's most pervasive political fact.

In the middle classes, the remark, "He made a lot of money," ends the conversation. If you persist, if you try to point out that that money was made by digging through his grandmother's grave to look for oil, you are met with a middle-class shrug.
— NORMAN MAILER, *THE PRESIDENTIAL PAPERS*, P. 233

IF HE HAD never written a single novel, we would have to call Norman Mailer a great talent, and even a great poetic talent, simply for the richness of his prose. If he had made himself the protagonist of twice as many embarrassing scenes, we would still have to call him disciplined: because in even the most fatuous of his written opinions he is capable of a phrase that opens up the depths of a subject on which he seems determined to sound shallow. He couldn't be trivial if he tried, and sometimes he tries hard. Mailer tried especially hard when he was young, with the result that no considerable writer sounded young so long. Henry Miller, whom Mailer generously elected as a precursor, was less a case of protracted adolescence than of premature senility. Miller, doddering and drivelling before his time, drooled much low-flown foolishness but never volunteered himself as a teenage fantasist. Mailer did, and well into what should have been his mature years: when he suggested, in cold print, that he had met Sonny Liston and seen fear in his eyes—meaning fear of the physical violence that the coiled Mailer might unleash—there was a sort of brilliance to it. (There might also, it should be said, have been an element of truth, although not in the way Mailer intended: professional fighters will go a long way to avoid a brawl with a civilian, because a human skull is exactly the wrong sort of thing to hit with an unprotected hand.)

But there is nothing very brilliant about Mailer's standpoint in this paragraph: it is the same blanket rejection of the bourgeoisie that Sartre tried to wish on Flaubert, and is self-refuting in the same way, by the social background of the man writing it. There is everything brilliant, however, about the comic illustration contained within it. The illustration is not even placed or timed for comedy: it is just thrown in, as if it were being thrown away. (Its introduction is decidedly casual, and even careless: he could have put "that the" for "that that," thus avoiding an awkward mouthful that always looks more mistaken than intended.) The illustration takes off from a cliché: the man who would sell his grandmother is already in the language. But Mailer's man digs though his grandmother's grave to look for oil. You get the sense that Mailer thought of that on the spot—on a flat spot that he saw needed livening up. Somewhere among his many writings about writing—perhaps in *Advertisements for Myself*—he speaks about the delight he felt when he revised a sentence in the last draft of *The Deer Park* and hit on the extra few words that brought it to life. With his usual combination flurry of modesty and conceit (Mailer's verbal version of the old one-two) he is enunciating a principle. The principle is simple, but only because its complexity is irreducible. It is the poetic principle. Mailer is no better at analysing it than any other poet who possesses the same gift. All he can do is tap into it when it comes. When it doesn't come, he has to wait; and he has said and done some silly things while waiting. But he has never had to wait long.

Randall Jarrell said that a poet must wait to be hit by lightning. Even in an otherwise demented essay, Mailer can be hit by lightning so often that you can hear his hair fizz. The effect is of brilliant conversation. You are having a drink with him, and he wants to describe someone who will do anything for money. The standard idea comes into his head of a man selling his mother or grandmother. Instantly he sees that the idea needs improvement. Sell her into white slavery? Not good enough. What about if she's already dead? Hallowed ground. Where is the money? Under the hallowed ground. So the man digs through his grandmother's grave to look for oil. Like the inspired talker, Mailer can put it all together in a moment. In jazz, the improvisation that most satisfies is the one that comes out better than it could be written. The quickness of the creative power deceives the intellect. No wonder the young Mailer saw himself as a jazz soloist. Writing like this, he is at his most American, and shows why America is at the heart of modernity—which would be arid if it were merely a sophisticated development, but is at its most rich when the sophistication returns to the emotions. One never stops writing about Mailer and neither does he. In both cases, however, the best reason to do so is that he takes us so close to the awkward reality about talent. It does not belong to its possessor. Its possessor belongs to it, and can find freedom only by accepting that he is a slave.

NADEZHDA MANDELSTAM

❧ ❧ ❧

Nadezhda Yakovlevna Khazina, known to us as Nadezhda Mandelstam (1899–1980), would have been sufficiently famous as the heroic wife and widow of Osip Mandelstam, one of the finest poets of twentieth-century Russia, and therefore one of the most illustrious of Stalin's victims among those luminaries of the old intelligentsia who had stayed on in Russia in the mistaken belief that the Soviet regime would be an opportunity for culture. As the naïvely non-political lyric poet soon found, it would have been an opportunity for him to starve, if Nadezhda's scholarly ability to translate easily out of the principal European languages had not helped to pay for the groceries. After the poet was arrested in 1934 (his "crime" had been to write a few satirical lines about Stalin), Nadezhda's translations from English were her only means of sustenance during her long banishment to the provincial towns, during which time, in 1938, her husband finally perished in the Gulag. Only after she was permitted to return to Moscow, in 1964, did she begin to write *Hope Against Hope*, the magnificent book that puts her at the centre of the liberal resistance under the Soviet Union and indeed at the centre of the whole of twentieth-century literary and political history. Some would place her book even ahead of Primo Levi's *Se questo è un uomo* (*If This Is a Man*—unforgivably known, in America, under the feel-good title of *Survival in Auschwitz*) and Jung Chang's *Wild Swans* as required preliminary reading for any prospective student enrolled at a university. A masterpiece of prose as well as a model of biographical narrative and social analysis, *Hope Against Hope* is mainly the story of the terrible last years of persecution and torment before the poet was murdered. Nadezhda and her husband are the most promiment characters, although there is a vivid portrait of Anna Akhmatova. The book's sequel, *Hope Abandoned*, is about the author's personal fate, and is in some ways even more terrible, because, as the title implies, it is more about horror as a way of life than as an interruption to normal expectancy. Both volumes are superbly translated into English by Max Hayward. Until the collapse of the regime, they were available in the original language only in samizdat or else from printing houses situated outside the Sovet borders. As with Akhmatova's permanently banned poem "Requiem," their final, free and full publication in Russia marked the day when the Soviet Union came to an end, and freedom—which Nadezhda, against mountainous evidence, had always said would one day return of its own accord—returned.

> We all belonged to the same category marked down for absolute destruction. The astonishing thing is not that so many of us went to concentration camps or died there, but that some of us survived. Caution did not help. Only chance could save you.
> — NADEZHDA MANDELSTAM, *HOPE ABANDONED*, P. 67

"ONLY CHANCE COULD save you" is the best thing ever said about life under state terror, and it took Nadezhda Mandelstam to say it so directly, bravely and unforgettably. Max Hayward chose the English titles well for his magnificent translations of her two great books. *Hope Against Hope* is about a gradual, reluctant but inexorable realization that despair is the only thing left to feel: it is the book of a process. *Hope Abandoned* is about what despair is like when even the memory of an alternative has been dispelled: the book of a result. The second book's subject is spiritual desolation as a way of life. Several times, in the course of the text, Nadezhda proclaims her fear that the very idea of normality has gone from the world. "I shall not live to see the future, but I am haunted by the fear that it may be only a slightly modified version of the past." The memory of what happened can't even be passed on without ruining the lives of those called upon to understand. "If any brave young fellow with no experience of these things feels inclined to laugh at me," she writes, "I invite him back into the era we lived through, and I guarantee that he will need to taste only a hundredth part what we endured to wake up in the night in a cold sweat, ready to do anything to save his skin the next morning." Well, none of us brave young fellows back there in the comfortable West of the late 1960s and early 1970s felt inclined to laugh at her. Schopenhauer had said that a man is in a condition of despair when he thinks a thing will happen because he wants it not to, and that what he wishes can never be. Nadezhda had provided two books to show how that felt. As such, they were key chapters in the new bible that the twentieth century had written for us. In a bible it is not astonishing that some of the gospels should sound like each other and seem to tell the same story. In Primo Levi's books, the theme is often struck that the only real story about the Nazi extermination camps was the common fate of those who were obliterated: the story of the survivors was too atypical to be edifying, and to dwell on it could only lead to the heresy that Levi called Survivalism and damned as a perversion. Survival had nothing to do with anything except chance: there was no philosophy to be extracted from it, and certainly no guide to behaviour. In Russian instead of Italian, Nadezhda said exactly the same thing about life under Stalin: Only chance could save you.

It was the dubious distinction of the Soviet Union to create, for the remnants of the old Russian intelligentsia, conditions by which they could experience, in what passed for ordinary civilian life, the same uncertainties and terrors as the victims who would later be propelled into Nazi Germany's concentrated universe. The main difference was that in Nazi Europe the victims knew from the start who they were, and eventually came to know that they were doomed. In the Soviet Union, the bourgeois elements could not even be certain that they were marked down for death. Like Kafka's victims in the *Strafkolonie*, they were in a perpetual state of trying to imagine what their crime might be. Was it to have read books? Was it to have red hair? Was it (the cruellest form of fear) to have submitted too eagerly? Other versions of the same story came out of China, North Korea, Romania, Albania, Cambodia. The same story came out of the Rome of Tiberius, but the twentieth century gave something new to history when societies nominally dedicated to human betterment created a climate of universal fear. In that respect, the Communist despotisms left even Hitler's Germany looking like a throwback. Hitler was hell on earth, but at least he never promised heaven: not to his victims, at any rate. It's the *disappointment* of what happened in the new Russia that Nadezhda captures and distils into an elixir. There were some mighty thinkers about the true nature of the Soviet incubus: Yevgeny Zamyatin, Boris Souvarine, Victor Kravchenko, Evgenia Ginzburg, Varlan Shalamov, Solzhenitsyn, Sakharov, Roy Medvedev and Aleksandr Zinoviev are only a few of them. Generally, however, the artists, if they lived long enough to speak, spoke better than the philosophers. But it was Nadezhda's distinction to speak better than the artists. With no lyrical world in which to find refuge, she commanded a prose more potent even than her husband's poetry, and perhaps that made her the greatest artist of all. She found the means to express how an unprecedented historic experiment had changed the texture even of emotion.

Even the incandescently gifted Anna Akhmatova, with whom Nadezhda had always been involved in intimate bonds of passion, jealousy and respect, never quite grew out of the romantic nature that helped to make her one of the most justly loved of the modern Russian poets. In her poem "Requiem," Akhmatova encapsulated the anguish of millions of devastated women when she wrote "husband dead, son in jail: pray for me." But a romantic she remained, still believing in the imaginative validity of a love affair beyond time. In *Hope Abandoned*, Nadezhda was able to say firmly that her friend was mistaken. Love affairs beyond time were impossible to take seriously when violent separations in the present had become the stuff of reality. With real life so disturbed, the nature of romanticism had been changed. In the new reality, all love affairs were beyond time.

It is important not to reach conclusions too quickly about whom she means by "we" and "us." An unreconstructed Stalinist, if we can suppose there were such a thing left, might say that she was identifying the class enemy. Quite early in the regime's career of permanent house cleaning—certainly no later than Lunacharsky's crackdown on the avant-garde in 1929—anyone stemming from the pre-revolutionary intelligentsia was automatically enrolled along with remnants of the bourgeoisie in the classification of "class enemy." Variations of the Sicilian Vespers multiplied. Civilized articulacy was as deadly a give-away as soft hands. (In a development that eerily echoed Shakespeare's scenes about Jack Cade, the Proletkult Komsomols were able to identify a victim's ability to defend himself verbally as certain evidence of guilt.) Eventually any kind of knowledge that had been acquired under the old order was enough to mark down its possessor. Just as Pol Pot's teenage myrmidons assailed anyone who wore spectacles, so the Soviet "organs" discovered that even a knowledge of engineering was a threat to state security. (Solzhenitsyn, it will be recalled, was especially poignant about the fate of the engineers.) Any field of study with its own objective criteria was thought to be inherently subversive. Given time, Stalin would probably have applied the Lysenko principle to every scientific field. To this day, scholars puzzle over the reasons for Stalin's purging the Red Army of its best generals in the crucial years leading up to June 1941, but the answer might lie close to hand. The fact that military knowledge—strategy, tactics and logistics—was a field of data and principles verifiable independently of ideology might have been more than enough to invite his hatred. In attacking his own army, of course, Stalin came close to demolishing the whole Soviet enterprise. But at the centre of the totalitarian mentality is the fear that the internal enemy might go unapprehended. Luis Buñuel gives a poetically condensed rendition of this truth in his *Discreet Charm of the Bourgeoisie*, when the chief of police, who has slept like a baby while dreaming of prisoners being tortured, wakes screaming and sweating when he dreams that one of them escapes.

A totalitarian regime's progressively expanding concept of the enemy is the thing to bear in mind when Nadezhda seems to be identifying herself as part of a class. She is really identifying herself as part of a category, and the category includes anyone who might offer a threat to the regime's monolithic authority—which means anyone capable of independent moral judgement. She does not go so far as to propose the possibility of independent moral behaviour: not even a hero can actively dissent if the penalty for recalcitrance is the suffering of loved ones. But she does believe that there is such a thing as independent moral judgement, a quality in perfect polarity with the regime, which can't tolerate the existence of independent moral judgement, and indeed has come into being specifically so as to eliminate all such values.

Throughout her two books, Nadezhda looks for comfort to those whose memories go back to the pre-revolutionary past. But her originality lies in her slowly dawning realization that decency is a human quality which can exist independently of social origins. Without that realization, she would never have been able to formulate the great, ringing message of her books, an unprecedented mixture of the poetic and the prophetic—the message that the truth will be born again of its own accord. She didn't live to see it happen: so the whole idea was an act of faith. Finally her inspiring contention is unverifiable, because when, after the nightmare was at last over, the truth was indeed reborn, it was hard to imagine that such a renaissance could have occurred without books like hers in the background. But there weren't many books like hers, and although it will always be useful to examine how the agents of change received their education in elementary benevolence, it might be just as valuable to consider her two main principles in the full range of their combined implications. One principle was that the forces of unreasoning inhumanity had won an overwhelming victory with effects more devastating than we could possibly imagine. The other principle was that reason and humanity would return. The first was an observation; the second was a guess; and it was the inconsolable bravery of the observation that made the guess into a song of love.

GOLO MANN

❣ ❣ ❣

Golo Mann (1909–1994), modern Germany's greatest historian, was the third child of its greatest modern novelist, Thomas Mann. After making a shaky start as the unbeloved son outshone by his brilliant siblings Klaus and Erika, the awkward Golo rose gradually to his later status as the family's scholastically most distinguished representative. Some of his historical works were written in the American exile that began in 1940, but by 1952 he was back in Germany for a succession of professorships and for the composition of his major books. *Wallenstein*, widely proclaimed as his masterpiece, is a hard read in the original and not much easier in English, but his monumental (a thousand pages plus) *Deutsche Geschichte des 19. und 20. Jahrhunderts* has the pace of a thriller and is easily seen to be the finest history of modern Germany. A separately published extract from it, *Deutsche Geschichte 1919–1945*, is probably the best single introduction to Germany's twentieth century tragedy, and an ideal book from which to start learning to read German. His memoir *Erinnerungen und Gedanken* (Memories and Thoughts) has the story of his youth and mental development under the Weimar Republic. As so often with the great historians, Golo Mann is perhaps best approached through his ancillary writings, where his opinions are high-lighted. The volumes of essays *Geschichte und Geschichten* and *Wir alle sind, was wir gelesen* (We Are All What We Read) show his capacity to get a book's worth of reflections into an article. His detailed trouncing of A. J. P. Taylor's chic views about the purportedly inevitable nature of Nazi foreign policy is a valuable instance of a serious political engagement knocking the stuffing out of a fad. If one writer could represent the recovery of liberal thought in Germany after World War II, it would be Golo Mann.

> To attribute foreseeable necessity to the catastrophe of Germany and the European Jews would be to give it a meaning that it didn't have. There is an unseemly optimism in such an assumption. In the history of mankind there is more that is spontaneous, wilful, unreasonable and senseless than our conceit allows.
> — GOLO MANN, *GESCHICHTE UND GESCHICHTEN*, P. 170

THROUGHOUT HIS distinguished career as an historian, Golo Mann tried to warn us against the consequences of attributing inevitability to what happened in Germany when he was growing up. This paragraph is one among many statements of that theme. What makes it especially notable is the way it traces a bad intellectual habit to a psychological propensity. Optimism, cocksureness, Professor Hindsight, call it what you like: there is a disposition of personality that likes to impose itself on the past and turn it into a self-serving cartoon. One becomes a seer in the safest possible way: retroactively. One predicts the past as a dead certainty. Golo Mann, who had been there when it happened, always remembered the uncertainty. According to him, the Weimar Republic didn't have to collapse: after it did, to say that it had to was yet another way of undermining it—sabotage after the fact. Similarly, the Jews didn't have to die, or even have to be classified as Jews. The classification was Hitler's idea, as was the massacre: the second thing following with awful logic from the first. But the first could have stayed in his sick mind, and he could have stayed out of power. If even one of the main factors had been subtracted from the Weimar equation—the inflation, the Depression, the unemployment—then out of power he would have stayed, to haunt the back alleys of lunatic fringe politics where he belonged. Facing the possibilities that were real even though they did not happen, Golo Mann found the most resonant and lasting application of his principle that the surest way to deprive an historical event of its significance is to abdicate from the task of tracing it back to its origins, which will be the more distant the more the event seems like ineluctable fate. And in that long chain of circumstances, anything could have been different.

Golo Mann's first book, published in 1947, was a treatise on the diplomat Friedrich von Gentz, the man whose claim to fame was that he was not as famous as Metternich. An historian's first book is characteristically rich in themes that will occupy him for the rest of his career, but part of the richness usually comes from their entanglement: he knows what he thinks, but tries to say it all at once. Golo Mann's book on Gentz is unusual for what can only be called a precocious maturity. To some extent this was imposed on him: because of the political disruptions in his early life, he was already in his late thirties when he began to publish. Undoubtedly his limpid view came from what he had experienced in the time of the Weimar Republic, and not from what he had read about the time of Metternich. He called the pre-revolutionary period before 1848 a hopeful time. People were full of ideas about how life could be more free and more just. *Aber diese Ideen hatten zu ihrer Verwirklichung durchaus nicht der Revolution bedurft.* But these ideas didn't need a revolution to make them real. This is still a key sentence; and was, at the time he first wrote it, a marker put down for the view of history he would unfold throughout his books, culminating in his masterpiece—which, in my view, is not his *Wallenstein* (1971) but his *Deutsche Geschichte des 19. und 20. Jahrhunderts* (1958). Without question *Wallenstein* is a mighty book. Its true worth is hard to assess in English because Golo Mann's prose style, when he wrote the book, was at its most dense and therefore at its least susceptible to being translated with decent respect for its unfaltering rhythm. Like his father Thomas, Golo Mann was accustomed to writing a sentence at the full length allowable by German grammar. Like any other language with arbitrary genders, German permits far longer flights of unambiguous coherence than English. The translator of *Wallenstein* fatally attempted to translate block-long sentences without breaking them up. The result is a meal of nougat, with molasses to wash it down.

But even in the original, where the style is merely condensed, *Wallenstein* suffers from its inclusiveness: the points are buried in documentary detail, and in the effort to isolate and remember them you feel that your enemy is the book itself. *Deutsche Geschichte* isn't like that. Memorable from paragraph to paragraph, the book sends you back to itself before you have finished it, just for the enjoyment of seeing complexity put so clearly. *Deutsche Geschichte* was one of the books from which I taught myself German, and we always have an immoderate affection for the books that brought us into another language. But since I first read it right through with dictionary to hand, I have re-read it twice from cover to cover, and am always using various bits of it as starting points for opening up a specific topic. At its height, Golo Mann's prose approaches the ideal of the continuous aphorism: you find yourself learning it like poetry. In the fascicle marked *Deutsche Geschichte 1919–1945* his analysis of the Weimar Republic's permanent crisis centres on a single formulation. He says that the split between capital and labour was at the centre of politics—the centre from which "the public was indeed governed, but always in a divisive manner." That was the fissure Hitler got in through, like a plague rat through a crack. Not that Golo Mann found the collapse of the Weimar Republic inevitable. There were many times it could have consolidated itself, if circumstances had not conspired against it. In an essay collected in *Gecshichte und Geschichten* (1963), he excoriated A. J. P. Taylor for Taylor's pernicious certitude on the subject. Taylor said that from the viewpoint of foreign policy the advent of the Nazis meant a return to political realism from the previous liberal dreamland. Golo Mann knew that the liberal dreamland had contained all the real hopes, and that Hitler's political realities were lethal fantasies.

In his *Zeiten und Figuren* (Times and Figures) (1979), Golo Mann expounded his key concept of *Offenheit nach der Zukunft hin*—openness to the future. He didn't just mean it as a desirable trait of personality but as a necessary qualification for the historian. By an effort of the imagination, the historian must put himself back into a present where the future has not yet happened, even though he is looking back at it through the past. If a narrator knows the future of his hero, he, the narrator, "is bound to tinge even the simplest narrative with irony." Succumbing too easily to the ironic mode is a cheap way of being Tacitus. The true high worth of Tacitus depended on his being always aware that tragic events had been the result of accidents and bad decisions, and the depth of the tragedy lay in the fact that the accidents need not have happened and the decisions might have been good. In a predetermined world there would be no tragedy, only fate. With his revered Tacitus as an example, Golo Mann was able to form the view that fatalism and frivolity were closely allied: to be serious about history, you had seriously to believe that things might have been otherwise.

Golo Mann could have his weak moments. Too quick to understand Ernst Jünger's flirtation with the idea of a powerfully rearmed Germany, he allowed the possibility of Jünger's genuine detachment from the awfulness of Nazi reality, as if Jünger's aesthetic refinement had been a part excuse for his political indifference. But the part excuse was wholly a defence mechanism. Jünger's *Tagebücher* should have revealed to Golo Mann—otherwise the most acute of stylistic analysts, on top of his other virtues—that Jünger took refuge in the exquisite as a way of not thinking about the obvious. One is reminded of the indulgence Gitta Sereny extended to Albert Speer: she convicted him only of not wanting to know. But he did know. He always knew. To be civilized is not a hindrance to recognizing the barbaric. The hindrance is the barbaric within oneself. Jünger was wedded to the idea of a strong, militaristic Germany. The wedding made him slow to see what the Nazis were actually doing. Why Golo Mann should have been slow to see what Ernst Jünger was doing is another question. The answer might have had something to do with Golo Mann's long passion for putting a liberal German intellectual tradition back together. He didn't want to throw away an attractive fragment.

It could have been that he just didn't like the idea of denouncing a misfit bookworm. He had been one of those himself. The Manns were not a dysfunctional family, but they were a family of dysfunctional people, and the young Golo had been an oddball even among the Manns. There is a desperately touching passage in his memoirs *Erinnerungen und Gedanken* (1986) when he recollects, as if it were yesterday (and obviously he always felt as if it were), how he was shut out from some yodelling youth movement. He had an urge to fit in. When he volunteered for the crucial job of going back to Munich to save Thomas Mann's compromising private diaries from the Nazis, he became indispensable at last. But his homosexuality always troubled him more than the same condition troubled his elder siblings, Klaus and Erika. Fractured character is probably what made him an artist among historians. Artists complete themselves in their works. Golo Mann's works are not so much the expression of a complete personality as of a personality completing itself as it writes: he is working himself out before your eyes, the way artists do. With an internal scope to energize his view of the external world, he set the measure for all the liberal German historians to come. E. H. Gombrich's irascible but useful complaint that his generation of assimilated Jews did not regard themselves as Jewish was already there in Golo's writings, enshrined as a principle. (It should be noted that Golo and his siblings were only quarter Jews, which might have got them by; but their mother was a half Jew, which would surely have meant trouble; so he had reasons near home for pondering the matter as the Nazis came closer to assuming power.)

By imposing a racial definition, Hitler did not reveal a reality: he created one, out of his own poisonous obsessions. Similarly, the pundits on the revisionist side of the *Historikerstreit* in the 1980s had already been discredited by what Golo Mann had written before they were ever heard from. Ernst Nolte and Andreas Hillgruber wanted to call Hitler's wars of extermination inevitable because Hitler was only reacting to what the Soviet Union had already done. Golo Mann had established in advance that there was no such historical tendency except in retrospect. In retrospect, the reader of history is apt to wish that less history had been written, but we are unlikely to feel that when reading Golo Mann. Second only to Thomas in the Mann clan, Golo wrote even finer expository prose than his father. It is sad that Thomas Mann did not live long enough to see the full glory of his most loyal son, but perhaps he guessed that it would come. We are all allowed to predict the future: it is one of the imagination's privileges. But predicting the past is a mischievous habit, and Golo Mann was the first to spot just how pervasive it was becoming, as historians presumed to impose upon events a baleful shape that had stolen into their minds: a shape that was a self-protective reaction to the events themselves—one more version of the small man's revenge for helplessness.

> It was no belief: it was a crime committed
> because of bad literature.
> — GOLO MANN, *DEUTSCHE GESCHICHTE*
> *1919–1945*, P. 138

Golo Mann is the greatest German historian of the twentieth century by a long mile, but when he said this he gave a hostage to fortune. He was trying to say that the Holocaust didn't have to happen. He was certainly right about the bad literature. Anti-Semitism was the claim to profundity of almost every literary halfwit in Germany during the years when Hitler, posing dramatically in front of a cheap mirror, was rehearsing his role as the man with the magnetic eyes.

Unfortunately Golo Mann's idea about the bad literature gave precursorial support to Daniel Goldhagen's suggestion, forty years later, that a whole culture, saturated with what he called "eliminationist" anti-Semitism, had necessarily been bent on the annihilation of a race. Both opinions, Golo Mann's and Goldhagen's, need to be discounted; and Mann's, unexpectedly enough, is more insidious than Goldhagen's, which has the sole merit of refuting itself. Mann's doesn't. Some of the top Nazis can indeed be portrayed as opportunists who did not really believe their own doctrine. By the end, Himmler and Goering were both ready to do a deal to get out; Goebbels, though a dedicated fanatic at the last day, was merely hopping a bandwagon on the way in; and there is even a possibility that Heydrich's hidden motive might have been to offset the rumours about own Jewish background by building up a sufficiently impressive record of eliminating everyone else with the same drawback. (A rumour was all it was, but he might have been able to imagine circumstances in which a rumour would have been all it needed to do him damage.) One question remains, however, and it is about Hitler. If Hitler's anti-Semitism wasn't a belief, what was it?

The less attention we pay to Hitler's mysticism, the more we must pay to his practicality. In the days of the ugly birth of the SS, Hitler just wanted the new elite corps to be a bodyguard. It was Himmler who wanted the SS to be a new order of Germanic knights. At Wewelsburg, his castle in Westphalia, Himmler played King Arthur. Each of his twelve companions at the round table had a suite decorated differently: thoughts arise of Las Vegas and the Playboy Mansion West. Hitler thought all the mystical stuff was nonsense. His fanaticism was entirely on the practical level: what one might call, must call, a true belief. Unencumbered by any metaphysical junk apart from his deluded root perception into the Jewish origins of Bolshevism, Hitler's convictions were unshakeable. Himmler's, on the other hand, were flexible. The same man who talked sinister tripe about a Nordic peasant aristocracy in the east was ready to listen when the Sicherheitsdienst, after two years of intense research into the blindingly obvious, concluded that the extermination policies in Poland and Russia had defeated the political purpose. No doubt with a sinking feeling, Himmler saw the point. But there is no reason to suppose that Hitler didn't see the point as well. He just didn't let it impress him. For him, the exterminations *were* the political purpose. Self-defeating or not, mass murder was his belief. And he didn't get it from bad literature. Most of the bad literature he read was by Karl May, inventor of a Western hero called Old Shatter-hand, who was deadly in pursuit of Indians and rattlesnakes, but not of Jews—a species thin on the ground among the cactus and the sage-brush. Any other literature, no matter how bad, Hitler only pretended to read. He probably didn't even read the anti-Semitic pamphlets. What he did do was listen to their authors shouting racist filth. They shouted it because they believed it, and he got the idea immediately because it is not an idea. It's a belief, and precedes its attendant ideas as the stomach ache precedes the vomit.

HEINRICH MANN

❡ ❡ ❡

Heinrich Mann (1871–1950), four years older than Thomas Mann but doomed never to catch up, won few of the literary rewards that came the way of his world-famous younger brother. Heinrich's voluminous fictional writings earned him a reputation as the German Zola but were rarely taken seriously as works of art. Though he was never less than a celebrity, he had to watch the laurels he would have liked for himself go to his less prolific but better organized sibling. He did, however, achieve one thing uniquely his: he gave the world a universally appreciable mythical figure. His novel *Professor Unrat* (1904) featured a respectable schoolmaster who was lured to destruction by a seductive female creature of the demi-monde. Filmed in 1930 as *The Blue Angel*, the story made Marlene Dietrich a star and, through her, gave Heinrich Mann a purchase on the international popular psyche that Thomas Mann would never equal: Aschenbach, in *Death in Venice*, is for an intellectual audience, whereas Dietrich's soubrette *fatale* works her destructive magic in all men's minds to this very day. Critics who dismiss Heinrich as glibly prolific should be reminded that Thomas, though Heinrich's slapdash facility dismayed him, was always generous enough to praise his brother's talent when he saw signs of its coming into focus. Thomas's main trouble with Heinrich was Heinrich's erratic behaviour, which was only intermittently embarrassing when they were both still in Germany, but became a real problem when they were both in exile. Heinrich did not take easily to being a displaced person. In Europe he had enjoyed less prestige than Thomas but at least he was well-known. In America he was a nonentity. Whereas Thomas's books became more famous than ever in translation, Heinrich's got nowhere. He ran easily through the money that he borrowed from Thomas, drank heavily, and his unwise choice of mistress led to the kind of social awkwardness that Thomas—always conscious of his exalted position in the glittering refugee society of wartime Los Angeles—found threatening. Just because Thomas was snobbish, however, is no reason to suppose that Heinrich was some kind of wonderful free spirit. He was the kind of knockabout bore who makes things worse by apologizing for it. But perhaps his erratic sensibility gave him insight. At any rate, it was Heinrich, and not Thomas, who guessed as early as 1936 that the Nazis had an atrocity in mind beyond all reasonable imagining.

The German Jews will be systematically annihilated, of
that there can be no more doubt.
—HEINRICH MANN, *DIE DEUTSCHEN UND*
IHRER JUDEN, COLLECTED IN *POLITISCHE*
ESSAYS, P. 146.

As always in any German writings of the modern period, everything depends on the year. In 1936 there were very few intelligent people who wanted to believe that Heinrich Mann's prediction was anything except an hysterical exaggeration. And indeed it was a guess; but what he guessed was the truth. He was able to do so by taking a general view of how the repressive laws had been applied with increasing severity. He deduced the destination from the momentum. Among the people who were already suffering so severely from those restrictions, there were not yet many who were ready to draw the same conclusion. Victor Klemperer's diary from the same year provides an instructive comparison. Klemperer could guess things would get worse, but he didn't yet see that the progressive turning of the screws could end only in death. There were Nazis who didn't see it. The idea of resettling the remaining Jews on Madagascar or some similarly outlandish destination had not yet been abandoned. Historians who, for various reasons, would like to believe that the idea of extermination was hatched much later would never countenance 1936 as a year in which the threat could be realistically conceived of. In Joachim Fest's biography of Hitler, the Holocaust is not precisely a side issue, but it would be fair to say that it is not presented as Hitler's main initial aim. Once in London I met Fest at a launch party and mentioned this essay by Heinrich Mann. Fest said that he had never heard of it, and that he found it hard to believe it had been published in 1936.

Looking back on Fest's books, it might seem strange to suggest that he soft-pedalled the Holocaust. Fest's picture of Heydrich in *Das Gesicht des dritten Reiches* (The Face of the Third Reich) remains the most penetrating we have, and in his study of the July 1944 plot against Hitler's life, *Staatsstreich* (Coup d'état), he pays proper tribute to the twenty or so conspirators who told the Gestapo that revulsion against the treatment of the Jews was their main reason for getting into it. Nevertheless, over the broad span of his writings, Fest's concern with the Nazis' most defining crime has an oddly soft focus. In the case of his Hitler biography, the soft focus can only be called damaging, and it is hard to see how his hefty book, apart from its chronological completeness, is much superior, for its psychological insight, to Konrad Heiden's pioneering work (*Hitler: Das Leben eines Diktators*) published in the same year as Heinrich Mann's essay, 1936. Hugh Trevor-Roper, among post-war historians the first in the field with his *The Last Days of Hitler*, was necessarily unarmed with the subsequent scholarship but still got closer to the nub of the matter. (In 2002 Fest reprised Trevor-Roper's crepuscular theme with his short book *Untergang*, which had some nice maps of the bunker: but I saw no reason to think that Trevor-Roper's pioneering study of the man cowering inside it had been replaced.) Coming after Trevor-Roper, Alan Bullock did the first full-length biography that mattered, and it continues to matter most. Bullock reprised his theme with the relevant portions of his stereoscopic *Hitler and Stalin*, but students should not excuse themselves from reading his first monograph: one of the essential books of the modern world. J. P. Stern's short book of 1975 (*Hitler: The Fuhrer and the People*) offers useful sidelines, but he stands on Bullock's shoulders. Ian Kershaw's recent two-volume effort has not really replaced Bullock, who packed longer judgement into a shorter distance. Though simplicity of heart must always present the danger of obfuscation, there is an even greater danger in too much finesse. While their foul subject was fresh, the first post-war English historians, in early before the smoke had cleared, smelt the Devil. They were right. The lasting merit of Heinrich Mann's prescient statement is that it disarms the defence mechanism by which—even today, and looking back—we would rather classify murderously threatening language as mere rhetoric. As the historians' picture of Hitler becomes more and more elaborate, there is a greater and greater tendency to suppose that his lethality grew upon him in the course of events. But it caused the events.

MICHAEL MANN

❦ ❦ ❦

Michael Mann (b. 1943) is a director famous mainly for giving his films, no matter how violent their subject matter, a soothingly diffused and pastel look, as if their contentedly vacationing audience were wearing sunglasses even at night. Though Mann had already made movies before he became executive producer of the globally successful *Miami Vice*, it was for the brushed and powdered episodes of that television series that he first achieved the full development of his characteristic look, which made a hero out of Don Johnson's tailor and turned Florida into an advertisement for itself. Like most film directors with an early history of earning their keep in television, Mann was obliged, however, to learn that the look of the thing came second to the story. (One of his first jobs in show business was writing scripts for *Starsky and Hutch*.) As a consequence, his feature films, pretty as they are to look at, are invariably made coherent by a strong narrative line, and not just by their tasteful mise en scène. *Manhunter*, for example, is by far the best plotted of the Hannibal Lecter movies, and would be recalled now as the benchmark for the franchise if it had not been sunk in advance by the comparative anonymity of its leading actor. (Later on—"ironically," as they say in Hollywood—the film's obscure leading man William Petersen became, as the face of *CSI*, one of the most recognizable actors on Earth.) The look of movies helps to form the stock imaginative patterns of the world, and to that extent the director often really is the formative influence. This remains true even though, in the main production centre, there is scarcely such a thing as a successful commercial movie which is not a collaborative venture controlled by a studio that can fire anybody concerned, the director included. Just as the atmospherics of Ridley Scott's *Blade Runner* now affect the appearance—and even, through the music of Vangelis, the soundtrack—of any movie made anywhere whose subject is the future, so do the atmospherics of Michael Mann's *Heat* affect the look of any movie made about crime: other directors, whether working out of the United States, Latin America, Europe or Hong Kong, either go with him, towards glamour, or go against him, towards grunge, but they always have his look in mind. What concerns me here, however, is not what happens to the pictures, but to the words. By definition, they are not in a universally appreciable language. But are they in English either? The answer has large implications, especially for international politics. If the troops who come to bring you freedom can't understand even each other, you had better hope that they know what is meant by a white flag.

Let's violate his ass right now.
— MICHAEL MANN AND OTHERS, *HEAT*

THE INFORMER IS being unforthcoming. The informer is on parole. Hard-driving police captain Al Pacino and his faithful sidekick grow impatient. The sidekick suggests to Pacino that they punish the uncooperative informer by arresting him for violating his parole. "Let's violate his ass." That's the way the sidekick says it. Did you get it straight away? Confess.

An extremely advanced foreign student of English might have

enough information to realize that "let's violate" is cop-talk for "let's arrest him for violation of parole" and that "his ass" is a standard jive-talk way of saying "him." But a merely advanced student—advanced enough to know all the words in the sentence without even consulting a dictionary—might forgivably conclude that the angry sidekick and the angry captain are on the point of sodomizing their uncooperative informer. The merely advanced student would translate the line accurately and get it hopelessly wrong. (There is even the chance that a slightly less than merely advanced student, educated by correspondence in some region of central Asia where any version of a horse can buy a bride, would fail to realize that "ass" is the American version of "arse," and so get the impression that the two cops are about to commit bestiality with a valuable animal belonging to the informer: but let's leave that one out.) It follows that there is more to translation than transliteration: you need the whole cultural context. It also follows that American cultural imperialism is so powerful it doesn't need to care whether you have absorbed the cultural context or not. It just wants you to see the movie.

British and Australian audiences—to name only two English-speaking markets for the American mass media—are in the position of merely advanced students. For them a line like this might as well have a subtitle. I myself, when I first saw *Heat* in 1996, had been absorbing the American mass media for fifty years at least. I had seen hundreds of cop shows in which the words "violate" and "parole" had been used in close connection. But when I heard "violate" without "parole" I had to stop and think—not an activity that *Heat* otherwise encourages. It is a highly enjoyable movie. (I mean as opposed to a lowly enjoyable movie like *Where Eagles Dare*, in which the fun comes from the stupidity.) Michael Mann's movies are well planned and look very good. His years in the glossy sweatshop of *Miami Vice* gave him a feeling for compressed narrative and a mastery of pastel composition transferable to any setting, including the morgue. Both qualities are well on display in Mann's *Manhunter*, the first and by far the most interesting film that draws on the dubious charm of the serial killer Hannibal Lecter. Mann is a director who can make even cannibalism into a fashion statement. With *Heat* he attained his apotheosis. Unlimited mayhem never looked so balletic. The gun battles are sensational: rather more sensational, one is bound to reflect, than any gun battle could ever be in real life, where a flak jacket would not be enough to protect Al Pacino's head if even one bank robber were shooting at him with a pistol. In the film, Val Kilmer and Robert De Niro both shoot at him for minutes on end with automatic weapons. Fusillades of bullets swerve around his head by magic. In real life he would have only his admittedly formidable hairpiece to keep the hurtling slugs out of his brain. But the director isn't transcribing life, he is choreographing its myths, and especially the myths of male conflict: Mann is a *mano a mano* man. He thinks in battles. In a Mann film, even when the hero is alone on screen with a telephone, he battles with the telephone.

In *Heat*, the most sensational battle of all is the hamming contest in the coffee shop between Pacino and De Niro. These two actors have never faced each other on screen before. Each actor knows that this is the shoot-out the audience has been looking forward to for years. Each actor fights with his best weapons. Al Pacino's standard weapon is to SHOUT AT RANDOM. Elsewhere in the movie he employs it freely, but in this key scene he abandons it. Robert De Niro's standard weapon is to repeat a line half a dozen times with slight variations of emphasis. "Clean up and go home," he tells Ashley Judd. "Clean up and go *home*." Hypnotized by this mantra, Ashley Judd cleans up and goes home to Val Kilmer, so thoroughly has her will been sapped. De Niro's power of repetition is a tried and tested standard weapon. A standard weapon, tried and tested, is what it is. Tried and tested. Tried and *tested*. But in this scene he abandons it.

In the coffee shop, the two knights of the screen have taken off their helmets and laid aside the axe and mace. They have upgraded their weaponry. They are about to go nuclear. They will fight in close-up. Pacino fights with ruminative pauses and a new, noiseless smacking of the lips: a deadly weapon. De Niro fights with a new pout. It is not as extreme as Val Kilmer's pout, but Val Kilmer was born pouting, like June Allyson: Val Kilmer can't *not* pout. De Niro's new pout is a vestigial, almost subcutaneous pout, a pout more thought than deed. He is proving that he can pout without moving his lips. He also looks sideways without moving his head. He looks sideways only with his eyes: a new subtlety. (All modern screen actors look sideways as much as possible while speaking. There is one called Michael Madsen who will face away from the camera while speaking, giving you a close-up of the back of his head.) Gradually you realize that Pacino and De Niro, like the characters they are playing, will both walk away from this battle. The fix is in. The two characters they are playing respect each other. But the characters could not possibly respect each other as much as the actors playing them respect each other.

Pacino and De Niro have each grown used, during a long career, to acting any interlocutor off the screen. They have met at last only on the tacit understanding that they will act each other *on* to the screen. Exactly measured by the number of close-ups, their mutual respect will be made exhaustively manifest. The outcome will be a draw. But they have to make it look good. Making it look good, indeed, is the only reason for doing it. Making it sound good is a secondary consideration. To prove this, each man reaches for the deadliest weapon of all: silence. Personally I find this a relief from the dialogue, which isn't bad, but is not very good. In the age of *The Big Sleep* and *The Maltese Falcon*, a similar exchange would have been over and done with in a minute at most, with each actor delivering a line memorable forever. But that was then, and this is now. Now the actor does not deliver lines. He delivers himself, usually like a truck full of eggs being unloaded one by one. *Heat* has a structure, and each of its carefully assembled component scenes has a mood. What it lacks is lines, and why not? It is after something bigger than verbal quotability. But in that case, why throw in a line like "Let's violate his ass"? The only conclusion you can reach is that *nobody knew it was difficult*.

Nobody knew, or nobody cared: it amounts to the same thing. In films, dialogue is a secondary source of narrative, not the primary one. If this seems a cause for grief, it can only be said that there are bigger things to grieve about. (A film has to star Steven Seagal or Chuck Norris before it begins to pose a bigger threat to the language than yellow journalism.) When a semi-literate film-maker proclaims the supreme importance of structure, it might sound like opportunism: but literate film-makers proclaim it too, and are not likely to be wrong. That capable screenwriter William Goldman has written entertaining books to demonstrate how even the most entertaining film can't be written like a book. If the story is not first worked out to make cinematic sense, no amount of excellent dialogue will save it from going straight to video.

For those of us who will see any film that Ashley Judd appears in—the definition of star power—*Kiss the Girls* is a must. The procedural police dialogue is of the highest class: anything Morgan Freeman gets to say once you want to hear twice. But the story is out of shape, so the movie was a box office dud. In *Wag the Dog*, the dialogue is even better: it is up there with the scripts of pre-war screwball comedy, which is as high as you can go. The film, however, would have joined *Kiss the Girls* on the long shelf of modern flops if the story had not been so satisfactorily worked out. Quite often the process of making the story work will marginalize even the cleverest writer, and even more often make him or her part of a team, any member of which can be unknown to the others. As S. J. Perelman pointed out in his valuable *Paris Review* interview, F. Scott Fitzgerald's personal tragedy in Hollywood centred on his deadly knack for failing to spot, at the time, that he was not the sole author of the script he was working on, and for being devastated when he found out later. Though there are writers with star power—Robert Towne when he doesn't want to direct, Joe Eszterhas when he can stay under the top, Richard Price, Tom Stoppard and David Mamet all seemingly without fail—the practice of calling in extra writers is unlikely to change. Nor is a star director necessarily the author, though he might strive to be thought so. A successful movie is usually its own author, like a little city. My favourite example is *Tootsie*, which I admire as a whole and in every detail, especially from line to line. Like thousands of *Tootsie* fans I can practically recite the dialogue from start to finish. But I have met very few among my fellow devotees who can name its writers, and I am not even sure that I know all their names myself.

There is no point complaining about the working conditions in an industry which must resolve so many powerful forces if it is ever to produce art. Better to be grateful that it sometimes does. The first credited writer on *Shakespeare in Love* is probably still cursing Tom Stoppard, whom we bless, because he made the film a delight to listen to. But not even the first credited writer was really the first writer, who was, or were, an uncredited duo: Caryl Brahms and S. J. Simon, joint authors of *No Bed for Bacon*, a comic squib from the days before Penguins had picture covers. Stoppard never read the book, and probably still believes that some of the ideas he inherited from the first credited writer (the idea of Shakespeare practising his signature, for example) were not lifted from it, along with the basis of the plot. It scarcely matters, because the real first writer of the film was Shakespeare himself, and his co-opted spirit energizes the whole thing: *Shakespeare in Love* really does make language the true hero of a film, just as he made it the true hero of a play. Film scripts are developed properties, and their written origins can lie far back in time. (Some of the properties are remade over and over: that perfectly shaped late Cold War thriller *No Way Out*, with Kevin Costner and Sean Young, was built to a verbal template already perfected before World War II.) The confusion arises from the too-persuasive fact that since *The Jazz Singer* films have used words, and those of us who love literature are always looking for the author of them, because the films we love have words we love too. But if words were as important for the people who make movies as they are for us, those same people would be trying to write books. Filming a documentary in Los Angeles, I met George Peppard at a charity event and made the fan's standard mistake of trying to impress him with one of his own memories. In *Breakfast at Tiffany's*, he had the privilege of delivering one of George Axelrod's most intricately crafted speeches: three short lines that captured the elegance of Capote's novella, compressed it into a small space, and demonstrated why Axelrod was the first-choice Hollywood scriptwriter of his time. Remembering, as I had always remembered, the precision with which Peppard had hit the stresses, I tried it on him. "I've never had champagne before breakfast before. With breakfast, often. But never before before."

Peppard had forgotten he ever said it. In retrospect, it is hard to blame him. He was in the movie for his face and his acting, not for his sensitivity to language, which, had he let it rule his head, would later have kept him out of *The A-Team* and its attendant retirement money. At least, when he got something good to say, he showed that he knew it by saying it well. In *Indecent Proposal*, Robert Redford, in full control of the movie, delivered a speech that pitiably ripped off one of the most cherishable moments in *Citizen Kane*. The pastiche he permitted himself to deliver was miserable stuff; he must have known it was; but he was working on the principle that he didn't have to impress me. He just had to look as if he might impress Demi Moore. In screenplay terms, the heist made sense. None of this means that the words in movies never count. They can: sometimes a single line can sum up the whole screenplay, but only if the screenplay exists as an experience that can be summed up. In *Bullitt*, the central conflict between the characters played by Steve McQueen and Robert Vaughn takes the whole film to reach the point where it can be epitomized in a single word. McQueen says it. The word is "bullshit." In the version edited for television in Great Britain, that one word was snipped out by a blockheaded censor. All you saw was McQueen saying nothing. You could call it a momentary return to silent movies, but it was no return to purity. A good picture had a tiny but vital piece of its heart taken out of it with a pair of scissors. Years later, when *Bullitt* was on TV again, the contentious word had been magically restored. So the words do count, after all. They just don't count the way we would like them to, as if nothing else did. But they don't in life, either.

What we call a good movie is the product of collective talent. Occasionally it is the product of collective genius. In *Singin' in the Rain*, the absolute concentration of an entire popular culture at its most powerful, every line of dialogue, and each line of every lyric, is as good as it could be from one end of the miracle to the other. Both in its book and in its songs, it is the best writing by the best writers for film musicals there have ever been, and in order for those writers to even exist, Broadway and Tin Pan Alley had to work like factories on a double shift for more than half a century. But not a word would mean a thing if the people on screen didn't look the way they do while singing the way they do and dancing the way they do. It is hard to imagine the movie without Arthur Freed, its producer, or Stanley Donen, its director, or Betty Comden and Adolph Green, who concocted its marvellous story; but it is impossible to imagine it without Gene Kelly. Not even Fred Astaire would have fitted the same spot, because the character has to be absurdly good-looking. Gene Kelly was an absurdly good-looking man who danced sensationally well, as well as acting well and singing well enough. It took the whole of America, including all of its modern history, to produce one of him. Because he was there, the cast is there, and the immense confluence of productive effort is there, and all those unforgettable words are there. As it happens, *Singin' in the Rain* is the one film that comes close to the writer's ideal of being written into existence: the whole thing started from a single line, which in the end even turned out to be the title. It was a writer's dream: a film

born from a phrase. But Gene Kelly had to be born first. The right face
in the right place at the right time in the story—it means that the
movies, in their essence, are still silent. In *Heat*, it has to be Natalie
Portman who tries to kill herself, and Al Pacino who discovers what
she has done; and all with scarcely a word spoken. The hardest thing
for a literary critic to accept about the movies is that the writing in
them is finally beyond analysis, because a large part of the writing is in
genetic code. Finally, if the casting is right and the emotion is unmistakable, it doesn't matter what the characters say. They can say "Let's
violate his ass" and we will pretend to understand, because we have
already understood.

THOMAS MANN

❦ ❦ ❦

So enormous at first glance that he might convince us he can safely be read about rather than read, Thomas Mann (1875–1955) is nevertheless the twentieth-century cultural figure most likely to keep coming back into the student's life. We begin by thinking we can do without him, and end by realizing that there is no getting rid of him. In his life and in his art, he incorporated every question about the history of modern Germany, and its place in Europe and the world. He began as a conservative believer in Germany's national strength, a belief that was an early source of conflict between himself and his radical elder brother, Heinrich. His novel *Buddenbrooks* (1901) was the story of a prosperous family that declined *because* it became artistically more sensitive: still a usefully original emphasis, even today. The student would do better to begin, however, with the brief and easily memorable *Death in Venice* (1912), and then move on, taking the journey by easy stages, to the monumental novel that set Mann on the path to world fame and the Nobel Prize, *The Magic Mountain* (1924). In the lofty setting of an Alpine TB clinic, the intensity of what does not happen between the young hero Hans Castorp and the bewitching consumptive Claudia Chauchat raises the subject of Mann's sexuality, which remained a nagging question throughout his career. (The quickest answer is that Thomas Mann the solid paterfamilias also led a fantasy life cast with handsome young men, most of them barely glimpsed in reality: a smile from a waiter could get him started on a novel.) In the early 1930s, when he had already made his opinion well known that Hitler was a threat to all values, the incoming Nazis would have dearly liked to brand their most conspicuous literary enemy as a homosexual. Though Mann's wife, Katya, was a half Jew, Mann himself was all Aryan, but Reinhard Heydrich had correctly identified him as a friend of Jewish culture and had put his name high on a list of those absentees to be dealt with if they came back to Germany.

Mann, out of the country on a reading tour when Hitler came to power, sensibly kept going. Eventually he went all the way to America, where, in exile, he completed his seemingly inexorable rise to prominence as Germany's most exalted cultural figure since Goethe. That he himself thought in those terms should not be allowed to detract from our estimation of him. Like his snobbery, thin skin, theatrical fastidiousness and insatiable hunger for honours, his towering pride was a functional element in his ability to focus his creative energy in circumstances that deprived many of his fellow exiles of their capacity to work at all. Even when occupied with such a huge task as his sequence of novels about Joseph and his brothers, however, he found time to help some of his fellow refugees (Jews included: the idea that Thomas Mann was anti-Semitic is a calumny) and to record radio broadcasts to Germany about what the Nazis were really up to. His long novel *Doktor Faustus* is often thought of as his final confrontation with the totalitarian menace. The student is likely to find that its subject matter, the composition of music, yields no clear indication of the contending forces. A possibly more valuable, and certainly much more immediately enjoyable, late response to the history he had lived through was *The Confessions of Felix Krull*. Against all expectation, Mann, unshakeably established as the icon and titanic artist, the man of destiny and responsibility, produced, with his time ticking away, a counter-jumping con man of a character with no substance except his own vitality. *Felix Krull* is even funny, and therefore should be read early on, to provide the student with a lifetime reminder that the sometimes ponderous gravitas of Thomas Mann's career did not necessarily come from within himself, but was imposed on him by an historical distortion that he would have given a lot to avoid. He would have preferred Germany to stay as it was: but it had already stopped doing that when he was a child.

There are several good biographies, but for readers of German there is nothing to beat Marcel Reich-Ranicki's sparkling book about the Mann clan, *Thomas Mann und die Seinen* (1987). Readers of German also have the advantage of a splendid, lavishly captioned picture book, *Thomas Mann: Ein Leben in Bildern* (1997). Luckily the real treasures among the ancillary writings by and about Thomas Mann, namely his *Tagebücher* (*Diaries*), have by now nearly all been translated and annotated. Read in sequence, they are one of the most fascinating ways of following the history of the Third Reich from day to day, and of understanding why, in the end, it was doomed never to prevail. At the very time of the battle of Stalingrad, Thomas Mann, alive and well in Los Angeles, could make an appointment for a manicure. Post-war German commentators who berated him for never coming home (both the West and East German governments offered him every enticement) had a point, but he had the answer. He had never left Germany. Germany had left him. The shelves of any bookshop in Germany today will show the extent to which the nation realized its mistake.

❦ ❦ ❦

Turn aside, turn aside! Confine yourself to the personal
and the spiritual.
— THOMAS MANN, *TAGEBÜCHER*
1937–1939, P. 291

*A*BWENDEN, ABWENDEN! Turn aside, turn aside! He felt it; he believed it; but luckily he did otherwise. At the time of the disastrous Munich conference in 1938, Thomas Mann's impulse was to put the political world aside forever. Earlier, he had thought that the internationally famous writers could still do something if they teamed up. In Geneva with Paul Valéry, Gilbert Murray, Karel Čapek and Salvador de Madariaga, he had seen a possible mission for the heavyweight manifesto adorned with multiple signatures of the eminent. But after Munich he wanted to quit, and obviously thought that the resignation could be permanent. Disengagement has always been the artist's temptation and has the advantage of looking like a claim to seriousness as well as a right of refuge. Witold Gombrowicz never questioned it. In the third volume of his *Journal* (pp. 134–35) we see him reading Sartre's *Situations*, picking out the sermon on political engagement, and tearing it to shreds. Thomas Mann had arrived at the same conclusion partly from permanent instinct, partly from bitter experience.

Thomas Mann had taken a nationalist political position at the beginning of World War I and it had earned him, in the long term, a reputation as a warmongering reactionary. In the chaotic aftermath he built himself a suit of armour as the unbiddable literary eminence, becoming more and more reluctant to open his visor. His own children execrated him for his slowness to make a public condemnation of the Nazis. (Actually he had several times cried out in warning, but when the time came he thought it prudent to fall silent.) Undoubtedly there was a sense in which he would have preferred never to make a stand at all, even when he was safe abroad. Californian exile suited a personality so theatrical that it could make even retreat into a performance. In April 1941, with a rampant Hitler already on the point of turning east, Mann's idea of a pertinent note in his diary was: *Der Pudel gesund.* The poodle is healthy. He wasn't talking in code. He meant the family dog.

We could hardly be blamed for thinking him a bit of a poodle himself, if we did not have, from the same source, evidence of how much time and effort he was putting into his role as the master spirit of the emigration. He was keeping it alive with his prestige, his connections and, quite often, with his money. The eminent refugees were in his house, taking his hospitality, his advice and, above all, his precious time. In addition, he spoke for them all at a level they could not reach: on the international stage. He was wearing himself out. *Abwenden!* Turn aside! Forget about it! But against all his inclinations towards a studious solitude, he felt compelled to do the opposite, and when he did, nobody was more effective. As early as September 1942 he was making broadcasts about the massacres of Jews in the east. Having, of course, no access to the Ultra decrypts, he had to put the story together by himself, partly from the detailed reports that were showing up in the Swiss press: but he was transmitting the information in a clear voice at a time when the Allied governments were still using the soft pedal. (The story is ably told by Walter Laqueur in his *The Terrible Secret*.) Later on, there would be plenty of Germans, resident in Germany, who would be ready to claim that they had had no idea of what was going on. Thomas Mann, a German resident in California, knew exactly. His claim to represent the real Germany thus became as unassailable on the political level as it had always been on the artistic one. It had been a long time since he had wanted the idea of art to be connected to the idea of a nation. But finally, at a higher and better level, he was forced back into the identification with which he had begun, and he might even have realized that the historical disaster which had diverted him into an uncomfortable, time-consuming and uncharacteristic position of generosity had also made him a greater artist. If he had immured himself untouchably in Pacific Palisades and Brentwood he might still have given us his *Joseph*. But to give us *Felix Krull* he had to rejoin the world. The seductive, amoral fabulist Felix Krull is the invention of a man set free; and Thomas Mann was set free by submitting to the bonds of duty.

> An epic is a sublimated boredom.
> — THOMAS MANN, *TAGEBÜCHER*
> *1935–1936*, P. 23

Thomas Mann had a knack for the short statement that demands an essay to back it up. Frequently the essay was supplied by him, but the above statement sits unaccompanied in his diaries, seemingly waiting to be joined for dinner. He said it in a restaurant, perhaps while waiting too long for the reappearance of a dish he had sent back. There is truth to it, because it brings in the self-congratulatory element that helps drive the reader or listener to complete the task set by the visible dimensions of a long work. Simply by its outline, an epic demands of us that we submit to having our time consumed, and be conscious of it. There are long works for which this bargain need not be made. *War and Peace* I would have read in a breath if I could have held my breath long enough. There is nothing boring about it except the overtly philosophical passages at the end, which are tedious in the same way as Chaplin's exhortations at the end of *The Great Dictator*—they are not only superfluous to the purpose, they betray it by falling below the standard set by the creativity that precedes them. In all other respects, *War and Peace* works like an ordinary novel—it's just extraordinarily rich. A true epic works in other ways, but always by setting terms for the bargain: the reader must pay in pain. There are Wagnerians who claim to have become so well acquainted with the *Ring* cycle that they cease to feel the pressure on their behinds even during *Siegfried*, but they are hard to believe. The *Ring*, however, is transparent excitement punctuated by the occasional stretch of opacity, like the Homeric epics and the *Divine Comedy*. More problematic is the *Aeneid*, which reverses the proportions: the Dido episode, and the journey into the under-world that succeeds it, add up to an oasis in a carefully landscaped desert, and it takes a lot of thirstily summoned dedication to convince yourself that those parched miles of dunes, elegantly arranged though they might be, are worth crossing just for the prospect of getting to Troy and watching it burn. The Orpheus and Eurydice episode in *Georgics IV* shows the intensity of dramatic talent that lay within Vir-gil's reach, but that only makes things worse when we find out how lit-tle drama the *Aeneid* has, compared with the long swathes of beautiful language with nothing in particular to be beautiful about. As it has come down to us, epic poetry in Latin is a misfire. The great classical historian Ronald Syme spoke the truth in passing, when he said that Tacitus wrote the Roman epics that the poets didn't. One poet did, but his name was William Shakespeare.

Benedetto Croce made a distinction—a fundamental concept for his aesthetics and a handy ad hoc proposition for us—between *poesia* and *letteratura*. Applying it to the *Divine Comedy*, he concluded that the bits you like are poetry while the other stuff is merely literature. The same criterion applied to the *Aeneid* would give you very little poetry amongst all that impeccably crafted verse. In Homer, the Catalogue of the Ships is only an interruption, and is even fascinating: a list of ships and tribes is, after all, likely to be inherently more sonorous than a shopping list of groceries. Though Homer can take his time to get his chores done, you will never have to read far to find something nearly as electrifying as the episode in which Odysseus, washed ashore, wakes up on the beach, looks up into the dazzle of the sun, and sees the outline of the nymph Nausikaa. You can call such moments the stuff of Homer's epics. You could say the same about Dante: stretches of theology are not its norm. Scholars warn us we should be slow to assume that drama always mattered more for Dante than theology did: but there can be no doubt that it matters more for us. Luckily for us, the *Divine Comedy* is thronged with human beings poetically alive. If only the same could be said for *Paradise Lost*. But except for Adam and Eve, Milton's characters are not of this Earth, and by restricting himself to a superhuman cast-list he faces the insuperable problem that nice angels are not interesting. Lucifer is the hero *a fortiori*. The forces of good are necessarily lacking in vitality, and the poem imposes upon itself a narcotic identification of virtue and bathos. The results are not ridiculous (Philip Bailey's long and justly forgotten poem *Festus* is ridiculous) but their dignity is all they have, in a language whose heightened decorum is its only purpose: stilt-walking in a toga.

In a monoglot literary context it can be fatal to call *Paradise Lost* a fizzer—there is no examination school in which it would be wise even to hint at such a thing. (There are plenty of examination schools in which Milton doesn't even get a mention, of course, but that isn't because he is thought no good: it is because he is thought too hard.) Keats didn't like the language of *Paradise Lost* but he might have lived to think differently, as T. S. Eliot did at a later time. Hazlitt is probably sincere about praising Milton's language; but there is something dutiful about the sincerity; he seems so much more relaxed when praising the language of Shakespeare, or even of Burns. Nevertheless the case for Milton's "high style" has accumulated too solidly to be wished away. There has never been any real liking for the poem's story, however, because there isn't one. It is just an outline, wished into existence out of the desire to write an epic. Even more damaging, the stories within the story are not up to muster either: the saving graces that make the *Aeneid* worth the space are hardly there. Most damaging of all, there is very little that demands to be remembered. There are lines and even passages that can be memorized, but that's a different thing. I have a friend who studied *Paradise Lost* at Oxford and has read it constantly ever since. But I have heard him quote Milton only twice in all the years I have known him, whereas he quotes Shakespeare all the time, and as naturally as breathing. There's the difference: *Paradise Lost* is unspeakable. Virgil should have been a warning for Milton: a got-up epic is not only hard to write, it reads that way. Virgil should also have been a *vade mecum*: if you have stuck yourself with so schematic a project, get some interesting digressions in at any cost. It was a pity that Aeneas had to leave Carthage, but at least we are given a taste of why Dido wept. Milton's hero should have got himself a girl.

Goethe didn't make Milton's mistake. In *Faust* the heavenly battle takes place on Earth. Goethe was as infatuated with Mephistopheles as Tacitus was with Tiberius, and with the same artistic result: evil energy was given intense language. As Satan's terrestrial representative, Mephistopheles has the persuasive human voice of Iago, and the divine virtues with which he is at war are incarnated as *ewig-Weibliche* women you can touch. Faust is occupied with his reasons for touching them, and with what he should do afterwards.

> *Denkt Ihr an mich ein Augenblick'chen nur:*
> *Iche werde Zeit genug an Euch zu denken haben.*

Think about me for just a little moment: I will have time enough to think of you. So says Margarete, and Faust must look into his conscience. What male reader never has? The poem's grand, overarching drama is not about Rome's imperial destiny or a schism above the clouds over Protestant England, but about how we live and think, whatever our circumstances. Only when the witches of *Walpurgisnacht* rave on too long does *Faust* run out of human incident, and thus out of interest. It thus offers few opportunities for the reader to score brownie points for endurance. But it does offer some: nearly all epics do. Authors of epics are almost certainly right to suppose that the reader will want to congratulate himself on having stayed the course. Anthony Lane has written entertainingly about how his young love affair with *The Lord of the Rings* began before he had read the first page:

it began when he glanced at the last page and realized that the book was 1077 pages long.

Tabulated through all their various editions, sales statistics for the individual volumes of *À la recherche du temps perdu* reveal that *La Prisonnière* has always been the point where most readers call it a day. Those of us who love the book, and never finish re-reading it, must still admit that Albertine's captivity is sublimated boredom with a vengeance. But we don't just admit it: we insist on it. We are proud of our battle honours. And there is even something to the argument that we have to find out how long Proust can go on before we can appreciate how brief he can be. At base, Proust is aphoristic. The pregnant conclusion is at least as characteristic of him as its long preamble. The same is true of Thomas Mann himself. We trust the slow unfolding of a block-long sentence in *Doktor Faustus* because we know about his knack for the neat statement. It was a knack he could overdo. In 1914 he said, "Germany's whole virtue and beauty . . . is unfolded only in war." Later on he realized he should never have said that. Chastened by the fateful specificity of a youthful certitude, he took refuge in a style that got in all the nuances at once, but the ability to speak about emotions on the human scale was always at the heart of it, and in his last years he proved it triumphantly by finishing (or anyway continuing: for once it was a terrible pity that he didn't go on forever) *Bekenntnisse des Hochstaplers Felix Krull*, the book we know as *The Confessions of Felix Krull*. It is not in Felix Krull's nature to put up with a moment of boredom, and his creator caught the mood. We catch it along with them both: the delight of the most impetuous of Thomas Mann's books is to be swept away at the speed of the hero's counter-jumping ambition. But we can give ourselves no credit for enjoying Krull's company: the book that enshrines his scapegrace charm is not an epic. To enjoy Hans Castorp's company in *The Magic Mountain* is a harder trick. It helps if we realize that Castorp, as he sits around in the health resort mainly doing nothing, isn't meant to be interesting: if he were more so, Claudia Chauchat would be less so, because Claudia's only dramatic function is to represent the vitality to which he might aspire if he could only concentrate his energy. But he doesn't have any energy. There is no uniqueness to him: he is a character without character. The same goes, and goes double, for Dr. phil. Serenus Zeitblom in *Doktor Faustus*. His grinding ordinariness is there to make Adrian Leverkühn light up. In the epic, flat patches can be functional. They are counterproductive only when we see no relief ahead.

John Motley's *Rise of the Dutch Republic* is the only long book that I have ever read right through to the finish in the certain knowledge that it would never come good. In three tremendously uninspired volumes, Motley never writes a memorable sentence until the end, where the little children weep in the streets. I have never forgotten that sentence, but perhaps I set myself that task too, to compensate myself for the insane plan of reading ten pages a day until it was all over. It was an extreme case of what a long work can do for us: etch its highlights into our tired brains by the pressure of its average weight. It helps if the average is high: a passage in Dante about nothing except dogma is still fascinating for its craft. But an average is something any tolerable epic is bound to have, because it can't do without low points. An epic must have historical sweep, in its frame of reference if not in its narrative sequence; and exposition, beyond a certain level, can't be made exciting. The question will always arise more acutely about the poetic epic than the prose epic, because if we find a prose epic disproportionately dull we tend to dismiss it, no matter how good an argument can be made for the longeurs. (Joyce's *Ulysses* would be a less successful prose epic if it had an even longer stretch of deliberately dud prose brilliantly reproducing the mannerisms of hack journalism.) Our tolerance of the uneventful poetic epic is more elastic from the start, because we have learned to expect less. Spenser is only the third most gifted exponent of the stanza named after him (Byron comes first and Shelley second) and his vast poem *The Faerie Queene* has a way of concentrating the reader's attention on everything except itself. When I was reading it I had to sit facing away from the window, or I would find myself counting the people on a passing bus. Whether by Ariosto, Tasso, Camões or Mickiewicz, an intermittently fascinating poetic epic might need explication and excuse, but no defence. Scholars must go on defending *The Fairie Queene* because no common reader can get through it without setting himself a daily quota. Other epics in English are easier on the eyelids, but they all leave Dante safe. Tennyson's *The Idylls of the King* is nothing beside Malory's *Morte d'Arthur*, and even in Malory there are roads of dross between the golden castles. Browning's *The Ring and the Book* is as unspeakable as *Paradise Lost*: the same greatness, yet the same resistance to being incorporated into memory. But the catalogue could go on, like Homer's list of ships, except that all the ships are holed below the waterline. The only serious epic that is entirely, lyrically successful from line to line is *Eugene Onegin*, which is really a verse novel. All the other entirely successful epics are comic: in English, they are *The Canterbury Tales*, *The Dunciad* and—the pick of the bunch, and the Cullinan Diamond of poetry in English after Shakespeare—Byron's *Don Juan*. An epic that mocks itself can make virtues of its own mechanisms. Otherwise it is doomed to creak forward like a siege engine in a landscape short of citadels. Any attempt to divest it in advance of its necessary dullness will destroy its coherence. An epic compiled from nothing except images is a contradiction in aims. Ezra Pound tried it, and the *Cantos* is, or are, there to remind us that nobody can make a meal out of condiments, or a statue out of sparks.

> Last night I finished reading Heinrich's *Henry IV*,
> a unique book . . .
> — THOMAS MANN, *TAGEBÜCHER*
> *1935–1936*, P. 179

Thomas Mann could be generous even about his older brother: something worth remembering when we face the persuasive evidence of just how self-centred the great writer could be. On page 413 of *Tagebücher 1937–1939* we find the Pacific Palisades *Hausherr* and his brilliant children locked in a delightfully catty argument about which of the émigré writers should be awarded *die Palme der Minderwürdigkeit*—the palm for mediocrity. Should it be Stefan Zweig, Emil Ludwig, Lion Feuchtwanger or Erich Maria Remarque? Even in exile, they all had big sales. It was easy for Mann to feel threatened. Contrary to the opinion about him that has since become commonplace, it took Mann some time to establish himself as the unchallenged literary representative of the eternal Germany. During his first Amercan years, he was often prey to the fear that things were going too slowly for him and too smoothly for others. (This was before Remarque won the affections of Paulette Goddard, but *All Quiet on the Western Front* had already been a best-seller in English on a scale that Mann was never to know.) Emil Ludwig alone was more than enough to make all the other exiled German writers feel that they were bound for oblivion. Ludwig's biographies of the great made him famous, influential and rich. They also inculcated in their author the preposterous notion that he was some kind of great man himself, a delusion he backed up by living in an appropriate style. Ludwig's Wagnerian standards of comfort were evoked scathingly by Alfred Polgar, an incomparably better writer with an incomparably smaller bank balance. But Polgar was not the only observer to spot the discrepancy between Ludwig's self-esteem and a just measure. Mockery for Ludwig's pretensions was standard throughout the emigration.

It is sad, however, to find Stefan Zweig's name on the list of mediocrities. Zweig thought Mann was an admirer. Mann was the master of the diplomatic letter that took people at their own estimation. He could effortlessly mislead them about his true opinions. But at his best, the diplomacy *was* his true opinion. He was generous about the importance of other writers in the emigration even if he did not much admire their individual works. The Palm for Mediocrity game is a useful reminder that shared adversity did not necessarily make people into saints. But the adversity was the culprit: the characters were its victims. Among the less immediately spectacular of Hitler's cruel tricks was his ability, at long range and by remote control, to drive different personalities into the same airless trap, where, struggling for a share of oxygen, they found out the hard way that they had never belonged together. After all, for writers to help each other beyond the bounds of friendship is no natural condition. In normal life, they are more likely to be at odds, and if they don't much like each other's work the usual response is not to talk at all. In the emigration, gifted people whose normal destiny would have been to despise each other were put at each other's mercy. Some, like Joseph Roth, were kind to those in adversity. But some behaved badly. Walter Mehring, whose memoir *Die verlorene Bibliothek* was one of the many inspirations for the book you are reading now, acquired a reputation for accepting financial help but forgetting to be grateful for it. Whether or not the reputation was earned, it still follows his memory. No such accusation has ever attached itself to Thomas Mann. Chronically behind schedule on his latest enormous novel, he hated to be bothered, but he did his duty.

Given all that, Mann deserved his status as a lion. He showed he had the heart for it, and all the more so because it was against his nature. One of his many reasons for hating the Third Reich was that it forced him to be a better man than he really was. Left undisturbed, he would have been a monster of conceit. But when thoughtfulness was forced on him, he rose to the occasion, and it would be conceited on our part to assume that the perennial thespian was just being careful not to look bad in the eyes of posterity. Literary pygmies are always making pronouncements about what goes on in the head of a giant, and the pronouncements always sin through over-confidence. They can't really tell what's going on up there. The worst you can say about Thomas Mann is that his ego was so big he took even history personally; but at least he knew it was history. "Poor Čapek!" he lamented during the war, "He died of a broken heart . . . and Menno ter Braak, the Dutch creator of precious criticism, shot himself on the night Hitler's troops occupied Amsterdam. Two friends, who were lights of my life—and National Socialism murdered them" (*Altes und Neues*, pp. 11 and 12). This is actually made stronger, not weaker, by the German reflexive verb: *und der Nationalsozialismus mordete sie mir.* Murdered them for me. Michael Burleigh's admonition in his marvellous book *The Third Reich* should not be forgotten: the destruction was not just of the creative and the prominent but of the ordinary and the unknown—millions of them. It can be said, safely from this distance, that Thomas Mann did not think enough about them. But he could certainly think of anyone who was a bit like him. Possibly, like most egotists, he thought everyone else was an egotist too. If he had been the egomaniac he is sometimes painted as, however, he would have had no concern even for the prominent: especially not for them, since they were rivals for the limelight.

Heinrich always spelled trouble for Thomas, and not just because Heinrich had made so much noise in earlier times. In fact Thomas would probably have liked it better if everything Heinrich did had scored a hit like *Professor Unrat*, the book that eventually gave us *The Blue Angel*. Artistically, however, the older brother, by the fastidious standards of the younger, was pathologically facile: a geyser with its own self-renewing supply of soap. All too wearily often, Thomas had to strain his criteria of worth to say that Heinrich had done well. There was also the problem of Thomas's bourgeois propriety: his domestic stability and prosperous façade were essential parts of his armour. Heinrich was a bohemian by comparison, and the more so the older he got. Later on, in Los Angeles, Heinrich's batty mistress was regarded *chez* Mann as an even bigger embarrassment than Heinrich's indigence, which could be judiciously compensated for, whereas there was no disguising her fathomless capacity to throw scenes. It would have suited Thomas to write off the crumbling Heinrich as a liability who had brought ruin on himself. But Thomas was too aware that Heinrich has come to his final grief only with Hitler's help, and finally there was always the consideration that Heinrich had done some good things despite all. Thomas had thought *Henry IV* was one of them, had said so, and continued to rate Heinrich at that level of possibility, if not of consistent achievement. In honour of artistic standards, Thomas Mann could put even his own ego into perspective: a Mount Everest yes, but with a picture of itself as only one mountain in the Himalayas, although admittedly the tallest. We should restrain our scorn then, when in Donald Prater's excellent biography of Thomas Mann we see, on page 237, the master spirit praising "my worried modesty." It sounds like comic self-deception, but it was justified by his behaviour. Even without his behaviour, it would have been justified by his art: nobody incapable of humility bothers to rewrite a sentence. Careful composition is an act of renunciation in itself. Thomas Mann wrote too well to be a true monster of self-regard. But with the help of the invaluable diaries we soon find out that in his everyday dealings he could be selfless too, and didn't always need that to be known. After his death, journalistic opinion tried to make an ogre out of him, but that said more about journalism than it said about him. He was one of the first victims of a modern cultural trend: mass therapy for the semi-cultivated, transmitted through supposedly edifying examples of the idol with feet of clay.

MAO ZEDONG

❦ ❦ ❦

The full evil of Mao Zedong (1893–1976) is continually being rediscovered, because it is continually being forgotten. In 2005 it was rediscovered all over again when Jung Chang, previously the author of *Wild Swans*, the book that blew the gaff on the Cultural Revolution in the 1960s, brought out, together with her husband, an account of Mao's career that pitched the body count of innocent civilians where it belonged, far beyond the total achieved by Hitler and Stalin put together. Jung Chang's Mao biography was greeted as ground-breaking in the Western press. But with due credit for its passion, there was little about the book's factual material that was new. Most of it had been in the previous book that rediscovered Mao's perfidy, Philip Short's *Mao: A Life*, published to wide acclaim ("A ground-breaking biography"—*The Sunday Times*) in 1999. As one who thinks that *Wild Swans* is an essential twentieth-century book for which Jung Chang deserves our unending gratitude, I nevertheless think that Short's book about Mao has the edge on hers, mainly because it is ready to contemplate the awkward possibility that Mao's thirst for blood might have been acquired over time, rather than inbred. Short, whose languages include Russian and Japanese as well as Chinese, is also

much sounder in the field of foreign policy. As to the bottom-
less squalor of Mao's personal behaviour, especially in his
lethal old age, Jung Chang is pre-empted by *The Private Life
of Chairman Mao* (1994), a stomach-turning memoir by Mao's
personal physician, Zhisui Li. None of this means that Jung
Chang and her husband do not deserve credit for their long
endeavours. But the idea that they stand at the beginning of a
studious tradition, instead of at a further stage in one well
established, is itself a straw in a sad wind. Why doesn't this
story stick when told?

Those of us who were at university in the 1960s can remember the vociferousness with which otherwise sane and sweet-
natured students professed to believe that the Cultural
Revolution was a message to the corrupt West. Yet the facts
about Mao's China had already, at that stage, been rediscovered several times. Quite early on after Mao took unchallenged
power, the true situation could easily be deduced from the way
that useful idiots like Edgar Snow endorsed the regime's official lies. Always, however, the rediscoveries were succeeded by
a further forgetting, and the same holds true today, not just in
the West, where the pseudo-left has too great an investment in
anti-Americanism to admit that there can be a reason for evil
independent of Washington's control, but also, and tragically,
in China itself, where Mao's image is still not to be mocked
without penalty. Eventually Lenin's statues went the way of
Stalin's, to the scrapyard. But Mao might well stay up there
forever, simply because there is such a thing as horror so great
that it can't be assessed even when the facts are known. The
truth sinks down when it sinks in, leaving the mind free to
operate a more tolerable economy. From the art lover's viewpoint, this might even be a good thing. The catchy opera
Nixon in China, for example, could never have been written if
its authors had fully realized that the picure they were painting
of Nixon's relative lack of dignity vis-à-vis Mao was hopelessly
compromised by the real discrepancy between the two historic
figures. Nixon, when he killed innocent people, did so as the
price of political success. Mao killed them as the condition of

it, and killed more by many, many times. Why Mao should have been the more difficult one to despise is a key question for an as yet untapped academic subject: the sociology of the international intelligentsia.

Let a hundred flowers bloom, let a hundred
schools of thought contend.
—MAO ZEDONG, APRIL 1956, AS QUOTED
BY PHILIP SHORT IN *MAO*, P. 455

THE PRETTY RUBRIC looks so harmless even today, now that we have some idea of what it cost. Halfway between a poem and a slogan, it is a small thought that would fit on a big T-shirt. It doesn't even sound wrong. Mao designed it to sound right. For the trick to work, millions of people had to believe the words meant what they said, even though the Party, within long memory, had never rewarded a contentious voice with anything except torture and death. Anyway, the suckers fell for it. The flowers bloomed, the schools of thought contended, and Mao's executioners went to work. The slogan had the same function as the Constitution of the Soviet Union, which Aleksandr Zinoviev tellingly defined as a document published in order to find out who agreed with it, so that they could be dealt with.

The hideous outcome of the Hundred Flowers campaign is described in Philip Short's book about Mao, a political biography from whose long march of horror no student should excuse himself a single step. You can get the essence of Jung Chang's *Wild Swans* in a few chapters, although you owe it to yourself and the author to read the whole thing. But Short's book has no essence; or, rather, it is all essence; you need to ponder the whole lot. For one thing, Mao was not the same man in the beginning as he was later on. Hitler and Stalin both were: in the early days, all they lacked of their later, epidemic awfulness was the power to exercise it. But Mao, who ended by killing a greater number of innocent people than both of them put together, started off as a benevolent intellectual: a fact which should concern us if we pretend to be one of those ourselves. Mao was no Marxist when he began. He scarcely could have been: Marx was not translated into Chinese until

1918, and Mao had no foreign languages. Nor, it seems, did he have a violent streak. He seems to have believed in a sort of peaceful anarchism. When he took up communism, he was the first Communist leader to break out of the orthodox view about the revolution depending on the urban proletariat. He saw the importance of the peasants, and in 1927 published a thoughtful document on the subject, *Report on the Peasant Movement in Hunan*. When the fighting started, he made his troops behave well, apparently in the belief that a measure of decency would earn credit for the movement.

His first attack on his own Party members did not occur until 1931–1932, by which stage Stalin was exterminating whole populations. Mao was a long while cranking himself up to anything on that scale, but when he really got going he kept up the tempo. The Hundred Flowers campaign was rare only in that it depended on a trick. At all other times, the state just went steaming on with its permanent purge. It didn't need trick questions, because nothing a potential victim thought of saying could possibly be of any use anyway. At the time of the Cultural Revolution, when Liu Shaoqi published his *How to Be a Good Communist*, it was greeted as "a big anti-Marxist-Leninist and anti-Mao-Zedong-Thought poisonous weed." No good Communist could be good enough. Liu was sixty-seven years old when he was driven to his death by the Cultural Revolution, after a dedicated lifetime of carrying out Mao's homicidal orders to the letter. All this was happening while some of my fellow undergraduates in Cambridge were under the impression that Western values were being challenged by whatever was happening in China. They were indeed, and I, for one, had sufficient suspicion of absolute power to guess in what way: but I nowhere near guessed the full horror of the reality. The only explanation is that Mao had even less imagination than we did in the matter of fatalities occurring among Chinese. There are so many of them, so how much does it matter when a few hundred thousand of them go missing?

Perhaps our best hope of understanding what was going on in his mind is to suppose that it was a version of what goes on in ours. Old men continue in their sins because to stop would be to admit them. But to concentrate on Mao's late-flowering monstrosity is surely a misleading emphasis. His early-flowering humanitarianism is a much more useful field of study. When it became clear that there were no demo-cratic means by which it could attain its object, he started thinking about the undemocratic means. The message seems to be that when the possibility of critical discussion is withdrawn, anything can happen, and everything is altered. Among the things altered is logic itself. As Swift foretold and Orwell analysed in detail, totalitarian obsession dis-torts the logical element within language, cancelling and even revers-ing its power to specify. Towards the end of Mao's reign, when there was—as there had to be by then, with the whole country in ruins—yet another version of a Leninist New Economic Policy, it was once again discovered that "small scale production engenders capitalism." Any moves towards rehabilitating the unjustly condemned were attacked as a "right deviationist wind of reversing correct verdicts." Correcting reversed verdicts would have been more like it. When Zhou Enlai died, there was true grief: at least he had not been insane. When Mao died, the grief was mainly feigned, except among the young, who knew noth-ing. It needs to be remembered, however, that to have some idea of what had gone on it was not enough to be older, and to have survived. One needed information, and Mao had so organized his colossal abat-toir of a state that information rarely travelled further than a scream could be heard. But that was inside China. Outside China, the story went everywhere, and there was never any excuse for not hearing it. The idea that there was is part of the lie—the part fated, it seems, to last longest.

CHRIS MARKER

❧ ❧ ❧

The name Chris Marker (b. 1921) is a fiction. His real name
was Christian François Bouche-Villeneuve but he preferred to
operate under a false identity. Fiction and falsity, by some
alchemy never fully explained, conferred on him, according to
his many admirers, a greater power to handle his raw material,
which was made up of fact and truth. It was a tribute to his talent that this absurd proposition looked quite plausible when
you saw his first documentaries on screen. (Some commentators prefer to call a Marker movie an "essay," but they are perhaps too influenced by their memories of when the word
"documentary" meant box office death.) *Cuba Si!* (1961) was
especially effective. Framed closely in black and white, the
Bearded Ones looked wedded to authenticity. Marker struck
foreign observers as being by far the best mind of the movement that became internationally famous as the *nouvelle vague*.
Admittedly the competition wasn't strong. From the political
angle, Jean-Luc Godard was an obvious featherbrain, and
François Truffaut had more sense than to make any overt
political statements beyond the usual ones about alienation:
The 400 Blows incited rebellious youths to become film directors, not to revolution. Later in the decade, when the Paris

événements were making world news, Marker came readily to mind as one of the serious voices that prepared the way. Even those of us who suspected that his Marxist world view was as frivolous as everybody else's were impressed by his tone of voice, most notably rich and confident in his must-see movie *Letter from Siberia* (1957). His documentaries *sounded* great. They therefore had a big influence on some of the young writers who would later earn a crust in British television. When I was a TV critic in the 1970s I tried to point out, armed by my memories of how Marker had bewitched me, that the filmed documentary was a blunt instrument. Later on, when I was filming documentaries of my own, I took care to disclaim, by making my commentary as self-deprecating as possible, the apparent omniscience that the written voice-over automatically conferred.

Today, documentaries win red-carpet coverage. Almost always, for good reasons, the documentaries that make the biggest noise stem from the left. Usually they lack Marker's spare, literate elegance, but what they inherit from him is his loose relationship with the truth. Even when filmed on the spot, with real people really suffering, the atmospherics tend to the specious and the arguments to the fraudulent. "Actual" hardly ever means factual. Michael Moore's documentaries are conspicuous examples of these failings. In *Bowling for Columbine* there is a scene in which he inveighs against U.S. planes taking off. He brands their mission as imperialist. But the planes in the footage were taking off for Kosovo, where they saved the lives of thousands of Muslims who would otherwise have been murdered. So that particular stretch of Moore's supposedly factual documentary is saying the opposite of what is true. The big difference between Moore and the founding father of his art-form in modern times, Chris Marker, is that Moore must know that he is telling an untruth. When Moore says that the poor of the world could have clean water overnight if the advanced nations agreed to it, he must know that he is talking nonsense. Marker really did believe that there was a collectivist answer to the troubles of the world.

He was the post-war French *gauchiste* artist-intellectual in a pure form, with the ingenuous version of Sartre's disingenuousness. By the time Marker became well-known, in the early 1960s, the bulk of his most vital work was already behind him. Whether or not Vietnam broke his heart, it certainly cramped his style. Later still, as his dreams retreated, he faded away into guru status. *La Jetée* (1962), a film composed almost exclusively of stills from which everything is absent including him, was really a premature epitaph, although the lasting strength of his influence demands that attention should be paid to his later showpiece *Sans soleil* (1982), a brave attempt at the synthetic work that gets everything in. Such a mind-scrambling attempt to say everything at once was a powerful hint that he was really born for the Internet, but had arrived in the world of universal information a few decades too early. Many of us who were floored by his first brilliant works, however, never really got over them.

There isn't any God, or curses: only forces,
to be overcome.
— CHRIS MARKER, *LETTER FROM SIBERIA*

SUCH, IN FRENCH, are the closing words of Chris Marker's 1957 masterpiece *Letter from Siberia*, which I saw at the National Film Theatre the year I arrived in London in the early 1960s, the decade that was to be visually embodied by the French *nouvelle vague*, of which Marker's cinema was a central element, the item of intellectual prestige. But I didn't know any of that yet. All I knew, at the time when I first heard it, was that Marker's closing paragraph was a thing for wonder. On screen, there was a big rocket going up, and the total, complex effect of words and pictures was to make what he was saying sound simultaneously lyrical and oracular. But I didn't quite believe what he was saying even as it overwhelmed me. It sounded like a slogan from the anti-God museum in Moscow. I could already think of several forces that were unlikely to be overcome in my lifetime, and indeed could scarcely be dealt with at all unless God and curses were kept well in mind. One of the forces was the force of disintegration still bursting out from the detonation points of contemporary history.

I was in Australia for the *Tampa* incident in late August and early September 2001. The *Tampa* was a Norwegian container ship that had picked up a cargo of asylum seekers from their sinking vessel. The asylum seekers had been heading for Australia and they naturally wanted to complete their journey. The Australian government thought otherwise. In the quality press, hundreds of thousands of words were uttered in condemnation of Prime Minister John Howard's insistence that the rescued boat people should not be allowed to land on Australian territory. There was outrage that he had put the arithmetic of controlled immigration ahead of the moral imperative of humanitarian generosity. Some of the outrage aspired to the status of philosophy. Here is an example, from the pen of Richard Flanagan, one of the established writers whom the Australian broadsheets regularly co-opt in their quest for a profound opinion when a matter of moment swims into view—or, as in this case, heaves into sight. "In the end, politics is not about focus groups and numbers; it is about the power of stories to galvanize and forge the thinking of societies" (*The Sunday Age*, September 2, 2001). As a novelist, Flanagan has the right to use the language as creatively as possible. But this is a creativity that belittles the truth. Though politics is indeed concerned with more than just numbers, it can't do without them. More important, in the light of events that have happened within living memory—my living memory, if not Mr. Flanagan's—there is nothing reassuring about his contention that politics is concerned with "the thinking of societies" being forged, galvanized or shaped in any way by "the power of stories."

After World War I, the right wing in Germany continued its struggle against democracy by using the power of a story. The story was that the armed forces had been the victims of a *Dolchstoss*—they had been stabbed in the back. Many ex-soldiers, understandably reluctant to accept that their sufferings had been for nothing, believed the story. How could it not be true, when they felt so much pain? Added to the realities of the inflation and the Depression, the fiction of the stab in the back prepared the thinking of a society for the advent of a sorcerer. Hitler expanded the *Dolchstoss* story by alleging that the Jews had held the dagger. Many civilians, their lives ruined by financial instability, were ready to believe that their hard-won savings had been stolen by international Jewish financiers. How could the story not be true, when there had been so much grief?

Stalin and Mao each had a similar story, about the rapacious bourgeoisie. Peasants and proletarians were keen to believe it until their turn came to be exterminated. All the tyrannies of the twentieth century were introduced by powerful stories, usually subscribed to by intellectuals before the event—and, in the case of the Communist tyrannies, long after the event. Writing as an intellectual, Mr. Flanagan ought to have been aware of that. But he was too exercised by the supposedly emblematic fate of the people on the *Tampa*. The power of the story was too much for him. It obliterated all sense of numbers, even though the real story was "about" numbers and nothing else. The first number to remember was the number of boat people stuck on the *Tampa*. There were 433 of them, and every one of them was a queue jumper with aspirations to a place reserved for a legal applicant. So if the illegals got onshore and stayed, 433 people who had already been kept waiting would be kept waiting longer. The distress of those in the queue was not seen on television. The distress of those on the ship was all over the media. Though the refugees were kept below decks, the Australian reporters were able to tap into their bewilderment by dint of telepathy, X-ray vision and other paranormal powers traditionally conferred by compassion.

Certainly the condition of the people on the *Tampa* was not enviable. In the course of the incident their despair, rage and uncertainty became the common property of Australia's intelligentsia, who didn't hesitate to place the blame squarely where they thought it belonged: on the Australian government. Since the Labor opposition seemed to share the Liberal government's intransigence, the opportunity was taken to condemn all politicians as a class. Australian politicians are used to that, but there was a further step: since the overwhelming majority of the electorate seemed to agree with the politicians, the opportunity was taken to condemn the people too. The people had not been so roundly condemned since the referendum of 1999, in which they had declined to embrace manifest destiny and vote for a republic. This time, indeed, they were condemned even more roundly because there were more of them, in the sense that the proportion of the people who were against the illegal immigrants being allowed to land was far larger than the proportion which had been reluctant to accept the necessity for constitutional reform. Once again the intelligentsia found no discomfort in its separation from the people. The people, it was made clear, should have found discomfort in their separation from the intelligentsia. If the people didn't, it went to show how far things had gone. Here was a country which owed so much to the contribution of asylum seekers, and it had so far forgotten its heritage that its population was refusing succour to these new asylum seekers, the ones on the Norwegian ship.

But they weren't asylum seekers. When they were processed, if they ever were, some of them would no doubt turn out to be asylum seekers, in the sense that if they were ever forcibly returned home they would face violent punishment for having left. Most of the contingent were from Afghanistan, where the psychotic Taliban were exerting a tyranny calculated to export the already devout population by millions at a time. But all of the Afghans could have sought asylum in Pakistan, where two million of their fellows had already found safety from the Taliban's thinking about society. Failing that, the Muslim voyagers could have sought asylum in their first main staging point, Malaysia; or in the second, Indonesia. They chose not to do so because their main object was economic advantage, in Australia. There is good reason to believe that the successful incursion of such enterprising people, who had already proved their acumen by raising the exorbitant fare demanded by the people smugglers, would, in the long run, be to Australia's economic advantage as well as their own. (I should say here that the economic case for uncontrolled immigration, with no distinction between asylum seekers and destination shoppers, is made with daunting eloquence by Mario Vargas Llosa in his collection of essays *El lenguaje de la passion*.)

But none of that altered the fact of their real status: illegal immigrant. They had been illegal immigrants when they were still on their original ship, the one that got wrecked after leaving Indonesia. The Norwegian ship had picked them up in order to save their lives. There had been excellent Christian reasons for saving their lives, and at first glance the same reasons seemed to apply to bringing them ashore on Christmas Island. The first glance was all that the Australian *bien pen-*

sant intellectuals needed. A second glance would have told them that the rescued illegals could have been returned to Indonesia, and that the Norwegian captain headed for Australian waters only because some of his new passengers threatened to kill themselves if he did otherwise. (It was a falsehood that some of the adults threatened to throw their own children into the water, and later the government spokesmen were much vilified for repeating the falsehood as if it had been true: but it was a quite plausible falsehood.) The first glance provided a simpler story, one of those stories that change the thinking of societies. In this story, the illegal immigrants were all instantly elevated to the status of asylum seekers: a bonus for the people smugglers, who thus became humanitarians, like those beret-wearing French Resistance heroes in British and American war movies who smuggle our downed flyers past the patrolling Germans. In reality, people smugglers are no more humanitarian than white slavers, drug dealers or standover men, but if you happen to hold that all refugees have automatic rights superseding the sovereignty of their asylum of choice, then anyone who manages the traffic must be the Scarlet Pimpernel. Such is the power of a story, and this story was *Waterworld* by way of *A Tale of Two Cities*.

The Australian government, meanwhile, had to deal with the intractable facts. If the illegal immigrants were allowed in, it would be hard to throw any of them out without attracting further opprobrium from the watching world. There was already plenty of that. The Australian press was eloquent about the obloquy which the government's instransigence had attracted from centres of humanitarian opinion all over the world. One of the centres of humanitarian opinion was the World Anti-Racism Conference in Durban, which was unlikely, if you thought about it, to reach any other conclusion. Some of the Australian quality papers ran photographs of "youths" demonstrating in the streets of Durban against racial discrimination. The "youths" looked awfully like Robert Mugabe's "war veterans" expressing their disapproval of white farmers in Zimbabwe. Another centre of humanitarian opinion was Kofi Annan, secretary general of the United Nations. The normally astute Paul Kelly of *The Australian* cited Annan's ringing pronouncements against John Howard's hard-heartedness as clear proof of the damage done in the world's eyes. This was a strong point if you thought that Annan's disapproval of poverty and racism was ever likely to diminish either of those things. (The poverty of his son has diminished, apparently, but we are assured that Annan had no direct responsibility for that.) Yet another centre of humanitarian opinion was Mary Robinson, quondam president of Ireland and now a big noise with the U.N. Robinson asked the Australian people to look into their hearts. Howard assured her that the Australian people had already done that. He kindly forebore from adding that the last time the Australian people had looked into their hearts they had elected him. Robinson's remarks amounted to a libel on a country, Australia, whose record of hospitality had been very good ever since World War II, in which Ireland— Howard didn't mention this either—had declined to fight against enemies whose ideas of immigration control were rather more drastic than anything she could now find to deplore on Australia's part.

Libel was by now the power of the story. There would be plenty more of it to come if the *Tampa* people were allowed in and then thrown out. If they came in, some of them would stay in, and the precedent would be set for the people smugglers to scuttle a ship anywhere near Australian territorial waters and leave the next bit to the Australian navy. There was also the consideration that Australia has a procedure for accepting prospective immigrants. The result—if it seems monotonous to hear this again, imagine what standing in line must be like—is a queue, and successful queue jumpers inevitably push legal applicants back nearer to the starting point, thereby disappointing them in their legitimate hopes. Paul Kelly published an explanation of why this was not so, but I did not undertand his explanation, although there is no quarrelling with the assumption that the illegal immigrants have more enterprise than the legal ones. In Chicago, Al Capone had more enterprise than the average Italian shopkeeper. It can even be said that he contributed more to the economy, although I understand that there was some argument about tax.

Apart from gumption, courage and determination, what the illegal immigrants have that the legal applicants haven't is money. No doubt the illegals have made great efforts to save it. Nevertheless, they've got it. If you reinforce the principle that illegal immigrants can pay a people smuggler to put them in a position where the Australian government will have to either admit them or leave them to die—many dreams have been brought to your doorstep—you also reinforce the principle that the queue is merely a mechanism for reducing hope to despair, one more mockery for people who have been mocked already. When the Australian intelligentsia had this explained to them, they were ready with their answer: there ought not to be a queue. Everybody should be allowed in. Think of the misery of all the world's injured and deprived. Think of the power of the story.

There is something to it, but only just. For those Australian commentators with an historical perspective—it has lately become fashionable to rent one of these by the hour—the *Tampa* sailed in the troubled wake of the *St. Louis*, the liner full of Jewish refugees that left Europe in 1939, was never allowed to land anywhere else, and ended up back where it started, delivering many of its desperate passengers to their untimely deaths at the hands of the Nazis. Most of the *Tampa* people, however, were simply in search of a better life. It was hard to blame them for that: so were my grandfathers. When you heard the journalists talk about racist Australia, however, it was just as hard to see why anyone should be thought unlucky not to be allowed in. The power of that story—the story about racist Australia—kept on growing until the Bali nightclub bomb took some of the puff out of it. Even then, some commentators managed to convince themselves that the bombers were students of history who were registering their dissatisfaction with the nearness of Australia's foreign policy to that of the Bush administration. But what never weakened the story, strangely enough, was that most of the people who were initially turned away eventually got in. They were diverted to Nauru, they spent time in detention camps in Australia, but eventually they got in. Yet the story persisted. If it did so, it was partly because there is nothing pretty about the detention camps. But here again, the intelligentsia shows invidious haste in holding the Australian population responsible. When adult refugees sewed their lips together in silent protest, it was indeed a daunting sight. Why, however, should their children do the same, unless encouraged to by the parents? The Australian population was asking a question about culture.

The intelligentsia, ever on the lookout for signs of intolerance, regards all questions about culture as racist at the root. That the common voters should ask such questions is taken as evidence of Australia's role as a source of the world's problems, and not as a refuge from them. Luckily the refugees themselves do not agree. They are in flight from a different story. They might not fully understand it as yet, but they have certainly felt its power. In the late 1950s, a man as intelligent as Chris Marker could still feel that there might be such a thing as a totalitarian answer to the world's miseries. That was the story told by his beautifully made little films. But the story wasn't true. Gradually he realized it, and, being at heart an honest man, he steadily lost the capacity to make the same sort of films again. Art had not been enough. When it takes politics for its material, that's the danger that it always runs.

JOHN McCLOY

❦ ❦ ❦

During and after World War II, John McCloy (1895–1989)
was a key member of the East Coast foreign policy elite, whose
story is told in one of the best modern books about American
politics, *The Wise Men*, by Walter Isaacson and Evan Thomas.
The foreign policy elite is often looked on as an old-money
nest of privilege in the europhile style, with its members all
born into the same lofty social stratum, and attending the same
prep schools and colleges. But the fact that it included a man
like McCloy, who could, and did, later lay proud claim to having been born on the wrong side of the tracks, is an indication
of its true strength: it made room for social mobility impelled
by talent and ambition. The other Wise Men were Robert
Lovett, Averell Harriman, Charles Bohlen, George Kennan
and Dean Acheson. After the defeat of Hitler, the elite, operating through the State Department and its dependent agen-
cies, built the globalized American system of influence and
alliance that expressed the principle of containment, the per-
ceived necessity to block the hegemony of the Soviet Union—
the necessity which had first been expressed by George
Kennan. A complete and final reversal of America's traditional
isolationism, this world-embracing U.S. foreign policy is the

one that we still live under today: after the collapse of the Soviet Union, the America of global reach might have found itself off balance, but was unable to draw back. A denigrator such as Gore Vidal calls the elite's creation the Security State, but the foreign onlooker needs to remember that Vidal himself comes from the elite's milieu, thus reflecting a far-reaching truth about its power: that it generates even its own contrary forces.

By now, little more than half a century later, the elite's heritage generates not only most of what is said in favour of its policies, but most of what is said against them. Almost everything that matters on issues relevant not just to U.S. interests, but to the world entire, is written within driving distance of Washington. Armed by close contact with polticians and officials, elegant writers such as Elizabeth Drew, and less elegant ones such as Bob Woodward, have given us, in their shelves of books, the history of how the United States has shaped the modern world. This tradition of higher political journalism goes back to Henry Adams, but by now it has got beyond the status of a useful individual study and become both indispensable and all-embracing. Two of the best recent books about the larger conflicts in the world, Fareed Zakaria's *The Future of Freedom* and Paul Berman's *Terror and Liberalism*, were both written in the United States. So was Samantha Power's *A Problem from Hell*, a book which was taken by some grateful foreign critics as evidence of the U.S.'s modern history of imperialistic interference. Actually Power's main conclusion, one she probably didn't want to reach, was quite different. She concluded that nothing stops a genocidal government except armed interference, which, usually, only the United States provides. Whether providing it means inflicting it is the question.

The answer that matters will eventually be arrived at in Washington itself, or else it will not be heeded. The answer, however, will be arrived at through argument, if not through congressional debate. American power is not monolithic. Nor was it in the crucial period after World War II, when there were plenty of voices within the elite who realized that to make

anti-communism a popular cause, in order to get the Marshall
Plan through Congress, would open the way for McCarthyite
demagoguery. They had a right to feel sure, however, that the
Marshall Plan itself was benevolent, at least in the sense that it
was in America's long-term interests to be disinterested in the
short term. There are those who, in retrospect, and with some
plausibility, condemn the Marshall Plan, NATO and the rest
of the U.S.'s post-war initiatives in Europe as the elements of
an imperialist campaign. But plausibility becomes absurdity
when they try to frame the United States with a single purpose, as if it had been totalitarian. They would have a better
chance of doing this if they confined their attentions to Latin
America, where the U.S.'s anti-Communist strategies were
truly disastrous: but even then, its agonized internal reaction
to a string of public embarrassments (truly unprincipled states
never blush) proved that it was not a totalitarian power.

It wasn't and still isn't. It would be easier to analyse if it
were. Trying to analyse America and its position in the world,
we can't do without the copious literature that is supplied by
America itself. Least of all can we do without that literature
when it comes to examining America's faults, mistakes and
crimes: it's not as if anyone in Europe is going to do a job like
Gary Wills or Seymour Hersh. The student in search of a
world view can plausibly read in no other language except the
English written in America. Doing so, the student could very
easily get the idea that America is the world. But at the source
of all that literature lies the story of the Wise Men like John
McCloy, and they had another idea. Standing sadly victorious
in the ruins of older civilizations that they understood and valued, they really did want to bring a complex world back to life,
not just to make it over in the image of their own nation. Nor
was their grief, and their hope for a better future, confined to
Europe. McCloy had an infuential hand in the July 1945 Potsdam Declaration that offered Japan something less harsh than
a fully unconditional surrender. If the Japanese war council
had spotted the significant gap in the wording that left the way
open for negotiation about the Emperor's fate, they might

have accepted the offer, and the atomic bombs need not have been dropped. After they were dropped and Japan surrendered, U.S. foreign policy towards Japan was predicated entirely on an occupation designed to dismantle itself after the country had recovered. Whatever the subsequent developments might seem to say to the contrary, at the end of World War II the last thing the American foreign policy elitists had on their minds was a post-war American empire ruled by force. To misinterpret their essential generosity as an assertion of power is to go beyond cynicism into wilful distortion, by which it becomes impossible to give a realistic account of America's actions even when we find them offensive.

An economically stable Europe, with the impetus it can give to free ideas, is one of the greatest assurances of security and peace we can hope to obtain.
—JOHN J. MCCLOY, MEMO DRAFTED WITH HENRY STIMSON AT POTSDAM, QUOTED IN *THE WISE MEN* BY WALTER ISAACSON AND EVEN THOMAS, P. 306

ONE OF THE stars of the group of American diplomats and civil servants that was later to become known as the East Coast foreign policy elite, McCloy had just been driven through the ruins of Berlin, where he saw women and children pulling apart a dead horse with their bare hands. The McCloy-Stimson memos on the subject of rebuilding Europe with economic aid were a big stimulus to what eventually happened, but essentially all the members of the East Coast foreign policy elite reached the same conclusion: whatever the putative merits of an isolationist attitude pre-war, a post-war isolationist attitude was impossible for the United States, and the best way of taking a political initiative in Europe would be to help its devastated nations to recover economically. Nor did common compassion allow any other course. Some of the elite's members—certainly Dean Acheson, "Chip" Bohlen and Averell Harriman—thought initially that the Soviet Union should be among the nations offered help. No members of the elite, not even

George Kennan, favoured a purely military answer to Soviet encroachment, even as the reports coming out of the Soviet-occupied East
European countries became more and more dismaying. Kennan's
famous Long Telegram, sent to Washington from his post in Moscow
in March 1946, is sometimes interpreted that way. At the time it was
being read, indeed, disquiet engendered by Stalin's behaviour in the
satellite countries had grown to the point where Kennan's emphasis on
"containment" was seen as the only theme the telegram had.

But Kennan's analysis, although distrustful of the USSR's political
intention, never depended on purely military means to contain it. They
scarcely could have contained it, since the United States, at the conclusion of the war, had pretty well disarmed. It is hard to remember at this
distance—mainly because of the success of a long *gauchiste* programme
to rewrite history—that the Marshall Plan did not need to be imposed
on the European nations at gunpoint. Nor were there any guns to
impose it if it had. It is also hard to remember at this distance that Kennan's distrust of Stalin's intentions, as it was interpreted at the time,
would have been understandable even had it been wholly meant. On
February 9, 1946, at the Bolshoi Theatre, Stalin made a speech that
blamed World War II on the inherent contradictions of capitalism. Lip
service was paid to the "freedom loving" Western allies, but only as a
preliminary to the renewed emphasis on the time-honoured bugbear
"capitalist encirclement." For many of the encircling capitalists,
Stalin's Bolshoi speech had a more dramatic effect than Churchill's
Iron Curtain speech was to have later on. Churchill's speech merely
confirmed them in the impression that Stalin's speech had already created. Stalin's speech itself was merely confirming an impression; the
impression given by the Soviet Union's unyielding ruthlessness over
Poland; the impression that it would allow no concessions to democracy in any territory it saw as falling within its sphere of influence.
Apart from Kennan, who had never believed that "a community of
interest" with the Soviets was possible, the foreign policy elite were
honourably reluctant to give up their hopes of cooperation with the
Soviet Union, especially on the subject of the atomic bomb. Acheson
and Stimson were both for international control, which would have
entailed giving the secret to the Soviet Union. (It was not yet known
that the Russians already had the secret.) International atomic energy

control was an aim not ruled out even as the Marshall Plan idea grew closer to reality. Harriman can be called the father of the Marshall Plan but really it had multiple paternity: almost the whole of the foreign policy elite were in on it.

The only real split was over the question of whether the Russians should participate, and even that split was less over the if than the how. Even Kennan thought they should be invited in, at least in the first instance. (He thought they would withdraw when they realized that not only would they have to give up their claim to reparations, they also would be helping to create what they would see as an encirclement by capitalist countries; but at least the invitation would be on the record, so that the United States would not have to take the blame for dividing Europe.) As it happened, the Russians decided the issue. Molotov could have killed the Marshall Plan by joining it. Instead he walked out, on Stalin's instructions. Poland and Czechoslovakia, which both desperately needed economic support in order to recover, were plunged deeper into cold night, and Europe was divided. It remains tantalizing to wonder what would have happened if America had found a way of imposing its economic generosity on the Soviet Union, but we must remember that Tantalus, tied to the stake, was never granted that drink. Stalin's obduracy was the historical fact that defeats imagination. Given his intransigence, no other scenario than armed confrontation was really possible. The idea that the United States chose to fight the Cold War can be discussed, but only in the context of the reality that it could not have chosen to call it off. The Soviet Union had been fighting it since Lenin took power. That was what the Comintern propaganda offensive had meant, and all the deeds that lived up to it. The members of the East Coast foreign policy elite can scarcely be blamed for taking Soviet foreign policy pronouncements at their word.

Nor can they be blamed for subsequent military developments in the European area. A more powerful American military presence was never something that the elitists wanted. Exhausted, like most Americans, after years of tension, they didn't want to maintain the military presence they already had. It was the European countries who wanted the American presence, so that the Soviets could never start something against them without killing Americans. The effective atomic force of the United States in Europe in 1946 was nil. Later on, after a scraping of the barrel, a single squadron of B-29s arrived, but they could not have delivered an atomic bomb even if it had been divided among them. From the beginning, Europe was an economic battlefield, and remained that way even as it filled up with weapons over the course of decades. When trying to decide what kind of economic battle it was, it helps to remember that the argument stressing American economic imperialism is not very good. As in the case of Japan, America did less to penetrate foreign markets than to finance foreign competitors. But there can be no question about the military battle: there wasn't one. From the Berlin airlift until the arms race passed its danger point—which was the point *before* mutual destruction was assured—all the military developments were logical. Western satirists had fun mocking the gung-ho language from the American side of the face-off (since most of the satirists were American themselves, few of them had any idea of what the Soviets sounded like when *they* were being gung-ho) but the idea that America's security state grew according to the principle of some sinister initial plan was a fiction in the minds of novelists. It grew, but it grew like Little Topsy. The real danger zone was never Europe, where the two main antagonists were debarred from fighting each other directly. The danger zone was everywhere else, and on this point the East Coast foreign policy elite really was vulnerable to criticism. It had been since the Marshall Plan was formulated, because there was no means of getting the Marshall Plan through Congress without the aid of a Red scare.

The elite had enviable access to the quality press. Acheson leaked information to James Reston, Chip Bohlen to Joe Alsop, James Forrestal to Walter Lippmann: this was an old boy network that left the United Kingdom's looking atomized. The elite had all been to the same prep schools and colleges and they had large influence in the corridors of Washington. But the United States is a democracy, the separation of powers is a fact, and a measure the size of the Marshall Plan could not be pushed through without the consent of Congress, in which, finally, the voice of the people is the voice of God. If Congress had never needed to be persuaded to finance aid to Greece and Turkey, America could have done without the rhetorical commitment to anticommunism which was mandatory from thence forward. (Here lies the fallacy in Gore Vidal's otherwise persuasive argument that in the Security State the American people are not consulted: the American foreign policy measure that troubles us most was launched on a wave of demagogic hot air, for no other reason except to secure the allegiance of the people.) The rhetoric opened the way for the suppurating reality of the junior senator from Wisconsin. Though the sum total of injustices brought about by Joe McCarthy in his whole madcap career scarcely amounted to a single day's depredations in Bulgaria, those who disliked America were given reason for their dislike, and—worse—those with reason to be grateful were given an excuse to express the resentment that the person helped to his feet always feels. Worse still, the domino theory came into operation.

Kennan had been perfectly right about the Kremlin's intention of subverting democratic government anywhere it could be reached: the Kremlin had never had any other intention, nor—to give it points for honesty—had it ever tried to disguise its aim. But it was a big and presumptuous step to assume that if communism became victorious in any country the countries next door would be toppled by the shock. The step once taken, the temptation was very large to make retaliation preemptive, cooperating with incumbent authorities, however brutal, against left-wing protest however justified. What François Furet was later so usefully to deplore as America's "limited inventory of evil" came fatally into play. The United States went to war against socialism in all its forms. In Europe it could hardly eliminate social democrat governments once they had been constituted. But in Iran in 1953 it could certainly cancel an attempt to nationalize the oil fields, and in Guatemala in 1954 it could certainly influence an election. From Guatemala to the debacle in Vietnam was a direct road. Bob Woodward tells the story of the CIA's part in this sad process in his lumpily written but vitally informative book *Veil*. But we need Isaacson and Thomas's book to face the full tragedy of the East Coast foreign policy elite's role in putting the country they had served so well on the path to a disaster. Acheson, in particular, could be seen as a figure of Greek tragedy if the true tragic figures were not to be found among thousands of dead soldiers, murdered peasants, and burnt children. But Acheson had been a hawk since long before the first fateful steps down the jungle path into Vietnam. The time when he could envisage cooperating with the Russians was far in the past, at the other end of a long active life. It had been, however, a real desire. What made it impossible was the intractable fact that the Soviet Union was not under the control of the United States.

During the Cold War, a side effect of the antipathy of many Western intellectuals towards U.S. foreign policy, and their distrust of its physical power, was the belief that the United States could change the world in any way it liked. The only brand of American imperialism to which that belief even remotely applies is cultural imperialism. In the long term, U.S. cultural imperialism, wherever in the world it is brought to bear, is bound to be influential. But in the short term, for a smaller country to suppose that it can do nothing to resist U.S. cultural imperialism is a policy of despair, and equally it is a policy of arrogance for us to suppose such a thing on the small country's behalf. When the Japanese army marched into Singapore and ended the period of British dominance in Southeast Asia, the film showing at the fanciest cinema in the city was *The Philadelphia Story*. In her novel *In the Eye of the Sun*, Ahdaf Soueif tells us what everyone in Egypt was watching on television on the evening of the Six Day War in 1967. It was *Peyton Place*. But America was not influencing the decisions of the Japanese army, and in the region of the eastern Mediterranean it has been a continuous lapse on the part of intellectuals in the Arab countries to think that Israel's foreign policy is exclusively an American creation. One particularly deleterious consequence of that last assumption is that the Arab nations might fail to realize that Israel, rather than be dissolved as a state, and whatever the United States might think desirable, would rather bring the world to an end. Those who credit the United States with a monopoly of powers for working mischief are making the same mistake as those who credit it with a monopoly of powers for doing good. Both sides of the assumption arise from the historical accident that America emerged relatively wealthy from a war that reduced Europe and Japan to poverty for at least a generation, while the Soviet Union, except in the military sense, had been reduced to poverty from its inception and couldn't recover from it unless it changed its ways.

The East Coast foreign policy elite had large powers of discretion in uniquely favourable circumstances, at a time when their initiatives could palpably alter the world. They were cultivated men, many of them of formidable intellectual and scholarly prowess: they did an impressive job of keeping their heads. But it was inevitable that they should fall prey to the sin of pride, which is at its most insidious when dressed as destiny. As I write, the elite is in its last phase, where it begins to forget the car keys through the effort of remembering the door keys. My mentor Gore Vidal is a case in point. He has forgotten that he was born and bred as a member of the very elite whose evil deeds he castigates in his brilliantly written polemics. The way he remembers it, the elite was even more powerful than it was in reality. In 2001 he published an article in the *TLS* by which he managed to suggest that the foreign policy of the United States tricked the Japanese Empire into a war in the Pacific. With some reluctance I tried to rebut that contention in the paper's letters column. Clearly he took exception to a pupil's rounding on him. But as an Australian I had a good reason. Though Australia's own foreign policy sometimes tries to give the impression that the country's future is bound up with the wholesale burgeoning of the region called the Pacific Rim, this glittering dream could not even be dreamed unless in the presence of a seldom spoken-of reality—the reality of a liberal democratic Japan. In view of this indispensable condition, nothing should be done to favour the belief of Japan's ever-hopeful right wing that it was tricked out of military power by the machinations of Washington. Japan went to war on its own initiative. The reasons went far enough back to look inevitable, but when it came to the point, the Japanese government, such as it was at the time, could have done something else. The same is rarely untrue anywhere in the world. It would help if the world's very large supply of anti-American commentators could decide on which America we are supposed to be in thrall to: the Machiavellian America that can manipulate any country's destiny, or the naïve America that can't find it on the map. While we're waiting for the decision, it might help if we could realize the magnitude of the fix that America got us out of in 1945, and ask ourselves why we expect a people rich and confident enough to do that to be sensitive as well. Power is bound to sound naïve, because it doesn't spot the bitter nuances of feeling helpless. The East Coast foreign policy elite were as bright as could be. In their young manhood, they had seen a lot of the world in which America, they correctly guessed, was bound to play a big part, although not even they could guess how big. They had the mental resources to sound as sophisticated as Talleyrand and Metternich put together. If, in retrospect, they look like big, clumsy children—well, they didn't yet know what it was like not to get their way.

ZINKA MILANOV

❦ ❦ ❦

Zinka Milanov was born Mira Teresa Zinka in Zagreb in 1906, and died in New York City in 1989, after a long career as one of the Metropolitan Opera's most beloved sopranos. When she retired from the stage in 1968 she had sung a full twenty-nine seasons in New York, to which she had migrated from Europe at the end of what she later called her "lucky year" of 1937. After a preparatory decade of hard work in the Yugoslav and Czechoslovak opera houses, her lucky year had included her debut in Vienna, starring in *Aida* for Bruno Walter. Walter's recommendation got her an audition with Toscanini for the Verdi *Requiem* in Salzburg, but her American career was already under way, because she had a contract with the Met in her pocket. She made her New York debut in December 1937, three months before the *Anschluß*. A whole political study can be made about what happened to European musicians and singers in the Nazi era, but we should not ignore that America had its attractions even before the event: a striking instance of the power of American cultural imperialism, which, even in the high arts, already shaped, from the angle of consumption, the world of classical music as it shaped the world of painting. (That the angle of consumption would eventually determine the angle of production was not yet evident.) All of them made for American labels, Milanov's recordings date from the second part of her career—she was already forty before she stepped into a studio—but they can be recommended as dazzling events for anyone making a start on grand opera. A born mezzo who added her top notes later, she had a voice as rich as blackberry juice in the middle, with champagne sparkling in the upper register. Beginning listeners should avoid boxed sets of entire operas, in my opinion: it is too easy to nod off before the fireworks start. The thing to go for is what used to be called "highlights" records. Milanov singing the showstoppers from *Tosca* (with Jussi Bjoerling) or *Il Trovatore* (with Jan Peerce) should be enough to get anyone addicted to opera straight away. Because singers lead very physical lives, what they have to say about the art they practise tends to be refreshingly down-to-earth. Zinka Milanov said something which, if quoted at the right moment, can come in handy for interrupting the momentum of anybody who is dragging too much technical information into the discussion.

> Dollink, either you got the voice or you don't got the
> voice: and I got the voice.
> — ZINKA MILANOV (ATTRIB.)

THE VOLCANIC SOPRANO had grown stroppy with an interviewer who badgered her too long on abstruse questions of vocal technique. In her moment of impatience, Milanov produced a nice variation on Duke Ellington's "It don't mean a thing if it ain't got that swing." I have never been able to find out when she actually said it, or to whom: a standard item of operatic folklore, it had gone from mouth to ear a million times before it got to me. Perhaps every word was wrong. But the idea had clearly remained unaltered, because any artist will say roughly the same thing if bored too long. At the National Film Theatre in London in the early 1960s I heard Jean Renoir say something similar to a questioner who had burdened him with a long analysis of one of the crane shots in *Le Crime de Monsieur Lange*. Renoir said that he made a point of forgetting about technical problems once he had solved them.

In a later generation, film directors became less inclined to forget anything. When a pyramid of explanatory journalism builds up around an art-form it is easy for a practitioner to become so impressed by his own entombment that he starts breathing the rarefied air and relishing the dust. It would happen to trail-bike champions if the media cared. It happens to film directors because the media care about almost nothing but the movies. The movies are as fascinating as a war, and the directors are the generals. There are very few people with the logistic ability to organize a battle between a bunch of averagely talented actors and a computer-generated army of trolls: when such a man is told that he is Michelangelo reborn, he finds little evidence to help him disagree. He soon forgets that he has almost no detectable talent beyond getting other people to combine their talents in accordance with his wishes. Singers, on the other hand, have the advantage of being kept fundamentally humble by the personal, individual and directly physical nature of their gift. Zinka Milanov had a gold-rush chest-voice that practically brought her body along with it when it soared into the grand circle. Quite a lot of that she could do when she was fifteen.

Apart from the very rare exception like Rosa Ponselle, singers must have their voices trained if they are ever to sustain a career beyond the first week. But there is still such a thing as talent, and finally, as initially, it is what matters. There were plenty of singers in Callas's generation who could do what she couldn't: make a transition from the upper register to the middle register without showing the join. But even in the later part of her life, when her upper register was in tatters, she could come powering back into the middle register with a hot roar that boiled the wax in your ears. She made a drama of it, and that was her talent. In her master classes she would try to show how it was done, but her pupils could never learn her unique trick of turning up the voice's darkness like a light as she plunged like a returning space shuttle into the stave.

Nijinsky got all his master classes over in a single line of explanation. When he was asked about the technical secret of his jump, he said: "I merely leap and pause." (Either you got the pause or you don't got the pause.) With all this said and insisted on, however, it should be remem-

bered that the idea that there can be an unstudied, perfectly spontaneous art is an idle dream. Zinka Milanov was merely seeing off a pest
when she made her most famous statement. It was true that she had
been born with a beautiful voice. But her voice had been trained from
the moment its quality was detected. At the Zagreb Academy of Music
she spent an entire year on nothing but exercises. For her first *Trovatore* Leonora, sung in Croatian, she prepared for two years, working on
each page a hundred times, note by note. This hard curatorial work
went on all her life, even after her retirement from the stage: as a
teacher, she stayed in training. She was right to say that she "got the
voice," but the essential counter-statement was given in an interview
she granted to the magazine *Étude* in 1940, when she said, about
singing well, that "the attainment of this goal is a full life's labour": a
dull truth, but true for all the arts. (Prodigies like Rimbaud merely
have their full lives early.) It's more fun to talk about amazing talents,
and indeed they exist. But the real miracle is the work that goes into
fostering them. In movies about artists, that aspect is usually dealt with
in a montage sequence two minutes long, because even a hint of the
real labour that goes into improvement would take an hour of screen
time at the very least. For that one reason, there will never be a credible movie about the making of an artist. Interior concentration doesn't
translate to the screen. Exterior impact does. For just a moment, Zinka
Milanov was a Central European actress delivering a line in a Hollywood movie, like Zsa Zsa Gabor. The line played well but it was only
half true. The true version, however, wouldn't play at all. "Artistic talent is indeed a gift from God, which the artist is obliged to match with
the gift of his life."

CZESLAW MILOSZ

❦ ❦ ❦

Czeslaw Milosz (1911–2004) was born in Lithuania and grew up speaking Polish. In 1934 he reinforced his career as a poet and freelance writer by taking a law degree. As a contributor to radio he got into trouble under the pre-war right-wing government for his left-wing views. Under a more ruthless regime, his experience at dodging official opprobrium came in useful when he wrote for the underground press in Nazi-occupied Warsaw. Representing post-war Communist Poland, he was a diplomat to the United States and, in 1950, to Paris, where he asked for political asylum. He spent ten years in Paris, and students of his writings will often get the sense that he was later more comfortable having his Polish translated into French than into English. In 1953 he published *The Captive Mind*, a bitterly disillusioned analysis, from the inside, of the influence of Marxist orthodoxy on his generation of idealists. The book, which students should regard as essential reading even today, can now be seen as an early blow at the foundations of the Warsaw Pact. Written before the Berlin Wall went up, *The Captive Mind* was a key factor in eventually bringing it down. At the end of his decade in Paris, Milosz left for California, where he became established as professor of Slavic lan-

guages and literature at Berkeley. In 1980 he received the
Nobel Prize, and after 1981 his writings began to be published
in Poland: not all at once, and seldom without official doubts,
but inexorably. For the regime in its long final crisis, Milosz's
international prestige was just too big to ignore, like the
Pope's. Milosz wrote poetry, essays and political analysis as if
they were all in the one medium, a genre beyond a genre.
From the technical angle, this now looks like the next breakthrough after Ortega, early in the century, identified the newspaper article as a vital medium for serious thought. The genre
beyond the genres had already been established by Milosz's fellow Polish-speaking exile Gombrowicz but nobody pursued it
with quite the copious fluency of Milosz, whose poems and
esssays flow into each other as if they belong to the one river
system. John Bayley, in his useful introductory essay on Milosz
collected in *The Power of Delight*, says, "By writing in every
form, he writes virtually in one: and he instructs in all." Milosz
had a wealth of personal experience to base his instruction on,
much of it tinged with remorse. As with Marcel Reich-Ranicki,
another future liberal who was a servant of the Polish Communist regime after the war, the supposed puzzle of Milosz's
unfortunate allegiance can be quickly solved: the Poles had no
reason to trust anyone. With his background so thoroughly
poisoned, the miracle of Milosz's writings is his range of
fellow-feeling: he can talk about modern history and the contradictions within liberalism as if we, his listeners, had been
made wise by the same childhood.

The scriptures constitute the common good of believers,
agnostics and atheists.
— CZESLAW MILOSZ, *VISIONS DE LA BAIE
DE SAN FRANCISCO*, P. 224

THAT THE BIBLE, for a Western civilization, is the common
good of believers and non-believers ought to be obvious, but for
some reason it is a truth hard to see except when that same civiliza-

tion is at the point of collapse. Milosz had seen a civilization collapse: like any of the post-war Polish writers awarded the privilege of growing to adulthood, he had been obliged to wonder whether a national culture can be said to have any roots at all after the nation itself has been obliterated. It has to be remembered that the typical Polish writer was Bruno Schulz. But for that to be remembered, Bruno Schulz has to be remembered, and the main reason he was so easily forgotten is that a Gestapo officer blew his brains out. It happened in the Drohobycz ghetto in 1942, when Schulz was only fifty, with the best of his career ahead of him. Schulz's little book *The Cinammon Shops* had the promise of a genius that would take time to realize itself, because the nature of time would be one of the things it would define. Even if he had never written a word, he would have been a hope for Poland's future just for how he could paint and draw. He was a walking fountain of talent, and the flow was stopped almost before it started, by one bullet in the right place. But at least he was heard of. Among the younger elite obliterated by the Russian firing squads before the Nazis even arrived, there were probably more like him. There were certainly more in the Warsaw ghetto, where the cultural life (plangently evoked by Marcel Reich-Ranicki in his long interview *Die doppelte Boden*) was like a university of dreams. Alas, the university had a direct rail connection with the slaughterhouse, and all that beautiful promise went into smoke. It took Roman Polanski, by his very existence, to remind us of what had ceased to exist: a whole generation of young talent was destroyed, and if Polanski had not been blessed with an inconspicuous personal appearance even he would have shared the fate of his mother. When the war was over, the memory of all this was not: for the artists who had come through, the pit was only a step behind them. When they looked over their shoulders, they could see right into it. In that direction, there was little else in view, except rubble. Milosz was living with that knowledge when he said this about the scriptures.

Looking for something to count on, he found the Bible in the ruins. For us, blessed with a more comfortable set of ruins—even if the streets are more dangerous, most of us live better now than we did in the houses we grew up in—there seems less to be afraid of: we can persuade ourselves that history is a linear development, in which even the eternal can become outdated, and be safely forgotten. Perhaps our own catastrophe will never come in any readily intelligible form, so it will never matter if there is nothing to go back to, no past to legitimize the permanent present, which will legitimize itself by doing us no evil except by its puffball bombardment of triviality. There is always the chance that our confident iconoclasts are right. Milosz is telling us not to bet on it, but perhaps he was unlucky. Like the Polish intelligentsia that was wiped out half by one set of madmen and half by another, he was just caught in the squeeze, and had his heart broken even though his body walked away.

You can be a non-believer, however, and still be amazed at how even the believers are ready to let the Bible go. In England, the most lethal attack on the scriptures has been mounted by the established Church itself. The King James Bible is a prose masterpiece compiled at a time when even a committee could write English. The modern versions, done in the name of comprehension, add up to an assault on readability. Eliot said that the Revised Standard Vesion was the work of men who did not realize they were atheists. The New English Bible was worse than that: Dwight Macdonald (his hilarious review is collected in his fine book *Against the American Grain*) had to give up looking for traces of majesty and start looking for traces of literacy. Those responsible for the NEB probably did realize they were atheists: otherwise they could scarcely have been so determined to leave not one stone standing upon another. For those of us unable to accept that the Bible is God's living word, but who believe that the living word is God, the successful reduction of once-vital language to a compendium of banalities was bound to look like blasphemy, and the perpetrators like vandals. When I joined in a public protest against the rejigging of the Book of Common Prayer, a practising Christian among the London editors—it was Richard Ingrams, editor of *Private Eye*—accused me of being in bad faith. He hated the new prayer book even more than I did, but thought I could have no reason for sharing his contempt. But it was my book too. I had been brought up on the scriptures, the prayers and the hymns. I had better reasons than inertia for deploring their destruction. Milosz had the same reasons. The scriptures had been his first food. For me, the scriptures provided a standard of authenticity against the pervasive falsehoods of advertising, social engineering, moral uplift, demagogic politics—all the verbal corruptions of democracy, the language of illusion. But for Milosz, the scriptures provided a standard of authenticity against a much more dangerous language, the language of legalized murder. We have to imagine a situation in which the state was so oppressive and mendacious that the Church looked like a free institution, and its language sounded like the truth. Milosz was well aware that the record of the Church in Polish politics had not been brilliant. One of his many braveries, post-war, was to give an unflinching account of Poland's institutionalized anti-Semitism, a strain of opinion in which the Church had always been implicated. We should also strive to remember that any German lover of his Bible must cope with the knowledge that its classic translation was the work of Martin Luther, whose loathing for the Jews was well up to Nazi standards. But we are not talking about our love for a Church, whether Catholic or Protestant. We are talking about our love for a book, and what we love is the way it is written. Rewriting it is not in the realm of the possible, and any attempt to do so should be seen for what it is: the threat of destruction.

Sooner than become the enemy of its own classical texts, the Anglican Church would have done better to seize the first opportunity of disestablishing itself. However tenuous, its offical connection to the state has been enough to saddle it with the doomed ambition of maximizing its popular audience, like a television channel in desperate search of more viewers who eat crisps. Separated from a fully secularized state, it might have fully enjoyed the only civilized condition for a religion, which is to provide a spiritual structure for private life. Only a secular state can be democratic; although the democracy will soon be in trouble if the private citizen is deprived of a spiritual code, to be acknowleged for its moral example even if he does not believe in its divine provenance.

With the possible exception of Buddhism, no religion we know about is capable of allying itself to the state without working to the destruction of liberty. Less commonly noted is that it will also work to the destruction of itself, by trivializing its own teachings, or rendering them obnoxious in the attempt to impose them legally, instead of by exhortation, example and witness. In its proper sphere, private life, a religion can keep its teachings as pure and strict as it likes, as long as they do not break the law. It is also free to protect its own sources of spiritual nourishment against the fatal obligation to make them universally intelligible. We can be sure that one of the consolations the Pope brought to Poland in 1979 was a few words of Latin. That he spoke Polish helped him to be understood, but that he also spoke Latin was the reminder, thirsted for by the faithful, that there was an eternal language which the years of the captive mind had not managed to corrupt. There were many among the faithless who were glad to be reminded too.

Evelyn Waugh's correspondence teems with bitter complaints at the time when the Church adopted a vernacular liturgy. He hadn't, he said, become a Catholic in order to applaud the Church's clumsy adaptation to the modern world. He wanted it not to adapt. He wanted, that is, a refuge. Those of us brought up as Protestants, but who later lapsed, found out, when the doors closed behind us, that we hadn't lapsed quite as far as we thought. We had lapsed into unbelief, but not into stupidity, and the spectacle of our one-time cradle rocking to the clappy-happy rhythms of half-witted populism was a betrayal of something that had once impressed us at least enough to invite rebellion. I don't want the teachings of Jesus taken from me. He might no longer be my redeemer, but he is still my master. If I no longer know that my redeemer liveth, I know that he speaketh not like Tony Blair. It is true that Jesus never spoke the language of the King James Version of the New Testament. But the language of the King James Version is of a poetic intensity congruent with the impact Jesus must once have made on simple souls, of whom I am still one: simple enough, anyway, to need my sins forgiven. Now that there is nobody to do that for me, I must try to do it myself. Like most men with a conscience, I find that very hard, and spend much time feeling absurd. But without the scriptures we poor wretches would be lost indeed, because without them, conscience itself would become just another disturbance of the personality, to be cured by counselling. We are surrounded by voices telling us that everything will come right if we learn to love ourselves. Imagine the torments of Jesus in his passion, if, on top of the sponge of vinegar and the spear, they had offered him counselling as well. Exiled in California, Milosz saw enough of America's culture of personal fulfilment to wonder what he had got himself into. But he never forgot what he had got himself out of—a repression so arid that it left him thirsty for a language he could respect, even though it came from a book he couldn't believe.

EUGENIO MONTALE

❣ ❣ ❣

Eugenio Montale (1896–1981) was Italy's most famous poet
after World War II, and eventually established himself beyond
challenge as the living embodiment of his country's humanist
culture in modern times. Immediately memorable even when
he was obscure, he was the nearest thing to a national lyrical
voice since D'Annunzio, and a distinctly more enticing
prospect. Whereas the posturing D'Annunzio had been one of
the harbingers of Fascist hysteria, Montale, growing up in the
Fascist era, was a portent of the more level tones of the liberal
democracy to come. Educated in the fine shades of love, loyalty and emotional truth during histrionic times, he gave
everyday sanity a lyrical voice for which his recovering country was grateful. His Nobel Prize in 1975 was welcomed as a
sign of restored national prestige. Every educated Italian
knows at least a few lines of Montale. People familiar with the
standard episodes of Dante and lyrics of Leopardi can usually
quote from Montale's famous poem about the sunflower
("Bring me the sunflower mad with light"). Beginning readers
of Italian can be confident that a few hard hours spent between
a dictionary and Montale's first, reputation-making collection,
Ossi di seppia (*Cuttlefish Bones*), will promote them directly to

the hub of Italian literature in the twentieth century, and give them a phrase or two that everyone will be delighted to recognize. One of the young Montale's principal objects was to tame rhetoric, the verbal inflation to which an over-musical language is prone. (The hardest trick in an Italian poet's book is to avoid rhyme: Montale could dodge it forever.) There have been many attempts to translate the masterpieces in Montale's main body of lyrical poetry. All have failed, but at least they have provided a wealth of parallel texts. For a long while the task of translating his exemplary critical prose looked equally doomed, but Jonathan Galassi finally did an acceptable job with *The Second Life of Art* (1982). Galassi sometimes misses the easy rhythm of a Montale sentence, but he always catches the dry neatness of its argument. Widely read in several languages but devoted to the value of common experience, the urbane and affable Montale was an enchantingly down-to-earth writer in every form he touched: even his most difficult poetry is full of concrete detail. He was also a singer (his early training provided the bedrock for his superb music criticism) and a painter. Alas, it was revealed after his death that a certain knack for sleight of hand had been among his talents: some of his reviews of English books had been written by a student, with whom he split the take.

Art destined to live has the aspect of a truth of nature, not
of some coldly worked out experimental discovery.
— EUGENIO MONTALE, *AUTO DA FÉ*, P. 81

IN HIS CRITICAL PROSE, Montale often reminds you of Flaubert's insistence that we don't love literature. Montale didn't love literature either: not in the sense of drawing his principles from it. He practised literature. As a practitioner, Montale was ready to countenance experiment. He had time for Ezra Pound. When he said, in reference to Pound, that talent presupposes dignity for anyone on whom it is conferred, he was being forgiving about Pound's politics. He knew he was being generous: Pound flagrantly represented the sort of capitulation

to Fascist rhetoric that Montale had not made. But Montale felt no
need to be generous about Pound's technical experiments in fragmen-
tation and panscopic allusiveness. Montale simply thought they were
legitimate: as he said much later of Auden, it didn't matter how lyricism happened as long as it happened. In his own era there were her-
meticists in whom he was determined to detect the lyricist even when
they themselves had given up. What Montale loved was music, and that
was where this cry from the heart came from. He was born and raised
as a musician—he could sing at professional level—and was there as a
critic at most of the first nights that counted in the long last gasp of the
classic Italian opera. Budding critics of television or the movies, if they
really want to know how the response to a cultural event can be turned
into a critique of the whole society behind it, should get a reader of
Italian to take them through a few paragraphs of *Prime alla Scala*, Montale's splendid compendium of the best pieces he wrote about the *teatro
lirico* on its way to exhaustion. What destroyed it—or anyway, what
marked its destruction, since cause and effect were hard to distinguish—was intellectualism. Late in his life, Montale was in the audience when the avant-garde composer Luigi Nono tried to persuade the
Italian musical public that he had been sent to make their lives more
significant with a Marxist arrangement of notes. Early in his life, Montale had also been in the audience when the great last operas of *verismo*
had made the audience's lives more significant without Marx getting a
mention: all it had taken was melody, orchestration and thrilling theatrical effect. Montale was thus ideally placed to point out that Nono
was a brain in a bottle.

We should concede, however, that the contrast between the truth of
nature and the experimental discovery is not always clearly marked.
Stravinsky, when he ventured into the atonal, did not sacrifice feeling:
and presumably he would not have gone there unless he felt the need
for a new range of opportunity. The Impressionist painters thought
they were being scientific, and in the matter of the analysis and combination of colours they actually were. In the Renaissance, perspective
was an experimental discovery, and must, with its chambers and mirrors, have looked cold enough until you saw the results. Vermeer's studio probably looked more like an optical laboratory than the simple
rooms he sets in front of us. In all the arts, and at all times, there have

been technical experiments. Rhyme must have felt like a technical experiment when it was being discovered, and probably sounded like it when its discoverers were exploring its possibilities beyond the immediate bounds of sense. In modern writing, I have had it explained to me, by admirers of John Ashbery in his later phase, how the stutters and elisions of his diction are a release mechanism for modulations of tone. To me they sound like the merest gesture towards complication, but so did the repetitions of Philip Glass until I listened harder. (The harder I listened to Stockhausen, however, the more his repetitions remained merely repetitive.) The real problem with Montale's protest is that in the earliest days of his poetry—at the time of *Ossi di seppia* and *La bufera e altro*—he might have been vulnerable to his own suspicions if he had come back from the future. In the lush context of Italian lyricism, his acerbities of diction were an experiment. They just happened to be a fruitful one. In his heart of hearts, he knows that the two terms of this statement are not as polarized as he makes out. He was just finding a polite way to say how much he hated self-consciously modern, wilfully unseductive, sedulously rebarbative, proudly repellent, unapologetically giftless music. In any kind of bad art, it is when the gift is gone that the experiment really does take over—the eternally cold experiment that promises to make gold out of lead, and bricks without straw. Leaving coldness aside (and we should leave it aside, because barren artistic experimentation can also be done in a white hot frenzy), it might be useful to mention that Montale, in another essay, came up with the perfect term for a work of art that had no other subject except its own technique. He called it the seasoning without the roast.

> True culture is what remains in a man when he has
> forgotten everything he has learned. This, however,
> presupposes an absorption, a profound penetration
> of his character.
> —EUGENIO MONTALE, *AUTO DA FÉ*, P. 313

Montale was careful to say that we should take it in before we forget it. Ezra Pound is famous for saying roughly the same thing (he said culture begins when we forget what book a fragment came from) but the idea is easier to accept from Montale. We can safely assume that his vast reading got into his writing, as a distillation if not as a frame of reference. After his death it turned out that the vast reading had not been quite as vast as we thought. He read widely in foreign languages and made the citations to prove it, but some of his reviewing of books in English had owed an inordinate amount to an assistant, who not only read those books, but wrote the pieces about them that were published under Montale's name. Montale had always modestly called English *una lingua che non si impara mai*—a language that one never learns—but here was evidence that he had found it even harder than that. It was an almighty scandal even by Italian standards, but eventually died down in the Italian way. Nobody ever supposed that Pavarotti sang worse for having finagled so much tax money, and in the long run it was tacitly conceded that Montale, after a lifetime of hard work, had a few easy hours coming to him in the bar while some young hopeful knocked out the article for tomorrow's *Corriere della sera*.

Scandals aside, Montale's learning in languages other than his own (including in English: he really had read a lot of it at first hand) was an abiding astonishment, and in Italian he had quite simply read everything that counted. On top of his knowledge of literature, there was his knowledge of painting: his praise of Roberto Longhi's art criticism is an act of communion with the great scholar that could beguile any lucky Italian student of art history and lead him by an enchanted route into the principality of literature in the next valley. Longhi knew how to write about painting; Montale knew how to write about writing about painting; and the chain of response has no weak links until it gets to you. Your turn, and welcome to civilization. And to cap his knowledge of literature and the plastic arts, there was his knowledge of music, which amounted to something far beyond expertise: if not the incarnation of the art, he was the incarnation of its appreciation. Take all his critical competencies together, and you get an enchanting picture of a man who illuminated his life by saturating his mind with the arts. It is quite easy to convince yourself that the results show up in his poetry. But don't we have to take the connection on trust? His poetry is not notably allusive to the arts. How do we know that his character was profoundly penetrated by them? What if he not only, in the superficial sense, forgot everything he learned, but actually and radically forgot the lot?

In conversation, Martin Amis once disturbingly suggested to me that no matter how much you admire a novel, after about a year you forget everything in it. He was proposing a rule of thumb, not a law of thermodynamics, but judging from my own experience he had a point. The reason I keep on reading *Lucky Jim* and *The Great Gatsby* is that otherwise I would be certain to forget them, and I know it's time to read *Madame Bovary* again when all I can remember is (a) Emma's lewd cab-ride in Rouen, (b) her being impressed by the physical glossiness of the landed gentry, and (c) her husband's lack of success with his operation on somebody's—whose?—foot. When so much goes, what is it that remains, and can it usefully be called an absorption? It might be better to call it a habit. Perhaps we just get into the habit of passing good things through our minds, and the better the things, the better the habit. It might also be that the passing through is the essential event: a polishing of the pipe, like El Dorado's throat.

We all know trainspotting types who remember useless things. They can have fun with it when they meet a fellow sufferer. But there is nothing amusing about the man who has hurled himself at an exalted art-form and remembered it all. Some of the worst cases have had it hurled at them in early life, and so are not really responsible, but you do meet near-maniacs who chose their fate in the years of maturity. I knew a man once—knew him briefly—who could refer to every aria in every opera by its first line, and always in the original language. He couldn't just do it for Verdi and Puccini. He could do it for Janáček and Moussorgsky. Worse than that, he couldn't *not* do it. During a single interval in the Crush Bar at Covent Garden you would see people departing from him as if launched by a catapult. I knew another man who remembered not just the full cast but all the technical personnel of every film he had ever seen. I wished the two of them in hell together, but at various times each chose me for a victim, and it was an ugly reminder that when it comes to art, forgetting is almost as important as remembering. I love memorizing poetry, but only the poetry I love, and I pity anyone who, without even trying, remembers all the poetry he reads. At Sydney University, one of my contemporaries had that affliction, with the result that his early career was distinguished by his winning a prize with a poem which had previously, in a large part, been written by someone else—a very public embarrassment. Without the capacity to forget, we would not be able to go back to something we love with the delicious twin certainties that it will yield a familiar pleasure of the highest quality, and still be new all over again. The triumph of Proust is that he can give you that feeling on first reading. He can do it because he set himself, in his earliest years, to remembering what it felt like to forget.

Memory tests: in Michael Frayn's novel *Towards the End of the Morning*, what does the hero say to reassure himself when he notices the rust eating the paint-job of his car? (It's the good strong brown undercoat showing through.) (But what is the name of the hero?) In *Portnoy's Complaint*, what does Portnoy say his real name is when he is trying to convince the Wasp girl skater that he is not Jewish? (Porte-Noir.) And what is his name for the fantasy girl who puts out every time? (Thereal McCoy.) (But what is the real name of the fashion model he calls the Monkey, and why can't you remember that, if you can remember the title of the Yeats poem he recites, or half recites, to win her favours?) (It was "Leda and the Swan"). You can remember the name of the weekly show that J. D. Salinger's Glass children appeared on (*It's a Wise Child*) but was it radio or television? And at the end of *Franny and Zooey*, how many of the Glass children are dead? Is it "Sergeant X" or "For Esmé—with Love and Squalor" that features the Dostoevsky quotation "Gentlemen and teachers, I ask you, what is Hell? I submit it is the agony of being unable to love"? Was it inscribed by a Nazi official, by his wife, or by the protagonist? In which novel by Evelyn Waugh does Mrs. Stitch drive her little car down the steps of the men's lavatory? What kind of little car?

In the paragraph above, there is not a novel, novella or short story mentioned that I have read fewer than three times, and in every case I am not only dimly aware of things I half remember, but painfully aware of things I have forgotten. It gets even more painful when it comes to painting. When the Courtauld collection was still in Bloomsbury I must have looked at Manet's *A Bar of the Folies-Bergère* at least a hundred times. There is a man in the mirror: probably he wants her for a mistress. On which side of her head does his image appear? I am damned if I can remember. But perhaps, if one could remember everything, one would be damned indeed. In the last weeks of a slow dying, it might be better to forget. One hopes that there will be a saving mechanism to it, a kind of mental economy. In my prime I thought that H. L. Mencken's fate—semantic aphasia—was the most cruel possible affliction for a man who had given his life to words: a punishment for love. But from the inside looking out it might have felt like a release.

A release from memories of beauty might be just the ticket: what else, after all, would they make you do, except long for what you can't have, more life? Perhaps we will forget what was lovely and remember what was true. Already, at no great age, I sometimes fancy that I can feel that happening. Recently, for the tenth time at least, I sat through a video of Kenneth MacMillan's ballet *Winter Dreams*, in the brilliantly sensitive television production by Derek Bailey. All over again I was ravished by what MacMillan did to make Darcey Bussell and Irek Mukhamedov dance as if they were mad about each other. Yet once again I am already forgetting the steps, while remembering better than ever what I have never forgotten since I first saw the work: the unsensational and quietly desperate *pas de deux* in which Darcey Bussell and Anthony Dowell act out the extinction of their marriage. When the lovers dance, they fly: they fly into a passion. When the married people dance, they die—almost nothing happens. But their doomed little movements are the work of MacMillan's choreographic imagination at its dizzy height. At one time, by his invitation, I was going to write for him a spoken ballet about Nijinsky. I suppose the project never really had a chance, but it paid off in that I saw a lot of him. Since the first time I saw *Mayerling* I had always thought he was a genius, and in the other full-length ballets evidence went on accumulating that any MacMillan *pas de deux* for lovers was an ignition point of modern art—a floodlight on the possibilities of human movement as a plastic equivalent for poetry. He was an easy man to embarrass, so I had to be careful how I told him what I felt, and when he declined into his last illness I shamefully ran out of things to say. I would like to think that this is a way of saying them. (A tip to young writers for when they grow old: if you have felt gratitude for a fellow artist's life, don't content yourself with telling him personally: say it in public—someone who knows neither of you might take heart.) I thought MacMillan's talent so great that it got beyond the beautiful. When his lovers danced sublimely, you could take it for granted. But when he found a steady poetry for slow heartbreak, he gave us something to remember at the point of death. You get no prizes for seeing that his first *pas de deux* for the lovers in *Mayerling* is beautiful. But there is a prize for seeing, in *Isadora*, that his *pas de deux* for Isadora Duncan and Paris Singer grieving for the accidental death of their children is beautiful too. If it ever came to the point where a lifetime's memories of artistic exaltation shrank to nothing except a single image, an image of dignity would be a good one to see. One would want to retain at least that much. But Montale must have had that idea in mind, or he would not have talked about the inevitability of forgetting in a way that emphasized the quality of what is remembered.

MONTESQUIEU

Charles Louis de Secondat, Baron de La Brède et de Montesquieu (1689–1755) is one of our ambassadors in history. Like Thucydides, Tacitus and Montaigne, he represents us in the depths of time, as if his mind were a space station built by the modern world and positioned in an observational orbit above the surface of the past. His well-known commemorative medal, on the other hand, makes him look like a projection into the future from the Senate of ancient Rome. The real man was a creature of his age, and very good at being so. Noble birth helped, but his brilliance was not of the kind that precluded sociability. He was a hit in the grand salons and no stranger to frivolity. *The Persian Letters* (1721), his first famous book, started as something of a joke. A measure of his success is that today we regard its central trick as commonplace: foreigners observe our society and find it strange. The French society that Montesquieu's two imaginary visiting Persians described was in fact heading downhill towards revolution, but it was delighted to be so wittily told that it was in a mess. Montesquieu was a Persian visitor himself when he spent two years in England, moving at the highest level, fêted everywhere: a period of observation that was to yield crucial results for his later work. First, however, came his *Considerations on the Causes of the Greatness of the Romans and Their Decline* (1734), a thriller which is probably the best port of entry for the new reader. His undoubted masterpiece is heavier going: *The Spirit of Laws* (1748). One of the formative books of the modern world, it is still, in a hundred different ways, relevant today. Perhaps, at the moment, it is most conspicuously relevant in the critique it implicitly delivers of its ostensible subject, multiculturalism. Montesquieu had practically invented the concept that all cultures evolved in different ways from separate imperatives; and in *The Spirit of Laws* he continued that theme, but by then he had seen the danger. In allowing the suggestion that all cultures might be equally valuable, room had been left for supposing that they might be equally virtuous. To guard against this, he advanced the further proposition—buttressing his argument with reference to the British constitution he had studied at first hand—that beneath cultural variety there were, or should be, values that did not change. In modern terms, he was concerned that a legitimate delight in the multiplicity of cultures should not develop into an ideology, multiculturalism: an ideology that would entail the abandonment of any fixed concept of justice. Seemingly in the face of his own cultural relativism, Montesquieu declared that justice was eternal. There is a fine introductory essay to Montesquieu by Isaiah Berlin (collected in his *Against the Current*), but Berlin strangely failed to see that Montesquieu's point had deep consequences for liberalism, which Berlin thought a matter of contending values. Montesquieu thought the same, but he thought there was a fixed point. Proposing, at least by implication, a liberalism dependent on a hard core of principles, and not just on tolerance, Montesquieu thus made a decisive pre-emptive intervention into the debate that we are having now.

It is not impossible that the things which dishonoured him most served him best. If he had shown a great soul from

the start, the whole world would have distrusted him; and
if he had been hardy, he would not have given Antony time
for all the extravagance that led to ruin.
— MONTESQUIEU, PLÉIADE EDITION,
VOL. 2, P. 137

AFTER FINALLY LEARNING enough French to put myself in a
condition where he might teach me more, I found Montesquieu
too big to begin at the beginning. The above citation was the passage
that addicted me to him. Dipping at random into one of his Pléiade
volumes, I chanced on this characterization of Augustus, and knew very
soon that I would be occupied with Montesquieu for a long time into
the future, so I put the books away in full confidence that when I came
back to them later I would be reading nothing else for days on end.
That was how it worked out, except that the days turned to weeks. (I
own two complete sets of the Pléiade Montesquieu now, one to be
occasionally carried with me on my travels, the other to be kept always
safe at home against a rainy day, such as might happen at the end of the
world, an event that would have left him sad but not stunned.) Decades
before, when I was first a student in Sydney, North's Plutarch had had
the same effect. The big, ugly Modern Library edition was hard to love
from the outside, but hard to leave once you were in. I could see
straight away what Plutarch had done for the posters on Shakespeare's
marquee. Even today, I can't believe that the lists of dramatis personae
for *Julius Caesar* and *Antony and Cleopatra*—my favourite plays on a
Shakespearean roster in which almost all are favourites—would strike
us as quite so rich if Shakespeare had not already found Plutarch to be
a crowded bench of well-established characters all looking for what
Hollywood used to call Additional Dialogue. Beyond that obvious connection, would all the other Shakespeare plays be the same as they are
without Plutarch: that is, without the idea and the example of character being destiny? Montaigne, said Stefan Zweig (in his *Europaisches
Erbe*—The European Heritage), read history not in order to become
learned, but to see how other men had handled events, and so set himself beside them. By assessing the behaviour of prominent characters in
history we find a measure for ourselves. But one of our first assessments of ourselves is that we would be unlikely to attain such a mag-

nificent objectivity on our own: we need our guides to the human soul, and among them Montesquieu is hard to beat, because he can withhold his moral judgement to the cracking point without letting go of it. Obviously he does not much admire Augustus as a man; but he can see Augustus's greatness as an emperor; and finally he can see the connection between Augustus's greatness and his not being much of a man. This is quite a feat of detachment. Most of us would table our decision long before that.

Montesquieu can delay his judgement on Tiberius: a forbearance that not even Tacitus could show. Montesquieu, it should be said, thought the world of Tacitus, "*qui abrégeoit tout parce qu'il voyoit tout.*" ("He abridged everything because he saw everything." Perfect.) Tacitus was charmed by Tiberius, but only as a maiden with a soft neck is charmed by the approach of a trained vampire. Like Tacitus, Montesquieu could appreciate Tiberius as an artist of bastardry. "There is no crueller tyranny," said Montesquieu, "than the one exercised in the shadow of the law, and with the colours of justice." A connoisseur of murderous casuistry, Montesquieu was impressed by the efficiency Tiberius brought to the business of perverting the judicial system. From a distance of sixteen hundred years, Montesquieu rewarded the imperial perpetrator with the quality of his prose: "*les couleurs de la justice*" is a magnificent phrase, one of those perfect formulations that should be left in its original language as a tribute to the culture from which it emerged. Tacitus had seen that Tiberius not only wanted the Senate to be servile, but despised it for flattering him. Yet Tacitus, as much fascinated as repelled, had his sense of irony exhausted by a satanically gifted individual. Montesquieu, less emotionally involved, saw a point about Tiberius that extended to all mankind. "Like most men, he wanted contradictory things; his general politics were nowhere in accord with his particular passions. He would have liked a Senate free and capable of making its government respected, but he also wanted a Senate to satisfy, at all times, his fears, his jealousies and his hatreds: finally the statesman gave way contentedly to the man." We are left free to deduce a universal principle. Unless constrained to do otherwise, the statesman will always give way to the man. Lord Acton's later observation about the corrupting nature of power is already there, and already expounded in apprehensible human terms. Part of the impact comes from our recognition of what has happened so often within ourselves: the feeling of relief and release as we slip from a rigid civic obligation into a spastic self-assertion.

Montesquieu was well aware, however, that the dolorous road of arbitrary imperial power led far past the point set by the demoralization of the sane, and that beyond the corruptible personality there was such a thing as the outright psychopath, demented from the womb, or anyway from the cradle. Montesquieu had no doubt that Caligula was crazy. But Montesquieu is able to enrich his condemnation—to make it an analysis, and not just a bleat of anguish—by examining how Caligula's blatant insanity did not preclude subtlety of intellect, and might even have encouraged it. He drew Caligula as a sophist of cruelty. Descended from both Antony and Augustus, Caligula said he would punish the consuls if they celebrated the day of rejoicing established in memory of the battle of Actium, and that he would punish them if they didn't. (For the puzzled or the innocent, here's how it worked: Antony lost the battle of Actium to Octavian, the future Augustus. Therefore, those who celebrated the battle dishonoured Antony, while those who didn't dishonoured Augustus. The way was thus left open to punish everyone.)

By entertaining the possibility that cruelty could be allied with a kind of artistic ingenuity, Montesquieu pioneered a field of study that we by no means exhaust by reading the Marquis de Sade: if only it were so. Many of de Sade's effects were merely cumulative, and anyway they were almost all fictional. They were ideas he masturbated to in gaol, and the quill was the only conduit between his imagination and reality. He didn't have an office with a telephone. In the twentieth century, alas, one of the ways that the same brand of madness proved itself in power was by the ingenuity which added, to physical tortures unseen since medieval times, a range of psychological tortures which had been thought to have died with the nuttier Roman emperors. If Saddam Hussein needed to acquire by education what he did not have from instinct, he could have learned from Stalin the techniques of mentally destroying parents by attacking their children. ("My handsome son Uday," we can imagine him saying, "is looking forward to meeting your daughter.") But not even Stalin's ingenuity was without precedent in ancient times, and Hitler's fondness for *Sippenhaft*—the German term for punishing the innocent family along with the guilty criminal—was a direct hand-on from Tiberius. (Stalin's penchant for obliterating the entire family of an Enemy of the People was not really *Sippenhaft*, because he was cleaning up a whole bourgeois element anyway: i.e., they couldn't *not* be guilty, so there was no arbitrariness to the punishment.) On a less exalted level in the infernal Nazi world, Victor Klemperer, in his diaries—*I Shall Bear Witness* and *To the Bitter End*—records the exquisite dilemma of the Dresden Jews in the years when they supposedly still had a life, before the Final Solution officially got under way.

Victor Klemperer is sometimes given a niggling press because he seems lost in everyday detail. But when everyday detail was so horrible, to record it was an act of heroism, and nobody who has read his diaries should lose an opportunity of pointing out to anyone who hasn't that they constitute one of the great documents of the twentieth century. At the heart of the document is the perception that the Jews were placed under designedly intolerable psychological pressure from the first day of the new regime. When they were still granted the luxury of travel by tram to their increasingly distant places of decreasingly remunerative work, they were permitted to ride only on a platform which could not be reached except though a compartment they were forbidden to enter. Their dilemma was between either walking to and from work, which was steadily less possible, or boarding the tram and facing almost certain punishment. The "almost" made things worse: if there had been no alternative to staying at home and starving yourself and your family to death, it might have been easier to face. But there was an alternative. The alternative, however, was to face the dilemma. A more delicately calibrated mechanism for inducing neurosis in human beings could scarcely have been devised. But devised it was: though it would be a relief to hear that the idea had simply evolved without a creator, there can be no doubt that some perversely talented Nazi factotum sat down to a desk and thought it out. Like Tacitus only more so, Montesquieu deserves our thanks for preparing us to face our own time. Tacitus thought that there were arguments for the use of torture. Montesquieu agreed, but said that there was something in our nature that cried out against it. Tacitus predicted what we have to face, but Montesquieu predicted us facing it, and thus ranks even higher among those men of the past who tell us that the future was always there—or anyway that enough of it had already happened to reassure us that the rest was not really unprecedented, just anachronistic. There is thus a kind of solace in reading them, saddening though it is; and with Montesquieu the solace becomes an inspiration, as if our doubts had met their voice.

> I believe that the thing above all which ruined Pompey was the shame he felt to think that in having elevated Caesar the way he did, he had lacked foresight. He accustomed himself to the idea as late as possible; he neglected his defence in order not to avow that he had put himself in danger; he maintained to the Senate that Caesar would never dare to make war; and because he had said it so often, he went on saying it always.
> — MONTESQUIEU, PLÉIADE EDITION,
> VOL. 2, P. 127

Apart from the hundred ways that this is better than anything in Gibbon, think of its pedigree. The psychological analysis of powerful men was already there in Thucydides: our Alcibiades is his Alcibiades first and foremost. It was there again in Sallust and Suetonius, and above all in Plutarch: through discovering in North's Plutarch the minds of other great men, Shakespeare discovered his own. If there had been no translation of Plutarch, Shakespeare might have learned the same possibilities from Montaigne alone, because Montaigne was saturated with the absorbed judicial powers of everyone we have so far mentioned, and nothing is more certain about Shakespeare than that he knew Montaigne by heart. Add all these names together, however, and even including Shakespeare you still do not reach a sum of political analysis that touches Montesquieu, of whom it can be said that not even his supreme artistic talent could lead him to a premature conclusion, and that he could find within himself the wellsprings of all human behaviour while yet maintaining a benevolent sanity. Pompey, when he became champion of the people, sacrificed his influence among the aristocrats. Unlike Julius Caesar, he lacked the instinct to hedge a bet. The two men were equally charismatic and equally ruthless, but eventually Caesar took control of the end-game. It could have happened only because Pompey had a psychological weakness. Without denigrating Pompey's intelligence, Montesquieu tells us what the weakness was, and makes the story of a mentality as gripping as a thriller. (The same thrill is what the numberless readers of a book like *The Da Vinci Code* are really after: they have just chosen arid territory in which to seek it.)

The mind perfectly open is usually vacuous: Montesquieu's is full of linked perceptions, a warehouse of networks in which truths connect with each other seemingly by themselves, because the medium, his prose, is so transparent. But the best way of knowing that psychology is not a science is that Montesquieu was its master, and was such an artist. There is a truth about mentality that Montesquieu would have taught us if Shakespeare hadn't: somewhere behind even the most universal comprehension there must be an individual mind. To take the two of them as a single example: they could not be so like each other if they were not so different. Here is Shakespeare being Montesquieu, in *Timon of Athens* II: 2. Flavius, for what must be the millionth time, is trying to make the prodigal Timon see prudent sense.

> *Ah! When the means are gone that buy this praise*
> *The breath is gone whereof this praise is made:*
> *Feast-won, fast-lost . . .*

That would be Montesquieu if it did not sound like Shakespeare, and it sounds like Shakespeare not just because it is in verse, but because, in the third line, its otherwise uninterrupted prose argument is momentarily condensed beyond the point where we can go on failing to notice that it is something written in transcendence of the power of speech. Shakespeare, even in prose, has the essence of a poet; and Montesquieu takes his prose always towards the unalterable interior balance of poetry; the extremes touch. The power of generalization is the same, because in each case it is energized by an unsleeping gift for specific psychology. Whether or not Montesquieu was right about Pompey, for example, he was right about you and me. Once we invest our opinion, we hang on to the investment; so the more we have at stake the more we risk, even by doing nothing. And the more powerful we are, the more likely we are to stick to our rusty guns: because it was firmness of purpose that made us powerful.

Montesquieu's Pompey resists being told the obvious, and answers by his behaviour the question why: he is obtuse in the matter because he is Pompey. Montesquieu has traced the blind spot to the centre of the character's vision. Degas developed a fault in his eyesight which eventually meant that he could not see when he looked straight ahead. Pompey has a dead patch in the centre of his moral retinas, and it makes him Pompey. In the same way, Shakespeare gives us the essence of Timon, who can't see that his generosity will destroy him; and of Coriolanus, who can't see that he must either woo the people or else decline to be their tribune. These are big things not to see and it takes big men not to see them.

Or it can take a big villain. In my time—this actually happened while I was alive, although fortunately I was not able to be present at the scene—Josef Stalin refused to believe that Nazi Germany would attack the Soviet Union. There is some doubt about the initial motive for his folly, but the best guess is that it sprang from the madness which placed ideological considerations above all others, even above the ability to maintain a state over which he had spent the best part of his life manoeuvring in order to assume control. Stalin had purged the Red Army of its best generals: deprived it, in fact, of its entire operating elite, and therefore of the ability to fight. If he had engineered the Molotov-Ribbentrop pact in order to give himself an opportunity to finish carrying out the purge, that would have been a logical chain of events, even if it started from an unhinged premise. If he thought, however, that there would not be a battle because his army could no longer fight it, there was no logic to his course of action at all. Under scrutiny, the second and stranger thought process seems the more likely, because everything he did next was equally deluded. Stalin staked his by now worldwide reputation for infallibility on his judgement that the Molotov-Ribbentrop pact meant what it said, and that Hitler would not attack him while it was still in force. If Hitler had not already proved that a document signed by himself meant nothing to him whatsoever, Stalin's own behaviour—in which no promise had ever outranked expediency—should have warned him that his opponent might repudiate a bargain which both of them had reached in the first place out of nothing but the cynical desire to share the spoils of a ravaged Poland while putting the democracies at a potentially ruinous disadvantage.

Yet Stalin, of all people, put himself in the position of declaring his faith in Hitler, of all people: and Stalin stuck to it even as the dissuasive evidence became overwhelming. By the eve of Operation Barbarossa, the Soviets had been supplied from the West with intelligence that described the German preparations in detail. The Ultra decrypts, fed to Stalin by personal order of Churchill, gave the German order of battle all the way down to the individual units. The Soviet intelligence authorities had long overcome their suspicions of a Western trick. Even without Ultra, they had plenty of evidence from inside German-occupied Poland and from inside Germany itself that an invasion was imminent. High-echelon Soviet intelligence officers continued trying to put the evidence on Stalin's desk even after it became clear that they were risking his wrath, and therefore their lives, by doing so. The spectacle of otherwise impeccably ruthless men ready to commit suicide in order to tell him the truth did nothing to shake Stalin's convictions. Instead, they were confirmed. His orders that the forward troops were to give no signs of being ready to defend themselves—lest the signs provoke the Germans—were not rescinded. They were reissued, up to and beyond the hour of attack. As a result, the invaders rolled forward almost unopposed. The attack was a long way into its first day before the flood of information at last gave Stalin pause for thought. When he paused, he collapsed.

As a measure of how well he had organized his monopoly of power, his disgusted colleagues felt that even in those circumstances they had no favourable opportunity to kill him. To the world's enduring loss, they fed him pabulum on his cot instead of smothering him with a pillow. In consequence, he was given the chance to recover from his nervous breakdown and resume the leadership, with a characteristically unlimited surplus of lies, wasteful violence, stupidity and perversion. Though he had enough sense to kick the propaganda effort screaming into reverse and transform the catastrophe from the Party's blunder into the Great Patriotic War, the illusion that the Communist Party saved the nation was to flourish from an early date. Mainly because of the immense mental investment by Western intellectuals in the Soviet Union's existence, the truth has taken more than half a century fully to emerge, but it was widely known in the Red Army from the first weeks of hostilities. Stalin not only came close to losing the war in its opening stages by his arrogance and ignorance, he found, later on, the most expensive possible way of winning it. From start to finish, there was not a single successful battle that could not have cost a fraction of its casualties: a fact attested to even by the Stalinists among the officer corps who managed to survive not only the war, but the peace. The peace proved almost as dangerous as the war, because finally Stalin had the temerity, once again and with not a tinge of irony or common shame, to purge his own army, which had got above itself by being indispensable to him: the very thing, probably, which had led him to purge it in the first place. From the end of World War II until the present day, it has been a constant source of bilious entertainment to hear desk-bound Western intellectuals, all of whom know even less about strategy than I do, praise Stalin as some kind of military genius: an opinion exactly coinciding with his own, and just as utterly divorced from reality. It ought not to matter, but there were too many good Russian soldiers who found out the hard way that the German army was only the start of their troubles. Their souls cry out from the snow, the minefields where they were used as human detonators, and above all from the prisoner-of-war pens, where, given up by the hundred thousand to please the will of a ruler for whom they mattered less than dirt, they were starved to death by another maniac who achieved the difficult feat of caring for them even less. I still can't believe that these obscenities happened in my time, and that during the Anzac Day march through Sydney in 1946 I was actually wearing a forage cap with a badge on it celebrating Stalin's heroism and genius. Now sixty years have gone by and my heart is with the young Russian soldier who starved to death in one of the prisoner-of-war compounds. I don't know his name, and by the time hunger and the weather had finished with him not even his mother would have known it. The words of the Persian general at Salamis are still with me: "Where are the names of those who perished?" Stalin, of coure, had a very good memory for names on death warrants: we ought to grant him that. But of the broad judgement and the detailed knowledge that it took to run military operations, Stalin had not a trace: not a scintilla, not a smidgin. Any historian who contends otherwise is simply incapable of giving up an illusion, for fear of the exertion that might be brought by reappraisal. What kind of history is that? Alas, it is scarcely even therapy.

A similar obstinacy to Stalin's was shown by Hitler, although Hitler had a better excuse. In his early campaigns, Hitler really did seem to know more than his generals. But it was mainly because he had a better estimation than they did of the state of mind prevailing in the opposing armies. When, in the second phase of the war, the opposing armies were better prepared to resist, Hitler's inflated conviction that his own general staff didn't know what they were talking about proved fatal. (The best argument for the general staff's being even more at fault than Hitler is provided by Alan Clarke's *Barbarossa*, a book which should not be belittled merely because its young author later grew rather too doe-eyed at the Führer's memory.) Though all the surviving generals pretended after the war that they had tried to dissuade him from his folly—the smart ones, spotting the danger of seeming to hanker after a more successful Nazi Germany, pretended that they had tried to dissuade him from war altogether—there were in fact few at the time who dared to say a word. Rundstedt and Guderian were both sidelined for telling him that his "no retreat" policy did nothing but rob the armoured formations of their mobility and ensure defeat. Manstein, the most able soldier of the lot but also the best psychologist, rarely raised his voice because he knew that Hitler would pay it no heed. In his book *Verlorene Siege*—Lost Victories, and thank God they were—Manstein says a great deal about how frank he was with Hitler. Even though the success of his fighting withdrawal prolonged the war, we ought to give Manstein credit for getting his way in the matter of the retreat from the Caucasus. But the officers who approached him in hopes that he might join a coup were all informed that what he had to offer Hitler was loyalty, not opposition. How Hitler had earned such loyalty remains in question, but bribery might have had something to do with it. Certainly it had nothing to do with Hitler's military understanding, which Manstein found out the hard way was a bigger threat than the enemy. (It was while Hitler was visiting Manstein's forward headquarters that the Russians, by refraining from an air attack, offered tacit evidence of their opinion that Hitler's continuing in supreme command would serve their interests.) Hitler proved incapable of listening to advice, even to the advice that might have saved his reputation from disaster. Insanity won't do for a reason: he was already insane while winning his victories, but he could listen then. The most likely explanation seems to be the one Montesquieu discovered for Pompey. Because he had said it so often, he went on saying it always.

There can be a stubborn investment even in cruelty: Daniel Goldhagen, in his unfortunately famous book *Hitler's Willing Executioners*, is too much startled by the not very amazing fact that the Nazi concentration camp guards went on maltreating their victims even when the game was up. They had always done so: to stop voluntarily would have meant admitting that it had all been useless. The most spectacular example of blind stubbornness in the World War II period was the behaviour of the Japanese officers in high command who not only wanted to go on fighting after the war was clearly lost, but actually seemed to believe that some kind of victory could still be won. Or it should have been the most spectacular example, but the palm belongs to Stalin. By a quirk of personality, being right about military matters was so important to him that he added millions of innocent lives to the total his political vision had already cost his unfortunate nation. For his ideological crimes there might have been some justification: certainly foreign observers as intelligent as Jean-Paul Sartre thought so. But for Stalin's pig-headedness in the face of towering evidence that he had made a mistake there was no justification at all. The consistent irrationality of his behaviour from the eve of the war to its end is well recorded by Dmitri Volkogonov in his indispensable biography of his father's murderer. What concerns us here, however, is its normality: the pre-emptive, silent tantrum that we call a refusal to listen, and the disabling consequences of realizing that we ought to have done so. Montesquieu transfixes the issue with that single word, *honte*. It is the shame of the child who has been caught out. Though Montesquieu understood all evils, it was not because he could trace them to suppressed propensities for evil in his own nature. He was too good for that. It was because he could trace them to memories of childhood: those memories which reading helps us to outgrow, but not to forget. Not even the uproar in the nursery, however, could make Montesquieu despair of human nature. He said he had a better opinion about himself when he read Marcus Aurelius, because Marcus Aurelius gave him a better opinion about people. One feels the same about him.

ALAN MOOREHEAD

❡ ❡ ❡

Alan Moorehead (1910–1983) was among the most prominent
of Australian cultural exports after World War II, when his
books of non-fiction such as *The Blue Nile* attracted a wide following in the United States and the United Kingdom as well
as in his home country. His rise to international fame had
begun during the war itself. He was one of several Australian
war correspondents who took the opportunity to employ, on a
wider stage, the journalistic proficiency they had developed
after several years of hard slog in the newsrooms of Sydney and
Melbourne, along with the fluent, easily correct prose that
they had learned to write in the Australian school system.
Moorehead was there for the battles and the conferences
through North Africa, Italy and Normandy all the way to the
end. The hefty but unputdownable *African Trilogy*, still in print
today, is perhaps the best example of Moorehead's characteristic virtue as a war correspondent: he could widen the local
story to include its global implications. By extension he later
did the same for his home country: resident in Italy, he inau-
gurated the era of expatriate Australian writers which continues into our day. There were Australian musicians and
theatrical figures who lived abroad before the war, and in

recent times Australian artists in every field have colonized the
world, but the post-war waves of expatriate Australian writers
would have been less confident about their adventurous enterprise without Moorehead's pioneering example of the confident interloper who showed how it could be a positive advantage
to come from somewhere else. No writer did more than
Moorehead to put Australia into the world picture as the most
striking example of the old empire's having produced, in its
disintegration, vital new centres of creativity. When Moorehead was starting off, most Australian artists in any field
thought of Britain as "home," the infinitely richer mother-
culture whose approval would validate them. Today the position is reversed: the British would like to know Australia's
secret. This demonstration of how colonialism can turn back
on itself was well understood in advance by Moorehead, who
set up his post-war European camp in the full knowledge that
it was an advance post for Australia's forthcoming cultural
expansion, although not even he could guess how successful
the expansion would be.

   A startling amount of the productivity was his. Of his many
books written in his self-imposed exile, *No Room in the Ark*, a
charming tribute to the African wild animals, is a good example of his knack for getting there at the right moment and
spotting the trends: in the Africa from which the old empires
were at last retreating, the animals had become a resource, and
the resource was threatened by mismanagement. Typically, he
had spotted a theme which would be important in the world's
immediate future. The final effect of Moorehead's accumulated work, so much of which stays as fresh as when it was
written, is to convince you that to be born and raised in a prosperous liberal democracy not only confers the energy to see
the world as it is, but the obligation to make sense of it, on
behalf of all those deprived of the opportunity.

   Outside, the street vendors came by, and the cries of the
   Cairo street vendors are just what you would expect them

to be—entertaining and romantic in the evening and
merely damnable in the early morning when you are trying
to work. There was one man who brought such nameless
pain and misery into voice that I was forced to the open
window to listen. He was selling bath mats.
— ALAN MOOREHEAD, *AFRICAN TRILOGY*,
P. 189

BEFORE THE LATE 1930s there had been individual Australians
who had sailed away to make a world impact both in the high and
the popular arts—Nellie Melba, Robert Helpmann, Errol Flynn—but
with the opening of World War II it started to happen in waves, and
the first wave consisted of the war correspondents. Of those, the most
dazzling was Alan Moorehead. Counting as Australia's first really conspicuous gift to international English prose, Alan Moorehead achieved
the peak of his fame after the war, with his two best-selling books about
nineteenth-century African exploration, *The White Nile* and *The Blue
Nile*. But he was building on a solid reputation laid down during the
war itself, when he was writing at his best. Though the Nile books have
their merits, I have always found them shapeless, just as their author, I
suspect, found the explorations indeterminate: nothing much was
decided, argument was endless, and narrative was defeated. Moorehead
retraced the steps of the explorers but all the paths were overgrown and
didn't tell him enough about what things had once been like. The
African Trilogy, on the other hand, has a neatly monumental story to be
told in the present tense. From being down and almost out, the Allied
forces in North Africa came back against the Italians and Germans,
brought them to battle, and defeated them. Moorehead was there to
see it all. In this latter respect he had a big advantage over another star
Australian war correspondent, Kenneth Slessor, who had made the
hideous mistake of allowing his demanding wife to encumber him with
her presence during the biggest assignment of his life as a journalist.
While the battle of El Alamein was being fought, Slessor's wife
required his presence in Jerusalem to help her go shopping. The most
important Australian poet of his generation, Slessor had linguistic gifts
outranking even Moorehead's, but there was no substitute for being
there: Slessor wrote the best poem about the North African campaign,
"Beach Burial," but he wrote it after the event.

Moorehead was almost always there for the event. Travelling light, he had nothing except the official censorship to interfere with the flow of his prose as it went back to Fleet Street in the form of dispatches. His copy was world-famous at the time and has stayed good: it represents the best title to the encomia that the late-twentieth-century Australian prose writers, with Robert Hughes in the van, have lavished on him ever since. They are quite right. Moorehead could control his tone even when the circumstances were at their most intense: the hardest thing for a correspondent to do. To take the most obvious comparison, he was a far better reporter on combat than his friend Ernest Hemingway, whose cadences he sometimes borrowed, and always to his detriment. But he never made the mistake of borrowing Hemingway's self-importance. Hemingway always wrote as if the action revolved around him. Moorehead wrote as if he had just happened to wander into it: the common experience of the war. Paradoxically, he sometimes had to feign this knack for happenstance. His *sortable* qualities of charm, good looks and cultivation gave him the entrée everywhere. (Then as later, the simplest classical tag from an Australian would stop the show with an English upper-crust audience, and Moorehead could quote from Theocritus and Horace until the officers' mess was drunk dry.) On top of the parlour tricks he was a terrific fixer, showing the Australian lurk-man's perennial talent for hitching a ride into the forbidden zone.

For reporting a modern war, Moorehead's only but irritating drawback was a lack of sympathy with machinery. Even about weapons he had a nose for the big picture—he was able to tell Beaverbrook personally that when the Allied tanks came up against the German ones after D-day, the Allied tanks would be outclassed—but when it got down to nuts and bolts, a shape in metal did little for his senses. He was the sort of writer who said "microphone" when he meant "loudspeaker." Another Australian, Paul Brickhill, aiming unerringly at an empire-wide audience of bright schoolboys, wrote a series of hit books (*The Great Escape*, *The Dam Busters*, *Reach for the Sky*) that inadvertently showed up the extent to which Moorehead had failed to penetrate the mentality of all the young men who had been propelled by the war into a new, classless world of high technology. (It was to be of high social significance that there were few English-born popular authors capable of duplicating Brickhill's achievement either: but what matters here is that Moorehead didn't.) To that extent, Moorehead was stuck in the mud. His renowned social mobility was employed mainly among the upper classes. There was another story emerging from the machine shops, but he missed it. (In the next generation of Australian social historians, a sympathy with technology and industry would put Geoffrey Blainey in the forefront: but his emphasis was regarded, and regarded correctly, as an initiative without precedent.) Though Moorehead had marvellous powers of evocative description—*vide* the passage about the anthills in chapter 5 of *Rum Jungle*—they just weren't aroused by anything technical, which meant that a whole dimension of tone was missing from his reportage, because World War II was a technical war.

The dimensions that were present made up for it. For a world war, he had a world mind. He understood the global interconnections of the battle zones from the start. He had a fully European intelligence as only a colonial can have: a cosmopolitan view that enabled him to assess the European tragedy without lapsing into chauvinism. Few Australian intellectuals, then or later, could match his capacity to see that Australia, far from frittering away its military resources, was making a necessary contribution to its own defence by throwing its efforts into the battles in the Middle East. In recent years, as the revisionist interpretations of Australia's connection with Britain reached an apotheosis of myth-mongering in the seductive theory of Other People's Wars, a position like Moorehead's became hard to understand. Now that the tide of politically inspired fable is receding, his view should look coherent again, and even more intelligible, because it outlined a recalcitrant set of facts, and if the facts had not been so awkward, the urge to deny them might never have arisen. Moorehead was one of the first Australian intellectuals able to overcome their cleverness and see what their much-patronized politicians saw: that there was no question of a world war leaving Australia out. A nose for grand strategy put him miles ahead of any other Australian reporter on the beat. (A possible precursor was indeed antipodean, but from New Zealand: the cartoonist David Low, although he, we should remember, was spectacularly wrong about the war before it actually started.) Moorehead's own country was not the only one to reap the benefit of his fair-mindedness, but a compatriot can be forgiven for attending first to what he said about the Australian troops. He reported faithfully and truly that in the long, hard preliminary slog to Benghazi they were crucial in reducing the Italian army from a fighting force to a liability. Moorehead blinked no details of the fiasco on Crete. Naturally if there had been less censorship he would have been able to be scathing about the blunders, but he left room between the lines for his bitterness to show. He was firm, however, on the critical point: the Australians had participated in an action which, though it failed, played a vital role in delaying Operation Barbarossa, and thus influencing the war in Russia. Seeing how the defeats fitted into the victories, he never made the intellectual's characteristic error of searching through a jigsaw as if it had a key piece. With *War and Peace* as a knapsack book, he was able to complement Tolstoy's key insight—everything depends on morale—with an insight of his own: morale depends on everything.

At this range it might be hard to imagine how important it was to be a good writer stating such complex and vital truths. In World War I, with Keith Murdoch's fanciful press campaign placing such disproportionate emphasis on the Dardanelles, there was no comparably imaginative prose available to stress what the Australians achieved on the western front. To this day, few Australians, even when they are students of modern history—alas, especially when—have any idea that their countrymen played a significant role in the final breaking of the deadlock in the trenches at the end of World War I. (Philip Knightley has been almost the only popular historian to mention the matter.) Thanks to Moorehead, however, the importance of the 9th Division at Tobruk in World War II is not as easily overlooked. Without the Australians and New Zealanders, the Germans might have prevailed in the desert, and thus been far more free to act decisively in Russia. Only for Hitler was North Africa a sideshow. Rommel knew better. So, to his lasting credit, did Moorehead. He could see how each part of the war affected every other part—the hardest aspect of a world war for a writer to deal with, since writers are so likely to get lost in particulars. In a war, however, the particulars resonate across the world, and the penalty for not being able to follow them is to miss the picture.

Later on, when the centre of attention switched to the European mainland, Moorehead was careful not to let his cat burglar's gift for access affect his broader judgement. After the war another Australian expatriate, Chester Wilmot, capped a brilliant success as a BBC war reporter by emerging as a literary heavyweight in many ways comparable in stature and ability to Moorehead. Wilmot, in his best-selling book *The Struggle for Europe*, gave a partisan view favouring Montgomery's thesis that he could have thrust straight through to Berlin if Eisenhower had not stopped him. Wilmot had allowed Montgomery to bowl him over. Moorehead did not. Moorehead had befriended Montgomery in Sicily, had secured unequalled access to his headquarters in Normandy, and was eventually given the green light to write a biography. Montgomery kept back some of the most explosive stuff, including his diaries, but on the whole he gave Moorehead the inside track. It would have been easy for Moorehead to overdo the gratitude. In retrospect, he might seem to have done so: he swallowed Montgomery's preposterous line that the delay in pushing on beyond Caen was deliberate, and wrote almost nothing about Arnhem's magnitude as an unnecessary disaster. But for the time, Moorehead's 1946 *Montgomery* was a probing book, and remains a well-balanced one. Moorehead proved himself capable of spotting the fatal flaw in Montgomery's technique at his wartime press conferences: Montgomery patronized the correspondents by forever trying to pre-empt their job of turning technicalities into simplicities. Over and above the question of Montgomery's merits and deficiencies, Moorehead was well able to see—as Wilmot calamitously didn't—that Eisenhower was Montgomery's superior in character and judgement. Finally, Moorehead was not seduced by the cosy glamour of the nearness that had been granted to him. He was too successful a seducer himself.

When dealing with stars, it helps to be a star. All the Australian war correspondents were gifted operators, but Moorehead had that invaluable extra attribute of being at his ease in a grand headquarters. High plaster ceilings and marble floors did not overawe him. He was one of those colonials who, through being hard to place, can place themselves anywhere as long as they are given a few minutes to dust their shoes and straighten their ties. In Cairo he was given letters from Auchinleck and asked to deliver them to Wavell in Delhi. In Delhi he had a long close-up of the brilliance of Sir Stafford Cripps—whom he might have overestimated, if Denis Healey was right in calling Cripps "a political ninny of the most superior quality" (*The Time of My Life*, p. 471).

Moorehead also recorded an unsettling insight into the intransigence of Gandhi. Challenged about the possible effects of relying on passive resistance to dissuade the Japanese, Gandhi was forced into his fallback position of averring that not even the Japanese could kill every Indian. Moorehead, who already had some idea of what Nazi Germany and the Soviet Union added up to in terms of population control, clearly had his own opinions. At such points, the *African Trilogy* is not just about World War II, but about twentieth-century history in its grim totality. But rather than claim too much for a book that already holds more than we have a right to expect—it was, after all, written on the spot, and often on the run—the reader probably does best just to enjoy the neatness of detail and the refreshing flow of common sense, the clear water supply of sound judgement from a young man who had realized, without having his head turned, that the world's crisis was his opportunity. The sense of destiny is in the dignified vigour of his prose, not in the magnitude of events. In that respect, he was the harbinger of the Australian voice that the world has since come to know, value and envy: the voice of common eloquence, speaking the way the Man from Snowy River used to ride. Unaffectedly confident, content to evoke without straining for effect, Moorehead described "the wonderful turquoise sea at Alamein, when the sunlight strikes the white seabed and is reflected back to the surface so that the water is full of dancing light and colour." Thus having established that he knew how to say just enough, he had the authority of tone to say what was profoundly and lastingly true about the Australian 9th Division that came into the Alamein line after two years of fighting.

"Tobruk had discovered the Australians to themselves." It was a piercing historical insight, which I had the privilege of echoing with a whole heart while reporting the Sydney Olympics more than fifty years later; and I was well aware whose voice I was copying. One way or another, all the expatriate writers in my generation have found themselves paying their tribute to a majestic progenitor. He could have handled success better. He should never have allowed *The New Yorker* to cripple him with the notoriously arrhythmic restrictions of its house style, but he had a Mediterranean house to keep up, and money talked. His first book about a world war, however, was the start of something for the country he left behind. In a few pages, Moorehead placed himself at the centre of the discussion about Australia's relations with England—such as they had been, and such as they would be in the future. Proponents of an Australian republic have a good case, but it will remain incomplete until they take in what Moorehead wrote. It was surprising to find that Robert Hughes, so convinced and convincing an admirer of Moorehead's, should have forgotten what his mentor said on the subject. He said what good writers always say: that history is the field to which you must first submit if you would turn it to use.

PAUL MURATOV

❦ ❦ ❦

Paul Pavlovich Muratov (1881–1950) shows just how brilliant somebody can be and still be a forgotten man. Essayist, critic, novelist and playwright, he was also the most learned, original and stylistically gifted Russian art historian of his time, and he wrote at least one book well equipped to last beyond his time and ours as well; but today it is as if he had never existed. What went missing wasn't him, but the Russia he grew up in. As with Diaghilev, he had all the artistic wealth and burgeoning energy of pre-revolutionary Russia as a context, but unlike Diaghilev he had no means of taking the spiritual substance of his context with him when it was time to run. In 1914 Muratov edited the magazine *Sophia*, promoting his ideal of a perennial classicism. He had already written a travel book meant to embody that idea: *Obrazy italii*, a title which is usually translated as The Images of Italy, although The Forms of Italy might be a better way of putting it, because he talks about much more than just paintings, taking in sculpture, buildings, gardens and the layout of cities. (We have a certain latitude in translating the title because the book itself has never been rendered into English.) The Revolution in 1917 was a powerful hint that the idea of a perennial classicism had a shaky basis in reality. The hint soon became a storm. After 1918, Muratov was associated with the only bookshop in Moscow which remained unregulated by the state. Called the Writers' Library, it was a wonderland of a market in which the bibliographical treasures of Tsarist Russia were exchanged for grain, clothes and firewood. (Readers of Italian can find the story on pages 4 and 5 of Muratov's Google entry, where Michael Osorgin, with the help of Claudia Zonghetti's suitably elegant translation, tells the almost unbearable story of the writers and the scholars shaking from cold and hunger as they traffic in their doomed treasures.) Banished in 1922, Muratov went on the road, deprived for the rest of his life of any scholarly resources except his memory. In the 1920s he was in Berlin, as a valued member of the vibrant émigré community evoked by Nina Berberova in *The Italics Are Mine*, the best single book written about Russian culture in exile. Berberova played chess with him, and always remembered him as "a whole and accomplished European": large praise from her, who was so conspicuously that very thing herself. (Berberova said a beautiful thing about Muratov. "He was always in love in a balanced and quiet way." She also said that he was "a man of inward order who understood the internal disorder of others.") At some point, along with several other books, Muratov managed to publish *Obrazy italii* in the definitive edition mentioned below. In the 1930s he was in Paris, where he acquired a reputation among left-wing intellectuals as an anti-Bolshevik—a very plausible development. During the war he was in Ireland, pursuing an incongruous new career as a military journalist: he wrote an account of the Russia campaigns for Penguin, thereby telling the almost laughably ironic story of how the Nazis were defeated by the same forces that had earlier ruined his life. As far as I can piece his story together, Ireland was his last stop. I could have left him out of this book and nobody would have noticed. The history of humanism in the twentieth century has managed to bury *Obrazy italii*, and nobody cares. Our idea that if a book is good enough it can never disappear is thereby proved false, because *Obrazy italii* is one of the most dazzling books of its type ever written. Can something so wonderful be allowed to vanish? Muratov himself was probably reconciled to the possibility. In that tragic bookshop called the Writers' Library he had seen a whole culture breaking up, like a stricken submarine in the abyss. So he had no illusions. But he didn't give in, and his subsequent career as a wandering scholar proved that there can be such a thing as a heroism of the mind.

☡ ☡ ☡

Del Sarto's golden arms don't make us forget for a moment
his everlasting internal mediocrity, just as Wölfflinn, by
laying bare with such clarity the laws of "classic art" in del
Sarto's composition, tries vainly to discover in it for us one
of the heroes of the High Renaissance.
— PAUL MURATOV, *OBRAZY ITALII*,
VOL. I, P. 277

CAN A GREAT book vanish? The fate of Paul Maratov's *Obrazy italii* (which I prefer to translate as *The Forms of Italy*, exercising my prerogative as one of the few people alive who have ever picked up a copy of it) suggests that it can. The book is seldom mentioned now, and the name of its author does not crop up often even in histories of the Russian emigration after 1917. (From all the Russian departments of all the universities in the world, the Web reveals a grand total of three scholars, one French and two Italian, who are on his case.) For a long time, when I began to read in that field, I never knew Muratov had been there. Looking back on it, however, I am glad to have discovered Muratov comparatively late in my life. His taste was too sure, and his view too wide, to have been much use to me earlier. It was his bad luck, and indeed the whole of modern history's, that one of the most accomplished of all writers on art remained almost unknown to the international reading public: but it was my good luck, because when I found him I was ready, and his masterwork *Obrazy italii* hit me like a long and beautiful poem. Ostensibly, the work is a three-volume prose treatise, published in the original Russian by the Leipzig émigré publishing house Z.J. Grschebin-Verlag in 1924. But for the mature student armed with patience and a sufficiently large Russian-English dictionary, Muratov's first few paragraphs have a surprise in store. Cool as equations, they are as rich as lyrics, and when it transpires that there are thousands more of them to come, the enthralled reader finds it hard to believe his good fortune.

There are many unknown masterpieces in the world, but they usually get that way because they were never very good. The Forms of Italy is a genuine unknown masterpiece. As a book on the Italian Grand Tour it not only stands directly in the tradition of Goethe, Gregorovius, Burckhardt and Arthur Symons, but it is better than any of them. (Better than Goethe? Yes, better than Goethe.) Muratov went to all the towns and cities, knew everything about the art and literature, had unfaltering judgement, and packed the whole complex mental and physical experience into tight, clear paragraphs saturated with meaning and sensitivity. The book is just too good to be true, and until somebody translates it into appropriately neat English the enthusiast will always run the risk of being thought to have made it up. It exists, though. I own two sets, and one of them is in front of me now. The three volumes are tiny, in a unique format which was probably specified by the author himself: shorter and squarer than crown octavo, bound in faded red linen, they slot into a maroon paper-covered cardboard box. There are black-and-white photogravure illustrations of some of the more famous paintings, frescoes, fountains and buildings, but mainly all you can see as you flick through is creamy white little square after creamy white little square of tightly packed black Cyrillic letters to a grand total of about a thousand pages of text. The magic is in the writing, and magic it really is; not flowery, but lavishly fruitful; sense and sensibility in their most condensed yet fluent congruity of form. It would be almost a relief if his judgement had sometimes lapsed. An ephemeral element might have been a comfort. But uncannily, indeed hauntingly, he spoke with an authoritative timbre that seemed to come from the future rather than the past, as if his testament, published in exile, was the harbinger of a time when the devastation of modern history would be put into reverse.

When I was first in Florence in the 1960s I swallowed Heinrich Wölfflinn's line on Andrea del Sarto hook, line and sinker. The Phaidon edition of Wölfflinn's *Classic Art* was with me as a handbook when I toured the churches, cloisters and galleries. It enshrined his proto-structuralist thesis that the artists of the Cinquecento had been engaged in a quasi-architectural approach to composition in the form of a steadily more compact pyramid, with the logical development—a Leonardo cartoon was here adduced—that several members of the Holy Family should end up sitting on each other. Andrea del Sarto, according to Wölfflinn, brought this monumental formal trope to a *ne plus ultra* climax. After him, the aberration of Mannerism began, with Pontormo as a particularly flagrant example of incipient monumentality sabotaged by neurasthenia. With the aid of Wölfflinn's treatise I became a scolding bore on the subject of the Cinquecento. On the Quattrocento, less hindered by academic assistance, I was capable of the odd independent judgement—I could see that any developmental theory that denied a high place to Paolo Uccello must have something wrong with it—but when it came to the High Renaissance I had a seeing-eye dogma, and the snorting beast was provided by Wölfflinn. Pontormo was right there in front of me (I was lodging only a few blocks from Santa Felicità and could see one of his supreme achievements every day just by stepping through the front door) but I had managed to convince myself, by repeated shouting over too many beakers of cheap chianti, that del Sarto was the last true exemplar of the titanic impulse. I doubt if even Muratov could have impinged on an obtuseness so well ingrained: unless, of course, he had got there first. But his book lay far in my future: far enough, luckily, to give me the remorseful but acute satisfaction of having expanded my view before his opinion had the chance to endorse it.

Over the years I came to appreciate Pontormo and Bronzino without benefit of clergy. The impact was all the sweeter when I found Muratov echoing my enthusiasm about the young Pontormo's fresco cycle in the Medici villa called Poggio a Caiano. He called the fresco cycle "one of the most surprising and beautiful productions of Italian art." The key word is "surprising." In a serenely dazzling ten-page stretch of prose, Muratov responds with a whole heart and mind to the *unexpectedness* of Pontormo; to the way a youthfully fulfilled and tirelessly original career like his just shouldn't have been there at that point in time; to the unanticipated refreshment, through one prodigiously gifted young man, of a tradition already buried by success. Muratov also seemed to take Bronzino at the same estimation I did, as a hard-edged paradigm of iconic excellence with an unplanned but inescapable literary application, someone who painted in a way one would like to write, presenting the clean-cut relief of a cameo no matter how large the canvas, his unoccupied planes of colour as precisely calculated as his embroidered detail: a unique combination of the broad brush and the engraving tool.

But the true revelation of Muratov's book was how his high standard of aesthetic judgement extended into the society and politics of the artistic context. He wasn't the first writer who had treated Italian cultural history in this way, but nobody, not even Gregorovius or the mighty Burckhardt, had come near Muratov's ability to compress an encyclopaedic erudition into a dramatic prose narrative. The consideration did not escape me that this was what Marxist cultural analysis ought to have looked like but conspicuously didn't, even when it came from the pen of Walter Benjamin. (What did escape me was that Diaghilev's writings on art, at the turn of the century, had already established the cultural parameters within which Muratov later wrote: that not even Muratov, in other words, had sprung full-blown from the head of Zeus. In culture there is *never* an innovation that does not spring from a tradition, because the interweaving of innovation and tradition is what culture is.)

How could, how can, such a prodigy of a book go missing? Egon Friedell's *Kulturgeschichte der Neuzeit*, a comparable effort in a field where few comparisons are possible, was threatened with death but proved impossible to kill. Unlike its author, it was invulnerable. Too many refugees took a copy with them in their baggage. Friedell's lifetime testament was surrounded with affection and protected on its journey. Muratov's equivalent achievement was forgotten. The Russians in exile, except to the limited extent that they, too, were a Jewish émigré community, did not provide a framework in which the book might be remembered. Nor did Russian émigrés of a conservative background, or even a merely liberal one, necessarily find favour among the Western intelligentsia, which for the next fifty years devoted enormous resources of inattention to helping ensure that the Soviet Union's official trivialization of the bourgeois heritage would be carried by default. There was no émigré publishing house of Russian provenance that could equal the success of Phaidon or Abrams in

translating itself into English while still preserving the core achievement of its origins. It might have helped if Muratov had gone to America, like, say, Ernst Kantorowicz, the fabulously erudite author of a
book about Frederick II that achieved the piquant distinction of finding favour with Mussolini, Hitler and Goering. But as a student of current events Muratov was last heard of in Ireland during the war, writing
and editing the Penguin volume on the Russia campaigns. No American university ever put money and effort into codifying his reputation
and achievement with an appropriate archive. The Phaidon archive,
alone, would be sufficient to ensure the continued existence of
Friedell's key works: but I wonder if there is a proper shelf of Muratov's
books anywhere in the world. As well as my two separate sets of *Obrazy
italii*, bought in London and Buenos Aires, I own his *Fra Angelico*,
translated from French into English in 1928: since all the plates were
monochrome, it nowadays rates as junk even in those doomed second-
hand bookshops that have mainly scrap for stock. During the late
twenties and early thirties, he brought out several books in French: I
have his book on Russian icons, *Trente-cinq Primitifs russes*, published in
Paris in 1931. There was at least one other book in Russian, a little
pamphlet on Cézanne. (It was published in Berlin in 1923, perhaps as
a rehearsal for *Obrazy italii*: I bought my copy in Oxford, and it already
looked as if it had been chewed at the corners by two different sizes of
rat.) His Penguin on the World War II battles in Russia is on the shelf
too, and I suppose it gives his career an unlooked-for illumination,
such as Max Friedländer, say, might have provided for himself if he had
spent the last year of his life writing a treatise about ice hockey. But
looking at my undocumented grab bag of Muratovian scraps, I can't
help wondering how to make sense of it all.

The point is that I shouldn't have to do the wondering. It ought to
be a task for scholarship. The thing I *really* wonder about is what the
Russian departments of the British universities have been doing with
their time. Unlike their American equivalents they haven't got much
money, but even now, as the Cold War demand for interpreters has
shrunk, they have had the benefit of dozens of Ph.D. students all
requiring to be given suitable subjects. Surely the scholars and creative
artists who were lost to the terror and disenfranchised by the emigration constitute a reservoir of potential theses that might have actually

contributed to knowledge instead of just furthering careers. On the walls of my library are three Suprematist paintings by Nina Kogan, who taught on the faculty of Malevich's Unovis art collective in Vitebsk from 1920 through into 1922, at the very time when Muratov, in the Writers' Library in Moscow, was engaged in the melancholy task of measuring out the country's literary heritage by its weight in black bread. Though Malevich at that time was keen on the idea that the work of his colleagues should all look the same, Kogan's looked different: she used the standard Suprematist kit of squares, oblongs and floating bits and pieces, but she gave them a pastel lightness hinting at the airborne boudoir of a futuristic angel. She stood out, even though Unovis was an outfit dedicated, in all lack of irony, to the precept that the artist's individual personality should vanish. No Unovis artist at the time, of course, had any conception that the state would eventually take steps to guarantee just such a result. By late 1922, however, the official cultural organs were making it clear that the opinion of the artists would not necessarily be heard first in the question of which direction the arts might take. (It was about this time that Muratov was lucky enough to be expelled from the country.) A woman of integrity surrounded by men with the souls of gangsters, Kogan stayed on in Russia, sincerely believing that she had a duty to her country's future. Her faith was rewarded with the inevitable persecution and eventually, most likely during the siege of Leningrad, she disappeared into the whirlwind. In my wishful thinking, she starved to death along with all the poor souls who weren't awarded the survival ration: but there was a purge on as well as a siege, and it is more likely that the hoodlums got her. The final judge of the relevance of her airily lyrical art to the monolithic purposes of the state was probably an NKVD slave driver in Siberia. There is one slim monograph about her, published in Zurich in 1985 to accompany a retrospective exhibition. The booklet was given to me by the proprietor of the Paris boutique Petroushka, where, over the course of years, I bought several of her strangely lovely little pictures. "Nina Ossipowna Kogan" says the title page. "1887 Vitebsk–1942(?)" In that bracketed question mark lies the tragedy. *Sunt lacrimae rerum*, and the tears are a frozen lake with no clear shore: no wonder they get into everything. But at least, for Kogan, there is a booklet. Where is there anything about Muratov?

In one of his more charming fits of silliness, William Saroyan once said of George Bernard Shaw, "I am that man by another name." I am not sure if I am Paul Muratov by another name: he knew much more than I do, and to the extent that I can construe his Russian fast enough to catch its rhythm, I have a dreadful suspicion that he wrote better as well. But I am very sure that I am that man with another fate. When I leaf through the tiny volumes of his magisterial book, I see the love of art rewarded by the distortion of a life, and the quietly desperate affirmation of creativity in the face of unrestrained destruction. I would like to think that I had the same passion, but except from hearsay I know little about the same destiny: not even enough, perhaps, to be sufficiently glad that I know no more. To die guessing that you will be forgotten is one thing. But what would it be like to know that you have been forgotten before you die?

N

❧ ❧ ❧

Lewis Namier

LEWIS NAMIER

❧ ❧ ❧

During what he called the Nazi era, and in its thoughtful after-math, Lewis Namier (1888–1960) was a figure of immense prestige in British academic and intellectual life, to the point that many of his fellow historians were able to call their country civilized simply because it had given him refuge: they didn't have to like him. Of Russian heritage, born Lewis Bern-stein in Poland, he was a Jewish refugee in search of a home-land. To his adopted country, Britain, he devoted microscopic attention. The mark of his historical method was to study the written records of Britain's representative institutions right down to the level of the names on the electoral lists, an approach which yielded a body of meticulous factual material that tended to overwhelm the conclusions he drew from it, thus making his major books hard to enjoy now. His journal-ism, on the other hand, was, and remains, a model for acerbic style and pointed argument. Namier's knighthood makes him sound like an etablishment figure, but his professorship at Manchester between 1931 and 1953 tells the truth about how the Oxbridge mandarinate preferred to keep him at a distance. In their own defence, they could say that his frustrations stim-ulated his productivity: a classic argument of the genteel anti-

Semite. A better defence was that another Jewish academic, Isaiah Berlin, scaled the heights of both the intellectual world and polite society. The truth of the matter probably lies there. Namier simply lacked charm. But he could write Engish prose with an austere beauty that leaves Berlin's sounding verbose. The influx of talented Jewish refugees was one of Europe's most precious gifts to Britain in the twentieth century, but Namier's career, which dramatized the story in almost all its aspects, reminds us not to be sentimental about it. A gain for the liberal democracies was a dead loss for the countries left behind. Poland's twentieth-century tragedy was already there in Namier's rise to success in his new homeland, and if he had possessed a light touch to ease his course, the disaster would only have been more evident.

Historical research to this day remains unorganized,
and the historian is expected to make his own instruments
or do without them; and so with wooden ploughs we
continue to draw lonely furrows, most successfully
when we strike sand.
— LEWIS NAMIER, *CROSSROADS OF POWER*

COMING TO ENGLISH as a second language, there were twentieth-century political refugees who wrote it with mastery: Joseph Conrad could do almost anything with his adopted tongue that any native writer of discursive prose had ever done before. There were even those who wrote it with primal, poetic genius, as if they had been born and grown up bathed in the richness of its etymology and idiomatic nuance. Vladimir Nabokov is the first example that springs to mind, and the last to be eliminated from discussion, because there will always be equivocal admirers who think that the beauty of what he could achieve with English was the real reason he could never tear himself way from the mirror.

But the exiled European writer who really got the measure of English, with the least show and the most impact, was Lewis Namier. Early to the field, he arrived in England in 1906 as a refugee from the pogroms in Poland. His stylistic achievement has never been much remarked because he was not thought of as a writer. He was thought of as an historian—which, of course, he was, and a renowned one. He would have been a less renowned historian, however, if he had not written so well: as with all truly accomplished prose styles, his was a vehicle for emotion and experience as well as for a sense of rhythm and proportion—the griefs and hard-won knowledge of a lifetime are dissolved into his acerbic cadences, and his neatness of metaphor epitomizes the gaze long grown weary but which misses nothing. His prose had hooded eyelids, but they were never quite closed. You can see his alertness in the single sentence quoted above. For primitive, improvised instruments, "wooden plough" is already good. For an isolated, not very well rewarded endeavour, "lonely furrows" is a pretty development; and "most successfully when we strike sand" is a poetic climax that drives a prose argument deep into the memory. The line of thought is a trek into pessimism: he is really saying that the historian's research tools work only when the work they do is not worth doing. But by the distinction of his style he exempts himself from the stricture, and by implication he exempts anyone else who can see the problem—and if it is put as clearly as this, who can't? So there is a game being played here, for high stakes. Hence the drama.

Namier was always dramatic, although in some of his central work he tried his best not to be. With his capital piece of original research *The Structure of Politics at the Accession of George III* he piled up impeccable credentials. The book was a hard grind to write and proved it by being a hard grind to read: like the tireless counting of heads that Ronald Syme brought to the study of ancient Rome, Namier's archival burrowings left no doubt that he was serious. But even here, with the air full of dry dust, he was establishing a dramatic principle: he was talking about the individual people who made up a class. He was doing the exact opposite of what the Marxists did, which was to talk about a class as if it formed its individual people. Though a convinced determinist, Namier had no time for big ideas. He hardly had time for the arts and sciences, about which he was unusually dispassionate for one of his background. Namier studied the parish registers and the electoral rolls in the urge to know about the individual lives which, he was convinced, were in the end unknowable. In a lifelong flight from the murderously abstract, Namier was making the other European contribution, which was pre-eminently the contribution of the émigré Jewish intellectuals—the contribution which could see developments in history but refused to accept that they tended towards a culmination. He had already seen how they could tend towards tragedy.

In his incidental writings that dealt with the diplomatic and political prelude to World War II, and the issues raised by the war itself, Namier brought his gift for drama to its fullest flower. It is meant neither as an insult nor as a paradox to say that he did journalism the favour of writing it like a journalist. Fifty years later, his buttonholing immediacy remains a shining example of what journalism can do. Contributed to the whole range of British upmarket publications—the *Times Literary Supplement*, the *New Statesman*, the *Listener*, etc.—his pieces were collected into a row of books which any serious student of modern English prose, let alone of history, should seek out and treasure, because more than any other books by anybody they give you the full weight of the event even when describing only a fragment. I have a row of them before me now; substantial demi octavo volumes bound in black or dark blue linen and stamped with silver titles: *In the Nazi Era, Europe in Decay 1936–1940, In the Margin of History, Conflicts*. One of them, although written as a set of instalments for the magazine *Political Quarterly*, was conceived as a complete book: the marvellous *Diplomatic Prelude 1938–1939*. Much of it was written before the relevant official papers were released, but his guesswork was dauntingly good, and remains penetrating to this day. Namier's academic contemporaries often punished him in print for his tendency to wander off the point into a forest of footnotes, but on the strength of his journalism you would say he had cogency in the blood. Put together, the books constitute a short but weighty shelf of some of the most vivid higher journalism in English since Hazlitt, although behind them is a far greater depth of learning—an extravagance of mental impulse for an arresting economy of effect. Writing at the time instead of later, he couldn't always be right, but he was never less than pertinent, even when, the circumstances being what they were, he faced the task of matching with his style a sadness that shrieked to heaven. In 1942 he was saying—saying without crying, and God alone knows how—that the Jews would have to be withdrawn from Europe after the war and go to their new home. He couldn't yet be certain, or didn't want to be certain, that Hitler and Himmler had concocted a radical new way of withdrawing them from Europe, but his fine essay is certainly written in the context of that terrible possibility. As Walter Laqueur has convincingly argued, the code-breaking unit at Bletchley Park was getting the news about the massacres in the east almost from their inception; and though circulation of the news was restricted to the very highest levels in order to protect the Ultra secret, it was definitely talked about. Namier, a born stalker of corridors, was not the sort of man to miss a significant word—or, for that matter, a significant silence. Though Namier never wrote a single book about the Holocaust, its significance permeated all his work from the moment he got wind of it.

With the war over, Namier showed his unusual powers of character analysis when it came to assessing the suave special pleading of the surviving German bigwigs who directed their appeals towards a higher tribunal than the one at Nuremberg. ("The factual material in these books," he wrote in *In the Nazi Era*, "is mostly of very small value." He meant that they were lying.) He wasn't fooled for a moment by Halder's claims that Hitler had buffaloed the Wehrmacht into an unwanted war. Fifty years later, Carl Dirks and Karl-Heinz Janssen in *Der Krieg der Generale* were able to quote chapter and verse from the military archives to prove that the German armed forces were always a long way ahead of Hitler in their expansive ambitions. Namier guessed the truth just from listening to the denials. He respected the decency of Beck but correctly spotted that the other surviving generals were looking for an alibi by blaming Hitler for the army's build-up to aggression in both west and east. Namier blew a melodious but piercing whistle over Halder's niftily calculated pamphlet *Hitler als Feldherr*. Namier had been warning the world since the 1930s that the Nazis were backed up by a German political culture whose authoritarianism would always amount to savagery if given the green light. He could be thought of as a sort of reverse anti-Semite on the subject, if it were not such a bad joke.

At Cambridge, the gusto and the speakable narrative style of J. H. Plumb rubbed off on a whole school of young historians. Nowadays, by consulting the chronology, I can shamefacedly compute that while I was dancing to mainstream jazz in the annexe of the Red Lion in

Petty Cury, the real action was in the bar, where Simon Schama was listening to Plumb—or, more likely, Plumb was listening to Schama. Namier had no such influence. Lacking Isaiah Berlin's personal charm and clubbability, Namier was slow to gain status as an establishment figure. A. J. P. Taylor found academic preferment elusive because of his opinions, the flamboyance with which he expressed them, and his Fleet Street outlets, which were deemed undignified. Namier missed out on the grand invitations for more personal reasons. An honorary fellowship at his beloved Balliol came late and might never have come at all. The drawback of academic fellowship in the ancient English universities is that fellowship means what it says. An Oxbridge college is like a London club with slightly less miserable food and wine. Conviviality counts for at least as much as gravitas. The chaps are supposed to get on with one another. With a thick accent that didn't always make his dogmaticism sufficiently hard to decipher, Namier was unusually disagreeable in a context where merely to disagree was to be disagreeable enough. He was a wet weekend in Lwów. In the long run this was probably a lucky break for both him and us. Isaiah Berlin—the truth must still be whispered—wasted far too much time at grand dinner tables. Like F. R. Leavis, Namier was condemned by his personality to the monastic dedication that the college system nominally favours but in fact frustrates. His mere presence at Manchester helped to put the redbrick universities at the heart of post-war intellectual achievement in Britain. His solid brilliance helped to give the writing of history in post-war Britain a weight of seriousness that not even the United States could match. America had the power: in the East Coast foreign policy elite, a scholar-diplomat like George Kennan was shaping the world. But Namier was understanding it: there was a difference, and part of the difference was conferred by Namier's prescient awareness that to draw up a balance sheet was Europe's privilege, and precisely because its power was broken. Namier obviously found that fact at least as liberating as inhibiting. The title of one of his later books, *Vanished Supremacies*, was not entirely a lamentation: vanished supremacies could mean values reaffirmed. One of the old man's strengths was that he was a realist without being a materialist: abstract ideas were never his strong suit, but the concrete idea of a spiritual value was not alien to him. So-called *realpolitik* had destroyed the world he came from but had not infected him. He was not a plague carrier.

What was he, apart from an historian of unquestionable eminence? For most of us, the eminence is unquestionable because we are never going to know much about his special subject. Eventually he cut down on his journalism and went back to parliamentary history, where he disappeared into the archives and never emerged alive, so that only a specialist can decide whether he was valuable or not. But his achievement as a stylist is apprehensible to all. He was one of those refugees—Sir Nikolaus Pevsner was another—who helped to make an exhausted Britain conscious of its lasting strengths. Pevsner did it through listing the buildings, and Namier through reaffirming the supple empiricism of the language. The war having been decided by the New World's gargantuan productive effort, the United States should logically have become the centre of the Western mind as well as of its muscle. Men like Namier ensured that the Old World would still have a say. With their help, it was English English, and not American English, that continued to be the appropriate medium for the summation and analysis of complex historical experience. With Namier's example to the forefront, Britain became the natural home for a language of diplomatic history, which is essentially concerned with that range of events, beyond America's ken, in which power can't be decisive. The echo of Namier's voice can be heard in Abba Eban's enthralling book *Personal Witness*, perhaps the most remarkably sustained work of intricate diplomatic exposition ever published. When Eban talked, it could have been Namier talking. Eban said of Yasser Arafat that he never missed an opportunity to miss an opportunity. Namier said things like that. Though he said them in the thick Polish accent that he never lost, they all depended on his croquet champion's mastery of an adopted syntax. It was Jewish humour, but it employed all the resources of the English language, as once it might have done with German. You couldn't call it a shift of power, because there was no power involved. It was a realignment of civilization.

One of the measures of our commitment to civilization is the extent to which we realize that material strength can never be more than a part of it, even if the part is essential. (An admirer of Talleyrand's cunning, Namier nevertheless found his craving for money not only pathological, he found it—a telling word—"pathetic.") Namier died as he had lived, largely unloved. There was nothing cuddly about his person, and nothing charming about what he said, except if we are charmed by a style adequate to the grim truth. We ought to be. What finally matters is the holy books, and how they are kept. If I had to choose a tone of voice in post-war expository prose that was commensurate with the importance of what had just happened to the world, I would choose the tone of Sir Lewis Namier. At Cambridge a history don once caught me reading the essays of Lord Acton. The don considered that Acton had deserved his high reputation at the time but "of course he's out of date now." I suppose it is possible that Namier's researches into the structure of politics at the accession of George III will eventually go out of date. But it will be a fateful day if historians cease to read Namier's incidental prose, because incidental was the last thing it was: it was vitally concerned with all the issues of his age, many of which are still the issues of ours. And one of those issues, by implication, is the most troubling that faces the humanist heritage: how are we to pass it on in its full complexity, and what can transmit that except style? Namier said of George Canning's letters to George IV that they were "brilliant, incisive, at times even boisterous." Although it is not the first word we think of in relation to Namier himself, "boisterous" must eventually be used for him too. He saw, and indeed foresaw, the whole European tragedy in modern times; yet somehow he persuaded it to give him energy. There was something biblical in that, like a prophet drinking oratorical inspiration from the splendid cataclysm of a sinful city punished by divine fire. Sometimes an artist is measured by the steadiness with which he holds himself when history leaves him no alternatives except to speak or weep. If he speaks, he is a seer: but when there is grief in his voice even though it does not break, we call that poetry.

❦ ❦ ❦

Grigory Ordzhonokidze

GRIGORY ORDZHONOKIDZE

❣ ❣ ❣

Grigory Konstantovich Ordzhonokidze (1886–1937) is sometimes given retroactive credit because he died mysteriously
during Stalin's terror campaign in the late 1930s, and therefore
might have been some sort of proto-liberal who, despite his
curriculum vitae as an Old Bolshevik, had been secretly at odds
all along with the course towards absolutism. There can be no
doubt that in the year of his "suicide" he protested directly to
Stalin about the free hand given to the NKVD, and it seems
probable that in the mid-1930s he had more than once
expressed doubts about Stalin's excesses: a sign of independence which certainly spoke for his bravery, and might well
have ensured the subsequent mysterious death all on its own.
But his earlier record was of a factotum thoroughly implicated
in repressive measures that neither he nor other grandees of
his rank thought excessive at the time. Indeed he wasn't just
implicated in those measures: in many cases he planned them.
One of the few non-Russians ever to serve in Stalin's government, he was born in Georgia, joined the Bolsheviks in 1908,
and during the Civil War was instrumental in bringing the
Caucasus under Soviet control, with appropriately firm methods of persuasion. Moving to the economic sphere, in the

1920s and early 1930s he led the forced march to industrializa-
tion, with an impact on the civilian populace that would have
looked excessive enough if he had not been so confident about
acting as one of the instruments of history. If he did indeed
become a member of the "moderate bloc" that some historians
would like to think made an attempt to rein Stalin in, his
motives for joining it would have had to be the result of considering some of his own past actions, about which he was on
record as being unrepentant, if not untroubled. From our position now, at a safe distance from the ideal State which at one
point he was proud of having helped to build, we can see that
his true historical role was to provide us with a standing joke.
He really did believe, and really did say, that the people who
inflicted the suffering suffered most.

> Our cadres who knew the situation of 1932–1933 and who
> bore the blow are truly tempered like steel. I think that
> with them we can build a State the like of which the
> world has never seen.
> — GRIGORY ORDZHONOKIDZE TO SERGEI
> KIROV, JANUARY 1934, QUOTED IN LE
> LIVRE NOIR DU COMMUNISME, P. 239

NATURALLY ENOUGH, this immortal statement was first made in
Russian, and had to be translated into French for its appearance in
Le Livre noir du communisme in 1997. Further translated into English,
it needs more translation yet: into its true sense. When Ordzhonokidze
talked about the cadres who "bore the blow," we need to know that the
blow they bore was the supposed necessity to *inflict* injustice, not to
suffer it. (They had been inflicting it since Lenin decreed that the
Party would have to rule by terror.) In other words, we are being asked
to sympathize with the butchers, not the victims. As Primo Levi was to
warn the world after the Holocaust, it will always be in the interests of
the perpetrators, after a great crime is identified, to say that they, too,
were helplessly caught up in it, and also suffered. But Ordzhonokidze

was saying more that that. He was saying that the perpetrators were the true victims.

In the period 1932–1933 Stalin staged the first of his great massacres: the immense disaster comprising the collectivization of agriculture, the liquidation of the kulaks, and famine exploited as a social weapon. His second great massacre was still ahead: the Yezhovchina, the comprehensive terror of which the 1938 show trials were merely the small component that the world heard about. But the two-year jamboree of repression euphemistically cited in Ordzhonokidze's grotesque letter was bad enough. The upper-echelon officials, many of them the very same Old Bolsheviks who later on would be eliminated almost to a man by the bureaucrat they had foolishly allowed to inherit Lenin's keys of office, had faithfully carried out their orders to mow down the innocent. Anyone who had qualms did not allow them to affect his trigger finger. Ordzhonokidze should really be talking about the ruined lives of hundreds of thousands of blameless citizens. But the only suffering that interests him is the supposed wear and tear on the nerves of those deputed to carry out the destruction. By implication he includes himself and Kirov among their number: a brotherhood of martyrdom. This brand of sentimental fellow-feeling is not uncommon among mass murderers and presumably helps to sustain them in their shared memories. One of the Einsatzgruppen chiefs, Paul Blobel—the distinguished leader of Einsatzkommando 4A—said after the war that the liquidators were the real unfortunates. "The nervous strain was far heavier in the case of our men who carried out the executions than in that of their victims." (Quoted, along with much other similarly noxious testimony from the hard-done-by, on page 364 of Heinz Höhne's *The Order of the Death's Head*. Not a book for the beach.)

It is not recorded that Kirov declined the honour of being addressed as one who summoned up his bravery for the challenging task of making war on the defenceless. Because Kirov was later murdered in his turn (in 1934, the year the letter was written) we tend to forget that his own record as a murderer was exemplary, with the White Sea Canal—which efficiently depleted the number of those prisoners who built it but was never dug deep enough to float a ship—as his masterpiece. But the fact might be remembered when the Kirov ballet company next comes on tour to a theatre near you. Petersburg is no longer called Leningrad, but the Maryinsky company, when on tour outside Russia, is still called the Kirov, presumably on the assumption that the ballet audience abroad remains clueless enough to believe that Kirov had once had some sort of background in the fine arts, like Sir Kenneth Clark or Sir Jeremy Isaacs. Kirov's background was one of unrestricted power and the extermination of blameless human beings. A measure of our slowness to face up to the real history of the Soviet Union is that the expression "Kirov Ballet" does not strike us as obscene. The expression "Himmler Youth Orchestra" would. So, to be fair, would "Pol Pot Academy of Creative Writing" or even "Madame Mao School of Calligraphy." The subsidiary Communist regimes have been stripped of their prestige: acquired late, it was quick to go, and it would be an uncommonly servile Western ideologue who still said, or even thought, "hands off democratic Kampuchea." But the Soviet Union, an earlier and more massive event even than Communist China, has retained its legitimacy, at any rate to the extent that some of its historical figures are still granted a stature that was always ludicrously at odds with their true significance. The regrettable tendency of intellectuals to worship power is exemplified by their readiness to attribute dignity to men who could prove their seriousness about politics only by slaughtering anyone who might disagree with them, as if ruthless nihilism were a testimonial to dedication, and an utter lack of mercy a mark of strength: if you can't stand the blood, get out of the abattoir.

Few among the intellectuals of the civilized world ever made a comparable investment in the future of Nazi Germany, so they had no trouble condemning it even before it fell, and showed no reluctance to analyse its workings. As a result, we are well acquainted with the retroactive soul-searchings of Nazi functionaries who were obliged by circumstances—circumstances beyond their control, according to them—to list mass murder on their curriculum vitae. Whereas we tend, erroneously, to think of the Soviet Union's Ordzhonokidzes and Kirovs as rare birds, we know that for the Nazis an upstanding blockhead like Gustav Franz Wagner was standard issue. As second in command under Franz Stangl, Wagner was the man in charge of the day-to-day business of the extermination camp at Sobibór. The place was supposed to be a bad dream but Wagner made sure that it was even worse than it needed to be. Rather distinguished in his personal appearance, he had a talent for supererogatory sadism that made the few survivors of his hellhole grateful for the relative humanity of those among his myrmidons who were content to devote themselves to mere murder instead of prolonged torture. Interviewed on film in his old age, he was full of the difficulties of the "hard task." Such language echoed Himmler's with the cold precision of a pistol shot in a brick-built barracks. Himmler was always telling his lovingly nurtured young SS officers how hard it would be for them to overcome their natural compassion. He had the same grim news for senior members of the party. At the October 1943 Posen conference (the one where Albert Speer was present according to eyewitnesses but absent according to himself) Himmler wrung all hearts by painting a picture of how the high-ranking party officials sitting to attention in front of him would have to put their civilized German values into abeyance while they continued to face the seemingly endless challenge of obliterating the sub-humans infesting Europe. "The hard decision had to be taken to have this people disappear from the face of the earth." Touring an alfresco prisoner-of-war pen near Kiev, Himmler demonstrated his own fragility by fainting dead away when he was accidentally confronted with real blood instead of a statistic. But he nerved himself to the job. He made the sacrifice. He bore the blow.

In both the Soviet Union and Nazi Germany, the class of professional exterminators divided fairly neatly into homicidal perverts who couldn't get enough and routinely squeamish placemen who had to get used to it. The second category necessarily outnumbered the first by a long way: under both regimes, there was a large reservoir of men and women who were not much more insane than us but who, in extreme circumstances, could be talked into, or could talk themselves into, extreme behaviour. In that respect the regimes were mirror images of each other. When the long reluctance of the world's intellectuals to admit this disturbing fact was at last overcome—and until the collapse of the Soviet Union the admission never looked like happening—the pendulum swung the other way. The first and loudest voice of the *Historikerstreit*, the acrid verbal battle between German historians that broke out in 1986, Ernst Nolte was only the most conspicuous example of a scholar who wanted to argue that the Communist ideology had brought the fascist ideologies into being, by a process more like cloning than parturition. On the whole, however, we have gained from the two great streams of unreason being seen in parallel: a full body count has at least had the merit of depriving apologists for the left (necessarily the more eloquent, because nobody except a psychopath ever apologized for the right) of the opportunity to excuse communism by saying Nazism was quantitatively worse.

But the drawback of bringing the two main ideologies closer together has been to encourage the assumption that a system of belief can explain the killing. Such an assumption springs from the familiar tendency—and in some ways it is a commendable one—to invoke a complex mental preparation for an elementary human act. The absurdity becomes manifest in the political sphere when its proponent, as he must, finds himself trying to establish similarities between the mental processes of a sophisticated intellectual like G. Y. Zinoviev and a lumbering maniac like Saddam Hussein. Zinoviev said—and therefore, presumably, thought—that the Revolution should wipe out innocent people as a matter of course. Saddam Hussein seems to have believed something similar. But really it doesn't matter what such different men believe, or think they believe. What matters is that they behave the same way, hence allowing us to deduce that what really interests them is unchallenged power, for which the necessity to commit murder is seen as a small price.

Here one ought to put the best possible construction on things and assume that most of the desk-bound mass murderers arrive at such a solution only in answer to problems clogging the in tray. In harsh actuality, there is plenty of evidence to suggest that some of the great killers became political figures in the first place for no other purpose except to wipe out their fellow human beings when they got the chance. Like Stalin, if with a touch more charm, Lenin was always vicious: a fact which, for more than seventy years, was the very last to be admitted by the international left intelligentsia even though men who had known him personally, and believed in his cause, had said so from the earliest days of the regime—even though Lenin himself had said that the regime must rule by terror. But as always, the psychotic cases are morally less edifying than the apparently normal ones. Ho Chi Minh is a more instructive exponent of state terror than Pol Pot because Ho could rein himself in: leaving aside the routine massacres through which he established himself in unchallenged power, he didn't start the class war against his bourgeoisie while the military battle remained unwon. But after his death, with the battle decided, his successors resumed the business of class war in accordance with his known wishes. Pol Pot dismantled his own victory straight away by killing everyone whose help he needed: probably because he needed their help, and found the dependency an unbearable challenge to his endlessly spiteful ego. From that angle, perhaps the most instructive example of all was Mao Zedong. The great leader began as some sort of anarchist who eschewed violence in the belief that reform could be achieved by example and persuasion. When he decided otherwise, he began killing people in large numbers. Eventually the numbers grew so large that they outran imagination. It wasn't even enough for them to be innocent: they had to believe what he believed, and thus be guilty of no other crime except the crime of not being him. It wasn't even enough for them to die: they had to die in agony, and the climate of fear worked best if they could be induced to inflict the agony on each other. In my ideal university, Jung Chang's *Wild Swans* and Philip Short's *Mao* would both be on the course, but there would be a danger of making the young student despair of life. Even at my age, the story of modern China can make me wonder if my life was worth living.

But there was good news. After Mao's death, somebody put the brakes on. Those blandly smiling Chinese authorities who wonder aloud why Western liberals are so concerned with the Tienanmen Square incident of June 1989 are not quite so cynical as they seem. By Mao's grandiose standards, an atrocity on so diffident a scale—the dead scarcely added up to a village, and Mao was accustomed to obliterating people by whole cities at a time—was truly less than nothing. No doubt any of us exposed to even half an hour of life in a present-day Chinese re-education camp would emerge gibbering if we emerged at all, but the truly orgiastic frenzy of torture and killing that went on under Mao seems by now to be a thing of the past. The juggernaut looked unstoppable, but it was stopped. The only possible conclusion is that someone knew which levers to pull, and wanted to pull them. The great mystery of the socialist totalitarian regimes has been not how they grew into killing machines—in retrospect, nothing seems more logical—but how the machines were put into reverse. When Khrushchev denounced Stalin at the Twentieth Party Congress in 1956, it was remarkable enough. More remarkable still was that Khrushchev came to think that way, having started out as a standover man of impeccably murderous credentials. He still didn't think that way entirely, as the Hungarians found out later the same year, but he was a different man from the Khrushchev who had carried out Stalin's bidding in the Ukraine: a "task" which necessarily included extermination on an epic scale.

Khrushchev began his career as an apparatchik capable of any crime the state ordered. But when the time came and he saw the glimmer of a chance, he didn't want to live that way any longer. Nor did Brezhnev. In contrast to Khrushchev, who was bright for a thug, Brezhnev was a dim bulb, but once safe in his appointment he could have done something to steer the Politburo back towards the cult of personality if he had really wanted to. Instead, he resolutely submitted to the restrictions of "collective leadership"—the only term or phrase in his pitiably mendacious official biography that means exactly what it says. Khrushchev and Brezhnev, with their sordid background in the classic massacres, are even more instructive exemplars than Andropov, the man who changed everything. Andropov could never have changed everything had not his immediate predecessors first changed something. For him it was comparatively easy: no doubt he had signed the orders for a few hundred young hotheads to be given the treatment in the psychiatric hospitals, and he had certainly been active in the re-education of the Czechs in 1968; but in his deeper past there were no stretches of permafrost or pine forest with thousands of bodies under them. It was easy for him to print off a special edition of *Nineteen Eighty-Four* and make his bright young officers read it. He wasn't going to get into trouble with the KGB. He *was* the KGB. The real breakthrough was further back, when the first mass killers got tired of killing. Against all the odds, it happened. When you think of the blood on their gloves, it doesn't seem much of a comfort: but if you want to live in hope, you have to deal with some very raw material. And if you want to see an end to the kind of "State the like of which the world has never seen," you have to accept that for some people there is nothing more habitual than to do their worst, and that the sole function your fine opinions might perform, and always at a tangent, is to affect those people at the moment when they begin to wonder whether being ordered to torment their fellow human beings might not indeed be a blow, and scarcely to be borne any longer.

P

❧ ❧ ❧

Octavio Paz

Alfred Polgar

Beatrix Potter

Jean Prévost

Marcel Proust

OCTAVIO PAZ

❣ ❣ ❣

Octavio Paz (b. 1914) is not only the great poet of modern Mexico, but the great essayist. Nobody in any of the main Western languages does more to demonstrate the closeness of those two forms. His every poem opens up a topic, and his every essay glows with treasurable turns of phrase. In his capacity as essayist he can be approached with confidence by the beginner in Spanish, because Paz's prose style might have been put on earth specifically as a teaching aid to that language. Attractively wrapped in coated white paper by the Spanish publishing house Seix-Barral, his collections of essays are almost beyond counting and cover every artistic subject. They leave the reader amazed that their author ever found time to be a poet. That he found time to be a man of action as well beggars belief. In the Spanish Civil War he fought on the Republican side. In the 1960s, in his role of diplomat, he was Mexico's ambassador to India. His engagement with the politics of his own country was unceasing and often tempestuous. All his artistic enthusiasm, and all his political experiences, yielded material for poetry: he was the embodiment of Goethe's principle that there could be no event in life without the golden shadow of a poem. In the light shed by this active

volcano of high-quality creative activity, the award of the
Nobel Prize in 1990 made his admirers wonder why some previous recipients were not shamed into handing their prizes
back. Of the old imperial European countries, Spain has been
the most conspicuous example of a homeland having its energy
restored by the creativity of its colonies. From Rubén Darío
onwards, the writers of Latin America were conscious of their
mission to restore the intellectual force of the Spanish world.
We can pick favourites among the twentieth-century exemplars—Sabato and Vargas Llosa are among mine—but Paz is
up there with Borges no matter what we think of either. As it
happens, I think Paz's homage to Sor Juana Inés de la Cruz is
one of the most romantic books in the world, and would still
have made him a master if it had been the whole of his work,
instead of only a hundredth part.

Faced with the disappearance of the correspondence of Sor
Juana, the melancholy provoked inevitably by the study of
our past is transformed into desperation.
— OCTAVIO PAZ, SOR JUANA INÉS DE LA
CRUZ, P. 181

IN OTHER WORDS, he was in love with her. Any man who reads the
book will feel the same way about its heroine, and wish for himself
Paz's Camusian good looks, the dark charm with which he has always
carried his immense learning. He had all the qualifications to think of
himself as her saviour from the solitude of the cloisters. Luckily he
remembered, as we must remember, that the lyrically gifted beauty's
life as a nun was a life she chose. Our own salvation is to reflect that it
was not necessarily the love of Christ that drew her to the convent in
the first instance. In Mexico, in the age of the Baroque, learning was a
man's business. Colonial Mexico had been founded by the conquista-
dores, and their suits of armour were still standing in the hallways of
the haciendas. Mexico is still a macho culture today. Imagine what it
was like then. In her childhood, Juana de Asbaje y Ramirez de Santi-
llana was so gifted that she taught herself Latin in a breath. She

dreamed of going to university and at one stage planned to pass herself off as a boy so that she could enrol. Finally the would-be Yentl had to face facts. Her grand name had no money to back it up. Much courted for her beauty and lively personality, she could have picked a rich husband and so gained the leisure to read and write. But she didn't want to sell herself. The convent was the only recourse. Though her faith was real, it undoubtedly came in handy. If we can't look on her lifelong piety as lip service, we can see it as a part expedient, and so dream of joining the long line of suitors who came to her at the convent. One of them might have succeeded, although, as was bound to happen, there has always been much speculation about her sexuality. Some believed that she was a man all along.

Even Paz thought she had a male mind. Women dream of her as men do, and might even be closer to the truth. There was a direct connection from the convent to the viceregal palace, where her poems were valued as evidence of the colony's growing place in the world. One of the vicereines was as attentive as any male suitor. She was the splendidly named and titled Maria Luisa Manrique de Lara y Gonzaga, Condesa de Paradis y de la Laguna. This time the big name had all the accoutrements, but with the wealth and the position went blue stockings. The accomplished and superior Condesa de Paradis was drawn to Juana Inés as one intellectual aristocrat to another. Since the nun could not go to the palace drawing-room, the Countess of Paradise and the Lagoon went to the book-lined convent cell. The nun wrote poems in praise of the noblewoman's beauty. The vocabulary of adoration was standard for the day, but there is no mistaking the passion, even after the lush lilt of her Spanish is cut and dried into English.

You are the queen of the flowers
Hence even the Summer begs
The pinks of your lips
The roses of your cheeks.

When the movie is made, undoubtedly they will grapple, albeit discreetly. In real life, they almost certainly didn't, but Sor Juana wrote some of the loveliest poems of her career, which means that she enshrined her passionate appreciation at the apex of Spanish poetry from all eras. When talking of her talent, the first thing to do is throw caution to the winds. In a single sonnet by her, there is a single moment that suffices to put Mexico in the centre of the Spanish literary world. The sonnet is the one which seeks to dismiss the praises ("*desmentir los elogios*") lavished on her portrait, and the moment is the last line, an inspired, legitimate and dazzling variation on Góngora: "*es cadaver, es polvo, es sombre, es nada.*" (It is a corpse, it is dust, it is shadow, it is nothing.) The moment would carry less weight without the argumentative solidity of the thirteen lines leading up to it. Her sense of form was monumental even when playful. As in her life, in her poetry she brought the Renaissance to the Baroque: in the first fully self-conscious artistic age, she rediscovered the sense of discovery.

How could so free a spirit have shut itself away from the world? Perhaps to get a better perspective, and anyway her solitude was strictly a metaphor. For year after year, her cell teemed with visitors, most of them bearing new books for her library. It was like a coffee house in there. Her *tertulia* was the hub of literary life in the colony. But the Church was a long way yet from tolerating the idea of a secular civilization. At forty, but already near the end of her life, she was called to order by her confessor and by her archbishop: she had to renew her vows. The Condesa de Paradis, her best mentor and protectress, had already left for Spain, never to return. In Madrid, the countess financed the publication of the first volume of Juana Inés's poems. Juana Inés was launched on her journey to the future, but in the present she was finished. In the same year that she renounced the world all over again, she dispersed her beloved library. Her papers and letters were scattered with the books. Paz's grief about the correspondence is hardly excessive: if we had the letters, we would have the whole story of a Creole culture becoming aware of its strength. Surely the letters would have been populated with all the voices of her *tertulia*. Books will be written endlessly in speculation about what her informal writings would have contained. Paz's was far from being the first book on Sor Juana, and there will be many more. But there will never be a book quite as exciting as his, because he is a poet at her level of intensity, and a prose writer who can get his poetic intensity into a paragraph. Her correspondence, he goes on to say, would have been a document to place her with those of her seventeenth-century contemporaries—not in Madrid or Lima or Mexico but in Europe proper—who were inaugurating the modern era. The correspondence was lost through sheer carelessness: the Spanish carelessness that Paz defines in scathing terms. "It is said that the passion that corrodes the Spanish peoples is envy; but worse and more weighty is carelessness: the creator of our deserts." When he brings in a phrase like *creadora de nuestros desertos*, Paz shows us the transatlantic cable that runs from Unamuno and Ortega to himself and Vargas Llosa: the charge of energy that brought Spanish civilization to life again, offshore in the Americas. Spanish expository prose in the twentieth century was a miracle that these men created, but they didn't dream it up out of the air. There was already a long heritage of rhetorical strength in the poetry, where the telling phrases lie separate that would later be strung together in a coruscating style.

One of the many virtues of Paz's continuously thrilling magnum opus about the brilliant creature Juana Inés is his success at bringing out the prose qualities in her poetry: the concentration of intelligence, the toughly argued sentence. For any beginner in Spanish, his book about her is one of the texts to put beside a big dictionary and construe line for line and word for word, in full confidence that none of the effort will be wasted. You will hear two people who never met each other talking across time, and realize once and for all that the reason most critical biographies fail is that the biographer falls out of love with his subject. Paz falls further and further in, and we go with him.

ALFRED POLGAR

❦ ❦ ❦

Alfred Polgar was born in Vienna in 1873, educated in the cafés and established himself early in his adult career as the unsurpassable exemplar of German prose in modern times, even though he never, strictly speaking, wrote a book. In 1927 his success as a writer of reviews, essays and articles took him to Berlin, and in 1933 the success of the Nazis almost deprived him of his life. He escaped the day before he was scheduled to be arrested. As a journalist dependent on the size of his audience, Polgar still had outlets in Vienna, Zurich and Prague, but his position steadily became more desperate. "I love life and I would never willingly leave it," he told a friend, "but it is leaving me." In 1938 he left Vienna on the night train to Zurich only a day before the *Anschluß*. Luckily he was able to follow the exile trail—Prague, Paris, Spain—all the way to America, although he knew before he got there that he was ill equipped to flourish. He was set in his ways, and he had nothing to sell. On the American market, his approach to writing would have been useless even if it had not been confined to the German language, because it was also confined to German-speaking society: his prose and its subject matter were aspects of each other. In Hollywood he was a beneficiary of the MGM programme that paid refugee writers for screenplays that would never be filmed. Well aware that this was tantamount to being given a free ticket to a soup kitchen, he was ashamed to take the money, but he had no choice. He was no longer young enough to master Engish in the way he had mastered his mother tongue.

On his home ground, Polgar had made German the ideal instrument for a body of prose so charged with the precision of poetry that it gives a picture of his era no other writer could match for wealth of registered detail and subtlety of argument: not even the magnificent collected journalism of Joseph Roth is quite in the same class. Polgar's prose is probably fated to remain accessible only to readers of German, who can approach it through several one-volume selections. The best of these, chosen by Polgar himself from the nine separate volumes of his writings, was published in West Berlin in 1950 under the title *Auswahlband* (Choice Volume). Another selection, with the conspicuous omissions that you might expect, was published in East Berlin in 1975 as *Die Mission des Luftballons* (Mission of the Air Balloon): Polgar had too much prestige to be repudiated as a bourgeois writer. There is an excellent biography, *Alfred Polgar*, by Ulrich Weinzierl. After the war Polgar returned to Europe but felt unable to settle in Austria or in either version of Germany, despite his being greeted as a hero wherever he went. He died in Zurich in 1975, with his immortality already established by a whole constellation of *kleine Schriften* (small writings) that Marcel Reich-Ranicki rightly defined as "an immaculate unification of tact and intellect, conscience and taste." Marlene Dietrich wanted Polgar to write her biography. Sadly, the project came to nothing.

Abel, if he had fled from the murderous attentions of his brother Cain, would as an emigrant have had to put up

with an even more bitter inconvenience. He would have
had to wander the world for the rest of his life with the
brand of Abel on his forehead.
— ALFRED POLGAR, PART OF THE
FRAGMENTARY ESSAY "TOWARDS A
CONTEMPORARY THEME"

IF I HAD what it took to translate the separable remarks of Alfred
Polgar and collect them into a book, *The Brand of Abel* might be the
title. Most of his remarks, however, don't separate out: they are bonded
into his feuilletons, a form that Karl Kraus hated so much he blamed
Heine for inventing it. But Kraus couldn't write an essay, for a reason
that Polgar nailed in a single, ostensibly praising antithesis: "He wasn't
a constructive talent: he was a critical genius." (Polgar also said of
Kraus that if he had lived, he would have had no-one left to attack.)
Polgar could write an essay. His every piece forms a rhythmic unit
from start to finish. Occasionally, however, a sentence can be carried
off on its own. Those were the sentences Kurt Tucholsky was probably
thinking of when he said that Polgar wrote filaments of granite. (*Filaments of Granite* wouldn't be a bad title either, but it would fudge the
point.) The brand of Abel is one of the filaments. The brand of Cain
belonged to the scriptures we already possessed. The brand of Abel
belongs to the scriptures that the twentieth century wrote for us: the
books, the articles and sometimes the single statements that evoke
the human disaster. In that new book of the holy word, witnesses to the
modern multiple apocalypse speak with precise resonance. The qualifications for having even a single statement recorded in that sacred text
are punishingly high.

But the man who is there a thousand times over is Alfred Polgar. A
measure of how dreadful his era was is that it took everything he had
to express it. A measure of what he had is that he could. It should never
have happened, of course. So much lyrical talent should never have
been required to deal with such an artificially contrived misery. At the
most it should have been occupied with the tragedies of ordinary life,
the events that Nadezhda Mandelstam was later to subsume under her
concept of the privilege of ordinary heartbreaks. But as things happened—as Hitler made them happen—Polgar was presented with the

dubious opportunity of gathering all the gifts with which he had so brilliantly reflected life in the German-speaking civilization and bringing them to the task of recording its disintegration. It would have been a daunting enough task for a much younger man. But when he went into exile he was already sixty-five. In Vienna and Berlin he had been at the top of his profession. Leaving it all, he was penniless. What little money he had made from selling his library was used up, and he had reason to believe that he would never make any more. Where he was heading, they spoke English, and he was too old to master it.

When the *New Hellas* left Portugal for New York on October 4, 1940, among the passengers were Heinrich Mann, Golo Mann, Franz and Alma Werfel, and Alfred Polgar. It was a convocation of the talents, but it is fair to say that even the imperious Alma, who had been loved by every important man in Vienna, knew which among her attendant male companions on the ship of the saved had a gift from heaven. Polgar was the one who could raise their tragedy to poetry. "Many attempt without success to make up for their lack of talent with defects of character." He could afford to say so, because his strength and depth of character were in everything he said. "A commonplace soul is often uncommonly spirited. But dreck is still dreck, even when phosphorescent." He could afford to say that too, because he was never flashy. Most of his best effects were achieved with nothing more than a subtle shift against a prepared expectation. Sometimes you can barely hear the swerve. "To reform an evildoer, you must before anything else help him to an awareness that what he did was evil. With the Nazis this won't be easy. They know exactly what they're doing: they just can't imagine it." Drawn with a single calligraphic stroke from a fine brush, the distinction between knowing and imagining was crucial to him. Armed with that, he could make literature from the bare facts, however sad. "The striking aphorism requires a stricken aphorist." We can almost convince ourselves that he welcomed disaster.

He hated every minute of disaster. "It is the destiny of the emigrant that the foreign land does not become his homeland: his homeland becomes foreign." Along with his books, he had left everything that sustained his imagination far behind. "When everything has left you, you are alone. When you have left everything, you are lonely." In Hollywood Polgar was too proud to accept his helplessness without an interior rebellion. As Hannah Arendt records, there was a phrase among the refugees for how they felt about America: *Dankbar aber ungülcklich* (thankful but unhappy). Polgar was too gracious to say it, but he felt it. (Sometimes he almost said it: he was the one who called Hollywood a paradise over whose door is written "Abandon hope.") Those who would like to believe that Thomas Mann was an anti-Semite have to deal with the undoubted fact that he reached deep into his pocket at a crucial time to save Polgar, who he realized was his equal as a guardian of the soul of the German language. (It was Mann who said Polgar's prose was marked by a lightness that plumbed the depths.) Throughout the war, Polgar wrote for such German publications as there were; and after the war he went back to Europe in a kind of belated triumph; but he was never again the force he had once been, and today he has no international reputation whatsoever. He foresaw the reason. "My spiritual handwriting can't be translated."

In the doomed attempt to translate it, we should switch our attention from his last phase to his early glory, in which his exuberant sensitivity to the scope of civilized life can still be appreciated even if the English words chosen to duplicate it are clumsily assembled. Among his other talents, Polgar was a theatre critic who could write a weekly review that chronicled a whole society. Our own greatest theatre critic, Shaw, was limited as well as focused by his playwright's agenda. Polgar, though he had dramatic gifts of his own (with Egon Friedell he wrote the most successful full-length cabaret script of the years between the wars), had no such limitation. He could see the whole play, and the whole world with it. To pit one critical genius against another, hear him on *Pygmalion*: "A comedy about a man who turns a girl into a lady, but in doing so overlooks the woman." Writing about his beloved Büchner, Polgar pulled off a character analysis so penetrating that we have to go back to Coleridge to find an equivalent. Polgar said this of Büchner's Danton: "His withdrawal from blood and terror is no moral withdrawal. His capacity for political murder has simply ceased, fallen out of his soul like an object out of an open hand grown tired of holding." Polgar thought Büchner's talent had been on the Shakespearean scale: high and knowledgeable praise from a critic whose interest in Shakespeare knew no limits. Polgar said of Shakespeare's Richard II: "He was, with God's blessing, a weak, empty king, and becomes, with

God's ill-will, a full, fruitful man, out of whom necessity presses sweetness and wisdom. He falls upward into depth." First the argument, then its compression. Polgar said of *The Merchant of Venice*: "Among empty masks made lifelike for a single evening by Shakespeare the master wig-maker, Shylock is the only face." Year upon year, Polgar would track every production of plays by Shakespeare, Ibsen, Shaw, Hauptmann, Pirandello. Wonderful is the only word for his long comparison of Ibsen to Wagner. His sequence of essays on Ibsen leaves Shaw's equivalent effort looking thin. Polgar never gushed; he was discriminating even in his worship; but the wellspring of his enthusiasm was a grateful love.

We should think of that first before we begin to enjoy his limiting judgements. Critics are always remembered best for how they sound when on the attack. *Schadenfreude* lies deep in the human soul, and to read a tough review seems a harmless way of indulging it. But the only critical attacks that really count are written in defence of a value. It was because of his admiration for competent practitioners that Polgar assaulted the incompetent. He could be hilarious while doing so, but never for the sake of being funny. Lesser critics look for opportunities to pour on the scorn. Polgar would rather have avoided them. When forced to the issue, however, he left no man standing. Witness the neatness with which he evoked Hermann Bahr's Napoleon turning back defeat with a strategic master stroke. "He emits the deathless words 'All battalions forward!,' draws his ceremonial dagger, and exits stage left in the direction of Lombardy, which he is seen in the next act to have conquered." The young Kenneth Tynan would have been proud of that. Polgar's demolitions were usually instantaneous. He called Sacha Guitry's *Desirée* "a *jeu* even older than *vieux*." He said of *Man and Superman*: "the audience gets an exhausting idea of the inexhaustibility of the subject, and is bored brilliantly." Of a young actress: "She is pretty, and tactfully concerned that the optical pleasure she provides shall not be disturbed by technical requirements any more than necessary." Of a bad playwright: "Saying nothing is the mother tongue of his art." But occasionally Polgar decided that a bad playwright, especially if he had earned an unwarranted reputation, needed something more effective than a skewering: he needed to be rubbed out. One such unfortunate was the fashionable darling Raoul Avern-

heimer. Polgar granted him the favour of a complete paragraph. At the
risk of interfering with its remorseless build-up, I will try to render it
in English:

> Civilization and culture, if they are left in peace long enough by
> war and pestilence, generate mould. And over this mould a layer
> of dust forms. And in this layer of dust microscopic life-forms set-
> tle. And these microscopic life-forms generate excrement. And in
> the breakdown-products of this excrement even less visible life-
> forms find their domicile. And these life-forms, as long as they are
> resident within the periphery of Vienna and eligible to vote in
> the central electoral district, generate the world portrayed in the
> comedies of Raoul Avernheimer.

Let it be said again that Polgar could write that way not because he was
cruel, but because he was comprehensive. The proof is in the subtle
judgements he made between the two extremes of praise and blame.
He admired Max Reinhardt's independence and industry, but knew
where to find fault. Some of Reinhardt's productions Polgar found not
only stylized, but sterilized. (The alliteration is there in the original.)
Bound in ties of friendship with Egon Friedell, Polgar greeted the
polymath's *Judastragödie* with only two cheers. He noted his friend's
"peculiar fencing stance: on the tip of the sword with which he attacks
flutters the white flag with which he surrenders." Friedell could have
done without Polgar's praise for his brains: "High intelligence, from
which the blessing of refreshing words falls in a shower, offers here a
rich substitute for art." In his letters, Schnitzler reveals how wounded
he was by Polgar's criticism. He would have been wounded less if Polgar had called him a bad writer. But Polgar called him a good writer
who was doing the wrong thing, indulging himself in "the opal tint of
his half-bitter, half-sentimental scepticism." Werfel would not have
enjoyed hearing that his diction was "palate-irritatingly over-spiced."
(Werfel forgot the imputation long enough to grant Polgar one of the
best things ever said about his style: he said that Polgar had the gift of
catching deep-sea fish on the surface.) If Schiller could have come back
from the dead, he might have wondered why he made the trip when he
heard Polgar point out that *William Tell* "isn't a protest against tyranny,

only against its misuse." When we call a critic deadly, it should be because he knows about life, and will not accept its being falsified. Polgar was suspicious of the theatre, which he called "a charlatan that works real magic." His love for it was an intelligent love. He tested it against the world, not by its own standards. Hence the permanent validity of his mocking advice to a bad critic: "Take aim, let loose. And when your arrow sticks in, draw a target around its buried point. That way you will score a bullseye every time."

Alfred Brendel put me on to Polgar. Brendel knows everything about the Viennese coffee-house wits, and carries in his pocket an anthology of their best sayings, individually typed out on slips of paper. Away from the piano, Brendel's fingertips are usually wrapped in strips of Elastoplast. (So would mine be, if they were worth ten million dollars each.) When you see those bits of paper being hauled from his pockets by his plastered fingers, you realize you are in the presence of a true enthusiast. Brendel gave me the name of every card in the pack, but told me to be sure of one thing: Alfred Polgar was the ace of diamonds. The advice saved me years. I probably would have got to Polgar eventually, but by getting to him early I was granted the entrée to a whole vanished world, because Polgar is the gatekeeper. Though a shy man, he knew everyone, because everyone wanted to know him; and he had their characters summed up. As for his own books, they put me on the spot. The way he wrote about everything at all levels confirmed me in what I had been trying to do, but the quality with which he did it was a poser. A single dull page would have been a relief, but there wasn't one. Travelling a lot at the time on filming trips, I found his titles in second-hand bookshops all over the world: wherever the refugees had gone to die in peace, and their children had sold the books because the old language was the last thing they wanted to hear again. On Staten Island I found half a dozen, and there was a bunch of three in Tel Aviv. Strangely enough, Munich teemed with them: despite instructions, fewer Jew-infected books were burned than the Nazis would have liked.

The original Polgar volumes are delectable to look at. Usually they are bound in light cardboard of a primary colour made pastel by time, and the format is small enough to fit the pocket. But the bindings are fragile, and easily crack. It was encouraging to discover, in the 1980s, that Rowohlt was putting out a multi-volume complete edition on thin paper, strongly bound. The editor could not have been better chosen. It was Marcel Reich-Ranicki, a long-time admirer of Polgar who was unlikely to muff the job. Nor did he, but the edition is unsatisfactory in one crucial respect. Each piece comes to an end without a sign of its provenance: to find out when it was written, you have to turn to the critical apparatus at the back of the volume. There was some reason to divide his work into its genres, although it would have been better arranged in a pure chronology, to show how his diversity was operating all the time. But to leave the dates off the pieces was to connive at a trick of wish fulfilment. German literature in the twentieth century was fated to lose its self-sustaining monumentality. The point came when everything depended on which year a piece was written, and then which month, and even which day. Glossing that over, you miss the story of how politics invaded art and came close to killing it. The complete edition would be a tomb if Polgar did not have a spirit that can shine through marble. You can see that I am unable to stop borrowing his tricks. But the real trick is to borrow his tone. Nobody should try who can't write English as well as Polgar wrote German, and I'm afraid that lets me out. It was hard enough, for this note, taking him on a sentence at a time. But he could write a whole essay like that: joined-up writing *in excelsis*.

BEATRIX POTTER

❧ ❧ ❧

Beatrix Potter (1866–1943) is as much belittled as flattered by her reputation of being the children's author that adults should read. What child would be impressed by that? She herself was not amused when Graham Greene wrote a semi-serious article about her. She wasn't interested in being a semi-serious subject. W. H. Auden was nearer the mark when he praised her outright as an artist of prose. So she was, and her little books would have been treasurable even without her drawings. Her stories attract tweeness towards them—the Peter Rabbit ballet must be hard to take for anyone except a very tiny child—but are never winsome in themselves, mainly because of her tactile, yet quite tough, feeling for language. She could luxuriate in the polysyllabic without making froth of the meaning: a rare, and strictly poetic, discipline. Some of the post–World War II writers for children got their poetry from rhyme and rhythm: James Thurber in *The Thirteen Clocks*, Dr. Seuss *passim*. Others got it from atmospherics: Maurice Sendak notably, Roald Dahl less tastefully, and J. K. Rowling by ransacking a sorcerers' warehouse stocked with all the magic gear since Grimm's first fairy tales. (In Harry Potter's world, it's only rarely that the *language* is magic, although Durmstrang would sound like a witty

name for a school to any twelve-year-old reader familiar with
the history of German literature.) Beatrix Potter got her
poetry from prose: which is to say, from speech, concentrated.
Written in an age when it was still assumed that children would
not suffer brain damage from hearing a phrase they couldn't
immediately understand, the books are plentifully supplied with
elevated verbal constructions. The bright child sees unfamiliar
phrases going by just overhead, and reaches up, while the parent is reminded of the historic privilege of being born into a
civilization where the morality of children's books, even at their
worthily meant worst, has evolved through supply and demand,
and not been imposed by the state according to a plan. In the
old Soviet Union, there were children's books that preached the
virtues of informing on one's parents. Beatrix Potter had her
own ideas of civic virtue, and most of them are still ours,
although we might be more inclined than she was to ask what
happens to those animals who go to market involuntarily.

Pigling Bland listened gravely; Alexander was
hopelessly volatile.
— BEATRIX POTTER, *THE TALE OF PIGLING
BLAND, P. 25*

PEOPLE WHO DID not have Beatrix Potter read to them as a child
soon learn to envy their own children. The luxury of her diction
seems an unfair treat for the young to those of us who meet it for the
first time in later life. My daughters didn't mind being compared to the
hopelessly volatile Alexander, as long as I kept saying it. Children like
to hear good things said a thousand times, so it helps if the good things
are as good as this. *The Tale of Pigling Bland* is especially rich in pointe-
shoe examples of Potter's gift for exquisitely elevated linguistic deport-
ment. In the next paragraph to the one in which this sentence occurs,
we find that Aunt Pettitoes gives to each piglet a little bundle, "and
eight conversation peppermints with appropriate moral sentiments in
screws of paper." Bright young listeners will savour the "appropriate
moral sentiments" as if they were the peppermints. More important,

they will savour the appropriate moral sentiments even when they aren't quite certain what appropriate moral sentiments are. If you, as an adult, happen to be there when the meaning teeters on the point of sinking in, it can be quite a moment. Poets, especially, are likely to be humbled: this is the transitional point where the art they practise begins and ends.

The only flaw in *The Tale of Pigling Bland* is that the piglets are going to market, yet there is no mention of the probability that they themselves will one day be on sale there in altered form. Bacon is frequently mentioned, but its significance is not alluded to by the author, which rather leaves it to the reciter: a difficult moral decision. In the story of Timmy Tiptoes, Potter is more straightforward about the fate of mice: cats kill them. With that much admitted, the *deus ex machina* that saves Timmy Tiptoes is saved from sentimentality. Timmy Tiptoes gets stuck in the trunk of a tree because the Chipmunk has tempted him to eat too many nuts. Potter finds two ways of being unforgettable about Timmy's nut-eating. The Chipmunk " 'ticed him to eat quantities." The reciter will find that his audience is suitably curious about "enticed" being reduced to " 'ticed," but is fascinated beyond delight by the "quantities." (For days afterwards, hopelessly volatile small people will be discovered to have eaten "quantities" of whatever it is they eat at all.) The *deus ex machina* is "the big wind" that blows the top off the tree. There is no suggestion that a big wind could save Timmy from a cat. There is, however, an implicit suggestion that something will save Pigling Bland and the hopelessly volatile Alexander from becoming bacon. No doubt there had to be such a let-out. Potter was, after all, writing children's books. It is a mark of how good the books are, however, that the merest hint of ordinary uplift is a shock, as if Jane Austen had forgotten to mention money.

JEAN PRÉVOST

❦ ❦ ❦

Of all the casualties among the French Resistance, Jean
Prévost (1901–1944) was possibly the most damaging loss to
the future of French culture. Before the war he had stood out
as a journalist with a wide range of enthusiasms, and, in a startling number of them, solid credentials: someone who could
write so well had every reason to consider himself a literary
figure, but his writings about sport were given additional
weight by the fact that he was a sportsman as well. He enjoyed
every aspect of a productive democracy and might, had he
lived, have run into trouble with the left, because his range of
enjoyments suggested that a capitalist society might be more
fruitfully various, and less alienated, than Marxist theory
allowed. Alas, the question of his future never arose. He joined
the Resistance as an active member and was killed in the fighting. As I try to contend in the following note, his brave death,
and not his conformist history, might have been the real reason his name took so long to come back to life. Jérôme
Garcin's *Pour Jean Prévost* is the essential, and still virtually the
only, book devoted to a career short of time but long on implication. Suggesting as it does that one of the duties of a writer

might be to place himself in danger, his life is probably fated to be more of a curiosity than a model.

But my soul is a fire that suffers if it doesn't burn. I need three or four cubic feet of new ideas every day, as a steamboat needs coal.
—JEAN PRÉVOST, QUOTED BY JEROME GARCIN IN *POUR JEAN PRÉVOST*, P. 111

JEAN PRÉVOST WAS forty-three years old when he was killed in battle against German troops in the Vercors on August 1, 1944. He was one of the few writers who were verifiable heroes of the Resistance and thus he was fated to die a double death, because in the post-war period the French intellectual world's climb back to health was long and slow and at a shallow angle. Figures who had been compromised were found less challenging to deal with than those who had been truly admirable. The admirable, indeed, became the negligible. Neither Prévost nor Marc Bloch was granted a tenth of the attention lavished on such flagrant collaborators as Drieu la Rochelle, Rebatet or Brasillach, whose graves were heaped with wreaths of understanding, sympathy and, all too often, outright approval, as if to have had friendly dealings with the enemy had somehow been evidence of an adventurous commitment. I wish I was exaggerating the case, but anyone who doubts it would only have to measure the short list of material written about Prévost against the whole shelves written about Drieu.

Before the war, Prévost had combined within himself, and seemingly without effort, two different writing careers, one as a student of literature and the other as a journalist writing at a high level on subjects which had not previously always enjoyed the quality of attention he brought to them. His studies of Stendhal and Baudelaire remain important to this day. (He had not yet quite finished the book about Baudelaire when he died fighting.) His journalism about cinema and architecture was better informed than most academic opinion on the subject, and far more engagingly written. He was a champion boxer who knew sports from the inside. As Jérôme Garcin notes in the study that rescued Prévost's reputation from its oubliette, "he was not pardoned for wanting to talk about everything and to be read by everybody." As the junior prodigy at Gallimard, as the whizz-kid of the *Nouvelle Revue Française*, he was looked down on by the established writers even when they were honest enough to admire his verve. Mauriac piously warned him against "*cette prodigeuse facilité.*" To get a picture of Prévost's personality, you don't have to put together all the ways his contemporaries approved of him. All the ways they disapproved of him would do it. Prévost was humanism reborn: its hunger, its scope, its vitality and its inner light—an inner light produced by all the aspects of life illuminating one another, in a honeycomb of understanding. As Garcin says, for Prévost *encyclopédisme* was a way of being. Behind the relaxed good looks, his interior mood was "a ferocious appetite nourished by a permanent anguish." None of it would have worked without his pure heart. A passion for justice and a genuine sympathy with the common people—much of his concern about architecture was on their behalf—ruled out any ideological commitment. After the war, pure hearts were hard to find. Sartre had the unmitigated hide to look down on Prévost's memory. The reason for Prévost's "failure," opined the all-comprehending philosopher, was that Prévost had not been confident enough to follow his star.

Unlike his fellow Resistance hero Sartre, Prévost had been confident enough to follow his star in the direction of the German soldiers, but Sartre left that bit out. There was a lot, after the war, that everyone wanted to leave out. The spontaneous universalism that Prévost had so ably represented in the thirties was irrevocably passé. The division of labour once again became the rule in clerical work. What a man like Prévost had once integrated into a single joyous effort was now broken up into separate specialities, each with its resident panel of shamans and charlatans. The once very real prospect of a widely curious humanism had decayed and separated into literary theory, bogus philosophy and ideological special pleading on behalf of political systems which had, as their first enemy, the irreducible complexity of a living culture. The separate practitioners in these fields all had their own reasons to forget that a man like Prévost had ever existed. But the single thing about him that everybody wanted to forget was his clear, clean decision about fighting the Nazis. That decision had been of a piece with the unpretentious nobility that marked all his work, including the popular journalism, which never flattered his readers except by making them feel talented. You can see what Sartre was afraid of. First of all, Prévost really was the Resistance fighter that Sartre only pretended to be—a pretence we could forgive him for, if he had not later on accused others of cowardice. But what must really have scared Sartre was the lingering memory of Prévost's literary personality: the liberal, humanist, democratic gusto which would have ensured, had he survived the war, his ascent to the status that Sartre, after the accidental death of Camus, was able to enjoy unchallenged—the savant, the philosopher, the critic of life and literature. On that last point alone, the point of literary criticism, the books that Prévost did not write after the war are a lost library to break the heart. As with Marc Bloch in the field of history—but even more sadly because a gift like Prévost's is harder to come by—a gap opens up that the imagination can't fill. You find yourself unable to calculate the damage. Perhaps we can get an idea by trying to imagine what would have happened to critical journalism in English if Orwell had been killed in Spain

MARCEL PROUST

❣ ❣ ❣

Marcel Proust (1871–1922) wrote a long book that even the most casual reader usually makes longer by adding notes on the endpapers. *À la recherche du temps perdu* exists to be annotated. A commonplace book in the classic sense, it is, itself, a set of annotations to all the works of art that Proust has read, looked at, listened to or otherwise enjoyed—and to everything he knows about nature, natural science, love, sex and the workings of the mind. This book you are reading now could easily have been ten times as long if it had contained nothing else but expansions on the notes I have made from reading Proust in several editions over the course of forty years. (In view of that threat, I have confined myself to a single short essay at this point, but you will have noticed, elsewhere in the book, that reflections on Proust tend to creep in when other writers are under consideration: a ubiquity of relevance by which, when it is acknowledged, one of his admirers will often spot another, whereupon they will start discussing Proust in lieu of the previous topic.) Forty years and no end in sight. *War and Peace* is big book too, but you are through it comfortably in a week, and all set to start again one day. *À la recherche du temps perdu* is never done with, because it keeps growing while you are reading it. Like no other book in the world, Proust's book leads everywhere: a building made of corridors, and the walls of the corridors are made of doors. The student can happily find an entrance through the Modern Library's six-volume *In Search of Lost Time*. This covetably handsome set, bravely decorated with photographs of the author, is basically the 1920 Scott Moncrieff translation (published serially throughout the 1920s under the title of *Remembrance of Things Past*) which was revised in the 1980s and 1990s by Terence Kilmartin and D. J. Enright. The whole enterprise took three-quarters of a century fully to materialize in English, and no student's bookshelf should be without it. But it might not be long before the urge arises to read the text in the original.

This urge should not be resisted. Pedants and snobs are fond of declaring that only accomplished French speakers can catch Proust's tone. That might be so, but the tone is only one of the things to be caught. There are whole levels of complexity that can be opened up by an elementary knowledge of written French, and the elementary knowledge is likely to expand usefully as the *recherche* goes on. I myself learned what French I have from reading Proust. It took me fifteen years before I could read confidently during the day without a dictionary, and even then I took home a list of words to be looked up in the evening. (A Larousse is essential to back up an ordinary dictionary: as Pasternak said of Pushkin, Proust is full of *things*.) But the mental improvement was well worth any feelings of inadequacy. The idea that your French needs to be perfect in the first place if you are to appreciate France's greatest writer is as absurd as the idea that you need to be able to read music in order to appreciate Beethoven's late quartets. If Beethoven had thought that, he would never have written them. Similarly, with Proust, a book entirely dependent on its language would not have interested him. When he was younger he was preoccupied with style, but always as a measure of compression and intensity; and he put the preoccupation behind him when he matured into a freedom that was all discipline, and a discipline that was all freedom.

Even his social climbing was dedicated to his art. There can be no doubt that he found the high life fascinating, but nothing is too mundane to get into the book, and its true aristocrats are artists. In Britain up to the present day, even in the work of such a clever critic as John Carey, it is often assumed that the concept of high art, because it was once the property of the landed gentry, is part of a traditional mechanism to repress the common people, and should therefore be denied its prestige. The Americans suffer less from that idea, but if it ever needed countering, the mere existence of Proust would be enough to do it. He places art firmly in the possession of those who love it, whatever their origins might be. His gentry, in fact, are those most likely to succumb to the epidemic Philistinism of the prejudice against Dreyfus. Zola was the most famous liberal commentator on the Dreyfus case but it was Proust who saw the matter through. In foreseeing the corrosive effects of licensed anti-Semitism on the civil order, Proust opened yet another door, the one leading into the accumulating political disaster of France between the wars. How so frail and troubled a man could have had all this strength and wisdom in him is a mystery. The mystery has been often explored, but George D. Painter's two-volume biography *Marcel Proust* is still the book to read about his life. (William C. Carter's single hefty volume is a valuable corrective but not a replacement.) The best single critical book is Jean-François Revel's *Sur Proust*, if only because Revel firmly warns us off the standard wild goose chase of looking for the novel's structure. It might have one, but only in the sense that we think we have learned something about the structure of the universe when we are told that space is curved.

"There is no man, however wise," he said to me, "who has
not, at some time in his youth, said things, or even led a
life, of which his memory is disagreeable and which he
would wish to be abolished. But he absolutely should not
regret it, because he can't be assured of becoming a sage—

to the extent that that is possible—without having passed through all the ridiculous or odious incarnations that must precede that final incarnation."
— MARCEL PROUST (ELSTIR'S ADVICE TO MARCEL), À L'OMBRE DES JEUNES FILLES EN FLEUR, P. 457

I N PROUST THERE are few figures that the narrator finds lasting cause to trust, but Elstir, the veteran and venerable painter, is one of them. The sage, said Elstir, must forgive himself his past faults. Elstir forgot to add that the sage should also correct them. Proust says it for him elsewhere: those we like least are those most like us, but with the faults uncured. It is always dangerous to say *"This* is what we read Proust for." There are people who read Proust just for the clothes. But those of us who read Proust for his remarks about life will always be wondering whether *À la recherche du temps perdu* is really a work of art at all. A work of imagination: yes, of course, and supremely. But is it a novel? Isn't it a book of collected critical essays, with the occasional fictional character wandering in and out of it? After the composer Busoni read *Du côté de chez Swann*, he complained to Rilke that although he had quite enjoyed the opinions about music, he thought the rest of the book was a bit like a novel. Isn't it a work of encyclopaedic synthesis? Thomas Mann, in his diaries, took notes on the way that Proust had taken notes. He especially praised the detail of Proust's interest in flying beetles. Isn't it a work of philosophy? Jean-François Revel, in his brief book *Sur Proust*—the commentary on Proust that almost gives you the courage to do without all the others—is clearly fascinated with the possibility that Proust might have restored philosophy to its position of wisdom. Often, in the long shelf of his writings, Revel argues that philosophy, having ceased in the eighteenth century to be queen of the sciences, has, in modern times, no other role except to be wise. In *Sur Proust* he casts his author as a character in a drama: the drama of philosophy reborn. Revel calls *À la recherche* one of the rare books that even in their weaknesses offer an example of "totally adult thought."

Proust's example drives Revel to philosophical aperçus of his own. Passion, says Revel, consists of seeing in the finite an infinity that doesn't exist. Revel floats the notion that Albertine might have been an even more interesting jailer had she been faithful: the thin end of a wedge into Proust's view of sex and jealousy. (E. M. Forster, from closer to home, had similar reservations, and erected them into a principle designed to cover Proust in general: he said that Proust's analytical knife was so sharp it came out the other side.) On the political plane, Proust is praised by Revel for keeping a level head against collective barbarism through his moral intransigence and his *perspicacité psychologique*. The collective barbarism was the anti-Semitic nationalism already poisoning French politics when Proust the social butterfly was preparing to write his novel. Revel is only one reader of Proust, but his readings are enough to hint at the richness that *À la recherche* would offer us even it were only a collection of critical remarks. It is, of course, much more than that: but one of the reasons it is much more than that is that it is never less. These qualities of non-fiction are useful to remember when we realize how many qualities of fiction the longest of all novels does not possess. It has, for example, no structure worth speaking of, and probably would not have attained to one even if Proust had been given another ten years to work on it. Characters would still have shown up twenty years too young at the last party, or twenty years too old, or simply still alive when they should have been dead. Devotees who say that *À la recherche du temps perdu* reminds them of a cathedral should be asked which cathedral they mean. It reminds me of a sandcastle that the tide reached before its obsessed constructor could finish it; but he knew that would happen, or else why build it on a beach?

Q

❣ ❣ ❣

Edgar Quinet

EDGAR QUINET

Edgar Quinet (1803–1875) was born in the aftermath of the French Revolution and lived out his life in its long shadow. Nowadays he is hardly ever read for himself, and only rarely cited, and then usually for a single remark. In his lifetime, however, he was a public intellectual of the type we know today, his opinions argued over by everyone who had an opinion. An admirer of religion who drew the line at the Jesuits, he gave lectures on the latter subject that caused so much controversy they were suppressed by government order. In the next revolution, in 1848, he was on the barricades, and voted with the far left in the National Assembly. Exiled to Brussels after the coup d'état, he settled in Switzerland in 1857, not returning to Paris until the fall of Napoleon III. During the siege of Paris in 1870 he was conspicuous as a patriot. Before he died in bed, five years after the Commune, he had written a shelf of books about the philosophy of history. Apart possibly from his autobiographical fragment *Histoire de mes idées*, published in 1855, most of his books now excite no-one. But a single line, the one quoted below, made it all the way to the 1990s, because it had presaged an idea whose time had come.

But this success, where is it?
— Edgar Quinet, quoted by Jean-
François Revel in *Fin du siècle des
ombres*, p. 246

QUINET'S CELEBRATED single line came from a less celebrated
single paragraph, but the paragraph is worth quoting in full,
because it evokes a specific context that has refused to go away. He
wasn't just giving us a handy witticism to trot out every time somebody
made a mess and called it a triumph. He was talking specifically about
the connection, in the absolutist mentality, between claims and crimes.

> The persistent illusion of the terrorists is to invoke a success in
> order to justify themselves before posterity. In effect, only the
> success can absolve them. But this success, where is it? The ter-
> rorists devoured by the scaffolds that they themselves erected, the
> Republic not only lost but rendered execrable, the political
> counter-Revolution victorious, despotism in place of the liberty
> for which a whole nation swore to die: is that success? How long
> will you go on repeating this strange nonsense, that all the scaf-
> folds were necessary to save the Revolution, which was not saved?

But we need the paragraph only to remind us of the context. With that
given, the line stands alone, ready to be imported into any argument
about the event that did most to shape modern poltical history.
Quinet's unsettling sound bite about the French Revolution was
echoed by Jean-François Revel and François Furet, both of them careful to give Quinet the credit. "Far enough from the revolution to feel
only fleetingly the passions that troubled the view of those who made
it," said Tocqueville in *L'Ancien Régime et la révolution*, "we are yet still
close enough to be able to enter into and comprehend the spirit that
brought it about. Soon one will have difficulty doing so: because the
great revolutions that succeed make the causes that produced them disappear, thus becoming incomprehensible through their very success."
But the question "Where is the success?" was already being heard
under the Second Empire, from a few awkwardly sceptical voices of

which Quinet's was one. There had always been aristocrats to ask it, but Quinet was an intellectual. Had the French Revolution been worth the agony?

"Where is the success?" is another version of Orwell's answer to the contention, vis-à-vis the Soviet Union, that you can't make an omelette without breaking eggs. Orwell asked: "Where's the omelette?" Nobody sane seriously doubts that in the case of eighteenth-century France, democracy had to come: but was the Revolution the best way, and didn't it help to ensure that the democracy was incomplete? The question has always turned on whether the Jacobinist terror was inevitable. (The most gargantuan expression of Jacobinist terror, the massacre in the Vendée, did not become a question until late in the twentieth century: the bones were a long time coming to light. Nowadays, mass graves can be seen by satellites.) The same question divided the *gauchiste* left and the independent left in modern France, and still does divide them everywhere in the world. If you can't have a revolution without Jacobinism, then it becomes a matter of how to have reform without revolution. Anyone who "accepts the necessity of Jacobinism" wants to try his hand at it. When François Furet hinted at this conclusion in his truly revolutionary book on the French Revolution, he found himself immediately tagged by the left as a diehard spokesman of the reactionary right. It was assumed that if he was against the Terror, he was against the people. His contention that the Terror had been against the people was not accepted. More than a hundred years had passed since Quinet had contended the same thing, and the idea was still considered too paradoxical to be entertained. One can safely conclude that the impressive combined death toll of revolutions in the last century will go on being considered as justifiable well into the next.

R

✧ ✧ ✧

Marcel Reich-Ranicki

Jean-François Revel

Richard Rhodes

Rainer Maria Rilke

Virginio Rognoni

MARCEL REICH-RANICKI

❧ ❧ ❧

Marcel Reich-Ranicki (b. 1920), by far the most famous critic in Germany between World War II and the millennium, continues, into the twenty-first century, to exercise, over the German literary scene, a dominance which some writers prefer to regard as a reign of terror. Actually there can be no real argument about the fairness of his judgements—a fact which, of course, makes his disapproval feel even worse for those found wanting. He writes so well that his opinions are quoted verbatim. Victims of a put-down are thus faced with the prospect of becoming a national joke. Most of those writers whose later books were savaged by him had their early books praised by him: those are the writers who become most resentful of all against him. Well equipped to look after himself, he is hard to lay a glove on. Watching magisterial figures such as Günter Grass vainly trying to get their own back on Reich-Ranicki is one of the entertainments of modern Germany. Even those wounded by him would have to admit, under scopolamine, that he can be very funny when on the attack. Hence their intense enjoyment of the moment when history caught him out. Deported from Berlin to the Warsaw ghetto in 1938, Reich-Ranicki survived the Holocaust but stayed on in Communist Poland after the war, and first pursued literary criticism under East German auspices. When he finally defected to the West he forgot to tell anyone that he had been a registered informer under the regime he left behind. Almost everybody was, but he made a mistake in letting someone else say it first. The scandal whipped up on this point did something to offset his impeccable wartime track record as a Jew on the run from the Nazis. But despite the extra animus aroused by what was taken to be his lack of contrition when discomfited, common sense eventually prevailed and his story as a survivor of Nazi horror returned to the centre of attention, especially after he published, at the turn of the millennium, his autobiography *Mein Leben*, which became a best-seller. There was an English translation, called *The Author of Himself:* but understandably it made little impact, his name being so little known outside Germany. Within Germany, he is as well-known as any chancellor, and more likely to last in office. Few critics in any country have ever so outstripped the poets and novelists in being literature's living representative, but there is no mystery about the reason. Vastly and yet vividly learned, his judgement alive in every nuance, he writes with a wonderfully seductive clarity which will be especially appreciated by the beginner in German, who could learn the language from this one writer, just from the way he writes about other writers. His favourite form, the short essay, makes for an easily digestible bite-sized chunk. Collections of these short pieces fill a shelf, and there couldn't be a better way into German literary culture, from the poetry to the politics and vice versa. He writes even better in praise than in dispraise, but, as usually happens, the dispraise is more fun. Reich-Ranicki, well aware of that fact, has often pointed out that a literary culture deprived of rigorous criticism would soon die of niceness. He is obviously correct, but that doesn't stop other writers hoping that he will be nice to them, and from protesting loudly when he isn't.

> We shouldn't call a critic a murderer just because it is his
> duty to sign death certificates.
> —MARCEL REICH-RANICKI, *DIE ANWALTE
> DER LITERATUR*, P. 88

A T THE VERY END of the twentieth century, Germany caught a lucky break. The best-seller lists were dominated for an entire year by *Mein Leben*, the autobiography of Marcel Reich-Ranicki. Germany's toughest literary critic had written a life story to entrance the nation, but the lucky break didn't come just from the remarkable fact that a man of letters with an unchallenged title to a marble plinth was encamped on top of the best-seller list as well. It came also from the fact that he was a Jew. A large part of his story was about the quirk of chance by which he had survived the Nazi era. It became part of Germany's story, however, and against all the odds, that the most dreadful century of its history was rounded out by an act of redemption. New generations were rushing the bookshops to find out about the crimes that the older generations had committed. Anti-Semitism had been officially over since 1945. Now, in 2000, it was culturally over as well. It might still be said to taint the culture, or even to permeate it: but not to dominate it. A Jew was in the driving seat. So that, at last, was the end of that.

Reich-Ranicki himself was unlikely to burst into tears of joy at these signs of atonement. One of the factors that made his best-selling triumph so satisfactory to the onlooker was that here was no figure of affection being handed a lifetime achievement award. Throughout his career as a critic—which, if you count in his first journalism written in Poland and East Germany, covers the entire post-war period—he has been notoriously unbiddable. A characteristic collection of pieces was published in 1984 as *Laute Verisse*, which pretty well means "Naked Hatchet-Jobs." In actuality he has a wide range of literary sympathy and is one of the rare critics in any language who can be as enjoyable in approbation as in the opposite. He has always had a way of recommending a book that sends you flying to find it: try *not* to read Theodor Fontane's nineteenth-century classic novel *Effi Briest* after Reich-Ranicki has got through praising it. But there can be no denying that he is a tough customer, and some of the living writers on whom he has passed negative judgement have made their wounded feelings known. There have been pitiable whimpers and loud squeals from the injured, and when MR-R (just as the *Kaiserliche und Königliche* Austro-Hungarian Empire used to be called *k.u.k* in print because it had to be mentioned so often, Reich-Ranicki is customarily referred to by his monogram) was caught up with by his pre-Western past, there were plenty of literary onlookers who found it hard not to enjoy his discomfort. The facts said that he had never done much for the Communist government of East Germany except to go through the motions of informing on people who had no secrets to keep, but for once MR-R was on the back foot, and fellow scribes who had been decked by him were glad to see it, especially if they lacked his gift of being vitriolic. One of his abiding flaws is to suppose that writers offended in their dignity have the expressive power to answer him if they wish. Commendably eager to avoid praising himself, he is slow to realize that his easy habit of buttonholing an audience through a newspaper is more than just a trick, it's a talent.

But the gift for being vitriolic counts for nothing unless it is contained within the larger gift of being appreciative. Nobody minds being knocked by the kind of critic who does nothing but knock. What hurts is being knocked by the critic whose praise you would like to have, and every living writer in the German-speaking countries would like to have MR-R's endorsement. The same would probably go for the dead, if their opinion could be consulted. MR-R is a critic who has always written as well as any writer, so even his most bitter enemies are aware from the starting gun that his own literary status is already settled, although he has never claimed such a thing for himself. He has always held to the principle (which was also favoured by Stefan Zweig) that great artists are disqualified from being objective critics, because they are always thinking of how *they* would have done it. Following Friedrich Schlegel, MR-R said it of the greatest German writer, Goethe. To say of the author of *Faust* that he was too much of a poet to know much about the arts was pretty bold, when you consider how much Goethe knew about everything, but it was characteristic of MR-R to take on the biggest example and make his argument stick. What he really meant was that Goethe's critical judgements were all self-serving, and that the fact should be remembered when you are under the intoxicating impression that Goethe, to make a single point, is invoking the whole aesthetic world. MR-R has always held that the business of judging a book is strictly ad hoc: he professes not to like the criticism that sets itself up as "an alternative airfield" and uses the subject as a pretext to stage an airlift of everything the critic wants to bring in to prove himself powerful. For MR-R to take this line was an act of self-denial, because he himself was very well equipped to play the *uomo universale*. Just because he has an incurable knack of making himself sound arrogant shouldn't deafen us to the truth of his humility. Advancing the principle that the great artist can't criticize with a pure heart, he has been ready to live by the unspoken corollary, that no objective critic can be a great artist. He has been ready to live by it, but he could never make it stick. He writes too well. No wonder he is feared.

Marcel Reich-Ranicki writes so well that he can point a critical judgement and make poetry of it, so that you remember the prose aperçu like a balanced line of verse. In his book *Nachprüfung* he calls Joseph Roth a "*Vagabond mit Kavaliersmanieren*" (p. 210). A vagabond with the manners of a cavalier: the perfect way to remember Roth, of whom we can be sure that when he was drinking himself to death in Paris in the late 1930s, he made no disturbance. Here is something more about Joseph Roth from the same source, and this is even better, because it captures what made the texture of Roth's writing so enchanting: "He always made it easy for his readers and often made it hard for his interpreters." But in the German the antithesis is less ponderously arranged: "*Er hat es seinen Lesern immer leicht und seinen Interpreten oft schwer gemacht.*" MR-R, as you can see, does the same: his German is so plainly carpentered that a beginner feels at home in it, and so neatly joined syntactically that it is hard to translate without pulling it to pieces. To round out the subject of MR-R's admiration for Roth, it should be said that MR-R also possesses the creative critic's essential gift of being able to quote from any source but always to the purpose. The man of letters Karl Heinz Bohrer said that Roth was a moralist out of stylistic purity, and a stylist out of moral sensitivity. Not even MR-R can improve on that, so he quotes it: just what a good critic should do, but it takes humility to do it—the kind of humility that needs an air of arrogance to protect its Delphic mission.

MR-R has never been just a stylist judging style, although there are worse things to be than someone who can do that. He can get to the heart of a writer and stay there, sometimes for decades. In the heart of Thomas Mann he set up shop. His book on the Mann family is the first thing to read on the subject (although first you should read the subject, which takes a good chunk of a lifetime) but if he had never talked about any of them except Thomas Mann he would still have done a lot to get the titan in context—and from the inside, which is the hard part. "*Er hat fast nichts erlebt und fast alles beschrieben.*" He experienced almost nothing and described almost everything: it was too true to be cruel. MR-R takes that truth as an invitation to extend his enquiries, not to shut them down. He has never stopped being interested in, or being interesting about, Thomas Mann; but always on the understanding that Thomas Mann devoted his life and art to needing no such assistance. So why is a critic necessary? Well, there are all those other critics who aren't, and they will hardly shut up unless contested: someone has to speak plain sense. There was a lot Thomas Mann could do, but he couldn't always do that. In the style of a great creative writer, too many clarities collide and make rainbows: sorting out the spectral maelstrom is a long job.

There have been other great names that MR-R has felt no compulsion to cling on to. He has always been a great one for echoing Tallulah Bankhead's vocal judgement during a self-consciously advanced production of a play by Maeterlinck: "There's less in this than meets the eye." Admirers of Walter Benjamin were disconcerted to find that MR-R thought him short of the very thing he was supposed to have in abundant stock: profundity. MR-R thought Benjamin the critic made a mistake in trying to think like a writer. MR-R skewered Benjamin's character on the basis of Benjamin's snobbish remarks about Walter Mehring's social background. (Mehring was a catchpenny writer of lyrics and sketches under the Weimar Republic, and in exile he was a bit of a liability, but he was also a genuine lover of books, as his lament for his lost library, *Die verlorene Bibliotek*, subsequently revealed.) When you consider that Benjamin's prestige as a pundit continues to be almost as high within Germany as outside it, you begin to grasp just how brave MR-R can be, or at any rate how cocky he can sound. On his ZDF television talk show *Das literarische Quartett* he regularly advances the outrageous opinion that no contemporary novel longer than 500 pages can possibly be worth reading. (A book of transcripts from the show, collected under the snappy title ". . . *und alle Fragen offen,*" comes in at 768 pages, but is very much worth reading.) Though his fellow panellists and most of the television audience secretly agree with him, they all delight in ascribing such opinions to his choleric impatience, and indeed he always looks as if he is about to bite the book he is holding in half, even if he says he likes it. But the short shrift he customarily extends to the profundities of *Kunstwissenschaft* ought not to be ascribed to the supposed brevity of his attention span. He has taken the time to understand what the higher criticism is on about. He just doesn't agree with it.

MR-R wants the critic's job kept down to earth. Really he wants the writer's job kept down there too. In a culture where the sublime has always seductively beckoned, his has been a useful corrective emphasis: a shift of direction towards talking turkey and away from *Mumpitz*, that useful German word for exalted twaddle. There is a danger of know-nothing savagery, but he offsets that by knowing everything. Politically clued up, he has always been able to approach contemporary German writers through what tends to be their blind spot, which is their attitude to liberal democracy. In a cockfight whose flying feathers have not yet settled, MR-R leapt on Günter Grass for flirting with the notion that at least the old DDR had had a system of belief. (Graham Greene used to peddle the same line about the West's deficiency in faith, but apart from Dwight Macdonald there was no Reich-Ranicki to tear into him.) Contrary to the received opinion among MR-R's more embittered opponents in Germany, he has always been hospitable enough to any writer who has found the capitalist West deficient in human values. He just punishes any lingering suggestion that the totalitarian East might have had a surplus of them. His credentials were impeccable: the East was where he came from. The credentials looked less impeccable when it turned out that part of the price he paid for staying in the East at the end of the war was that he had to turn stoolie, but his personal history—though he made a mistake in not admitting it before it was revealed—couldn't invalidate the attacks he launched on writers in the East after he himself had made it to the West. Regretfully but firmly, he dismantled the claims to seriousness of those East German writers who did not, as he did, take it on the lam, but who stayed on, compromised with the State, and flourished. He argued, surely correctly, that the compromise not only turned their opinions to apologetics, it turned their literature to propaganda. But the unyielding strictness with which he said so has understandably been held against him, and raises the question of whether a critic should ever throw a stone without remembering his house is made of glass.

When we look at the quoted statement carefully, however, we see that MR-R is claiming no such right. The death certificate is signed by a doctor. It is the death *sentence* that is signed by a judge. The judgement MR-R is talking about is the diagnostic one about whether the work presented to him is alive or dead, not about whether it should live or die. As long as this is borne in mind, it seems to me that the irascible arch-critic is on strong ground. He is often called *Henker*, hangman, but it's a nickname. At most he is a grave-digger, and what would we do without those? We have a right, though, to ask grave-diggers for a modicum of tact. Hamlet met one with the saving grace of humour. MR-R's humour is real and often hilarious, but he would do better to make his fellow-feeling more obvious more often. In old age, heaped with honours and uncontested in his position, he continues to write as if he had not yet made it. One of the most piquant complaints in his autobiography is how he was not made to feel at home in the German literary world: it is a complaint that goes all the way back to Jakob Wassermann, whose case is cited in MR-R's indispensable pocket book *Der doppelte Boden* (The False Bottom). Under the Weimar Republic, Wassermann was nationally famous but felt he did not belong. MR-R, nationally famous in a democractic Germany half a century after the Holocaust, still feels the same. If it is the condition of the Jew in Germany, then the condition is historically incurable. (There is a lot to prove that the German intellectual world has done everything in its power to make amends.) But it might be just personal. Not many artists feel secure in their posts, and Marcel Reich-Ranicki is an artist if anybody is: an artist of criticism if you like, but for anyone who can write a sentence the way he can, the option to rule himself out is not open. As MR-R has always been the first to insist, a critic is not a scientist, because there is no Golden Yardstick: no *Metermass*. That leaves the critic as either artist or factotum. MR-R claims the lower status, but the way he writes condemns him to the higher. I came to German late, and it has sometimes been a hard tussle with my thick wits: but knowing what I know now, if I had never learned it to read anyone else, I would have learned it just to read him.

JEAN-FRANÇOIS REVEL

❦ ❦ ❦

Jean-François Revel (1924–2006) was the man who defined the Communist world as the first society in history condemned to live behind walls in order to stop people getting out. The best way of defining his style as a writer is to say that there is something as good as that in every paragraph. No political commentator anywhere is so consistently entertaining on such a high level. Revel's youthful beginnings were as a courier in the Resistance. After trading in his thorough academic preparation as a philosopher for a career as a working journalist, he set out on a long attempt to bring French political journalism back towards philosophy, by developing, over the course of twenty-five or more books, a dense consistency of liberal views always underpinned by both a deep background in historical reading and a close observation of daily events. The close observation fed a good memory, which made him the bugbear of his *gauchiste* opposite numbers, because he remembered things they preferred to forget: to the end, he retained an impressive knack for tracing the latest progressive fad back to its roots in the orthodoxy before last.

In succession to Raymond Aron, and on a par with the eloquent ex-Communist François Furet, Revel was part of

France's comeback from the depths of glamorous but perilously self-deceiving radical chic. Several of his books, most
notably *How Democracies Perish*, earned international fame. It
could be said that in the United States at least one of his opinions made him too famous: his notion that democracy might
have to give up some of its liberties in order to protect itself
was, when translated into English, far too popular on the
American neo-conservative right, as Hendrick Herzberg
pointed out at the time. But Revel is at his most rewarding
when read in his own language, which he writes in a style that
the beginner will find gratifyingly clear in its structure, memorable for its vivid imagery, and consistently funny. Revel is
brilliant in attack, but always remembers to dismantle the
man's position and not the man. He has a lively appreciation of
how people can get stuck with a view because it has become
their identity. In 1970 his book *Without Marx or Jesus* was an
early guess that America would not be universally admired for
making a totalitarian hegemony impossible. After the collapse
of the Soviet Union, Revel was prescient about how nostalgia
for a collectivist social solution would continue to infect the
left. By extension, he foresaw the crisis that would be brought
to liberal democracy by an ideology of multiculturalism,
because it would automatically undermine liberal values at
home without even needing to pay allegiance abroad. Perhaps
Revel's single best book about the world picture is *L'Obsession
anti-américaine* (2002, translated as *Anti-Americanism*), which
ranges far more widely than its title suggests, persuasively tracing the development of globalized terror from its origins in the
threat, not that the Palestinians might be denied their own
state, but that they might gain it in a way that accepted the
existence of the state of Israel. The best book about him is by
him: his 1997 autobiography *Le Voleur dans la maison vide* (The
Thief in the Empty House). It is impossible to imagine any of
his dogmatist opposite numbers writing anything so human,
self-deprecating and charmingly troubled. No wonder they
loathe him. Outwritten, outpointed and outraged, French
gauchiste commentators have always consigned Revel to the far

right, but they find it hard to make the classification stick. When it comes to the welfare of the common people, he was all too clearly more to the left than they are, never having succumbed to the intellectual opportunism that cherishes a non-existent class struggle as the motor of social progress.

During the preparation of this book for the press, Jean-François Revel, full of years and honours, died at the age of eighty-two. Though the pseudo-left throughout the world went on calling him a right-winger to the very end, it was always apparent, to anyone with an ear for his sardonic music, that he was a popular champion in the very best sense of the term. He began on the left, and, in the only sense that really matters, on the left was where he finished: vigilant against all powers that hold the common people in contempt, including the power that claims they can be coerced into being free.

There are no genres, there are only talents.
—JEAN-FRANÇOIS REVEL, *LE VOLEUR DANS LA MAISON VIDE*, P. 311

R EVEL, WHEN HE wrote this in the late 1990s, was defending the status of journalism against lofty minds who presumed to despise its immediacy. In France, the philosophers, the sociologists and the savants in general had always enjoyed an automatic superiority to journalists, because for the savants the unit of thought was the book, whereas for the journalists the unit of thought was only the article. Books outweighed articles. Revel had good personal reasons to question this hierarchy. The philosophers in particular, with Sartre always in the ascendant, had an impressive record of getting the post-war world wrong, whereas Revel and some of his fellow journalists had been getting it right. Revel was too modest, however, to quote from his own works in order to demonstrate that the mainspring of this talent was a capacity for compression that left the philosophers sounding vapid. They weren't just peddling falsehoods, they were pumping the life out of the language while they did so. Revel pumped the life in. He could do so from an historical perspective, which always helps. On the matter of Malraux's inflated prestige as an omniscient pontifex of the visual arts, for example, Revel could go all the way back to Hegel for evidence that real knowledge about art sounded less like a tinkling cymbal. Hegel, said Revel, actually looked hard at paintings and judged before he theorized. Revel found the French art-history tradition critically short of of Jewish scholars. Elie Faure, august author of that platitudinous tome *L'Esprit des formes*, had emerged not from a proper scholarly tradition but from a vacuum, and Malraux represented the same vacuum with better publicity. Revel scorned that kind of highfalutin cultural globetrotting for its second-hand world-historical verbiage (*"le verbiage historico-mondial de deuxième main"*—the sandbag swings more elegantly in the original). He called it vulgarization in an ampule. But the phrase that counted was *déclamatoire prétentions métaphysiques*. It was the claim to philosophical status that riled him.

Well schooled in philosophy himself, Revel thought the philosophy that mattered most had always begun from the level of well-written journalism, which was in touch with the world and had a professional imperative to keep the contact while making specific propositions. He put a premium on the thinking that did not give itself a licence to get above writing. The danger of that position is to overvalue simplicity: its proponent had better be able to suggest everything else while he zeroes in on a neat precept. Revel could, and can: we need the two tenses because he gets better as he gets older. His prose, right down to the epithet, demands to be unpacked, and it is a long time before we see the bottom of the suitcase. He is the master of the nonmoronic oxymoron. In any language, practitioners of broadsheet commentary love the oxymoron as a device, because it hints at a pipeline to profundity. But an oxymoron from Revel always pays its way. He was the first to come up with a two-word formulation for the miraculous ability of pundits to deduce that a past event had been inevitable: "retrospective clairvoyance." In an everyday piece for a newspaper, he called terrorism "systematized delirium." Most authors of a treatise on the subject would be very glad to think of an expression as rich with implication as that.

Even in straight expository prose—no rhetorical devices, no tricks— he has the gift of putting a large argument into a small space, usually when he is summarizing what he has just been expounding. In a sear-

ing article on the deliberate dumbing-down of the French education
system, he encapsulates the possible consequences: "a non-selective
diploma is a passport to unemployment." (Note the resonance of the
buried metaphor: a passport implies a foreign land, which is what
unemployment is.) In Britain, Kingsley Amis got into the language
with a phrase about the same theme: *More will mean worse*. (He actually
wrote it in italics, which helped the op-ed journalists to home in on it
without the tax to their poor brains of reading it in context.) But the
strength of Amis's point depended on his treating education specifically, as an absolute; and the strength was also a weakness, because he
had no inclination to extend his view to a social tendency. Revel's
phrase leaves the way open for an argument about whether a proposed
cure for social ills might not exacerbate them. Always characterized by
the *bien pensant* left as a diehard right-winger, Revel was fruitfully
obliged to go on pointing out that he was in fact a liberal democrat who
was genuinely concerned that doctrinaire *gauchiste* measures would
leave the underprivileged less privileged than ever. Being misrepresented can be a stimulus, and in France Revel could depend on being
misrepresented from all directions. He was energized by a vivid knowledge of what the states in the East had been like when their official
thinkers had been in a position to translate their vilification of a dissident into practical action.

As things are now, it is getting hard to imagine just how reluctant
the French intelligentsia was to give up on its righteous commitment
to the international anti-capitalist dream. "A school of thought that
knows itself to be in decline," said Revel in *La Connaissance inutile*,
"fights all the more furiously to conserve its identity." As it became
clear that the West, in order to bring communism to ruin, didn't have
to do anything except exist, the French left became more vindictive,
and not less, against liberal democrat commentators of Revel's stamp.
The left actually intensified, instead of diminishing, its insistence that
the Communist world was beseiged by hostile forces. Revel got his
answer into a nutshell: "The Communist world is indeed a fortress
besieged, but from within." His critics might conceivably have one day
forgiven him for thinking like that. But they have never forgiven him
for writing like that. They would prefer to call his way of putting
things irresponsible: mere journalism. At the end of 2001, Bernard-

Henri Lévy published his portentously titled *Réflexions sur la guerre, le mal et la fin de l'histoire*. A commentator with philosophical credentials, Lévy is so madly fashionable that his new book appeared in the vitrines of the fashion boutiques along the Boulevard St. Germain. More than three decades having elapsed since the events of May 1968, Lévy has had the time, and the good sense, to work his way to an acceptance of liberal democracy. But from the way he states the position he now holds you wouldn't know that it had been held from the beginning by men like Revel, who never gets a mention.

Later in the same passage from *Le Voleur dans la maison vide*, Revel goes on to confess that whenever he wrote an article he was always thinking of how it would fit into a book. This confession might seem contradictory: if talent matters and genres don't, why should a journalist publish books at all? But the question answers itself. The attraction of journalism is that one runs no lasting risks. But that's just what encourages the sloven. I prefer to be encouraged by a man like Revel, who has always written even the most fleeting piece as if he might need to defend it on the day of judgement—and for any craftsman proud of his work, of course, the day of judgement is always today. *Ce jour*: journalism. In French the connection is obvious. In English, we tend to forget that journalism means today, and we are seldom encouraged to remember that history is made of nothing else except one today after another.

> Ideology functions as a machine to destroy information,
> even at the price of making assertions in clear
> contradiction of the evidence.
> —JEAN-FRANÇOIS REVEL,
> LA CONNAISSANCE INUTILE, P. 153

This is an example of Revel restraining himself, rather than letting fly. The propensity of left ideologists to argue from a sense of history while lacking a sense of fact has always got his goat, but he has managed to stay coherent. Sometimes one wishes that he would sideline the suave sarcasm and give way to a bellow of rage. On the same page of the same book, Revel quotes Regis Debray's ringing assurance, dating from 1979, that "the word Gulag is *imposed* by imperialism." (The italics are there in the original French, where they have even more the effect of a proud smile from a man in tights who has just farted a blue flame.) Debray's confident pronouncement would have been bizarre enough in 1959, when even Beauvoir must have been having doubts, but for 1979 it was a striking example of the determination of the French far left to call their retreat an advance. Revel was the first to spot that those ideologists who did give up parts of their position became very angry if it was suggested that they had done so in response to criticism. "Those who hold the monopoly of error reserve to themselves the monopoly of rectification."

Revel had always been good at cutting a section through the mechanism of the totalitarian mind so that you could see the cogs turning. Raymond Aron had begun the job in his *L'Opium des intellectuels*, where he pointed out the essential difference between a sense of history and an ideology. A sense of history reveals variety, and an ideology conceals it. Revel made an advance on Aron by picking up on the bullying aspect, the set of coercive mental habits that made an ideologist a totalitarian even in his way of thought. On a later page of *La Connaissance inutile*–and also, with the appropriate scholarly back-up, in *Pourquoi des philosophes*—he pinpoints Heidegger as a case of *totalitarisme dans le démarche discursive*, tirelessly and needlessly accumulating affirmatives: "terrorist tautology" in the style of Hitler and Stalin. In *Le Voleur dans la maison vide*, Revel drew sad conclusions about the ideologists in general: "The intellectuals have the opportunism of the exterminator" (p. 231). After the verbal battle of a lifetime, he had come to accept that the reason for the readiness of the intellectuals to connive at mass extermination was that their language was itself a totalitarian instrument. Hence the hollowness of what he called the eternal dream of the *bien pensant* left: *un totalitarisme végétarien* (p. 557). The reluctance of ex-ideologists like Bernard-Henri Lévy to acknowledge their debt to Revel is quite understandable. He isn't telling them that they were bad writers because they thought that way. He is telling them that they thought that way because they were bad writers.

RICHARD RHODES

An American journalist with showbiz status, Richard Rhodes
has a diva-like shyness about revealing his precise age, but the
records show that he graduated from Yale in 1959, which
probably means that he was born somewhere around 1938.
Like many of us who were children during World War II and
found out while we were growing up that the world we inherited had been shaped by technology to an unprecedented
degree, Rhodes pursued a fascination with machines and systems. Most of the eighteen books published under his name
are about technical matters at a high level of complexity, which
he can talk about with professional expertise. At various times
he has been a visiting scholar at both Harvard and MIT. On
subjects other than science and technology he can fall prey to
catch-all sociological theories—for the machine buff, there is
always the temptation to think that society is a machine too—
but on purely technical matters he has a rare knack for putting
difficult topics in clear, and even self-effacing, prose. He is also
a novelist. With his work in that area I won't pretend to be
familiar, but at least two of his non-fiction works are compulsory reading, and one of those is a book that every student of
liberal democracy should know in detail. *The Making of the*

Atomic Bomb (1986) depends on a thoroughness of research that would scarcely have been possible without the author's being supported for five years by the Ford Foundation and the Alfred P. Sloan Foundation. (The availability of aid on such a scale is probably the chief reason that the United States produces so many more of this type of writer than say, Britain: it isn't just their unabashed can-do attitude, it's the depth of their back-up.) Rhodes deserves personal credit, however, for having done an unusually judicious job in tying the story together.

In a still rarer feat, he has managed to dramatize a technical story without fudging the science. The spectacular nature of some of the human material on display might have helped in this dramatization. The minds assembled at Los Alamos were often histrionic characters even when they shrank from human contact, and the way Robert Oppenheimer marshalled their talented and sometimes temperamental efforts was a theatrical event. But finally the object they were all after depended on physics and engineering, and Rhodes's real triumph is to make a drama out of those things too. The narrative catches the reader up in an excitement that is unlikely to suit his proclivities, unless he believes in advance that it was necessary not only to build the bomb, but to drop it on a city.

On the latter issue, Rhodes lays out the case without fudging the arguments on either side. Those who think there is only one side, against the bomb's use, will discover that Oppenheimer was never among their number. Even though the war against Germany was over, he thought there was a case for using the bomb to bring about a quick and certain end to the war against Japan, and he presented the case with logic hard to fault. Oppenhimer's sensitivities about the nuclear weapons he had been instrumental in bringing into existence were concentrated not against the uranium bomb but against its successor, the hydrogen bomb. Rhodes, again with the aid of a couple of large foundations, tells the story of the hydrogen bomb too, in *Dark Sun: The Making of the Hydrogen Bomb* (1995). The second book is as uncompromisingly thorough as the first but necessarily less fascinating, because the moral problem remained notional. The hydrogen bomb was too destructive to be used in war, and the fact was plain to any given government, which would rein in its own military leaders if they thought it could. As it happened, it was in the United States, during the Cuban missile crisis, that the military got closest to starting a global thermonuclear war on its own account, when the air force, and especially its Strategic Air Command, tried to provoke the Soviet Union into action, against John F. Kennedy's clear orders as commander in chief. The Constitution held, but only just. Since the end of the world came that close, it is easy to argue that the development of nuclear weapons was evil in itself: even those ready to contemplate that the nuclear strike against Japan might have been an acceptable price for shortening the war are usually less ready to concede that the threat of a fried planet might have been the price of freedom. But liberals should face two uncomfortable possibilities; first, that it was a necessary evil; second, that nothing else, in the Cold War years, could have stopped the two major powers from fighting. The left is always at its weakest when it argues for an alternative past, administered by better men. They can only mean men like them. (This assumption of personal superiority is where the perennial left comes closest to the classic right.) But the past was administered by men as clever as they were at the very least. The chief virtue of Rhodes's book about Los Alamos it to give you the feeling of how a group of the cleverest men on Earth combined their best efforts in the belief that building a bomb to kill a hundred thousand people at a time was the only thing to do. There can be moral discussions of the modern world that don't take that fact in, but they won't be serious.

Enrico Fermi and Edward Teller were not, however, the first to conceive of using a nuclear chain reaction to initiate a thermonuclear reaction in hydrogen.
— RICHARD RHODES, *THE MAKING OF THE ATOMIC BOMB*, P. 375

IN HIS *The War Against Cliché*, Martin Amis hilariously demolishes—
nukes, to use one of his favourite verbs—a book about sex written by
this same Richard Rhodes. On the evidence of the quotations adduced
by his reviewer, Rhodes's sex treatise must indeed be a disaster. I can't
bring myself to read it, but partly because I would like to retain my
respect for the author of two of the best books I have ever read about
science and technology, *The Making of the Atomic Bomb* and *Dark Sun*.
Though it might not apply to sex, where some of the secrets are buried
deep, Rhodes has a nose for the enriching detail. The immediate consequence of reading the above quotation is to find out who *was* the first
to conceive of a thermonuclear reaction in hydrogen, and thus of the
device that we later came to know as the hydrogen bomb. Guess forever and you will never guess.

It was the Japanese physicist Tokutaro Hagiwara. He gave a lecture
on the subject in Kyoto in May 1941, seven months before the Pearl
Harbor attack. Hagiwara was also very early in the field on the subject
of uranium isotope separation, with particular emphasis on plutonium
(*Dark Sun*, p. 77). Later on, the plutonium option was to become the
biggest single Allied secret of the war, outranking even the secret of the
code-breaking operations. Though Rhodes doesn't say so—he doesn't
need to say so—Hagiwara's precocity raises interesting questions about
what Japanese physics might conceivably have achieved if the initial
strategic plan of Japan's armed forces had worked out and America had
been quickly brought to terms. We can tell ourselves that the strategic
plan would never have worked out. We can also tell ourselves that
Japan would never have been able to match its physics with a concerted
technological effort comparable in its vastness to the one with which
the Americans were able to back up the brain-work in Los Alamos: but
we can't tell ourselves the second thing with quite the same confidence
that we can tell ourselves the first. Post-war, after a defeat amounting
to total destruction, Japanese technology got itself together again well
enough. If there had been an early truce, leaving time to get organized,
there is no telling what might not have been accomplished, although
even the Japanese now commonly say that there would have been no
fully modern reform of their science and industry if it had not been for
the defeat and the occupation. Rhodes is probably right, however, to
stay off those paths. His best gift is to present the facts and let the

reader do the awed speculating. (The disqualification of justly forgotten techno best-sellers like Robert Jungk's *Brighter than a Thousand
Suns* is that their authors, short of information but long on excitable
prose, stifled the reader's reaction by trying to echo it in advance.)
Rhodes, aware that he is dealing with genuinely high drama, goes easy
on the theatrical effects. We learn that when Niels Bohr was in Cambridge he brushed up his English by reading *David Copperfield*. When
Fermi was building the first reactor in Chicago, the graphite slabs were
hefted into position by the college football team in mufti. (Captain
Future, block that kick!) At Bikini on March 1, 1954, the Castle Bravo
H-bomb shot was a fifteen-megaton runaway. The merit of Rhodes's
books is that he withholds moral judgement long enough to bring out
the creative atmosphere generated by brilliant people working
together on vast, novel projects. In *The Making of the Atomic Bomb* he
can even make you see how an ugly customer like General Leslie
Groves might be just the man to have around if you are trying to build
an atomic bomb that will work. The awkward implication is that if you
want to do without the company of General Groves, you must organize a world free of conflict. Such a world is hard to imagine, but perhaps Rhodes thought that establishing the principles of stress-free sex
was the way to start.

RAINER MARIA RILKE

❦ ❦ ❦

For those who look on the arts as a kind of celestial sports competition, Rainer Maria Rilke (1875–1926) is up there with Bertolt Brecht for the title of German Poet of the Twentieth Century. The standard view of the contending couple is that Brecht's poetic art was dedicated to social revolution, whereas Rilke's poetic art was dedicated to art. There is a lot to be said for that view as it applies to Rilke, because few writers who have died so young covered so much aesthetic ground. Born in Prague, he studied art history there and also in Munich and Berlin. The personalized melancholy of his early verse gave way to an overt quest for God after he made two trips to Russia, where he met Tolstoy and the Pasternak family. (Lou Andreas-Salomé, a recurring figure in his life as she was in the lives of many other famous men of his time, was along for the ride up the Volga.) In Paris he got himself appointed secretary to Rodin. An ideal aestheticism took over from mystic revelation in the poems of *Neue Gedichte* (1907). Some would say that his strongest and least self-consciously ethereal verse was to be found in that volume. Showing signs of believing that he had arrived at the apotheosis of art, he ascended to the empyrean in his *annus mirabilis* of 1922, when he wrote all of *The Sonnets* to *Orpheus* and all of *The Duino Elegies*: works in which the Poet is elected (some might say self-elected) as the only shaping force capable of dealing with natural energy. Rilke's verse is hard to translate but some of the middle-period verse comes across in parts. The prose is a better bet, especially the deliberately approachable *Letters to a Young Poet*. When he actually had so much to say that he wanted to be understood, Rilke turned out sentences that you could write a book about.

❧ ❧ ❧

Fame is finally only the sum total of all the
misunderstandings that can gather around a new name.
— RAINER MARIA RILKE,
GESAMMELTE WERKE, VOL. 5

THE MOST OFTEN quoted thing Rilke ever said in prose, this was his equivalent of Mae West's "Come up and see me some time." She never said it quite that way, just as Bogart never quite said "Play it again, Sam." But Rilke did say, pretty well exactly, this. He said it, of course, in German, where it sounded even more stately, because in German "fame" and "name" do not rhyme, so there is no cheap chiming of start and finish. Neat as it is in either language, however, here is a good example of a sentence begging to be misunderstood. The idea behind it is at least half right, although it would have no force unless it was partly wrong. To take an example: the actress Marion Davies remains famous only for being the mistress of William Randolph Hearst. The facts, however, say that she was an extremely talented comedienne, well capable of earning a high salary in her own right; and that she genuinely loved Hearst, who was in awe of her. It did him credit: though he could have had any woman who was available for money, he loved talent.

But the facts are hard to get at. Her films are not in circulation. The film that makes the myth is *Citizen Kane*, which, since the title character is based on Hearst, reinforces the idea that Marion Davies was a casualty, because Kane's mistress in the film is an insufficiently gifted singer forced to humiliate herself to gratify Kane's egotistical dreams for a young woman he loves like a toy. The cumulative power of a myth, and the difficulty of dispelling it, are both demonstrated by how generations of high-IQ film society attendees have prided themselves on their knowledge of *Citizen Kane*'s biographical subtext, down to and including the supposed fact that "Rosebud" was Hearst's pet name for Marion Davies's clitoris. In Rilke's sentence, *Inbegriff* could possibly be translated as "essence," but since the dictionary gives us the alternative "sum total" we might as well use it, because in myth-mongering the driftwood helps build the edifice. The *Inbegriff* of misunderstandings about Marion Davies would be very hard to shake even if a showreel of her comic moments on film were to be tacked on to the end title of *Citizen Kane*, however it was reproduced in whatever medium. Orson Welles did a terrible thing to William Randolph Hearst. To assault the tycoon's reputation was one thing, and no doubt Hearst deserved it. But to belittle the woman he loved was cowardly, and it is worth wondering whether the crime remained on Welles's conscience, and thus helped to explain some of his self-destructive behaviour in later years. Whatever the truth of that, there can be no doubt that Welles contributed mightily to the corroboration of Rilke's remark. The fame of Marion Davies survived her death, but it had little to do with the woman who had once been alive. It was a sum total of misunderstandings.

Fame can be polarized between two contrary distortions and leave its true human subject untouched in the middle. Brecht is a classic case. As the poet and playwright of the international left he was revered by the progressive intelligentsia across the world. After Stalinism at long last became questionable, the international left was only reinforced in its fashionable authority, and Brecht's reputation along with it: he was thought to represent what had been permanently valuable in the socialist world view. Apart from the operas, whose value was seldom challenged (only Lotte Lenya ever dared to say that Brecht would have been nothing without Kurt Weill), the plays were thought to be profound analyses of world capitalism in crisis. In my time as a student in Sydney in the late 1950s, *The Good Woman of Setzuan* was mounted with reverence and greeted with awe. The amateur actors concerned with the production, many of them my friends, had no idea that the body count of Mao's Great Leap Forward was still mounting even as they fretted over trying to remember their lifeless, hectoring lines about the difficulty of jolting Chinese peasants out of their selfish ways.

(It was from the producer of *The Good Woman* that I bought my set of the Brecht-Weill opera *Mahagonny*, on the understanding that if he had not been strapped for cash by the inescapable effects of world capitalism in crisis, nothing would have induced him to part with it.) Even as late as my undergraduate years in Cambridge, Brecht's unswervingly charmless *A Man Is a Man* was one of the Cambridge Theatre Group's gifts to the Edinburgh Fringe, the production having been given into the keeping of an earnest young theatrical vagabond on the grounds that he had once been with the Berliner Ensemble.

On subsequent investigation it turned out that he had been with the Berliner Ensemble only to the extent of sweeping the stage, but the mere connection was enough, such was the blinding effect of Brecht's renown. The Berliner Ensemble was a long time turning into a bad joke, and indeed the joke was never as bad as all that: when the ensemble's touring company of *The Threepenny Opera* visited London in the early sixties, Wolf Kaiser as Mackie Messer showed what a decade or so in the same role could do for an actor's polish. (He also showed, with his perfectly believable naturalistic impersonation of Mackie's charismatic *savoir vivre*, that Brecht's theories about the alienation effect were balderdash; but that's by the way.) In the long run, however, there was no reversing the erosion of Brecht's shamanic prestige as the personification of radical theatre. Friedrich Torberg's post-war criticisms of Brecht's plays could not be dismissed as right-wing propaganda, although Torberg's connections with publications partly financed by the Congress for Cultural Freedom were naturally used to blacken his name. (We have to imagine an intellectual climate in which it was thought that only a secret payment from the CIA could explain a sceptical reception for Brecht's views on the Western conspiracy against socialist benevolence.) It had been apparent since *The Resistible Rise of Arturo Ui* that Brecht had never had any intention of telling the truth about the central facts of politics in his own time. He knew what the truth was: nobody knew better, he just wasn't going to bring it in, even by implication. Above all, the main truth was left out. According to his dramatic works, Nazism, not just at the beginning but throughout its career, existed because capitalism willed it so, and communism was the soul of freedom. In the end, there was no considerable audience left anywhere, west or east, for such a fantastic interpretation, and Brecht's reputation as a seer melted away in good time to be replaced by a contrary reputation based on the repellent details of his real-life biography.

He emerged as an ice-cold, ruthless, self-serving egomaniac contemptuous of all decencies, and especially pitiless to the women who made the mistake of paying him allegiance. Even people who admired his work have given pen-portraits that turn the stomach. The psychologist Manès Sperber never lost respect for Brecht's dedication to his gift, but Sperber was a witness to Brecht's ruthless manipulation of actors and despised him for it. Marcel Reich-Ranicki's admiration for Brecht went far beyond Brecht's gifts as a poet: Reich-Ranicki really thought that Brecht was a force in the theatre. But Reich-Ranicki has given us an account of a face-to-face meeting from which Brecht emerges as such a titanic pain in the arse that you wonder why Reich-Ranicki didn't reverse his lifetime opinion on the spot. That he did not is a tribute to Brecht's aura. It might also, however—and here is the crucial point—have been an instance of accurate critical estimation. Somewhere in between the thoroughgoing con man Brecht was in real life, and the hollow prophet he was as a man of the didactic theatre, Brecht was a great poet. In the twentieth-century annals of German poetry, he shares pre-eminence with Rilke, who was no paragon of humanity either.

Rilke's fame, however, was based on the assumption that he embodied art for art's sake. Since the evidence for the assumption was overwhelming, his fame was impregnable. He had no other allegiance, and certainly no political one, to distract him from his pursuit of the exquisite. Everything in his life had to match up to the refinement of his wife, and if his wife didn't fit the picture, she had to go. His notepaper was as beautiful as his handwriting. He was as careful in his dress as Beau Brummell. The various settings in which he wrote poems were chosen from a catalogue of the great houses of Europe. Titled women who owned the houses found themselves in receipt of his finely judged letters, delicately suggesting that if hospitality should be extended to him when the wind was in the right direction, masterpieces would ensue. The famous Schloss Duino, where he wrote the elegies, was not the castle that its name implies, but an Italianate palazzo with suitably comfortable quarters in which elegies could be written in lieu of rent. Rilke's perfect taste accompanied him beyond death. Volumes of Rilke correspondence are still coming out from the publishing house Insel Verlag, all of them in the same prettily proportioned format. By now I have a five-foot shelf of books just by Rilke himself, let alone of books about him; and still there is no end in sight. I could never throw the stuff away. It looks too good.

And somewhere in the middle of it all is the relatively thin sheaf of poetry that justifies the bustle. Poets in English continue to line up for the inevitable failure of translating his short lyrics. The best translations I have seen are from Babette Deutsch but everyone falls short, even J. B. Leishmann, who devoted his life to translating Rilke poems both big and small. Though Rilke would be a bad reason to learn how to read his language, after you have done so he rewards you by proving, especially in such short lyrics as "*Das Karrussel*," that he really was a wonderful poet. But you can't chase up all the ancillary stuff without getting as precious as he was, and there is dangerous moment when, in the elegies, "the tear trees, the fields of flowering sadness" start sounding like fine shades of meaning, instead of forced exercises in sentimentality. Rilke had too much civilization, just as Brecht had too little: their matching deviations from normality make both of them toxic company. Take the two of them together and you barely end up with one man you would want to have a drink with. You also get a pretty fair idea of just how important it is to estimate a writer through his own language, and not through the language that gathers around him. Hannah Arendt has been much criticized for "Forbidden to Jove," her essay about Brecht collected in her book *Men in Dark Times*. (This could be the moment to print a health warning: while Arendt's journalism is nearly all valuable, her formal philosophy is nearly all unreadable.) John Willett, one of Brecht's principal devotees and translators, vilified Arendt for that essay. At first glance, there is indeed something absolutist in the way Arendt assures us that Brecht ruined himself as a poet by praising Stalin. It reminds us of her thesis about the desk-bound bureaucrats who drove the Holocaust: an explanatory idea that left too much unexplained.

But a second glance is advisable. Even as a poet, as a master of lyric forms in which he could say anything, Brecht was inhibited by all that he could not bring himself to say about real life in the East. If his poetry is a tree, there is a whole side of its trunk missing. But we would hardly care if it were not for the sky-filling majesty of what is left. For most of his readers in English-speaking countries, the way to his poetic achievement was not open until the great parallel text came out in 1987. His use of German had always been colloquial, compressed, innovative and ("*in der Asphaltstadt bin ich daheim*"—I am at home in the city of asphalt) street-smart: hard to get at for a foreigner. In other words, there were no other words: even Rilke had been easier to translate. Thanks to the devotion of his translators to social minutiae, the supremely sociable courtier's relentless preciosity of diction was something that a non-German reader could get a handle on, whereas Brecht's tap-room argot remained strictly a foreign language. Even a linguist like Michael Frayn benefited from the new crib. I know that because he must have read through it in the same week I did. Meeting at a first night—one of his, as I remember—we got to the subject within a minute. Frayn said Brecht's poetry had astonished him. I had to agree; and by then, perhaps rather piously, I had thought that nothing could astonish me about a man I had long since identified as the creepiest major talent of modern times. In the long view of history, Brecht's fame as a creep will prevail, as it ought to. An unblushing apologist for organized frightfulness against the common people whose welfare he claimed to prize above his own, he was really no nicer than Sir Oswald Mosley, and a lot more dangerous. Brecht's fame as a poet will depend on a wide appreciation of what he could do with language, and there lies the drawback: because the more you appreciate what he could do with language, the more you realize how clearly he could see, and so the more you are faced with how he left things out. You are faced, that is, with what he did *not* do with language.

Talent usually earns forgiveness, but there are good reasons that linguistic talent earns it least. Auden was right to pardon Kipling and Claudel (as his rhyme had it, he pardoned them "for writing well") and eventually Orwell would have pardoned Auden for so glibly sanctioning "the necessary murder": but nobody would have forgotten what anybody *said*. There is something about words that sticks. Painters are usually given the benefit of the doubt by writers: i.e., writers patronize painters. Picasso, for his backing of communism, is seldom given the same bad marks that we give to Brecht. Picasso was late to the game; he occasionally had the grace to be embarrassed by the outrages of

Soviet foreign policy vis-à-vis the satellite countries; and anyway, he was "only" a painter. His character is more likely to be judged by the way he treated his women than by the way he read the newspaper: judged and then excused. In writing, talent intensifies crimes. In painting it dissolves them. Picasso will never be famous as a painter who abused his women, any more than he will be famous for having given aid and comfort to a totalitarian regime. He will always be famous as a great, protean painter—the great painter of his time, with only Matisse as a rival.

In that respect, Rilke's statement needs to be amplified. Fame is not only the sum of the misunderstandings that can grow around a name, it also depends on the understandings that do not grow around it. Somehow Picasso's domestic behaviour and political allegiance have not adhered to his central reputation. We are probably not wrong to be thus lulled. When a noxious idea turns up in a painting, it is more likely to make us smile than retch. Like painters but even more so, musical performers are issued at birth with a get-out-of-jail-free card. In my first year in London I heard Walter Gieseking play at the Festival Hall. I was not much bothered by his connection with Nazi Germany. If I had known then just how much of a Nazi he had been, I might have walked out, but I would have missed some good Beethoven. At least Gieseking was a German. Alfred Cortot was a Frenchman, and therefore would have been something worse than a Nazi sympathizer even if he had just played the piano at Parisian soirées well peopled with grey and black uniforms—a Sacha Guitry of the keyboard. Actually he did more: he was an active collaborator, denouncer and thoroughgoing rat. But he is not famous for it and probably shouldn't be. After Rubinstein, two of the major players of Chopin are Rachmaninoff and Cortot. Rachmaninoff fled from totalitarianism and Cortot stayed to profit: but they both sound wonderful. At Covent Garden and the Festival Hall during my first years in London, you could hear German conductors who had been forced to flee and others who had chosen to stay: I heard, among others, Rudolf Kempe, Karl Böhm, Hans Knappertsbusch, Herbert von Karajan and Otto Klemperer. Everyone knew that Klemperer went into exile and that Karajan had a Nazi party number, but who knows now, of Kempe, Böhm and Knappertsbusch, which one stayed on in the Third Reich? (Trick question: they all did.) And who cares?

Well, of course we should care. The question is how. In the brains department, and therefore in the area of moral responsibility, conductors traditionally rate above performers. Hearing and watching Elisabeth Schwarzkopf sing Strauss's "Four Last Songs" with maximum purse-lipped projection of the umlauts, I had no trouble resisting the impulse to throw her a Hitler salute as a reminder of the sort of audience she had once wowed in Berlin. But if Furtwängler had been conducting the band it might have been a different matter. Ronald Harwood wrote an excellent play about Furtwängler (*The Dividing Line*) raising all the moral issues, and there were plenty to raise. The only point Harwood missed was Hitler's 1944 offer to build Furtwängler a personal mini-bunker as a reward for his staying on in Berlin to conduct morale-building concerts. Furtwängler turned down the offer, generously suggesting that the bunker might be built for a few workers instead. The prodigiously gifted old ass seems genuinely to have done his best to keep civilized values alive. He just never realized that his services to an ideal world of art had been co-opted in advance by a force dedicated to its ruin. He was not alone in the anomaly. There were Aryan conductors who saved Jewish orchestra members from death, or at least delayed it. Unfortunately there were no Aryan conductors who, by lending the regime their prestige, did not aid its legitimacy. And over and above the conductors, at the exalted level of composer, the argument is even less equivocal, although still not quite as clear-cut as with the writers. The playwright Gerhart Hauptmann stayed on, first of all because he was adulated; second because he was too old to run if he didn't have to; and third—he said so himself— because he was a coward. (*Weil ich feige bin!*) His reputation was ruined, as it deserved to be: but we should be sorry for its being so ruined that we can no longer appreciate just how revered he was before the Nazis came to power. (Marcel Reich-Ranicki, a raging theatre buff when young, saw everything of Hauptmann's and generously records the euphoria in his autobiographical writings.) Understanding, not misunderstanding, became part of the *Inbegriff* of Hauptmann's fame, and destroyed it utterly.

But the same thing never happened to Richard Strauss, who stayed on for two of the same reasons: he was at the height of his renown, and, as an Aryan who didn't have to run, he felt old enough to excuse himself from doing so by choice. The third reason, cowardice, he was always too arrogant to plausibly claim, although his bravery soon evaporated when the Reichskulturkammer leaned on him. Stefan Zweig, whom Strauss had invited to write the libretto of *Die Schweigsame Frau* (The Silent Woman), was disinvited in a tearing hurry when the Nazis got to hear about it. Like Heidegger but perhaps more plausibly, Strauss took pains later on to pretend that he had never been part of the Nazi landscape. The landscape he preferred being part of was the apocalyptic heap of rubble down which he strode in 1945 to tell the GIs that he was the composer of *Der Rosenkavalier*. While Wagner was alive, there were no mass exterminations of Jews at German hands. While Strauss was alive they died by the million. It was Wagner who took the rap. Strauss got away with it, partly because he was shrewd enough to look a bit daffy when the conversation got awkward, but mainly because his music proposed no analogy more embarrassing than *Also Sprach Zarathustra*, and was mainly about love, usually between a couple of sopranos, one of them in velvet pants. Filming once in Chicago, I called on Georg Solti at the opera house during a break in his afternoon rehearsal. I was trying to nail him down for an interview about Chicago, not about his own career. Clearly this was not a diversion of emphasis that he particularly relished, but he invited me to his dressing room to discuss the matter further. I was able to tell him, truthfully, that I thought his *Eugene Onegin* was one of the greatest opera sets ever recorded. He took unbridled praise no worse than I did and sent me out into the empty auditorium with the assurance that I had a surprise coming.

He was right about that. Strolling on to the stage came the Chicago Symphony Orchestra. The maestro appeared in front of it, raised his baton, and launched into the opening measure of *Also Sprach Zarathustra*. Being Solti, he didn't get further than the first eight bars before he brought the whole thing to a halt in order to re-educate a violinist, but I was already carried away by the magnitude of an historic moment. Here was a man whom the Nazis would have killed on the spot, and he was playing one of their tunes. But of course it wasn't just theirs: that was the point. It was ours—something that Strauss must have realized, even while the Nazis were trying to bend him to their odious purposes. After all, he wasn't a fool: just old, conceited and weak, and at some time in our lives we are all of us those things, although not, if we are lucky, all at the same time. The writers know straight away when they are being weak, whereas the composers can kid themselves for decades at a stretch. We think of the Soviet Union's favourite epic novelist, Sholokhov, as a shameless liar, but of the composer Khachaturian as just a hack. Perhaps we should think worse of Khachaturian, since all the evidence suggests that for a true musician in the Soviet Union the price of seriousness was to suffer unmistakeable humiliation through being obliged to kiss the badly barbered behind of one cultural commissar after another. Shostakovich, on his own anguished confession, was a case in point. (And lest there be any doubt that Solomon Volkov's recension of Shostakovich's memoirs, even though largely a fantasy on Volkov's part, had solid roots in reality, it should be noted that Ashkenazy settled the question in an article he wrote for the May 5, 2000, issue of the *Financial Times*. He wrote it because he had grown sick of listening to clueless debates about the basic facts of the regime from which he, unlike Shostakovich, had been lucky enough to find a way out.)

It remains a moot point, however, whether there was ever any such thing as specifically totalitarian music. Watching a couple of well-built slaves doing their love dance in *Spartacus*, it is hard not to think of all those people freezing to death in Vorkuta while pig-eyed Presidium members at the Bolshoi were doting on the ballerina's bare thighs, but that was scarcely Khachaturian's fault. (The divine Plissetskaya, incidentally, as her memoirs written late in life reveal, was well aware that she was dancing for murderers: but she was a dancer, and where else was there to dance?) In Sydney when I was first a student, Carl Orff's *Carmina Burana* was introduced to me by a European refugee who probably had no idea that its composer found favour with the kind of people who had gassed her family: there was nothing in the music to tell her, except perhaps a certain predilection for bombast. If Prokofiev had never gone home to Russia, he might not have written *Romeo and Juliet*, but he would still have been Prokofiev, not Stravinsky. There is enough historicist determinism in the world without our straining our wits to attach it to people who think up tunes. *Doktor Faustus* has some of Thomas Mann's most marvellous writing in it, but there is something crucial it does not include: we get no idea of how Leverkühn's bargain with the devil shows up as music. The safest bet is that it showed up as boredom.

There is a marvellous piece by James Thurber about an heroic solo aviator who earns the worship of America before anybody realizes that he is a prejudiced buffoon who will be a public relations disaster if sent abroad to represent his country. Finally he has to be pushed out of a window. Clearly Thurber meant Lindbergh. In real life, Lindbergh could never be manoeuvred close enough to a suitable window, but in the long run something more drastic happened. He was justly famous for his bravery and skill as a lone flyer. But when his baby was kidnapped and killed he showed a kind of courage that the media didn't like: reticence. The way was prepared for his reputation to collapse when the isolationism he favoured (the America First movement) was discredited by the attack on Pearl Harbor. Understanding, it seemed, had gathered around his name, and certainly, on close scrutiny, there was nothing noble about his fondness for the dictators. (Gore Vidal, while making a good case for Lindbergh's isolationism, neglects to explain why anti-Semitism had to be part of the package.) But there was a later phase, less known, that ought to be part of the picture. Lindbergh tested high-performance aircraft, probably shot down a Japanese aircraft in combat, pioneered long-distance routes for Pan Am, and generally lived out a productive life. His fame is in two parts, like Brecht's: he is the hero and the villain. For the thoughtful, it is in three parts: he is also one of the first victims of the celebrity culture. (There would have been no kidnapping if he had not been so publicized that even a stumbling halfwit had read about him.) But it ought to be in at least four, because behind all the personae determined by events there was a personality that remained constant. He valued self-reliance, and possibly valued it too much: it made him hate collectivism so blindly that he thought fascism was the opposite, instead of the same thing in a dark shirt. Yet there is something magnificent about a man who could make a success out of any task he tackled. To complete Rilke's observation—and it is an observation, because it answers visible facts—we must accept this much: to measure the distortion of life we call fame it is not enough to weigh the misunder-standings against the understandings. We have to see through to the actual man, and decide whether, like so many artists, he is mainly what he does, or whether he has an individual and perhaps even inexpress-ible self, like the lonely flyer.

VIRGINIO ROGNONI

❣ ❣ ❣

Virginio Rognoni was born in Corsica in 1924. A student of
law and a practising lawyer after World War II—the period in
which the new democratic Italy was transforming, sometimes
insufficiently, the embarrassing inheritance of the Fascist legal
system—he rose to prominence as professor of institutions of
civil procedural law (a typically Italian mouthful of an academic title) at the University of Pavia. In 1968 he was elected
to parliament as a Christian Democrat. After the kidnapping
and eventual assassination of ex–Prime Minister Aldo Moro by
the Brigate Rosse (Red Brigades) in 1978, Rognoni was put in
charge of the Ministry of the Interior, his chief task being to
defeat the terrorists. The job took him five years, and produced enough dramatic action to keep the Italian movie and
television industry supplied with plot lines until the present
day and presumably beyond. At the time, however, the tension
was all too real. Neo-fascist bombers got into the act on their
own account and the legal system looked like an unarmed
prophet. But Rognoni's chief triumphs were in court. Historians from either wing generally agree that the Red Brigades
were finished from the moment that the American General
James Lee Dozier, whom they had taken hostage, was recov-

ered alive in 1982. After his success against the terrorists, Rognoni went on to a number of political posts, the most important of them concerned with legal reform. His effectiveness as vice president of the Consiglio Superiore della Magistratura (Superior Council of the Magistracy) can be argued about indefinitely by sceptical critics of Italian politics, who suffer from no shortage of subject matter, those on the left always able to detect the hand of the CIA, those on the right always alert to the revival of Communist subversion in a new disguise. But nobody can seriously deny that Rognoni played the crucial role in confronting a genuinely dangerous threat to democracy and neutralizing it by reasonable means. Right-wing theorists continue to believe that there was a terrorist mastermind ("*grande vecchio*"—grand old man) who escaped. Left-wing theorists continue to believe that the terrorists were right-wing *agenti provocantori*. Sensible people prefer to concentrate on what Rognoni thinks of the matter. Luckily his opinions, closely allied to his vivid memories, are available in print, providing a crucial text for all humanist students beginning to grapple with the question of how a liberal democracy can maintain its integrity when forced to defend itself against misuse of the freedoms it exists to cherish. Since Lincoln himself wondered aloud how a state dedicated to liberty could be strong enough to protect it, there is no blame attached to not having a ready answer. As Rognoni found out, however, the answer is, or had better be, there within ourselves, waiting to be discovered. When faced with an ideology of opportunist violence it helps to have some principles in advance, before the pressure of events starts reinforcing the idea that expediency might be a principle in itself.

In whichever way a democratic system might be sick,
terrorism does not heal it, it kills it.
Democracy is healed with democracy.
—VIRGINIO ROGNONI, *INTERVISTA SUL
TERRORISMO*

IN ITALY, THE publishing firm Laterza puts out an attractive series
of booklets devoted to interviews with leading cultural, scientific and
political figures: Alberto Moravia, Gianni Agnelli, Enrico Fermi, Federico Fellini and many more are among my own collection. To the new
student of Italian, I can recommend the series as an *autostrada* into the
culture. You can hear the language being spoken at its top level, and the
subject matter is real: sometimes all too real. This interview with Virginio Rognoni is one of the best. He had impeccable credentials to
pronounce the opinon quoted above. As minister of the interior
between 1978 and 1983, Rognoni was the man on the spot in the
period the Italians still call *gli anni di piombo*—the years of lead. It was
a period in which the extreme right and the extreme left staged a
shooting and bombing competition which held the spectators on ten-
terhooks, because they were among the targets. As the death toll
mounted, Rognoni was under tremendous pressure to arrogate emer-
gency powers to himself: not least, of course, from the terrorists, who
would have liked nothing better than for the state to adopt illiberal
means. Rognoni resisted the temptation and settled in for a long battle. The blessed day when a full thirty-two leaders of the Red Brigades
were sent to gaol—it was Monday, January 24, 1983—happened on
his watch. Terrorism in Italy wasn't over, but its back was broken.
Rognoni, a prime target himself, had done his job. Though he was
accused by the left of pursuing left-wing terrorists harder than he pursued right-wing terrorists, the facts prove his neutrality. He was a good
Catholic, but so were plenty of the terrorists, even among the Marxists. His enemy was not the left, but terrorism *tout court*, which he, better than anybody, knew was cherished by many of its adherents as an
end in itself, rather than a means to justice. In other words, evil had
become a career for the otherwise unemployable, and there would be
no end to it unless it was stopped.

Accusations of police torture were frequently made, but Rognoni
sounded convincing when he rejected them. Occasionally he could not
reject them, and had to explain. He said that some agents had got angry
because of atrocities and had exceeded their authority. That sounded
convincing too. The impression he gives is of a man to whom terrorism was so repugnant that the planned use of counter-terror to fight it
would have been inconceivable. We can safely draw a clear line

between him and the "dirty war" *caudillos* in the Americas: sadists who, when it came to leftist insurgency, had no other idea than of getting their frightfulness in first. What we have to ask ourselves is whether Rognoni's attitude to terrorism makes sense as a universal principle. It certainly made sense for Italy, which, however sick (*malato*) it might have been, was a functioning democratic system. The Brigate Rosse, if they had had their way, would have converted their country from a producer of wealth, however badly distributed, into a producer of poverty. But it isn't hard to name countries, calling themselves democracies, in which injustice, to the idealistic young, seemed so deeply institutionalized that terrorism occurred to them as the only workable response. They might have been wrong. They might have done better to choose exile, or direct martyrdom. (When they were detected, they were martyred anyway.) They were bound to find themselves among strange bedfellows. It takes a very confident onlooker, however, to suppose that he could never have found himself harbouring the same impulse. One of the strengths of the most unsettling works of art ever devoted to the subject, Gillo Pontecorvo's *The Battle of Algiers*, was that some of the terrorists looked convincingly inspired by idealism when they were getting ready to sacrifice themselves. They were all too willing to sacrifice innocent people as well—Pontecorvo didn't gloss that over—but inspired they were. Desperation had brought them to it, but inspiration was what it was.

Religion makes inspiration easy. Young Hamas and Al Qaeda suicide bombers of today are promised a place in paradise, as of tomorrow. It sounds more attractive than dying for dialectical materialism. But even a nominally Marxist terrorist is seldom likely to risk his life for communism. He risks his life for the oppressed. (Should he succeed, they will almost certainly end up more oppressed than ever, but he is too young to have read the books that prove it.) Our revulsion comes from his readiness to kill innocent people other than his own, but the mathematics might seem convincing. Kill a few innocent people in a nightclub now, and that will save the lives of thousands later. (In the 1960s, the mathematics were put into a book, Robert Taber's *The War of the Flea*: a little classic of casuistry which can be recommended, with a health warning, to anyone who doubts just how dangerous the French intelligentsia could be in that period.) He assumes that there can be an economy of killing, and the awful truth is that he is not entirely absurd to think so. An economy of killing was in the minds of the terrorists who helped to found the state of Israel. Britain, the mandatory power, was a democractic state within the meaning of Rognoni's definition. Theoretically, it was open to persuasion by democractic means. Practically, the Israeli activists didn't think it was. (It should be remembered that British foreign policy had spent years looking as if it had been designed to support their view. The pre-war quotas set against Jewish immigration into Palestine had retained their lethal effect even after the war, with British Foreign Minister Ernest Bevin's ill-disguised self-satisfaction being remembered in Israel as a particularly offensive insult.) The terrorists of the Stern Gang, and the more militant members of the Irgun, saw no means of dissuading the British from their tutelary mission except by terror. The strategy was assumed to have worked because Britain gave up: *post hoc ergo propter hoc.* (We can be sure that this apparent chain of cause and effect has been in the minds of IRA strategists ever since.) When the Irgun massacred the Palestinian inhabitants of Deir Yassin—the empty houses could still be seen in my time, only a short walk into the suburbs of Jerusalem—officers of the Haganah protested. Bar Lev, Haganah commander in the area, wanted to arrest the Irgun leaders, one of whom was Menachem Begin. David Ben-Gurion didn't listen. It seems a fair inference (I have heard even anti-Zionist Israeli liberals implying it) that terrorizing the Palestinian population into flight was a deliberate policy.

These considerations need to be kept in mind by anyone who, like myself, believes in the state of Israel's right to exist and regards the concerted attack by the Arab nations in 1948 as ample reason for Israel to be concerned in perpetuity about defensible borders. But it was worse than unfortunate, it was tragic, that the apparently efficacious use of terror threw a long shadow. When the Arab countries had their man of the hour in Anwar Sadat of Egypt, the man of the hour in Israel was none other than Menachem Begin, whose pedigree went back to Deir Yassin. Actually it went back further than that, into an experience under the Nazis which taught him that the only answer to threatened extermination was to fight with any means: moral considerations were a culpable luxury, for which your own innocent people would have to pay. The two major totalitarian earthquakes of the twentieth century—

the Soviet Union and Nazi Germany—had a seismic influence on the Middle East: wave after wave of distortion, the waves interfering with each other in a pattern so complex that it looks like chaos.

But there was one influence easy to isolate. The state of Israel was built by people who knew all too much about terror. Failure by the Arab powers to grasp this fact led them to the supreme stupidity of threatening extinction to people who had been threatened with it already by experts. But Israeli leaders who take a hard line against Palestinian insurgency are asking a lot if they expect automatic moral condemnation from onlookers for the latest suicide bomb delivered by a young Palestinian with a ticket to the beyond. The PLO has a suitably disgusting track record in which the Black September massacre of the Israeli Olympic athletes in 1972 was merely the most attention-getting point. Hamas will probably top that sooner or later. But the state of Israel's own track record goes back far beyond Ariel Sharon's dubious achievements in the Lebanon refugee camps. (All he did was stand by, but it was a murderous indifference.) It goes back to an act of terror by the Irgun. It goes back to the King David Hotel collapsing in Jerusalem. When it did, the perpetrators got what they wanted.

Now their descendants must convince the Palestinians that similar means will never work. The Palestinians would be easier to convince, of course, if their activists, and the Arab nations that stand behind them, had any real idea of the continuous historical tragedy that led up to the installation and consolidation of a Jewish settlement in Palestine. Unfortunately the standard of informed commentary on the Arab side has been kept ruinously low by the absence of an independent, secular intelligentsia. I met Edward Said, and liked him as anyone would. He had distinction of mind written all over him. He must have been already sick by then, but he looked haunted as well, and I don't think it was just by his outrage at Israel's behaviour. He was haunted by the ironic fact that his only natural allies were liberals within Israel. An inch away from Amos Oz and a thousand miles from Vanessa Redgrave, Said was an isolated figure, and he himself could never admit in print that the Arab nations dished their cause in advance by not persuading the Palestinians to accept their own state in 1947, and by combining to attack the nascent Israeli state in 1948. If he had, he would probably have been assassinated. (As the assassination of Sadat proved, the Arab irredentists, like the Zionist ultras, have always been unerring in picking off any incipient mediators.) In the Israeli press, a constant feature is a *sottisier* of what the official Arab publications, including school textbooks, say about the eternal iniquity of the Jewish race and the holy necessity to eradicate it from the face of the Earth. The Israelis scarcely need to quote any of that stuff out of context. Most of the remarks could have come out of the divinely inspired mouth of the Grand Mufti of Jerusalem at the time when he was in Berlin urging Hitler to get on with it.

Compared with terrorism in the Middle East, terrorist campaigns elsewhere in the world tend to strike us as half-hearted: Low Intensity Operations, as regular forces are wont to call them. We should resist that emphasis, or lack of emphasis. There has been nothing half-hearted about terror in Northern Ireland. But there again, ambiguity looms. The Republic of Ireland owes its existence to terror. Terror worked. It was a terror campaign that forced the local constabulary and the British forces to counter-terror. Not only the nauseating activities of the Black and Tans, but what the British army felt compelled to do to maintain order, was sufficient to demoralize the London government and bring about Home Rule. Since partition, the IRA in the North, even when apparently dormant, has worked for the same result, and not entirely without success. At one stage even Conor Cruise O'Brien was suggesting that a further partition was the only solution. It was possible to imagine the Protestant enclave being driven in upon itself to the point where its members would go home. Certainly the terrorists were dreaming of something like that. If the Protestants had not been a majority in the North, it might have worked. Confined by a shorter perimeter, no longer a majority in the North but still a minority within an almost united Ireland, the northern Protestants would be reduced to the position of the *pieds noirs* in Algeria, who pointed out in vain that they *were* home: they were born there, and had no other home to go to. But there was always France, where the new man in charge, Charles de Gaulle, having first pretended to listen to them, yielded to the inevitable. The inevitable had been made so by terror. Without the terror, the French army would not have been driven first to torture, then to demoralization, and finally to subversion. Democratic means would never have changed the domocracy's mind: or so the National Liberation Front strategists, armed with a plenitude of historic evidence, preferred to believe.

For Latin America, the situation has been analysed by Mario Vargas Llosa with clarity, subtlety and an admirably firm hand. A one-time leftist himself—his years at Sartre's feet turned his head, until Camus began to set it straight—Vargas Llosa found on his return to the Spanish world that the arguments in favour of Marxist insurgency were a confidence trick. New students of Spanish (who would be wise to start with books of essays anyway) could hardly do better than to track Vargas Llosa's long series of articles on the subject: they run right through his landmark collection *Contra il vento y marea* and on into his late-flowering, consistently brilliant *El lenguaje de la pasion*. He paints a repetitive but startling picture—the same thing happening again and again, like successive frames in a strip of film—of insurgent groups such as Peru's Tupamaros subverting the institutions of their countries to the point where a militarized junta launches terror in its turn, with the result that the institutions erode, underdevelopment plunges to new depths, and the oppressed in whose name the insurgents acted end up more helpless than ever. He gives a classic account of a remorselessly recurring pattern. But not even Vargas Llosa can quite bring himself to face the possibility that if the institutions weren't working in the first place then a convulsion was what they needed.

The standard promise of the terrorist is to reveal the true nature of the state by unmasking the police force as militarists and the military as fascists. In the Americas, that was roughly what terrorist insurgency did. In Argentina, for example, it was only when the bourgeoisie found its own children being taken and tortured that it woke up from its habitual complacency: and the complacency had been complicity, in corruption, exploitation and the deeply damaging sleep of reason. Throughout the Americas, after the CIA's ground-breaking adventure in Guatemala in the 1950s, there were many young idealists with good cause to believe that the oppressor, drawing on support from Washington, would go on robbing the common people forever. The results of that belief were disastrous, and particularly so for the common people. But the belief can't be dismissed. Vargas Llosa, with an artist's mind and a politician's practical knowledge, is understandably reluctant to reach the philosopher's uncomfortable conclusion that chaos might have been constructive. But terror, if it was criminally foolish in presuming to dramatize the true nature of states, was historically functional in dramatizing the desperation of societies content to call themselves moribund rather than admit themselves unjust. Luckily, apart from all the dead Indians, everyone involved spoke the same language. When a proper dialogue started at last, they all understood each other. It is some comfort to realize that bright young idealists in Latin American universities today are reading about these matters in the crystalline Spanish of Vargas Llosa rather than in hasty translations of Regis Debray's inexcusably irresponsible diatribes. But the voice of a man like Vargas Llosa rings so clearly now only because the air was cleared in the first place of its perennial miasma. If the Americas had waited until the United Fruit Company had evolved into a benevolent institution, they might still be waiting. Finally the disastrous pro-strongman foreign policy of the United States was reversed under President Reagan. When Reagan came to office, only two of the U.S.-favoured states in Latin America were democracies. When he left office, there were only two that weren't. It was one of the great foreign policy revisions in recent history, but it didn't happen because Reagan was a genius of sympathetic perception. It happened because there had been telegenic chaos. None of this means, of course, that dead terrorists should be venerated as heroes. Most of them were ruthless dogmatists and many of them were homicidal maniacs. But the problem remains of the ones who were neither.

We have to go a long way down the world's scale of enormities before we find a terrorist scenario that looks like pure farce. When we do, it's probably because we don't know enough about it. Already we forget that the fantasy politics of Germany's glamorous young terrorists in the Baader-Meinhof era had real victims. In the Basque area of Spain, the terrorists are currently collecting what they call "war tax" from their own civilians: pay up or get shot. It looks like the reductio ad absurdum. At one time a regular holiday-maker in Biarritz, I was very glad when a Basque bomber from south of the border, taking a rest from his little war while he constructed a new device, blew himself through the front window of one of my favourite bars and wound up in pieces all over the Rue Gambetta. (Don't think it didn't strike me that I would have been less glad if I had been in the bar at the time.)

On top of my holiday from London, I got a holiday from pity. To the onlooker, the Spanish government would appear to have done its best to give the Basques everything they want. It seems, however, that they want their own country, coterminous with their own language and culture. When the Slovaks wanted that, Vaclav Havel gave it to them. (Some of his own colleagues thought he was foolish to do so, and that he permanently impoverished the Czech Republic as a result.) But the Spanish government, we are told, is not in the same position to be generous. Too much of Spanish industry is in Basque territory. It is the mission of the ETA terrorists to persuade the Spanish government that their cause is just. It doesn't seem so to me: it doesn't even seem sane. But there are some young Basques who are ready to face torture for it. To steel themselves, they torture each other. Faced with that kind of determination, the first idea we must give up is that terrorists are not serious.

The idea we must never give up is that they are not rational. Not even Israel was necessarily a unique case. The Irgun could have wrought suitably unacceptable havoc on a target that was not alive. But it would have taken more resources than they had, and anyway the chances were good that the British, exhausted from the war and with the will to empire fading fast, would pack up and go home. In all other cases, the consequences of killing the innocent are predictable only in the sense that the terrorists will alienate the best elements among their own political sympathizers. The IRA put its own cause back by years when it blew up a London bandstand that contained nothing military except musicians. The whole idea of a soft target is a misconception. Insurgents could choose the hardest target, themselves. All the evidence suggests that if dramatization is the aim, there is nothing more dramatic than a suicide in the right spot. When the Vietnamese monks set themselves alight in central Saigon, the flames were seen in Washington. When Jan Palach set himself alight in Prague in 1968, the flames were seen in the Kremlin. There was no immediate effect—the sequel was years of oppression in each case—but suppose there had been twice the number of human torches the next day, and twice as many again the day after that, and so on? In recent years the use of demonstrative suicide has expanded to include innocent victims. So far it hasn't worked: probably because it can't, in the sense that those groups wedded to it as a weapon have no clear aims that can be granted. (Palestinian suicide bombers, for example, want the dissolution of the state of Israel, a wish that will be granted only on the understanding that the whole area is dissolved along with it, by the atomic bombs that the Israelis would presumably use if the state caved in.) It hardly needs saying that if suicidal terrorists returned to leaving the innocent out of the equation they would no longer be terrorists. But by confining violence to themselves they would be dramatizing one thing for certain: the sympathy for the oppressed that made them ready to give their lives. Young people who see *The Battle of Algiers*—and they should all see it, although not, I think, before they are old enough to vote—will identify that sympathy as a creative force, and they will not be wrong. In the bar afterwards, however, we might find it hard to resist asking them what they suppose Algeria is like to live in now, almost half a century after the oppressor was put to flight. It isn't like Italy, that's for sure. But there lay Rognoni's big advantage: he was starting with a country that knew what it wanted to get back to, before it went anywhere else.

S

❧ ❧ ❧

Ernesto Sabato

Edward Said

Sainte-Beuve

José Saramago

Jean-Paul Sartre

Erik Satie

Arthur Schnitzler

Sophie Scholl

Wolf Jobst Siedler

Manès Sperber

ERNESTO SABATO

❡ ❡ ❡

Ernesto Sabato was born in Buenos Aires in 1911 and studied physics and philosophy at the University of la Plata. For the first part of his long career he combined science with radical politics. In 1930 he joined the Juventud Comunista and by 1933 he had risen to become secretary of that embattled organization, but his doubts about Stalin had already begun. Reluctant to let the Party go, he eventually sought renewal of his faith by enrolling at the School of Leninism in Moscow. Luckily he had got only as far as Brussels when news of the Moscow trials led him to break a journey which, he later admitted, would surely have ended in his premature death. At the Curie Laboratory in Paris he went on with his study of physics, and was present when the French did enough work on the atom to give an idea of the destructive power that was on its way. Sabato, always prone to thoughts of suicide and large questions about life and death, was suitably impressed by the prospect of doom for all mankind. After 1945 he did no more physics, giving himself full-time to writing, painting and education. But when he wrote articles in dispraise of the Peron regime, the public education system was no longer a field open to him, and he had to transmit his ideas by writing. His nov-

els—most famously *The Tunnel* (1948)—are important, but
unwieldy for the beginning reader. His essays provide the ideal
approach to his teeming range of opinion, almost all of it reasonable, even when camped beween the dream world and the
world. During the war over the Malvinas in 1982 he took
Argentina's part but that didn't stop him burying the last credentials of the junta with his editorship of *Nunca Mas* (Never
Again, often called simply the Sabato Report), which detailed
and analysed the atrocities of the military regime. He was even
better than Borges at being interviewed, so when they talked
with each other they could cut out the middleman. The transcripts of their dialogues are delightful. Sabato's non-fictional
prose is collected in half a dozen attractively presented volumes of essays which he himself, as a pedagogue, might have
designed as magically unputdownable textbooks for foreigners
learning to read Spanish. In his later years, after he was med-
ically declared to be too blind to read and write, he has concentrated on his painting: a typically category-busting gesture
from a writer so good at convincing the rest of us that we aren't
looking hard enough, and especially not into our own memories. Sabato's memory of his radical years has served him well.
Protected against snobbery, he never fell for the illusion, rife
in the elevated Argentinian literary world, that art was only for
the elect. He thought that even humble journalists could share
the glory of a genius, simply by pointing out that he was there,
and thus offering him the consolation of understanding.
Sabato has a phrase for it: *la infinita liberacion de no saberse solo*.
The infinite liberation of knowing that one is not alone. I
should add, in fairness, that there are young intellectuals in
Argentina who find my admiration for Sabato incomprehensible. They remember that he, too, like Borges, sat down with
the generals. But I rememer that he stood up again; and his
prose, which they find stifling, I find lucid. But that could be
the usual effect of reading in a language not one's own: one is
too easily impressed.

> Only a thick skin can defend itself, and the characteristic of
> an artist is an extreme delicacy of skin.
> — ERNESTO SABATO, *ENTRE LA LETRA Y LA*
> *SANGRE*, P. 126

I F I HAD my time again, I would never react publicly to criticism, no
matter how unjustified. Unless the point in dispute is a point of fact,
all you can do by doing so is to cooperate in your assailant's aim of getting you onto your back foot and keeping you there. But this is mainly
a tactical consideration. The injunction that you should not *feel* criticism is an impertinence. After all, when you criticized other people, it
was on the assumption that they would feel it, or anyway ought to have
done. Savagery of critical expression can often be put down to the
critic's belief that his subject, having become renowned, has attained a
position of power, and might not be troubled unless well whipped; with
the conscience-saving clause that the hurt will not go deep, because its
recipient is too well-armoured with the world's rewards. Success has
given him a thick skin. But as Sabato was right to point out, for an artist
there is no such thing as a thick skin. Sometimes his thin skin has to
bear the weight of complete steel, but it will suffer from that too: the
burden of seeming toughness is hard on the nerves, and you can't wear
a suit of armour to bed without losing sleep.

In his diaries, Thomas Mann made what sounded like anti-Semitic
remarks about the critic Alfred Kerr. Mann was no anti-Semite, but he
flew off the handle because Kerr had belittled him in print. (Mann,
with some justification, thought that he was Goethe, so making him
feel belittled was easy: all you had to do was suggest that he was only
Schiller.) Proust's invariable response to adverse criticism was to write
to the critic at great length. When the first volume of *À la recherche du
temps perdu* came out, it was panned in *Le Temps* by a blundering hack
called Paul Souday. Proust wrote to him in detailed protest, and over a
period of years invited him several times to dinner. Souday later
claimed to have discovered Proust. In effect, Proust had disarmed his
tormentor by taking him at his own absurdly exalted estimation. From
my experience as a critic, I would have to conclude that no writer of
any kind or degree is content to be taken any other way. Anthony
Powell and Patrick White had in common an elephantine capacity to

remember the perpetrators of an unfavourable notice: White sincerely believed that they were all in touch with one another. He kept a list. When I heard that I was on it, I wondered if he would send his seconds, or some large man carrying a tyre iron. I was also struck by John le Carré's private reaction to a bad notice I gave his long novel *The Honourable Schoolboy*, which I thought, and said, was a put-up job. Le Carré did not react in public, but in private he spread the opinion that I was conducting a vendetta. Since, in the same article, I had called *The Spy Who Came in from the Cold* a masterpiece, it would have been a strange vendetta.

Le Carré would have been on solid ground if he had confined his annoyance to the industrial fact that a negative notice in the *New York Review of Books* could be of no help to his new book's prospects in America, and might well have damaged them. I would guess, however, that he threw his toys out of the pram because I had suggested that his new book was a dud by his own standards. The compliment involved in that kind of condemnation never registers. I once saw a famously cool literary friend of mine turn angry enough to commit murder. A collection of his critical pieces had just been dismissively reviewed in the *Times Literary Supplement*, the burden of the review being that somebody of my friend's high talents should not be wasting his time writing journalism. The paper's reviewers were still anonymous in those days but my friend knew who the culprit was: a notorious dullard. The victim pronounced anathema not only against the dullard for writing the review, but against the editor for printing it. Clearly he would have liked to see the guilty pair lashed back to back with cable and used as landfill in the Thames estuary, but only after being toasted to the point of death with a flame-thrower. I was so shaken by the spectacle of his white lips and clenched fists—one of the fists had a pint of beer in it, so there was danger from flying glass—that I had trouble remembering three pertinent facts. The dullard's sedulous mediocrity was fully revealed in his piece for all to see; almost every piece in the book that he had reviewed was more intransigent than the review; and it had been scarcely twenty-four hours since the victim, in that same pub, had given me a withering lecture on my absurd sensitivity to criticism.

But injured pride knows no reason: a fact I know from my other experience, as an author. It took me many years to grow out of the assumption that any adverse criticism was a personal attack. It *felt* like a personal attack. Sometimes it was meant to feel like that, but common sense should have told me at the time that a limiting judgement can be written out of regret as well as spite. After all, I would have been outraged if anyone had dared to suggest that my own limiting judgements on other authors were written out of anything except an objective care for literature. The fly in the ointment (what W. C. Fields called "the Ethiopian in the fuel supply" until he was stopped from doing it) is that an author's work *is* his personality, so he can't help feeling that any aspersions cast on it are cast on him. Realizing this to be so is one of the secrets of survival in the literary world: as so often happens in life, the strength that matters is gained from recognizing your weakness. Without going so far as to forgive yourself for it, you have to get it in perspective. The price of not doing so is a disabling petulance. Confidence must be preserved somehow, but to assume that everyone who criticizes you is out to get you is a bad way of preserving it.

One once-famous contemporary playwright always operated on the assumption that any hostile critic was motivated by envy of his fame, money, house and wife, all four of which were on display in the colour supplements from week to week. He missed out on listening properly to advice he should have heeded, because the day came when his major revenue stream consisted of royalties from Norway. I learned my own lesson when someone I knew and loved told me that I should be counting my syllables along with my stresses. We were having a huge fight at the time and I thought that everything he said against me was meant to wound. Some of it was, but on that point he was right. I learned another lesson when I finally realized that the point he had been right about was the hardest one to forgive him for. Even when they are confined to private interchange, these prickly sensitivities amount to the most uncomfortable thing about the creative life. One of the many advantages conferred by a general knowledge of the arts is the evidence it provides that not even the greatest figures are immune. What makes them great is that they are not disabled. Verdi longed for Wagner's praise, but eventually wrote *Falstaff* without it. Renoir was right to be mortified when Degas found him wanting. (Where Renoir went wrong was in dismantling some of the strengths of his technique in an effort to correct the weaknesses: he should have trusted his public.) Keeping

an eye on yourself is a hard but necessary task. Much as it hurts, criticism can help you do it. A thick skin, taking nothing in, turns dry and
cracks. The thin skin is the strong one. It wasn't just generous of
Sabato to say so: it was realistic.

> The tango . . . is the strangest popular song that mankind
> has ever produced, a popular song which is also the one
> and only introverted, even introspective, dance.
> — ERNESTO SABATO, *ENTRE LA LETRA Y LA*
> *SANGRE, P. 131*

About the tango, Sabato intuited what Borges didn't: that this strangest
and most lovely of all dances is a self-assessment made compulsory by
music. Borges is often given credit for a love and understanding of the
tango, but the sad truth is that he declared it dead by the way he loved
it, and missed its meaning by the way he understood it. When he came
back from Europe to Buenos Aires in the twenties he did some leg-
work in the low-life haunts of the *compadrito*, the bad guy of the bars
and brothels. He concluded that the best of the music and the dancing
was already over, when in fact it had just begun. But Sabato, if he said
more than Borges ever did about the tango, still did not say much.
Sabato sometimes gets the credit for the famous definition of the tango
as a sad thought, dancing. It is nice to know that he was sensitive to the
idea, but the idea was not his. As he was always careful to acknowledge,
the definition was coined in the 1930s by a vernacular poet, Enrique
Santos Discepolo. There were many gifted tango lyricists in Buenos
Aires. Some of them were more celebrated than he was—Carlos
Gardel was world-famous—and a few of them were almost as prolific,
but nobody was both as gifted and prolific as Discepolo. All the literature that will ever really matter about the tango is in his lyrics. The
acid jealousy is in them, and the dirt and the danger. They can be read
with profit as an example of what an unrecognized poet can do with his
freedom from respectability. But they can't be read with as much profit
as they can be listened to. Even with Discepolo, the words take you
back to the music, and the average lyric by a less inventively observant
writer never leaves the music, because it is too thin and predictable.
The usual tango text is a sob story that clinches almost every quatrain

with the word *corazon*. (Try substituting our non-resonant little word "heart" and you'll see straight away why most tango lyrics don't translate.) Accumulating over decades, the treasury of tango lyrics, repetitive though it is, already represents a large potential distraction from the music, and hence from the dance.

Unfortunately scholarship, which rarely dances, has an imperative of its own, and has been inexorably crowding into the act. In one language or another, there is a new book about the tango every month. There are whole sociological treatises on how the dance started. Was it a ritual parade of mutual ownership staged by a hooker and her pimp? Was it an elaborate ruse by two gay gauchos to placate a fractious steer? The one thing certain is that the news first leaked out from La Boca, the low-life port district of Buenos Aires. It definitely didn't come in from Africa with the slaves, because there weren't any. If the denizens of the bars and brothels did not actually invent the *milonga* and transform it into the tango, why did people of such low expectations develop an art-form so infinitely, so incongruously, so *needlessly* elaborate? (Because the tango's improvised steps, like the moves in chess, rapidly extrapolate towards infinity, you will never dance the same tango twice unless you repeat the whole pattern from memory, on an empty floor.) How did it all happen? Since the origins are blurred, the opportunities for speculation are endless. As happened with jazz, the main threat posed by scholarship is that it will raise the tango to the level of respectability, and thus drain away some of the excitement. But comfort can be taken from the piquant fact that the tango has never become socially acceptable in its country of origin. For the upper classes of Argentina, the tango is a low-life event, and President Carlos Menem, by his avowed passion for the dance—in the ten years of his presidency from 1989 to 1999, he must have mentioned it a thousand times—only proved that his origins were on a par with his hairstyle and stacked heels.

To hear Menem tell it—and I heard him tell it, when I interviewed him in his office—he is a *tanguero* born and bred. In fact he can dance about three steps, which at least puts him ahead of Eva Peron, who never danced the tango in her life. Since her death, of course, she has been dancing it more and more all the time. In the movie of *Evita*— fun fascists burn the boards!—the tango goes on all around her, as if it had been the national dance of Argentina. It never was, still isn't, and probably never will be as long as there are young females of good family who want to look as if they are saving themselves for a suitably elevated marriage. Strangely enough, there *is* a country which has the tango as its national dance: Finland. But an Evita story relocated to Finland was never on the cards.

If the tango has yet to complete its conquest of the country that gave it birth, it has certainly conquered the rest of the world, almost certainly because of its unique combination of beauty and difficulty: it is lovely if done well, but doing it well takes intense application. In Japan, for example, where ballroom dancing is taken very seriously, the tango is correctly judged to be the dance that leaves all the other dances looking elementary. It should be said in haste that the Argentinian tango is not really a ballroom dance at all. For a long time, the ballroom version of the tango was the only version the world knew about. Hence the impression, still widespread, that the dance is assembled from struts and poses, with a rose being passed from one set of bared teeth to another, as in *Some Like It Hot*. Gradually the touring tango shows from Argentina have supplemented that impression with a more subtle one, and among dancers all over the planet the tango is now seen to be a truly international culture in itself, with a full attendant panoply of legend, protocol, dress code and scholarship. Quite a load for a mere dance to carry.

And a dance is all it is. It's *the* dance, and you have to take it seriously or you'll never dance it, but if you can't laugh at yourself along the way you'll crack up before you get there. This is especially true for a man. A woman can learn the steps with reasonable ease, but a man, because he must lead, will be face to face with his own character when he finds he can't. Previous experience in any form of dancing which entails holding on to a partner will be a help, but it won't be enough to keep him from despair as he once again, for the tenth time that evening, steers a woman into trouble. Apart from her twitching hand and trembling back, the thing to grasp is that a minute's dancing is worth a month of talk. A lot of what comes with the dance is fascinating, yet still irrelevant. What's unequivocally worthwhile is the music, but it's possible to go overboard even for that. By now even the wax cylinders of the first tango bands are on compact disc, proving that the sumptuous texture of the tango sound was there from the start. The sound has always had a drive that needs no drums: the bass fiddle, the pacemaker guitar, the staccato sob of the *bandoneon* squeezeboxes and the plinking pizzicato of the strings combine to provide the inexorable momentum. On top of the momentum the melodic interplay gives continually varied signals for the leader to alter his steps and for the woman to decorate hers with a kick or flicker of her free foot. The texture has always been an invitation to musical talent, and to trace the achievement of the individual composers and bandleaders like Anabal Troilo, Enrico Cadicamo, Oswaldo Pugliese or Carlos de Sali is almost as rewarding, in each case, as following Duke Ellington through the late thirties and early forties.

Standing at the post–World War II peak of the tradition, Astor Piazzolla was certainly a prodigy, but he might also have been a portent, not to say a nemesis. As a working member of Troilo's orchestra, Piazzolla was boiling with so many of his own out-of-tempo ideas that he had roughly the same effect as Charlie Parker on Jay McShann's sax section. When Troilo warned Piazzolla that people didn't come to listen, they came to dance, he might not have been wrong. Piazzolla pushes the characteristic rubato of the tango to a point where only an expert dancer can respond to it, and tango music is dead if it loses touch with the dance. Collect the records by all means. A Japanese tango fan who goes by the name of Baba has accumulated more than five thousand of them. Several times a year, Baba makes the thirty-five-hour trip from Tokyo to Buenos Aires in order to bury himself in the record stores on and around the Avenida Corrientes. By my calculations he will never finish listening to the discs he already owns even if he spins them only once each, but one salient fact saves him from being a clinical case of *tango loco*: he must be practising his moves while he listens, because he dances pretty well. Several times in Buenos Aires after midnight, I have seen him dancing to the music he loves so much. He has a nice long tread and a neat swerve that he must have perfected while dodging around his free-standing stereo speakers back there in Japan.

Baba has been listening with his feet, and so should we all, because they are trying to tell us something. They are telling us that we can't hear that bewitching music in its full whining, weeping, surging succulence until we see it danced. What was once true of jazz is still true of the tango. The rhythmic measure of pre-bop jazz was the human heartbeat, and the way to feel it fully was to watch dancers fling each other about. The rhythmic measure of the tango is the human breath, and you can feel it fully only when you watch dancers perform the visual equivalent of a sigh of regret and a moan of bliss. You have to see the sad thought, dancing. Even if I had been a mere onlooker, my own involvement with the tango would have been worth it for what I have seen. Not just in Buenos Aires but in London, Paris, Berlin, Madrid, New York, Nijmegen, Sydney, Melbourne, Adelaide and Auckland I have seen men and women, right in the middle of a jammed salon, create something for which only the word "poem" can serve the turn: the word "sculpture" would be too static. If I hadn't been present, I would never have known, because these were poems written to be thrown away. No minicam will ever be able to capture those moments, even if it follows the dancers through the crowd. The observer has to be there, with the thing observed.

As to the question of how a man of my generation feels about women, I detect, at the eleventh hour, signs of improvement. Undoubtedly it was the sight of old goats with pretty young women in their arms that helped draw me into the tango world, a man in winter longing for a touch of spring. It is also inescapably true that sex and the tango are in close connection. But to be connected, things first have to be separate, and the beginner soon finds out that if he regards the salon as a make-out mall he will not get far. The attractions are real and the jealousies are awful, but they are usually more about dancing than about desire. In Buenos Aires, I have danced with women old enough to be my mother, and got furious when they danced better with their husbands. So if the passion to possess has not been quelled, at least it is operating on a scale less narrow. On the whole, I have seen few fields of human activity where the deep urge to love has come closer to being tamed and civilized. I am not even sure, any longer, that the urge to dance might not lie just as deep. On those terrifying nights of compulsory jollity in Stalin's dacha, when the maidservants had been dismissed and the crazy old killer kept his drunken ministers awake until dawn, he would make them dance, and occasionally join in himself. His madness and their fear had reduced them all to a condition so primeval that they might as well have been wearing skins, yet dancing is what they did. There is a neutrality to dancing, if only because people, while they are doing it, can't easily do anything else. Even a war dance happens before the war, not during it. Hitler and Goebbels both heard a tango orchestra, and quite approved. A pity they never got addicted, because as any man who tries it is bound to discover, it can't be done without humility, and if you haven't got much of that, you have to get some, or else give up. Sabato was right about the introspection. A man who wants to find out who he really is should try watching the woman he loves as she dances the tango with a maestro.

EDWARD SAID

❦ ❦ ❦

Edward Said (1935–2003) was the most spectacular intellectual asset of the Palestinians in exile. Because he had been exiled all the way to Columbia University, where he was professor of english and comparative literature, it was possible to say, as the perennial crisis in the Middle East continued to shape his scholarly and critical work, that he was caught between New York and a hard place. But there is no call to doubt his integrity just because he had been raised in transit on luxury liners, laurelled at Princeton and Harvard, and otherwise showered with all the rewards that Western civilization can bestow. What can be doubted is his accuracy. His influential book *Orientalism* (1978) painted a picture in which Western students of African, Arab and Eastern cultures had practised racist imperialism under the guise of a search for knowledge. The book was hugely influential: its "narratives of oppression" became the tunnels through which non-Western academics came to preferment in the West. Said's ideas found such favour on the international left that he became a whipping boy for the right, but it is important to say that there were some Arab thinkers who equally found *Orientalism* a wrong-headed book. According to them, it encouraged a victim mentality by enabling failed states to blame the West for their current plight: a patronizing idea, common to the Western left, which the emerging non-Western intelligentsia would find that much harder to rebut when endorsed by someone with Said's credentials and prestige. Though most of Said's Western admirers were never aware of it, this ambiguity marked Said's written work thoughout his career: he was continually telling the people he professed to be rescuing from Western influence that they were helpless in its embrace. A quality of self-defeating ambiguity also characterized Said's role as a practical diplomat. In 1988 he helped secure the breakthrough by which the Palestinian National Council finally recognized the State of Israel's right to exist, but in 1991 he resigned in protest at the Oslo peace process, before Arafat had even had a chance to scupper it. If a solution had been secured it could well have meant that the lives of everyone involved on the Palestinian side of the negotiating table would have been forfeit, but Said was unlikely to be put off by Arab extremists, who for a long time had been threatening him with death in one ear just as loudly as extreme Zionists had been threatening him in the other. Yet Said was exemplary in his insistence that Israel had an historic claim in Palestine and that anti-Semitism, with the Holocaust as its centrepiece, had better be understood by the Arab nations or there would be no end to the conflict. When he simplified history, it wasn't because he was a simpleton: though many a buffoon hoped to acquire points for intelligence by sitting beside him, his dignity was unimpaired, and he still looked wise even when accompanied by Tariq Ali looking serious.

Said's writing on the arts, at its best, has the exuberance that his writing on one art, music, always has. He played the piano to professional standard: a piquant demonstration that the Western and non-Western worlds of creativity had not been symmetrical. But his answer to that was convincing: if both sides had not created the music, they could both perform it. After his death, his orchestra plays on: the West-Eastern Divan, founded by him and Daniel Barenboim, has performed in the Occupied Territories. Said was an accomplished and charming man who presented his admirers on the left with the dangerous illusion that by appreciating his writings they were being fast-tracked to an understanding of the history of the Middle East in a refined form, without having to study it in further detail. There were non-Western scholars who thought that he had the same illusion about his nominal subject, and that no Orientalist has ever been more damagingly superficial than he. There can be no doubt, alas, that some of his themes were cartoons. His argument that every Orientalist racist imperialist scholar since the Enlightenment was furthering the territorial ambitions of his home country broke down on the obvious point that the best of them came from Germany, which before the twentieth century had no colonies to speak of. Simply because they believed in the objective nature of knowledge, the great European students of foreign cultures were all humanists before they were imperialists, and often defended the first thing against the second, out of love and respect. Today's Indian scholars of Indian languages further the work of English scholars whose names they revere, one fact among the many that Said found it convenient either not to mention or never to know. Also his idea that Napoleon had wrecked Egypt's advance into the modern age was not one shared by Naguib Mahfouz, who said that Egypt had Napoleon to thank for everything modern it possessed. Said was right to this extent, however: Occidental intellectuals find out very little about what is thought and written in the Oriental world. Very few of Said's admirers in the West could begin to contemplate the fact that there are some bright people in the East who thought of Said as just another international operator doing well out of patronizing them, and with less excuse. I finished writing the piece that follows not long before Said finally succumbed to cancer, and I have left it in the present tense to help indicate that I was treating him as a living force, brave in a cause that was very short of his kind of soldier.

I pressed harder. What about the admiring caresses
lavished by the camera on Mathieu marching into Algiers?
— EDWARD SAID, *REFLECTIONS ON EXILE*,
P. 286

ANNOYINGLY UNDATED except for its opening phrase, "A few
months ago," Said's essay on Gillo Pontecorvo is the account of a
personal meeting that probably took place in the late 1990s, by which
time Pontecorvo had not made a film in many years. But he had once,
in 1966, made a film that Said continues to admire as a masterwork of
political analysis: *The Battle of Algiers*. I feel the same, but for different
reasons, and by focusing on the second of these two quoted sentences
it is easy to make the difference plain. Said wants the film to be an outright condemnation of imperialism, with no concessions made to the
forces of oppression. Said thinks that the French claims to have
extended civilization to Algiers had nothing to be said for them, and
that the rebellious native Algerians, whatever atrocities they might
have committed, were well within their rights, considering the magnitude of the atrocity that had been committed against them. I want the
film to be what it is. It certainly does condemn imperialism, but it
shows that the French imperialism in Algeria was the work of human
beings, not automatons. It need hardly be added that Said is right
about how their apparently successful colonial efforts in Algeria corrupted the French into illusions of manifest destiny. Elsewhere in the
same book, Said gives an exemplary caning to Tocqueville, who was
respectful enough about the repressed minorities in America, but who
chose to despise Islam when he became gung-ho for a French Algeria.

Said's only mistake, but a crucial one, is to question Pontecorvo's
directorial emphasis at the exact moment when Pontecorvo is being
most sensitive. At his most sensitive, he is at his most comprehensive,
and comprehending. In letting the camera, and thus the audience, be
impressed by the French general's heroic stature as he marches into
Algiers at the head of his paratroopers, Pontecorvo shows why he ranks
with Costa-Gavras as a true *auteur* of the political film. In Costa-
Gavras's film *The Confession*, there is a similarly penetrating moment
when Yves Montand, released from gaol, meets his torturer in the
street, and can show nothing except embarrassment, while the torturer

(Gabriele Ferzetti) assumes that the victim will join him in blaming the whole episode on unfortunate circumstances. These are human reactions, in all their ambiguity. In *The Battle of Algiers*, the paratroopers' commander, Mathieu (in real life he was General Jacques Massu), is greeted with rapture by the *pieds noirs* as he leads his soldiers down the main street. They cheer, weep, do everything but lay palm fronds before his polished boots. He is greeted with hosannas because he looks like a saviour. Here is the man who will take the necessary measures to ensure that our innocent children are no longer blown to pieces in the nightclubs and restaurants. When the camera is on him, it has the eyes of his worshippers. If the camera bestows admiring caresses, it is because the crowd is doing the same.

Since 1834, generations of the French in Algiers had grown up believing they inhabited part of France. In 1963 they believed de Gaulle when he said that Algeria would stay French. To them, the paratroopers looked like the guarantee that it would do so. The paratroopers believed it too, and the film, in its tragically logical unfolding, shows that belief being undermined by horror at the tenacity of the other belief that they encountered, and at what they must do to fight it. "*Non siamo sadici,*" the general tells the press: "We are not sadists," and one of the measures of the film's unique subtlety is that we believe they are not, even as they set about doing sadistic things. There is a key moment when a couple of the paratroopers say a respectful "Courage!" to the man who is about to be tortured. Said might legitimately have objected to that. In any military group conducting interrogation by violence, no matter how reluctantly the policy is pursued, there are always a few genuine enthusiasts who relish the opportunity to make their sinister dreams come true. But Said's objection is directed elsewhere, at the very idea that the French in Algeria might have had a point in thinking that they had something to protect.

Wedded to his conviction that imperialism is always and exclusively a force bent on destruction, Said writes as if the French could have had no reason to believe in their *mission civilisatrice*. He writes as if they would only have had to take thought to see the truth. But they had been bred to believe that there was something to it. In the opening sequence of the movie, Pontecorvo showed that their belief was an illusion. As the future insurgents look on silently from the gaol window, an anonymous colleague, with frightening efficiency and speed, is executed in the courtyard. Civilization means the guillotine. But the *pieds noirs* thought the repression of the natives was incidental, not fundamental. They had developed a culture, had some reason to believe in its superiority, and were concerned to protect it. (There is a constant assumption behind Said's writings that multiculturalism, in imperial times, was an *a priori* view that had to be suppressed by propaganda, rather than a view which grew out of the imperial experience as a result of the contact.) For the French in Algeria, their mission to rule by right was an understandable belief. Even Camus shared it to a certain extent: he could be single-minded in despising Nazism and communism, but he was in two minds about Algeria until his last day. How would Said have had Pontecorvo film the scene in question, the one about the paratroopers arriving in Algiers like redeeming heroes at the striding heels of their suave commander? Should the actor playing him have been uglier, even though Massu looked like a film star in real life? Should his dialogue have been less subtle, even though Massu was well aware that a holding action was the best that could be hoped for, and said so? Should he have been wearing a swastika armband?

Said has similar objections to the glamour of the Marlon Brando character in Pontecorvo's other big political statement, *Quemada!* The imperialist looks too good. This bothers Said even though *Quemada!* like *The Battle of Algiers*, is scrupulous in attributing all the impetus and justification of history to the insurgents: scrupulous, relentless and disturbingly convincing for those of us who doubt the efficacy of the outcome. Said doesn't doubt it, yet he detects in Pontecorvo a lingering tendency to admire the envoys of established power. The same tendency can't be imputed to Said. One detects in him a puritanical determination to remain unsullied by the blandishments of his own cultural sympathies. As a critic and man of letters he has an enviable scope, but it is continually invaded by his political strictness. It would be foolish to blame him for this. If he had a secular Islamic intelligentsia behind him, he could leave a share of his self-imposed task to others. But he is pretty much on his own, and needs his absolutism if he is to fight his battle. Though his aesthetic judgements are often finely nuanced, there can be few nuances in his basic political position, so he is easily put out when the same turns out not to be true for an established West-

ern radical he would like to admire without reserve. At the end of his
encounter with Pontecorvo, he is disappointed to discover that Pontecorvo has been making commercials without telling anybody. The
implication is that if Pontecorvo had lived up to the seriousness of his
early masterpieces, he would now be living in a tent, and proud of it.
But Pontecorvo, until 1956, was a Communist, and Said has underestimated—or, rather, overestimated—the grandees of the Italian Communist intelligentsia. Few of them ever embraced the privations of the
proletariat. The Italian intellectuals of the post-war *sinistra* might have
paid lip service to Gramsci but their true models were among the
perennial left-leaning artists of Europe: the Picasso who disguised his
limousine as a taxi, and the Brecht whose rough-looking blue work-
shirts were tailored for him out of matted silk. The luminaries of the
Italian left were concerned with taking their place in a current society,
not a future one. Fundamentalism was corrupted by the temptations of
civilization, and Said might eventually reach the conclusion that it
would be better if the same thing could happen in the Islamic world.

In his fine long essay "Nationalism, Human Rights and Interpretation" (appearing as chapter 36 of *Reflections on Exile*) there is an encouraging sign that he has already reached it. He notes that the Lebanese
writer Adonis, like Salman Rushdie, was reviled for suggesting that a
strict literalism in the reading of sacred texts kills the spirit. Said is only
a step away from saying that no text is sacred. He is brave enough to
take that step: he is used to having his life threatened. His other fear is
the disabling one: the fear of giving aid and comfort to the automatic
enemies of Islam. But one is not necessarily an enemy of Islam for saying that although all good books are holy, no book is the word of God.
Even the greatest books are the work of human beings, in all their
frailty. Without the frailty, there would be no art, or even any thought.
When Said saw the general up there on the screen looking so seductive, he thought that he had caught Pontecorvo in a weak moment. But
the weak moment was a moment of strength. Pontecorvo had asked
himself: "How would I have reacted, if I had been a French Algerian,
and had been there in the street for the arrival of the strongman who
had come to reassure me that my life had not been wasted?" By looking into himself, he was able to see everything else: the sign of the
artist. As for Pontecorvo the ex-artist, he made those commercials in

order to maintain his way of life as a figure of prestige, a man who counts. And after all, the prestige was impressively brought into play when Pontecorvo strode forward as a headline act in the demonstrations against the bombing of Afghanistan. There he was, up there on the screen: the great director, being lavished with the camera's admiring caresses. One imagines that Said was pleased enough to see that.

SAINTE-BEUVE

Charles-Augustin Sainte-Beuve (1804–1869) was the illustrious nineteenth-century French man of letters who got a bad press from a long line of good writers, from Flaubert through Proust to Vladimir Nabokov: it was his bad reputation, rather than his renown, that outlived him. The student should be slow to join in the denigration. Sainte-Beuve really was the greatest literary critic of his time, even though he sometimes gave too much praise to mediocrity, and not enough to genius. Nor did he miss out on every genius. His advocacy and understanding of Victor Hugo led to a close friendship, although his love affair with Madame Hugo was not calculated to reinforce it. That was probably the best thing about Sainte-Beuve's multifarious energy (he was poet and novelist as well as critic): he was willing to live outside the categories. He had a nose for the everyday, and he found the everyday everywhere. For such a writer to make criticism his main creative effort was without precedent. Throughout his life, the weekly essay was his characteristic form, and finally it was the wealth of observation, invention and reasoning that he was ready to pour into an apparently casual piece that marked him out. Read today, his volumes of weekly pieces are still a good way of building up strength in one's reading of French, because even when the subject was ephemeral he gave it permanence with his registration of contemporary detail, so the reader is usefully driven to the dictionary and the Larousse. (The presence of that latter volume on your desk is a sure sign that you are on the right track.) As a literary grandee, Sainte-Beuve took a prominent place at the celebrated Parisian restaurant Magny's, where all the literary world came to dine and the brothers Goncourt surreptitiously wrote down the conversation. (*Dinner at Magny's*, by Robert Baldick, can be recommended as ranking high in the sumptuous genre of gossipy books about Parisian artistic life.) The concept of a literary world—a milieu which surrounds the outstanding literary figures, ameliorates their natural isolation and incidentally provides an honourable and useful life for those who are not outstanding—was represented for nineteenth-century France by Sainte-Beuve, as it was represented for eighteenth-century England by Dr. Johnson. The literary world turns the café into a campus, with conversation as a permanent seminar. Sainte-Beuve's triumph was to have his conversations with the public as well as with the writers. In the universities he was less uniformly successful. Appointed by Napoleon III as professor of Latin poetry at the College de France in 1854, he was shouted down by rebellious students. Later on, as a senator, he retrieved his reputation as a champion of liberal thought. He had set the style for the public intellectual speaking through a newspaper column to an audience of those either literate or aspiring to be so. The role was open to abuse, but it became the natural centre of critical energy, and modern civilization owes Sainte-Beuve a permanent debt for having played his part without stinting his talents.

Every circle of society is a little world apart; to the extent that one lives in it, one knows everything and believes that everyone must know the same things; and then, ten years, twenty years, thirty years having gone by, the circle is broken and vanished, not a sign is left, nothing is written

down, and one is reduced to guessing about the whole
thing, to bringing it back on the basis of the vaguest hear-
say and through feeble echoes.
—SAINTE-BEUVE, FROM A LETTER
COLLECTED IN VOL. 17 OF HIS
CORRESPONDENCE GÉNÉRALE, AS QUOTED
IN *TIMES LITERARY SUPPLEMENT*,
OCTOBER 3, 1975

QUITE APART FROM its manifest truth, this is Sainte-Beuve at his
best: a best we can't afford to ignore. Plenty of his critics—critics
of the critic—have striven to help us forget all about him. Ernst Robert
Curtius thought that Sainte-Beuve's long critical career had given
French literature a coherence and a continuity that were absent from
German literature because no comparable figure to Sainte-Beuve
existed. But very few figures comparable to Curtius have ever shown
the same enthusiasm about Sainte-Beuve, and many of them have
decried him as a shameless puffer of journey-work, the exemplar and
protector of the second-rate. Nabokov, always on the lookout for novelists unjustly praised, loathed him, and with some reason. Sainte-
Beuve certainly had a gift for slighting the gifted while rabbiting on
endlessly in praise of mediocrities. Flaubert poured the energy of
genius into the job of demonstrating how thoroughly Sainte-Beuve
had misunderstood him in the matter of *Salammbô*. As for Proust himself, it can be said that his whole career was one long version of his
polemic *Contre Sainte-Beuve*. The music critic Edward Hanslick carried
a comparatively slight burden: as the object of Wagner's scorn, he was
the involuntary model for Beckmesser in *Die Meistersinger von Nürn-
berg*, but at least he had only one opera aimed at him. Sainte-Beuve was
the target for the whole of *À la recherche du temps perdu*. He was lucky
to be dead.

But in literature there is, or ought to be, such a thing as a right of
precedence, and the chronological facts say that Sainte-Beuve sounded
like Proust before Proust did. At one stage I read all the way through
the collected *Causeries du lundi* columns in a bunch of disintegrating
paperbacks I bought from a *bouquiniste* on the Left Bank. With torn
and faded yellow wrappers thinner than their pages, the books were
sadly battered little bundles that fell open anywhere and eventually fell

apart. It was one of the ways I learned French: a *lundi* a day, underline every word you don't know, keep going for as long as you get the sense, look up the hard words afterwards. Later on I replaced those tatty collections of Sainte-Beuve's weekly output with a glistening Pléiade set, and although I never took the Pléiade volumes down from the shelf with the same alacrity, they had their use, principally for checking up on just how completely the star critic had missed the point of most of the great writers of his time. Had Nabokov exaggerated about Sainte-Beuve's peculiar tolerance for the uninspired? Not really. Eventually, in a fit of madness, I supplemented the set of Sainte-Beuve's literary criticism with a complete Pléiade three-volume set of his unwieldly sociological masterpiece *Histoire de Port-Royal*, just in case I ever wanted to get on top of whatever he had had to say about Jansenism. It hasn't happened yet, but might. My point now is that with all these books of his on my shelves, I still would have missed this particular paragraph, because even though I read him for his tone rather than as a guide, and therefore could have read him writing about anything, it still would have been unlikely that I would have read the correspondence through. I have all the correspondence of Voltaire, and enjoy dipping into it: but I will probably never read it through. You need to be very mad about an author to follow him down all his alleys, because you will be spending time on his minutiae that you could be devoting to someone else's main event. (Sometimes the correspondence *is* the main event: Madame de Sévigné put everything she had into her letters, and there is nowhere else to find out who she really was.)

The blunt truth about all the attendant writings of even the greatest writers is that we must almost wholly rely on the machinery of scholarship, publishing and reviewing to draw our attention to the little things that piece out the big picture. Somebody had to edit at least seventeen volumes of Sainte-Beuve's general correspondence, and somebody else had to read them with reasonable thoroughness, before a piece could appear in the *TLS* from which I could seize this paragraph and copy it out into my journal. I did so for two reasons: for the truth of what it said, and because it reminded me of Proust. At the time—more than a quarter of a century ago—I had not yet lived with Proust long enough to realize that the connection might go a long way beyond mere coincidence, or the fact that the two men wrote in the same language. As the years went by, however, the way Proust's mind worked became a more open book—his book, always, but less puzzling, if even more daunting. Proust the great writer stood more and more revealed as Proust the great critic. He was a great critic because he responded to all the arts at the level of their creation. He could not see a painting, hear a piece of music or read a stretch of prose without joining in with the painter, the composer or the writer. It was always as if he had been there, collaborating.

He had been there even with the despised Sainte-Beuve. In Sainte-Beuve's prose, the vehicle for opinions Proust found fatuous, he had found something profound that he could use, as he found something he could use in everyone to whom he paid attention, even if all they did was make cakes. With Sainte-Beuve I think it was the additive measure: the way the paragraph steadily unfolds an argument. In Sainte-Beuve's weekly grind of journeyman judgement, most of the arguments did not reach very distinguished conclusions. He said himself that he praised the dullards because "for me it is truly an affair of equity." A pretty damning confession.

But a judge's opinion can be wrong and still have distinction in the way it incorporates observations about life. The distinguishing mark of Sainte-Beuve's opinions was the confidence of generalization he could put into them. In that, the young Proust saw a possibility. He would not have seen it in this letter, which he could not have read: but the letter—and this is why I seized on it—is a distillation of Sainte-Beuve's characteristic manner, which Proust might have abominated but could not avoid, because it was part of the landscape. Somewhere in Sainte-Beuve's steady outpourings that chugged away reliably like *les égouts* beneath the streets, Proust saw a way forward for himself. Later on he might have forgotten where he saw it. He was not a mean man and would not have belittled Sainte-Beuve just to discredit the source of a debt. It is a diverting mind game to imagine how Sainte-Beuve would have reviewed the complete (more accurately, the never-completed) *À la recherche du temps perdu*. He probably would have missed its significance. But he might well have spotted the rhythm of his own prose, transformed in the taking over and put to a more ambitious use, yet undeniably, in his opinion, pinched.

Great writers get away with absorbing the discoveries of lesser writers. If the great writer is great enough—T. S. Eliot, for example—he can even get away with saying outright that he steals them. The person stolen from is seldom heard to complain, being already dead; but sometimes he is almost the star's contemporary, and on a few occasions there is no almost about it. Robert Graves went through an embarrassing phase of being hopping mad about how W. H. Auden had helped himself to the cadences of Laura Riding. Graves, who had the misfortune to be Riding's husband, was thought to be slightly potty on the subject, but it is quite possible that Auden had seen her verses, absorbed some of her rhythmic quirks, and incorporated them into his upcoming work. Only one critic ever blew the whistle on Hugh MacDiarmid's flagrant thefts from E. E. Cummings: the Scottish critics thought their man had *droit de seigneur*, and hardly anybody else cared. MacDiarmid was probably speaking the truth when he said he never consciously stole from anyone. He could steal hundreds of lines without batting an eyelid. Only the psychopathic plagiarist counts on getting caught. Most plagiarists are just submitting themselves to influence. It isn't even necessary for the raptor to lift a finished idea: a mere suggestion can be enough. Among my acquaintances, there are at least two novelists who will nick any good phrase they hear in conversation, and at least one who knows he is doing it. His justification, as far as I can make out, is that he would have thought of it eventually anyway. He is probably right. Proust would have ended up writing like Proust even if he had never read Sainte-Beuve. But without reading Sainte-Beuve, Proust would have been a bit slower to realize the way that Proust was meant to sound.

JOSÉ SARAMAGO

❦ ❦ ❦

José Saramago (b. 1922) is a Portuguese writer who won the
Nobel Prize, whereas Fernando Pessoa was a Portuguese
writer who didn't. Since Pessoa was without question the outstanding literary figure in his language, the anomaly tells you
all you need to know about the true value of the prize: but
Saramago is not without an importance of his own. His novels
present the kind of straightforward allegorical provocations
that journalists enjoy treating as problems. In *The Stone Raft*,
Portugal breaks off and puts out to sea, thereby demonstrating
its isolation: in *The Gospel According to Jesus Christ*, the Jesus
story is rewritten to give him a sex life, thereby anticipating
Martin Scorsese in the challenge to standard religious sensibil-
ities; and in *Blindness* almost nobody can see what life is really
like, thereby supporting the notion that bourgeois society
demands blind obedience. The rehashed gospel did most to set
a Catholic country by the ear, but the book about mental
myopia was really the more outrageous statement in a country
waking up from military dictatorship, because Saramago was
still proposing what he had always proposed: that liberal
democracy wouldn't be democratic enough, and only communism could give life its full value. This latter conviction on his

part should be kept in mind when reading his notebooks. Written in his idyllic retirement on the island of Lanzarote in the Canaries, the *Cadernos* give us a beguiling account of how a literary giant handles his life. But the enchantment ought to carry a health warning. Saramago joined the Communist Party in 1969. The Party had been banned under the military dictatorship, which no doubt seemed a good reason for joining it once the regime had melted away, but to join up in the year after the Soviet Union had stamped on Dubcek took a brass neck on Saramago's part. There is no reason to think, however, that Saramago has ever especially admired the coercion exercised by all Communist regimes, without exception, against the common people they claim to champion. He just seems never to have heard of it. What he has heard of is the inadequacy of democracy. His Nobel Prize in 1998 might have been awarded for his proven inability to advance his position by so much as a nuance. In *Le Monde Diplomatique* for August 2004 he published an article pointing out that no ruling party elected by the people ever truly represents them. The possibility that an unelected ruling party would represent them even less he left unexamined. "I am not against parties (I am a militant member of a political party). . . ." Yes, but that party is against parties, isn't it? One could go on: almost everything he so confidently states to be true would be thought to need less absurdly guileless language even by those who share his views. Politically, Saramago is a writer whose fluent readiness to explain the world is unimpeded by the embarrassing fact that he has somehow managed never to hear the real news. A functioning democracy represents the people mainly by ensuring that no one group can maintain its power over them without being subject to displacement at their whim. Saramago's impressive reluctance to consider this principle is perhaps evidence that a military dictatorship is a bad place in which to get an education in the politics of either wing, but there are plenty of Portuguese intellectuals among Saramago's contemporaries who would say that the native land of Pessoa didn't cease producing intelligent people just because the thugs were in charge. With Saramago, as with so many other writers and intellectuals of his stamp, we should be careful about attributing a deep seriousness to inflexible error. To be reasonable is not to be frivolous: it's the very opposite. Saramago the Nobel laureate, however, deserves credit for making sure, especially in his highly readable notebooks, that the reader never loses sight of the turbulence where culture and politics meet.

> I am a Eurosceptic who learned his scepticism
> from a professor called Europe.
> —JOSÉ SARAMAGO, *CUADERNOS DE*
> *LANZAROTE (1993–1995)*, P. 486

AT THE TIME he wrote this, Saramago was a distinguished old man snugly busy with his notebooks (*cadernos* in Portuguese, *cuadernos* in Spanish) on Lanzarote, his volcanic island in the Canaries. He was only a few years short of winning the Nobel Prize in literature for Portugal. No doubt it was Portugal's turn: by the same standard, Fernando Pessoa should have won it six times, once for each of his multiple personalities. But some of us who enjoy Saramago's expository prose found it hard to suppress a snort of derision at the general agreement by the international culture-page press that the prize committee, in paying its respects to literature, was justified in tacitly conceding that his political stance might have had something to it. It was a false equation: Saramago is a charming diarist, but his political stance has nothing to it beyond a formidable inbuilt capacity to gloss over its own consequences. Europe might have taught him Euroscepticism. There was a whole ruined world that should have taught him to be sceptical about communism. He never got the point. As a diehard believer who had refused to give up his faith even in the face of limitless evidence that it was a pack of lies whose first victims were the people it claimed to benefit, Saramago was reminiscent of Pablo Neruda and Nicolás Guillén: he had to be taken seriously because there was no other way to take him.

Beyond the ludicrous, the scale of the preposterous starts coming back in the other direction, so that we return to the point where a mind can be granted a kind of dignity for its persistence in folly. (This was the defence that was often made for the Scottish nationalist poet Hugh MacDiarmid, who joined the Communist Party *after* the repression of the Hungarian uprising in 1956, at the precise moment when everyone else was leaving: you can't deny that he stuck to his principles.) Neruda and Guillén can both be given points for sticking with communism if you concede that democracy might never be capable of bringing justice to Latin America: and there will probably continue to be dark moments when we want to concede that. But as in the case of Africa, these are moments of despair on our part, and by succumbing to them we grossly patronize the people on the spot, for whom a drastic solution will be no relief at all for their suffering, and will almost certainly intensify it. Similarly, Saramago's long intransigence was a measure of the fix Portugal had got itself into with its tenaciously self-renewing tradition of salon fascism, a tradition that was by no means extinguished by the retirement of Salazar in 1968. When democracy finally arrived in 1974, Saramago didn't trust it.

Saramago had good reason to suspect that justice would never come by reasonable means. But when it finally showed signs of doing so, he did nothing in his discursive writings to justify his position in the only way it could have been justified. He could have said that without the critique mounted from people like him who had been driven by exasperation to the far left, the far right would never have been eroded in its confidence. It would have been partly true. But it was wholly untrue to go on claiming that the far left offered an alternative in itself. The price of sticking to such a proposition was to restrict his frame of reference to the size of his own study. There was a world elsewhere in which the common people, all around the planet, had been massacred by the million over the course of decades, and all in the name of the cause he remained proud to represent. None of that taught him anything. It couldn't because he didn't want it to. Europe taught him Euroscepticism because he did want it to: because he thought that the idea of a united Europe was a stratagem for capitalist hegemony. But the people who hatched the idea had more creative aims in mind than that. They wanted an end to violent conflict. The people who hatched the ideas at the base of Saramago's declared faith never wanted anything of the kind. For any deliberately withdrawn writer who would like to be encouraged in his isolation, Saramago's journals make pleasant reading, but if you compare them to the journals of, say, Gombrowicz, the difference comes howling out of the page. When Gombrowicz ignores the world, he knows what the world is. Saramago doesn't want to know. It wouldn't matter if he were just a creative writer. But he wants to be taken as a political philosopher. It is a pose about which we are entitled to be sceptical, having learned our scepticism from a professor called history.

JEAN-PAUL SARTRE

Radiating contempt for its bourgeois liberal conformity, Jean-Paul Sartre (1905–1980) looms in the corner of this book like a genius with the evil eye. For the book's author, Sartre is a devil's advocate to be despised more than the devil, because the advocate was smarter. No doubt this is a disproportionate reaction. Sartre, after all, never actually killed anybody. But he excused many who did, and most of those never actually killed anybody either: they just gave orders for their subordinates to do so. There is a moral question there, of the type with which Sartre was well equipped to deal, had he chosen to do so. He was a brilliant man: the first thing to say about him, although unfortunately not the last. After the liberation of Paris in 1944 he called, in his capacity as a Resistance fighter, for punishment to be vented on those among his fellow literati who had collaborated with the Nazis. The question of how much Resistance fighting he had actually done did not impede his postwar climb to prominence. As philosopher, novelist, playwright, social commentator and political analyst, Sartre was the preeminent French left-wing intellectual of the Fourth Republic and beyond, reigning supreme in the Left Bank cafés with Simone de Beauvoir the queen at his side. The pair made intellectual distinction into a media story: the celebrity enjoyed now by a glamour-boy philosopher such as Bernard-Henri Lévy has its precedent in that post-war connection between serious thought and media dazzle, a Parisian microclimate which helped to give France a sense of luxury at a time when food and fuel were still in short supply. After Camus died prematurely in a car crash, Sartre's true rival, Raymond Aron, was a long time in attracting the allegiance of the independent left, and in the meanwhile Sartre's *gauchiste* vision was the style setter of French political thought, founding an orthodoxy that still saturates French intellectual life today, and, to a certain extent, continues to set a standard of *engagement* (the word, especially when detached from any real connotation, looks better in the orginal) for intellectual life all over the world. A key principle in this vision is that the Communist regimes, no matter how illiberal, had serious altruistic intentions in comparison with the irredeemably self-serving capitalist West. (Acadmics in the capitalist West greeted this brainwave with awed approval, failing to note that their society could hardly be self-interested if it allowed them to do so—unless, that is, freedom of expression is a sly trick played by capitalism to convince the gullible that they are at liberty.) When Sartre broke with the Communists, he retained respect for their putatively benevolent social intentions, and was ready to say something exculpatory even if what he was exculpating was the Gulag network, whose existence, after he finally ceased to deny it, he never condemned as a central product of a totalitarian system, but only regretted as an incidental blemish. This manoeuvre, implying a powerful ability to deny the import of a fact even after he had acknowledged it, was hard to distinguish from duplicity.

Sceptics might say that a knack for making duplicity look profound was inherent in Sartre's style of argument. Students who tackle his creative prose in the novel sequence *The Road to Freedom* or the play *Kean* (his most convincing illustration of existentialism as a living philosophy) will find clear moments of narrative, but all clarity evaporates when it comes to the discursive prose of his avowedly philosophical works. It should be said in fairnesss that even the English philosopher Roger Scruton, otherwise a severe critic of Sartre, finds Sartre's keystone work *L'Être et le néant* (*Being and Nothingness*) a substantial work; and Jean-François Revel, who took Sartre's political philosophy apart brick by brick, still admired him as a philosopher who earned his own credentials, without depending on the university system for his prestige. But those of us unfettered by being either professional philosophers or patriotic Frenchmen can surely suggest that even Sartre's first and most famous treatise shows all the signs not just of his later mummery, but of the mummery of other pundits who came to later fame. Foucault, Derrida and the like shouldn't have needed scientific debunking to prove them fraudulent: the pseudo-scientific vacuity of their argufying was sufficiently evident from the wilful obfuscation of their stylistic hoopla: and the same could have been said of their progenitor. Where Sartre got it from is a mystery begging to be explained. It could have had something to do with his pre-war period in Berlin, and especially with the influence of his admired Heidegger. In Sartre's style of argument, German metaphysics met French sophistry in a kind of European Coal and Steel Community producing nothing but rhetorical gas.

But the best explanation might have more to do with his personality. Perhaps he was over-compensating. It would be frivolous to suggest that Sartre's bad eye was a factor determining personality, like Goebbels's bad foot; and anyway, Sartre's physical ugliness in no way impeded his startling success with women. It might be possible, however, that he was compensating for a mental condition that he knew to be crippling. He might have known that he was debarred by nature from telling the truth for long about anything that mattered, because telling the truth was something that ordinary men did, and his urge to be extraordinary was, for him, more of a motive force than merely to see the world as it was. This perversity—and he was perverse whether he realized it or not—made him the most conspicuous single example in the twentieth century of a fully qualified intellectual aiding and abetting the opponents of civilization. More so than Ezra Pound, who was too crazy even for the Fascists; more so even than Brecht, a straight-out cynic who kept his money in Switzerland. Sartre was never corrupt in that way. Like Robespierre, he had an awful purity. Sartre turned down the Nobel Prize. He was living proof that the devil's advocate can be idealistic and even self-sacrificing. Minus his virtues, he would be much easier to dismiss. With them, he presents us with our most worrying reminder that the problem of amoral intelligence is not confined to the sciences. It can happen to culture too, which suggests that on some level being a humanist means not being like Sartre. His admirers might say that we are in no danger of that. But usually, when they admire him that much, they make his sort of noise. The tip-off is the sentence that spurns the earth because it fears a puncture.

❦ ❦ ❦

> The Cogito never delivers anything except what we ask it to deliver. Descartes never interrogated it concerning its functional aspect: "I doubt, I think," and by having wanted to proceed without a guiding thread from this functional aspect to its existential dialectic, he fell into the substantialist error. Husserl, instructed by this error, remained fearfully on the plain of functional description. By that fact, he never superseded the pure description of appearance as such; he remained fixed on the Cogito; he merits being called, despite his denials, a phenomenist rather than a phenomenologue; and his phenomenism borders at all times on Kantian idealism. Heidegger, wanting to avoid the phenomenism of description that leads to the megatic and antidialectic isolation of essence, directly tackles the existential analytic without passing through the Cogito. . . .
> —JEAN-PAUL SARTRE, *L'ÊTRE ET LE NÉANT*, QUOTED BY JEAN-FRANÇOIS REVEL IN *POURQUOI DES PHILOSOPHES*, PP. 69–70

BUT ENOUGH, AND more than enough. Language which makes such a show of saying everything at once is usually concealing something important, and in Sartre's case, Revel knew exactly what it was. Revel could have hung Sartre out to dry, had he wished. Revel had the credentials and the information with which to expose Sartre's imposture as a Resistance hero. Sartre's nauseating theatricality in that regard (he didn't mind implicating de Beauvoir in the charade either: for once they were a couple) was finally laid bare in 1991 by Gilbert Joseph in his blood-curdling book *Une si douce occupation*. But it could have been done years before, by people who were on the scene and knew the truth: people like Revel.

Revel contented himself with pointing out what ought to have been self-evident: that anyone who could perpetrate a passage of balderdash like this had done a pretty thorough job of detaching philosophy from wisdom—and wisdom, according to Revel, was the only thing that philosophy could now concern itself with, and had been since the rise of the sciences cancelled the last possibility of philosophy being a science to itself. In France, where the language offers no automatic defence mechanism against the flummery of scientism, this argument needed plenty of putting until quite recent times. Finally it took a pair of scientists, writing in French but with a thorough background in American scepticism, to produce the book that blew the whistle on Jacques Lacan, Julia Kristeva, Jean Baudrillard and the other artistes in the flouncing kick-line of the post-modern intellectual cabaret. But the two sceptical critics, Alan Sokal and Jean Bricmont, did not extend their catcalling to management level. Their justly praised but not really very revolutionary book *Impostures intellectuelles* (1997) should not have come as such a bombshell. It did so because critics well qualified to assess the health of French intellectual life had been pussyfooting for decades, uncomfortably aware that the infection of pseudo-scientific casuistry was not peripheral to the main fields of humanist speculation, but central: exalted balderdash was their common property. Revel knew all too well that Sartre was peddling a system for betting on the horses. But the interesting question was how a serious customer like Sartre got himself into such a comical fix, and that was the question that Revel couldn't bring himself to tackle.

Surely part of the answer is that Sartre couldn't do for himself as an analytical thinker what he was bound to do for himself as a creative artist—live out his bad faith. Sartre is high on the list of the writer-

philosophers who were more writer than philosopher. Montaigne, Pascal, Lessing, Lichtenberg, Schopenhauer, Nietzsche—it is exalted
company, but Sartre earns his place as a stylist who could make the language speak. The actor lucky enough to take the title role in Sartre's
play *Kean* (in the original production it was the mighty Pierre Brasseur,
he who was Frédéric Lemaitre in the Occupation's escapist masterwork, the film *Les Enfants du Paradis*) gets better things to say about
existentialism than are ever said in Sartre's formal writings on the subject. In its later life, Sartre's play *Huis clos* is too much praised for having been an act of political daring when it was written. Its original
production was officially allowed by the German Occupation authorities, some of whom came to see it. They allowed it because they knew
its appeal to liberty was camped in the air, and they came to see it
because they knew they were in safe company. The moral problems
with which the play's supposedly trapped personages elegantly wrestle
are woefully abstract compared with those which were currently
drenching even the proclaimed fascist sympathizers among French
intellectuals in cold sweat every night. (Sartre might really have had
something if he had set his play in the *wagon-lit* that took the minor
writers Jacques Chardonne and Marcel Jouhandeau on their 1941 trip
to Germany, or if he had set it in the swastika-decorated salon of the
Vienna hotel where they were joined not only by the French collaborators Drieu la Rochelle and Robert Brasillach but by the Nazi hier-
arch Baldur von Schirach in full dress uniform.) As for the moral
problems waiting to be faced by French intellectuals who fancied that
they were resisting tyranny by assenting to its demands with sufficient
reluctance, those had not yet arisen in perceptible form, and in the
conspicuous cases of Sartre and Beauvoir they were never to do so.
Huis clos is a play absolutely not about its time—a time when the case
for humanity was being heard not behind closed doors but with the
doors wide open, so that everyone could see, but only at the price of
weeping tears bitter with the salt of shame. It is, however, a play *of* its
time, and perhaps most flagrantly so because of what it ignores. In
other words, the inner turmoil gets into the action somehow. Why else
would these etiolated personalities be pretending ordinary life is hell,
unless somewhere, in the real life outside, real personalities were
encountering a hell without pretense? What could not be said in the

street was there in the theatre in the resounding form of what could not be said on stage. As a writer, in short, Sartre was unable to escape history, because his use of language could not keep it out.

As a philosopher, to escape history was Sartre's chief concern. There was almost no salient truth about the Occupation period that he was able to analyse directly at the moment when it might have mattered. When it was safe to do so, he nerved himself to say that anti-Semitism was a bad thing. *Réflexions sur la question juive* even contains a good epigram: armed with anti-Semitism, he said, even an idiot can be a member of an elite. Though the trains had already left from Drancy—by the time he wrote the pamphlet, the Nazis were gone as well—at least his opinion was published. He slammed the stable door. But he never made a beginning on the question of how the writers and intellectuals who continued with their careers during the Occupation could do so only at the cost—precisely calculated by the Propaganda Abteilung—of tacitly conniving at Nazi policies, all of which radiated from one central policy, which was the extermination of the Jews. No moral issue was ever more inescapably real; even the cost of ignoring it was directly measurable in lost lives; there could be no philosophical discussion of any subject on which *that* subject did not intrude. If Sartre wanted to avoid examining his own behaviour—and clearly he did—he would need to develop a manner of writing philosophy in which he could sound as if he was talking about everything while saying nothing. To the lasting bamboozlement of the civilized world, he succeeded, at least on the level of professional prestige. Working by a sure instinct for bogus language, a non-philosopher like George Orwell could call Sartre's political writings a heap of beans, but there were few professional thinkers anywhere who found it advisable to dismiss Sartre's air of intelligence: there was too great a risk of being called unintelligent themselves. *Effectivement*—to reemploy a French word that was worked to death at the time—Sartre was called profound because he sounded as if he was either that or nothing, and few cared to say that they thought him nothing.

How did he work the trick? There was a hidden door. From the writer committed to transparency it might go against the grain to say so, but there is such a thing as an obscure language that contains meaning, and there is also such a thing as a meaning too subtle to be clearly expressed. Karl Popper made a heavy commitment to what he called "ordinary language philosophy." But in *Unended Quest* (subtitled "an intellectual biography") he registered his telling, last-ditch concessions that ordinary language is conservative; that "in matters of the *intellect* (as opposed, perhaps, to art, or to politics) nothing is less creative and more commonplace than conservatism"; and that although "common sense" is often right, "things get really interesting just when it is wrong" (p. 125: the italics are his). Because Popper is the doorman, we can believe that there really must be a door, and that it is a very large one to be left open. The legitimate inference seems to be that an expository language pushing deep into originality might not necessarily sound readily intelligible; with the niggling corollary that a language which does not sound readily intelligible might conceivably be exploratory.

Revel, heartening in his impatience with Sartre's ponderous folderol, usefully records Kierkegaard's threat to Hegel: that he would send to him a young man who was in search of advice. Kierkegaard's menacing insinuation was that Hegel would have to either get down to brass tacks or be responsible for the young man's bewilderment. Revel also, and even more usefully, suggests that we should make the same threat to Heidegger. One says "even more usefully" because although there is something to be said against the belief that Hegel's obscurity is never meaningful, there is nothing to be said against the belief that Heideggers's obscurity is always meaningless. Hegel was trying to get something awkward out into the open. Heidegger was straining every nerve of the German language to do exactly the opposite. More than half a century later, the paradox has still not finished unravelling: it was Heidegger's high-flown philosophical flapdoodle that lent credibility to Sartre's. It was a paradox because Heidegger was an even more blatant case than Sartre of a speculative mind that could not grant itself freedom to speculate in the one area where it was fully qualified to deal with the concrete facts—its own compromises with reality. But merely to call Heidegger a "more blatant case" shows what we are up against. The case is still not clear, and in the years when Sartre and Heidegger were in a supposedly fruitful intellectual symbiosis, it was still not even a case: Heidegger's involvement with the Nazis was thought of as a flirtation. The means scarcely existed for anyone—philosopher, philologist, literary critic, journalist or clinical psychologist—to point out the truth which has since become steadily more obvious, even if it does not appear axiomatic yet: that these two men, Heidegger and Sartre, were only pretending to deal with existence, because each of them was in outright denial of his own experience, and therefore had a vested interest in separating existence from the facts. Will it ever be realized that they were a vaudeville act? Probably not. Even George Steiner, who can scarcely be accused of insensitivity to the historical background, persists in talking about the pair of them as if they were Goethe and Schiller. Those of us who think they were Abbott and Costello had better reconcile ourselves to making no converts.

There are plenty of philosophical works that writers should read, starting with the Platonic dialogues if not before. Life being short, however, and full of things that an artist should know, there is only so much time to read books *about* philosophy. Bertrand Russell wrote a great one—his *History of Western Philosophy*—and there are many more, some of them very seductive: Bryan Magee's handbook about Popper is an introduction much more entertaining than the subject it introduces. But *caveat lector*: life is waiting, and to read about someone who writes about life is getting far from it. Reading Schopenhauer when he tells you to watch out for reading too many books is already getting far from it, and at this moment you are reading someone who is telling you about how Schopenhauer said that you should not let reading come between you and life. In philosophy, the infinite regress is a sign that someone has made a mistake in logic. In ordinary life, it is a sign that someone is hiding from reality.

Sartre hid. Of course he did; and if *he* did, anybody can, including us; although I think that if we hide in lies, the lies should not be blasphemous. Sartre blasphemed when he took upon himself, and kept for the rest of his life, battle honours that properly belonged to people who ran risks he never ran, and who died in his stead. All his other weaknesses can be comprehended, and easily pardoned if not dismissed: most of us would have shown the same frail spirit. Many of the traumatized French soldiers who were allowed to go home from German POW camps pretended they escaped: it sounded less feeble. To get a play put on, Sartre bent his knee to the Occupation authorities. In one of Beauvoir's novels, a character otherwise obviously based on Camus is portrayed as doing the same, whereas the character based on Sartre is braver than a lion. Sartre was genuine (conveniently genuine) in granting Beauvoir her individuality, so he can perhaps be excused for not feeling responsible for her: but on that point an apology to Camus might not have come amiss. To question himself, however, was not in Sartre's nature. For a man whose Resistance group had done nothing but meet, he was a haughty inquisitor during *l'Épuration*. Memories of the French Revolution were not enough to tell him that there might be something wrong with the spectacle of a philosopher sitting on a tribunal instead of standing in front of it.

But many a mouse came out roaring during *l'Épuration*: it was what that performance was for, a fact de Gaulle recognized by closing it down as soon as possible. Sartre should have called it a day after that. Camus did: decently aware that his resistance had not amounted to much (though he took many more risks than Sartre), he was out of the hero business long before his death. But Sartre could never let it go. He pretended that he had been brave: the single most shameful thing a man can do when other men have been brave and have paid the price. Sartre, the philosopher, the man of truth, lied in his teeth about the most elemental fact of his adult life all the way to the end, so it is no wonder that his philosophy is nonsense. Revel valuably noticed how modern philosophy denies from the start that "the level of the essayist and the critic" should be its departure point. He must also have noticed that in Sartre's case it couldn't be, because Sartre, as an essayist and critic, was almost exclusively concerned in concealing the truth instead of revealing it. As Solzhenitsyn pointed out in *The Gulag Archipelago*, Sartre on his trip to Moscow was at one point standing only a few feet away from the living refutation of all his mendacity on the subject of the Soviet Union: a black Maria full of innocent prisoners. If the back door had accidentally swung open, he would probably have said the people inside were criminals, or actors—anything except what everyone in Russia knew they were. Nobody serious in the ex–Iron Curtain countries ever thought Sartre the Philosopher much better than a solemn buffoon. But in his homeland Sartre's national prestige was too enormous for anyone to think of undermining it completely. Mockery was permitted, but only within the limits of throwing eggs at the Arc de Triomphe.

Not even Revel, by far the most penetrating critic of Sartre's bombastic philosophical style, could quite bring himself to say that it was a mechanism devised not only to ape meaning while avoiding it, but by avoiding it to conceal it. As Egon Friedell noted, the true philosopher is close to the artist, except he has only himself for a character; so that any deeply felt philosophy is an autobiographical novel. The converse holds: Sartre's autobiography was the last thing he wanted us to know, and so his philosophy was never felt, but all a pose.

ERIK SATIE

✲ ✲ ✲

Erik-Alfred-Leslie Satie (1866–1925) was the eternal figure of
the brilliant young French composer in rebellion against
everything at once: the social order, bourgeois gentility, even
music itself. Wagner had opened the way for Debussy, but for
Satie Wagner was an oppressor, simply because he had become
accepted. Satie successfully made it his mission to save
Debussy from Wagner's influence. With his goatee, pince-nez
worn askew, and pumiced fingers—he had a Howard
Hughes–like obsession about clean hands—Satie was the kind
of eccentric who unites normal men by making them feel protective. Debussy and Ravel, never generous to each other, were
both generous to him. Whatever was orthodox, Satie hated:
his ballets were not like ballets, his lyric dramas were not dramatic, his chamber pieces were designed to make the chamber
uncomfortable. Dropping out from the Paris Conservatoire
after a single term, he started his career as a piano player in the
cabarets of Montmartre, but as a composer he soon lost any
wish to appeal to a wider audience. On the contrary, his aim
was to trim the audience down to a select few, and perhaps to
zero, by making his programme notes and general presentation as off-putting as possible. When he published his first set

of piano pieces he called it opus 62. After living in poverty he went back to school at the Schola Cantorum, but took care to hide the seriousness of his subsequent compositions with suitably demented titles: *Three Pieces in the Form of a Pear* was typical. Some of his fellow composers were not fooled: Darius Milhaud and the rest of Les Six all kept tabs on what he was up to, the impressionism of his *Sarabandes* and *Gymnopédies* anticipated Debussy and Ravel, and his determination to get the emphasis away from harmonic lushness and back on to a spare melodic line went on influencing music in France after his death. Today's admirers of advanced music who find even John Cage an historical figure, and think that there must be unexplored paths of development beyond his pieces for "prepared" pianos, deliberate passages of silence, etc., might care to study Satie's brief but frenziedly original career, in which they will find everything they could desire except electronic effects. Satie was too early for those, although he was in time for the telephone, which he incorporated into the orchestra for *Parade*, the 1917 Diaghilev ballet that unleashed Satie, Cocteau and Picasso on the public all at once, setting standards of innovation that have been hankered after in vain ever since: to get an effect like that, you don't just need all those people, you need the war they were ignoring. In the score of *Parade*, Satie's instrumentation was competing with the western front. Finally, however, Satie's lyrical talent was victorious over every nonsensical idea that he could throw at it. A quarter of a century after his death, his piano pieces were rediscovered, joined the standard repertory, and became so popular—really popular, Chopin popular, Rachmaninoff popular—that they might have been mistaken, by him, for the kind of sonic wallpaper he so despised. Satie would have had something to say about that: his killing wit never failed him, especially at inappropriate moments. Students of Dada from Tristan Tzara through to Yoko Ono sometimes yearn for jokes with genuine laughs. Satie's jokes were really funny, probably because he was really gifted. The grand gesture of throwing it all away depends for its effect on having something to throw.

❦ ❦ ❦

Ravel refuses the Legion d'Honneur
but all his music accepts it.
— ERIK SATIE, QUOTED BY ROLLO MYERS,
ERIK SATIE

AND RAVEL WAS one of his friends. At the height of his productive period that stretched from the teens of the twentieth century until the early 1920s, Erik Satie would throw his completed compositions behind the piano, either trusting the important ones to emerge from the mulch by themselves, or just not caring. The composer important enough to influence both Ravel and Debussy had no regard for his own dignity. He was ready to insult even himself. In our time, Barry Humphries is a Satie figure, but one who is glad to incorporate the conventional life even while making war against it: one of the secrets of his creative longevity. Satie incorporated the war. Self-destruction was the surest sign of his rebellion. Among the tanning factories and market gardens of Arcueil, Satie looked up to no-one except the phantom Madonna he called *Notre-dame Bassesse*: Our Lady Lowness. Like Baron Corvo (real name: Frederick Rolfe), Satie would sign his name as a bishop, but just for the gag. Unlike Baron Corvo he had no hankerings to be Pope. All the facts are in Myers's book, but many of them—according to Robert Orledge, our best qualified scholar of that effervescent period in French music—were lifted with insufficient acknowledgement from an earlier book of the same title by Pierre-Daniel Templier. Satie would probably have approved of the misappropriation. In every department except his compositions, even in their performance, he was out to sow the seeds of anarchy.

Lydia Sokolova in her memoir of the Russian ballet records the meeting of Satie and Cocteau for *Parade*: the conjunction of two hierarchs in the minor but vital French tradition of taking frivolity with uncompromising seriousness. For Satie, however, there was no hierarchy: his superiority was unassailable. "Those who are unable to understand are required by me to adopt an attitude of complete submission and inferiority." He said it before the premiere of *Socrate*, and the "by me" tells you everything. This confidence in the importance of his mereness—the melody unadorned, stripped even of harmony—

remains the most shocking thing about him, though the confidence was justified. Today his music is a case of once heard, never forgotten. But he was determined to be forgotten first, and succeeded. His written directions to the performance of his pieces ("Play like a nightingale with toothache") were designed to help them go out of date. He knew that nothing takes on verdigris faster than a determined novelty. By a trick of coincidence—surely it was not a planned echo—Ring Lardner exactly reproduced the cracked tone of Satie's surreal annotations in the stage directions of his, Lardner's, little plays: "The curtain descends for seven days to denote the passing of a week." In that regard Satie, like Lardner in the same mood, was out to make nothing but mischief. Edmund Wilson hated it when Lardner called a book of short stories *How to Write Short Stories*. Why put up barriers of nonsense? In Satie's case, it was probably a dread of having so transparent a secret penetrated by the solemn. Nobody unqualified to open the casket should clap eyes on its contents of water-drop jewellery. Here the precursor of Dada outflanked the whole movement, because the Dadaists had no secret: the protection was all there was. Satie's defences marked the route to treasure. No writer who has heard and loved Satie's piano pieces (they came back in a big way only in the early 1960s) will be proof against the urge to strip from prose everything except its melody, as if, in the necessary interplay of word and thought, there could be a purely lyrical essence. There can't. But in music Satie made a vivid reality out of the hopeless ideal of a central, primal thread. He makes babies of us, except if we are distracted by his words, in which case we do not qualify.

ARTHUR SCHNITZLER

Arthur Schnitzler (1862–1931) was the giant of literary Vienna in its most fruitful era. A practising physician before he turned professional writer, he brought a view steeped in the harsh realism of the consulting room and the surgery to his stories, novels and plays. The most conspicuous, and most enduringly controversial, element in this clinical realism was his exploration of the erotic. As a physician he knew a lot about it at second hand. At first hand, he was an energetic young man physically attractive to women of all classes. The addition of fame to his natural advantages made him hard to resist, and one of the commendable things about his private life is that he somehow managed to forge a moral sense out of limitless opportunity. It was the plays that made him famous: as a man of the theatre he ruled the city. Though he is still respected internationally as a dramatist, the plays remain notoriously difficult to capture in English, even though playwrights as accomplished as Tom Stoppard have tried. (Some of the plots from his plays turn up constantly in the movies.) Schnitzler is probably most easily approached through his stories, but one of his full-length novels, *Der Weg ins Freie* (often translated as *The Road to Freedom*, although *The Path into the Clear* is less likely to get him mixed up with Sartre), should not be ignored by anyone studying the relationship of culture and politics at a key place in a crucial time: none of his writing, in any genre, was more penetrating about the Jewish identity crisis in Austria. A Jew himself, Schnitzler was not blinded by his own huge success to the pervasive nature of anti-Semitism in Viennese polite society: his play *Professor Bernhardi* dealt with that very subject. But the glittering theatregoers sat still to watch the play. Schnitzler was quick to notice, however, that he had another bunch of overdressed spectators who were less disposed to sit still while their prejudices were examined. The Nazis, vocally active against Jewish cultural Bolshevism long before they took power in Germany, found it easy to calumniate Schnitzler as a cosmopolitan pornographer. Schnitzler was much quicker than Freud to spot that the Nazis would bring everything in Viennese civilization to an end. There is a lingering misapprehension about Schnitzler: because his memoirs of youth are so unflinchingly realistic, he is thought to have been irredeemably coarse. But his realism, even about previously unmentionable matters, was made possible by sensitivity, not by obtuseness. He had a lyrical awareness that penetrated everywhere, even into the truly sick minds of those who called his honesty an illness, and wanted to kill him for it.

❦ ❦ ❦

There are all kinds of flight from responsibility. There is a
flight into death, a flight into sickness, and finally a flight
into stupidity. The last is the least dangerous and most
comfortable, since even for clever people the journey is not
as long as they might fondly imagine.
— ARTHUR SCHNITZLER, *BUCH DER
SPRUCHE UND BEDENKEN*, P. 78

WHEN RAYMOND ARON, in *Le Spectateur engagé*, said it was a mistake to underestimate the role of obtuseness in human affairs, he was merely making a useful statement. These lines from Schnitzler amount to a true aphorism, and all his warnings against the aphorism as a literary form duly apply. (Shake an aphorism, he said, and in most cases a lie falls out, leaving only a banality.) But Schnitzler's own aphorisms are guarded and enriched by his lifelong distrust of the merely paradoxical. If they were not, they would be more popular, like Wilde's. Schnitzler was really out to get at the truth, and this bold linking of cleverness and stupidity is typical of how bravely truthful he could be.

Is stupidity a mere absence of mind, or has it a mind of its own? If the second thing is true, then stupidity is a force in itself. But it would be a hard force to study, because it always seems to be mixed up with something else: cleverness, for example. In the field of geopolitics, Hitler provided at least one glaring case of what seems, at first glance, to be stupidity in its pure state. After the launching, in June 1941, of Operation Barbarossa, he terrorized millions of people in the Soviet Union who had already been terrorized for years by their own government, and who would willingly have smoothed the path for his armies and administration if he had behaved with even the bare minimum of benevolence. A light hand would have been in his interests as a conqueror; but the heavy, murderous hand was the only one he would contemplate. It was one of the many points at which he guaranteed the loss of his own war. But there's the hint: the many points can all be traced back to the beginning, and their root found in his irrational obsession with racial hygiene. For him, by his nature, mass extermination was an end, to which the creation of a Greater Germany was only a means. His opening anti-Semitic campaigns after the *Machtergreifung* in January 1933 subtracted the Jewish effort from the German physical sciences—a self-inflicted handicap which would have ensured that he could never have been victorious in the long run. Even that basic point, however, although hard to argue with in retrospect, needs qualification. Though Germany's pure science was crippled, applied science and technology still got an awfully long way under the Nazis, and it is an act of retroactive trust to suppose that Heisenberg and the other Aryan physicists would never have been able to build an atomic bomb if they had been given time, although they would not have been able to deliver it before the Allies did, because Germany's long-distance bombing capacity had not kept pace. Hitler's Germany had all the potential for world domination. Leaving aside the question of whether world domination is a sane aim—we usually don't call Alexander crazy—Hitler need not necessarily have pursued it in an insane manner. It is just our dubious luck that he did. It was his principles that dished him. If he could have sacrificed them to expediency, he might have won.

Within the parameters of his apoplectic *Weltanschauung*, Hitler could be ingenious and even brilliant. His ideology depended on extermination, but some kind of ideology it undoubtedly was, and although, as Raymond Aron said many times, no ideology can be realistic, that does not necessarily mean that an ideologist need be stupid in all areas. Hitler's abiding fault, indeed, lay in his cleverness. Demonstrably clever in the machinations of mass politics, he was encouraged by his own success to embrace the delusion that he was omniscient in any field of which he possessed knowledge. Far from being ignorant of what a Russian campaign had done to Napoleon, Hitler had made a study of the subject, and had seen merit in the general agreement among historians that Napoleon should not have occupied Moscow. Hitler also knew enough about Germany's requirements for raw materials to decide that the oil fields in the Caucasus were a more important target. His reasoning was clever on the level of grand strategy. But on the level of military strategy it ignored a fact which had had no relevance in Napoleon's time, but was now crucial: Moscow was the Soviet Union's communications centre. If Hitler had concentrated his forces and gone all out for Moscow in the autumn of 1941, he could have had all the oil and minerals he wanted not long after. But he was too smart: or, if you like, too stupid, except that it strains the meaning of the word.

Schnitzler's point about one of the flights from responsibility being a flight into stupidity looks clearer cut when we move from Hitler to Stalin. Admirers of Stalin always liked to think that he was never stupid. There was some evidence to back up their faith. Long before the final accounts came in, it should have been obvious that Stalin's rule was self-defeating for socialism. But if we can grant that he had nothing like socialism in mind, and thought only of an exercise in pure power, the regime he perfected looks like a work of genius. So acute an observer as Isaiah Berlin gave him credit for a master plan behind his succession of purges. Aleksandr Zinoviev, in his *The Reality of Communism*, overstated the later Soviet regime's coherence—a coherence inherited from Stalin—only in suggesting that it could incorporate, while still remaining stable, all recalcitrant phenomena up to and including dissidence. (If Zinoviev had really believed that, of course, he would not have written his dissident books; but he felt it, and wrote them from deep pessimism.) While Stalin ruled the Soviet Union, however, his one and only creation, the Party apparat, showed few faults as a mechanism for preserving a single aim: that he should rule. He even seemed to have heeded Seneca's warning that you can kill as many people as you like but your successor will be among those who survive. Stalin acted as if he intended nobody to survive.

Mao Zedong acted the same way. It can be called stupidity only if you think such behaviour threatens the state. But it didn't threaten *his* state. On that measure, Ho Chi Minh showed Pol Pot the way, and Pol Pot was the stupid one because he failed to pay heed. Ho's delayed and selective ruthlessness against his bourgeoisie—actual, potential, or notional—weakened his economy but preserved him in power. Pol Pot's instantaneous wholesale massacre of anyone who could read and write destroyed the state he had created before he had a chance to rule it. Attacking with a chainsaw the branch he sat on, he was a figure from a diabolical cartoon. But few of the longer-lasting Communist despots were so dense. Ceauşescu was a maniac, but so is an ordinary serial killer; an ordinary serial killer doesn't run a state. It could be said that Castro is the cleverest person in Cuba because anyone cleverer swam to Miami, but it's a joke. Castro is not stupid and it is most unlikely that the material decay of his country has surprised him. He simply preferred personal rule to national prosperity, and stifled the second in order to reinforce the first. As Lenin proved, you can't have a socialist economy without the occasional NEP (a New Economic Policy that allows a measure of free enterprise); you can't continue as a socialist dictator without the dexterity to dismantle the NEP as soon as it becomes productive; and to balance the resultant hope against the inevitable deprivation is the secret of success. Maintaining yourself in power is the only thing you succeed at, but the time soon comes when the balancing act becomes your *raison d'être*. Castro had the knack, and remained in power while his beard grew grey.

If the United States had been able to find a way of burdening Castro's early socialist aspirations with help, the Communist regime in

Cuba might never have formed in the first place. But America had committed itself to a foreign policy which viewed any hint of socialism as an invitation to communism. The policy was stupid, but here again it was not necessarily the product of stupid men: the East Coast foreign policy elite constituted the cleverest collection of political brains in America. Otherwise known as the Wise Men, after World War II they gave an unwise policy its initial impetus because there was no other way of getting a genuinely beneficial measure—the Marshall Plan—through Congress. They needed a Red scare as an appeal to the masses: always an uncomfortable position for any intellectual elite to be in. Appeals to the masses are better managed by big business.

Schnitzler's flight into stupidity might look like the only explanation for the sort of newspapers, magazines, television programmes and movies that make us ashamed to be living in the West. At first blush, the mass media seem to offer the ideal chance of examining stupidity in isolation. But once again the trick is not easily worked. There is a possibility, amounting to a probability when the really big money is involved, that the stupidity is being manufactured by clever people whose commercial motives put their taste, scope and integrity into abeyance. This non-anomaly becomes most obvious in the case of Hollywood's blockbuster movies, where the long haul of creative intelligence takes a spiral route towards the big haul at the box office. Every onlooker who fancies his powers of discrimination has a wonderful time when a blockbuster flops on the opening weekend. But the blockbuster that we actually have a wonderful time watching is a more equivocal case. *Where Eagles Dare* has always been my favourite example: since the day I first saw it, I have taken a sour delight in rebutting pundits who so blithely assume that the obtuseness on screen merely reflects the stunted mentalities behind the camera, and I go on seeing its every rerun on television in order to reinforce my stock of telling detail—and, all right, in order to have a wonderful time. There is something precious about the intellectual squalor of *Where Eagles Dare*: it is a swamp with a surface of green pulp squeezed from emeralds. You can't get the same charge from Delta Force movies, or from the adventures of Jean-Claude Van Damme in the brainless universe where men with guns are helpless against a man fighting with his feet. *Where Eagles Dare* is the apex of a form: it shows that there is somewhere to go beyond *The Guns of Navarone*, a numbskull stratosphere in which not even *The Wild Geese* could fly. Where eagles dare, the sense of the ridiculous winks out to a dot, and the vision is filled with the vaulting pretensions of latterday schoolmen who believe, if only *ad hoc* and *pro tem*, that cinematic sense can exist *in vacuo*: detached, that is, from any other sense; a voluntary brain-death. The whole complex phenomenon is epitomized by Richard Burton's hairstyle.

Schnitzler, let us remember, said that the flight into stupidity is a flight away from responsibility. But soaring beyond any human absurdity that even Schnitzler could imagine, Richard Burton's hairstyle in *Where Eagles Dare* is a flight into stupidity and away from the barber. Burton plays a British agent who is possibly also a German agent, although we can be fairly sure that he will turn out to be a British agent in the end, because Richard Burton's agent would never agree to a deal by which his client was shot at dawn. Burton the almost certainly British agent is sent, with Clint Eastwood and other agents—some of whom actually do turn out to be German agents—on a mission to a castle deep behind German lines, there to rescue, or possibly confirm the credibility of, or perhaps betray the real identity of, an actor pretending to be an American general in possession of the Plans for a Second Front. The actor playing the actor need not detain us, and considering how he acts it is a wonder that the Germans have detained him. (There is a lot more to wonder at about the behaviour of the Germans, but we'll get to that later.) The actors who matter are Richard Burton and Clint Eastwood. Clint, already a top box office draw at the time, has been cast as the simple, straight-talking American assassin who helps the fiendishly ingenious British spy: it's the same relationship as Felix Leiter to James Bond, but beefed up to equal status to meet the requirements of the American marquee. Apart from saying "hello" so as to make Germans turn around before he shoots them with his silenced pistol—if he had merely mouthed "hello" before shooting them in the back, it would have been a different kind of movie, i.e., a realistic one—Clint's character has nothing anachronistic about him except his cataleptic taciturnity, which we are glad to recognize as a minimally equipped actor's career-long habit of overdoing the understatement. Burton's own style of acting is equally dissonant with the time, but in the opposite direction: he always overdid the overstatement, and from the beginning to the end of his career on screen he looked exactly like a stage actor projecting to the upper circle, except when a director with animal-training skills (Martin Ritt in *The Spy Who Came in from the Cold*, to take one of the few examples) either whipped him into submission or else slipped a sedative into his morning triple. Burton always moved his lips so much when he enunciated that they would stick out past the end of his nose, and there are episodes in *Where Eagles Dare* in which they practically leave the frame, as if yet another triple were waiting out there, begging to be imbibed.

It isn't the stuff he does with his face, however, that makes Burton look out of place in this castellated anteroom of World War II. It's the stuff on top of his head. It's his hairstyle. It was probably still all his own hair at that stage, but it's a hair*style*: an item, that is, which not even women found it easy to obtain during World War II, and which for men was unknown. (In the movie, Mary Ure has obviously taken a hairstylist into action with her, but we never see him: although if he had wandered into shot holding a crimping iron he would have looked no more futuristic than her miraculously smooth coiffure, shining with a blonde lustre that Eva Braun, even with her connections, could only dream of.) The high command of the Romanian army did indeed issue an order that no officer below the rank of major should wear makeup, but the British army and the German army both made a policy of short back and sides for all ranks, and the German army was particularly close-cropped. Yet Burton, intending to be accepted as a German officer in order to penetrate the enemy redoubt, has gone into action sporting a pageboy hairstyle so fulsome that it spills abundant curls and waves below the back of his collar. Burton had a big head anyway. I interviewed him once, and found out why he always looked so stocky on screen: it was because his upper works were so broad you had to lean sideways to see past him. Even if close-shorn he would have had to wear a cap rare for its size in the whole of the Wehrmacht. But with his hairstyle added to his massive cranium, his cap has to be big enough for a buffalo, and it still does nothing to disguise—does a lot, indeed, to emphasize—the anomalous abundance of hair protruding at the back. On several occasions in the movie he has to pass a German checkpoint, and you can only deduce that the garrison has been recruited from an institute for the blind. Later in the war, when the

regular German forces were in a state of collapse, *Volkssturm* units were
organized from the old, the adolescent, the lame and the sick, but I
can't remember that very many sightless people were issued with a
Panzerfaust and asked to shoot in the direction of the noise kicked up
by Allied tanks. Here at the castle there is no discrimination against the
optically handicapped.

Whether as a single, double or triple agent ("Triple, please," you can
imagine him saying) the Burton character would have been barely free
of his parachute harness before being placed under arrest. He would
have been locked up on the basis of his appearance alone. Every other
anachronism is explicable, within the screenplay's purely cinematic
parameters. In the Geman pub below the castle, Burton, Eastwood and
the other agents—the others are notable chiefly for their expendability—talk very loudly in English. Yes, English is their chosen language
when they discuss their plans about fooling the Germans, and they do
not lower their voices when members of the garrison pass by closely
behind them. It could be said, however, that a convention is being
observed here, and that our agents are really speaking German. (It
could also be said that if they *were* speaking German, the closely attendant Germans would be even more likely to notice that plans to fool
them were being loudly discussed, but let that pass.) There is also the
consideration that English seems to be the adopted language of every
German in the area. Similarly it could be put down to an equally hallowed cinematic convention when the German commandant arrives in
the castle courtyard by helicopter. There were no operational helicop-
ters in World War II, but there were no operational cannon in ancient
Rome either, and Shakespeare still put a few in. Shakespeare pioneered
Hollywood's flexible attitude to temporal authenticity, as any Hollywood mogul with a tertiary education will be glad to tell you. For every
howler in the movie there is a good justification, the principal one
being that the people who made the movie must have known it was a
howler, but correctly judged that nobody they cared about would
notice. In the majority of big-budget war films since World War II, and
in all the small budget ones, the enemy has always fired a special kind
of bullet that goes around, instead of through, the actors on our side,
occasionally penetrating only at the shoulder or in a sexually neutral
section of the upper thigh. In *Sands of Iwo Jima* John Wayne finally got

killed by a Japanese bullet while he was sitting down, but only after the Japanese machine-gunners had vainly fired thousands of bullets at him when he was running very slowly. In *Where Eagles Dare*, whole German machine-gun nests equipped with multiple examples of the lethal MG42 (rate of fire: 1200 rounds per minute) are unable to graze Richard Burton's hairstyle. Big enough for a slowly moving cow to graze it, for cinematic reasons it is impervious to speeding lead. But there are precedents for that. There is no precedent for the hairstyle *per se*.

This is where the pundit clinches his seemingly open-and-shut case for Schnitzler's flight into stupidity as the principal motivation of the film's creators, or perpetrators. He might concede that some of the perps are technically clever, but in that case he will insist that there is still a collective perp: the system itself. And he will be right, but not as right as he thinks. He has overlooked the factor of star power, which is what made him see the movie in the first place. Letting Burton keep his everyday hairstyle was the studio's only chance of getting him into this sector of World War II. (He kept a bit less of his thatch for his cameo appearance in *The Longest Day*, but it still wasn't buoyant enough to get him arrested by his own side, let alone by the enemy.) And Burton wasn't being stupid either. He had realized that the point was not to look like a British agent plausibly pretending to be a German officer: the point was to look like Richard Burton. The reality of star power depends on exactly that. Malleability is for actors. For screen stars, recognizability is what matters. Much later, and in a better movie, Robert Redford proved it all over again by declining at the last moment to adopt an English accent when he played Denys Finch Hatton in *Out of Africa*. He was right. *Out of Africa* was a serious venture, but it was still a blockbuster, and it needed Redford as a draw on the marquee, not as a paragon of authenticity on the screen. Redford was content to leave all that to Meryl Streep and Klaus Maria Brandauer. He wasn't just content, he insisted. And it was by making such demands that he became Robert Redford. If we doubt the value of that, we should remember that he would never have been in a position to set up the Sundance Festival, and thus alter the whole course of independent and intelligent film-making in America, if he hadn't been Robert Redford in the first instance. He is a very clever man, and so, between drinks, was Burton, who could recite English poetry by the mile. Burton was clever enough to intuit a deeply awkward truth, and incorporate it in the hairstyle he carried into action in one of the most lucrative movies he ever made. To one side of the world's great events, there is the interpretation of them. To one side of the interpretation, there is entertainment. And to one side of entertainment, there is absurdity. But if the absurdity is correctly judged, it will be found entertaining, even by those who are well aware of the real importance of the events being travestied. There can be a willing, mass participation in the flight into stupidity, because there can always be an agreed moment when the flight away from responsibility becomes irresistible. To pick that moment takes a kind of talent. It might be a spoiled talent, but mediocrity will never make it.

In all those big, bad movies that ought to have been better (I don't mean the big, bad movies that couldn't be worse, like *The Avengers* or *Pearl Harbor*) the stupidity is institutionalized, and you can take it for granted that if they make a big score on the opening weekend, almost everyone concerned is very clever indeed, and often dauntingly cultivated. But these masterminds are smart and suave enough to know that their target audience for the opening weekend is neither of those things. The masterminds are after the young, who know nothing. It is usually a mistake to overestimate their degree of dumbness—the movie has to make some kind of sense—but to overestimate their ignorance is impossible. The disparity of intellect between the manufacturers and the consumers would be frightening if the manufacturers were not at the consumers' mercy, instead of vice versa. Hence the tendency of Californian film moguls to revel in their own superiority: they have nowhere else to hide from the consequences of a mistake. Their flight is not into stupidity, but into sophistication. In the British cinema you can meet plenty of people who know something about Frank Lloyd Wright, but only in Los Angeles can you meet a movie executive who lives in a house that Frank Lloyd Wright built, and who devotes time, taste and knowledge to restoring it. His name is Joel Silver, and he is the same man who, in *Die Hard*, sent Bruce Willis hurtling barefooted through a plate-glass window to settle the hash of two dozen combat-trained terrorists instead of slicing himself to hamburger. Luckily the guns of the terrorists were loaded with the standard magic bullets rigged to swerve around any actor on our side with star billing, and nobody virtuous got killed except a Japanese executive, possibly as a payback for Iwo Jima.

These functional anomalies of the mass media teach us to look out for whether the rules of the game induce clever people, in other fields as well, to behave in stupid ways. In the year when Senator John Kerry challenged President George W. Bush, the question of why Bush pretended to be able to speak English was never as interesting as the question of why Kerry pretended not to be able to speak French. In the United States, the free democracy whose electoral system most nearly approximates a free market, an historical consensus of extremely clever operatives has decreed that a candidate should not only keep things simple, but seem simple himself. Cultural memory is difficult: too much detail. Cultural amnesia is easier. Eventually there will be nobody alive who knows for certain that there was never such a thing in World War II as Richard Burton's hairstyle in *Where Eagles Dare*, so why don't we forget it straight away? President Bush's speechwriters encourage him to forget that World War II even existed before Pearl Harbor was attacked. Not even he could not know that: but it is deemed expedient that he should seem not to. How these decisions about utilitarian ignorance are taken is a study in itself. But it is the very study that intellectuals as a class are least equipped to make. For past catastrophes, dull intellectuals try to blame a dumb individual: hence the notion that all the soldiers in the trenches of World War I were murdered by Field Marshal Douglas Haig. Slightly smarter intellectuals try to blame a dumb collectivity: hence the notion that the escalation in Vietnam was the work of the CIA. (In fact, the CIA warned JFK not to commit troops on the ground: he ignored the warning.) Clever intellectuals can analyse a complex event, but tend to attribute a simple motive: hence the notion that the Cold War and the arms race were American inventions designed to stifle the socialist aspirations of liberated Europe. It takes a very smart intellectual, however, to accept that those vast, costly and even criminal stupidities were brought about by people no less bright than he. Clever contemporary thinkers who proceed on the assumption that their predecessors were stupid are apt to write the superior nonsense that works mischief. It is a consideration that Schnitzler left out of his aphorism: there is indeed a flight from responsibility into stupidity, but the flight from responsibility into cleverness can be equally destructive.

> "But what if," said Leo, "the execution fires
> should be lit again?"
> "In that case," said Heinrich, "I solemnly promise
> I will come straight to you."
> "Oh," George objected, "those times will never return."
> —ARTHUR SCHNITZLER, *DER WEG INS FREIE*

On some unspecified day around the turn of the nineteenth century into the twentieth, the three Jewish boys have been lolling on a well-appointed hillside. They have been conducting a long, lazy argument about whether to dream of Palestine is really an appropriate response to the petty, everyday anti-Semitic snobbery of Vienna. After all, none of them is religious. But the argument gets quite heated, and they break the tension with this joking exchange. Looking back across eight decades, we can see it as one of the most prophetic moments in modern literature. But it should also remind us of the dangers of historicism: hindsight is not a view of the world, it is an indulgence of the self. It puts us in control of history, whereas the first thing we should realize about history is that we are not in control of it: not by looking backward, and still less by looking forward. Only one of the three young characters believes that assimilation is a dangerous illusion, and even if all three of them did, they would still be characters: they would not be Schnitzler. If Schnitzler himself had really thought that the future was cut and dried, he would never have written another line. But the idea of a possible disaster is undoubtedly being floated, and it comes from the author's heart. Schnitzler understood Theodor Herzl's views about the *ignis fatuus* of Jewish assimilation. He himself was about as assimilated as someone of Jewish background could well be. Even after World War I, with the old empire broken up, Schnitzler's prestige in Vienna's cultural life was on the scale that Mahler's had been when Franz Joseph still ruled. At the Burgtheater Schnitzler, the unchallenged master playwright, was accustomed to multiple curtain calls for every successful first night: sometimes he seemed to be on stage almost as long as the actors.

But he also knew what it meant to feel insecure even in his eminence. Some of his best plays have that for a subject. *Professor Bernhardi* is a play about a man of Schnitzler's prestige finding out how little his prestige avails him against the perennial hatreds. Schnitzler never betrayed the same sort of nervousness as, say, Jakob Wassermann, a novelist who despaired of a social acceptance to match his big sales. Schnitzler took his popularity as a sign of approval. But he knew that the contempt was always there, a tincture in the culture. For two reasons, he was particularly stung by the essayist Alfred Polgar's critical notices. One reason was that Polgar wrote so well: limiting judgements hurt most when they come from a writer of talent. The other reason was the one that barely shows up even in Schnitzler's private correspondence, but it is detectable between the lines. Polgar was a Jew, and should, Schnitzler felt, have found less hostile language for his belittling judgements. Franz Werfel had a right to feel the same way about Karl Kraus. In the first year of the twenty-first century, the eminent art historian E. H. Gombrich, nearing the end of long life, protested against the misguided consensus of commentary which seemed to assume that there had ever been such a self-conscious body as The Jews before Hitler so portentously invented it. Solidarity had to be imposed, and was never really felt even then. Among the prosperous, fully assimilated Jews of the professional classes who found themselves bewilderingly subject to Nazi proscription, there were plenty who went to their doom still convinced that the whole thing would never have happened if not for the resentment aroused by the influx of all those strangely dressed and unsociable *Ostjuden* refugees from the accursed east. But you can still see why a prominent Jewish artist who was cut down to size by a Jewish critic should feel betrayed: things were tough enough without being done down by your own people. Things were even tougher if, as an assimilated Jew, you had rejected the idea of there being such a thing as your own people. Like so many stars who have been told too often and too glibly that they embody the hopes of a race, Schnitzler wanted to be an individual, not a representative. The anguish aroused by your own principles is hard to take.

If Schnitzler, who was lucky enough to die of natural causes when Hitler was not yet in power, had lived long enough to see Nazism begin to make actual the atavistic threat that his characters laughed off, what would he have thought? Luckily, such speculations are useless, because they make an inadmissible presumption about the continuity of personal psychology. Schnitzler was an unusually perceptive man, but his perceptive powers might have withered with further age, or even rejected the evidence of his senses. Karl Kraus lived long enough to say that he had nothing to say about Hitler. The implication was that Hitler's unspeakable awfulness had been beyond the scope of even Kraus's satirical view. The truth was that Kraus, largely because he thought the institutionalized Viennese anti-Semitism of the late 1890s was as nasty as things could get, hadn't seen Hitler coming, and his blindness was at least partly wilful. Later on, the gifted satirist Kurt Tucholsky, desperate in exile, doubted if his persistent mockery of the Weimar Republic had ever been wise. Kraus had come too far to have the same doubts about his own activities in post–World War I Austria. He was too tired to adapt his forces to the new challenge. The same thing might have happened to Schnitzler. By the time of his death in 1931, Schnitzler had heard Nazi voices in full cry: they found the Jew plutocrat and erotomaniac Schnitzler a tempting stimulus for their own literary efforts. Some of the stuff written about him is too horrible to quote.

But he didn't make a subject of it. That these voices in the alley would ever take power was hard to imagine even for him. He had been through all that back at the turn of the century. (My copy of *Der Weg ins Freie* is dated 1922, but he was working on the manuscript in 1903.) He had poured into a great novel all his reflections on Jewish identity, on assimilation, on its impossibility in less than a thousand years, on how everyone affected would have to find his own path into the clear. Since then, he had found his: through achievement, success, fame, the rich emotional rewards of his private life. If he encountered anti-Semitism in grand drawing-rooms, there were few grand drawing-rooms he could not enter. It was hard to imagine that all those subtle, stylishly insidious old parlour prejudices would gain an entirely different order of force when restated by maniacs. In Freud's last diary we can see that even the great student of the primitive subconscious was slow to acknowledge the scope of the Nazi challenge to civilization. Freud, Kraus, Schnitzler—they were all at the apex of Viennese cultural intelligence. But for all three of them, there was no Jewish Question in the Hitlerite sense. The question they had dealt with had been about anti-Semitism as a stain on a living culture. The new anti-Semitism *à la* Hitler was a culture all by itself: a culture of death. Theodor Herzl had prophesied its advent, but on the evidence of what had always happened in the east. To accept that the same order of destruction might be possible in the civilized west, a prophet was what you had to be, with the prophet's vulnerability to suggestions by reasonable people that he might be mad. Prophecy and creative intuition might have something in common: they both depend on a consideration of possibilities that does not censor itself in advance. Schnitzler's richness as a writer depended on his capacity not to censor the reports from his own instincts: in writing about desire, he established a tradition that comes all the way down to Philip Roth, who owes more to Schnitzler than he does to Kafka, because it was Schnitzler who opened up the subject of how desire can saturate the imagination. (One of Roth's most memorable book titles, *The Professor of Desire*, fits Schnitzler exactly.)

Similarly, Schnitzler did not censor his insecurity. In all aspects of his adult life he made himself the complete figure of bourgeois solidity: he was practically part of the Ringstrasse, the great circuit of buildings in central Vienna that really amounted to a theatre whose sets, as it were, were set in stone. But he maintained access to his unease. He had grown up and flourished in the tolerance of the old *k.u.k* society. But it was the tolerance that bothered him. Tolerance could be withdrawn. If one of the boys on the hillside—it is Leo who sees deepest—points out to the others that the age-old hostility runs deeper than they think, he is certainly expressing the author's unsleeping doubt, if not his overmastering conviction. The whole allure of Schnitzler's extensive range of work depends, like human beauty, on the ineluctable reality of evanescence. Read in the original, his plays rank him with Ibsen and Chekhov, but most particularly with Chekhov, and not just because Schnitzler, too, was a doctor by his first calling. The dynamic in Ibsen is of chickens coming home to roost. In Chekhov it is of the falling leaves. Schnitzler's short stories, sketches and novellas rank him with Chekhov again, although *Leutnant Gustl* makes you think also of Joyce, because it exhausted the possibilities of the interior monologue before

Joyce had even begun to explore them. Schnitzler's paragraph-sized aphorisms are philosophical essays in themselves. And if he had written nothing else, *Der Weg ins Freie* would make him one of *the* novelists of modern Europe. In my shelves, the thin-paper volumes of Schnitzler's complete works form one of those points in space where gravity increases to draw light in so that it can't get out: get near and you will go in with it.

But the illumination in there is phosphorescent. Schnitzler knew that he was writing about a social order in decay. He never gave up on the world—he thought that civilization, no matter how it transformed itself, would continue—but he did say a clear goodbye to the social order into which he had been born. He described it in such loving detail that we are tempted to think of his emotional imperative as nostalgic. But it wasn't. He was a realist. The wonderfully named American critic Joseph Wood Krutch said about Cervantes that only a romantic can be realistic enough, and there is something in what he said. Schnitzler's romanticism, however, was not a self-serving overlay but part of his perception of the world, which for him, because he was an attractive man lucky in love, was always full of sexual adventure even into his old age. From that aspect, he was a small boy in a sweet shop. But he had no illusions about the sweet shop's proprietors. He didn't let the strength of his personal satisfactions blind him to the general fragility of the world in which he enjoyed them. There lies the main difference between Schnitzler's Belle Époque and Joseph Roth's. Schnitzler was there, and told the truth. The compulsive liar Roth looked back on it, nostalgic for its lost coherence. Roth's *Radetzkymarsch* is a great novel. You don't have to know much about the Austro-Hungarian Empire to see that. The more you do know, however, the more you see that *Radetzkymarsch* is a beautiful dream. Schnitzler is the man to show you the reality—the one and only path into the clear.

> No spectre assails us in more varied disguises
> than loneliness, and one of its most impenetrable
> masks is called love.
> —ARTHUR SCHNITZLER, *BUCH DER*
> *SPRUCHE UND BEDENKEN*, P. 117

In 1927, in Vienna, the Phaidon Press, as one of its first publications, brought out a little linen-bound collection by Arthur Schnitzler whose title can be translated as Book of Sayings and Thoughts. I found my copy, in a house full of books sold by the children of refugees, on Staten Island in 1983 and have been reading it ever since. No taller than the length of my hand or wider than the palm, it can be carried easily in a jacket pocket. I think it is one of the great books of the modern world. In not many more than two hundred small pages of Bodoni bold print, it contains the summation of a lifetime's introspection by a man who travelled into his own psychology with the same bravery that men later showed when they travelled into space. The difference is that everything he found was alive. You could call the book's paragraphs aphorisms—he sometimes used the same term himself—but I prefer to call them essays, bearing in mind that Montaigne called it an *essai* when he tried to draw conclusions from the endless titration of his experience and his reading. Schnitzler had lived everything he wrote down: the longer ago he had lived it, the more he had thought about it, so the book often gives the impression of light at great depth, with colours leaping to surprised life, as if they were not used to being on show. (When Jacques Cousteau first took powerful sources of light down to shelves of coral that had never been illuminated before, he asked: what is all this colour doing down here?) Some of the most disturbing essays are about love, which for Schnitzler always started with physical love, even when he was getting on in years and had become a bit less capable. When he was young he must have been capable indeed; and even, by his own account, indiscriminately predatory. But in the long run, multiplicity of experience didn't coarsen his perceptions. It refined them, often against his will. There is no element of consolation in this single-sentence essay about love and loneliness. But there is no despair either. Quite apart from the surrounding anti-Semitism that aroused his constant fury, there was a lot about Viennese life that drove Schnitzler to recrimination—he took a bad review no better than any other playwright—but he never quarrelled with love just because it left him lonely. He counted himself lucky to find it at all: surely the sane attitude.

Was he right about the impenetrable mask? Wrong at the start, and right in the end: because love, unlike loneliness, is more of a process than a permanent condition. In the German, the "most impenetrable masks" are *undurchschaubarsten Masken*—the masks you can't see through. (We might note at this point that "loneliness" is feminine: arbitrary genders really are arbitrary, but in this case it's a nice coincidence.) When love comes, there is no mask: or shouldn't be. There is nothing to see through, because you are not lonely. There really is another person sharing your life. But later on a different truth—one you are familiar with, but hoped to have seen the last of—comes shining through. Unlike light in space, it needs a medium to do so, and the medium is the mask itself, seen in retrospect. You are lonely again. You were really lonely all along. You have deceived yourself.

It would have been a desolating view if Schnitzler had been quite sure of it. But if he had been quite sure of it he would not have gone on worrying at it. On the same great page—great books have great pages, and in this book page 117 is one of the greatest—he tries again. "That we feel bound by a steady longing for freedom, and that we also seek to bind someone else, without being convinced that such a thing is within our rights—that is what makes any loving relationship so problematic." The question here is about possessiveness, and the first thing to see is that there would be no possessiveness if there were nothing real to possess. So this is not loneliness concealed by an impenetrable mask. This is the other person, whom you love enough to be worried about her rights. You are worried, that is, about someone who is not yourself. You want to be free, and assume that she does too: but you want her to be yours. You could want that with a whole heart if your heart were less sympathetic. There have been men in all times, and there are still men all over the world, who have no trouble in believing that their women belong to them. But those men are not educated. If Schnitzler's writings on the subject can be said to have a tendency, it is to say that love provides an education. What is problematic about the relationship is essentially what tells you it is one. It might not be an indissoluble bond, but as an insoluble problem it gives you the privilege of learning that freedom for yourself means nothing without freedom for others. When you love, the problem begins, and so does your real life.

Still on the same page, but at the top—I have taken the paragraphs in a different order here, to restore a sequence that he might have deliberately scrambled—he develops the theme of love and loneliness in a blood-chilling direction. "Each loving relationship has three stages," he says, uncharacteristically sounding rather like Hannah Arendt or W. H. Auden setting out a philosophical fruit-stall, "which succeed one another imperceptibly: the first in which you are happy with each other even when silent; the second in which you are silently bored with each other; and the third in which silence becomes a form that stands between the lovers like an evil enemy." This would be a less terrible thing for him to have said if it had no truth in it that we recognized. But most of us will acknowledge the familiar declension of a passion gone sour. Some passions, of course, ought to go sour, to make room for a fresh one that might even stay fresh. It should be said in a hurry that Schnitzler himself was nothing like Proust in this respect. Proust says, over and over in *À la recherche du temps perdu*, that love always intensifies into jealousy: that it doesn't just convey within itself, but actually consists of, the seeds of its own destruction. For Proust things seem to have been like that in real life.

Schnitzler's real life was different. As far as one can deduce from Renate Wagner's exemplary biography *Arthur Schnitzler*, he was never promiscuous in the usual sense of not caring who the woman was. Until a good way into his mature years, he seems to have been moved to end an affair early mainly out of fear that the woman might get the same idea first. Once he got used to the probability that he would not be betrayed, he formed enduring relationships. The memory of Olga Waissnix stayed dear to him after her untimely death. He might never have let go of his wife (the other Olga, born Olga Gussmann) if she had not insisted on her freedom so as to pursue her career as a singer unimpeded. She was a bit of a Zelda, as things turned out: she started her career too late, failed at it, and they had been too miserable together for him to want her back in the house. But they stayed close. His love for the young actress Vilma Lichtenstern was as enduring as it was intense: her death in a car crash left him devastated. Clara Pollaczek consoled him in his old age, although she might have been less loyal if she had known that the old man had yet another young lady tucked away in the wings. Though he did not enjoy telling lies, he was a master of tactical silence. But it would be a big mistake to suspect him of stunted feelings. His feelings were large, and very generous: if you compare him to a truly selfish Pantaloon like Bertrand Russell, the difference is decisive. Schnitzler was a verifiable believer in female liberty and fulfilment. He wanted his women to become themselves for their benefit, and not just for his.

Nevertheless he was an exponent of what the therapists of today would call a compartmentalized emotional life. The subversive element, however, was in how he drew creative energy from the compartments. He thought that men's minds worked that way and he did an impressive job of dramatizing his view, to the extent that Thomas Mann and Sigmund Freud both thought him a master psychologist. But very few psychologists of today would agree, expecially if they were working as counsellors; and by the American measure, which demands a married couple, volubly happy for their whole lives, his idea of the silent enemy sounds like the Fiend incarnate. The American measure of the eternally happy couple requires two people with half a personality each. Schnitzler worked by the European measure, in which two complete individuals might or might not get on. Which of these measures we take for a paradigm could be a matter of choice. But Schnitzler, although he did not go so far as to insist that all men were like him, believed that there *was* no choice. For him, the civil convention and the impulse in the soul were at odds, and out of the conflict he made his drama. Artistically, it was a decision beyond reproach: but the result was a body of art incomprehensible in America, which is the real reason he has never become world-famous. Ibsen, yes, and even Strindberg. In America, Strindberg can be Edward Albee's acknowledged ancestor: the two lovers in *Who's Afraid of Virginia Woolf?* can tear each other apart right there on Broadway. They are, after all, a married couple, together forever, like a pair of turtle doves with brass knuckles. But only the novels of Philip Roth acknowledge a mental world in which Schnitzler might be a master, and Roth's heroes must concede the misery and confusion at being in the expensive, shameful grip of lust in action, as if they were Henry Miller's crapulent bohemians in better suits. Schnitzler conceded no such thing. He thought that the battle between imagination and fidelity was a fact of life. Even today, more than seventy years after his death, those who think he had a point must still reach up for his works as if to the top of the rack, where dangerous publications are shrink-wrapped in cellophane. The civilization whose pent desires he did so much to explore is still not ready for him.

SOPHIE SCHOLL

About Sophie Scholl (1921–1943) there are few facts to record, because she did not live long. In Munich in 1942, Sophie's brother Hans did his best to keep his sister out of the White Rose resistance group. Sophie, however, was very good at insisting. Apart from their father, the Scholl siblings (*Geschwister* is the useful German word) had few adult companions in their little group. It was a bunch of kids. Not surprisingly, there was not much resisting they could do. But to print and distribute handbills was daring enough, because there could be no doubt about the penalty if they were caught. Sophie could have been spared that penalty had she wished, but once again she insisted. The example set by the *Geschwister* Scholl is of high importance in Germany and beyond, because as Aryans they were protesting against the fate of the Jews purely out of common humanity. Daniel Jonah Goldhagen made a serious mistake when he left them out of his book *Hitler's Willing Executioners*: his thesis that the whole of the German non-Jewish population was devoted to "eliminationist" anti-Semitism was bound to look shaky if it deliberately ignored a group of young non-Jews who avowedly were not. There are several books about the White Rose. One of the best is an edition of the relevant documents by Sophie's sister Inge, *Die Weiße Rose* (new enlarged edition, 1993), which contains transcripts of the handbills, records of the Nazi court, memoirs from friends and acquaintances, and, on page 32, a photo of Sophie fit to break the heart. The Nazi decision to soft-pedal the publicity about the Scholl case paid off. In her excellent book of memoirs *Berliner Aufzeichnungen* (Berlin Notes), Ursula von Kardoff reveals that hardly any of her bright young friends in Berlin, sceptical about the Nazis though they were, got to hear about the Scholls even a year later. Their fame was a post-war event, steadily growing until now, with, it is to be hoped, no end in sight. Could a nation that has never plumbed the same depths put so much value on such a story? In 2005 a movie about Sophie came out in Germany, called *Sophie Scholl: Die Letzten Tage* (The Final Days). More than a million people went to see it. Whether a Hollywood movie will ever be made for a world audience is another question.

Finally, someone has to make a start. We only said
and wrote what many people think. They just don't
dare to express it.
— SOPHIE SCHOLL AT THE WHITE ROSE
TRIAL IN MUNICH, QUOTED BY RICHARD
HANSER IN *DEUTSCHLAND ZULIEBE* (FOR
THE SAKE OF GERMANY), P. 15

S HE DIDN'T STAND a chance anyway. The mere fact that the reliably fanatical Roland Freisler had been sent to preside over the court sealed her doom. But once again in her young life she was bearing witness, and to such effect that even the clinically insane Freisler was momentarily rendered speechless. When he got his breath back, he used it to remind her of his mission, which was to render her speechless permanently. Sophie Scholl was guillotined by the Nazis at Stadelheim prison in Munich on February 22, 1943, at five o'clock in the afternoon. She was twenty-one years old. In life she had been reserved with strangers but full of fun with those she loved. Without being especially pretty she had radiated a moral beauty that left even her Gestapo interrogators self-consciously shuffling their papers, for once in their benighted lives hoping that the job of killing someone might pass to someone else. If there can be any such thing as a perfect person beyond Jesus Christ and his immediate family, Sophie Scholl was it.

Sophie's brother Hans, the leader of the little resistance group that called itself the White Rose, was already pretty much of a paragon. The Scholl family weren't Jewish and Hans could have had a glittering career as a Nazi. He even looked the part: with a face whose measurements fitted the Aryan ideal to the millimetre, he was a page from the sketchbook of Arno Breker. Yet in spite of a standard Third Reich education, including membership in the Hitler Youth, Hans figured out for himself that the regime whose era he had been born into was an abomination. By the time he reached this dangerous conclusion, armed insurrection was out of the question. A few Wehrmacht officers were the only people with guns who didn't think that Hitler ruled by divine right. Any effective opposition was going to have to come from them. The only means of resistance open to Hans and his like-minded fellow students was to hold secret meetings, write down their opinions and spread them surreptitiously around under the noses of innumerable snoops. There were a few adults in the White Rose, but mainly they were just a bunch of kids. They could never hope to do much more than circulate their skimpy pamphlets. Long before the end, Hans had guessed that even to do so little was bound to mean his death. He died with an unflinching fortitude that would have been exemplary if the Nazis had let anyone except his executioners watch. Plans by the Munich party office to have the young conspirators publicly hanged in the courtyard of their university had been scrapped on orders from Berlin, doubtless for fear that a show of courage might be catching. Philip II of Spain had once taken a similar decision when he heard from the Low Countries about heretics delivering defiant speeches from the stake. He issued orders that they should be drowned in secret. The brains in the Wilhelmstrasse were thinking along the same lines.

You would have thought to be as good as Hans Scholl was as good as you could get. He did what he did through no compulsion except an inner imperative, in the full knowledge that he would perish horribly if he were caught. Yet if moral integrity can be conceived of as a competition, Sophie left even Hans behind. Hans tried to keep her ignorant of what he was up to but when she found out she insisted on joining in. Throughout her interrogation, the Gestapo offered her a choice that they did not extend to her brother. They told her that if she recanted she would be allowed to live. She turned them down, and walked without a tremor to the blade. The chief executioner later testified that he had never seen anyone die so bravely as Sophie Scholl. Not a whimper of fear, not a sigh of regret for the beautiful life she might have led. She just glanced up at the steel, put her head down, and she was gone. Is that you? No, and it isn't me either.

She was probably a saint. Certainly she was noble in her behaviour beyond any standard that we, in normal life, would feel bound to attain or even comfortable to encounter. Yet the world would undoubtedly be a better place if Sophie Scholl were a household name like Anne Frank, another miraculous young woman from the same period. In addition to an image of how life can be affirmed by a helpless victim, we would have an image of how life can be affirmed by someone who didn't have to be a victim at all, but chose to be one because others were. At present, Sophie's story is not widely known outside the country of her birth: a big light to hide under a bushel. The recent movie about her has so far not, like *Downfall*, resonated beyond Germany. A Hollywood movie about her life would make her world-famous, but until recently it was difficult to think of an actress who might be given the starring role. Then Natalie Portman came along. At this point I will seem to digress: but I hope to make a connection later on.

A lot of people must have sat there with their fingers frozen in the popcorn as they watched the then thirteen-year-old Natalie Portman in *Leon* (known as *The Professional* in the United States) and thought this girl isn't just good, she's *good*. Apart from the happy accident of her enchanting looks, what she emanated was something much more rare: natural moral stature. It could be said that a movie like *Leon* had to get its natural moral stature from somewhere. But who cared, when the man with the flak emplacement under his raincoat was taking out the sleazeballs a bunch at a time? While Leon, the taciturn French terminator weirdly resident in New York (How did he score his green card? Did he marry Andie MacDowell?), wordlessly massacred swarms of heavies, the audience, including myself, chuckled its endorsement in the dark. In those days, undimmed by the shadow of recent events, apocalyptic body counts in the streets of New York were popular film fare. Yet I can remember being disturbed by, even a bit disappointed by, the fact that little Natalie Portman was there to complicate the story— the nice way of saying she spoiled the fun. Usually I enjoy movies about loner hit men using wit, guile and lovingly maintained ordnance to wipe out creepy people who deserve to die. Value free? *Tant pis*. I even enjoyed the original French version of *Nikita*, which was just about as value free as the genre can get. In *Nikita*, the hit person of the title didn't even know whether her targets deserved to be iced or not. She was just an instrument, a curvy part of her own gun. I still had a whale of a time.

I'm not even sure if movies like that are bad for me. Clearly my pleasure in them taps into the same current of fantasy by which, finding thieves in my apartment, I ensure that they do not leave alive. In reality, if I found thieves in my apartment they would probably leave with everything of value I possessed. But in my imagination I suddenly remember that old souvenir Japanese ceremonial sword stashed behind the partition between my bedroom and the *en suite* bathroom. Having begged for permission with a craven mien superbly feigned, I slink off to take a leak and come back as Toshiro Mifune in *Sanjuro*, scaring the daylights out of them before I even take a swing. What follows is a whirlwind multiplication of the strict Sharia penalty for theft. An idle reverie no doubt, yet without such fancies I would feel even more helpless about the way the world is going. Like all those young Chinese suit-wearing lower-echelon businessmen scattered through the world who dote on the omnipotence of some kick-boxing ham actor and thus brighten lives in which they are at the mercy of their own mobile telephones, we need these dreams to live, or we think we do. What was so bothersome about Natalie Portman's mere presence in *Leon* was that it set another standard, one which is no dream at all. It's a reality; the reality of uncompromising goodness; the unreal reality we find it worrying to hear about, because it would be so hard to live with. Embodying sensitive decency in a role which asked her to be mad keen about guns and to bare her tiny midriff to the ambiguous gaze of a mature imported assassin with a bad shave, she certainly made the film more interesting than it might have been, but a touch of quease was hard to wish away. What's a girl like you doing in a joint like this?

She did it again—or at any rate she did it again for me—in *Beautiful Girls*, a movie I knew nothing about when I first happened to switch it on during some long plane ride. I missed the opening titles and at first didn't realize that the perfect little dream girl was Natalie Portman again. It's a good film. I own a video of it nowadays, and I still find it hard to watch any of it without watching it all. But there can be no doubt that her scenes stand right out of the picture. In some respects they are designed to. For one thing, they're written that way. Everywhere else in the picture, everyone talks the standard, scabrous demotic of any movie about a gang of young American friends growing older, from *Diner* through *The Big Chill* to forever. *Beautiful Girls* is an especially deep reservoir for that kind of talk. I love it: it always was the quality of the slang that made me envious of America. But Natalie Portman's character, Marty, talks another language entirely. Marty (when she tells Timothy Hutton her name, you have to be my age to think no, *you're* not Marty—Ernest Borgnine is Marty) talks the mandarin dialect of a J. D. Salinger Wise Child. "I just happen to be the tallest girl in my class." Where have we heard that proud precocity before? Of course: it's the upper-crust young English girl in the title story of *For Esme with Love and Squalor*, the one who heals the war-ravaged American soldier's soul with the benevolent rays of her crystal spirit.

Randall Jarrell had a phrase that exactly jibed with Salinger's diagnosis of the sick place in the American dream: "a sad heart at the supermarket." Salinger's pot of balm for the sad heart was the elevated chatter of the pre-teen, pre-sex alpha-nymph, unearthly in her potential understanding, limited only by her lack of experience, desperate to grow up. Faced with her bewitching purity, the damaged veteran, himself too holy for this world, has only two courses of action: to accept his karma with renewed humility or to blow his brains out. In "A Perfect Day for Bananafish," Seymour Glass chose the second path. Though there are cynics who think he did it from remorse after exposing his penis underwater to his angelic interlocutor, it seems far more likely that Salinger's version of the Dalai Lama offed himself because, after meeting the incarnated Godhead, he had nowhere else to go. The bananafish wasn't a euphemism, it was a mantra. Similarly with Marty: her upmarket vocal articulation while she mashes snow with her tiny gloves is a guarantee of her heavenly credentials. Her snowballs are pills to purge melancholy. She's a script-conference pitch dressed up as a pixie.

After meeting Marty, the sapped, self-doubting Will ("You've really got to chill, Will," trills Marty cutely) can at last face up to the life in which his dreams of being a great jazz piano player won't come true. He'll still be the saddest heart at the supermarket, but he'll be a good citizen. Marty's barely pubescent love for him, and the vision of her that he will take away, are his consolation prize, a wish fulfilment pure and simple. Or rather, not so pure and by no means simple: a bill of spiritual goods, a high-tab product marketable to every small-town dilettante who wants to convince himself that he has been sent into the world to suffer for his sensibility. But if that's the kind of vision we need in order to be better than we are, then Natalie Portman is the girl to embody it. The thoughtfulness of her screen presence—you practically hear those little wheels turning—can raise an average part to the mental level of the heroic. In the years to come she is doubtless destined to make many serious movies look profound and many that are shallow look serious. Her function, and perhaps her fate, will be to sanctify anything they hand her. At best (at *their* best, because it will always be her best) she will turn a well-written role into a poetic epiphany, as in *Closer*. At worst she will breathe life into bathos, although not, we hope, into any more than three stipulated Star Wars prequels, of which the first, *Star Wars Episode I: The Phantom Menace*, wasted her gift with such casual indifference that I would not see the second if I were paid. Even in that tongue-tied clunker, as she visibly struggled with the unrewarding role of Amidala, Queen of Naboo, the Bad Hair Planet, she almost managed to humanize what looked like the central character in the first all-zombie production of *Turandot*.

In addition to her talent, Natalie Portman has another conspicuous qualification for playing Sophie Scholl. As far as one can tell from reading her print interviews, Natalie is leading a good life—an important requirement for pretending to be a good person. She has already played Anne Frank on Broadway. Better than a career move, her taking of the role was a testament to her fundamental seriousness, and to the unflashy professionalism of the people around her. The gifted girl seems to have sensible parents: there is no Culkin factor. As a college student, she emulates Brooke Shields and Jodie Foster in her admirable determination to have a life of the mind beyond the exiguous parameters of the entertainment industry. Apart from the mad hairstylists of Naboo, no professional freaks have so far succeeded in sidetracking her very far down their sinister alley. For too many of her magazine-cover photo shoots she has been caked with makeup, but probably her parents weren't to blame. Photographers can be persuasive. (Whatever Annie Leibovitz was thinking of when she rouged and lipsticked Natalie's defenceless face for *Vanity Fair*, it reminded me of how Brooke Shields was dressed and lit by Louis Malle for *Pretty Baby*, his justly neglected movie about a New Orleans whorehouse.) The frozen poses are against Natalie's nature. When she talks, you can hear her thirst for learning, as if that were her only passion. As our sad Babylon of a Western world goes, the kid is still a virgin.

Yes, if a Hollywood movie about Sophie Scholl gets made for the international market, it has to be with Natalie Portman. Myself, I kind of hope it never happens, and not because I distrust Hollywood *per se*. The place has come a long way since the era when it could guarantee to miss the point. In the bad old days, it wouldn't have been hard to imagine the first preview when the cards came in negative about how Sophie's story ends. ("We can't snuff the muffin. It's a reshoot, people.") But that couldn't happen now. At worst you would get the smoothest, most literate possible rearrangement of the recalcitrant historical facts, always in the name of pressing home the dramatic point. In reality, Sophie and the nice boy she loved—he was a fellow conspirator—never slept together. In the movie they would have to at least do a bit of heavy petting: you know, to show what she's going to miss by this crazy choice of hers? Pity we can't *call* it *Sophie's Choice*, but there it is. And we can't have her dying before the boys do, the way it actually happened. The prison officers took mercy on her and killed her first because they knew from experience that waiting was the worst part. Merciful Nazi prison officers? It's confusing, like those Gestapo heavies who don't even do any torturing because the kids spilled everything as soon as they were sure there was nobody still free out there that they had to protect. A lot of script points to iron out, but it can all be done with a clear conscience as long as the main point is left intact: the girl dies.

And that's where the dream movie falls apart, because if Natalie Portman plays the role, the girl won't die. Natalie will go on after the end of the movie with her career enhanced as a great actress, whereas Sophie Scholl's career as an obscure yet remarkable human being really did come to an end. The *Fallbeil* (even its name sounds remorseless—the falling axe) hit her in the neck, and that was the end of her. Her lovely parable of a life went as far as that cold moment and no further. It's a fault inherent in the movies that they can't show such a thing. The performer takes over from the real person, and walks away. For just that reason, popular, star-led movies, no matter how good they are, are a bad way of teaching history, and you don't have to be an oaf to get impatient when they try to. Most of us, when sitting in the dark at the multiplex, would rather be entertained than instructed. Instruction is for the art house. If every tent-pole movie we saw gave us the full complexity of existence, we'd be living twice. My own ration for a movie like *Gods and Monsters, Lone Star* or *Breaking the Waves* is about three a year. And it seems cruel to say so, but if Emily Watson, playing the central figure of *Breaking the Waves*, had been more famous, we would have found the story easier to take, and thus harder to assess at its true high worth. The same would be true if Natalie Portman were to play Sophie Scholl. Simply because it would be she saying them, her lines of dialogue would get into the common interchange of civilized speech, and eventually into literature. But part of the sad truth about Sophie Scholl is that nobody remembers a thing she said, and in her last few minutes alive she said nothing at all. If she had said something, the man who bore witness to her bravery would have remembered it.

WOLF JOBST SIEDLER

❧ ❧ ❧

Wolf Jobst Siedler (b. 1926) would be a fair choice for the title of Most Civilized Man in Post-War Germany. In 1943 both he and Ernst Jünger's son were sea cadets when they were caught making sceptical remarks about the future of the Nazi regime. At the personal intervention of Dönitz their lives were saved, but Siedler spent nine months locked up before he was drafted as a *Luftwaffenhilfer*—a dogsbody in a flak battalion. After the war he studied sociology, philosophy and history at the Free University of Berlin before spending ten years as a literary journalist. He then rose to an influential position in publishing with the houses of Ullstein and Propylaen, before, in 1980, starting his own house. Siedler Verlag became such a successful property that the Bertelsmann conglomerate eventually bought it, but Siedler continued in place as the most high-toned publisher in Germany. His own writings helped his glossy image. There was a series of beautifully produced picture books about the foundations and fate of the architectural heritage. (The picture book with long, well-informed captions can be a delicious form in the right hands, which his were.) But his most valuable contribution has always been as an essayist. He wrote a whole series of essays emphasizing the cleverness of the Nazis in leaving the high bourgeoisie able to feel that nothing much had changed. Some of Siedler's critics on the left thought that he had underestimated the anti-Semitism of the cultivated class before the Nazis came to power, and over-estimated its ignorance afterwards. But Siedler's immense learning and faultless taste—best sampled in his volume of selected essays *Behauptungen* (Opinions)—gave his views weight. As the publisher of the historian Joachim Fest, Siedler can perhaps be held accountable for aiding and abetting Fest's effect of displacing the Holocaust as a central theme in Nazi history. When it comes to the case of Albert Speer, however, there is no "perhaps" about it. There can be no doubt that Siedler aided and abetted Speer's post-war campaign of self-rehabilitiation. As Speer's publisher, he attended on Speer as one civilized man attending on another, and Speer's pose as a man who never really knew what the Nazis were doing to the Jews was given extra plausibility by his being so welcome in Siedler's ambience. Siedler's credentials to play host look impressive. From his student years onward he was decorated with all the favours of post-war democratic German culture, right down to the signed presentation copies of Ernst Jünger's books and the fond letters from Thomas Mann. Persuading us that even the unthinkable can be finessed from the centre of our attention and normalized as a source of growth, his finely judged tone of voice gives comfort. But we should be cautious when we spot comfort creeping into the historic memory: if it climbs the wall like a stain, it could be a sign that the truth is being drowned.

As well as the most spooky and unsettling, the most misleading thing about this State was that on the very evening of the burning of the synagogues, an event which brought the Eastern Europe of the Middle Ages into the Germany of the twentieth century, everywhere in the cities of our country festively clad people went to operetta, theatres and symphony halls, and that, six hours after the

deportation wagons left the station platforms of Berlin, the
trains for the seaside left also.
— WOLF JOBST SIEDLER, *BEHAUPTUNGEN*,
P. 72

MOST OF SIEDLER'S books have been published under his own
class-act imprint. I have a collection of his lavishly illustrated and
finely printed monographs about architecture in Berlin and the Mark
Brandenburg, and about how that architecture was restored or further
wrecked—usually the latter, wherever the Communists were in
charge—after the war. On the left of the right, Siedler is a very civilized, quietly persuasive voice. One of his most seductive themes is the
idea that the Nazis were the militant arm of bourgeois taste: that they
never really radicalized a comfortable, well-stuffed patrimony, but
instead co-opted it for their purposes. Care for the end phase of the
bourgeois era, he says at one point, doesn't really contradict the law of
tyranny: it expresses it. There is something in what he says. Though
there was plenty of very bad, very kitsch Nazi plastic art—much more
than Siedler can be bothered to contend with—there was never very
much specifically Nazi literature, and it would probably have been
swept aside if it had ever existed. As things were, Germany had no Vil-
fredo Pareto, Georges-Eugène Sorel, Charles Maurras or Giovanni
Gentile. As an approved literary pet of the Nazi regime, the dud scribe
Hans-Friedrich Blunck thought that an enthusiasm for Fascism might
threaten a diversion of National Socialism in the direction of un-
German intellectualism. Blunck was not alone among Nazi thinkers in
finding Fascism dangerously novel and far too concerned with the brain.

The more cultivated among the Nazis proved their cultivation by
knowing the traditional names: minus, of course, the names of Jews.
When a production of a Mozart opera came to occupied Poland, the
soundtrack of the newsreel celebrated the occasion thus: *Auch so, auf
tanzenden fussen, kam Deutschland in diesen Land.* ("Even so, on dancing
feet, Germany came to this land.") No mention of the Stukas and
Panzers: it would have spoiled the mood. Siedler is unbeatable in his
evocation of the regime's anti-modern, thatched tone. He practically
makes you taste the cream cakes that were Hitler's fast food of choice.
But Siedler's final effect is to overstate his case by underplaying the

facts. Perhaps because he thinks that everybody else has already done it, he doesn't make enough of the enormous, raucous, radically perverted creativity represented by the Nazi system of Führer worship and mass murder. There was nothing normal, snug or unchallenging about the filth coming out of the radios and the loudspeakers. The instantly disgusting *Der Stürmer* was on sale at street corners, not in cellophane packets on top shelves. By putting such an emphasis on the bourgeois normality of the Nazi period, Siedler retroactively creates an ambience in which an intelligent man might be lulled into thinking that things were not so abnormal after all. It was certainly the message that a man like Albert Speer wanted to hear. In 1973 at his villa in Berlin-Dahlem, Siedler, in his role as publisher, hosted a launch party for Joachim Fest's biography of Hitler. Speer was the guest of honour. Marcel Reich-Ranicki was invited without being told that Speer would be present. In *Mein Leben* (p. 482) Reich-Ranicki records how Speer, to establish an atmosphere of chummy colloquy, gestured at Fest's black-bound 1,200-page book where it lay on a table and said: "*He* would have been pleased." Reich-Ranicki went home, and his friendship with Siedler was never the same again.

Speer was also a social hit at his own launch parties, especially in London; and probably for the same reason: reassurance. His suavely barbered poise helped to persuade civilized people that on the Nazi question there might have been no clear choice. Perhaps we all would have fallen for it, especially if there were a few men in well-cut suits like him around. That was the lazy assumption that the post-war Speer counted on. But it was also the assumption that the Nazis counted on: none of the good, dependable things in life have changed, you can have your nationalist dream and eat your cream cakes too. Siedler has done us a service by bringing out the cosiness that the Nazis offered the middle class in return for its quiescence. He could have done more to bring out the Nazis' cleverness in offering the lower orders, set free to climb by the radical social programmes, a point of aspiration that would recompense them for any horrors they might have to endure or inflict: membership of the middle class. But what he scarcely brings out at all is that nobody with half a brain, whether the brain was bourgeois or plebeian, could have failed to notice for five minutes that the whole Nazi state was a raving madhouse.

MANÈS SPERBER

❦ ❦ ❦

Manès Sperber (1903–1984) was psychologist, philosopher, epic novelist and fascinated eyewitness to both of the main twentieth-century European tidal waves, which collided right in front of his eyes. Like Sartre's *Road to Freedom* novels, Sperber's fictional trilogy, *Like a Tear in the Ocean*, can be read as a saga of the politically engaged conscience, but Sperber's enduring testimony as a writer is another trilogy, the set of autobiographical books that record his own story directly, without benefit—or anyway with less benefit—of imaginative reconstruction. Non-fiction in the truest sense, Sperber's auto-biography makes a point of shirking nothing about the author's initial Communist convictions and the long and bitter business of disillusionment. Born in Galicia, Sperber first picked his political side in Vienna, and was an active Communist organizer when he moved to Berlin in 1927, by which time the Communists and Nazis were already fighting it out in the streets. Doubts about Stalin had set in even before he transferred to Paris, but they did not reach fever pitch until news came through of the Moscow trials. Even as late as 1939, however, Sperber was still writing articles in which he called Nazism an extension of capitalism: he developed that view to

the point of explaining the Molotov-Ribbentrop pact as proof
that the two totalitarianisms had both become forms of "state
capitalism" at root. A tenuous position, but by that time
nobody was listening anyway, because events had outrun theories. Lucky enough to be granted domicile in Switzerland,
Sperber emerged after the war as one of the most prominent
analysts of a period he had been very lucky to get through
unhurt by one or the other of the popular forces dedicated to
destroying all notions of the liberal democracy which he himself never quite got around to taking seriously. The three
books of autobiography, collectively called *All das Vergangene*
(usually translated as All Our Yesterdays), are *Die Wasserträger
Gottes, Die vergebliche warnung* and *Bis man mir Scherben auf die
Augen legt*. They can be found in English translation, called,
respectively, *God's Water-Carriers, The Unheeded Warning* and
Until My Eyes Are Closed with Shards. In the original language,
in paperback, they can be handily carried as pocket books. The
complete work can be confidently recommended as a guide to
the times. Above all it gives disturbing credibility to the view
that so many serious young people of Sperber's age had no
choice except to decide that democracy was doomed.

A bad conscience, an ineradicable feeling of responsibility
for the crimes committed in the name of Germany, could
be found only among men and women who had always
been opponents of Nazism and had suffered from its rule.
These, the guiltless, had overcome either late or never
their shame for what had happened.
—MANÈS SPERBER, *BIS MAN MIR SCHERBEN
AUF DIE AUGEN LEGT (UNTIL MY EYES
ARE CLOSED WITH SHARDS)*, P. 260

THE QUICKEST WAY to praise the inexhaustibly unfolding wisdom
of Manès Sperber's three-volume intellectual autobiography *All
das Vergangene* (All Our Yesterdays) would be to say that almost every
moral judgement in it is as good as this. At this point he is talking about

the Germans he was meeting in the French zone of occupation after World War II, where the German Communists were playing the same cynical game as in the American zone. (The game was "cynical" even if the anti-Communists said it was: one of the easiest points to forget when reading about European politics in the aftermath of World War II.) The German Communists, denying all vestige of their real allegiance, were masquerading as democrats in order to persuade the occupation authorities that the Social Democrats were the enemies of civil order. In the French zone the tactic succeeded to the extent that an Antifaschistichen Kampfbund (Anti-Fascist Battlegroup) was set up, whose cover remained unblown until 1948. (In the Russian zone there was no need for pussyfooting, and the Social Democrats could be sent straight to Buchenwald, which was kept open for business specifically to accommodate them.) Sperber was an adept at working out what was really going on because he had known the Communist Party from the inside. It was not until very late in the 1930s that he started making the break. There is a telling confessional passage early in *Bis man mir Scherben auf die Augen legt* (a better translation would be Until They Put the Pennies on My Eyes) in which he lays bare, through bitter hindsight, the psychological mechanism that enabled him to predict in June 1934 how the massacre of the SA leadership in the "Röhm purge" would strengthen Hitler's position rather than weaken it. As a Communist, Sperber was obliged to debate the point with his comrades. As always, they were certain that the Nazis had overreached themselves and would shortly disappear from history.

Unusually blessed with realistic insight, Sperber guessed that such confidence was moonshine. But while doing his best to convince his comrades that the opposite was true, he never once brought forward the example that weighed on him and from which he shrank with a reflex of fear—namely, the way Stalin's elimination of the left social revolutionaries, the worker-opposition and the Trotskyists had bolstered his dominance. Sperber wrote his intellectual autobiography near the end of his life. The great psychologist was at last ready to ponder the mental subterfuge by which, long ago, he had failed to admit even to himself the significance of what he already knew. The news about the brutalities of Soviet rule had been reaching the socialist movements in Europe—and especially the Germans—since the 1920s.

Sperber had known all about it. But he was not yet ready to think about it. The third volume of his fascinating experiment in self-examination is especially useful for showing us how intelligence can work to defeat itself for as long as any kind of grip is maintained on the wrong end of the stick. If he had been more dense, he might have found fewer mental tricks with which to go on convincing himself that his faith had never been misplaced.

Arthur Koestler's horrifying personal experience in Spain—loyalty to the independent left almost got him killed by the Stalinists—was a big influence on Sperber's eventual reappraisal of his own historic expectations. Before its publication in 1940, Koestler showed Sperber the manuscript of *Darkness at Noon*. Sperber was convinced by the book's central idea that a figure like the Old Bolshevik Bukharin could have made such absurd confessions at the 1938 show trials only out of duty to the Communist ideal. This notion remained popular among ex-Communists until the Twentieth Party Congress in 1956, when Khrushchev convincingly pointed out what should always have been obvious: that the confessions had been obtained by torture. ("Beat, beat, beat!" shouted Khrushchev, who knew all about it, because he had actually done it.) Sperber analyses the process by which those who had held the illusions were so reluctant to be disillusioned completely. "Many years had still to go by after our break with so-called Marxism-Leninism before we were finally free from all illusions and from many picture-book imaginings [*Bilderbuchvorstellungen*] that despite everything we almost unconsciously, and anyway without willing it, had held on to" (p. 172). One of the picture-book imaginings had been the consoling notion that a bloodstained old ideologue like Bukharin, with his perpetrator's knowledge of monstrosity on the grand scale, might have been some kind of idealist despite all. Even the hard-bitten Koestler— one of the first to realize, and to say, that communism was the god that failed—had cherished that pious wish at some level. The pious wish had helped to give *Darkness at Noon* some of its complexity and force, but it was nonsense. The secret of the show trials was that there was no secret—they were an exercise in unlimited violence.

Another reason for Sperber's slowness to accept this might have been his temperament. For Sperber, "absolute negativity" was a horror (*ein Greuel*), a death in life, a forecast of extinction (p. 185). In one of

Sperber's novels, a Yugoslav partisan refuses to believe that cruelty is deeper than sympathy, or more real than love or even than the need for justice. Sperber was simply—or rather, not simply, but firmly—a lover of life: a pretty generous reaction when you consider the range and determination of the forces that were always conspiring to bring about his death. He escaped the scythe, but plenty of people he knew and loved did not, and he saw them go. No survivor's writing could be further than his from the cheap consolations of ordinary uplift. His tone is "positive," but the affirmation has been hard won. The strength comes from the admission and examination of weakness. Without aligning himself with the perpetrators—which would be another indulgence—he can plausibly suggest that most of them got into a life of crime because they were human, and were therefore unable, on the occasions when it mattered most, to face the truth even when it was staring them in the face. He can suggest that from his own self-knowledge, but only because he has the rare gift of being honest about how his mind once worked: often too slowly, and always far more wisely after the event than before. The only point he misses is the one still missed by reformed Communists all over the world. What about all those liberal democrats who never fell for the voodoo in the first place, and will their tormented shades ever be offered an apology for being called social fascists while they were alive?

> When a woman asked me, at an evening meeting a few
> days later, how I could have presented an opinion that was
> so obviously contrary to likelihood, I defended my
> conviction aggressively. But I read in the eyes of this
> woman that she did not believe me, and I was so struck
> by it that I remember that evening, and that scene,
> exactly, even today.
> —MANÈS SPERBER, *DIE VERGEBLICHE WARNUNG*
> (THE UNHEEDED WARNING), P. 182

The evening meeting in 1931 took place a few days after Sperber had spoken publicly in a debate following the first Berlin screening of the Soviet film *The Way to Life*. The film, famous at the time, purported to show that the Soviet problem of homeless children (the *besprisorny*) was over, because they were all being re-educated in special schools to lead a useful life: they went into the school as wastrels and came out as scholars, heroes of labour, future leaders. Sperber was not long back from his first trip to Moscow, where, in a single square near his hotel, he had seen dozens of homeless children sleeping rough, with nothing but an asphalt-melting oven to keep them warm. At the time, Sperber managed to convince himself that these must be the last of the homeless children still on the loose, because it would have been easy for the government to sweep them out of sight. They were still there only because there were so few of them, and they would soon be sent to the special schools. (Sperber had been taken to see a special school, where he swallowed the assurance that it was only one of many: the old Potemkin village trick worked again.) A Russian psychologist at the psychological conference he had been attending tried to convince him that the government's promises on the subject had not been fulfilled, and that the same was true for every other promise in the first Five Year Plan. She could back up this argument with the evidence of her own life. As an academic of rank she had been allotted barely enough living space and nourishment to maintain a decent existence. Sperber rationalized all her objections, even though she was the woman on the spot. Even as early as 1931, he was well capable of seeing that the Soviet leadership was lying, especially about Stalin's benevolence. But he still thought that without the Party's leadership there could be no chance of rescuing Germany from the obscenities of unemployment and the coming collapse of capitalism. It bothered him that the Soviet Union seemed to be suffering from shortages and privations even worse than those haunting his homeland, but he wanted to believe the Soviet Union had a future, whereas Germany was dying in the grip of its past. So he understood the sardonic objections of his Russian friend without taking them in.

But this other woman, the one at the evening meeting in Berlin, shook him. He knew at the time that he already had his underlying doubts, but he had been able to keep them in balance against his need to believe in the Soviet mission. Her disapproving look was instrumental in the long process by which the balance tipped towards disbelief. The process took all of ten years, but this was where it started. A mind that knew it had been massaging the facts was altered towards facing the consequences. Sperber's trilogy is full of such moments, and their quietly dramatic presentation as turning points in a long road puts his masterpiece on a level with Bowlby's three-volume work *Attachment and Loss*, except that Sperber's emphasis is on the mechanisms of political allegiance rather than of neurosis. Belief is made concrete as the memory of a woman's glance. Not long after I read this passage for the first time, I was watching one of the later episodes of *Band of Brothers*. The crucial moment of morally revealing behaviour involved a woman's glance. Deep in Bavaria on their way to Berchtesgaden, Easy Company of the 82nd Airborne is billeted in a small town. In a grand house, the American captain, an alcoholic in search of a drink, deliberately drops the framed photograph of a Wehrmacht officer so that the glass breaks. The Wehrmacht officer's well-born wife stares at him accusingly and he wordlessly admits his embarrassment. Next day, a company scout finds a slave labour camp nearby in the woods. In keeping with the facts, the scenes are horrific. (This much we owe Spielberg and his visual achievements in *Schindler's List* and *Saving Private Ryan*: whatever his Disneyland impulse towards last-ditch uplift, the look of the thing had never been so true to the facts before.) Again in keeping with the historical reality, the good burghers of the town are put to work dragging the ruined corpses to the burial pits. One of the appalled citizens put to work turns out to be the Wehrmacht officer's wife. The same captain sees her at her labours. He catches her eye, and this time it is she who registers shame before she looks away. Again there are no words, but everything is said, and it will all be remembered.

If I look carefully at my own memories, many of them centre on the humiliating moment when shabby behaviour was observed and correctly judged by someone else whose face I still recall exactly, and for no other reason. Other people tell me that the same is true for them. If there is such an automatic and unceasing system of moral accountancy in the mind, Sperber was one of its first scholarly explorers, although of course it had been explored in literature from the beginning. Shakespeare's ghosts are memories that haunt living minds. Tolstoy is full of such moments. When we read his biography, his egocentricity seems monstrous. But when we read *him*, we see that his soul was examining its memories constantly, and assessing them all according to a moral test. When, in *War and Peace*, Zherkovim makes a condescending joke about General Mack and is chewed out by

Andrey, why is Zherkovim's humiliation so vividly presented? Almost certainly because it happened to Tolstoy himself. He was laying a ghost to rest. The conspicuous merit of Sperber's great work is that these admissions about the mind's embarrassments are not offset on to fictional characters, but are faced fair and square as personal experience. Writing in that vein, Sperber is like Freud transferred into the political dimension that Freud himself fought shy of by focusing his attention on character traits formed in infancy. Nobody can entirely supplant Freud: but he can certainly be supplemented, and Sperber triumphantly does. Sperber would probably have given the credit to Adler, but he would have been too generous: his honesty about his own mind was born in him, like a poetic gift.

That being said, we are entitled to point out a gaping hole in his analysis of the political forces contending in the last years of the Weimar Republic. He is good and honest about saying why he believed in communism against all the evidence that was coming out of the Soviet Union, and even in despite of the Comintern's incomprehensible instructions that that the Communists should join the Nazis in voting against the Social Democrats. But he doesn't say enough about the Social Democrats. There were always more people voting Social Democrat than voting Communist, right to the end. Why did not the Social Democrats see the Party as the only hope? Sperber doesn't tell us. One can only conclude that even while he was writing his monumental autobiography, at the end of his life, he still clung to the belief that the people who fell for neither of the political extremes weren't fully serious about politics. Such is the long-term effect of an ideological burden: when you finally put it down, you save your pride by attributing the real naivety to those who never took it up.

✿ ✿ ✿

Tacitus

Margaret Thatcher

Henning von Tresckow

Leon Trotsky

Karl Tschuppik

TACITUS

❣ ❣ ❣

Throughout this book, Tacitus (ca. A.D. 55–ca. 120) is the voice behind the voices. In Greece, Thucydides had already given the world a way of talking about democratic politics, but Tacitus gave the world a way of talking about the despotism and terror that so often succeed the collapse of a representative system—a familiar pattern in recent times. The tone of voice he found to deal with these matters has remained a paradigm for almost two thousand years. From Montesquieu through to Golo Mann, pre-modern and modern heroes in this book measured the fulfilment of their responsibilities against the grandeur of Tacitus, his powers of condensed expression. Born and raised under the Empire, Tacitus never saw the old Republic except as an ideal, although his first work praised his father-in-law, Agricola, as an exemplar of the lost virtues. The first career of Tacitus was as a pleader at the bar and as a praetor. But his formative experience, and the source of his secret as an analyst of the totalitarian mentality, was under the tyranny of Domitian: a reign of terror that gave him his retroactive insight into the age of Tiberius, which had happened before his time, but whose influence, he correctly assumed, had generated a lingering infection. When the relatively benevolent

Nerva dispelled the climate of fear created by Domitian, Tacitus returned to public life as a consul, and was able to continue his career as an historian without threat of reprisal. After the useful *Germania*, his third major work was the indispensable *Historiae*, an analytical narrative covering the period from the accession of Galba in A.D. 68 to the death of Domitian. Only the first four and a fragment of the fifth of its twelve books survive, but the student should regard the *Histories* as a necessary port of call, and as a reason, all on its own, for learning to read some Latin. For students acquiring Latin in adult life, the language is most easily approached through those historians who really wrote chronicles—Cornelius Nepos, Sallust, Suetonius and Livy—but with the *Histories* of Tacitus you get the best reason for approaching it at all. There are innumerable translations but the original gives you his unrivalled powers of compression. (You can pick this up from a parallel text, always remembering that the purists, when they warn you off the Loeb Library, are giving you the exact reason you should hold it dear—it's a painless dictionary.) What Sainte-Beuve said of Montaigne—that his prose is like one continuous epigram—is even more true of Tacitus. His last capital work, *Annales* (*Annals*), is a still harder nut to crack: even experts in the ancient languages find it as difficult in the Latin as Thucydides is in the Greek. Tacitus's already elliptical style becomes so tightly wound that it seems impenetrable. But the narrative is a must. It concerns the Julian line from Tiberius through to Nero. Only about half of the original work survives, but what we have would still be essential reading if it contained nothing else except Tacitus's reflections on the reign of Tiberius, which was the single most startling ancient harbinger of twentieth-century state terror, just as Tacitus's account of it remains the single most pentrating analysis of what we now see as the morphology of limitless power. If, below, I presume to offer a critique of a great critic, it is only on a single point, and in the full knowledge that I would not even possess the viewpoint from which to attempt it if Tacitus had not first lived and written. This whole book of mine grew out of a single sentence of his:

"They make a desert and they call it peace." More than fifty years ago I heard that line quoted by one of my schoolteachers, and I saw straight away that a written sentence could sound like a spoken one, but have much more in it.

❡ ❡ ❡

But in Rome, the consuls, the Senate, the knights, rushed
headline into servitude.
— TACITUS, *ANNALS*, BOOK 22

ALONG WITH THUCYDIDES, Tacitus by his mere existence pushes us hard up against the central conundrum posed by the realistic political thinkers of the ancient world: if they were so like us, why weren't they more like us? Though his characteristic technical device was the pregnant statement rather than the extended argument, Tacitus showed powers of analysis that we are unable to take for granted even among political writers of our own time. *Solitudinem faciunt, pacem appellant.* They make a desert and they call it peace. As a four-word encapsulation of a counterproductive political policy and a campaign of euphemistic propaganda, it identifies each and condemns both. Not many writers now could match it for compression. (What makes the line even more impressive is that Tacitus gives it to a German leader speaking against Roman policy in general, not just against a specific abuse.) In the *Annals* book 22, his picture of the Roman upper orders volunteering for subservience goes to the root of the Republican tradition's irretrievable collapse in the time of Tiberius.

You would think that a man who could see that could see anything. And indeed Tacitus saw the tragedy in every aspect of the old order's vulnerability: when virtue had been declared a crime, there was no refuge even in reticence. The more nobly behaved the family, the less chance it stood. Psychological torture had become a weapon in the emperor's hands more effective than military violence. Fathers had to choose between giving up their daughters to concubinage or condemning the whole family to death. Tacitus was so alive to all this that he had to develop a new kind of prose to contain his despair: the prose of the crucible.

Yet he could never see anything wrong with the legal precept by which a slave's testimony could be taken only under torture. It would have been too much to expect that he might have seen something wrong with the institution of slavery itself. But he might have seen something wrong with torture. Rome, after all, was not Greece. In Athens, both Aristotle and Demosthenes had regarded torture as the surest means of getting evidence. But they were only Greeks. *Autres temps, autres mœurs*, and Rome prided itself on being a step forward. In Rome, even Cicero—by every measure a lesser mind than Tacitus, and certainly the greater opportunist—managed to figure out that torture had something wrong with it. By this important parameter, then, Cicero, and not Tacitus, became the precursor of Montaigne, Montesquieu, Voltaire and Manzoni, who all condemned torture, and of the less famous but far more efficacious Cesare, Marquis of Beccaria, the reforming jurist who not only wrote against it but actually managed to introduce the practical measures that cleared it out of Tuscany in 1786. Cicero the infinitely malleable advocate had the right idea. Tacitus, the man of steel, didn't. It seems never to have crossed his mind. By mere intuition, with no means of observation, Nicholas of Cusa guessed right about the movement of the planets, Lucretius guessed right about atoms, and Heraclitus guessed that the whole of existence was an endless flux. Tacitus, whose opportunites to observe were ample, never guessed right about the morality of putting slaves to the torture. He heard the screams, and must have been revolted. He just never worked out what his revulsion meant.

But we should avert our gaze from the spectre of what Tacitus never did, and fix it on the reality of what he could do, because without the reality we never would have seen the spectre. Tacitus did not invent the cruelties of his age, though such is the force of his prose that he inevitably seems to have done: he invented the pity for them. Somehow, as if a tunnel had opened through time, our feelings go back to join his voice. In the *Annals*, the young daughter of Sejanus is taken away to be killed. "What have I done?" Tacitus has her say. "Where are you taking me? I won't do it again." We have heard that voice before, but it was later: it was only yesterday, in the Ukraine, at one of the Dubno shooting pits, on October 5, 1942. All the victims were naked. The German engineer Hermann Graebe recalled one moment particularly. "I still clearly remember a dark-haired, slim girl who pointed to herself as she passed close to me and said, 'Twenty-three.'" It is the same horrific event, dramatized with the same helpless voice, and just as we can't admire it as an artefact in the modern instance, because it is too real, we should not admire it in the ancient instance either, because it was real then. If it had not been for Hermann Graebe, we would not have heard the girl at Dubno speak; and we would not have heard Sejanus's daughter speak if it had not been for Tacitus.

It is quite possible that Sejanus's daughter said nothing, and that Tacitus made up what she said, as all the Roman historians made up the speeches of their emperors and generals. But the emotion he registered, both hers and his, was a true one, and puts us beyond aesthetics. Great writing is not just writing. As we can see in the troubling case of Ernst Jünger, even the most gifted writer can hide from reality in his art, and it might well be true that the more gifted he is, the more he is tempted to do so. Jünger, in his notebooks before July 20, 1944, had already said enough about Hitler to get himself executed if the Gestapo had seized them. We can see from his notations that he had been told everything that mattered about the Final Solution. But he couldn't address the dreadful reality in his writing. After the failure of the attempt on Hitler's life, while people Jünger knew well were being tortured and strangled for their complicity, he turned his full attention to Monet's country studio at Giverny, and gave one of the best ever literary descriptions of the cycle of paintings we call the *Waterlilies*. After visiting the Groult Collection in the Avenue Foch, he voiced his sensitive concern about the holes in the roof caused by flak splinters. The holes might let in the rain, to damage the treasure house of Fragonards, Turners and Watteaus. You can hear his full concern about a threatened civilization. But the threat to civilization had already gone far beyond that, and he had declined to deal with it, as if it was beneath his art.

It wasn't beneath his art; it was beyond his art; and Tacitus is there to prove it. We know now, in retrospect, that even worse things happened in the time of Tacitus than he could realize. But he did face up to the worst thing he knew. Though it took the whole of his art to write it down, his art was not the first thing on his mind: the first thing on his mind was to register the intractable fact of an innocent, unjust death. He could not make the girl immortal. When we say that she has never ceased to speak, we speak metaphorically. She died. In fact, as he tells us, it was even worse. Because virgins were safe from the executioner, she was raped first, so that no laws would be broken. The Nazi execution squads in the east were obeying the law too. The paradox had already been identified by Tacitus, and traced to its origin, in the mind of a tyrant. Great writing collapses time by freeing us from illusions, one of which is that the aesthetic impulse can be a law unto itself. An advantage of being able to write criticism in the wonderfully copious English language is that we are not stuck with an inappropriate word to register the impact of art at its height. Hearing the voice of Sejanus's daughter, we are not obliged to say, "That's beautiful." In Italian, even the mighty Croce could only have used the word *bello*. Croce painted himself into a corner with an aesthetic vocabulary that he inherited but fatally neglected to expand. The warning is clear. An aesthetic vocabulary is only part of what we need. Criticism needs a complete vocabulary, or else the rare art that responds to the whole of reality will leave us helpless; and far from being able to appreciate Tacitus, we won't even be able to appreciate Hermann Graebe.

MARGARET THATCHER

❦ ❦ ❦

Margaret Hilda Thatcher (b. 1925) read chemistry at Oxford but went into politics, a field in which she succeeded to the point of becoming prime minister of Great Britain. Her ascent to this post was a crisis for Britain's ideological feminists, who could no longer maintain that there was a glass ceiling to rank attainable by women. (Some of them said she was not really a woman at all, but a view which had had little plausibility when applied to Elizabeth I had none whatsoever when applied to someone with a husband and children.) Though very few of those males in attendance upon her ever managed to complete a sentence without being interrupted, it was not true that nobody could get her ear. Some of those who did were intellectuals. This fact could be disturbing if you were an intellectual of another persuasion. "There is no such thing as society," a statement of hers which was held up by her enemies as an example of her callousness, was in fact a summary of a recognized philosophy of individual responsibility. It could well have been planted in her ear by one of her closest advisers, Sir Keith Joseph. But it was undoubtedly her fault not to realize how it would sound if released as a sound bite. She let such gaffes happen only because she almost entirely lacked tact. Her rule was unchallenged for just so long as, and no longer than, that lack was thought to be a virtue. But her lack of verbal guile made her praise, when she gave it, doubly flattering. Once, in her presence at a soirée in No. 10 Downing Street, I managed to complete the thought that the great advantage of the British constitution, vis-à-vis the American constitution, was that it had never been written down. She was so emphatic in endorsing what I said that for a while I thought the idea was mine. In 1990 she was forced out of the leadership of her party by Sir Geoffrey Howe. Having grown far too confident of her own infallibility, she had been ruling without a cabinet, and with typical lack of diplomacy had assumed that those cabinet members whose opinions she had brushed aside would not mind. But they did, and that was the end of her reign: although she stuck around close enough and long enough to make life miserable for several luckless males who later got the job of leading the Conservative party, usually to defeat.

Solzhenitskin.
— MARGARET THATCHER, IN A
CONSERVATIVE PARTY POLITICAL
BROADCAST, APRIL 1978

SHE MUST HAVE got Solzhenitsyn mixed up with Rumpelstiltskin, and the result was a composite character of a kind unseen since that unjustly forgotten 1950s Hollywood musical *The Five Thousand Fingers of Dr T.*, whose fans will remember two roller-skating old men joined by the one beard. Most things that Prime Minster Thatcher is remembered for saying were not said very memorably. They are remembered because she said them. One of the Conservative party's tame writers, probably Robin Douglas-Home, later handed her the catchphrase "The lady's not for turning," which she delivered to the waiting television cameras with typical over-emphasis. She might or might not have realized that the line was a variation of Christopher Fry's ringing title *The Lady's Not for Burning*. Probably not: on her own proud insistence, her literary tastes ran mainly to the novels of Frederick Forsyth, read more than once so that she could savour their vigorous prose. A quasi-biblical phrase "Let us rejoice at this news"—she delivered it to the surrounding press at a key moment in the Falklands war—probably came to her from memories of the Book of Common Prayer. But this single word, "Solzhenitskin," was a truly original coinage, so startling and resonant that I have employed it ever since, and think of it every time I see her picture. As she charges forward into her bustling, interfering dotage, an old party still haunting her old party, she has even become, in her appearance, a fitting companion for Solzhenitskin—whose Russian component, Solzhenitsyn, also lived to see the day when his intransigence began to erode his legend. In my mind's eye I can see the helpless Solzhenitskin with this untiring crone yammering in his ear, telling him what he already knows, interrupting him in mid-sentence even as he struggles to agree. When I was in the press party that trailed her through China in 1982, I never heard a man in her company get six words out in succession, except perhaps for Zhao Ziyang, and even with him it was only because she had to wait for the translation. So she had to interrupt the translator.

It would be a mistake to think that Thatcher got her basic ideas from her entourage. The same assumption is made about Tony Blair today, and it is equally untrue. What Thatcher got from her attendant spirits, when she was wise, was mainly her vocabulary. Somebody must have told her that the works of the Russian dissident Solzhenitsyn provided powerful backing for her dislike of collectivism, so Solzhenitsyn would be a good name to bring in. She tried, and invented Solzhenitskin. (The fact that whoever was in charge of the Tory party political broadcast could not bring himself to correct her pronunciation is a sign of either his ignorance or the blue funk she induced in her support group even at that early stage.) Admittedly, the Russian sage's real name is hard to handle without practice. Solzhenitsyn probably had the same sort of trouble when he tried to say "Thatcher." It was remarkable, however, that when the prime minister mentioned Solzhenitskin on television, it did not get a laugh. Normally all too ready to pounce on any slip she might make, the liberal press held back on that one: perhaps they didn't realize she had made a mistake. The liberal press at the time was already showing signs of a contracting frame of reference. When the Duke of Edinburgh mentioned that he had been reading

Leszek Kolakowski, his mere citation of the Polish philosopher's name was regarded by the *Private Eye* school of political commentators as conclusive evidence of pretentiousness. Obviously they found Kolakowski's name funny in itself, because it sounded so foreign. Equally obviously, they had no idea who Kolakowski was; that the critique of Marxism in his monumental three-volume *Main Currents of Marxism* was a standard item for anyone working in the field: and that its pertinence had long before spread his name to most readers who read seriously about politics at all. Viewed from Pseuds Corner, anyone who refers to a big book by a foreign author must be a fake. (One of the signs of the marvellous self-confidence that has always reigned in the *Private Eye* prefects' room is the unquestioned assumption that someone like the Duke of Edinburgh might be trying to impress *them*.) The view is limited, but has the large advantage of being easily expressed. All it takes is the written equivalent of an impatient snort and a wrinkled nose. Strangely enough, however, "Solzhenitskin" was greeted with a respectful silence. In my television column for the *Observer*, I was the only journalist of any kind who welcomed his advent, and I have to confess that I myself got Rumplestiltskin mixed up with Rip van Winkle, and ran around making cheap cracks about Thatcher's having suggested that Solzhenitsyn had been asleep for a hundred years.

In the long run, Thatcher's mistake, whose consequences we have all inherited, was to listen to her intellectuals not only on the level of slogans and smart remarks but on the level of their convictions. Her own fundamental notions would have seen her through. Her electoral base, for example, expanded into the working class as a natural result of her inbred conviction that people would look after council houses better if they were given the chance to buy them. With her widely admired passion for good housekeeping, she could have opened Britain to the free market without dismantling its civilized institutions, and so won kudos all round. The institutions had their representatives in her cabinet, but it turned out that they might as well have been speaking from the Moon. Her free market ideologists, on the other hand, could approach her in private, where they had access to her ear as her cabinet colleagues never did. The free marketeers convinced her that some of the institutions were a hobble for commerce. By herself, she would never have thought of removing the quality requirements for the Independent Television franchise bids. When she did, the predictable result was a stampede of the big money to secure the franchises through pre-emptive cost cutting, and a plunge down market once the franchises had been secured. The BBC, eager to placate the government, and afraid that it could not justify the television licence fee unless it kept its audience share, duly followed ITV in its swallow dive off the cliff. The long-term result was a ruined broadcasting system. By the time Mrs. Thatcher was remaking the state, Solzhenitsyn was preaching spiritual renewal: to the disappointment of his liberal admirers, he no longer seemed to believe that the West's free institutions were very much preferable to the Eastern authoritarianism he had helped to dismantle. But if the young Solzhenitsyn had been present, and could have got a word in edgeways, he might have told Mrs. Thatcher that the opinions of intellectuals might be an adjunct to sound government but are no substitute for it. The Russian Revolution was prepared by theorists who were able to persuade themselves, in a period of chaos, that their theories would be put into action. But the only political theories worthy of the name are descriptive, not prescriptive. If prescriptive theories have plausible hopes of filling a gap left by a decayed or undeveloped institution, the game is already lost.

She should have trusted her instincts and shut out the smart voices, which—as often happens when they at last get a hearing—turned out to be not smart enough. Her best instinct was to stick to a simple course of action once it had been chosen. That instinct became her enemy, and the enemy of the country, on those occasions when a simple course of action was not appropriate. In domestic policy it hardly ever is. But her instinct paid off in foreign policy, with far-reaching results. When she chose not to be faced down by the Argentinian junta, she followed through with the necessary consequence: war. There were yells of protest from the far left, which would have preferred to give a green light to the Argentinian fascists rather than resort to gunboat diplomacy. The far left preferred love-boat diplomacy: an interesting reprise of the Labour party's position in the late thirties, when the menace of Hitler was admitted but the menace of rearmament seemed greater. Over the Falklands, the parliamentary Labour party had no choice but to go with her—nobody pranced for war like the Labour party's leader, Michael Foot—but the first disaster would have put her on the block. There wasn't one; the British carried the day; and the junta fell as a direct result.

There was another long-term effect of her courage which is seldom considered. Later in the same year, 1982, she went to Beijing to face the Chinese leaders in the matter of the upcoming Hong Kong handover. Typically, the bonzes of Beijing announced their conclusions before the talks: Hong Kong would become part of China. But she had never thought any other result was possible. What was really in the balance was what would happen to Hong Kong *after* it became part of China. The Chinese might have reduced it to the condition of Tibet. They didn't do so, and have still not done so. It seems fair to conclude that Mrs. Thatcher obviated the possibility by her prestige. She had won in the Falklands, and had done so partly because of the firmness of Britain's alliance with the United States. (An important factor, in that regard, was undoubtedly the diplomatic effort of the British ambassador in Washington, Sir Nicholas Henderson.) Thus she was able to suggest to the Chinese leaders that the consequences of extinguishing Hong Kong's freedoms might be drastic. She probably didn't have to suggest it out loud: she had a way of glaring at the right moment that went through the language barrier like a bullet through butter. With the Americans behind her, Mrs. Thatcher was presenting the Chinese leaders with the possibility of atomic war. The freedoms of the Hong Kong citizens were not up to much, but they were better than nothing, and the colony's last governor, Chris Patten, in the final few years before the handover, did a lot to reinforce them. Beijing vilified him for his pains, even going so far as to call him a tango dancer: but such withering invective left him unshaken. He kept on reminding Beijing that the citizens of Hong Kong had rights and that the rights were inviolate. He did what the Foreign Office had never done. So did Mrs. Thatcher. Beijing sent in the soldiers but they never fired a shot. Nobody was arrested. The Trojan War did not take place. Since that blessedly uneventful day, a flourishing Hong Kong's influence on mainland China has already been huge. If the eventual consequence is an irreversible erosion of China's monolithic state, the transformation will have to be traced back to the same extraordinary year, 1982, in which the Red Army's tanks did not come to Poland. What didn't happen in Warsaw eventually influenced everything that did happen in Europe until the fall of the Berlin Wall. It could well be that what didn't happen in Hong Kong started the same sort of process in the Far East. It was the year that Thatcher flew to China to be faced with a fait accompli, but in fact accomplished everything by dictating what would not be allowed to occur. She couldn't pronounce "Solzhenitsyn," but in most other respects she knew how to say what she meant.

HENNING VON TRESCKOW

Henning von Tresckow (1901–1945) was the heart, the soul and
the brain of the July 20, 1944, plot against Hitler's life. After the
plot failed, Claus von Stauffenberg, who delivered the bomb to
Hitler's forward headquarters, was the name popularly associated with the attempt; but really Henning, the mastermind in
the background, was the man who mattered. Nor had he always
been in the background. In March 1943 he personally got a
bomb on Hitler's plane. The bomb should have gone off. Had
it done so, Henning would have changed history. Superficially,
he had all the characteristics of the ideal hero. On the revisionist left to this day, efforts continue to denigrate the July plotters
as aristocratic right-wing romantics who wanted the war
against the Soviet Union to continue, with better leadership
than the Nazis could provide. With regard to how the Nazis are
viewed in retrospect, the contest between the old aristocracy
and the far left is a perennial stand-off, mainly because both
sides were guilty, and therefore each had a permanent interest
in passing the buck to the other. Hitler would scarcely have
risen to power if the Weimar Republic had not been sabotaged
by the aristocracy. On the other hand the Communists sabotaged it as well, and in the crucial period between the signing of

the Molotov-Ribbentrop pact in 1939 and the launching of Operation Barbarossa in 1941 they gave Hitler aid and comfort by denouncing any attempts to resist him as "imperialist." The July plotters undoubtedly had questionable credentials as democrats. But a full twenty among them, when interrogated by the Gestapo after the plot failed, insisted that they had been motivated by revulsion at what happened to the Jews. Henning, had he lived, would have said the same. There can be no doubt that he despised the Nazis. There can, however, be a doubt about his views on the German army and its career of conquest. Like most of the career officers he enjoyed the idea of the army becoming strong again. Because only Hitler could make it so, Henning was in a dilemma. He finally resolved it by turning against Hitler. Henning's key role in the conspiracy depended on his ability to persuade senior officers that they should do the same, so that there would be some hope of taking Germany back from the grip of the SS after a successful attempt. He probably knew, before the critical day, that not enough of the senior officers had been persuaded. He then said the thing that mattered: the attempt should go ahead, at whatever cost. In other words, he was proposing a religious sacrifice. If modern Germany, as a liberal democracy, now recognizes the word "July" in that sacrificial spirit, it has a lot to do with Henning von Tresckow.

❦ ❦ ❦

Now the whole world will fall upon us and mock us. But I remain, as before, firmly convinced that we did the right thing. I regard Hitler not only as the arch-enemy of Germany, but as the arch-enemy of the world. If, a few hours from now, I stand before the judgement seat of God, and am asked for a reckoning of what I did or failed to do, I believe with a good conscience that I can represent myself by what I have done in the battle against Hitler.
— HENNING VON TRESCKOW, AS QUOTED BY BODO SCHEURIG, *HENNING VON TRESCKOW: EIN PREUSSE GEGEN HITLER*, P. 217

ENNING VON TRESCKOW said this to his fellow conspirator Fabian von Schlabrendorff at 2nd Army staff headquarters in Ostrów, northeast of Warsaw, in the early morning of July 21, 1944, the day after the plot failed against Hitler's life. Or anyway, Schlabrendorff *said* that Henning said all this: all this and more. It really doesn't matter, because it was undoubtedly what Henning thought. Before the attempt, he had said that it should go ahead *coûte que coûte*—no matter what the cost. After it failed, he made immediate plans to kill himself, because he knew too much and might, under torture, give everyone away. At one stage I was so struck with Henning's heroism that I thought of writing an opera libretto about him. The piece would have been written as a long flashback from the moment of his death, which Henning accomplished by walking into the forest and blowing himself up with a grenade. He was trying to make it look like a battle incident, in the hope that the Gestapo would be fooled into thinking he had not been a conspirator, and so lay off his family. It hardly needs saying that the stratagem didn't work, but Henning should not be seen as a blunderer on that account. Many of the conspirators were blunderers, but he wasn't. He knew that the coup d'état scheduled to follow the July attempt was so sketchily organized that it would probably come apart even if Hitler was killed, but he thought the attempt should go ahead because the sacrifice would mean something in itself.

He had a right to say so. Of all the long-term conspirators, he had come closest to killing Hitler on a previous occasion. On March 13, 1943, only a month after the Stalingrad defeat, Henning got a bomb on the four-engined Focke-Wulf Condor carrying Hitler back from Smolensk to Rastenburg in East Prussia. The only reason the bomb did not go off was that the Czech-made fuse was of a type sensitive to temperature. It froze at altitude. If the bomb had gone off, the modern history of Europe might have been quite different. Henning had been only a millimetre away from eliminating the arch-enemy. It might have been better if Henning had been in direct charge of all the attempts. Unfortunately he was also the ideal man for arranging the attendant coup: a necessary effort that involved a huge expenditure of time even when it got results. Most of the time it didn't. One of the lost dialogues of the war was the conversation he had with General Erich von Manstein—the embodiment of the old, pre-Nazi army—in

February 1943. Henning paid what was ostensibly a staff visit to von Manstein's headquarters at Saporoshje in Russia. From Alexander Stahlberg's book *Die verdammte Pflicht* we know that Henning and von Manstein were together for at least half an hour. What was said? Whatever it was, the canny von Manstein would not bet. Henning kept on plugging away at the senior officers. He had been plugging away at them since the launch of Operation Barbarossa, and had been winning the allegiance of the junior officers since well before that. After July 20, 1944, it was frequently said that the young officers had found reason to rebel only after the reverse at Stalingrad in late 1942 and early 1943. But Henning was already organizing his network of young rebel officers while Barbarossa was being planned in early 1941. Before the starting whistle blew in June of that year, he had recruited Schlabrendorff, Rudolf Freiherr von Gersdorff, Heinrich Graf von Lehndorff, Hans Graf von Hardenberg and Berndt von Kleist. Most of the names were from the *Almanach de Gotha*, and some of them had a romantic notion of making peace in the west so that the more dangerous enemy could be fought in the east: but on the eve of the invasion of Russia they were all capable of realizing that the most dangerous enemy was a single German.

For an opera libretto, Henning's conversations with the young officers would provide tempting opportunities for duets, trios, quartets and so on, with the additional attraction that everyone was in Wehrmacht uniform, with no SS insignia in sight: a stage full of fresh-faced idealism. If a certain element of fresh-faced naivety is hard to ignore, it should be remembered that these really were the flower of their generation, and even the most dense among them had realized that something had gone seriously wrong with Germany's historic mission. There were thousands of young officers who got all the way through the war—or anyway all the way to an early death—without realizing that the Jewish business was at the very least a mistake. Henning's conspirators knew better, even when they still believed that *Grossdeutschland*, conveniently rid of Hitler, might somehow be allowed to fight on beside the western allies in the battle to save civilization against the threat from the east. After July 20, 1944, the Gestapo included several of the young aristocratic officers on their list of conspirators who had confessed to having rebelled because of Nazi policies towards the Jews.

Henning chose his soldiers well. The question of why there were so few like them is largely answered by the fact that there were so few like him. The aristocracy was a network that had been there before the Nazis arrived. The aristocrats had a language they could share in private. They knew how to talk freely to one another. But anyone who wanted to get them organized had to trust them not to talk out of turn. Once there were more than a few involved, the contact man was living on borrowed time. In other words, a hero was required, and that cut the field right down: cut it down, in effect, to Henning von Tresckow.

Unfortunately for the librettist, there is a problem with Henning himself. In the first winter of the Russia campaign, it became apparent that if there were no quick victory the German troops, stuck in place, would freeze. They had no warm clothing. Behind barbed wire, hundreds of thousands of Russian prisoners still had their felt boots and overcoats. It was decided—in clear defiance even of German military law, let alone of the Geneva Convention—that the Russian prisoners should be deprived of their warm clothing so that it could be given to the German troops. In their book *Der Krieg der Generale*, Carl Dirks and Karl-Heinz Janssen show that one of the men who endorsed this sinister initiative was none other than Henning von Tresckow. Stealing the warm clothes must have seemed like common sense at the time. But it was common sense only in the context of the world that Hitler had created, and that was the very world that Henning had set himself against. Faced with this awkward information, one must struggle to remember that Henning had a long-term aim, which would have been impossible to achieve had he been removed from his staff post—and if he had refused to sign the order, he would probably have been removed straight away. Henning's stature as a hero just about survives the struggle. But the opera becomes a casualty. A baritone aria on the theme of "Let the Russians freeze first" would make a mess of Act One.

LEON TROTSKY

❦ ❦ ❦

After being murdered at Stalin's orders, Lev Davidovich Bronstein, alias Leon Trotsky (1879–1940), lived on for decades as the unassailable hero of aesthetically minded progressives who wished to persuade themselves that there could be a vegetarian version of communism. Trotsky could write, orate, loved women, and presented enough of a threat to the established Soviet power structure (admittedly showing signs of rigidity by then) that it should want to track him down to his hiding place in Mexico and rub him out. It followed, or seemed to follow, that Trotsky must have embodied a more human version of the historic force that sacrificed innocent people to egalitarian principle: a version that would sacrifice fewer of them, in a nicer way. Alas, it followed only if the facts were left out. It was true that Trotsky, in those romantic early days in Paris, was a more attractive adornment to the café than Lenin. In the Rotonde, where Modigliani settled his bill with drawings and paintings when he lost at craps, Lenin could at least defend "socialist realism" against Vlaminck, whereas Trotsky couldn't even get a job as an artist's model (too small). But the Russian Civil War that turned Trotsky into one of the century's most effective amateur generals also unleashed his capacities as a mass murderer. The sailors at Kronstadt, proclaiming their right to opinions of their own about the Revolution, were massacred on his order. In the vast crime called the collectivization of agriculture, Trotsky's only criticism of Stalin was that the campaign should have been planned more like a battle. The only thing true about Trotsky's legend as some kind of lyrical humanist was that he was indeed unrealistic enough to think that the secretarial duties could safely be left to Stalin. His intolerance of being bored undid him. But his ideas of excitement went rather beyond making love to Frida Kahlo, and at this distance there are no excuses left for students who find him inspiring. Trotsky's idea of permanent revolution will always be attractive to the kind of romantic who believes that he is being oppressed by global capitalism when he maxes out his credit card. But the idea was already a dead loss before Trotsky was driven into exile in 1929. He lost the struggle against Stalin not because he was less ruthless, but because he was less wily.

Under a totalitarian regime it is the apparatus that
implements the dictatorship. But if my hirelings are
occupying all the key posts in the apparatus, how is it that
Stalin is in the Kremlin and I am in exile?
— LEON TROTSKY, QUOTED BY DMITRI
VOLKOGONOV IN *STALIN*, P. 303

TROTSKY WAS GOOD at sarcasm. His journalism written in Mexican exile would have been enough reason on its own for Stalin to nominate him as a target. Pro-Soviet credulity among Western intellectuals was usually proof against logic, but Trotsky had rhetoric: a more penetrating weapon. If Stalin's emissary had not managed to smash Trotsky's head in, there might have been more such jokes to make the Moscow show trials sound less convincing. From that viewpoint, Trotsky's murder was not only horrifying, it was untimely. Treachery made it possible, and the subject is still surrounded with a miasma of bad faith. Pablo Neruda was instrumental in smoothing the assassin's path but never wrote a poem on the subject: something to remember when reading the thousands of ecstatic love poems he did write. They are full of wine and roses but no ice axe is ever mentioned. Admirers of Neruda don't seem to mind. The same capacity for tacit endorsement is shown by Trotsky's admirers, who even today persist in seeing him as some sort of liberal democrat; or, if not as that, then as a true champion of the working class; or anyway, and at the very worst, as one of those large-hearted Old Bolsheviks who might have made the Soviet Union some kind of successfully egalitarian society had they prevailed. But when it became clear that the campaign for the collectivization of agriculture would involve a massacre of the peasantry, Trotsky's only objection was that the campaign was not sufficiently "militarized." He meant that the peasants weren't being massacred fast enough.

Trotsky had previously shown the same enthusiastic spirit when leading the attack on the rebellious sailors of Kronstadt, and Orlando Figes's book *A People's Tragedy* proves all too thoroughly that Trotsky's talent for mass murder was already well developed during the Civil War. We can dignify his ruthlessness with the name of realism if we like, but the question abides of just how realistic his ruthlessness would have been if he had won a power struggle against Stalin and stayed on to rule the Soviet Union. As things turned out, there never was a power struggle. Trotsky wasn't interested in the hard, secretarial grind of running the show: leave that to Stalin. But—an important but—Trotsky yielded no points to Stalin in the matter of dealing with anybody who dared to contradict. It was a trick they both inherited from Lenin. Golo Mann said it went back all the way to Marx. Croce quoted Mazzini's observation that Marx had more anger in his heart than love, and that his whole temperament was geared to domination. We can still see it today, even when totalitarianism is no longer a thing for states, but only for religious fanatics. It is the trick of meeting contradiction by silencing whoever offers it. Trotsky's undoubted fluency as a polemical journalist does not mean that he wouldn't rather have had a gun in his hand. The humanist makes a big mistake in supposing that a literary talent automatically ameliorates the aggressive instinct. Osama bin Laden has several of Trotsky's characteristics. According to students of Arabic, he commands his native language with vibrant fluency, giving a thrilling sense of its historic depth; he can lead a simple life and make it look enviably stylish, as if asceticism were a luxury; and above all, he can inspire the young to dedicate their lives to an ideal. If the ideals of the caliphate tend to become more elusive on close examination, so did the ideals of communism: but they needed to be incarnated for that very reason. Trotsky lived on after Stalin, and to some extent is still alive today, not because young people want the world he wanted: a phantasm that not even he could define. What they want is to be him.

KARL TSCHUPPIK

Karl Tschuppik (1876–1937) was an historian whose major books were famous in post–World War I Vienna, along with his personal charm and a particularly sardonic version of Jewish coffee-house wit. His biographies of Franz Joseph and Maria Theresa attracted attention beyond the country (*Franz Joseph I: The Downfall of an Empire* appeared in America in 1930) and there was also a biography of Ludendorff that examined the role of German militarism in leading the Austro-Hungarian Empire to its collapse. Along with his prestige as a scholar, however, Tschuppik exemplified the dubious gifts of his friend Peter Altenberg at living from hand to mouth. A Café Herrenhof habitué by daylight, Tschuppik managed, like the journalist Anton Kuh, to secure a night-time billet in the luxurious Hotel Bristol, but whereas Kuh paid little, Tschuppik paid almost nothing. The manager regarded it as an honour to have him on the premises. In partial recompense, Tschuppik would conduct long philosophical dialogues with the doorman. Erika and Klaus Mann, who mentioned Tschuppik (too briefly, alas) in their indispensable memoir of the emigration *Escape to Life*, said that they loved to visit him when they were in the city. As a man of the left, Tschuppik assumed

that the erosion of democracy in Austria after 1932 could only
be the prelude to Nazism, and warned that his country would
soon "again wade through rivers of blood." He was lucky
enough to die a year before the *Anschluß:* lucky because, like
Kuh, he had been an early analyst of Hitler's oratorical style,
and the Nazis had a long memory for that branch of literary
criticism. His admirer Joseph Roth said, "Our friend Tschuppik chose the right time to die. . . . When he did, it was clear
to me that everything was lost."

☞ ☞ ☞

It is written with love and criticism.
—KARL TSCHUPPIK, FROM THE
INTRODUCTION TO HIS <i>FRANZ JOSEPH: DER
UNTERGANG EINES REICHES</i>

L ARGELY FORGOTTEN NOW, like its author, Karl Tschuppik's book
about the collapse of the Austro-Hungarian Empire is beautiful
even to look at. I read it in the library of Castolovice, the Sternberg
castle in Bohemia, and there I had to leave it, because the books still
belong to the state. It would have been a discourtesy to my hostess if I
had asked to borrow it. The request would have put her in the position
of allowing a national treasure to leave the country. Besides, the lovely
setting of the old library was where the book belonged. Bound in
brushed yellow linen, clearly printed on good paper, it was a product
of Avalun Verlag, one of the publishing houses that once flourished in
Hellerau bei Dresden. In my own library, some of my most cherished
books were printed in Dresden at that same time: the twenties were a
great period for fine printing of popular books. Wolfgang Jess Verlag
turned out a full set of thin-paper volumes devoted to the nineteenth
century scholar of the Renaissance Ferdinand Gregorovius—a set that
I managed to reassemble after breathless discoveries in second-hand
bookshops all over the world. At Castolovice the Tschuppik book
stopped my breath in the same way. It brought back Dresden as if the
bombs had imploded and gone back into the sky. It was the reintegra-
tion of two successive lost eras: the post–World War I efflorescence of
German-speaking pre-Nazi culture, and, before that, the old Austro-

Hungarian Empire whose last glories it examined *mit Liebe und Kritik*—with love and criticism.

Though Tschuppik was a committed democrat and no pushover for the erstwhile social order, his love for the old *k.u.k* society saturates the book. It reminds you less of Schnitzler, who guessed that the phosphorescence meant decay, than of Joseph Roth, whose nostalgia was incurable. The Austro-Hungarian Empire was, after all, not quite an empire like the others. It had conquered no foreign territories. It integrated several Central European countries without subjugating their populations. Ethnic minorities had reason to be grateful for its rule. Many of their intellectuals had the good sense to be grateful at the time, and Tschuppik, looking back on what had been a modus vivendi if not a grand harmony, was well justified in expressing a passion deeper than mere affection. But his criticism is equally all-pervasive. Tschuppik doesn't gloss over how different things would have had to be for the outcome to be otherwise. To begin with, there would have had to have been no great war. A war was bound to bring the empire down, yet Franz Joseph's deluded army of adminstrators walked straight into it. Their one excuse is that they walked in their sleep. Graf Stefan Titza was the only hero in the cabinet. He alone warned against what a war would do. When the day was upon them, however, even he came round. *Va banque*: the brave cry of the already bankrupt.

On the same weekend, in the same library, I worked through the two imposing volumes of Metternich's *Denkwürdigkeiten* (Things Worth Thinking About), published in Munich in 1921, more than sixty years after the master diplomat's death. Once again the modern typeface had the scrupulous clarity that marked the era. (It was not until 1933 that the fussy old black-letter typefaces returned, as part of the general cultural throwback by which the Nazis presumed to give the very look of thought an air of the Gothic: and even then they returned only to Germany. The Austrians kept their modern typefaces until the last day.) Metternich's prose is as neat as the type in which it is set. If Henry Kissinger, who has always seemed to like the idea of being styled our modern Metternich, could express himself like his role model he would be better equipped to defend his actions. For any liberal democrat, Metternich's own actions still need plenty of defending, but there was nothing wrong with his prose style. Metternich tied his powers of decision to his clarity of language. Here is a passage I translated into my notebook:

> I have always thought that the most important business for a statesman is the care with which he keeps a strict eye on the difference between things which he builds within himself and things imposed on him by the spirit of party during the course of time, and to keep them just as strictly separated. The most fruitful means for carrying out this business lies in the care to fix words to the things they are called on to signify, and hold them fast (vol. 2, p. 466).

But that doesn't get the vigour of his rhythm. He was an old man, but his prose was a stripling. Wittgenstein recommended the poetry of Mörike, in which, he said, the word does not exceed the thing. Metternich had reached the same conclusion long before. Some of his other conclusions, however, were not just conservative, they were reactionary, and therefore inadequate to facts he already knew. Try this:

> If the name of God, and the powers instituted by His divine decisions, are dragged into the mud, then the Revolution is already prepared. In the castles of the King, in the salons and boudoirs of certain cities, the Revolution had already happened while the mass of the people were still getting ready for it (vol. 2, p. 71).

He switches from the present tense to the past because he is switching from the general case to the particular instance: the French Revolution. The particular instance is the part that he brings alive, with a touch for rhythm that any translation is bound to miss: ". . . *war die Revolution schon vorbei, während sie bei der Masse des Volkes erst vorbereitet würde.*" It is always dangerous to praise sonic effects in a language not one's own: they might be cruder than one thinks. But surely *vorbei* and *vorbereitet* are deliberately linked in order to help the second part of the sentence launch itself from the first. A clear idea is expressed with verve. But the idea was wrong, or at least not exhaustively right. England's George III and his government, for example, were godly institutions; they were dragged in the mud with great thoroughness, not least by the pitiless caricatures of Gillray; and there was no revolution. (To make certain that there wouldn't be, in the next reign potential subversives were sent to Botany Bay, on the assumption that they and their progeny would never be heard from again.) Further back, the palace of Louis XIV was haunted by irreverent wit that felt no need to whisper: everyone knew that Louis abandoned a successful campaign in the Low Countries because Madame de Maintenon had burst into tears, and nobody forbore to say so. There was no revolution: not then. The revolution had indeed to be prepared, but it was prepared among the people, or anyway outside the palace. Lafayette was turned from duty by what he met in the streets, not by what he had heard in the corridors of Versailles or the Tuileries. Metternich had good cause to fear revolution: he had spent his life dealing with its consequences. But irreverent remarks had not been the cause of it, and he must have known that to be true. He just didn't like wit. There is a marvellous passage in which he tips his hand. To quote it is to quote a quotation, because he put the thought together from his reading.

> Talleyrand rightly says: "*L'esprit sert à tout et ne mène à rien.*" For Madame de Staël, her fame was a kind of power. The longer I live, the more I treat that power with mistrust (vol. 2, p. 166).

For the French, *l'esprit* is a wide-ranging term, but wit is at the core of it. Talleyrand is probably saying that verbal brilliance can be applied to anything but leads to nothing. It was the right proposition for Metternich to agree with: the man of concrete decisions had heard too much talk. But his contempt for Madame de Staël is a giveaway. She had an insight into power, having seen the frailties of the men who wielded it. On the day that Napoleon sent her into exile across Lake Geneva, she told her journal the lasting truth about her persecutor. She said that Napoleon possessed such an all-embracing talent that there was nothing he could not do, except understand the behaviour of a man of honour. Today she would have said woman of honour, but the most famous of all the first feminists—the first Germaine—was restricted by her inherited language. She was not, however, restricted in her thoughts, and Metternich was mistrustful of exactly that. She incarnated the only permanent revolution that counts: that of the critical intellect. Even today, her example can lead men of order to huff and puff. Vladimir Nabokov, in his long, detailed and half-crazed commentary on *Eugene Onegin*, dismissed her with a wave of his fastidious patrician hand. He forgot to say that Pushkin himself thought the world of her. But Pushkin was tuned to the feminine. He could see the strutting hypocrisy on the bastions of the state.

Metternich, who dismantled and reassembled kingdoms according to his personal judgement, called the state a divine expression: about as far as hypocrisy can go. Yet nobody now could surface from Metternich's book of reflections without a sense of loss. Those were the days; when men who could do things like that could write like this. You could see why such books were printed to be cherished in the years after World War I. Their publishers and editors were putting a world back together, in the hope that the new world would be something like it. Their publishers and editors thought that love and criticism would be enough. But the storm came. Not many of the books slept through it. They were strewn to the winds along with their owners, or were burned in the libraries their owners left behind. The library at Castolovice was lucky: the vandals passed it by. The family defied the Nazis but its castles were spared. When the Communists took everything, the family scattered to the outside world. Castolovice was turned into a factory for repairing refrigerators. Thought to be useful, the roofs were repaired too, after a fashion: so the acid rain of the red East did not get in, and nothing attacked the books except the dust of bad cement.

After the Velvet Revolution—which was less a revolution than a restoration of the old republic—one of the many commendable impulses of Vaclav Havel's civic order was to restore faith with the cultural heritage. Dispersed all over the world, some of the historic families were invited back to rebuild their castles, tend their estates, and thus, by offering employment, regenerate the villages which had grown up around their lands in the past. On a Machiavellian view, it was a neat way of getting the aristocrats to put their hard currency into the economy, if they had any. Some didn't: the patriarch of the Kinski family is back in his castle, but it will remain a ruin, because he spent the lost years not abroad but in the mines, paying the long price for never having fled. The plan has been only a partial success. It costs more than money to put a culture back together: it takes dedication and patience, because the old craft skills have all disappeared. Castolovice is one of the few success stories. The castle and the lands thrive, employing people for miles around. It was early spring when I was reading Metternich. The deer in the fields had dropped their horns, the imported emus were sitting on their eggs, and the castle was getting ready for the tourist season.

On a fine day in summer, it is not unknown for more than a thousand people to turn up. Most of the visitors are from the Czech Republic. They come to see what life was like a hundred years ago, under the old emperor: the era in which the future republicans grew up, nourishing their democratic dreams with the rich traditions that lay around them. The books I had been reading dated from the time of Masaryk and Beneš, whose own books were produced to the same standard. While a guest of honour at the Olomouc Festival of Documentary Film in 2001, I searched the second-hand bookshops and found a two-volume set of Masaryk's writings dated 1925, and matched it with a two-volume set of Beneš dated 1927. Each set carried the word *Revoluce* in its title, but of course it was not a revolution at all. Revolutions trample the past. The republic of Masaryk and Beneš grew out of the past organically, bringing the established cultural wealth along with it. You can see it in the look of their books: the proportion of the printing, the lustre of the linen bindings. When I got the four volumes back to London, I laid them out on my library coffee table and drank their appearance in. I opened them and caressed the thick, good paper that will never grow brittle. I did everything but read them. I can't read Czech: not yet, anyway. I am told that once you master the alphabet it is not as hard as Russian. It is certainly easier than Polish to pronounce. The prose of Beneš is famously unreadable but I would like to be able to judge that for myself, and Masaryk was such a man as few countries are given for a spiritual father: I would like to relish what he wrote in the way he wrote it. If I had the knack of Timothy Garton-Ash, I would be reading it by now. Those of us with more pedestrian powers of assimilation have to find the time, and at my age I am feeling a bit short of time altogether. But the books will go into my shelves anyway, where one day, if my library stays together, someone like me might come along and take them down—I hope without having to brush them free of cement dust, or whatever residue might characterize the next barbaric age.

u

❣ ❣ ❣

Dubravka Ugresic

Miguel de Unamuno

Pedro Henriquez Ureña

DUBRAVKA UGRESIC

❣ ❣ ❣

Dubravka Ugresic (b. 1949) might have been put on Earth for the specific purpose of reminding us that there is never anything simple about the Balkans. She was born in Croatia into a family of mixed ethnic origin, with a Bulgarian mother. She spent time at Zagreb's forbiddingly entitled Institute for the Theory of Literature. A graduate of Moscow State University, she did academic work on the Russian avant-garde. In 1993 she left Croatia, staying first in Holland and Berlin before taking up a succession of posts in American universities, among them Wesleyan and UCLA. Her novels, which I have not yet read, are usually described as the work of a writer's writer, or perhaps of someone who has been to the Institute for the Theory of Literature in Zagreb. One of them has, at least in English translation, the best title of the twentieth century's twilight years: *The Museum of Unconditional Surrender*. Her journalism, which I have read with respect, despair and delight, is essentially a refusal to surrender to the historically determined chaos of the area where she was born and grew up. As brave as Oriana Fallaci ever was but less burdened by ideology (so far she has not stuck herself with any large theories that she might need to repudiate, except possibly for the Theory of Literature), Ugresic is unbeatable at explaining the inexplicable entanglements of Balkan cultural traditions, particularly as they relate to the hellish position of women.

> One hot summer's day I stopped in the New York subway
> hypnotized by what I saw. A middle-aged couple was
> dancing an Argentinian tango, describing around them an
> invisible circle in which only the two of them existed, the
> man and the woman, and a dusty cassette player on the
> ground beside them. The man and the woman were
> neither ugly nor beautiful, neither young nor old. They
> were dressed in black, their clothes were tidy but worn, the
> man's black trousers shone with a greasy sheen. They
> danced seriously, modestly, without emotion, without
> superfluous movements, with no desire to please. The
> crowd around them was becoming steadily larger.
> — DUBRAVKA UGRESIC,
> *THE CULTURE OF LIES*, P. 131

T HIS IS WHAT the tango can give you: an atoll of bliss in a sea of turmoil. Just to watch it, let alone dance it, is a holiday from the accidental, and a free pass into the realm where the inevitable, for once, looks good. The dance is beautiful all by itself: the dancers don't have to be, and in this passage they obviously aren't. Ugresic goes on to ask rhetorically why a couple of tango dancers can make hard-bitten New Yorkers, who would otherwise hurry past, stop to watch and miss their trains. She deduced that they were being taken out of themselves. It was true for her. Like the moment it describes, the passage is an interlude made doubly sweet by what the rest of life is like. Her book is a cautionary tale for anyone who might think he can guess something about the Balkans without having been there. *The Culture of Lies* is really a collection of observations, many of them focused on the official abuse of language: the ghost in the background is Karl Kraus. What Kraus did for Austria and Germany in the pre-Nazi period, Ugresic does for Croatia in the Tudjman period, with the Bosnia of Milosevic looming in the wings; and she does it at least as well. Whereas Kraus's real measures of normality lay in the Austro-Hungarian Empire, whose last phase he lived through and never forgot, Ugresic's, unlikely though it may seem, lay in the vanished Yugoslavia of Tito. For her, Yugoslavia lingers in the mind and heart as the dreamed reality, whereas Croatia is the living nightmare. Tito's iron hand at least kept the ethnic minorities from each other's throats. The new iron hands want something else, and throats are their first target. Their second target, however, is the one that fascinates her, for reasons that become steadily more obvious. Whatever faction a man represents, the uninvited penetration of a woman seems to be his main reassurance of personal power. Beside and scarcely below the threat of murder, rape becomes a part of a woman's life expectancy. It is hard to think of another book in which a climate of casual violence incubates such a lucid concern for women's rights. Nadezhda Mandelstam's two books of memoirs add up to the great twentieth-century record of everyday frightfulness, but Nadezhda wasn't thinking about women's rights. She probably found Alexandra Kollontai absurd. Kollontai campaigned for women's rights to be granted by a state dedicated to the principle that nobody of either sex had any rights at all. Nadezhda would have been glad to have the old repressions back, and male chauvinism along with them.

But Ugresic is in a different place, a different time, and a different frame of mind. She knows what has come true for women in the West, and is ready to blame the whole mess in her country exclusively on the strutting male. She calls him Yugo-man and sometimes the Yugomaniac. She makes a very convincing job of it. Whether Serb, Croat, Slav, Muslim, Bosnian this or Herzogovinian that, all the men in the book carry on like wild animals whenever they see a skirt. She doesn't make enough of one of the saddest facts of all, perhaps because it didn't fully emerge until much later: Muslim women who had been gang-raped by Serbian men were scared to tell the Muslim men, lest they be punished for having submitted to dishonour. Apart from that, however, her readiness to distribute her scorn evenly makes her the writer she is, and surely she is one of the most interesting to come out of Eastern Europe in modern times. (Ugresic attended the trial of Milosevic, and I can hardly wait to see what she writes about it.) She comes from one of what Kundera memorably called the Kidnapped Countries, and she has given it its voice, which is the voice of a woman. The woman carries plastic bags full of the bad food and the thin supplies she has queued for by the hour while the men sit around in the square scratching their crotches and dreaming up their next war. In the course of their dimwitted conversations, the men refer to any given woman as a cunt. The twin functions of the cunt are to put dinner on the table and lie down when required. Most male readers will find this an uncomfortable prospect, as they are meant to. Multicultural ideologists, if there are any left, will find it even less comfortable than that. According to Ugresic, multiculturalism in rich countries abets ethnic cleansing in the poor ones. Try this:

> Proudly waving its own unification, Europe supported disintegration in foreign territory. Emphasizing the principles of multiculturality in its own territory, it abetted ethnic cleansing elsewhere. Swearing by European norms of honour, it negotiated with democratically elected war criminals. Fiercely defending the rights of minorities, it omitted to notice the disappearance of the most numerous Yugoslav minority, the population of a national, "nationally undetermined" people, or the disappearance of minorities altogether.

Residents of Britain will find such passages particularly embarrassing. It was British foreign policy, as propounded by men who thought they were acting for the best, that kept America from dropping its bombs on Slobodan Milosevic until it was almost too late to save anyone. The idea was to leave the area alone while things worked themselves out. (Long before, with regard to Biafra, Harold Wilson's government had pursued the same policy, and with the same results.) From those helpless civilians who were left alone while things were working themselves out, and who somehow managed to survive the experience, anger is the least we can expect. Ugresic's tone can be taken as a commendably moderate expression of the opinions she must have held while searching the sky in vain for the NATO aircraft that are held to be the worst thing in the world by those who have no idea how bad the world can get. If that's the way she wrote it, that's the way it probably felt, at the very least. No wonder then, if, on a brief holiday in New York, she found the tango dancers a holiday from history. If the Twin Towers had been hit at that very moment, it would have been no surprise to her. It would have been just a bigger version of the routine gang rape, or of a woman taking a hit from a sniper and falling on her plastic bags.

MIGUEL DE UNAMUNO

❦ ❦ ❦

Miguel de Unamuno (1864–1936) was a Basque, born in Bil-
bao. From 1891 he was professor of Greek at the University
of Salamanca, but his writings and influence extended far
beyond the academic world. In 1897 he had a spiritual crisis
in which he lost his faith: the most important personal event
in his life. From then on, every idea was a new struggle,
which he dramatized in his prose, on the principle that his
mind was the main character in a drama. With a twenty-year
head start on Ortega, Unamuno pre-empted the title of the
most style-setting philosopher of modern Spain, although
Unamuno's philosophy was avowedly anchored in a literary
context, whereas Ortega prided himself on an apparently
broader scope. But Unamuno's more diffident range gave
him a sharper focus. (And his humility gave him a deeper
realism: the son of a baker, Unamuno would never have been
capable of Ortega's contempt for the masses.) Unamuno's
sensitivity to what was vital in literature not only allowed him
to redirect the traditional evaluation of the literary heritage
of the Spanish mainland, it allowed him to detect that it was
about to be re-energized by what was happening in the
Americas, the key factor in the thrilling story of how the

Spanish world, in the twentieth century, came back from the dead. That was the vital analytical breakthrough, which we can now see should be counted as political as well as cultural, because the literary confidence in Latin America was the vehicle, for the countries below the Rio Grande, of a workable nationalism, a connection which the philologist Pedro Henriquez Ureña, one of the men on the spot, was able to establish from direct participation. Unamuno had enough to deal with in the mother country. Of Republican sympathies, he was exiled in 1924 to the island of Fuerteventura. After the founding of the Republic he returned in triumph to Salamanca. His mental independence, however, was incurable. He was soon at odds with the Socialist regime, whose doctrinaire aims and methods, he thought, confused the issue of a nationalist struggle; and he loathed the idea of foreign interference in Spain's affairs. Since the two biggest totalitarian powers on Earth, at the invitation of the infinitely cynical Franco, were both intent on interfering in Spain with no thought at all to the country's interests, he was thus in the position of being a witness to a tragedy. Luckily, in December 1936, he died before he could see the worst of it. But he might already have heard the worst. His death from a heart attack was brought on by a confrontation with a fascist general who drove the old professor out of his beloved university at gunpoint. The physical insult might have been bearable but the rhetoric wasn't. "Death to intelligence!" screamed the general. "And long live Death!" The general was living proof that his two propositions were valid; especially the first one.

Rather than reading a book in order to criticize it, I would
rather criticize it because I have read it, thus paying
attention to the subtle yet profound distinction
Schopenhauer made between those who think in order to
write and those who write because they have thought.
— MIGUEL DE UNAMUNO, *ENSAYOS*,
VOL. 2, P. 1013

A NYONE WHO HAD ever done any book reviewing will recognize the importance of the distinction Unamuno is making here. For a young writer, being asked to review books is an exciting business. Unless he is an unusually dedicated novelist with a well-organized budget—including, for preference, private means—he will find time to review a book when asked. He will also find that the time can be a dead loss: the book wasn't worth the effort. He might write a funny piece saying so, and the funny piece might lead him into a useful sideline: but even if for the best, his career will already be distorted. Further down the line, the man of letters who draws his principal income from book reviewing will find himself wasting his main asset. His main asset is to be well read, but if he spends too much time reading secondary books only for the sake of reviewing them, he will be adding little to his initial stock of useful erudition. Worse, he will be adding much that is useless. The activity dilutes itself automatically. In any literary editor's stable of regular contributors, the man who can be counted on for a thousand words by Friday about absolutely anything is always the most pitiable figure. The deadly combination of facility and impecuniosity did him in. In the 1930s, in *Enemies of Promise*, Cyril Connolly had already codified the dangers lurking in Grub Street for the too biddable bookman.

As often occurs, the worst case defines the ideal. Anyone faced with the deadly task of first reading, then writing about, a book he would not ordinarily have read in the first place, is brutally reminded of what he was really born to do: read books that can be felt, from page to page, to do nothing for his wallet but everything for the spirit. (At a publishing house, the best editor is always the one who physically suffers at the thought of how his daily labours are ruining his capacity to read for pleasure.) A good sign is the constantly welling urge to underline, to make notes in the margin, or to sketch a commentary in the endpapers. In the book you are reading now, almost any book mentioned has passed that test. Unamuno's pages cry out to be defaced. One hesitates, because his books are usually very pretty physically. Invariably published by Aguillar, his early collected editions on thin paper are hard to find now. I found most of mine in two very different Spanish cities: in Madrid, where they cost a bomb in the special-

ist bookshops, and in Havana, where they can be found on the open-
air stalls in the bookshop square. In Havana they cost little but are
seldom in good shape. Buying two sets of the essay volumes, one set
in each city, I was well equipped to make marks in the damaged volumes and keep the pristine ones for the bookcase. Mine were by no
means the first marks Unamuno's margins had ever received. At his
potent best he could put the aphorisms one after the other like the
wagons of an American freight train stretching from one prairie rail-
head to the next.

Unamuno first ambushed me in Mexico City. I had a date with Carlos Fuentes to do an interview. Turning up at his beautiful house, for a
while I was alone with his books. The whole of the Spanish literary
world was there on the shelves and lying around piled on tables. My
eye went straight to an open volume of Unamuno, from which, I
guessed, Fuentes was currently reading, because there was a pen beside
it on the table. I couldn't resist taking a peek at what he had underlined,
although it felt like snooping. He caught me at it. Slightly embarrassed, I said that he had underlined a lot. He flicked through the book:
there seemed to be at least one underlined passage on every page. He
said that when reading Unamuno it was rare when he didn't underline
an argument at the point where it was drawn to a conclusion. "Very
great Spanish writer. Very great writer *in Spanish*. Because he was one
of the writers who began to give us our sense of the Spanish world. The
essay as an art form. Unamuno."

I think his mention of the hero's name might have been a gentle
corrective to my pronunciation of it, which had been a bit hesitant.
(The third syllable should be stressed, but for an English speaker the
attraction of the word "unanimous" tends to drag the stress back to
the second.) My pronunciation must have been good enough,
though, for Fuentes to deduce that I had at least made a beginning on
reading his native language. Thus began the kind of conversation that
you could have before or after a TV interview but not during it.
Nowadays, when I have transferred most of my television interviewing activities to the Internet, those are the conversations that I seek
rather than avoid, but in the circumstances it would have been inconceivable to tape a conversation about Rubén Darío, Ortega, Octavio

Paz and Unamuno. It would have been inconceivable because it would have been self-defeating. Carlos Fuentes had only one reason for going on television with me in a "Postcard" programme, and the reason was good: he did it to talk simple sense on an elementary subject, the status of his country. There would be a mass English-speaking audience listening: millions of people who would never hear of Unamuno.

But the television programme wouldn't have happened if there had not been a democratic world, and that was where Unamuno came in. Voices like his had helped to restore the Spanish empire to civilization. Unamuno's message to a moribund Spain was that Spanish culture was alive in the Americas and would eventually come home. His essays had been worth writing in themselves—there were no utilitarian tests they had to pass, and none they could have passed in the long run if they had been written to short-term utilitarian requirements. But one of their uses had been to stay good. They had provided a measure of intelligence that could be referred to in times of confusion. By his own example, he had proved that Spanish is one of the languages of the modern world. Hence the special pleasure of finding his books in the sunlit marketplace of old Havana. With their gold-stamped spines flaked and crumbling and their onion-skin paper crinkled by the plaster-curdling humidity, they were still too expensive for the few book-lovers left among the local population. Spanish-reading tourists like myself do most of the buying, and I suppose that in the course of time almost every Aguilar edition that has ever gone into the marketplace has been taken back to Spain, where it was first printed. But some of the people who had first read the books were probably still alive somewhere. Perhaps a few of them were still in Cuba: not every bibliophile had taken to the rafts. Almost all of them had underlined something. Underlining means the determination to remember. The determination usually fades faster than the marks of the pen or even of the pencil, but the intention was good. All the readers had participated with the writer in the tradition of tolerant, receptive sense he had helped to found: a tradition which had made the critical essay part of the wealth of the modern Spanish language—the true and worthwhile residue of the Spanish empire, as the English language is of the British.

The eternal, not the modern, is what I love: the
modern will be antiquated and grotesque in ten years,
when the fashion passes.
— MIGUEL DE UNAMUNO, *ENSAYOS*,
VOL. 2, P. 1167

Unamuno, like Croce, was a critical writer with an instinctive grasp of
how the sublimities of the arts he loved were rooted in the mundane.
In his time, the febrile Spanish literature of the mainland, as opposed
to the burgeoning Spanish-language literature of the Americas, suffered badly from the aestheticist belief that a high calling required a
high treatment of (the fatal step) a high subject. In a magnificent linked
series of critical essays, he laid out an aesthetic principle that would
counter the final mutation of that belief into *modernismo*—which was
merely the latest version of the assumption that the right elevated artistic attitude would bring automatic results.

The quoted passage makes more sense when we trace what he meant
by *eternismo*, the eternal. He didn't mean an appeal to transcendental
values: he meant attention to the profane reality that is always there.
On the same page (once again a great book has a great page) he wrote
that the universal is in the guts of the local and circumscribed, and that
the eternal is in the guts of the temporal and evanescent. *Entranos*
could be more decently translated as "entrails" or "bowels," but I think
he meant to be arrestingly earthy. (Memo to myself and younger readers: all guesses about tone in a foreign language should be checked with
someone who speaks it for a living.) Two pages later, he glossed *univer-
salidad*. "Universality, yes: but the rich universality of integration,
brewed from the concourse and shock of differences." Or to put it
another way: not the universality of abstract ambition.

Unamuno took his concern with concrete reality all the way to the
basement, in the artist's personality. He didn't think it could be left
behind any more than a bird could spurn the air. What Unamuno
says—more than a thousand pages into the same rich volume—can be
borne in mind when we remember Eliot talking about the artist's striving after an ideal state of impersonality. Unamuno had already said that
there could be no choice involved. A true artist, he wrote, puts in his
personality even when he most wants to conceal it. Unamuno said that

with Flaubert you can see his personality even in his last novel, *Bouvard et Pécuchet*, which is all about clichés and pedantry. Unamuno meant that Flaubert, uniquely alert to language, could not create the character of a pedant without incorporating into the character the pedant within himself. The best writers contain within their souls all the characters they will ever create on the page; and those characters have always been there, throughout history; so the writer, no matter how modern he thinks he is, deals always and only in eternity.

PEDRO HENRIQUEZ UREÑA

❣ ❣ ❣

Pedro Henriquez Ureña (1884–1946) was the philologist who taught a generation of Latin American cultural figures that they weren't living in a backwater after all, but that they were actually—and precisely because of their historical position—at the forefront of the revival of civilization in the Spanish world. In other words, he told them that the small time was over and they were on to something big. His intellectual position was developed throughout his lifetime, but it depended on a proud confidence that he must have inherited. Born and raised in Santo Domingo, he moved to Cuba to write *Ensayos Criticos* (1906), his first book of critical essays. From the very start he was out to proclaim the essential oneness of the apparently fragmentary Latin American cultural achievement. He was doing so at a time when, apart from such a visionary poet as Rubén Darío in Nicaragua, no critical writers had been thinking that way in Latin America, or even in Spain: the only scholars of Latin American literature were English or German. He spent seven years in Mexico, where he pioneered a way of writing about the indigenous heritage and the Spanish heritage as simultaneous continuities: an emphasis that would be picked up half a century later by such writers as Octavio Paz and Carlos Fuentes. In 1915 Ureña went to New York, then to Washington, and then taught at the University of Minnesota until 1921: a period spent among the *norteamericanos* which increased his international prestige and therefore his influence in Latin America. During that period he spent time in Madrid, in fruitful conversation with the scholarly giant Alfonso Reyes and the philologist Menéndez Pidal, the man who invented the phrase "the spontaneous yearning after the totality of knowledge." Knowledge ruled Ureña's life but he couldn't keep politics out, especially after the United States invaded the Dominican Republic in 1916. Although he eventually tended towards socialism, his political position mainly became apparent in his teachings about literature, in which his guiding principle was that the colonial history, properly interpreted, could be taken as a strength, not a weakness: there was such a thing as "spiritual nationalism" which arose spontaneously from a complex historic memory and could be cherished with a whole heart.

A single sentence by Ureña can be taken as the epigraph for the whole history of the burgeoning of Latin American literature in the twentieth century: "*Todo aislamiento es ilusorio*" (All isolation is illusory). Ureña pointed out that even the culture of the ancient Greeks had not grown in splendid isolation, but on a basis of nourishment imported from other places. A generation of writers were inspired by Ureña's ability to reinterpret a history of failure and frustrated nationalism as a positive development. Not that his positive attitude was merely euphoric. He also warned them not to accept any patronizing foreign approval of their "exuberance." Most of the exuberance, he warned, was mere verbosity, the sure sign of a sparse culture. His own prose was a model of vigour made stronger by not being given its head. But beyond his key place in the story of Latin America's rise to prominence in the modern Spanish world, there is an important message for the entire world in his insistence that literacy was basic to all hopes of political maturity. His essays about the importance of teaching literature in the schools are classic statements of a true position from which liberal democracy will always be tempted to stray through its egalitiarian impulse towards making school easy. Ureña thought school should be demanding, but he had a convincing way of saying that the difficult could be delightful. Some of his best essays on the subject can be found in the two files under his complete name on the second page of his Google entry, one of which has an excellent summary of his career by the scholar Laura Febres.

After 1924 the constantly travelling Ureña came to rest in Argentina, first in La Plata and later in Buenos Aires, where he taught, among others, Ernesto Sabato: a fascinating example of the productive relationship between academic teacher and creative writer. Ureña died in Buenos Aires in 1946. In the Dominican Republic there is a university named after him but really his influence lives on in every good school south of the Rio Grande.

❡ ❡ ❡

Great art begins where grammar ends.
— PEDRO HENRIQUEZ UREÑA, QUOTED BY
ERNESTO SABATO IN ANTES DEL FIN

IN ARGENTINA JUST after World War II, Pedro Henriquez Ureña was a respected teacher of philology and Ernesto Sabato was one of his pupils. Later on, Sabato would become one of the most illustrious literary figures in Latin America's growing cultural dominance of the Spanish-speaking world. But even at the time, the pupil needed no telling that the above statement was true. In Spanish it is easier to give the idea its proper chronology: "*Donde termina la gramatica empieza el gran arte.*" It is always encouraging to hear what you know by instinct resoundingly formulated by an authoritative figure, so that you can draw upon the memory for a lifetime. Certainly Ureña's maxim is true for literature, and by extension for all the other arts: a thorough technical competence is the climbing frame for inspiration. Inspiration might never come, of course—there are plenty of well-schooled mediocrities in every field—but if it comes to the unprepared the result is a breech birth at best. The apparent exceptions are not really exceptions. If Moussorgsky had known more about orchestration there would have been no need of Rimsky-Korsakov's improvements, but Moussorgsky still knew enough to write down what he heard in his head, and to modify it meaningfully on the paper. The Douanier Rousseau got enough technique from somewhere to make his jungle shine in the moonlight, and the ruinous results of Renoir's belated thirst for school-ing—his *manière aigre*—merely prove that if he had studied in the first place it would have been a good thing. Just because Picasso sailed through art school doesn't mean that anybody else can sail past it.

Isadora Duncan's spontaneous dancing influenced the ballet. She herself could dance ballet only to the extent that she was able to absorb some of its disciplines by mimicry. (Tamara Karsavina, in her marvel-lous memoir *Theatre Street*, recorded her admiration for Duncan but insisted that while real ballerinas might have profited from copying Isadora, Isadora could not possibly have copied them.) Although there is always an argument for vigorous primitivism against academic tor-por, the argument is not very good, because the torpor is not really competent either: it has merely acquired one set of essentials while missing out on another. The trick is to see the art latent in the gram-mar, and to realize what the grammar can release when it is mastered: expression. In Franz Werfel's bleak novel *Verdi* there is an even bleaker sub-plot in which the ageing Verdi, nerving himself to confront Wag-ner in Venice, meets instead an impoverished, tubercular young com-poser who rudely proclaims that he has discovered the next thing: a music beyond music, an expression without laws. Rendered arid by the force of Wagner's example, unable to get started on his opera of *King Lear*, Verdi for once feels humble enough to give an ambitious upstart a hearing. For the sake of the young composer's suffering wife and son, Verdi hopes that he will hear something wonderful. But the young composer, flailing at the piano, merely proves that he knows nothing about music: all he has is the desire, a consuming passion that kills him along with his disease.

There is a consoling mythology, constantly being added to, which would have us believe that genius operates beyond donkey work. Thus we are told reassuringly that Einstein was no better at arithmetic than we are; that Mozart gaily broke the rules of composition while jotting down a stream of black dots without even looking; and that Shake-speare didn't care about grammar. Superficially, there are facts to lend substance to these illusions. But illusions they remain. There is always some autistic child in India who can speak in prime numbers, but that doesn't mean that Einstein couldn't add up; Mozart would not have been able to break the rules in an interesting way unless he was able to keep them if required; and Shakespeare, far from being careless about grammar, could depart from it in any direction only because he had first mastered it as a structure. Moreover, unless we ourselves know quite a lot about how grammar works, there will be severe limits on our capacity to understand what he wrote, especially when he seems to be at his most untrammelled. Take a single line from *Henry V*:

How ill white hairs become a fool and jester.

Here is a whole story in eleven syllables, but unless we grasp how an extremely compressed sentence can be put together, we won't get the story out; and if Shakespeare had not grasped it, he would not have been able to put the story in. Though they might look like it at first glance, "ill" and "white" are not a pair of adjectives. "Ill" is an adverb, modifying the verb "become." If this is not realized, the meaning is reversed. If Shakespeare hadn't realized the fundamental difference between an adjective and an adverb, he couldn't have written the sentence. A good actor will help him make the point, by emphasizing "ill" so that its effect carries over to "become." But it is quite easy to imagine a bad actor missing the point, and conveying the impression that ill white hairs make a fool and jester look good, or, even worse—two errors for one—allowing it to be thought that ill white hairs have *turned into* a fool and jester. This latter kind of misapprehension has become especially likely in recent times. There are now a whole generation who have never been required to understand the verb "become" in any other sense than the one for which I employed it in the preceding sentence: in a previous generation they might have heard a fragment of popular song ("Moonlight becomes you") and realized that there was another sense. But granted the slim possibility that a school pupil of today might encounter Shakespeare's line and be asked to explain it, there would be no reproof for construing a meaning that the writer did not intend. More likely would be praise for a valid response: valid for the reader. The school of permissive reading, which is the natural child of the school of permissive writing, would like us to believe that such misapprehensions are creative in themselves: we are extracting from the text even greater riches than its author planned.

One of the reasons I have found the theatre almost uninhabitable is that even the best actors are allowed to miss such points all the time, and especially if the text is by Shakespeare. There are few recent actors who can speak like Gielgud, but that was inevitable: what grates is that there are almost none who can think like him. (Peter O'Toole, Antony Sher, Ian McKellen, Simon Callow and Kenneth Branagh all stand out because they can read well enough to write.) When the National Theatre was finally transferred from the Old Vic to its hardened missile silo on the South Bank, one of the opening attractions in the Olivier Theatre was Peter Hall's production of *Hamlet*, starring Albert Finney. As the actors squeaked around the thrust stage in army surplus boots, I did my best to concede that it might be a legitimate production point: Elsinore might have looked more like a territorial army drill hall than a castle, and no doubt there was some pretty anachronistic footwear at the Globe. But Finney's line readings made you long for Sergeant Death to bellow in his ear and tell him to get a haircut. "The funeral-baked meats," droned Hamlet, "did *coldly* furnish forth the marriage tables." The false emphasis made "coldly" a mere adverb modifying "furnish." According to Shakespeare, "coldly" is doing service for a whole clause: "when they were cold." He might have been wise to put a comma on either side of the word, in order to tell the actors and producers of the benightedly enlightened future that something precise was meant. Properly isolated, the word tells us that the funeral was followed so closely by the marriage ("hard upon" as Horatio puts it) that the hot meat of the first event was eaten cold at the second: desecration as household economics. Hammered, the word tells us nothing except that the actor won't listen to advice, or that the director, with his thoughts on the décor, is too preoccupied to give it. (More charitably, one should allow for the likelihood that Peter Hall, a keen student of clear speech, told Finney the right way to say the line, but that Finney forgot.)

The notion that there is something spontaneous about an actor who tramples Shakespeare's grammar and syntax could have arisen only from the assumption that Shakespeare himself thought them peripheral to expression. There could be no greater mistake. An individual style can emerge only from firmly grasped universal principles, even if great writers themselves sometimes try to convince us of the opposite. Riled by pedantic reviewers in search of a solecism, Proust said that there was no correctness this side of originality. But he would never have countenanced the suggestion that there could be any originality without a preliminary grammar. The only question is about the best way of acquiring it: by prescription or by example? Shakespeare probably learned it at school. Stratford Grammar School certainly taught him the parts of speech: we know that from the way he makes Jack Cade threaten death to anyone who claims to know the difference between a verb and a noun. But Shakespeare might equally have learned it from his regular reading of the current English translations of Plutarch and Montaigne, although he would have needed an unusual capacity to transform passive into active knowledge. In the light of what else he could do, there is no reason not to grant him that, but a more likely explanation is that he mastered the rudiments in the classroom and then rapidly built on them through what he read: internal evidence from the plays and poems suggests a working knowledge of at least three languages.

Writers don't read just for the story: they read for the way the story is written, and the way the sentences are put together is the information that sticks. It helps, however, to have been taught in the first place what a sentence is: something that conveys information only by the rules it keeps. Grammar is a mechanism for meaning one thing at a time. Without it, you can't even manage to be deliberately ambiguous, although to be ambiguous by accident is a result all too easily attained.

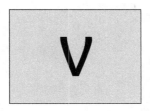

❦ ❦ ❦

Paul Valéry

Mario Vargas Llosa

PAUL VALÉRY

❦ ❦ ❦

Ambroise-Paul Valéry (1871–1945) presents many parallels with T. S. Eliot, especially in the proportions of his output. As with Eliot, there is comparatively little work in verse, but it is all of the very highest quality. Again as with Eliot, there is a large amount of ancillary prose, much of it ranking high among the critical work being done at the time. Where Valéry departs sharply from Eliot is in the amount of prose that never saw the light. From 1894 onward, Valéry kept a notebook, and by the time of his death there were 287 volumes of it. Even in French it has been published only in facsimile. Such semi-secret activity was typical of him. By the age of twenty he was already recognized as a promising poet but he repudiated the ambition and stayed almost silent for a full two decades. He was forty when he was persuaded to publish his early poems, a task he undertook only on the understanding that he would add a new, prefatory poem. This took him five years to write. Published separately in 1917, *La Jeune Parque*, together with a succeeding slim volume *Charmes*, worked to establish him as the most prominent French poet of his time. The highlight poem of *Charmes*, called "*Le Cimetière marin*," is recognized by French-reading poets all over the world as the untranslatable modern miracle of their craft. (It should be said that the Irish poet Derek Mahon has made a stunningly good shot at rendering its music into English.) Even without publishing the notebooks, Valéry still had a full eighteen volumes of prose to give the world, and scattered among them are some of the best essays written in his time. With solid mathematical training to back up his humanist erudition, he could take almost anything for a subject, but he was especially good at wrting about the arts: the essay on Leonardo, and the little book on Degas, are models of the genre. Malcolm Cowley translated some of his best early essays in 1926, and retranslated those, as well as translating some later ones, in 1958. Valéry was one of those rare poets who could write appreciative technical criticism. Kingsley Amis, an excellent technical critic with an unfoolable ear for diction, was at his best when proving that his subject poet was overrated. Robert Lowell and Elizabeth Bishop were at their best when praising each other. Ezra Pound could be informative about Browning's language but not without persuading you that his own was demented. Valéry kept a perfect sanity on that subject as on any other. The homage paid to Valéry by other writers is only fitting, because nobody could quite equal him at writing about the arts out of deep and unenvious love. He knew his notebooks were a doomed venture ("There sleeps the labour of my best years") but he also knew that the doomed venture helped to discipline his unequalled powers of exposition. Thankfully he was too old for the Occupation to catch him in any seriously compromising position, although he might have done better not to publish even once in the *Nouvelle Revue Française* under the editorship of Drieu la Rochelle. If there is an objection to be made to him, it is a milder version of the objection we make to Rilke: that the dedication to art verges on preciosity. Valéry, however, gives a better sense than Rilke of other artists than himself being fully alive. There was a generosity to him which his nation returned in kind, as if his capacity for appreciation were in itself a national treasure. General de Gaulle came to his funeral.

❣ ❣ ❣

Sometimes something wants to be said, sometimes a
way of saying wants to be used.
— PAUL VALÉRY, POÉSIE ET PENSÉE
ABSTRAITE, FROM MODERN FRENCH POETS
ON POETRY, P. 216

T HE SECOND PART of this statement is the striking one. It makes
explicit a trade secret that most poets would prefer were kept
under wraps. The English editor and anthologist Geoffrey Grigson
once said, with typical acerbity, that he didn't like "notebook poets,"
and that he could always tell when a poet had been writing down
phrases and saving them up for future use. Though it reminds you of
Malcolm Muggeridge's proclaimed ability to tell which women were
on the pill by the lack of light in their eyes, Grigson's complaint is a
good polemical point, but its epistemology is questionable: if the job
was well done, how could he tell? In my own experience, a phrase will
wait decades for a poem to form around it. Larkin kept one of his most
beautiful ideas ("dead leaves desert in thousands") for thirty years and
never completed a poem into which it would fit: strong evidence, if
negative, of how his mind worked. He found ways of saying things and
the ways led to poems. For all good poets, something like that process
happens. It is probably a stroke of luck, however, that the process is
becoming harder to study. When poets still had worksheets, a scholar
could presume to trace the course of the seed phrase to the full blooms.
I can't believe that any poet, no matter how dedicated a techno nerd,
could compose entirely on a machine, but it is a fact that there will be
fewer worksheets to study in the future: most of the *pentimenti* will be
deleted into cyber limbo.

One benefit of this will be that scholars will jump to fewer conclusions. A poem's binding energy can be supplied by its last retouchings.
Australia's first great modern poet, Kenneth Slessor, would carry his
next-to-final draft of a poem with him for weeks on end—a draft in
which all the alternatives for words on which he had not decided
appeared above and below it, like a club sandwich. Luckily no scholar
ever got his hands on one of these documents, or whole speculative

books would have been written on why and how he made his choices. In reality, the final choices are infinite and begin at the beginning. Sometimes the phrase that started it all is struck out at the finish, having done its work in a way that is beyond examination even by the creator. Gianfranco Contini loved the study of variants, but he was a qualified philologist, and his critical conclusions would be pale without their scientific content. Croce was probably overstating the case when he called variants *carteffaci* (waste paper), but he had a point. The critic does well to speculate about how a poet might have an idea and look for a way to say it. But the critic is on shaky ground when he intrudes on the real mystery, which happens when the poet thinks of a way of saying something and starts looking for a larger meaning to which it might contribute. There is nothing mysterious about the order of events: nobody is amazed that a composer thinks of a fragment of a melody, or of a harmony, before he thinks of a structure, and it would not be stunning if we were somehow to be told that Michelangelo had the idea of God touching Adam's fingertip long before Julius II had the idea of repainting the ceiling of the Sistine Chapel. But there is a mystery, and an insoluble one, to how the smaller unit of inspiration sets off in search of the larger one that will incorporate it. Artists spend a lot of time waiting for that to happen: while they wait they must trust to luck; and it is no wonder that some of them get very nervous, and fall into bad habits. Until now, what the nervous poet did in his notebook—changing a word, changing it back again—was available to the scholar. In the cyber age there will be no such archives of first and second thoughts, unless, as some strangely confident techno freaks assure us, nothing ever *really* gets deleted, and it is all still there somewhere. In which case, Valéry's idea will never cease to be a departure point for speculation.

> With the artist, it happens—this is in the most favourable
> case—that his internal urge to produce gives him, all at
> once and without a break between them, the impulse,
> the immediate exterior aim and the technical means to
> reach it. Thus there is established, in general, a
> regime of execution. . . .
> — PAUL VALÉRY, *INTRODUCTION À LA
> POÉTIQUE*, P. 58

But trying to translate this is hopeless: *un régime d'exécution* sounds like a firing squad, when what he means is a climate of possibility, a feeling on the artist's part that he knows what he wants to do and is already getting it done, simply by letting the general shape or tone of the project form unbidden in his head. I have heard poets call it "being inside the poem" and some of them even claim, plausibly, that it alters their rate of breathing. It can certainly alter their rate of smoking. In my own case, for what the news is worth, when a poem is completing itself—when the new ship on the slipway is fitting itself out, when every part insists on relating itself to every other part, and when nothing must be allowed to interrupt—I actually feel as if I am suffering from sunburn. The virtue of Valéry's brief treatise is that it makes you feel less absurd for having been so caught up. He gets at the soul of the subject through the body of the poet. He must be talking about the body because he is not talking about the conscious mind. "*Tout ce que nous pouvons définir se distingue aussitôt de l'esprit producteur et s'y oppose.*" (Anything we can define distinguishes itself instantly from the productive spirit and is opposed; p. 39.) In other words, the artist gets into a clever but clueless state where no amount of science can meet the case.

My copy of the little book *Introduction à la poétique*—a flat, floppy and not very glorious-looking glorified pamphlet by Gallimard—is from the tenth edition, published in 1938, on the eve of the nightmare. I bought it in Cambridge in 1967. It was one of the first books in French I ever read to the end. It helped that the text was very short. But even as I stumbled through with the dictionary ever present, I could tell that I was on to something. I underlined things, put stars in the margin, added knowing comments about the provenance of Valéry's ideas ("Croce was here!"). It was a book I loved, and I love it still. The author of one of the great modern poems, "*Le Cimetière marin*"—its play of tones is the nearest thing to a Degas pastel wired for sound—Valéry had generously given the succeeding generations the most valuable kind of encouragement, by saying that he had no real idea of how he did it. Better than that, he said that having no real idea of how to do it was the only way to do it. (In our own time, Tom Stoppard has said that the trouble with bad art is that the artist knows exactly what he's doing.) "One conceives, for example," Valéry says on page 27, "that a poet might legitimately fear altering his original virtues—his immediate power of composition—if he were to analyse them." It was a rationale for the irrational. He didn't mean that just getting yourself into a vague state would produce a poem, in the same way that, in the Impressionist era, untalented painters thought that if they let their eyes go out of focus and painted what they saw, they would produce Impressionist paintings. But he did mean that the state of being creative would always feel beyond analysis. After that, I learned to trust in my sunburn, and took its absence as a sign that the poem was not yet finished after all, no matter how long I had worked on it.

Valéry's famous assertion that a poem is never finished, only abandoned, is one I do not believe. Try and think of a way in which Shakespeare's sonnet "The expense of spirit in a waste of shame" is not finished. Valéry could talk precious nonsense. He was a bit of a dandy, and sometimes he got his pouncet-box too close to his nose, so that the aperçu came out as a refined sneeze. But on the whole he had the rare gift of talking concrete sense about the most complicated thing people do, and talking it as an insider. Later on his gift was born again, in Philip Larkin, whose critical writings are based on the insistence that true poems must come from instinct, even if the conscious mind is fully engaged on their way to realization. Larkin knew from introspection that a poem came of its own volition. Sometimes its will failed, whereupon he left it. To our loss, he never recorded his physical sensations when the fit of composition was on him. One guesses that the urge manifested itself as a tremendous determination not to do anything else: the best explanation for the circumscription of his pleasures.

Baudelaire, seeing Victor Hugo taking a walk along the boulevard, correctly deduced from Hugo's rhythmic gait that he was polishing alexandrines in his head. From all the testimony we have been given by the poets about themselves and about each other, the common theme which emerges is that everything else must be laid aside in the last phase, when the thing is integrating itself. This could be the reason women's poetry is on the whole a comparatively recent event in history. It used to be very hard for women to lay everything else aside. Unlike men, women were not allowed to be hard to live with. Poets have traditionally been hard to live with, and the tradition will probably continue. At the very moment when a poet is working hardest in his head, he looks exactly as if he isn't working at all. On the face of it, it's the ideal moment for asking him to do something useful. The answer is unlikely to be diplomatic, and probably wasn't even from such a smooth operator as Valéry.

MARIO VARGAS LLOSA

Mario Vargas Llosa (b. 1936) is the Latin American writer who best exemplified the course of the relationship between literature and politics in late-twentieth-century Latin America. Raised mainly in Peru, he graduated in Madrid before embarking on a dazzling literary career that took him to many European and American cities and universities, a path as a wandering scholar that he has continued to follow all his life. It was only in 1975 that he spent his first long period as an adult in Peru, when the military dictatorship that had begun in 1968 was still five years from its conclusion. The pattern of his life was to see Latin America's problems from close up and then reflect on them while he was abroad. The international network of hospitable universities was his second country. Of comparably influential writers—Carlos Fuentes, Julio Cortázar and Gabriel García Márquez (Vargas Llosa wrote his Ph.D. dissertation on García Márquez)—none, not even the suave Fuentes, was to so glamorously exemplify the new role of the boom-time Latin American writer as world citizen and acknowledged legislator of mankind. Only Octavio Paz can really be talked of in the same breath. All Vargas Llosa's novels are considerable but the cigar for sheer attractiveness must go to his fifth, *Aunt Julia and the Scriptwriter*: one of the best books about bright adolescence in any language, it is up there with *The Catcher in the Rye*, Alain-Fournier's *Le Grande Meaulnes* and Franz Werfel's *Die Abituriententag*.

Some of Vargas Llosa's admirers might say that attractiveness isn't the real point of his novels, and that they do best when facing the ferocious realities of Latin American politics, especially the horrors generated by the perennial figure (not yet completely out of the picture) of the Strongman. The true strength of Vargas Llosa, however, is undoubtedly in the essay. His collected essays written between 1962 and 1982, *Contro viento y marea* (Against the Wind and the Tide) come in either three-volume or single-volume form. The single-volume version makes the perfect pocket book for getting up to speed with how the bright baby-boom students of Latin America won their way towards a solid concept of liberal democracy through the miasma generated by the deadly friction between a self-defeating radical activism and a retrograde local nationalism, the latter backed up by U.S. foreign policy at its most witless. The only real progressivism, he convincingly reveals, is from revolution to reform.

For the beginner in Spanish, his essays are an enticing way in, and for the student of politics south of the Rio Grande there could be nothing better, because Vargas Llosa records, step by step, an intellectual odyssey that began on the left and, in the light of experience, steadily headed rightwards as far as reason could go. The nut left enrols him on the nut right, but really it won't wash. He never lost the humanitarian ideals he learned from his Left Bank heroes (especially Camus, always a good hero to have), and the long mugging he received from reality was delivered largely in the context of practical politics, which he was not afraid to observe from close enough to see the sudden space after people disappeared. Eventually he ran for the presidency of Peru in 1990 and lost to Alberto Fujimori: a throwback strongman with affinities to Rafael Trujillo, the subject of one of Vargas Llosa's later novels. Though he ended up firmly wedded to the belief that the failed states in

Latin America needed double-entry bookkeeping more than
they needed any ideology, he has never lost his initial commitment to the rights of the deprived. On the subject of open borders, one of the pet themes of the international left consensus,
the classic essay in favour of illegal immigration was written by
Vargas Llosa.

One of the many advantages of learning to read Spanish is
that a copiously productive writer like Vargas Llosa, who
responds to current history, can be read while the history is
still current. Despite the turmoil, the anguish and the frequent
desperation of his raw material, a Spanish word, *hechiceria*
(witchcraft, charm), and a Spanish phrase, *a sus anchas* (at one's
ease), both apply exactly to his prose, one of the more encouraging continuities linking two millennia.

❦ ❦ ❦

Nationalism is the culture of the uncultivated,
and they are legion.
— MARIO VARGAS LLOSA, *CONTRO VIENTO
Y MAREA*, P. 439

FOR THE NEW century, Australia might well become the world's
ideal nation. As an Australian by birth I can say that with some
pride, but also with trepidation, because Australia still has a lesson to
learn. Vargas Llosa is the man to teach it. Latin America in the late
twentieth century was a tragic laboratory for testing all the wrong ways
to think about a national culture. The foreign policy of the United
States was never a help. (In Latin America, the United States behaved
in the very way that Harold Pinter thinks it has always behaved everywhere.) But the real hindrance came from dreams of cultural autarky
on both the left and the right. In a long series of essays that constitutes
one of the key political documents of the modern era, Vargas Llosa
established that Latin America had no "dependent" cultures which
needed to be "emancipated": either they were already that, simply for
being cultures, or else they were folklore.

Speaking across a hundred years, a key contributing figure in Vargas
Llosa's position was the Nicaraguan poet Rubén Darío. Vargas Llosa

puts Darío's *cosmopolitanismo vital* at the centre of the Latin American cultural upsurge which went on to restore the literature of the Spanish world—a literature in which Vargas Llosa himself, although modestly he does not say so, is yet another key figure. Though personally I would put Octavio Paz first—perhaps because, by accident, I actually did—students who want to make a start with Spanish could do worse than to track Vargas Llosa through his essays. Short pieces of expository prose are the easiest route into a new language anyway, and Vargas Llosa's have the merit of being argued concretely from point to point, with scarcely a whiff of metaphysics even in his early phase when he was still impressed by the French left. It could be said—there are plenty who say it—that his rejection of the left has made him a cat's paw of the right, but it is a pretty strange right-wing cat's paw who favours the idea of unrestricted illegal immigration into Spain. For those of us who like his style, watching it mature into its full fluency over the course of decades has been an unmixed pleasure.

But unmixed pleasure should not imply unmixed agreement. His commitment to the *cosmopolitanismo vital* has its drawbacks. There is a measure of obscurantism lurking within the enlightenment: a dark angel in the sun, positioning itself for its classic attack. Like the philosopher E. M. Cioran, Vargas Llosa admired Borges for his world citizenship. Unlike Cioran, Vargas Llosa had no self-preserving ulterior motive for putting Borges's universal prestige above his questionable local politics. But you don't need a self-preserving ulterior motive to wonder if Borges did not give himself a free pass. In Vargas Llosa's view—an uncomfortable view we need to hear often if we are interested in politics at all—the Latin American countries which fought dirty wars against their radical insurgents had more reason than our compassion would like to grant them. Forcing the incumbent regimes into a criminal response was always among the insurgents' aims: a prophecy that could be coerced by terror into fulfilling itself. But to understand all should not mean to forgive all, if forgiving all entails to forget what matters. The obscenities came from both sides, but the obscenities perpetrated by the incumbent power were always the more reprehensible. To do him credit, Vargas Llosa keeps that possibility in mind, in his cultural arguments if not in his political ones. The regimes that dreamed of cultural autonomy were bound to be repressive. It

remains a pity that in the case of Argentina, for example, Vargas Llosa
has never considered that Borges and the other luminaries in the constellation that formed around Victoria Ocampo's magazine *Sur* might
have been promoting their *cosmopolitanismo vital* as a version of that
same dream, and thus indulging themselves in a detachment from reality, even while they seemed to be embracing a larger world.

Argentina actually had a national culture which, by Vargas Llosa's
definition, was international because vital: the culture of the tango. But
the *Sur* constellation never really went for the tango, any more than
the upper orders did, or, for that matter, the various governments
inhabiting the Casa Rosada. (Under the junta, the tango was forbidden
because people had to gather to dance it, and gatherings were banned.)
Borges, in particular, wanted an Argentina that belonged at the international level, whether or not it belonged to itself at the national level.
Until the end of World War II, Argentina and Australia were running
in parallel. Today, they separately demonstrate what a luxury it is to be
a stable, prosperous, democratic nation with a dependable constitution.
Australia is all that and more, and Argentina, after yet another implo-
sion of the civil order, is once again none of it and less. Australia can
afford to do without nationalism, because it is a nation. To do without
nationalism as a political force, you have first of all to satisfy all the
requirements which encourage that force to gather strength: the real
subject underlying Vargas Llosa's essays, even as he continues to present the true perception that liberal democracy is the indispensable
state of affairs for any country. But first of all it must be a country, not
just an area of conflict.

Evelyn Waugh

Ludwig Wittgenstein

EVELYN WAUGH

Evelyn Arthur St. John Waugh (1903–1966) was the supreme writer of English prose in the twentieth century, even though so many of the wrong people said so. His unblushing ambition to pass for a member of the upper orders was held against him by critics who believed that art, if it couldn't be an instrument of social reform, should at least not be the possession of a class that had enough privileges already. Even so irascible a representative of that position as Professor John Carey, however, felt obliged to enrol Waugh's first comic novel, *Decline and Fall*, among the most entertaining books of the century. By extension, students should be slow to believe that Waugh's most famous single book, *Brideshead Revisited*, is as self-indulgently snobbish as its denigrators say: usually they have a social programme of their own, and almost always, against their inclinations, they can quote from the text verbatim. The same might be said for critics who can find nothing valuable in his wartime *Sword of Honour* trilogy: the comic scenes alone are enough to place him in direct rivalry with Kingsley Amis at his early best, and rather ahead of Anthony Powell and P. G. Wodehouse, neither of whom came up with an invention quite as extravagant as Apthorpe's thunderbox. Really it takes blind prejudice to believe that Waugh could not write magically attractive English. But Waugh showed some blind prejudice of his own in believing that he wrote it perfectly. His apparent conviction that only those with a public school (i.e., private school) education in classics could write accurate English was a flagrant example of the very snobbery he was attacked for. It also happened to be factually wrong, on the evidence that he himself inadvertently provided.

❡ ❡ ❡

A little later, very hard up and seeking a commission to write a book, it was Tony who introduced me to my first publisher.
— EVELYN WAUGH, *A LITTLE LEARNING*,
P. 201

THE DECAY OF grammar is a feature of our time, so I have tried, at several points in this book, to make a consideration of the decline part of the discussion. Except in a perfectly managed autocracy, language declines, and too much should not be made of the relationship between scrambled thought and imprecise expression. Hitler did indeed abuse the German language, and there was many a connoisseur of grammar and usage who was able to predict, from what he did to the spoken word, what he would do to people when he got the chance. But Orwell set his standard too high when he called for clean expression from politicians: it would have been sufficient to call for clean behaviour. At the moment, the use of English in Britain is deteriorating so quickly that "phenomena," afer several years of being used confidently in the singular, is now being abetted by "phenomenon" used in the plural. People sense that there ought to be a distinction. Everybody *wants* to write correctly. But they resist being taught how, and finally there is nobody to teach them, because the teachers don't know either. In a democracy, the language is bound to deteriorate with daunting speed. The professional user of it would do best to count his blessings: after all, his competition is disqualifying itself, presenting him with opportunities for satire while it does so, and boosting his self-esteem. (When I catch someone on television using "deem" for "deign," it consoles me for having found out that I have spent fifty years stressing "empyrean" on the wrong syllable.) The most interesting aspect of the collapse is that the purist can do so little to stem it, and might even succumb to it himself, sometimes through a misinterpretation of his own credentials. Evelyn Waugh was a case in point. Nobody ever wrote a more unaffectedly elegant English; he stands at the height of English prose; its hundreds of years of steady development culminate in him. But he was wrong about how he did it. In *A Little Learning* he pronounced that nobody without a classical education could ever write English correctly.

Only a few pages away from that claim, he wrote the cited sentence, which is about as incorrect as it could be, because he ends up talking about the wrong person. He meant to say that it was he, Evelyn Waugh, who was very hard up, and not Anthony Powell. To make the lapse more delicious, Powell himself was the arch-perpetrator of the dangling modifier. At least Waugh had got over the influence of Latin constructions. Powell, to the end of his career, wrote as if English were an inflected language, and at least once per page, in Powell's prose, the reader is obliged to rearrange the order of a sentence so that a descriptive phrase, sometimes a whole descriptive clause, can be re-attached to its proper object. In a book review I once mentioned Powell's erratic neo-classical prosody. He sent me a postcard quoting precedent as far back as John Aubrey. He was right, of course: our prose masters have always been at it. But our prose masters, now as then, ought not to prate about correctness while leaving so much of the writing to the reader. Correct prose is unambiguous. There is no danger of the clear becoming monotonous, because opacities will invade it anyway. Even the most attentive writer will have his blind spots, although deaf spots might be a better name. Kingsley Amis, who was an admiring friend of Anthony Powell, was nevertheless well aware that Powell's grammar was all over the place. (In a letter to Philip Larkin, Amis made a devastating short list of Powell's habitual errors.) Amis himself was a stickler for linguistic efficiency. The only mistake I ever caught him making was when he overdid it. In *Lucky Jim*, which is a treatise on language among its other virtues, Gore-Urquhart, Jim's mentor in the art of boredom detection, unaccountably seems to approve of the paintings of the fake artist Bertrand Welch. "Like his pictures," says Gore-Urquhart. Since he says everything tersely, the reader—this reader, at any rate—tends to assume that he means "I like his pictures." But what he means is that he considers Bertrand a fake, *like his pictures*. The reader is sent on a false trail by a too-confident use of the character's habitual tone. The author should have spotted the possibility of a misinterpretation. But we, the readers, should remember that it is one of the very few possibilities of misinterpretation that Kingsley Amis didn't spot. He spotted hundreds of thousands of them, and eliminated nearly every one. If he had written without effort, many of them would have stayed in. (Exercise: find a complex interchange of dialogue in *Lucky Jim* and count the number of times you are left in doubt as to who is speaking. You are never in doubt. Now try the same test with a novel by Margaret Drabble.)

The main reason a good writer needs a drink at the end of the day is the endless, finicky work of disarming the little booby traps that the language confronts him with as he advances. They aren't really very dangerous—they only go off with a phut and a puff of clay dust in the reader's face if they aren't dealt with—but those aren't the sounds that a writer wants his sentences to make. Evelyn Waugh didn't really want this sentence to make this sound, but he relaxed his vigilance. He knew what he meant, and forgot that the descriptive phrase was closer to the wrong person than to the right one. If we correct the sentence, we can guess immediately why things went wrong. "A little later, very hard up and seeking a commission to write a book, I was introduced by Tony to my first publisher." But the correct order would have struck the writer as awkward, because the loss of "it was Tony" would have removed the connection to a previous sentence in which Powell had been talked about. In other words, it was Waugh's sense of coherence that led him into the error. With bad writers it is often the way. In their heads, it all ties up, and they don't fully grasp the necessity of laying it out for the reader. Even good writers occasionally succumb. Waugh, who was as good as they get, hardly ever did: but he did this time.

LUDWIG WITTGENSTEIN

❦ ❦ ❦

Born into a wealthy Viennese family, Ludwig Josef Johann Wittgenstein (1889–1951) was the glamour boy of English philosophy in the twentieth century, and in the new millennium his influence continues to be potent. If there are still English philosophers who seem to prefer it when nothing is discussed except the means of discussion, their memories of Wittgenstein are probably the reason. Before World War I, there was a period when only Bertrand Russell knew who Wittgenstein was. After valuable false starts as a student of engineering in Berlin and Manchester, Wittgenstein had come to Cambridge to study mathematical logic under Russell, who had the humility (a virtue of Russell's that offset many of his vices) to spot an intellect potentially superior to his own. During the Great War, Wittgenstein fought for Austria as an artillery officer. Captured by the Italians, in the prison camp at Montecassinao he completed the work we now know as the *Tractatus Logico-Philosphicus*, a set of aphorisms based on the principle that language is a combination of propositions picturing the facts of which the world is composed. Under the impression that he had brought philosophy to an end, Wittgenstein gave away his money and took up the simple life in Austria as a schoolteacher, a gardener's assistant and an amateur architect.

He resembled T. E. Lawrence both in his homosexuality and in his recurring desire to retreat from a stage whose centre he seemed born to occupy. Realizing, however, that philosophy was not over after all, he returned to Cambridge in 1929. First as a research fellow and then as a full professor, he developed a second philosophical phase, or emphasis, in which his original concept of language as a set of pictures was, if not repudiated, certainly elaborated into something more subtle—infinitely more subtle, because he now saw communication as a whole family of language games in which the meanings of words depended on their use. Usage, however, was not everything. A given line of argument could be outright wrong, especially if it sought obsessively for a unity that could not exist. Wittgenstein had thus constructed an instrument for discussing the totalitarian mentality, but he never used it. During World War II he voluntarily served as a hospital porter in London and a lab assistant in Newcastle, but he never said anything in print about the Nazis. Apart from the *Tractatus*, all his books, collected from notes made from his lectures, were published posthumously. No student should miss the key work of his second phase, *Philosophical Investigations* (1953), but not even in that otherwise electrifying book is there any sense of current events. His silence might not have been an act of will. It could have been that words failed him. There is evidence, however, that when he finally saw photographs of the hideous aftermath in the concentration camps he forgot his famous rule about being silent on issues of which one cannot speak, and broke down in tears. But in the few years left to him before his death from cancer, he still resolutely declined to say anything specific about the era he had lived through. He had helped to shape it, but only by ignoring it.

Not that Wittgenstein believed there was anything peripheral about his subject. As we know from one of his letters to the linguist C. K. Ogden, he thought nothing could beat the thrill of philosophy. Clearly, for him, close, penetrating reasoning was an aesthetic experience on the level of the Schubert C Major Quintet, which he thought possessed "a fantastic kind of greatness." But for Wittgenstein it was the thought that was seductive, not the language. A condition in which the thing said exceeded the thing talked about was not a condition he could admit, and especially not in poetry. He despised Bertrand Russell's attempts to write plain-language philosophy on a high aesthetic level. Russell wanted to be Spinoza, and Wittgenstein devastated him by telling him he was wasting his time. Wittgenstein was undoubtedly being sincere. He would have thought the same sort of aim a waste of effort even if it came from himself. Yet he himself was in the first rank of German writers. As an aphorist he had no superior and only a few peers: Goethe, Lichtenberg, Schopenhauer, Nietzsche, Schnitzler, Kafka, Polgar—the list is quite short, and for his almost unearthly detachment he can be said to dominate it.

Wittgenstein's requirement that we should not be seduced by language is understandable in the context of the rich second phase of his philosophy, whose aim we can find summed up for him on his brass plate in Trinity College chapel in Cambridge: "*Rationem ex vinculis orationis vindicam esse.*" (Reason must be released from the chains of speech.) The requirement that we should not be seduced by *his* language, however, is hard to meet. He had things to say that were as good as Hegel's line about the owl of Minerva. He was the poet without a context, the poet in the waste land. His chief fear was that philosophy would be dominated by science. David Pears—whose short book *Wittgenstein* (1971) remains valuable even in the flood of light cast by Ray Monk's magnificent biography of 1990—assures us that the whole aim of Wittgenstein's work was to prevent such a domination. But of course philosophy *is* dominated by science, if philosophy is thought of as a subject in itself. What Wittgenstein proved is that the dominance of science does not extend to language, and that philosophy, as a corollary, is present in all the considered language that is ever used. Far from it being hard to say something significant, to say something insignificant is almost impossible, even for a baby just old enough to know that babbling makes it popular.

❣ ❣ ❣

Philosophy, as we use the word, is a fight against the
fascination which forms of expression exert on us.
— L U D W I G   W I T T G E N S T E I N ,   *T H E   B L U E   A N D*
B R O W N   B O O K S ,   P.   2 7

P HILOSOPHY AS anyone uses the word, one would have thought. But for a long time few dared to think that, so Garboesque was Wittgenstein's glamour. When Wittgenstein was in the room, even Isaiah Berlin was at a loss for words. Wittgenstein placed such an emphasis on precision of language that he made the merely eloquent feel slovenly. To get Wittgenstein in perspective, it required first of all his death, and then some unsentimental reflection on the breathtaking scope of what he had never talked about. He received credit for giving away the large amount of money he had inherited, and thus detaching himself from his social privileges and from the involvements and distractions of everyday life. But he also detached himself from everyday life by ignoring what was going on in Europe. After his sufferings in World War I the detachment was understandable, but the result was a chilling hermeticism in his frame of reference. Neither in his philosophy nor in his ancillary writings did he ever say much about what subsequently happened in the German-speaking countries, at the very time when civilization was facing its greatest threat. It could be said that he was under no obligation to, but it is still a strange omission. The advantage to his philosophical position was that by not saying much he never said anything ill considered. His philosophical position was like a defensive aesthetic strategy by which a poet hopes to write poetry in which there is nothing that can be criticized for its looseness: every line a Maginot line.

In the fully developed form of his second phase, Wittgenstein's eventual position about language was so obviously right that it is hard to see, at this distance, how a whole school of philosophy could have grown out of it. *"Ein Ausdrück hat nur im Strom des Lebens Bedeutung,"* he said in his last days. An expression has meaning only in the stream of life. Could anyone doubt it? Generations of students learned not to ask for the meaning, but to ask for the use. Wittgenstein got the credit. If Shakespeare had ever believed anything else, he would never have written a line. (The drawback of the academic guru is that his students continue, long after graduation, to see him as the incarnation of the seriousness of their subject: but their subject incarnates its own seriousness, or it would never have been worth studying in the first place.) Wittgenstein's real power lay in the fact that he, too, was a literary prodigy. In all phases of his career Wittgenstein was an important writer in the rich German tradition of the aphorism. He favoured the epigrammatic, the dry, the tart. But he was slow—painfully slow, hour after hour slow, sweating and struggling in front of his own class slow—to accept the truth about the simple statement: the truth being that it is an *ignis fatuus*.

The simple statement was never a problem: or, rather, it was never anything except a problem. The difficulty of getting something said clearly was never news: except of course, to the latest intake of philosophy students, who gave Wittgenstein the credit for everything that would have struck them anyway if they had been left alone with the merest metaphysical lyric from the early seventeenth century. Expressing oneself clearly is the most complicated thing there is. Mature English is complicated in order to mean one thing at a time—the closest to the simple that it can ever get. Wittgenstein looked always to the moment when, with the rhetoric blown away and language reduced to the parameters of a children's language game, the "mental mist . . . disappears." It can never quite do that, but with the proper illumination we can tell it is a mist. Wittgenstein was closer to the pay dirt in one of his letters to the philosopher G. E. Moore, when he talked about thought with due attention to what fascinated Heisenberg on his deathbed: turbulence. "One can't drink wine while it's fermenting, but that it's fermenting shows that it isn't dishwater."

As Wittgenstein conceived it, and apparently wanted to conceive it, philosophy should leave everything as it is, after having flooded it with light and air. But there was a consequence of his principle of refinement and precision that was seldom considered within his lifetime, and is still not often considered now. The precise tool was never ready to be brought to bear on the world: only on philosophy itself, which increasingly, under his influence, defined itself as an activity whose references were all to its own ways and means. The completeness with which this exclusive preoccupation suited its professional practitioners should have tipped off the more talented among them that they were engaged in a system for betting on the horses. Few of them, alas, were as talented as Wittgenstein: they could do the logic, but they could not duplicate his sensitivity to language—a sensitivity that was essentially poetic. Like literary theory at a later time, however, analytical philosophy was a game hard to get out of after you had started drawing the salary.

> We acted as though we had tried to find the real
> artichoke by stripping it of its leaves.
> —LUDWIG WITTGENSTEIN, *THE BLUE AND*
> *BROWN BOOKS*, P. 125

This is the Wittgenstein that matters to a writer. There is a Wittgenstein that matters to professional philosophers, but they can prove it only to each other. The Wittgenstein that matters to a writer might be mistaken for his meaning by ordinary readers, but he can never be mistaken for his poetic quality, which is apparent even in his plainest statement. The precision of his language we can take for granted, and perhaps he should more often have done the same. His true and unique precision was in registering pre-verbal states of mind. In *The Blue and Brown Books* (p. 137) he proposes a "noticing, seeing, conceiving" process that happens before it can be described in words. That, indeed, is the only way of describing it. It sounds very like the kind of poetic talent that we are left to deal with after we abandon the notion—as we must—that poetic talent is mere verbal ability. "What we call 'understanding a sentence' has, in many cases, a much greater similarity to understanding a musical theme than we might be inclined to think" (p. 167). But he doesn't want us to think about music as a mechanism to convey a feeling: joy, for example. "Music conveys to us *itself*!" (p. 178). So when we read a sentence as if it were a musical theme, the music doesn't convey a separate sense that compounds with the written meaning. We get the feeling of a musical theme because the sentence means something. I thought he was getting very close to the treasure chamber when he wrote this. In 1970, reading *The Blue and Brown Books* every day in the Copper Kettle in Cambridge, I made detailed transcriptions in my journal every few minutes. It didn't occur to me at the time that his prose was doing to me exactly what he was in the process of analysing. It sounded like music because it was so exactly right.

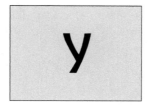

y

❦ ❦ ❦

Isoroku Yamamoto

ISOROKU YAMAMOTO

❡ ❡ ❡

Isoroku Yamamoto (1884–1943) was the son of a schoolmaster called Takano, and the famous surname by which we know him belonged to the family into which he was adopted. After his education at the naval academy he was wounded at the battle of Tsushima in the Russo-Japanese War. He studied at Harvard after World War I and served as a language officer in the early twenties, before becoming naval attaché at the Japanese embassy in Washington later in the decade. His wide knowledge of the United States extended to the factory floors, where he was impressed by American powers of production, and to the gambling joints, where he always fancied his chances. As chief of the aviation department of the Japanese navy in 1935, and as vice navy minister from 1936 to 1939, he argued both for a main force based on aircraft carriers and for avoiding any policy that would lead to a fighting alliance with the Axis powers in World War II. But after being promoted to Admiral and placed in command of the Combined Fleet, he dutifully planned the attack on Pearl Harbor. After his defeat at Midway six months later, and probably before, he knew that to continue fighting was a mere formality; the war was already lost. The idea that his death by enemy action was tantamount to suicide, however, is almost certainly part of the romance that continues to surround his name, not least in Japan, where he is a cult figure, and not exclusively on the political right. His distaste for a war with the Western allies has always rung a bell with post-war liberals aware that, if the enemy had been as pitiless as the Japanese High Command, the defeat could have been more disastrous, the occupation more humiliating, and the subsequent resurgence of both the culture and the economy much less impressive.

The Yamamoto romance benefits from his artistic tastes. Like America's General Patton, Yamamoto wrote accomplished poetry. Again like Patton, and like other romantic commanders such as Rommel and Guderian, Yamamoto probably experienced battle as an aesthetic event: the most likely reason for his participation in a war of which he disapproved. Superior military minds share with poets the uncomfortable position of waiting for lightning to strike, and having to act on it when it does. Yamamoto knew that World War II was the wrong war, but it was the only war he had. Strategy is a talent, and talent will out, even though it is hard to get the credit for it, since it becomes less possible to visualize the larger the scale grows. For that reason alone, the idea of a star strategist never transfers satisfactorily to film, because the action of even the smallest battle is too complex to be dramatized. (Hence the hero of *Patton* is shown to be decisive by the way he sorts out a traffic jam involving two trucks: the low moment of George C. Scott's career.) In *Tora! Tora! Tora!* and *Midway*, both of them Hollywood films but made with Japanese participation, the Japanese producers eked out the necessary paucity of hardware by casting, in each film, one of their most venerable actors as Yamamoto. In *Tora! Tora! Tora!* he was played by Soh Yamamura and in *Midway* by Toshiro Mifune. Both actors conveyed genius with a flashing glance and resolution with a fixed frown. In either case, the viewer was left hungering for a more detailed characterization. It can be found in the extensive literature that has built up around Yamamoto in his own language, but almost every general study in English of the Pacific war has a chapter on Yamamoto, usually concluding that although the Japanese navy might have done no better had he lived, it was bound to do worse after he was dead. For the Pearl Harbor attack itself, the Readers Digest picture book of 1966, *Tora! Tora! Tora!*, with a text by Gordon W. Prange, might sound like an elementary proposition but is still the first book to have, if you can find it.

The book was translated into Japanese and had a huge success in the hero's homeland. It seems a fair guess that the average Japanese reader got the same point as Yamamoto did: that the war with the United States was a wilful mistake. The idea that Japan was tricked into the war by the Americans is one held only by Tokyo right-wingers who dress up like Michael Jackson, by the priests at Yasukuni shrine, and by Gore Vidal in his dotage. Yamamoto would have laughed aloud to hear it. For young people who correctly suspect that a schlockbuster movie like *Pearl Harbor* dishonours the dead as well as insulting the intelligence of the living, most of the issues concerning Yamamoto and the opening shots of the Pacific war are covered in Prange's later, more complete historical work *At Dawn We Slept* (1981), but a warning should be attached: once the reader is launched on the study of a war so huge and horrible, he should be prepared at least to consider the unpalatable proposition that the quick ending of it by recourse to the atomic bombs was not only inevitable, but justified. Any revisionist historian who contends that the millions of Japanese soldiers based in the home islands would not have opposed a landing is obliged to believe that the military commanders, without a specific instruction from the Emperor, would have seen reason and surrendered. For those who hold that view, a close study of Yamamoto's face can be recommended. He knows your country well, admires its virtues, and doesn't even think he can prevail: but he wants to fight anyway.

> If we are ordered to do it, then I can guarantee to put up a
> tough fight for the first six months or a year, but I have
> absolutely no confidence as to what would happen if it
> went on for two or three years.
> —ADMIRAL ISOROKU YAMAMOTO TO PRIME
> MINISTER PRINCE KONOE, IN LATE 1940

O N AT LEAST two separate occasions, Prince Konoe asked Yamamoto what Japan's chances would be in a war against the United
States. Each time, Yamamoto gave roughly the same answer, which is
nowadays usually quoted and printed as if it had been given once. Variously translated into English, and variously rendered even into Japanese, Yamamoto's declaration of uncertainty is probably the second
most famous thing any Japanese of the Pacific war period ever said,
ranking only slightly behind the passage in the Emperor's surrender
broadcast which conceded, in impossibly high-flown court language,
that the war had developed in ways not necessarily favourable to
Japan. Yamamoto's advice to the government seems to have predicted
that the unfavourable developments would be inevitable in the long
term. Later on he was much criticized for not having expressed himself more firmly, but he must have felt that he didn't need to. He was
already on record as having advised that "Japan and America should
seek every means to avoid a direct clash, and Japan should under no
circumstances conclude an alliance with Germany." That last part was
in line with the *genro* Prince Saionji's advice to the Emperor: advice
which the Emperor ignored. Yamamoto never lost hope, however,
that the Japanese government, even when Tojo was running it, would
see sense and reach an agreement with the United States. He still had
hopes even as the Pearl Harbor operation got under way. His last
briefing to Admiral Nagumo was that if the negotiations in Washington were successful then the attack would have to be stopped even if
the aircraft had already taken off from the carriers, and that there
could be no arguing with such an order. Yamamoto, sometimes at the
risk of his life, had spent the whole of the thirties preaching the necessity of staying out of a war with the United States. He had studied at
Harvard, seen America's factories, and knew more than any other top-

ranking Japanese officer about America's war potential. What else could he advise Konoe?

Why, then, did Yamamoto consent to lead the Pearl Harbor attack? There are several possible answers, all leading by separate paths into the brain of a complex man. Speculations about the subtlety of "the Oriental mind" we can safely discount: they never amount to much more than ignorance and racism snuggling together under a duvet of rhetoric. Yamamoto would have been complex if he had been born and raised in Brisbane. First, he was a gambler anyway. He enjoyed gambling, possibly because he won almost every time. Second, he might have thought the chances reasonably good that the war would be short. If the Japanese diplomatic service had not botched the declaration of war, Pearl Harbor would still have been a surprise attack—an attack on Hawaii, a full two-thirds of the way across the Pacific from Japan, was not much more likely than an attack on Seattle—and might conceivably have brought America to terms, especially if the American aircraft carriers had been put out of action along with the battleships. Third, he was Admiral Isoroku Yamamoto, supreme commander, Combined Fleet, Japanese navy. That was his career, those were his orders, and he had a job to do, win or lose.

To hindsight, the third reason seems the most powerful. Like Nelson and Napoleon, Yamamoto was a short man whose military gifts had carried him to great heights. If you look at the press photographs of his funeral cortège arriving at the Yasukuni shrine, the coffin looks about the size of a shoebox. A coffin always looks smaller than the person inside, but Yamamoto, even for a Japanese man of his generation, was of small physical stature. His moral stature meant a lot to him, and long before the war it had already grown enormous. His tactical brilliance, organizational ability and nonconformist daring were legendary, and they were all in service of the navy. Japanese naval aviation was practically his invention. He had opposed the laying down of the last two great battleships, *Yamato* and *Musashi*. He was for more aircraft carriers and a lot more aircraft. He represented the transition from heavy steel to light metals—from deep keels to free air. The bright young officers adored him for it. Though he was always self-deprecating about his poetry, he was probably serious when he wrote this poem on New Year's Day, 1940.

Today, as chief
Of the sea guardians
Of the land of the dawn,
Awed I gaze up
At the rising sun.

He wrote the poem on board the battleship *Nagato*, his flagship as commander in chief Combined Fleet. So the rising sun would have been the ship's pennant. The land of the dawn, of course, was Japan: the two characters Ni-hon (usually pronounced Nippon) mean Sun Source, or the Land Where the Sun Rises. Yamamoto, if we may translate a subtle thirty-one-syllable Japanese poem into blunt English words, was on top of the heap. It would be foolish to imagine that he did not enjoy his eminence, even as he saw the looming threat of getting into a war with the wrong enemy. He enjoyed a battle as he enjoyed women, and might even have found a losing battle more interesting, just as he obviously found multiple love-trouble more interesting than a single alliance. On that last point, whenever the time came to quit Tokyo to join his ship, he had to set out early so that he could say his goodbyes without undue haste. He had big appetites, and they weren't just lustful. They were also emotional: a clue to his taste for drama. He might have quite liked the idea of being at the centre of a big story, and what could be a bigger story than working the miracle of saving Japan from the doom he himself had predicted? After all, going ahead with the attack wasn't his idea. He wasn't that crazy. He had, however, planned an excellent attack.

Or it would have been excellent, if it had caught the American aircraft carriers in harbour. When the returning aircraft reported that the American carriers had not been present, Yamamoto, supervising the operation at long range from the *Nagato* anchored at Hashirajima in the Inland Sea, knew straight away that the Americans had the wherewithal to go on fighting. He was also absorbing the dreadful information that the Japanese declaration of war had been sent too late; that his surprise attack had been transformed into a sneak attack; and that the Americans therefore had redoubled motivation as well as insufficiently depleted means. The deadly combination of the two factors was proved all too soon. In May 1942, only five months after Pearl Harbour, the American carriers fought him to a draw at the battle of the Coral Sea. At Midway, scarcely more than six months after Pearl Harbor, they destroyed him. He had been right about making things tough for the Americans for six months. Six months of supremacy were all that the Japanese enjoyed. After Midway, they had no chance of keeping the initiative. But we make a mistake if we think they were crazy not to admit defeat. There was always the possibility that they could bring their opponents to terms by making it too costly to go on fighting. Because Yamamoto died early, and because the English-speaking gambler is such a sympathetic character, we tend to enrol him in the ranks of those who would have seen reason and sought a sane way out. It is just as likely, however, that he would have gone on fighting to the end, in the manner of his comparably brilliant army equivalent, Yamashita. Though the army's lack of a victorious future in the land battle did not become apparent to all until much later, Yamashita was just as aware as Yamamoto, and just as early, that Japan's adventure was over from the day that supremacy on the sea, and therefore over the supply lines, was lost: and that day was the very first day of the war.

People of a literary bent tend to idealize the poet warriors, of whom, in modern times, Yamamoto must count as the most conspicuous apart from General Patton. But we need to ask ourselves whether a flair for the poetic might not be a limitation to generalship, in which a considered appreciation for the mundane is essential. A poetic flair has an impatient mind of its own: it likes to make an effect, and it has a propensity for two qualities that can easily be inimical to a broad strategic aim. One of those qualities is what A. Alvarez called the shaping spirit, and the other is what Frank Kermode called the sense of an ending. Yamamoto's plan for deciding the war on the first day was not only the equivalent of a roulette player's betting his whole bundle on a single number, it was also the equivalent of trying to cram the whole of *The Tale of Genji* into a single *haiku*. There was bound to be material that didn't fit. Even if the American aircraft carriers had been in harbor they would not have sunk far enough in the shallow water to be beyond salvage. One way or another, the American fleet was bound to come back.

It has been said in Yamamoto's defence that the six months' grace he promised was all the Japanese forces needed to consolidate the Strike

South. But there were senior officers who didn't believe it. One of them was Admiral Tomioka, who accurately assessed the risks Yamamoto was taking, and, more importantly, was doubtful about the efficacy of the outcome even if the plan had worked. (Tomioka's analysis is well outlined in Gordon W. Prange's *At Dawn We Slept*, a work by no means unfavourable to Yamamoto, but one from which Tomioka emerges as the voice of reason on the Japanese side.) If the Japanese command structure had been as well organized from the outset as America's command structure very quickly became, Tomioka would have been in a position to overrule Yamamoto. But the Japanese never did get organized at command level. The drawback of military government was that there was no government to control the military, whose commanders formed a perpetual discussion group from which policy emerged as the highest common factor of contending opinions. The Americans, on the other hand, appointed, as supreme commander in the Pacific, Admiral King, to whom both General MacArthur and Admiral Nimitz reported directly. Though MacArthur hogged most of the limelight, Admiral Nimitz was the key man. His unspectacular qualities, coalescing into an authority all the more daunting for being so reasonable, can be assessed from E. B. Potter's biography, *Nimitz*. The Japanese continued with Yamamoto, who wrote his Pearl Harbor poem all over again at Midway, except that this time the masterpiece came apart completely. In the Japanese language there is an expression to cover the concept of making an almighty hash of things: to serve the dish with bean paste. At Midway bean paste was the whole dish.

Spiritually, Yamamoto died at Midway. In the matter of his physical death, however, it seems unlikely that he committed suicide in expiation. Romantic interpreters sometimes favour the appealing notion that Yamamoto invited the American ambush that resulted in his being shot down into the jungle of Bougainville on April 18, 1943. While airborne on an inspection tour of the forward areas, he was caught by a flight of P-38s. In a big sky, they knew exactly where to find him. But it is a long step, even for conspiracy theorists, to argue that he had deliberately tipped off the enemy. At Midway, it was indeed true that Admiral Spruance, armed with signals intelligence, knew where to intercept the Japanese aircraft carriers. But the Japanese, like the Germans, were reluctant to accept that their military codes were being read: reluctant even when there was no other plausible reason for a defeat. When he saw the P-38s forming to attack, Yamamoto might have guessed that they were acting on information received: i.e., that the coded radio messages announcing his route had been read in Hawaii. He might even have guessed that the P-38s had intercepted from below—making it look like an accidental encounter—in order to protect the secret in case anyone escaped from the two aircraft carrying him and his staff, or from the escort of Zeros. But by then the guesswork could avail him nothing, and down he went. When the Japanese search party tracked down his corpse in the jungle, he was still strapped into his seat. His sword was beside him. If he had wanted to commit suicide, he would probably have done so on dry land or on the deck of a ship, included the sword in the ceremony, and written a poem first.

It is another romantic notion to suppose that Yamamoto would have become a voice for common sense had he survived. He had been ready to fight a war that he had long predicted was bound to be lost, and he would probably have gone on fighting it long after it became obvious that there was no hope even for a truce. That things were as bad as they could be was already evident on the day after Midway: so evident that the military tried to conceal the scale of the disaster from the Emperor. Talking about a Japanese national character might be pointless, but to talk about a Japanese military culture in the modern period is perfectly legitimate—and one mark of that culture was that its senior officers were ready to fight on far beyond the limits that might have been set by military sanity, let alone political reason.

Imminent defeat was always seen as the climax of the battle. There was even a valid idea behind that view. The idea was to make victory so expensive for the enemy that he would call a halt. The idea was not quite as crazy as it sounds now. In Europe, after the catastrophe of the second Schweinfurt raid in October 1943, the American 8th Air Force had to think twice about continuing with the daylight bombing of German targets. They thought twice and continued, but another massacre of air crew on that scale might have dictated a breathing space for the Luftwaffe to regroup. (It would never have had time to replace its lost fighter pilots, which was the real damage that the Allied air bombardment inflicted on the enemy; but the German fighter aircraft could have been switched to the eastern front, where they were sorely needed.) Similarly, in the Pacific, and very late in the day, Admiral Ohnishi's kamikaze strategy might well have done more than it did to slow down the American navy. Yamamoto, had he been on the scene, would have had no ships to fight with—a fact partly his fault—but he might have been fertile in ideas for how the kamikaze weapon could have been used to better effect. He was never against the concept: until his flight commander, Genda, came up with a less wasteful scheme, Yamamoto's plan for the Pearl Harbor attack entailed the expendability of the pilots. He might have flown a suicide mission himself, if he had ever learned to fly. Like General Yamashita, he might have remained dangerous to the end. When Tojo finally overcame his jealousy and brought Yamashita back from purdah to lead the defence of Luzon, Yamashita turned the expected American walkover into a protracted nightmare.

There is no reason to think that the Japanese home islands would have been defended with less tenacity. Revisionist historians and commentators who deplore the use of nuclear weapons against the two Japanese cities have a humanitarian case, but they weaken it by supposing that they have a military case to back it up. The same pundits who maintain that the bombing campaign against Germany was useless are fond of saying that the conventional bombing by B-29s would have been enough to ensure Japan's quick surrender. There is also a fond confidence that an invasion by the Russians would have brought the same result, although the consideration is usually ignored that the Red Army, which had no amphibious equipment, might not have been in an ideal condition to fight after its troops had swum to Hokkaido. The awkward truth is that the Japanese generals had correctly guessed which beaches the Americans would have used to invade Kyushu and Honshu. The Japanese had several million troops available to fight the battle. The only objection the Emperor raised to what would surely have been a long and bloody last stand was that the preparations were not going ahead fast enough. The atomic bombs changed his mind and he recorded his surrender speech. Some of the young officers tried to kidnap him before it could be broadcast. Older heads prevailed. The best we can say for Yamamoto is that he would almost certainly have been among them, but mainly because his loyalty to the Emperor was undying—the very factor that led the poetic admiral to write his miniature masterpiece in the first place.

Z

♀ ♀ ♀

Aleksandr Zinoviev

Carl Zuckmayer

Stefan Zweig

ALEKSANDR ZINOVIEV

❣ ❣ ❣

Aleksandr Alexandrovich Zinoviev (1922–2006) has suffered a fate predictable only in retrospect. When the Soviet Union finally collapsed, it buried the reputations of those who had tried to point out its flaws from the inside. Today there might seem nothing remarkable about what Zinoviev tried to tell us: but there was, and there still is, because nobody else carried penetrating criticism to quite such a depth. His *The Reality of Communism* (1984) is one of the key short books of political analysis in the history of its subject. It might stand out more in the memory if some of his other books—especially the satirical novels, of which *The Yawning Heights* attracted the most attention—had not been so long. But at any length, he was telling the story from the centre of the action, because he was a philosopher and sociologist who actually worked within the system until he figured out that it was broken. Handsome and energetic, a natural leader along Gagarin lines—he looked more cosmonaut than academic—Zinoviev was no rebel when he started off. During World War II he was a pilot, and afterwards a star student at Moscow State University, rising to academic posts both there and at the Institute of Philosophy of the Soviet Academy of Sciences. For his increasing anti-

Stalinism he was first of all harassed by the KGB and finally expelled from the Soviet Union in 1978, after being stripped of his rank with maximum opprobrium. He settled in Munich, where he continued to write copiously in his native language. His many books were usually published in Russian by Editions l'Age d'Homme in Lausanne before being translated, first into French and then into English. So his work was plentifully available: some might say too much so for its own good. Rarity value would have given him more impact.

After 1990 he entered a new, strange phase in which he backtracked on his own discoveries and declared that the Soviet Union had disintegrated not because of the internal stresses he had pointed out, but because of a brilliantly successful concerted attack mounted by the imperialist West. There was little market for this idea even among diehards. But what ensured the eventual fading of his name was that he had been so clamorously proved right when the yawning heights caved in. Suddenly everyone was an expert, and nobody wanted to be reminded of a time when he wasn't.

I know of no more pitiable spectacle in human society than
the Soviet people's intimate closeness to one another.
—ALEKSANDR ZINOVIEV, *KOMMUNISM KAKH
REALNOST*, P. 109

AFTER ALEKSANDR ZINOVIEV was expelled to the West in 1978, I met him briefly in London. I was reading a lot of Russian at the time—if you were reading only Zinoviev, you were reading a lot of Russian, because he was torrentially productive—but I couldn't speak enough of the language to sustain a meaningful conversation. His English was in the same transitional stage, so the encounter turned into a smiling competition. I had been reviewing his books as they came out. Some of the books were physically huge. There was a hell of a lot to keep up with. Zinoviev had been told that I was keeping up and he smiled with gratitude. I hope my smile of gratitude was as dazzling as his. I thought he had done mighty things, but I suspected already that his reputation in the West would rapidly plunge now that he had made himself available. An accelerated Solzhenitsyn scenario was easy to predict. The main difference was that Solzhenitsyn's principal message really *was* contained in his big book *The Gulag Archipelago*, rather than in the satellite works. Zinoviev's principal message was in his smaller books, especially this one, later translated as *The Reality of Communism*. His big books inflated into comic fiction what was perfectly apprehensible as a factual argument. Nor, indeed, was the comic fiction quite as funny as it might have been if the author had been given a strict word limit. In the not very long run, the big books duly flopped on top of the little ones, and Zinoviev's literary reputation slowed to a crawl. Today, very little of him is even in print.

But it should be remembered that the man who could write a sentence like this wrote hundreds more just as acute. Most of the dissident literature understandably stressed how hellish life was for the dissidents and their dependants. Zinoviev's field was the hellishness of everyday life. He was not an Englishman and had never heard the crack about every Englishman's dream being to travel alone in a first-class compartment. He was a Russian and had been brought up in conditions of enforced propinquity. His genius was to guess that there was something wrong with it. People were not meant to live on top of each other. He always wrote acutely on the subject of housing. While experts in the West were still arguing that a certain amount of overcrowding was the inevitable price of Russia's domestic accommodation being provided at low rent, Zinoviev pointed out that there was no question of the rent's being low: the rent was paid out of stolen wages. The same, he said, applied to the free medical care: not only was it no good, it cost the patient almost everything he should have been earning. All this was observation: visiting Western observers had done some of it, but Zinoviev had the advantage of being on the spot full-time.

What made him exceptional, however, was the theoretical structure that he erected on top of his observations. There was nothing abstruse about the structure. It was as carefully built as it was solidly based. He said that the living conditions could never be allowed to improve beyond a certain point because they were a control mechanism. The system packed everyone together but the resulting irritability had the useful consequence of minimizing human contact. People who spent a large part of the day either standing in long queues or pulling wires to dodge them would not only lack free time to conspire, they would never trust each other. As a theorist, Zinoviev overdid it only when he predicted that even dissidence would turn out to be part of the plan: a built-in safety valve. Commendably, he backtracked on that point not long before he packed his bags. He would probably never have said it if he had not been reduced to despair by the thuggishness with which he was stripped of his academic posts and honours. He was drummed out of the country through a shower of abuse. We tend to forget that the people who were bright enough to predict that such things would happen to them still needed a lot of moral courage to remain calm when they did. But Zinoviev didn't despair for long: not in Russia, at any rate. In the West, he went silent, sharing the fate of several of the prominent émigré dissidents, which was to find out the hard way that they had destroyed the glamour of their special subject by helping to deprive it of its power.

CARL ZUCKMAYER

Carl Zuckmayer (1896–1977) was a German dramatist born in the Rhineland who later settled in Austria, where the first of his two best-known plays *The Captain of Kopenick* (1931) made him part of the social landscape. After the *Anschluß* in 1938 he immigrated to the United States, where he wrote the second best-known play, *The Devil's General* (1946). Apart from these and other theatrical works, he also wrote poetry and two novels. At one time in the late thirties, before he reached the United States, he spent a brief period in England as a writer on Alexander Korda's doomed production of *I, Claudius*. While the film spent a fortune getting nowhere, the refugee from Hitler witnessed three other tyrants in action at once: Korda, the director Josef "von" Sternberg, and the self-damagingly childish actor Charles Laughton. It was a demonstration of where temperamental despotism belongs: in the arts, not in politics. Zuckmayer's most notable piece of ancillary writing, however, and perhaps his most resonant achievement, was the autobiography from which I quote below. Memoirs were the mainstream of what the émigré writers achieved, and much of what they recalled can reduce the reader to helpless grief. But Zuckmayer, perhaps because of an irrepressible good humour, remembered to say that the destruction of the old European culture could have been more complete. If all those who remained had behaved badly enough, there might have been less to long for. But most of them behaved quite well, thus allowing room to hope for mankind, even if also to regret all the more bitterly that their good character had not done much to stave off the oncoming disaster.

> Most of our friends and acquaintances in theatre, film and
> literature, who had no personal persecution to fear and
> could remain in their country, stayed true to us, the exiled,
> and let us know in every possible way that between them
> and us there was no division. A few, a very few, turned out
> to be opportunists, delators and traitors.
> — CARL ZUCKMAYER,
> ALS WÄR'S EIN STÜCK VON MIR, P. 387

THIS IS GENEROUSLY said, and it is a relief to know that it is said truly. Among those artists who, enjoying the dubious privilege of racial acceptability, were able to stay on in Nazi Germany if they wished, comparatively few took the opportunity to flourish. None of those could have guessed, before the battle of Stalingrad, that there would be a reckoning within their lifetimes. If they chose not to cooperate, it was a moral choice. The temptations were hard to resist, yet hardly anyone of real note succumbed. The playwright and Nobel laureate Gerhart Hauptmann agreed to speak well of the Nazis, but he did it because he was old; and even at the time he blamed his own cowardice. The case of the eminent actor-manager Gustav Gründgens, who was pleased enough to be patronized by Goering, is celebrated because it was rare, and the picture of him painted in *Mephisto* is far too dark: Klaus Mann had a mean streak. (Gründgens didn't help his case by the way he defended himself after the war: his book was self-justificatory, without showing any awareness that the necessary prelude to explanation was an admission that justification was impossible.) Nevertheless there were those who could not resist a place on the gravy train. Zuckmayer knew most of them personally. The quoted passage is not all he has to say on the subject. Without abandoning the philan-thropic restraint that marks his book of memoirs—its title, translatable as "As if It Was a Piece of Me," is meant partly as a signal that the friendships of a lifetime helped to form him—the great man of the Weimar theatre goes on to give an example of what one of the oppor-tunists managed to achieve.

His name was Arnolt Bronnen, and he was a friend of Brecht. Under Weimar, Bronnen's socially conscious plays attained enough acclaim for the sceptical Anton Kuh to find them fatuous. When the Nazis came to power, Bronnen faced an abrupt demotion from his success, because his father was a Jewish schoolmaster who had married an Aryan woman. Luckily for him, Bronnen's powers of dramatic inven-tion served the purpose. He concocted a deposition by which his mother had betrayed her husband with an Aryan man, and therefore he, Bronnen, was *ein rassenreiner Fehltritt*: a racially pure false step. Having thus armed himself with the proper dispensation, Bronner was able to get along under the Nazis, although they did not forget that his plays had been a success under the *Judenrepublik*, their typically oafish nickname for the Weimar democracy. Off the hook but not yet on the bandwagon, Bronnen tried to improve his position by publishing anti-Semitic articles. His piece called "Cleaning Up the German Theatre" featured a would-be nifty flight of punning word play about Max Rein-hardt: *"Jetzt aber nicht mehr Reinhardt, sondern rein und hart!"* ("But now no more Reinhardt: instead, clean and hard!" It loses something in translation, but there was never much to lose.) After the Nazis col-lapsed, Bronnen found another totalitarian bureaucracy to serve. He became an editor in East Germany. The function of an East German literary editor, it hardly needs saying, was to seek out fresh talent and make certain it did not get published.

Zuckmayer was even better acquainted with Hanns Johst, a mediocre man of letters who ranked as a big noise among the Nazi literati. (Johst, not Goering, was the original author of the crack about reaching for his revolver when he heard the word "culture": an instruc-tive example of a clever remark floating upwards until it attaches itself to someone sufficiently famous.) But Zuckmayer correctly spotted that Bronnen was the more interesting moral case. Accusing your own mother of adultery to save your skin is creativity of a kind so special it can almost be called a talent. Our challenge, however, is to convince ourselves that we would not have done something similar: perhaps a less shameless version, but equally self-serving. And the self-serving action becomes easier on the conscience if we can persuade ourselves we are serving our art, which would be impoverished without us. This process of mental deception seems to have proved especially prevalent among the musicians. Perhaps the writers, confined as they were to words, were quicker to spot it when they were telling themselves lies. Musicians could tell themselves that their art was not affected by the world of ideas. The conscience of Herbert von Karajan seems to have been unaffected, either then or later, by his Nazi party membership, which he applied for voluntarily, on the grounds that he needed it to get ahead. The unblushing readiness of the rising young soprano Elisabeth Schwarzkopf to sing for the Nazi hierarchs (her luxurious apartment had previously belonged to a Jewish conductor forced into exile) makes us doubly grateful for the memory of Marlene Dietrich, who could not sing from the operatic repertoire but had at least seen the nightmare coming, and made her attitude clear from an early date. As an Aryan, she could have gone home to Germany had she wished: but she never did until Hitler was defeated. Zuckmayer's point, however, is even more encouraging: most of those who stayed behaved with honour.

STEFAN ZWEIG

✞ ✞ ✞

Stefan Zweig (1881–1942) is a fitting name to introduce the coda of this book, because his life, work, exile and self-inflicted death combine to sum up so much of what has gone before, which is really the story of the will to achievement in the face of all the conditions for despair. Zweig's own achievements are nowadays ofen patronized: a bad mistake, in my view. Largely because of his highly schooled but apparently effortless gift for a clear prose narrative, he attained, while he lived, immense popularity not just in the German-speaking countries but in the world entire, and he is still paying the penalty for it. Except in France, where his major works are never out of print, it is usually safer to call him second-rate. Safer, but not sound. Most of his poems, plays and stories have faded, but his accumulated historical and cultural studies, whether in essay or monograph form, remain a body of achievement almost too impressive to take in. Born into Vienna's golden age, he took the idea of cultural cosmopolitanism to heart, and looked for its seeds in the past, in a series of individual studies that form a richly endowed humanist gallery, in which the first and still the most impressive portrait is his monograph *Erasmus*. Such names as Goethe, Hölderlin, Kleist, Nietzsche, Rilke, Herzl,

Freud, Schnitzler, Mahler, Bruno Walter and Joseph Roth
might have been expected to attract Zweig's attention, but he
also wrote a whole book on Balzac, as well as valuable essays on
Dante, Montaigne, Chateaubriand, Sainte-Beuve, Dickens,
Dostoevsky, Renan, Rodin, Busoni, Toscanini, Rimbaud,
James Joyce and many more. Full-sized books on Marie-
Antoinette, Mary Stuart and Magellan were international best-
sellers. For beginners who can read some German, his
collection *Begegnungen mit Menschen, Büchern, Städten* (Meetings with People, Books and Cities) is probably the best place
to start, and they will be reading much more German afterwards. His *Die Welt von Gestern* (*The World of Yesterday*) is—it
bears saying again—the best single memoir of Old Vienna by
any of the city's native artists, although George Clare's *Last
Waltz in Vienna* will always be the book to read first. A lustrous
picture book, *Stefan Zweig*, came out in German in 1993, and
in French the following year. Its dazzling pages prove that he
got some of his immense archive of documents and photographs away to safety. His magnificent library in Salzburg, alas,
was burned by the Nazis in 1938. They knew exactly what he
represented, even if some literary critics still don't. Stefan
Zweig was the incarnation of humanism, so when he finally
took his own life it was a persuasive indication that the thing
we value so highly can stay alive only in a liberal context.

> With whom have we not spent heart-warming hours there,
> looking out from the terrace over the beautiful and
> peaceful landscape, without suspecting that exactly
> opposite, on the mountain of Berchtesgaden, a man sat
> who would one day destroy it all?
> — STEFAN ZWEIG, *DIE WELT VON
> GESTERN*, P. 396

"HEART-WARMING HOURS" sound less corny in German: *herzliche Stunden.* Zweig had a house in Salzburg, and from the terrace he could see across the border into Germany, to the heights on

which the exterminating angel perched, gathering its strength. If Hitler had looked in the other direction, he would have seen, on Zweig's terrace, everything he was determined to annihilate, and not just because it was Jewish. There were plenty of gentiles who came to see Zweig. But they were all infected with *Kulturbolschewismus*, the deadly international disease that presumed to live in a world of its own: the disease that Hitler, in his role as hygienist, had a Pasteur-like mission to eradicate. Everyone who mattered in the European cultural world knew Zweig. It was one of his gifts. He believed in the sociability of the civilized. In the long run it was a belief that might have helped to kill him. When he committed suicide in Brazil in 1942, he already knew that the Nazis weren't going to win the war. But the Nazis had already won their war against the gathering on the terrace.

The question remains of whether Zweig had valued that gathering too much. Never a man for being alone in the café, he had staked everything on the artistic community and the mutual consideration which he supposed to prevail automatically within it. The artistic community, not his worldwide popularity, was the context of his success. When Hitler destroyed that success, Zweig quoted Grillparzer's line about walking alive in the funeral procession behind his own corpse. Zweig had no notion that the Nazi assault on the idea of an artistic community was not unique. As late as the year of his death, he was still saying that there was "no second example" of such murderous irrationality. Though he had once been on a train ride with the Bolshevik cultural commissar Lunacharsky to visit Tolstoy's old estate at Yasnaya Polyana, Zweig knew little of what had been going on in the Soviet Union, where the artistic community of Petersburg that had gone on flourishing between 1917 and 1929—a confluence of talent to match any gathering on his terrace—had been obliterated as a matter of policy. (The crackdown was announced by Lunacharsky himself, the erstwhile bohemian chosen by Stalin to put out the lights of bohemia.) To the bitter end, Zweig believed that the natural state of affairs between exponents of the humanities was one of affectionate respect: a professional solidarity.

He would have been horrified to find that Thomas Mann thought of him as a mediocrity. It would have been one horror too much; but, unlike the other horrors, it had not been invented by Hitler out of thin air. That Mann had uttered such an opinion was the simple truth. But we should not put too sinister a construction on a snide remark. Mann was never at ease with the idea that some other German writer might sell more books than he did in the world market. The natural state of affairs between exponents of the humanities is one of tension, suspicion, rivalry and, all too often, enmity. Only a catastrophe can bring about, among its survivors, any degree of the automatic mutual regard that Zweig dreamed of so fondly. A great deal of creativity arises from conflict between the creators, and it tends to be annulled when they are driven to make peace by supervening circumstances. Colin Thubron, who can read Mandarin, noted the blandness that prevailed in the literary aftermath of China's Cultural Revolution in the 1960s: when dissent had been alive, the dissenters had dissented among themselves. It is a misconception to think that the emigration from Germany produced nothing—the memoirs alone constitute a whole library of substantial German literature—but equally it would be a misconception to think that the émigrés achieved even a tiny fraction of what they would have achieved had they been left free to quarrel. (They quarrelled anyway, but on a drastically reduced scale: unable to disagree about Hitler, they could disagree only about Stalin.)

In my time, in both London and New York, there have certainly been gatherings on the terrace; and in Melbourne and Sydney they become more frequent and impressive by the year; but the *herzliche Stunden* can never for long be counted on as a sustaining context. Thomas Mann, a tougher nut in every way than Zweig, noted how in the Vienna of Brahms it was remarkable how the musicians, united only in their mutual suspicion, jealously protected their individuality. (The omniscient Fitelberg, one of Mann's best shots at the figure of the cultural ominivore, says it in *Doktor Faustus*: "Wolf, Brahms and Bruckner lived for years on end in the same city, namely Vienna, avoided one another the whole time, and none of them, as far as I know, ever met one of the others.") The same applies to the Paris of the great painters. Today their masterpieces hang together in the same galleries. We can find our ideal Paris in New York, Chicago, Moscow and Petersburg. While they were painting, in the real Paris, they would cross the boulevard to avoid each other. For understandable reasons, Zweig wished the world otherwise; but in that respect his World of Yesterday was a never-never land. He was always looking for concrete, tangible realizations of a coherence that can exist nowhere except in the spirit. His celebrated collection of autograph manuscripts, which was in display in the Salzburg house, brought the great artists of the past together: another gathering on the terrace. Typically, upon arrival in his last new country, Zweig wrote a book about it: *Brasilien, Land der Zukunft* (Brazil, Land of the Future). Quoting freely from the Portuguese, the book is a stunning tribute to his powers of almost instantaneous assimilation. But it also testifies to his corrosive grief. He tries to persuade himself that a land without a past might be a new start for civilization. The real theme, however, has all to do with what he has lost. In Rio de Janeiro the terrace was almost empty, and in Petrópolis, where he took his own life, there was no terrace at all. I have been there, and seen it; and it can be a beautiful place, when the purple *quarezmas* bloom against the green forest; but it isn't long before you starve for company.

> And I realized that for any man, much of the best of his
> personal freedom would be limited and distorted by
> photographic publicity.
> —STEFAN ZWEIG, *DIE WELT VON
> GESTERN*, P. 371

This was an early perception of how the destructive effects of fame in the twentieth century were spreading even to the world of art. Zweig knew more about success than any other serious writer of his time. No stranger to press scrapbooks and photo albums, he documented himself with care. He was always a mighty archivist. But he saw the danger, and might well, had he chosen to live, have chosen the next stage to fame: reclusion. (He could never have done without illustrious company, but might have been quite good at scaring them all to silence.) If he could have seen forward in time, he would have well understood the course taken by Thomas Pynchon and J. D. Salinger. He would have been an appreciative student of the minimax approach to the requirements of publicity, by which the star says just enough to keep the mill turning. Nowadays, everyone knows that fame must be managed, or it will do the managing. Marcel Reich-Ranicki, in *Der doppelte Boden*, says that Heine was condemned to world fame. The "condemned" is the modern word, but Zweig would have seen its force. Even earlier, Proust had foreseen that there would be a desirable status beyond being well-known, in which one was known only by those that fame did not impress. In *Sodome et Gomorrhe* he noted that the true stars of *le monde*—by which he meant high society—are tired of appearing in it. Zweig never got tired of it, while it was still a society. He enjoyed his stellar status, but his good heart made him slow to grasp that his very celebrity was one of the reasons the Nazis wanted him dead. The idea that the German-speaking culture was being so prominently represented by a Jew made them angry: a sign that Nazi ideology had only a tangential relationship with nationalism.

> We are a lost generation, who will never see a
> united Europe again.
> — STEFAN ZWEIG, QUOTED BY ERWIN
> RIEGER IN *STEFAN ZWEIG*, P. 112

The term "lost generation" had already been launched by Gertrude Stein. Zweig merely put it to a more appropriate use. Nobody was trying to kill Hemingway and Fitzgerald except the manufacturers of what W. C. Fields called spirituous fermenti. Zweig's generation was up against a more formidable enemy. Nevertheless his suicide in January 1942 will always be a bit of a mystery. It seems not quite to fit the circumstances: with America in the war, the Nazis no longer looked like winning, and there was no reason to think that he would not have resumed his glittering international position when the war was over. But we could be dealing with a disposition of mind. Despite his success and his huge range of prominent friends, he had been on the verge of despair for most of his life. As the date of this quotation shows, he already felt that way while the Weimar Republic was still in one piece. He had felt that way at the end of World War I. He had wanted a depoliticized world, and it was obvious that the war had had the opposite effect: it had shattered the foundations of society, but it had also reinforced politics to the point where nobody was exempt. By 1928, when Germany was enjoying an economic recovery which might have perpetuated the Weimar Republic if the Depression had not sealed democracy's fate, Zweig had reasons to modify his pessimism. But it deepened, because the political divisions in Europe were deepening too. From the start of his waking life, Zweig had staked everything on the concept of a coherent European humanist heritage. After the Nazis got in, there was nowhere for his pessimism to go except further into despair.

Franz Werfel said truly that Zweig was equipped to live in the countries of exile before there *was* an exile. He was multilingual, he was famous all over the world, his manners were perfect and there was nowhere that his stream of royalties did not reach. But his personal success meant little to him outside the ambit of its original context. His final breakdown can be seen well under way in the *Tagebücher* that he kept early in World War II. On page 410, we see that he was already carrying a phial of poison at the time of Dunkirk. On page 464, "*der Epoch der Sicherheit vorbei ist*" (the epoch of security is over). The word *vorbei* keeps cropping up. "It is over. Europe finished, our world destroyed. Now we are truly homeless." By "we" Zweig didn't mean just the Jews, a category in which he was reluctant to believe until he found out the hard way that Hitler did. Zweig meant everyone who had lived for the arts, for scholarship and for humanism. He was wrong, of course: Thomas Mann was angry at the selfishness of Zweig's suicide—too personal. But that was the way Zweig felt, even as it became clear that the forces of destruction would not win the war. He thought that they had already won the war that mattered. We who grew up in the aftermath have a right to say that his resignation was premature, but we would be very foolish to slight its sincerity. Our united Europe of today will be doing very well if it can restore the qualities of which he was the living representative, and which led him to destroy himself because he thought they were irretrievably *vorbei*. The price of studying the heritage that produced him is to be steadily invaded by the suspicion that he might have been right. Reader beware.

> That was why he read history and that was why he studied
> philosophy: not to educate himself or convince himself, but
> to see how other men had acted, and thus to measure
> himself beside others.
> — STEFAN ZWEIG, *EUROPAISCHES ERBE*, P. 53

Zweig always wrote wonderfully about Montaigne, with whom he shared the gift of summarizing and assessing the actions of historical figures, although Zweig probably did it to a different end. Montaigne could have been a man of action: there were many official attempts to lure him out of his library, and one of them secured his services for a diplomatic initiative that probably saved France from ruin. Shakespeare, our supreme student of Montaigne, actually *was* a man of action for most of his life: the theatre was no cloister, and nobody could have invented Timon of Athens who had not dealt with practical matters, kept the hirelings in line, and acknowledged the power of an account book. Zweig, however, was a man of letters in the most usually accepted sense: i.e., he was not a man of anything else. His gallery of portraits of the mighty, stretching through his writings like the Uffizi collection through its long corridor, does not lead to a paradigm of action, except to the extent that to achieve understanding is an action in itself. There is something passive about Zweig, and, human nature being what it is, the passive invites a kicking. Critics capable of being sensitive about anyone else still find it permissible to be insensitive about him. While he was alive, they found it mandatory. Is he really, they used to ask, any better than Emil Ludwig, who lives high in rented villas and plush hotels while cranking out glib historical success stories to convince Philistine businessmen that they are really Napoleon? Doesn't Zweig, by lavishing the same sympathy on both, reduce Erasmus to the level of Marie-Antoinette? Where is the man, behind that universal curiosity and suspiciously mellifluous style?

Well, the answer is that he is not behind them: he is in them. Zweig was the sum total of his appreciations, to which his style gave the spiritual unity that they never had in life. For those of us reading German as a language not our first, there is always a tendency to be too grateful for the writer who makes it easy. But Zweig makes it better than easy: he makes it effortless. There are whole pages that the beginner can sail through and leave the dictionary until later, because the impetus makes the syntax unmistakeable. Much of his prose rhythm is poetic in the raw sense of being laid out with the specific, point-to-point vividness of verse. Often you will find Zweig writing a clause that you could match to a line by Rilke. They were soulmates, although you can bet, as so often with Zweig, that the admiration was more selfless from his direction than from the other. Rilke and Zweig visited André Chénier's tomb together. Zweig was the one better equipped to appreciate the generosity of Chénier's last night on Earth, which he spent comforting an aristocratic young lady against the chill prospect of the morning, when they would both be taken from the Conciergerie to be guillotined. Rilke would have been more interested in her coat of arms.

The difference between Rilke and Zweig was crucial. Rilke was a mighty lover of the arts, but even that love redounded to his own glory. All that he adored was absorbed into his personal style. He glossed the world over with his own preciosity. Zweig was more humble. He could imagine a world without himself, and when the time came he made what he imagined real. (It is hard to conceive of Rilke committing suicide: how could the world have stood the deprivation?) Yet both of them are glories of twentieth-century literature in the German language. Their books are lined up in the most fruitful kind of competition, in which neither contestant can really replace the other. Collecting Zweig's books is made the more delicious by the variety of formats and publishers. Rilke, even after his death, went on and on in the standard format lovingly chosen for him by Insel Verlag. But the gulf between the physical uniformity of Rilke's books and the physical variety of Zweig's invites us to look for a deeper clue. We can find it in the dates on the title page. Insel Verlag was permitted to go on publishing Rilke in Germany right through the Nazi era. Zweig's books had no single home, and least of all were they at home in Germany and Austria while the Nazis were in power. While Goebbels ruled German culture, the state had no fundamental quarrel with Rilke's humanism. It proscribed Zweig's humanism because Zweig was a Jew. There is a reminder, there, that we should not get carried away by the idea that totalitarianism can't put up with the humanist love of the arts and learning. Josef Brodsky said that Osip Mandelstam was proscribed because his lyricism was intolerable to the state. No doubt it was, but it is even more likely that he was proscribed because he wrote something rude about Stalin. Even the Soviet Union, which was much more thoroughly censorious than Nazi Germany, put up with quite a lot of overt love for the arts. The pre-revolutionary repertoire of classical ballet, for example, was never taken away from the people. (In Communist China it was: one of the several measures by which the Maoists, and especially Madame Mao, were even more insane than the Stalinists). To avoid sentimentality, we should be ready to accept the possibility that an all-knowing state will know enough to co-opt the arts by letting people love them, as long as that love does not interfere with the state's ideological precepts. A smart bad state could afford to let the arts survive, because it would know that they are better at encouraging contentment than arousing rebellion. We should beware, then, of their seduction. Liberals and humanists are always saying that art is the soul of truth. But they are quite often ignoring the truth while they say so.

The most seductive thing about literature is the books. They are a token of how self-contained it all is, or at any rate appears to be. A printed book is actually a miracle of technology that took more than five hundred years to develop, but it does not look or feel impossibly far from the notebook and the pen that are all it takes for us to get a printed book started. For the musician, things are not always so portable. Some of the instruments are beautiful, and increasingly the instrumentalists are beautiful too—female violinists get spreads in *Vogue*. But a composer can't carry his orchestra around with him, and there were no good old days in which the composer for even a single instrument, except perhaps if he concentrated on the piccolo, could pull it out of his pocket. Chopin never pushed his piano into a café. The painters used to draw in the café but were rarely allowed to paint there. Not only can the writer read in the café, he can write. And the day might always come when the book he reads in the café is the book he wrote. When he looks at his own sentences in print, he will find them transformed. The better they are—let us suppose that he can tell bad from good even when reading his own stuff—the more they will sound as if he didn't write them. They will sound as if they were written by the single voice that all good writers seem to share when at their closest to the truth.

When children carefully inscribe their names at the front of their school-books they add their address to the name, and then add the information that the address is in a certain country, which is in the world, which is in the universe. They are trying to raise their names to universality. Print does all that for you. Print leaves your sedulously practised signature behind, along with your personal handwriting. Strangely enough, this process does not feel like the weakening of identity, but the strengthening of it. We must tread carefully here, because that feeling of having one's identity strengthened by being absorbed into a mass is at the heart of fascism's appeal in all its varieties. But the writers don't cease to be themselves: far from it. They aren't marching anywhere, they look implausible in uniform, and they have a petulant reluctance to give up responsibility for what they say. They might blend together in print, but they become, through being printed, more individual than ever. My heroes and heroines in this book would not only have been less famous if they had never been published, they would have been less defined as characters. It was being published, even after his death, that brought Franz Kafka alive: otherwise he would have been just a man who got nowhere with women. As things are, he defines the anguish of an epoch. Albert Camus would have been just a man who got everywhere with women. As things are, he is the exemplar of liberalism as the awkward truth. Anna Akhmatova would have been just a woman who broke men's hearts. As things are, she is remembered forever as the poet who answered the prayer of innocent victims to define the nightmare that had broken the heart of her country.

You can say, if you like, that in every case the private person was the real one. But it would be a very thin conception of what a person is, and a hopelessly impoverished version of reality. Our lives are enriched by people who create works of art better than their personalities: the best excuse for the rogues among them, and the best reason for our raising the virtuous to the plane of worship. The latter reaction might seem extravagant, but we should watch out for those who say so: they are much more short on reverence than we are on judgement. There is an unmistakeable continuity between holy scripture and the accumulated secular text we call literary culture. All we have to remember is that infallibility plays no part in it. On the contrary: fallibility is of the essence. The phrase "it is written" is automatically suspect, especially when the written words are printed. The authoritative typeface might be devoted to an insidious lie. Or there might simply be a misprint. My final quotation, the only anonymous one in the book, is chosen with that possibility in mind.

CODA

❣ ❣ ❣

Kun-Han-Su

ECKSTEIN AND THE
EGYPTIAN KINGHOPPER

❧ ❧ ❧

Kun-Han-Su
—AN ANONYMOUS TYPESETTER

WHEN THE Vienna newspaper *Presse* carried a story about the latest poem by Kun-Han-Su, nobody in the Café Imperial had ever heard of Kun-Han-Su except for Eckstein, who knew all about him. Eckstein, referred to always and only by his last name, was famous for knowing absolutely everything. Eckstein told his young admirers about the creative heights to which Kun-Han-Su had carried some of the ancient verse forms under one of the last emperors of the Ming dynasty. Next day the *Presse* regretfully announced that "Kun-Han-Su" had been a misprint for Knut Hamsun. It transpired that Eckstein had known all about the misprint, and indeed could give an account of misprints, in all languages, throughout the ages.

Eckstein's universal knowledge was also memorably proved when he was out walking with Hofmannsthal and Hofmannsthal's beautiful daughter, Christiane. They saw a hopping bird. Eckstein identified it as an Egyptian kinghopper. "It can't fly," he expatiated. "It can move forward only by hopping. It spends the winter in Egypt, hence the name." Hofmannsthal looked around, saw no persuasive evidence that this conversation was taking place anywhere except in Vienna, and mildly objected: "You said only just now that the bird couldn't fly." Eckstein said: "*That* far it can fly."

These stories about Eckstein are told by Friedrich Torberg in his *Die Tante Jolesch*, with due acknowledgement that Eckstein really was a very learned man. In his youth Eckstein was a pupil of Anton Bruckner, and later on he wrote an important monograph about his teacher. Eckstein was enormously well read. He just couldn't bear to admit that there was something he had missed. It is very easy to get that reputation. When strangers know that your speciality is books, their usual way of breaking the ice is to ask you if you have read such-and-such a book. The penalty for saying no is to hear a précis. The quickest way out of a potentially boring conversation is to say yes. But it only takes one smart-arse to test you with a fake title and you're cooked.

As the alert reader will have often noticed, this has not really been Eckstein's book, even when it most seems to be. I have not read everything, nor have I remembered everything I have read. What I tried to do was keep some of it with me and draw lessons from it. Hegel once said that neither a people nor its government could learn much from history. Had he lived to see the twentieth century, he would have found his belief confirmed after World War I, when the victorious powers, pooling their wisdom in the conference at Versailles, carefully laid down the conditions to ensure that the catastrophe which they had barely survived would be soon repeated. There were observers—John Maynard Keynes was one—who guessed what would happen next. But even among them, few were prescient about the scale of the horror. Thinkers who had seen a million soldiers die concluded that the enemy was war itself. They didn't foresee that millions of innocent civilians would die next. They thought that peace could be made a principle. But peace is not a principle: merely a desirable state of affairs. The only answer to Hitler was a contrary violence. There were intellectuals who refused to believe it. There were still more intellectuals who refused to believe that in the Soviet Union the real enemy of the people was the Communist Party: the enemy of its own people, and of any other people living under democratically elected governments. It would be wrong to conclude, however, that there was something about being an intellectual that precluded the seeing of the truth. There wasn't then and there isn't now. For all but the born prodigy of common sense, opinions are arrived at by the sifting of opinion. The process might occasionally lead to error, but ignorance will lead to error always. So we seek out the best of what is said on weighty matters, and naturally assume that the very best resides amongst what is said well.

There is a danger there, as I have tried to point out. Any effective writer of expository prose is an artist of a kind, and artists give shape to the facts. But facts are recalcitrant, and often they refuse to fit, especially when political. The artist who fancies himself above politics is tacitly conceding that the world is too much for him, even as the concession gives him freedom. It can be a fine freedom, but it counts for nothing beside the freedom of the common people, and when the discrepancy shows up with tragic force, we are right to call a halt to our admiration, and ask: is this really so well expressed, if reality is so very different? We question, that is, the earthbound soul behind the transcendental work. To say so might seem to let in the incubus of biographical enquiry, and thus issue a licence to every dunce who wants to make a living out of the elementary revelation that our idols have feet of clay. But there was never any humanism without humans. The only peril is that we will stop short, by failing to realize that the personality of the creator is a created marvel in itself, and all the more so for its weaknesses, which are close to the source of its inspiration. Fame is not the spur. Fame is the result. Creativity starts in the well of human feeling which for want of a better single word we call the soul. It is more glamorous and exciting to believe that creativity starts in the gift; but by what has happened to some gifts we can see that the soul is where they came from, and is what reaches us even when we fight shy of reaching it. Among my hero Alfred Polgar's fellow émigré writers who praised his accomplishments, most felt compelled to frame their encomia as aphorisms that would equal his for brilliance, as if style were the thing in question. And so it was, but the style came from a cast of mind, which the comparatively unspectacular journalist Hans Sahl had the simple boldness to define. He said that Polgar had a spiritual superiority that could transmit the terrible, and that he was not only clever and witty, but wise.

The getting of wisdom is a hard road. Most of us are not equipped by nature to travel it at high speed, and some of us must crawl like babies. Our chafed hands and knees can easily make us wonder if the journey is worth it. If I could go back in time and design my own birth, I would introduce the genetic material that might have made me a bit less of a dunderhead. Even today, in my seventh decade, I meet people forty years younger who are patently more sensible than I was when I set off on my great adventure. I was their age then, but they are my age now: old heads on young shoulders. What I had to learn by trial and error, they seem to have been born knowing. But perhaps they have had the luck to be born into a better time. If so, and if they are to stay lucky, the worse time had better not come back. For those it didn't kill or maim, it injured the air. Uncertainty was something we all breathed in, back then. The horrors of the past and present made us nervous about the future, and the habit is hard to shake. The young might do well to tie a handkerchief over the rear-view mirror and just get on with it. The world is turning into one big liberal democracy anyway. Terrorism will punch angry holes in it, but in the long run nothing will stop the planetary transformation. Even if armed with a second-hand atomic bomb, an obscurantist can do nothing for the poor. Most of the poverty on Earth is caused by the number of people being born who would ordinarily have never been conceived. Prosperity gave them life. All too frequently the life seems not worth living, but when we cry out at the injustice we are asking for more democracy, not less. Subsidiary populations that migrate into the liberal democracies are seeking a legitimate economic advantage in comparison to the homelands they left. They are understandably reluctant to accept that their economic disadvantage in the homelands they left might have been at least partly due to the culture they grew up in. In their adopted countries they are often encouraged in this reluctance by local humanitarians who think it illiberal for an imported culture to be criticized for its backwardness. But when the zealous young men of the imported culture begin to practise terrorism under the encouragement of their religious leaders, even the local absolutists for human rights come to see the point of restricting the freedom of religious leaders to preach violence against the adopted state. So eventually the rule of law under an elected, replaceable government will have even the humanitarians behind it. It can't lose. Why, then, bother to ponder how we got out of the mael-strom? Why be an Ancient Mariner, who stoppeth one in three and boreth them to tears? The only answer comes from faith: faith that the rule of decency—which at last, and against all the odds, looks as if it might prevail—began in humanism, and can't long continue without it.

How will we know if our earthly paradise is coming to pieces, if we don't know how it was put together? It was the human mind that got us this far, by considering what had happened in history; by considering the good that had been done, and resolving to do likewise; and by considering the evil, and resolving to avoid its repetition. Much of the evil, alas, was in the mind itself. The mind took account of that too. The mind is the one collectivity that the free individual can thrive in: which is lucky, because live in it he must. Even within ourselves, there are many voices. Hegel, when he said that we can learn little from history, forgot about Hegel, author of the best thing about history that has ever yet been said. He said that history is the story of liberty becoming conscious of itself.

ILLUSTRATION CREDITS

Many thanks are due Ruth Mandel at Images Sought and Found for her outstanding photograph research and perseverance in uncovering images of even the most elusive subjects.

Pierre Drieu la Rochelle, © Albert Harlingue/Roger-Viollet
Alfred Einstein, Smith College Archives, Smith College
Duke Ellington, © Bettmann/CORBIS
Federico Fellini, ullstein bild/The Granger Collection, New York
W. C. Fields, © Bettmann/CORBIS
F. Scott Fitzgerald, © Hulton-Deutsch Collection/CORBIS
Gustave Flaubert, © Hulton-Deutsch Collection/CORBIS
Sigmund Freud, © CORBIS
Egon Friedell, Hulton Archive/Getty Images
François Furet, © Sophie Bassouls/CORBIS SYGMA
Charles de Gaulle, ullstein bild/The Granger Collection, New York
Edward Gibbon, Portrait of Edward Gibbon (1737–94) (oil on canvas) (b/w photo) by
    English School (18th century). © Private Collection/The Bridgeman Art Library
Terry Gilliam, © Corbis
Josef Goebbels, ullstein bild/The Granger Collection, New York
Witold Gombrowicz, © Sophie Bassouls/CORBIS SYGMA
William Hazlitt, National Portrait Gallery, London
Hegel, ullstein bild/The Granger Collection, New York
Heinrich Heine, © Albert Harlingue/Roger-Viollet
Adolf Hitler, © Bettmann/CORBIS
Ricarda Huch, ullstein bild/The Granger Collection, New York
Ernst Jünger, © Sophie Bassouls/CORBIS SYGMA
Franz Kafka, ullstein bild/The Granger Collection, New York
John Keats, © Corbis
Leszek Kolakowski, Courtesy of the John W. Kluge Center, Library of Congress.
Alexandra Kollontai, ullstein bild/The Granger Collection, New York
Heda Margolius Kovaly, © John Foley Photographe Studio Opale
Karl Kraus, ullstein bild/The Granger Collection, New York
Georg Christoph Lichtenberg, Städtisches Museum Göttingen.
Norman Mailer, © Mark Gerson/Camera Press/Retna Ltd.
Nadezhda Mandelstam, © Gueorgui Pinkhassov/Magnum
Golo Mann, ullstein bild/The Granger Collection, New York
Heinrich Mann, ullstein bild/The Granger Collection, New York
Michael Mann, AP Images
Thomas Mann, ullstein bild/The Granger Collection, New York
Mao Zedong, AP Images
Chris Marker, Source: British Film Institute
John McCloy, W. Eugene Smith, Time & Life Pictures/Getty Images
Zinka Milanov, The Metropolitan Opera Archives
Czeslaw Milosz, AP Images
Eugenio Montale, © Ferdinando Scianna/Magnum Photos
Montesquieu, The Granger Collection, New York

Alan Moorehead, © Getty Images

Paul Muratov, reprinted from Neulovimoe sozdane: vstrechi, vospominaniia, pisma; by Inna Andreeva. Courtesy of the Slavic and Baltic Division, The New York Public Library, Astor, Lenox and Tilden Foundations.

Lewis Namier, Hulton Archive/Getty Images

Grigory Ordzhonokidze, © Sovfoto

Octavio Paz, Steve Northup/Timepix/Time Life Pictures/Getty Images

Alfred Polgar, Imagno/Hulton Archive/Getty Images

Beatrix Potter, Hulton Archive/Getty Images

Jean Prévost, © Albert Harlingue/Roger-Viollet

Marcel Proust, Hulton Archive/Getty Images

Edgar Quinet, © Collection Roger-Viollet

Marcel Reich-Ranicki, ullstein bild/The Granger Collection, New York

Jean-François Revel, © Sophie Bassouls/CORBIS SYGMA

Richard Rhodes, Courtesy of Gail Evenari

Rainer Maria Rilke, ullstein bild/The Granger Collection, New York

Virginio Rognoni, AP Images

Ernesto Sabato, Time & Life Pictures/Getty Images

Edward Said, © Jerry Bauer/Grazia Neri

Sainte-Beuve, Adoc-photos/Art Resource, NY

José Saramago, © 1998 Nobel Foundation

Jean-Paul Sartre, © Lipnitzki/Roger-Viollet

Erik Satie, © Collection Roger-Viollet

Arthur Schnitzler, Imagno/Hulton Archive/Getty Images

Sophie Scholl, Reprinted from Scholl, Inge, Die Weisse Rose: Erweierte Neuausgabe, Fischer Taschenbuch Verlag, Frankfurt am Maim, May 1955

Wolf Jobst Siedler, ullstein bild/The Granger Collection, New York

Manés Sperber, ullstein bild/The Granger Collection, New York

Tacitus, The Granger Collection, New York

Margaret Thatcher, © Camera Press/Retna Ltd.

Henning von Tresckow, ullstein bild/The Granger Collection, New York

Leon Trotsky, Courtesy of the Library of Congress

Karl Tschuppik, Reproduction of the title page of his work Marie-Thérèse, Éditions Bernard Grasset, Paris.

Dubravka Ugresic, © Jerry Bauer

Miguel de Unamuno, ullstein bild/The Granger Collection, New York

Pedro Henriquez Ureña, reprinted from Obra Fotografica en la Argentina; by Greta Stern. Art & Architecture Collection, Miriam and Ira D. Wallach Division of Art, Prints and Photographs, The New York Public Library, Astor, Lenox and Tilden Foundations

Paul Valéry, ullstein bild/The Granger Collection, New York

Mario Vargas Llosa, Time & Life Pictures/Getty Images

Evelyn Waugh, © Yousuf Karsh/Camera Press/Retna Ltd.
Ludwig Wittgenstein, Hulton Archive/Getty Images
Isoroku Yamamoto, AP Images
Alexandr Zinoviev, Hulton Archive/Getty Images
Carl Zuckmayer, ullstein bild/The Granger Collection, New York
Stefan Zweig, ullstein bild/The Granger Collection, New York

INDEX